ASSUMPTION COLLEGE
ECUMENICAL INSTITUTE

Presented by

FULLER FOUNDATION

MUIRHEAD LIBRARY OF PHILOSOPHY

An admirable statement of the aims of the Library of Philosophy was provided by the first editor, the late Professor J. H. Muirhead, in his description of the original programme printed in Erdmann's *History of Philosophy* under the date 1890. This was slightly modified in subsequent volumes to take the form of the following statement:

'The Muirhead Library of Philosophy was designed as a contribution to the History of Modern Philosophy under the heads: first of different Schools of Thought—Sensationalist, Realist, Idealist, Intuitivist; secondly of different Subjects—Psychology, Ethics, Political Philosophy, Theology. While much had been done in England in tracing the course of evolution in nature, history, economics, morals and religion, little had been done in tracing the development of thought on these subjects. Yet "the evolution of opinion is part of the whole evolution".

'By the co-operation of different writers in carrying out this plan it was hoped that a thoroughness and completeness of treatment, otherwise unattainable, might be secured. It was believed also that from writers mainly British and American fuller consideration of English Philosophy than it had hitherto received might be looked for. In the earlier series of books containing, among others, Bosanquet's *History of Aesthetic*, Pfleiderer's *Rational Theology since Kant*, Albee's *History of English Utilitarianism*, Bonar's *Philosophy and Political Economy*, Brett's *History of Psychology*, Ritchie's *Natural Rights*, these objects were to a large extent effected.

'In the meantime original work of a high order was being produced both in England and America by such writers as Bradley, Stout, Bertrand Russell, Baldwin, Urban, Montague, and others, and a new interest in foreign works, German, French and Italian, which had either become classical or were attracting public attention, had developed. The scope of the Library thus became extended into something more international, and it is entering on the fifth decade of its existence in the hope that it may contribute to that mutual

LIBRARY OF PHILOSOPHY

understanding between countries which is so pressing a need of the present time.'

The need which Professor Muirhead stressed is no less pressing today, and few will deny that philosophy has much to do with enabling us to meet it, although no one, least of all Muirhead himself, would regard that as the sole, or even the main, object of philosophy. As Professor Muirhead continues to lend the distinction of his name to the Library of Philosophy it seemed not inappropriate to allow him to recall us to these aims in his own words. The emphasis on the history of thought also seemed to me very timely; and the number of important works promised for the Library in the very near future augur well for the continued fulfilment, in this and other ways, of the expectations of the original editor.

H. D. LEWIS

MUIRHEAD LIBRARY OF PHILOSOPHY

General Editor: H. D. Lewis

Professor of History and Philosophy of Religion in the University of London

The Analysis of Mind. By BERTRAND RUSSELL. 8th Impression.
Analytic Psychology. By G. F. Stout. 2 Vols. 5th Impression.
Coleridge as Philosopher. By J. H. Muirhead. 2nd Impression.
Contemporary American Philosophy. Edited by G. P. ADAMS and W. P. MONTAGUE.
Contemporary British Philosophy. Edited by J. H. MUIRHEAD.
Contemporary Indian Philosophy. Edited by RADHAKRISHNAN and J. H. MUIRHEAD.
Contemporary British Philosophy. Third Series. Edited by H. D. LEWIS.
Development of Theology Since Kant. By O. PFLEIDERER.
Dialogues on Metaphysics. By NICHOLAS MALEBRANCHE. Translated by MORRIS GINSBURG.
Ethics. By NICOLAI HARTMANN. Translated by Stanton Coit. 3 Vols.
The Good Will: A Study in the Coherence Theory of Goodness. By H. J. PATON.
Hegel: A Re-Examination. By J. N. FINDLAY.
Hegel's Science of Logic. Translated by W. H. JOHNSTON and L. G. STRUTHERS. 2 Vols. 2nd Impression.
History of Æsthetic. By B. BOSANQUET. 4th Edition. 5th Impression.
History of English Utilitarianism. By E. ALBEE.
History of Psychology. By G. S. BRETT. Edited by R. S. PETERS. Abridged one-volume edition.
Human Knowledge. By BERTRAND RUSSELL. 3rd Impression
A Hundred Years of British Philosophy. By RUDOLF METZ. Translated by J. W. HARVEY, T. E. JESSOP, HENRY STURT. 2nd Impression.
Ideas: A General Introduction to Pure Phenomenology. By EDMUND HUSSERL. Translated by W. R. BOYCE GIBSON. 2nd Impression.
Imagination. By E. J. FURLONG.
Indian Philosophy. By RADHAKRISHNAN. 2 Vols. Revised 2nd Edition.
The Intelligible World Metaphysics and Value. By W. M. URBAN.
Introduction to Mathematical Philosophy. By BERTRAND RUSSELL. 2nd Edition. 8th Impression.
Kant' First Critique. By H. W. CASSIRER.
Kant's Metaphysic of Experience. By H. J. PATON. 2nd Impression.
Know Thyself. By BERNADINO VARISCO. Translated by GUGLIELMO SALVADORI.

Language and Reality. By WILBUR MARSHALL URBAN.
Matter and Memory. By HENRI BERGSON. Translated by N. M. PAUL and W. S. PALMER. 6th Impression.
Modern Philosophy. By GUIDO DE RUGGIERO. Translated by A. HOWARD HANNAY and R. G. COLLINGWOOD.
The Modern Predicament. By H. J. PATON.
Moral Sense. By JAMES BONAR.
Natural Rights. By D. G. RITCHIE. 3rd Edition. 5th Impression.
Nature, Mind and Modern Science. By E. HARRIS.
The Nature of Thought. By BRAND BLANSHARD. 2nd Impression.
On Selfhood and Godhood. By C. A. CAMPBELL.
Personality and Reality. By E. J. TURNER.
The Phenomenology of Mind. By W. W. F. HEGEL. Translated by SIR JAMES BAILLIE. Revised 2nd Edition. 3rd Impression.
Philosophical Papers. By G. E. MOORE.
Philosophy and Political Economy. By J. BONAR. 4th Impression.
Philosophy of Whitehead. By W. MAYS.
The Platonic Tradition in Anglo-Saxon Philosophy. By J. H. MUIRHEAD.
The Principal Upanisads. By RADHAKRISHNAN.
The Problems of Perception. By R. J. HIRST.
Reason and Goodness. By B. BLANSHARD.
Some Main Problems of Philosophy. By G. E. MOORE.
The Theological Frontier of Ethics. By W. G. MACLAGAN.
Time and Free Will. By HENRI BERGSON. Translated by F. G. POGSON. 6th Impression.
The Ways of Knowing: or The Methods of Philosophy. By W. P. MONTAGUE. 4th Impression.

Muirhead Library of Philosophy
EDITED BY H. D. LEWIS

LANGUAGE AND REALITY

By Wilbur Marshall Urban

THE INTELLIGIBLE WORLD

VALUATION

FUNDAMENTALS OF ETHICS

BEYOND REALISM AND IDEALISM

HUMANITY AND DEITY

LANGUAGE AND REALITY
The Philosophy of Language and the Principles of Symbolism

by

WILBUR MARSHALL URBAN

Yale University, New Haven, Connecticut, U.S.A.

LONDON. GEORGE ALLEN & UNWIN LTD
NEW YORK. THE MACMILLAN COMPANY

FIRST PUBLISHED IN 1939
SECOND IMPRESSION 1951
THIRD IMPRESSION 1961

This book is copyright under the Berne Convention. Apart from any fair dealing for the purposes of private study, research, criticism or review, as permitted under the Copyright Act, 1956, no portion may be reproduced by any process without written permission. Enquiries should be addressed to the publisher.

PRINTED IN GREAT BRITAIN
BRADFORD AND DICKENS
LONDON, W.C.1

PREFACE

THE title of this book, *Language and Reality*, may seem somewhat "ludicrous for a grave philosophical work," as did Campbell's *Philosophy of Rhetoric* to Dugald Stewart, but if so it is solely because the philosophical problems implicit in the title are not fully recognized. These problems are not only of perennial interest and importance in the history of philosophy, but, for reasons which will later appear, are of a special exigency at the present time. It is not too much to say that, for the time being at least, they bring to a head the main issues of philosophic thought.

In the epilogue to an earlier book, *The Intelligible World*, I mentioned a third part, already written, but which was left out in the publication of the work. One of the chapters, entitled The Language of Metaphysics, considered in detail the problems of the philosophy of language raised in various parts of the book. Again, in a paper in *Contemporary American Philosophers*, entitled Metaphysics and Value, I expressed the opinion that the basal problem of science and philosophy is the problem of a philosophy of language and symbolism, and stated that I hoped ultimately to contribute something towards the solution of this problem. It is out of these convictions that the present work has grown.

When first planned, the task seemed relatively limited and one that could be completed in a few years. In the meantime the situation was rapidly changing. The publication of Wittgenstein's *Tractatus Logico-Philosophicus* in 1922 had initiated a movement which was making itself felt in the widest philosophical circles and generating new problems which had to be met. It is, perhaps, safe to say that Logical Positivism has passed its zenith and has modified its original positions to such an extent that its sensational character is greatly softened and its initial force largely spent. But it is equally certain that it has left a residuum of significant problems which constitutes a permanent element in the philosophy of the present. Perhaps the best way to introduce the present study is to relate it to that movement. The writer shares with those of this way of thinking the belief that problems of language are basal for science and philosophy. If philosophy is not solely a "critique of language," as is frequently maintained, such a critique is certainly an indispensable *prolegomenon* to philosophy. Doubtless it cannot be said that that which cannot be expressed is not "real," but surely that which cannot be expressed cannot be said to be either true or false. The problem of knowledge is bound up with those of verification and confirmation, and these in turn with communication. On the other hand, the writer believes that the main positions of this movement on these fundamental issues are in many respects erroneous, and that the errors involved go back ultimately to unsound views of the nature of language and of its relation to "reality." It was partly for this reason that the present study was undertaken.

I have spoken of the peculiar exigency of problems of language at the present time. This is created partly by the movement of which I have just spoken. One uses the term crisis with great hesitation. In the present mood of Western civilization every tension becomes a crisis of civilization, if not of the universe. And yet it is difficult to avoid the feeling that something of the nature of a crisis in our culture is present and that preoccupation with problems of language is in a sense symptomatic. "Language," as Hegel said, "is the actuality of culture," and to question language is to question culture. The Sophistic movement in Greece and the nominalistic movement in mediaeval thought were symptoms of such crises, and both movements revolved, to a considerable extent, about the question of the validity of language. Something of the same character, although greatly aggravated, is present to-day.

There are those who seem to ascribe all our difficulties, economic, political, and social, to the "tyranny of words" which hide from us the realities of things. There are those, on the other hand, who find in "blessed words," with all their accumulated intension, the very actuality of culture and the embodiment of reality. It is not my object here to decide between these two extremes, but merely to suggest that what are called verbal questions are really not merely verbal but go to the heart of philosophical issues. In any case, I think it must be patent to all that a philosophy of language such as that of the New Positivists, which would eliminate whole areas of human discourse as meaningless and unintelligible, has significant implications for human culture. It might conceivably be the prelude to a brave new world in which the human spirit, having rid itself of the ghosts of Plato and Aristotle, and the impedimenta of the centuries, should enter into the full light of a wholly "scientific" era. It might, on the other hand, conceivably be a symptom of a decaying culture and a prelude to a scientific barbarism and a cultural nihilism. In any case, the issues presented by so untoward a situation constitute a challenge to critical thought.

A word may be said with advantage about the division of the book as indicated by the sub-title. Part I is entitled *The Philosophy of Language*. The science of language which developed in the nineteenth century proceeded upon naturalistic premises. A certain revision of its assumptions at crucial points has resulted in what is known as the philosophy of language. The development of the latter—notably in Europe—has led to the recognition of new problems and of new ways of approach to their solution. Chapter II is, in a sense, an *excursus* and might have been printed as an appendix, but it seemed to be a necessary stage in the development of the main thesis of the book. Chief among the problems of a philosophy of language are the relation of language to logic and of language to knowledge or cognition. The chapters dealing with these problems are obviously central to the entire treatment of the theme.

One of the points which chiefly distinguishes this attempt from others in the field is, then, the extended study of language from the standpoint of linguistic science and philosophy. I became increasingly impressed by the fact that logicians and philosophers continually made dogmatic statements about language concerning the truth or falsity of which I had no way of deciding. A long study of writings in this field, not only greatly extended the labours of the work, but opened up perilous paths. In cutting across boundaries in this way, it is impossible that a layman should not make blunders, some of them perhaps serious. I am under no illusions in this respect, but simply had to take the risk.

Part II is entitled *The Principles of Symbolism*. Problems of symbolism are also a burning point in modern theories of knowledge, and the emergence of these problems is not unconnected with the emphasis on problems of language. The actual occasion for renewed emphasis on the notion of the symbolic, as contrasted with the literal representation of reality, is the development of the symbol concept in modern science, more especially physics. One may indeed speak of "symbolism as a scientific principle" in the sense that for the copy or model theory of physical concepts of the nineteenth century, a doctrine of symbolic representation has been developed. But the problem of the principles of symbolism extends far beyond the scientific field. The time is ripe for an attempt to formulate a general theory of symbolism, and such an attempt has here been made.

This task, like that of the first part of the book, greatly extended the labours of the work, but it also opened up perilous paths. In trenching upon the special fields of art, religion, and science, it is impossible that the writer should have escaped making blunders, some of them perhaps serious—especially in the field of science. In extenuation it can only be said that it seemed more important that the present study should be adequate than that it should be without error. In any case, a general theory of symbolism is an important *desideratum* at the present time and such a theory is possible only if the nature and function of the symbol in these various fields are the objects of such comparative study. It may be that the basal rôle of symbolism in knowledge, as presented in this book, will not commend itself to the reader. But it is hoped that the effort to develop this thesis will at least leave, as a permanent residuum, contributions to a more adequate theory of symbolism.

Two ideas constitute, so to speak, the leading motives around which the secondary problems of the book are organized and which give it whatever unity it has. Whatever originality it may have also comes from the treatment of these two themes. These are the notions of *communication* and *intelligibility*. All knowledge, including what we know as science, is, in the last analysis, discourse. This is recognized, either explicitly or tacitly, by every theory of knowledge, and the conditions of intelligible communication become the basal problem of any philosophy. Moreover, the meaningfulness or intelligibility of our assertions is, as the logical positivists rightly see, in some way bound up with their verifiability which is, in turn, conditioned by confirmation and this by communication. The relations of these notions have, I believe, never been adequately worked out. It is hoped that some contribution toward the solution of this problem has here been made. In the course of this attempt the entire problem of verification has been examined afresh. Inevitably the relation of truth to intelligibility has been canvassed and some attempt made to form a satisfactory conception of "symbolic truth."

When Kant wrote his *Prolegomena* it was in the expectation and belief that it would constitute prolegomena to any future metaphysics. To claim for the present work any such function would be even more ludicrous than the title itself may appear to some. And yet of the philosophy of language itself—as it is now being prosecuted—it may be said that it does constitute prolegomena to any future metaphysic. If considerations of language and its logical analysis can, with any show of reason at all, be held, as by some, to eliminate metaphysics, and to reduce it to the level of the unmeaning, then surely the study of language itself, and more especially the language of metaphysics, if for no other reason than to refute such views, must be the preliminary of any significant metaphysics. It was suggested by Hamann that Kant would have done better to write a Critique of Language than a Critique of Reason. It has been suggested by others that this is precisely what he did. Much can be said for this interpretation. For one way of stating the Kantian problem is this. Our language, made to deal with the material world, the world of phenomena, has constantly been extended for discourse about the noumenal. Kant asked the question whether knowledge in this sphere is possible. He might just as well have asked whether discourse about such objects is meaningful or intelligible. Kant's questions are now being asked in this form and answers to them do therefore constitute "prolegomena to any future metaphysic."

The original occasion for the studies here undertaken was the problem of the language of metaphysics as raised by the positions of *The Intelligible World*. In the earlier work I maintained the thesis that *philosophia perennis*, which I described as "the natural metaphysic of the human mind"—with its subject-predicate language and its substance-attribute metaphysic—is the only one that speaks an intelligible language. This position is reaffirmed in the present work. A not insignificant part of the present study is therefore an examination of this natural metaphysic from the standpoint of language and, as a correlate, the critique of modernist tendencies from the linguistic point of view. Of these modernistic tendencies it is maintained that they presuppose an erroneous philosophy of language and become, therefore, in the end unintelligible. The book would, in a sense, be complete without the concluding chapter, but the theses therein developed serve to illustrate its main contentions in what seems to the author to be a significant way.

I am greatly indebted to the editor of the Library of Philosophy, Professor J. H. Muirhead, and the assistant editor, Dr. J. E. Turner, for their many valuable suggestions in the preparation of the manuscript for the press, and especially for their kindness in helping me with the reading of the proofs.

WILBUR M. URBAN

YALE UNIVERSITY
May 1938

CONTENTS

PART I

THE PHILOSOPHY OF LANGUAGE

CHAPTER		PAGE
	Preface	11
I.	Language and Reality: The Theme of a Philosophy of Language	21
II.	What is Language? Origin and Development. The Science of Language	57
III.	Language as the Bearer of Meaning: What it is to Understand	95
IV.	The Phenomenology of Linguistic Meaning: The Primary Functions of Language	134
V.	The Normative Problem of Language: Linguistic Validity	169
VI.	Intelligible Communication: Its Nature and Conditions	228
VII.	Language and Logic: The "Logical Analysis" of Language	268
VIII.	Language and Cognition: The Metalogical Problems of Language	330

PART II

THE PRINCIPLES OF SYMBOLISM

IX.	The Principles of Symbolism: The General Theory of Symbolism	401
X.	The Language of Poetry and its Symbolic Form	456
XI.	Science and Symbolism: Symbolism as a Scientific Principle	503
XII.	Religious Symbols and The Problem of Religious Knowledge	571
XIII.	The Language of Metaphysics: Symbolism as a Metaphysical Principle	629
XIV.	*Philosophia Perennis:* The "Natural Metaphysic of the Human Mind"	685

	PAGE
Appendix I. The Development and "Progress" of Language	731
Appendix II. The Problem of Translation in General Linguistics	736
Appendix III. Neo-Nominalistic Philosophies of Language	741
Appendix IV. Symbolism as a Theological Principle in St. Thomas	748
Index of Names	751
Index of Subjects	753

PART I
THE PHILOSOPHY OF LANGUAGE

CHAPTER I

LANGUAGE AND REALITY: THE THEME OF A PHILOSOPHY OF LANGUAGE

I

INTRODUCTION: THE PROBLEM

A

LANGUAGE is the last and deepest problem of the philosophic mind. This is true whether we approach reality through life or through intellect and science. All life, as Henry James has said, comes back to the question of our speech, the medium through which we communicate. Life as it is merely lived is senseless. It is perhaps conceivable that we may have a direct apprehension or intuition of life, but the meaning of life can neither be apprehended nor expressed except in language of some kind. Such expression or communication is part of the life process itself.

It is not different when we approach reality through knowledge or science. In a very real sense the limits of my language are the limits of my world. Science, in the last analysis, is language well made. It is true that science in some of its more sophisticated forms and stages may eschew natural language —may have recourse to graphs and equations, and may even deny that these either can or need be retranslated into words, but the fact remains that such graphs and equations are, after all, but means by which the mind takes possession of its objects and operates with them. Until they are interpreted they say nothing. The question as to "what science says" can be answered only in natural language.

It is not surprising, therefore, that reflection on language is one of the oldest and most constant preoccupations of the human mind. In the Upanishads we are told to meditate on speech. "If there were no speech, neither right nor wrong would be known, neither true nor false, neither the pleasant nor the unpleasant. Speech makes us understand all this. Meditate on speech." Now, whether it be true or not that if there were no speech nothing would be known, that there would be no such distinctions as true and false, right and wrong, is indeed precisely one of the fundamental questions of a philosophy of language. The relation of cognition to language is one of the central themes of the present treatise, as, indeed, it is of all present-day philosophy. In any case the problem of what we can know is so closely bound up with the question of what we can say, that all meditation on knowledge involves meditation on speech. It may not be true that, as Parmenides said, "Name is everything, everything that mortals have established in confidence that it is the truth," but it *is* true that until something has been fixed by names there is little if anything of which either true or false, or even meaning, can be predicated.

II

THE PROBLEM OF LANGUAGE IN THE HISTORY OF THOUGHT

Reflection upon language is, then, one of the oldest and most constant preoccupations of men. This preoccupation has been deepened at all critical points in human culture. It is precisely because we have reached such a turning-point that there has been a revival of interest in the philosophy of language.

Of such critical turning-points in Western European culture we may note five: (*a*) The period of the Greek sophists and sceptics; (*b*) the latter part of mediaeval scholasticism; (*c*) the epistemologists of the eighteenth century; (*d*) the idealistic reaction in the course of the nineteenth century, and finally these early decades of the twentieth century when the full effects of the Darwinian epoch of evolutionary naturalism are being felt.

A history of European thought and culture might well be written about this problem of language. It is not my purpose to attempt this history here. It will suffice to make clear the main outlines of this story and the outstanding characters of the epochs that are chiefly significant for its understanding.

A
High and Low Evaluations of Language

"Culture is the measure of things taken for granted." Among the most important of such things is language in which, as Hegel says, "culture is actualized." The relation of the word to the thing is, as Parmenides saw, the key problem about which all culture and all knowledge finally turns. The history of European culture is, accordingly, the story of two great opposing valuations—high and low evaluations of the *Word*.

It may be taken for granted, I suppose, that the notion of a traditional philosophy, of a *philosophia perennis*, in the sense of the Greco-Christian tradition, is more and more being accepted as a true description of the story of Western philosophy. However diametrically opposed the evaluation of the tradition, as, for instance, in John Dewey's *The Quest for Certainty*[1] and in the present writer's *The Intelligible World*, the account of the driving-force of that tradition and of the assumptions that give it unity and continuity does not in the two cases materially differ. I suppose that it would also be agreed that this same tradition is based upon a high evaluation of language; on a doctrine of reason which identifies it, in some degree at least, with the Word, the *Logos*. Bergson is certainly not far wrong when he tells us that this entire tradition is based upon a trust in language. This high evaluation of language is the underlying assumption of all periods of rationalism and is uniformly accompanied by some belief in the reality of universals, since the very naming of anything immediately universalizes it in some sense and to some degree.

As opposed to this high evaluation, with its trust in the word, there is the low evaluation which appears in all critical periods of culture. Scepticism is always ultimately scepticism of the word. If being *is*, so we find it in Gorgias, it is unapprehensible and unknowable by man; but even if it is knowable, it is inexpressible and incommunicable. Scepticism of the word is the underlying assumption of all periods of empiricism and is again accompanied by some form of nominalism—by disbelief in the reality of the universal, the reality of the universal being at once the condition of valid naming and of communi-

---

[1] Published by George Allen and Unwin Ltd.

cation of meaning. The inseparability of the word and the thing is, then, in one form or another, the postulate of all positive cultural epochs and the loosing of the word from the thing the beginning of scepticism and relativism.[1]

B

Sophistic Scepticism and the Reinstatement of the Word

Sophistic scepticism had already loosed the word from the thing. In the time of Plato, therefore, the relation between word and thing, name and object, had become a customary topic of conversation. In Xenophon's *Memorabilia* (III, 14, 2) we read that at a banquet in Athens the question of the proper usage of language was the topic of discussion. This is also the theme of the dialogue, *Cratylus*, of which more will be said in the sequel. The criticism of the Sophists by Socrates was in principle an attack on the conventional theory of language and an attempt to re-establish a trust in language. The doctrine of the Idea of Plato and, still more, the logic of Aristotle, were, on the whole, a reaffirmation of the natural trust in language which the scepticism of the Sophists could only disturb and not actually destroy. The Stoic philosophy of language, with its postulate of natural language and the *Ursprache*, signalized the final triumph. This scepticism of the word did not fail to leave its mark even on Plato. He found himself compelled to make a sharp distinction between two meanings of the *logos*, one which becomes of immense importance in the Seventh Letter, in which his philosophy of language is most clearly expressed, a distinction, namely, between the pure concept, the concept or idea as such, and the concept expressed in language. But this distinction tends to disappear in the main current of philosophic thought, its influence being largely felt in Neo-platonic mysticism. It is doubtless too much to say that Aristotle built his logic wholly on language, that the fundamental distinctions upon which his logic is built are determined en-

[1] A history of the philosophy of language is, as Ernst Cassirer remarks, still to be written. The best contribution to such a history is his own sketch, which is found in his *Die Philosophie der Symbolischen Formen*, Vol. I, Chapter I, entitled "Das Sprachproblem in der Geschichte der Philosophie."

THE THEME OF A PHILOSOPHY OF LANGUAGE

tirely by the Greek language. Nevertheless a trust in language is the basal supposition of that logic.

Viewed broadly, this trust in the word is the dominant note of mediaeval culture and one of the chief keys to its understanding. "In the beginning was the Word, and the Word was with God." This notion of the primacy of the word not only made inevitable the "realism" which is the basis of mediaeval culture, but made possible that trust in language on which the *via eminentiae* was built—that bridge by means of which, through natural language and its analogies, a way to the nature of Deity is found. Nominalism thus becomes, for this culture, the most fundamental of all heresies. The philosophy of common sense of classical scholasticism is essentially a philosophy of the *sensus communis*. The great contrast of this philosophy with the sophisticated epistemology beginning with Descartes' philosophy of doubt, is rightly seen to lie in the fact that it starts with the assumption that we *have* knowledge. But no less important is the "realistic" assumption that in language and its categories we have the structure of reality.

C

Nominalism and the Realistic Reaction

The nominalism of the late mediaeval period and of the Renaissance represents, then, a veritable crisis in culture of the same general character as that of the Sophistic period. Again, scepticism of the word is the key to the moral relativism and scepticism of the period. From our point of view, however, the attack on the Aristotelian logic which began at this time is highly significant. It was precisely with the philologists of the Renaissance—such figures as those of Lorenzo Valla, Ludovico Vives, and Petrus Ramus—that the attack began. By their linguistic and grammatical studies they sought to overthrow the scholastic-aristotelian philosophy as the exclusive systematic of the spirit. The rhetoricians join with the physicists in their attack on the dialecticians and in the demand for a return from the word to the thing.

Seen against this background, the philosophical rationalism of the Continent appears, on the whole, to be dominated by the spirit of the *philosophia perennis* and an attempt to reinstate that trust in language which is part of traditional philosophy. Descartes' *de omnibus dubitare* may indeed be viewed as expressing the scepticism of the Renaissance, but it may also be looked upon as an answer to that scepticism. The doubt of everything was not only a doubt of all knowledge, but also a doubt of language in which that knowledge is embodied or expressed. The meeting of the doubt and the reinstatement of innate ideas meant also the reinstatement of the trust in the word with which the idea is bound up. This was clearly seen by the sensationalist critics of the doctrine who denied innate ideas partly on the grounds of the non-innateness of language.

Descartes himself did not make language a special problem in his chief works, but in the single connection in which he refers to it (a letter to Mersenne) he gives it a particular turn which is highly significant and widely influential in the thinking of the rationalists. He insists upon the inseparable character of the relation of reason and language. As in all forms of knowledge, there is always one ground form of knowledge, the human reason, so there must be in all the different languages one language, the universal, rational, form of language. The mathematical ideal of knowledge, with its emphasis upon universality, brings with it also a demand for a universal language. The demand for a *Mathesis universalis* includes in it, for all parts of knowledge which are not mathematical, the demand for a *Lingua universalis*.[1] Herein we find the stimulus for the many systems of universal language which followed in swift succession, an activity in which Leibniz also took part.

One aspect of the rationalistic philosophy of language requires special comment. The trust in language which, as we have seen, dominated on the whole the preceding epochs of European culture, is in the main continued in the rationalistic movement. It is precisely from this trust that, from one point of view, the dogmatism which Kant ascribes to it proceeds. Such words as Self, external world, and God are not "empty words" but refer to objects. They embody an intellectual as opposed to sensuous intuition, that intellectual intuition which Kant later subjected to criticism. The doctrine of innate ideas

[1] Letter to Mersenne, November 20, 1829, *Correspondence*, ed. Adam-Tannery, I, 80 ff.

presupposes, as we have said, the trust in the word with which the idea is bound up.

D

Empiricism and the Transcendental Reaction

The critical point in the philosophy of language of modern times came with the empiricism of the eighteenth century. This movement naturally approached the problem in an entirely different spirit from that of rationalism in that, far from assuming linguistic validity, as in principle the rationalists did, the very heart of empiricism was the questioning of it.

Indeed, Locke was the first to have realized that meditation upon language must be, if not the propaedeutic, at least the constant accompaniment of philosophical reflection. Thus he confesses: "When I first began this discourse of the understanding and a good while after, I had not the least thought that any consideration of words was necessary to it. But when, having passed over the original and composition of our ideas, I began to examine the extent and certainty of our knowledge, I found it had so near a connection with words that unless their force and manner of signification were well understood, *there could be very little said pertinently and clearly concerning knowledge*; which being conversant about truth had constantly to do with propositions: and though it terminated in things, yet it was, for the most part, so much by the intervention of words, that they seemed scarce separable from our general knowledge."[1]

For the empiricist no less than for the rationalist, words are inseparable from knowledge, but the inferences drawn from that fact are wholly different. Add to this statement of Locke, the further thesis that all words originate in sense experience of physical things and are then carried over to the non-physical, a thesis which Locke develops in great detail, and the entire problem of the "force and signification of words" is set. All words "being ultimately derived from such as signify sensible ideas," the problem of their valid reference to non-sensible ideas is immediately raised. This is the systematic ground upon which all treatment of language problems within empiricism,

[1] *An Essay Concerning Human Understanding*, Book III, Chapter IX, Section 21.

from Locke to the logical positivists, is directly or indirectly based.

The empirical philosophy of language becomes the basis for a theory of knowledge which eliminates the universal. Berkeley seeks to show the impossibility of abstract ideas and he traces them to the source from which they flow, namely, language. He even proposes "to confine my thought to my own ideas, divested from words." He does not "see how he can then be mistaken." He even doubts whether language has contributed more to the hindrance or the advancement of the sciences.[1] This sceptical view of language Berkeley was not able himself to maintain, his doctrine of notions being in reality a reinstatement of innate principles in another form, but it continued as the basis of the entire empirical movement, and is in a sense the ultimate ground of the scepticism of Hume. In the mind of the empiricist this principle of the inseparability of knowledge and its expression in language becomes the final argument against innate principles and the extension of knowledge beyond the empirically observable. The "one irresistible argument," according to William Godwin, "proving the absurdity" of such principles is that it is impossible that a principle should be innate unless the ideas expressed in the proposition are innate also. The "near connection with words" of which Locke wrote makes that impossible.[2]

The philosophy of language of empiricism precipitated a crisis in culture as its theory of knowledge precipitated a similar crisis in the sphere of technical philosophy. As Hume woke Kant from his dogmatic slumbers, so the critique of language we have been considering gave birth, indirectly at least, to a new and higher evaluation of language connected with what is called the *Romantic* movement. The philosophy of language connected with this movement, as, for instance, expressed in Herder, is at the same time a reaction against this account of language and against the arid intellectualism of the later rationalism as exemplified in the logical investigations of Leibniz.[3]

---

[1] *The Principles of Human Knowledge*, Section 21.
[2] William Godwin, *Political Justice*, Book I, Chapter 4.
[3] The best single treatment of the philosophy of language of the Romantic period is that of Eva Fiesel: *De Sprachphilosophie der Deutschen Romantik* (J. C. B. Mohr, 1927). All the fundamental concepts of this philosophy, its notion of inner

E

Von Humboldt and Hegel: The Idealistic Philosophy of Language

Kant is then indirectly the answer to that scepticism of the word which constitutes the underlying assumption of sensationalistic empiricism. That answer is transcendentalism. But so far as the philosophy of language *eo nomine* is concerned, that answer is given by von Humboldt. In him we find the embodiment, so far as meditation on language is concerned, of that change in the *Zeitgeist* which marks off the nineteenth century from the eighteenth. This, of course, is not to overlook the contributions of Hamann and Herder and many others of lesser moment. It is merely to seek in one outstanding figure the key notions of this epoch.

Something of the spirit of this entire epoch is expressed in a letter of von Humboldt to Wolf, written in 1805. "Im grunde ist alles was ich treibe Sprachstudium. Ich glaube die Kunst endecket zu haben die Sprache als ein Vehicel zu gebrauchen, um das Höchste und Tiefste und die Manigfältigkeit der ganzen Welt zu durchfahren."[1] As for Locke, so also for von Humboldt, language and cognition are inseparable. But the important thing for him is that language is not merely the means by which truth (somehow already known without the instrument of speech) is more or less adequately expressed, but is rather the means by which the not-yet-known is discovered. Cognition and expression are one. This is the source and the assumption of all Humboldt's researches in language. Here, then, through the mediation of Kant and Herder, he returns from the narrow logical conception of speech of the later Leibniz to the deeper and more comprehensive notion of reason which underlies Leibniz's philosophy as a whole and which expressed the real spirit of rationalism.

The influence of von Humboldt's germinal ideas on the

form and of language as creative, together with its distinctive doctrines of the origin and development of language, are brought out with enlightening detail. An excellent presentation of Humboldt's conception of language is also given. Although not reckoned with the Romantics, the close relation of many of his fundamental concepts to this movement is shown.

[1] From a letter to Wolf (1805), quoted by Cassirer. For a fuller treatment of von Humboldt's entire philosophy of language, see *op. cit.*, Vol. I, pp. 98 ff.

science of language is not the theme of the present discussion. It is everywhere apparent and will receive attention in the appropriate places. We are concerned rather with the place of his "meditation on speech" in the cultural and philosophical life that followed.

The inseparability of *Geist* and *Sprache*, the organic conception of language, the reciprocal dependence of thought and word, all passed as necessary presuppositions into the idealistic movement which we associate with the name of Hegel. It would not be too much to say that the notion of language as the vehicle by which to reach the highest and the deepest is the unspoken assumption of the entire Hegelian philosophy, for which language is "the actuality of culture." It is not to be doubted that the Hegelian dialectic involved a critique of language. The principle of negativity by which the dialectic proceeds is, from one point of view, the denial of the adequacy of the word, but this is merely a step in a dialectic which finds *better words* for the expression of reality. The significant point is that reality *can be expressed*, that language is a vehicle for the exploration of the highest and deepest of the world. Hegel's doctrine of the categories differs from the Kantian primarily in that, while the latter takes as the key or the *Leitfaden* for the discovery of the categories of the real, the fundamental grammatical forms of language, denying a categorial character to those "ideas" which are merely "regulative," for Hegel the latter also are constitutive, *Leitfaden* which, through the dialectic, lead to an understanding of the real.

F

From Hegel to Darwin

It was when this philosophy of language was at the height of its influence that, like the general philosophy with which it was bound up, it collapsed and with its collapse precipitated a crisis in culture the full meaning of which is probably not yet realized. This we may describe as the step from Hegel to Darwin, from *Geist* to *Natur*, from idealism to naturalism. It was only to be expected that this crisis would, as heretofore, bring with it renewed meditations on language.

THE THEME OF A PHILOSOPHY OF LANGUAGE 31

From the more general cultural standpoint it is the complete "naturalization of the intelligence" which is the significant element of the movement. With this naturalization of intelligence followed the naturalization of language with which intelligence is bound up. The consequences of this movement for the methodology of the science of language will be considered in a later context.[1] Here we are concerned solely with its general significance. Scepticism of the word has returned with renewed virulence, but it is now a scepticism the like of which has not hitherto been seen.

The characteristic common to all these sceptical periods has been nominalism in one form or another and the distrust of language which inevitably follows. That which characterizes the present epoch is a form of nominalism which may be characterized as Neo-nominalism. Its distinguishing characteristics will engage our attention in the ensuing section. Here we shall emphasize a single point. The naturalistic and ultimately behaviouristic view of language which has developed of necessity from Darwinian premises, has brought with it a scepticism of the word, a distrust of language more fundamental than any hitherto experienced. The naturalization of language makes of it, in the last analysis, merely a method of adaptation to and control of environment, and denies to it *ab initio* all fitness for apprehending and expressing anything but the physical, all those functions which have belonged to it by virtue of its traditional association with reason and with *Geist*.

This low evaluation of language is, as we shall see, the key to the most significant movements of the present day in general culture and in technical thought. Against this evaluation and the premises upon which it is based, movements of reaction are evident. Even in the sphere of linguistic science itself, as we shall presently see, there are "idealistic" reactions against this naturalism. In the main, however, we are in one of those critical turning-points of human culture of which we have spoken, and here, as always, the philosophy of language has, as we shall also see, become a chief preoccupation.

[1] Chapter II, pp. 59 ff.

G

Summary and Conclusion

The preceding account is not intended to be a complete story of the philosophy of language or of those reflections upon speech which have been the inevitable accompaniments of the development of European thought and culture. To be complete it would need to be little less than the story of Western philosophy and science itself. It has served, however, it may be hoped, to make clear two things. It has justified, in the first place, our initial statement that preoccupation with problems of language has universally been deepened at all critical points in human culture. It has shown also that the story of that culture is not only bound up with reflection upon language, but must be understood as an age-old conflict between two great evaluations of the word, which we have described as the high and the low evaluations.

It is clear, in the second place, that throughout these movements, whether the valuations be high or low, whether the movements be rationalistic or empirical, one underlying assumption determines them all—namely, the inseparable relation between the problem of knowledge and the problem of language. For the Sophist, no less than for Plato and Aristotle, for Locke no less than for Descartes and Leibniz, for evolutionary naturalism no less than for the idealism of von Humboldt and Hegel—it is this assumption which creates the problem of language for the philosopher, and it is at this point, now as always, that the problems of the philosophy of language arise.

III

THE PROBLEMS OF A PHILOSOPHY OF LANGUAGE; LINGUISTIC VALIDITY

A

The revival of interest in philosophical problems of language is accordingly one of the outstanding features of the present cultural situation. The reasons for this revival are not far to seek. They are, to be sure, *mutatis mutandis*, the same fundamental issues as forced meditation on language at any of the crucial points of human thought and culture. In the present instance, however, the problems have been given a new turn by reason of two distinctively modern developments.

The first of these is the purely naturalistic view of language which followed upon the application of Darwinian principles to all cultural forms. The step from Hegel to Darwin, which, as we shall see, changed the face of linguistic studies in the nineteenth century, eventuated in a tendency not only to explain but to evaluate language in purely biological and naturalistic terms. Our language became "the cries of the forest corrupted and complicated by anthropoid apes," and the question was very properly asked how such a mere extension of the tool-making function of man, this mere organ of adaptation to environment, could become the vehicle even of "physical" knowledge, to say nothing of its being, in von Humboldt's terms, a vehicle for travelling through the highest and deepest and the manifold of the entire world! In short, what has been called the behaviouristic theory of language, of which more shall be said presently, has raised entirely new problems.

The second distinctively modern development has come from the physical sciences: the increasing elaboration of the technical, non-linguistic symbols of science, the ever-increasing divergence of these symbols from natural language and the ever-growing difficulty of communicating their meaning in ordinary language.

If we look about us, it is true, as Paul Valéry[1] writes, that "we see speech dwindling in importance in every field where accuracy is on the increase. . . . Undoubtedly common speech will always be used to teach the manufactured languages and adjust their strong and accurate mechanisms to minds as yet unspecialized. But by contrast speech has become more and more a means for the first rough approximations and is being ousted as systems of purer notation develop, each one more adapted to one special use. . . . A kind of picture writing is growing up to connect qualities and quantities, a language whose grammar is a body of preliminary conventions (scales,

[1] Paul Valéry, "Leonardo and the Philosophers," *The Hound and Horn*, Vol. IV, No. 2.

axes, quadratures, etc.), and whose logic is the dependence of figures or parts of figures, their properties in situations, etc. . . . Words doubtless call the graphs into being, give them meaning and interpret them, but words no longer consummate the act of the mind's possession."

This is, I take it, in the main a true picture of the present situation. The dwindling of speech in importance, its ousting by systems of purer notation, is part of the modern problem. It is, I think, becoming quite clear where this problem lies. In the sphere of physical science itself the issue is clearly understood. Can the physical object of science be connected with the physical object of "common sense," or have modern methods of analysis created a dualism which we must be content to leave unbridged? In terms of the philosophy of language we have the same problem in other words. Is there a dualism between the "manufactured" languages and "natural" language which we must likewise be content to leave unbridged? Must we be content to leave mathematical formulas uninterpreted? Words no longer consummate the mind's possession of its objects, so science bursts through natural language. But the fact remains that it is words that call these systems of purer notation into being, words in the last analysis alone give them meaning, and interpretation can ultimately be in words alone. In sum, we have here what Hönigswald calls the principle of the essential "Worthaftigkeit des Denkens." Whatever manufactured languages we may create, is not the ultimate symbolism from which they all come and to which in the last analysis they must all return, the language of words?

These two modern movements create a unique situation in the philosophy of language. They have united to form what I have described as neo-nominalism.[1] As distinguished from earlier nominalism, both that of mediaeval thought and of sensationalistic empiricism, its special characters are quite clear. In its earlier forms, nominalism denied the reality of universals; neo-nominalism is thoroughgoing and denies the reality of individuals also. In its more extreme forms, it denies reality to all except the flux of sensations and eventuates in a panfictionism, according to which to name a thing at all is to turn

[1] See my article, "Modernism in Science and Philosophy," *The Journal of Philosophical Studies*, Vol. V, No. 18.

it into a fiction. It is this neo-nominalism, in its varied forms and far-reaching ramifications, that has made the problem of language the central one in present-day philosophical thought.

B
Neo-Nominalism and "Modernism" in Philosophy

All types of philosophy are thus being forced to take up the problems of language again, and what is called the philosophy of language has become a special and relatively distinct department of philosophical activity. Language has, so to speak, become the *Brennpunkt* of present-day philosophical discussion.

There is scarcely a characteristic philosophical movement of our time which does not turn, at some crucial point, about its conception of language and the relation of language to reality. The Bergsonian philosophy is an outstanding illustration of the situation. The conception of metaphysics as the science that seeks to dispense with symbols is based upon a definite philosophy of language. Scarcely less significant, however, are the logical atomism of Bertrand Russell and the organic philosophy of Whitehead as developed in *Process and Reality*. For the latter the very possibility of a metaphysics rests upon the redesigning of our language, and an entire reconstitution of the categories embodied in our language.

The chief point, however, at which the linguistic issue appears is in the position of logical positivism, more especially with regard to metaphysics. As is well known, this form of positivism, like its progenitors, is characterized primarily by the wholesale elimination of large regions of so-called knowledge from the realm of actual knowledge and the reinterpretation of such knowledge as remains, namely, scientific, in a fashion not wholly acceptable to scientists themselves. The fields eliminated are those of morals, religion, art, and, above all, metaphysics. These are relegated to the sphere of feeling and emotional expression. The view of science maintained is that it is merely descriptive and that all "metaphysical" propositions are meaningless here also.

So much the old and the new positivism have in common.

The point of divergence of the new from the old, although from a more general point of view not important, is precisely that which, from our standpoint, makes it highly significant. The new positivism is based upon the "analysis of language" and ultimately upon a philosophy of language. For the older positivism, the statements or propositions within the spheres of discourse known as the value sciences and metaphysics were untrue—useful fictions perhaps, but still fictions. Such is, for instance, still the positivism of Vaihinger. For the new positivism, they are not untrue but meaningless. They deal with questions and assertions concerning which the problem of truth or falsity really does not arise, for the questions and assertions are themselves meaningless. The standpoint is well expressed in the well-known article of Carnap entitled *Die Ueberwindung der Metaphysik durch die logische Analyse der Sprache*.[1] The details of this position belong to later discussions; here we are concerned merely to indicate the way in which language has become the central problem in philosophy.

C

What is the Philosophy of Language?

What, then, is this philosophy of language the basal issues of which are, as we have seen, involved in all distinctively modern forms of philosophy and upon the solution of which all in the last analysis turn? What is the philosophy of language and how is it related to linguistic science? We may best approach this problem by considering a series of questions about language which, as we have seen, have been continually asked in all epochs of human culture and are still asked with increasing insistence to-day. Any field of knowledge may be defined by the questions it asks and by the type of answers which it gives.

What is the nature and function of language? Is it a God-given hand-maid of reason, as Schlegel says, or merely a form of animal behaviour—in the words of Anatole France, the sounds of the forest corrupted and complicated by anthropoid

[1] *Erkentniss*, Vol. II, No. 4.

THE THEME OF A PHILOSOPHY OF LANGUAGE

apes? Is its function to mirror the world, to be a vehicle by which the spirit comes to self-consciousness as Novalis says, or is it only at home when used to manipulate physical objects, for which manipulation it was primarily made? Are the powers of language limited to the practical functions for which it was "primarily made," or has it, in its development, achieved a freedom which makes it, in the words of Humboldt, "a vehicle for traversing the manifold and the highest and deepest of the entire world?"

Examination of these and similar questions makes it clear that there is a group of problems regarding language which have to do with its *evaluation*, with the determination of its significance in the total life of the human spirit and as a means for the apprehension and communication of reality. The philosophy of language, we may then say, to begin with, is concerned with *the evaluation of language as a bearer of meanings, as a medium of communication and as a sign or symbol of reality.*

This idea that there are distinctively philosophical problems of language and that these problems are problems of evaluation, is by no means unknown even in the field of linguistic science itself. No less an authority than Jespersen has said that the limitations of theories of language in the past, the lack of breadth of vision in modern linguistics, is due to the fact that linguists have neglected all problems connected with the evaluation of language.[1]

The philosophical problem of language is, then, the problem of its evaluation or the problem of *linguistic validity*. In its earliest form, as in the discussions of the *Cratylus*, it was, as we have seen, the problem of the "natural rightness of names." But behind this simple formulation there lies a deeper question which has been constantly restated in all the critical periods of culture. Do language and the word belong entirely to the realm of subjective "opinion" and convention, or natural process, or does there subsist between the realm of words and the realm of being some deeper connection? The Sophists denied, the Stoics affirmed such objective validity of the word. This denial and affirmation constitute two opposing valuations throughout the entire history of European thought. These have been called the high and low evaluations of the word,

---

[1] See Ogden and Richards, *The Meaning of Meaning*, p. vi.

and, although the opposing valuations have been always present, it is the high evaluation which has in the main dominated Western thought.

D

The Philosophy of Language and Linguistic Science

Philosophical problems of language are then, in the first instance, connected with the evaluation of language, or with the question of linguistic validity. But there is also linguistic science and it is also important to determine the manner in which distinctively philosophical problems are related to those of linguistic science. We shall consider certain specific problems of linguistic science in the following chapter. Here it is desirable merely to establish the general relation in a preliminary way.

The science of language may be clearly marked off both by material and method. What is language? asks Dauzac, a French linguist, in the introductory chapter of his *La Philosophie du Language*, and the answer given is distinctly in the terms of linguistic science. Language, he replies, is a collection of articulate sounds—that is the first aspect that strikes the linguist. The study of the sounds constitutes phonetics and it involves relations with physiology and physics. Language may, in the second place, be envisaged as an instrument of thought. This is the subject-matter of semantics and includes the analysis of grammatical relations, morphology and syntax, and the significance of the life of words. Here relations with psychology are important. Finally, language is social fact, as medium of communication, and at this point linguistics makes important contacts with the social and cultural sciences.

This answer by a linguist to the question, What is language? represents fairly adequately for our purpose the three main divisions of linguistic science. In the following chapter, we shall see that the scientific study of language has actually passed through these three phases. In the earlier stages the emphasis was on phonetics, with a corresponding emphasis upon physics and physiology. Later the turn was to problems of meaning, with a corresponding emphasis upon the psychology of language and its function as a social and cultural

THE THEME OF A PHILOSOPHY OF LANGUAGE

phenomenon. All this is a subject for later consideration; here we shall concentrate our attention upon the division of linguistic science known as semantics.

The meaning of words, which constitutes the subject-matter of this division, is, as has already been indicated, the point at which linguistics and psychology come together. It is also, however, the point at which the chief problems of the philosophy of language arise. The nature of meaning is, from one point of view at least, the central problem of both language and philosophy. The linguist cannot solve his problems without trenching on the philosophical, nor can the logician and philosopher solve theirs without linguistic analysis; it is for these reasons that the special field of the philosophy of language has been developed. Over against semantics in the linguistic sense we may set the field of philosophical semantics.

Semantics, in the linguistic sense, deals with the analysis of grammatical relations, morphology and syntax, and the "significance of the life of words." But all these problems have their philosophical aspect, for they raise the question of the relation of these words, forms, and relations to reality. The philosophical aspect of semantics may be seen specifically in the "empirical criterion of meaning" as formulated by logical positivism. The object of this criterion is to find a means of distinguishing the meaningful from the unmeaning in language, apparent words from real words, pseudo-sentences from real sentences. This criterion is found in the reference to observable entities, and, it is held, where such reference cannot be shown, language is meaningless. It is not our purpose to examine this criterion at this point, but merely to use it as an example of philosophical semantics—to point out that it is a criterion, and as such seeks to establish a norm in terms of which language may be evaluated. That the formulation of such a norm makes assumptions of a philosophical character is obvious—assumptions which it is the task of philosophical semantics to examine.

The general relations of the science to the philosophy of language have been well stated by Karl Vossler. After enumerating the various conceptions of language with which linguistic science makes us familiar—"a meaningful sound, a sociable noise, a passing to and fro of signs, which men make chiefly through the mouth and take in through the ears, and by means of which they communicate with each other—through gestures, hands, eyes, etc.," he writes as follows: "No one denies that behind this shifting pattern something is at work that may be called Force, or Meaning or Will, or Mind or Body or Soul of Man, or anything else. But as soon as we inquire what this 'something' is, opinions begin to diverge widely. The pious see in it the divine breath, the enlightened a natural disposition that is to some extent shared by animals. The origin of language is attributed by psychologists to the psychic part of this disposition, by phoneticians to the bodily part, by sociologists to the communal life of man. The clash of opinions becomes most violent when it comes to the problem of the *value* of language [italics the author's]. Overestimation stands against underestimation. On the one hand language is thought to be error and illusion, a veil hiding truth and self-deception; on the other it is looked upon as the first and most important educator of our thought. If we wish to pick our way among these clashing views, we have to realize that we need the help of philosophy and even metaphysics which will lead us to the ultimate foundations of the human spirit."[1]

It is not necessary to subscribe to this passage *in toto* in order to see the philosophical problems which inevitably arise in any adequate consideration of language. There are certain problems which linguistic science cannot itself solve. These problems culminate in that of the value of language or linguistic validity, and this problem can be solved only by reference to those wider considerations to which we give the term philosophical.

IV

THE SPECIFIC PROBLEMS OF A PHILOSOPHY OF LANGUAGE

We have now distinguished between the science and the philosophy of language. We have also determined in a general way the theme of the philosophy of language as that of linguistic validity. With these conceptions in mind, it is now possible to formulate more accurately the problems of language which

[1] *The Spirit of Language in Civilization*, London and New York, 1932, p. 1.

are more distinctly philosophical in character and implication. Linguistic validity is concerned with the problem of the evaluation of language as a *bearer of meaning, as a medium of communication and as a sign or symbol of reality*. The further development of this theme leads us, I think, to four distinct problems.

It is not easy to formulate these problems of language without using in the very terminology employed some theory of language and of its relation to reality, in other words, without begging the questions at issue in the very form of their statement. Thus Mr. Bertrand Russell, in his introduction to Wittgenstein's *Tractatus*, formulates the four problems I have in mind, but in his very statement there is assumed a conception of linguistic fact which is itself open to question. This is especially evident in his statement of what is called the logical problem of language. "What relation, it is asked, must one fact or set of facts, such as a sentence, have to another fact, the proposition, in order to be capable of standing significantly for them—of being a valid surrogate for them?" In this apparently obvious formulation is hidden a whole nest of questions, the chief of which is precisely the separation of the two sets of facts, the sentence and the proposition. Whether such a form of statement is valid or not, is not the issue here. The question is raised merely as a warning against so formulating the problems of a philosophy of language as to beg the issues involved.

A

Language as the Bearer of Meaning. Linguistic Meaning

There is then, in the first place, the problem of language as the bearer of meanings. In the words of Cassirer it is this: how in general a particular sensuous content, such as a collection of sounds, can become the bearer of a universal or spiritual meaning. It is at this point that linguistic science and philosophy first come together, for meaning is a central notion in both. It is precisely because the problem of meaning in the one cannot be answered without reference to the other that a philosophy of language is inevitable. The nature and differentiation of linguistic meaning is the primary problem, but the solution of it takes us far beyond the limits of linguistics themselves. The existence of "meaning" in some sense prior to the development of language, raises the further problem of the nature of this meaning and of the relation of linguistic meaning to it. A theory of linguistic meaning is but part of a larger problem of the nature of meaning and cannot be answered without an analysis of the "meaning situation" itself and the development of a general theory of meaning. The questions raised here are partly psychological, but they are also phenomenological and philosophical. Meaning is the first specific problem of a philosophy of language.

B

Language as Medium of Communication

The problem of language as a bearer of meaning passes directly into the problem of language as a medium of communication; for, as we shall presently see, it is part of the modern speech notion that language, *as language*, has no reality except in the speech community.

The problem here involved may again be expressed in different ways. We may, with Mr. Russell, ask how shall we use language so as to convey the meaningful rather than the unmeaning, the true rather than the false? Or we may ask, how is meaningful, intelligible communication possible? This may be described as a sociological problem, for it is in part concerned with language as social fact. But the problem is really more than this. Answers to questions such as these involve an examination of the entire process of communication, or of the conveyance of meaning, which is ultimately a philosophical, not a sociological problem.

The study of language as a medium of communication involves consideration of the relation of linguistic to other forms of communication and the determination of the nature and limits of such communication. In the pursuance of such questions subsidiary problems of far-reaching import arise. The fundamental notions of "expression" and "understanding" (*Das Verstehen*) must be examined and analysed—in short, the conditions of intelligibility and intelligible communication. It involves, finally, an examination of the entire problem of the

THE THEME OF A PHILOSOPHY OF LANGUAGE 43

relation of communication to knowledge; the relation of meaning to verification and verifiability, and the relation of these notions to communication.

C

Language and Logic

The third problem of a philosophy of language we may describe, following Mr. Russell, as the logical problem, or the relation of language to logic.

This problem has been an important one ever since logic itself came into being. As logic began with an analysis of language, so its development has involved a continuous analysis and critique of linguistic forms. The central character of this problem to-day arises out of the fact that the developments of modern logic have been in the direction of the detachment of logic from the linguistic matrix in which it formerly had its being. The logician has come to think of logical entities and relations as something wholly different from words and their grammatical relations. We have, therefore, the problem of language and logic stated in this way: What is the relation of the one set of facts—in the case of language the word or sentence—to another set of facts—in the case of logic, the terms or propositions? Or expressed normatively, what relations must the first have to the second in order to be capable of standing *significantly* for them—of being a valid surrogate for them?

This may not be, as we have suggested, the right formulation of the problem, but the problem, however formulated, raises the question of how far "logical analysis" of language may determine the meaning of terms and the sense of propositions as constitutive of discourse—in other words, how far logic is determinative of linguistic validity. The issue as here presented is, perhaps, the central one in present-day philosophy of language. For, as has already been made clear, on this issue turns, for many minds at least, the whole question of what shall and what shall not be included in meaningful or intelligible discourse.

D

Language and Knowledge

Finally, we have a problem which underlies all the others—a problem which I shall describe as the epistemological or metalogical problem of language.

As formulated by Mr. Russell, it is this: What is the relation subsisting between thoughts, words, and sentences, and that which they refer to and mean? This problem of *reference* belongs, he tells us, to epistemology. In similar fashion Carnap distinguishes this problem from the logical problem of language and describes it as metalogical. This problem of reference or of the relation of language to reality, I shall then, following Carnap, call the metalogical problem of language.

This is not the place to distinguish in detail between logical and metalogical problems of language; enough to emphasize the essential point of difference. It has been well expressed by Wittgenstein: Logic assumes that terms have meaning and that propositions have sense; it is not for logic to determine that meaning and that sense. Metalogical problems of language arise precisely at the point where we seek to determine this meaning and this sense. Meaning and sense are inseparable from reference to reality, and it is the nature of this reference which must here be investigated. The relation of sense datum or of idea to thing has always been the problem of epistemology, but if, as our historical orientation has shown, "knowledge is scarce separable from language," or if, in other words, language is involved in the intuitive process itself, the epistemological problem of language is the final problem of a philosophy of language.

E

A Synoptic View of these Problems: Problems of Intelligibility and of Truth

These four problems of the philosophy of language are recognized in one form or another by all who are engaged in the study of language, and they must be recognized and distin-

THE THEME OF A PHILOSOPHY OF LANGUAGE

guished if there is to be any intelligent discussion of language in the philosophic sense.

I have attempted to formulate them in such a way as not to beg the issues involved, the very questions which it is hoped our study will help to solve. In stating the problems of meaning and meaningful communication, I have avoided all assumption as to the nature of meaning, whether behaviouristic or causal, whether naturalistic or idealistic. In stating the problems of the relations of language to logic and cognition I have avoided, so far as possible, all assumptions as to the relations of words and sentences to terms and propositions, all assumptions as to whether there is or is not knowledge prior to language and description, and all theories, whether realistic or idealistic, as to the nature of knowledge. We have, so to speak, temporarily at least, put all these assumptions or prejudices "into brackets." Only so is any real solution of our problems possible.

The foregoing statement of the problems of the philosophy of language invites further comment at this point. In the first place, a more synoptic view of these problems shows that they may be naturally divided into two groups, namely, problems of intelligibility and problems of truth. The very formulation of the problems involved the use of both of these conceptions. What is it to use language so as to convey the meaningful rather than the unmeaning? What is it to use language so as to convey the true rather than the false? Problems of meaning or of intelligibility and problems of truth are closely related, but they must also be carefully distinguished. Meaningful, intelligible discourse *may* be one thing; discourse that conveys truth may be another.

Certain uses of language, it is often held, may convey meanings and yet have no reference to reality. The expressive language of poetry is often held to be of this type. Other uses of language, it is also sometimes held, express neither intelligible meanings nor contain references to reality. Such, on certain views of language, is the language of metaphysics, which is supposed to play with empty words which have no objects, and to attempt with these words to express meanings which in their very nature cannot be expressed. It is not our purpose to go into these problems here, but merely to indicate the relation between problems of intelligibility and problems of truth.

Enough has been said to make it clear that these problems which arise in the use of language cannot be solved without going into the philosophical question of the nature of meaning and truth and of their relations.

V

THE PHILOSOPHY OF LANGUAGE AND THE PROBLEM OF SYMBOLISM

A

The metalogical problem, as above defined, is concerned with the evaluation of language as a sign or symbol of reality. This aspect of the subject brings the study of language into close relations with the more general problem of the nature of symbols and of symbolism. The philosophy of language passes therefore inevitably into a philosophy of symbolism.

For any but the most primitive and naïve views of language the word is never identical with the thing, and the relation is therefore, in some sense and to some degree, symbolic. Whatever be our views of the origin and development of speech —questions which we shall consider in the next chapter—it may be accepted as certain that words and articulated speech have departed more and more from the "original source of their being." The movement of speech may indeed be described, in the formula of Cassirer, as a passage through three stages: the mimic or imitative, the analogical and the symbolic. How far this general account of the progress of language accords with the facts and conceptions of the development of language as understood by linguistic science is a problem for later consideration. It suffices for our present purpose to maintain that language, in its developed form at least, is a form of symbolism and that the philosophy of language becomes ultimately a philosophy of symbolism.

Language is, however, but one form of symbolism, and one of the problems which develops out of the philosophy of language is the relation of linguistic symbols to other forms of symbolism. Language, in the sense of articulate speech, is, we may assume, from the standpoint of practice and social communication the most important form of symbolism. But it is not necessarily the only one or, indeed, the most adequate.

THE THEME OF A PHILOSOPHY OF LANGUAGE

There are, so to speak, other "languages," the language of mathematics and the language of art. On one view of science, at least, mathematics is both a more accurate and a more ultimate symbolism than that of articulate speech. On some theories of art, forms and colours, tones and rhythms, may express the ultimate character of reality in a way that language cannot. In general it may be said that, on some views of language at least, it is both the inner tendency and the valid goal of experience and thought to burst through the "husk of language" to non-linguistic forms of representation and symbolization as more adequate means of expression. It is at this point that one of the most pressing, as it is one of the most fundamental, problems of the philosophy of languages arises—namely, the evaluation of language in its relation to other symbolic forms. The problem as it has arisen in science is the most striking, but in principle it is no more important than that of the relation of language to other symbolic forms, such as those of art and religion.

B

Symbolism in Science and Philosophy

We have seen how the problems of a philosophy of language pass over into the larger problems of a philosophy of symbolism. The same special conditions which have led to the revival of interest in the philosophical problems of language have led to a renewal of interest in problems of symbolism.

It is primarily because of far-reaching changes in the physical sciences that this has come about. The "copy" or model theory of physical concepts which dominated the physics of the earlier nineteenth century has, as is well known, gradually given place to a purely symbolic theory. From the time of Heinrich Hertz's *Principien der Mechanik*, in which this turning-point is most definitely marked, until the present moment, the symbol concept has continually grown in importance. This is the place neither to trace the stages of this development nor to investigate the notion itself—these are problems of a later chapter—but merely to register the fact of this change and of its far-reaching implications for philosophy.

The acknowledged symbolic character of our physical concepts inevitably raises the question of the evaluation, not only of the scientific symbol but of symbolic forms in general. It is for this reason, among others, that the problem of the symbol and of symbolic forms has become, as Cassirer says, the *Brennpunkt* of modern science and philosophy. So long as the copy theory of physical concepts prevailed, so long, in other words, as men were literalists and fundamentalists in science, the problem of symbolism and of symbolic knowledge was of but minor interest and might be left to the spheres of art and religion which, for the literalist, are not, strictly speaking, forms of knowledge. With the abandonment of this literalism in science, however, the entire problem of symbolic forms—of which science is but one—is again brought into the foreground of the theory of knowledge and of philosophy generally. A theory of the scientific symbol is an essential part of every philosophy of science, but it is also a necessary part of every general theory of knowledge.

Moreover, the influence of this change is felt in the sphere of metaphysics, and the problem of the meaning and possibility of metaphysics is being explored from new angles. Is, as Bergson holds, all science essentially symbolic while metaphysics is the science that claims to dispense with symbolism? Or is metaphysics itself a form of symbolism—that form of thought, indeed, which carries the symbolizing activities of the mind to their highest pitch? Here, again, the object is to indicate problems, not to solve them. Enough has been said to make it clear not only that the philosophy of language leads inevitably to a philosophy of symbolism, but that it is precisely the central place of symbolism in modern thought which has of necessity revived and deepened the philosophical study of language.

VI

THE FINAL PROBLEM OF A PHILOSOPHY OF LANGUAGE

A

Both the philosophy of language and the problem of symbolism, so closely related as we have seen, stand at the centre of modern culture. The reasons for this centrality should now be clear.

The two distinctively modern movements which have brought these problems into the foreground are the naturalistic conceptions of language and the symbolic theory of scientific concepts. These two developments have united to produce what I have described as neo-nominalism, and to generate problems which are distinctively characteristic of our epoch.

The centrality of the symbol-concept in modern science is undoubtedly the outstanding feature of the situation, but it is in language, after all, that the deepest roots of the modern problem are to be found. For language, in the sense of articulate speech, is that out of which non-linguistic symbols develop, and it is to this natural language that all conventional symbols, if they are to be understood and interpreted, must inevitably return. Language in the sense of speech may emerge from non-linguistic forms of expression and communication, to become a relatively autonomous form of activity. The spirit which embodies itself in this autonomous form may, in order better to achieve its ends, seek to burst through the husk of language. For the better realization and manipulation of its objects, and in the interests of a clearer notation, it may seek to substitute for language non-linguistic signs. But when we work with such substitute symbols we merely manipulate; we *say* nothing. In order to say anything about reality such symbols must again be translated into linguistic forms.

The fact remains, then, that mind or spirit is inseparable from language and linguistic form. To language it inevitably comes and to language, after all its alarms and excursions, it inevitably returns. Life, to be sure, is deeper than language, but that which is thus deeper is sense-less. I may have a sense of life, but life has no sense or meaning until it is expressed, and in the last analysis that expression must be verbal. Reality is in a sense, doubtless, beyond language, as Plato felt so deeply, and cannot be wholly grasped in its forms, but when in order to grasp reality we abandon linguistic forms, that reality, like quicksilver, runs through our fingers. In sum, language is the actuality of culture, as Hegel said. It is that alone in which both life and knowledge are actualized. In a very real sense science itself, in so far as it is defined as knowledge that is verifiable and communicable, is language well made. In an equally fundamental sense, the limits of my language are the limits of my world. All life comes back to the question of speech, the medium through which we communicate.

B

Language and Reality

It is here, then, that the real, the deepest problem of the philosophy of language is to be found. It is the critical problem of the relation of linguistic forms, and of symbolic forms in general, to the immediately given reality.

This problem arises from a fact which, however it may be interpreted, will be universally admitted. The richer and more energetically the human spirit builds its forms and symbols the more it appears to depart from the original sources of these forms and symbols. In so doing it seems also to depart from the original sources of its own being. More and more, it seems to find itself caught in the toils of its own creations. In language, in art, and in the intellectual symbols of science, it appears that, in Bergson's words, a veil has been woven between us and reality which only a *tour de force* of intellect can tear away. Now the fact itself—that reality as we know it is other than the hypothetical pure experience out of which our knowledge has developed, is an ideal construction in which language has been the chief creative force—is indeed beyond question. The only real problem is whether our creations have taken us to reality or away from it, whether they have become a veil to be torn away, or are, after all, when properly understood, the only road we have to reality.

The former view, in one form or another, is a common assumption of a large part of modern culture and philosophy. In the words of De Gaultier, "the existence of language, civilization, culture is at a price—an evil ideology."[1] This evil ideology is the theme of the new morality, the new logic, in fact of everything that is distinctively modernistic in both science and philosophy; and since language is the actuality of culture, it is precisely against language, which "takes the word for the thing," that this sceptical animus is chiefly directed.

[1] *La Fiction Universelle* and other works.

THE THEME OF A PHILOSOPHY OF LANGUAGE

In a sense this is the theme of Whitehead's *Process and Reality*, in so far at least as the problem of language is involved. Natural language, though valid to a certain extent for practice, has created a set of categories, an evil ideology, which distorts reality. The elimination of this ideology, and the redesigning of language to conform to reality conceived of as *events*, is the first condition of an adequate metaphysics. For the anti-metaphysical, on the other hand, it is this evil ideology which has made possible metaphysics *überhaupt*, and we have only to get rid of that to get rid of metaphysics.[1]

This is one possible answer to the question of the relation of language to reality. Language is *not* "moulded on reality," to use Bergson's terms. It is either a veil that has been woven by practice between us and reality, and which must be torn away, or else it is a distortion of reality which must be corrected by the invention of other instruments and symbolisms.

Suppose this entire assumption of a reality known independently of language, of a hypothetical pure experience, were itself an illusion; suppose reality, as we know it, is to an incalculable degree an ideal construction in which language itself is the chief organ of that construction. Then the problem would be wholly different and its solution must inevitably take another direction. The notion of a language moulded on reality would itself be a fatal metaphor and the so-called ideology of language, far from being necessarily an evil, would be the very source and stimulus of a critical dialectic by which alone experience could be interpreted and evaluated. In that case the solution of the problem of the relation of language to reality would consist, not in tearing away the veil of language, but in completing and perfecting the principles of expression and

---

[1] This theme of the evil ideology of language has even become grotesque in messianic hands. Count Alfred Korzybski, in his latest panacea, semantics (as developed in *Science and Sanity*, 1934), has apparently found not only the source of all evils in natural language and the subject-predicate logic, but also a cure for these evils, individual and social, in a true semantics based upon science. Wrong identification of words with things may, because of false evaluations, ruin human life, science or the entire social system. True identifications will cure insanity, create right social relationships, and eliminate from science the evil ideology which, in this case, is the survival of Aristotelianism. It would not be just to make too much of these extreme developments, but it is only fair to say that it is in principle the same theme which, in a more moderate form, underlies a large part of recent philosophic thought.

symbolism. It would proceed upon the assumption that the more richly and energetically the human spirit builds its language and symbolism, the nearer it comes, if not to the original source of its being, at least to its ultimate meaning and reality.[1]

These, then, are the two possible ways of solving this final problem of the philosophy of language. Which of the two is the valid solution it is one of the objects of this whole study to determine. In any case the statement of the problem serves but to emphasize from another angle the thesis of this entire chapter, namely, the central place of the problem of language in philosophy as a whole.

C

Plato on Language

Language, we ventured to maintain, is the last and deepest problem of the philosophic mind. It is to be hoped that this statement may now not seem so extravagant as it doubtless at first appeared. Plato's wrestling with the problem of language might well be taken as a gloss upon our theme.

The *Cratylus* has a sits main theme the problem of linguistic validity, or the relation of language to reality. Its real purpose was not the origin of language, but its nature and function, although, as Plato saw, the question of validity could not be wholly divorced from the question of origin. In this remarkable dialogue, in which most of the fundamental problems of language are already found in germ, "we see," as Jowett says, "grammar and logic moving somewhere in the human soul."

The basal problem is that of the *rightness of names*. Does knowledge of names give knowledge of things? Cratylus is inclined to think so. The way to the discovery of things is through the discovery of the meaning of names. Hermogenes doubts any natural rightness of names, any primary reference of name to thing. He wants to know wherein consists this natural rightness. Socrates admits that he cannot show it exactly, but he insists upon the fact. In our derivations we cannot go back indefinitely; somewhere we must come upon self-authenticating

---

[1] For a statement of this point of view, see Ernst Cassirer, *Die Philosophie der Symbolischen Formen*, Vol. I, Chapter I.

THE THEME OF A PHILOSOPHY OF LANGUAGE 53

words. All words are intended to show the nature of things, and the secondary derive their significance from the primary. Into the detail of the argument of the *Cratylus* we need not enter—either into the form of the copy theory which seems to be here proposed or into the fanciful etymology, which Plato himself recognizes as being very crude, an etymology in which he seeks to find the relations of names to things by the analytical way of breaking words up into letters or the primary elements of which they are composed. Enough for our purpose that in this dialogue Plato not only insists upon the basal character of the problem of language for knowledge and philosophy, but likewise upon the existence of some *intimate and primordial relation between the word and the thing*, as the necessary condition of there being any knowledge whatsoever. One may recognize fully the experimental and even playful nature of much of the thought of this dialogue and yet sense the seriousness that runs through it. If the view put into the mouth of Socrates may be taken as indicative of Plato's position, it is clear enough what that position is. "Confidence in names should not go so far as to lead us to develop a metaphysic from them, but on the other hand it would be equally fatal to deny a fundamental relation of language to reality."[1]

Thus the Plato of the *Cratylus*. The Plato of the *Seventh Epistle* is a different matter. Through what disillusioning experiences he must have passed to justify the almost peevish expressions of this letter![2] The statement that "no intelligent man will ever be so bold as to put in language those things which his reason has contemplated," and that "if he should be betrayed into so doing then surely not the gods but mortals have utterly blasted his wits," cannot but surprise us in one for whom discourse was the very actuality of reason and for whom the one way of attaining to truth was through communication from mind to mind. But let us see what lies behind these astonishing statements.

In this letter the attempt is made for the first time in the history of thought to determine the knowledge value of language in a purely methodological fashion. It is therefore of

---

[1] See A. E. Taylor on this dialogue: *Plato: The Man and His Works*, pp. 75 ff.
[2] On the genuineness of this epistle, see A. E. Taylor, *op. cit*, p. 15 f. and Wilamowitz, *Plato*, I, 641 ff., II, 282 ff.

outstanding interest to us and may, in a certain sense, set the problem for the ensuing studies. Language is indeed recognized as the first step in knowledge, but it is only the first step. For everything that exists, we are told, there are three classes of objects through which knowledge about it must come: the knowledge itself is a fourth, and we must put as a fifth entity the actual object of knowledge which is the true reality. There is something, for instance, called a circle, the name is the very word I have uttered. In the second place, there is a description of it which is composed of nouns and verbal expressions. . . . In the third place, there is the class of objects which are drawn and erased and turned on the lathe and destroyed, processes which do not affect the real circle to which these other circles are all related, because it is different from them. In the fourth place, there are knowledge and understanding and correct opinion concerning them; all of which we must set down as one thing more, that is found not in souls, nor in shapes of bodies, but in minds; whereby it differs evidently in its nature from the real circle and from the afore-mentioned three. Of all these understanding approaches nearest in affinity and likeness to the fifth entity, while the others are more remote from it.

Language is represented as the *first* step in knowledge, but only the first step and, so to speak, at fourth remove from reality. Language is, as such, representation—presentation of meaning by means of a sensuous sign. So long as philosophical thought remains in this sphere of "existence" which is language, it cannot reach true being. Language and the word strive towards the expression of pure being, but they never reach it because there is always mixed with the reference to the pure being a reference to another "accidental" character of the object, therefore that which makes language incapable of representing the highest, the content of purely philosophical knowledge.

We understand now why, according to Plato, no intelligent man will put in language those things which his reason has contemplated. Plato should then have kept silent regarding this true knowledge, for even if it is attainable to him, it is incommunicable. But not only was Plato not silent, but he felt compelled to communicate the points of difference between the word and the object. Such communication was possible only through language, and, if the communication is veridical, language itself must be capable of expressing something of true being. Evidently there is something radically wrong here. It is evidently impossible to escape the principle of the inseparability of language and knowledge, of intuition and expression, which as we have seen is assumed in different ways by empiricism and rationalism alike. It is with language that knowledge begins and to it it must inevitably return, if the notion of knowledge or science includes in it any conception of the verifiable and communicable.

There is apparently one way of escaping from this conclusion, that of mysticism, as developed in Neoplatonism and expressed in modern form by Bergson. Language, by reason of its lowly origin and nature, is incapable of apprehending and expressing reality. But language may be used in another way, not to *represent*, but to bring the hearer to a point where he himself may transcend language and pass to incommunicable insight. It is a dialectical ladder which, when we have ascended, may be kicked away. This view of the function of language, so beautifully developed in Bergson's *Introduction to Metaphysics* is, I take it, in principle the same as that of Plato. But the whole question is whether this insight and intuition, if wholly incommunicable, is *knowledge*. It is certainly unverifiable. It is true that there are other symbols than those of language, namely, the symbols of art and of mathematics, by means of which meaning may be communicated. But those symbols themselves require interpretation, and interpretation is only possible in terms of language. This, then, is only an apparent escape from the principle of the inseparability of language and knowledge. The Plato of the Seventh Letter should have been silent—even about the nature of language.

Thus Plato wrestled with the problem of language, and it is clear that, with all his wrestling, he failed to solve it. As all the fundamental problems of the philosophy of language are already in germ in his treatment of the question, so also the two possible ways of solving the problem of the relation of language to reality are already struggling for mastery in his mind. For him also language appears to be a way to reality. Some intimate and primordial relation between the word and the thing seems to be the necessary condition of there being any knowledge. But language also seems to him to be a veil woven between us and reality which must be torn away if we are to see reality face to face. Plato failed to resolve this contradiction. Perhaps it cannot be resolved. In any case it is this contradiction that makes language the last and deepest problem of the philosophic mind, the problem upon the solution of which, in the last analysis, all our philosophies turn.

CHAPTER II

WHAT IS LANGUAGE? ORIGIN AND DEVELOPMENT THE SCIENCE OF LANGUAGE

I

A

In Anatole France's *Revolt of the Angels* there is much argument on high matters. Arcade, "having at great length set up his scientific idealism in opposition to Zita's pragmatism, the beautiful archangel told him that he argued badly. 'And you are surprised at that!' exclaimed young Maurice's guardian angel. 'I argue, like you, in the language of human beings. And what is human language but the cry of the beasts of the forest or the mountains, complicated and corrupted by arrogant anthropoids. How then, Zita, can one be expected to argue well with a collection of angry and plaintive sounds like that? Angels do not reason at all; men being superior to the angels reason imperfectly. I will not mention the professors who think to define the absolute with the aid of cries which they have inherited from the pithecanthropoid monkeys, marsupials, and reptiles, their ancestors! It is a colossal joke! How it would amuse the demiurge if he had any brains!'"

In this well-known passage we have in peculiarly vivid form a characteristic philosophy of language of our time—namely, the determination of the nature, function, and limits of language in terms of its supposed origin. "Colloquial language," we are told, "is part of the human organism and is not less complicated than it. From it it is impossible humanly to gather immediately the logic of language."[1] Again, "language was invented to serve the uses of the familiar world: it may not readily be invoked to convey the meanings appropriate to another."[2] Even more important for our purposes are certain statements of Whitehead on this point. The basal thesis of *Process and Reality*, in so far as it concerns language, is also that language was invented to serve the uses of the familiar world, and that this "literary

---

[1] L. Wittgenstein, *Tractatus Logico-Philosophicus*, p. 63.
[2] C. E. M. Joad, *Philosophical Aspects of Modern Science*, p. 307 (Published by George Allen & Unwin Ltd.).

language breaks down completely in the task of expressing in explicit form the larger generalities." More specifically, certain notions, above all the notion of substance, have entrenched themselves in language. Useful as they are for many purposes of life, whenever we attempt to use them as a fundamental statement of the nature of things, they prove themselves mistaken. Pragmatically natural language is defensible; in metaphysics it represents sheer error.[1]

B

Quaestiones Facti and Quaestiones Juris

Such statements as these—about the nature, origin, and purpose of language—constitute the premises upon which philosophical evaluations of language proceed. We know, it is argued, what language is, that it is the sounds of the forest and the mountains, "a series of squeaks and grunts," or what not; therefore we know what it can and what it cannot do. We know how it began and "what it was made for"; therefore we know that it is incapable of doing certain things—of expressing certain meanings, of "defining the absolute." These things we say we know. They are questions of fact. If so, the only source of such knowledge, of such facts, is the science of linguistics. It is accordingly incumbent upon us to find out just what linguistic science has to say on these questions, to determine, in a summary fashion at least, the prevailing notions on these and allied questions. The philosophy of language cannot proceed without this reference to the science of language.

It is obviously neither possible nor desirable to try to cover the range of linguistic science in a single chapter. We shall therefore deliberately confine ourselves to certain problems upon which fundamental philosophical issues turn—to those points in linguistic science to which appeal is made as a factual basis for the philosophical evaluation and critique of language. There are, I think, three such main points: (*a*) The question of what language is; including the question of the fundamental speech functions; (*b*) the question of the origin and development of language, including such problems as that of the *Ursprache* and that of levels of speech development; (*c*) the

[1] *Process and Reality*, pp. 16, 122.

problem of the parts of speech, or the grammatical elements of language, including the question whether these forms or elements represent in any sense "a necessary intuitive analysis of reality, or merely our ability to compose that reality into a variety of formal patterns."

Our concern is, then, with the views of present-day linguistic science on these basal questions in so far as they can be ascertained. Current philosophical evaluations of language are uniformly based upon certain assumptions regarding these three points. Our problem is to determine, if possible, to what extent these assumptions are justified by linguistics. Before proceeding to these specific questions it will be well, however, to preface our discussions by some comment upon the general situation in present-day linguistic study.

II

THE GENERAL SITUATION IN LINGUISTIC SCIENCE

A

Problems of language are, we have seen, as old as human thought; the problem of the "word" is as old as the problem of the "thing," but the scientific study of language, in the modern sense, is largely a product of the nineteenth century. The step from Humboldt and Hegel to Darwin, as Cassirer describes it, which gave birth to linguistic science in this sense, was the step from *Geist* to *Natur*, the same step which was taken in all the humanistic sciences.

The underlying assumption of the new science of language was that language is a part of nature and must therefore be studied by the methods of the natural sciences. This general assumption included also certain further assumptions, namely, that, as part of nature, it must have not only a purely human, as opposed to divine, origin, but also a natural in the sense of animal or sub-human origin; secondly, that as all other parts of nature, it must be conceived as evolving through external forces, from the simple to the complex, and that changes in speech forms must be conceived as following laws analogous to the laws of other natural objects.

It was only natural that in the pursuit of this programme

the first approach to language should be through its physical and physiological basis. Whatever else speech is, it is a collection of sounds and sounds as such can be studied only physically and physiologically. Phonetics, or the study of the origin and changes of the sounds of the human voice employed in communication, proceeded on the assumption that here also natural laws of a mechanical character analogous to those of physical nature could be formulated. This was the first stage in the scientific study of language. That interesting and useful facts have been ascertained on this assumption no linguist would deny, but that it leads us far into the understanding of language is doubtful. It is, perhaps, an exaggeration to say with Vossler that "the belief that phonetic and analogical mutations are due to the operation of natural law" is exploded and that all purely mechanical explanations are discredited, but it is beyond question that in the general methods of linguistic science, such conceptions have fallen into the background and this phase of linguistic study has in a significant degree been passed.

Similarly the step from Hegel to Darwin brought with it Darwinian conceptions and analogies, so powerful in all the humanistic sciences of the nineteenth century. S. Schleicher maintained that the theory of evolution which Darwin had developed for the species of plants and animals must be no less applicable to the organisms which we call languages. On these assumptions concepts of origin and evolution by a kind of natural selection were introduced analogous to these notions in biology. Here again it would probably be an exaggeration to say that such notions are wholly abandoned, that "naturalism no longer really fools us in the guise of biology," but most linguists would probably agree with Ch. Bally[1] that all such extensions of Darwinian doctrine were mistaken, and although they almost succeeded for a time in directing linguistics along a wrong track, that danger is in general past.

That which in the first instance brought linguistics back from its false methods was the increased emphasis upon semantics, more particularly the study of meaning from the psychological point of view. For the psychologist the meaning of words is but a special case of meaning in general, and the way to

[1] C. Bally, *La Langue et La Vie*, Paris, 1913, p. 14.

WHAT IS LANGUAGE?

the understanding of linguistic meaning and its mutations is through the study of psychological facts and laws.[1] Add to this the field of social psychology (the *Völkerpsychologie* of Wundt, for instance), the study of language as "social fact," and the picture of linguistics at this stage of its development is complete.[2]

The psychological stage in the development of linguistics was of great importance. Even in the matter of phonetic laws (*Lautgesetze*) physiological causes tended to be displaced by psychological. Whether the psychology was that of Wundt or that of Herbart, as employed by H. Paul, the important point is that the key to language is found in mind and not in things. Significant as this change was, the limitations of the psychological point of view became evident. The revolt against *Psychologism* in the cultural sciences in general appeared in linguistics also. For one thing, language still remained a part of nature, for mind as conceived by psychology was still conceived more or less mechanically. But more important still is the notion of meaning. For meaning, while a psychological notion, is variously conceived by the different psychologies. For *Gestalt* psychology meaning is, so to speak, the primary fact, while for Behaviourism it is wholly secondary and in extreme cases extruded from psychology. But more than this. Meaning while a psychological notion is more than psychological. So soon as this truth is recognized the psychological standpoint is transcended.

---

[1] Pillsbury, *The Psychology of Language*, pp. 7, 14.

[2] The study of the languages of primitive peoples, such as that of Malinowski, may serve to give us not only quite different ideas as to what is necessary to language but quite different notions of its functions. The older purely intellectual notion of language, of its primary function as expression of ideas, gives way to the idea that it is indeed for communication, but not primarily for the communication of ideas. Again, such studies as those of Lévy-Bruhl in his *Fonctions mentales dans les sociétés inférieures* may make it clear that the "indication" of a person or an object, which to us seems the only function of a name, is in the eyes of the primitive something secondary. For him the meaning of the name does not lie in this. It expresses rather the relation of the individual to his totem group, with the forefathers whose reincarnation the individual totem is, with the individual totem or guardian angel who has revealed himself in dreams, with the unseen powers which protect the secret societies into which he enters. The name did not therefore originally express the individuality of a single being, but creates and at the same time indicates the community with other beings.

B

The Autonomy of Linguistics: The New Speech Notion

In his summary picture of the present situation in linguistic studies, G. Ipsen describes their development as having passed through three stages, the physical or physiological, the psychological and the phenomenological. And with this has come what he calls the "new speech notion" and the postulate of the autonomy of linguistic science.[1] Now I should not wish to say that the term phenomenological represents the standpoint and assumptions of the whole of present-day linguistic study—certainly not the term as used in a narrow technical sense—but that which Ipsen has in mind in the use of the term is certainly beyond dispute. The idea that language is an *Urphenomen*, neither reducible to nor explainable in terms of non-linguistic fact, seems to be a common assumption of linguistic study. In other words, language is a unique phenomenon and the phenomenological standpoint consists in studying it, in the words of Ammann, in its *absoluten Besonderheit*.[2] We shall have more to say in detail of the phenomenological standpoint in a later context. Here we are concerned only with one phase of the question, namely, the significance of this stage for linguistic science. This may be expressed as the principle of the autonomy of linguistics. This principle denies that language can be reduced to or explained in terms of non-linguistic fact, and that the science which deals with this fact can be made a part of the natural sciences—of physiology, psychology, or even sociology in terms of which it was earlier defined. This notion of the autonomy of linguistics is, to be sure, but a phase of that larger movement which has been called the decentralization of the sciences, and which is closely connected with the general doctrine of emergent irreducible levels of qualitatively different fact. In any case, this new speech notion, with its doctrine of autonomy, has fixed itself more and more in linguistic science and is part of the revision of the assumptions of linguistic science of which we shall presently speak.

---

[1] Gunther Ipsen, *Sprachphilosophie der Gegenwart*, 1930. An excellent account of the development of linguistic science and of the philosophical problems involved.

[2] H. Ammann, *Die Menschliche Rede*, Vol. I, pp. 10 ff.

WHAT IS LANGUAGE?

The key to the passage of linguistic study through these three stages and to the development of the present "speech notion" is to be found in the problem of meaning. It is the recognition of the fact that the essence of language is found in meaning and of the unique and irreducible character of meaning which constitutes the phenomenological standpoint.

This principle of the *Primat des Sinnes*, as Cassirer calls it, may be stated in this way. The sole entrance into the understanding of language is through meaning, for meaning is the *sine qua non* of linguistic fact. Language for modern linguistics is not the sound, nor again the motor and tactual sensations which make up the word—not even the associations called up by the sound or the motor processes; it is the meaning itself which, while conditioned by these, is not identical with any or all of them. The nature of this meaning is the problem of the next chapter; here we shall consider merely the significance of this principle of primacy for linguistic study.

This significance is far reaching. It means negatively, as we have seen, the denial of the adequacy of physical, physiological, or even psychological, approaches to language. But it involves also significant changes in methodology. Earlier methods proceeded from the elements to the whole—from the sounds to the words, from words to sentences, and finally to the meaning of discourse as a whole. The present tendency is the exact opposite—namely, from meaning as *Gestalt* to the sentences and words as elements. The spirit which lives in human discourse works as a totality constituting the sentence or proposition, the copula, the word and the sound.[1]

C

The Return from Nature to Mind: Revision of Assumptions

If, then, we attempt to envisage this movement within linguistics as a whole, it seems clear that, as Cassirer has said, methodologically understood, it has been a movement in a circle. So far as the assumptions underlying its procedure are concerned, a revision has taken place to such an extent that it is again approaching the standpoint from which it started. As it took

[1] *Die Philosophie der Symbolischen Formen*, Vol. I, pp. 110 ff.

the step from mind to nature, so now in a very real sense it is turning again from nature to mind.

Linguistic science, it was held, should be based upon natural science in order that it may attain the same certainty and the same exact character, with the same universal laws. But gradually these notions of physical and physiological, of biological and psychological "laws" showed themselves mistaken and untenable. The entire conception of nature and natural law upon which it was sought to build turned out to be merely a fictitious unity, including very disparate elements. Thus, as the naturalistic and positivistic scheme which constituted the programme of the science tended gradually to break up, there has also been a tendency towards a gradual return to the traditional notion of language. An outstanding representative of this tendency is Karl Vossler, who in his *Positivismus und Idealismus in der Sprachwissenschaft* (1904) and *Sprache als Schöpfung und Entwickelung* makes clear both the grounds and the stages of this return.

It is not our desire to over-emphasize the importance of this revision of assumptions or to exaggerate the extent of this change of view among linguists. The positivists are doubtless still many. For the purposes of our discussion it is enough that the opposition exists. For it challenges the dogmatic assumptions upon which so much of the philosophy of language has been reared.

III

WHAT IS LANGUAGE? THE MEANING FUNCTIONS OF LANGUAGE

A

With this general picture of linguistic science, we may turn to the more specific problems concerning which the philosopher must go to linguistic science for an answer. The first of these is, what is language? What, then, is this thing language about which philosophers and scientists make statements upon which so much hinges? This question is presented with certain grave difficulties at the outset. Is there any such thing as language as such? Are there not after all merely languages and not language? Is not language after all merely an abstraction made by the grammarians? It is often said that it is a paradox of

WHAT IS LANGUAGE?

linguistic science that it has come to doubt the existence of its own object. Now language, in the sense of a universal language, is doubtless an abstraction of the grammarians. Purely empirically there are only languages and not language. Nevertheless it is about language and not languages that the logician and philosopher talk. All their statements as to what language is and what it does are about language as such, not about the language of Hottentot or philosopher, of Greek or Chinese. There must be *some speech-notion*; otherwise we can make no statements about what language is or does. Has linguistic science anything to say about what language as such is? If so, it is important to know just what it says.

B

The Nature of Linguistic Fact: the Primacy of Meaning

Every field of study or science is concerned with a certain type of facts. What, then, are linguistic facts? By language in the widest sense is often understood any means of communication between living beings. It includes all expressive movements and all secretions.[1] Under the term language is often included non-linguistic means of communication such as the "language" of art, mathematics, and various forms of symbolism. These broader uses of language are justified in certain contexts. Speech as a form of "behaviour" cannot be isolated from other forms of behaviour with which it is closely connected genetically and functionally. Again, it is the character of communication and representation to break through the husk of speech and to develop other forms of symbolism. The functions of language in the narrower sense cannot be understood without reference to these non-linguistic "languages." On the other hand, a definition of language that is extended to cover all forms of communication and types of reference, becomes, as Sapir tells us, utterly meaningless, and linguistic science must start at least with speech, with expression through articulate sounds.[2] This, then, is the first element in the speech-notion as understood by linguistic science. This it is that constitutes "linguistic fact." What, then, is the nature of that fact?

[1] Pillsbury, *op. cit.*, p. 7.   [2] Edward Sapir, *Language*, p. 3.

We may best determine this notion by considering what language is not, by a process of elimination. First of all, language as *linguistic fact* is not the sound. The word "house" is not a linguistic fact if we understand by word merely the effect of the vowels and consonants that compose it. These latter may be studied by phonetics, and changes in the vowels and consonants may throw light on certain aspects of the development of language, but by themselves they do not constitute language. Nor is language the motor processes and tactual sensations that make up the articulation of the word. These, too, are important from the standpoint of the physiological and psychological studies of language, and in some extreme theories identical with linguistic fact; but while speech, as meaning, is closely related both to muscular reaction and tactile sensation, it is not identifiable with them.

On the question as to what linguistic fact is not, linguists are in general agreed. They are also agreed upon what it is that constitutes positively linguistic fact. The *sine qua non* of language is precisely the *meaning* of which the sounds, the motor processes and tactual sensations, are the *bearers*. This is the principle of the primacy of meaning of which we have already spoken. What, then, is the nature of this meaning? The answer to this question is of course possible only on the basis of the analysis of the following chapter and we shall not anticipate the results of that analysis here. Two points are, however, of importance in the present context. In order that we may understand what is involved in this new speech-notion these must be brought out clearly.

The first of these concerns the *differentia* of linguistic meaning, that which for ever differentiates the meaning of "words" from the meaning of "things." The essence of language is the representation, *Darstellung*, of one element of experience through another—the *bi-polar relation* between the sign or symbol and the thing signified or symbolized, and the consciousness of that *relation*.[1] Until this element of *Darstellung*, of predication in some form however potential arises, language and linguistic meaning cannot be said to exist. The significance of this con-

---

[1] The two most important influences in the development of this speech-notion are said to be F. de Saussure, *Cours de linguistique générale*, edited by Ch. Bally (1916, 1922), and E. Husserl, *Logische Untersuchungen*, second edition, 1913.

WHAT IS LANGUAGE?

cept of linguistic meaning will be brought out more definitely in the next section on the meaning functions of language and in our discussions of the origins of language. Here we wish merely to emphasize the fact that it is a necessary part of the present speech-notion.[1]

The second element of importance in the new speech-notion is that language and linguistic meaning exist only in the speech community. In other words, part of the notion of meaning in the linguistic sense is communication and communicability. In this connection linguists frequently distinguish between speech and language. This is the basal theme of A. H. Gardiner's book entitled *The Theory of Speech and Language*. The distinction is of such importance for the philosophy of language that it will be well to consider it briefly.

On this view, speech is the primary notion and language the derivative, the product of speech. Language is, then, the *petrifact* of living creative speech. This distinction, with its emphasis on the primacy of the speech-notion, has important consequences for both linguistics and the philosophy of language. It affects the methodology of the study of language, turning our attention to the wholes of meaning within living speech, rather than to the merely analytical study of the elements of a petrifact.[2] On this view the problem of the necessary parts of speech becomes, as we shall see, significantly different from that of the grammatical forms of languages. It throws doubt, as we shall also see, upon that artificial standpoint in logic which would relate words as things or entities with terms in propositions, also conceived as entities. All these consequences are of importance. Here, however, I wish to emphasize only one thing. Language, when viewed as speech, has reality only in a speech community. When abstracted from that it loses its reality. Meaning, we have seen, is the *sine qua non* of linguistic fact, and this meaning includes as part of its nature communicability. Meaning does not first exist and is then communicated; it exists only in communication. Intuition and expression are one.

---

[1] On this general point consult E. Cassirer, *op. cit.*, Vol. I, pp. 126 ff.; Vol. III, pp. 126 ff.; and G. de Laguna, *op. cit.*, p. 75 ff.
[2] *Op. cit.*, Chapters II and III.

C

The Meaning Functions of Language

To the question, What is language? modern linguistics answers uniformly in terms of meaning. Language in the sense in which the notion is used in present-day linguistics has as its central and determining concept that of meaning. It is *not* the sounds of the forests or mountains, however complicated they may be, but those sounds as the bearer of non-sensuous meaning. Moreover—and this is an equally important part of the notion—this meaning is a function of communication. The question now arises, what does this notion of meaning include? What are the meaning functions of language?

We have already seen that one meaning function, namely, that of representation, *Darstellung*, predication, is in general conceived to be part of the nature of language as such. To this is generally added two other functions which we may describe as the indicative and the emotive or evocative. Speaking generally, it may be said, I think, that present-day linguistics recognizes these three primary meaning functions of language, three types of meaning which are present in some form wherever there is linguistic fact, and which are irreducible one to the other. Different terms are often used for these three functions, but the notions underlying the terms are the same.

The significance of the question here raised is found in the fact that it is part of the question, what language is: the answer to it is in terms of what language does. But it has a further significance in the fact that in many quarters there is opposed to this conception one which we may describe as a theory of dual functions. In many philosophies of language it is assumed, either explicitly or implicitly, that language has but two functions, namely, the indicative and the evocative or emotive—any primary representative function, either intuitive or symbolic, being denied. An important element in this theory is the view that these "uses of language" are independent of each other in the sense that some uses of language are wholly indicative and some wholly emotive and evocative. On these assumptions, as to fact, certain normative conclusions, as to what language ought to be, are based and

WHAT IS LANGUAGE?

a critique of language is undertaken which involves vital issues for philosophy. The entire philosophy of language of Ogden and Richards is based upon these premises, and it is also a cardinal assumption of the so-called Vienna School being explicitly asserted by Carnap.[1]

This is not the place to go into all the issues raised by this dual theory, nor indeed to attempt to refute it as an element or assumption of a philosophy of language. The question will be considered more fully in the chapter on the Phenomenology of Linguistic Meaning and in other contexts. Here we wish merely to maintain that it finds no justification in linguistics —that from the point of view of linguistics a use of language which was purely indicative would be no language at all. Still less would a purely emotive. The *sine qua non* of language, according to the present speech-notion, is the presence of all three functions.

From the point of view of linguistics the question has both a phenomenological and a genetic aspect. The first aspect has to do with what is intrinsic to the speech-notion itself. Few would deny that developed language fulfils all these functions, and that these three functions are the *sine qua non* of linguistic fact. Ejaculatory words express feelings, emotions, inner states; names indicate objects and many words are distinctively representative in character—not only indicative but stand more or less adequately for objects. The modern "speech-notion" insists, however, that only when these three functions are present do we have language. In other words, there is no emotive expression without indication and representation in some degree; no indication without the other functions, and, similarly, no representation without expression and indication.

The genetic problem is, of course, of quite a different order. From the beginning one of the problems of linguistics has been the attempt to derive developed language, with all its meaning

---

[1] The origin of this theory seems to be in certain distinctions made by Hughlings Jackson in his studies in abnormal psychology (*Brain*, XXXVIII, p. 113), more especially of disturbances of speech functions. In these studies he distinguished between "emotional" and "propositional" language, between "inferior" and "superior" speech functions. Now, whatever value such a dual distinction may have for the purposes for which he made it, it serves merely to distort the picture when applied to linguistics and the philosophy of language. On this whole question, see E. Cassirer, *op. cit.*, Vol. III, pp. 246 ff.

functions, from one primary function. The interjectional, onomatopoeic, and other theories represent this attempt. Of these theories and their failure we shall speak briefly presently. As a result of their inadequacy, however, recent views stress the presence of all three functions on the lowest levels of linguistic development. Thus Professor de Laguna attempts to derive articulate speech from animal cries and stresses the presence of all three functions (implicitly) in these cries. Her thesis is that in the animal cry of the proclamation type all three functions are present. The cry proclaims the presence of the object and is thus indicative; it expresses an emotional attitude, as in the warning cry; and, finally, it has at least the *potentiality* of predication, in that it proclaims or "says" something about the object which it indicates. On this genetic aspect of the question we shall have more to say presently when we come to problems of origin. Professor de Laguna's theory at least serves to emphasize the general view of linguistics that all three functions are intrinsic to the speech-notion as such.[1]

D

Definitions of Language: the New Speech-Notion

The discussions of the present section are all subsidiary to the basal question, What is language? When one asks what anything—any subject of discourse—is, it is customary to answer with definitions. It is, however, precisely such things as religion, science, language, etc., which are hardest to define because of the plurality of contexts in which such terms are used. The chief difficulty, however, lies in the fact that if our definition is to be framed so as to cover all forms of the cultural phenomenon in question, it will take one form; if, however, it is to be so framed as to characterize intensively the developed forms of religion, science, or language, as the case may be, it will inevitably take another form. This it need hardly be said is peculiarly true in the case of language. We have no desire by definition to beg the very questions which the further discussions of this chapter necessarily raise, but merely by a tentative definition to indicate the general standpoint from which language is now viewed.

[1] *Speech: Its Function and Development.*

A definition given by Sapir represents in part at least this present standpoint. "Language is a purely human and non-instinctive method of communicating ideas, emotions, desires by means of a system of voluntarily produced symbols."[1] This definition is even more significant for what it denies than for what it affirms. It denies by implication the entire reductive point of view of the naturalistic approach and in so far expresses the tendency towards autonomy in linguistics. Positively it stresses the voluntary creative character of symbol formation in language and to that extent also expresses the present tendencies in linguistics.

This definition has been criticized by Professor de Laguna as belonging to the older intellectualistic tradition which defined language as a medium for expressing and communicating ideas and which therefore assumed a dualism between ideas and words, between content and medium. Such a conception, she holds, is wholly inadequate for a successful psychological study of speech and proposes a purely behavioural and objective conception.[2] The issue here is not what is language for the *psychologist*, but for the linguist. And from his point of view *expression* and communication are the *sine qua non* of language. The traditional conceptions may have over emphasized the idea side of language and made too sharp a dualism between content and medium, but the essence of that conception is still fundamental in the present speech-notion. Language, according to Humboldt's famous definition, is "the ever-repeated labour of the mind to utilize articulated sounds to express thoughts." That definition, properly interpreted, is as much a characterization of the new speech-notion as of the old.

IV

THE ORIGIN OF LANGUAGE

A

From the beginning reflection upon languages has been preoccupied with origins. In the *Cratylus* Plato was primarily concerned with questions of linguistic validity, but he could not separate them from questions of origin. In the latter part

[1] *Op. cit.*, p. 4. [2] *Op. cit.*, pp. 9 ff.

of the eighteenth century when language first became an object of special study and not merely an appendix to philosophical inquiry, a common title for such works was the origin and nature of language. In such classical works as Lord Monboddo's on *The Origin and Progress of Language* and Herder's *Abhandlung über den Ursprung der Sprache*, the two problems were never separated. Nor are they in fact separated to-day. As the quotations at the beginning of this chapter indicated, the questions of the nature, function, and limits of language are still answered in terms of their supposed origin.

Our present concern with questions of origin is limited wholly to their bearing upon philosophical issues—that is, solely to origins in so far as they are appealed to as a basis for evaluations. From this point of view it is important to recognize that the problem of origins has had very different meanings. Of these we may distinguish three, namely: (*a*) the problem of ultimate or metaphysical origin; (*b*) the problem of the *Ursprache*, or the original functions of human speech, and (*c*) the origin of articulate speech from non-linguistic expression.[1]

B

Meanings of the Concept of Origin

To the "pre-scientific speculators" on the subject of language the metaphysical problem was uppermost. Language seemed to them a structure of such marvellous perfection that it could not be conceived as the work of man, but must be God-given, of more than human origin. This notion passed, largely through the work of Humboldt, into a conception of origin which, while still metaphysical, displaced the notion of the Divine mind by that of over-individual mind or *Geist*. Language seemed to him to "spring out of the depth of humanity in such fashion that it forbids being conceived as the mere product or creation of peoples. It involves an independence or self-sufficiency, obvious although not explainable ultimately, and is, when viewed from this aspect, not a creation of our activity but

---

[1] Closely connected with the problem of origin is that of the development or "progress" of language. In so far as this notion is significant for the philosophy of language, it is treated in Appendix I.

an involuntary emanation of the spirit (*Geist*), not the work of nations but a gift of inmost fate or destiny."

With this metaphysical concept of origin is closely connected the question of the *Ursprache* or the character of original language. With the emphasis upon *Geist* and creativity, it was only natural that the original form of language should have been conceived as poetic and the emphasis put on the relations of myth and language. This notion was developed especially by Herder in his *Abhandlung*. On the basis of a cultural philosophy and a critique of modern science with its intellectualistic tendencies, he developed a conception of the *Ursprache* which had great influence in his own day and survives in the conceptions of language of Croce and Vossler to-day.

With the triumph of "scientific" conceptions of origin both of these problems receded into the background, and with the notion of evolution from simple to complex the problem for linguistics became that of the origin of the simple elements out of which the articulate complicated speech developed. The older problems receded into the background but, as we shall see, were still there, to reappear in new forms.

C

Scientific Problems of Origin: the Doctrine of Primitive Roots

The step from Humboldt and Hegel to Darwin transformed then, for the time being at least, the entire problem of origin. The methodological assumptions which resulted from that step were that language is but a part of nature and must be studied as such; that, as a part of nature, it must have a purely natural origin; and finally, that it must have evolved by purely natural laws from simple uncomplicated elements to complex and articulated forms. Theories of origin therefore took the form of a doctrine of primitive roots. The problem of linguistic science was to discover the most primitive and elementary sounds which are immediately intelligible and to develop all mediated and extrinsic meanings from them. In the words of W. D. Whitney, it is the problem of "immediately given self-significant and self-authenticating sounds." It is at this point that the famous theories known as the interjectional and onomatopoeic came into play. Their bearing upon our problems must be considered briefly.

The interjectional theory would explain speech in somewhat the following way. The interjection *ach* conveys an immediately intelligible emotive meaning. By a well-known process of association, this sound becomes a name for the mental state expressed and we have the noun *ache*. Now it is true that emotions constantly give rise to meaningful expressions, but few specific names of objects or even of mental states can be traced to these expressions. All attempts to explain the origin of language in this way have been fruitless. There is no tangible evidence, historical or other, tending to show that the mass of speech elements or processes has evolved out of interjections.

The onomatopoeic theory is in much the same case. Names given to objects, especially to animals, are often imitations of the sounds made. Evidence for this is found not only in the languages of primitives, but in that of children. Many words which we do not now feel to have a sound-imitative value can be shown to have once had a phonetic form which strongly suggests their origin as imitations of natural sounds, such as the English word laugh. For all that, it is quite impossible to show, nor does it seem reasonable to suppose, that more than a negligible portion of the elements of speech, or anything at all of its formal apparatus, is derivable from an onomatopoeic source. However much we may be disposed on general principles to assign a fundamental importance in the languages of primitive peoples to the imitation of natural sounds, the actual fact of the matter, as is generally recognized, is that these languages show no particular preference for imitative words. The most primitive peoples of aboriginal America, for instance, particularly the Alaskan tribes of the Mackenzie River, have languages in which such words seem to be nearly or entirely absent.[1]

Linguists are, accordingly, pretty generally agreed in their evaluation of this type of theory. The general position of linguistic science may perhaps be expressed in the following way. No one of these theories, taken by itself, is capable of explaining human language. Each explains part and there is nothing to hinder us combining them. But even when com-

[1] Sapir, *op. cit.*, p. 6.

bined, they do not explain everything, especially they fail to explain the central parts of language and its complex structure, the fundamental parts of speech and their grammatical relations. Moreover, all three theories make certain unconscious assumptions which are in harmony neither with the facts of recent linguistic science nor with our present notions of psychological functions. So far as the former are concerned, such theories assume that single words are the units of communication and develop in isolation, whereas it is probable that sentences and larger unities came first and that words are the result of analysis helped by written language. Psychologically also, the notion that sentences and larger unities came first and that single words are the results of analysis is more in harmony with the present notion of the primacy of *Gestalten* and of elements as the results of analysis. In all these theories a further assumption is tacitly made, namely, that up to the creation of language man was, so to speak, mute and inexpressive, whereas it is much more probable that he had already been able to communicate both by vocal and other organs through something which was not yet speech but might lead to speech. It is as a result of the reconsideration of these assumptions as much as of the inadequacy of the theories themselves that the theories of the origin of language in gesture and in animal cries arose.

Despite the inadequacy of theories of this type there is one notion which underlies them that must be noted and understood. They all assume the idea of the necessity of immediately intelligible self-significant elements or aspects of speech and that out of these the indirectly significant or symbolic forms develop. This assumption must, it would seem, be held fast to in some form. It is true, of course, that developed language is a racial acquisition, a non-instinctive method of communication, a system of *voluntarily* produced symbols. But the thesis that all language is convention is difficult to make intelligible —in plain words, nonsense. If we go back to any point at will and assume that no symbolic or representative element or means of communication were present at all, it is extremely difficult to see how it could ever arise. With regard more specifically to the onomatopoeic theory, it is undoubtedly true, as we have seen, that while imitative sounds actually play a slight rôle in primitive languages and that what is called the formal apparatus of language is not directly derivable from that source nevertheless the relation of the word to thing, implied in these imitative elements, seems to have been determinative in the primitive speech consciousness.

D

Speech and Gesture "Language"

The dispute over *Urworte* has then, as Cassirer says, largely disappeared from linguistic science. The doctrine of primitive roots is no longer the concept of real historical existents, but of pure abstractions. So far as the problem of origins remains in linguistic science, the problem has been transferred from the linguistic to the non-linguistic field. Modern theories of origin seek to derive linguistic from non-linguistic communication and to understand human language by carrying it back to non-human, animal forms of communication. With the development of activistic as distinguished from intellectualist conceptions of language, the problem of language was subsumed under the more general psychological problem of expressive movements and motor reactions.

Of outstanding importance in this movement was Wundt's theory of language developed in his *Völkerpsychologie*. Oral speech has arisen, according to him, as a modification of more general expressive movements of the body which constituted a sort of primitive gesture language. He points out that two main forms of gesture are to be distinguished, the imitative and indicative. With his hands man points and imitates or represents. If, therefore, the intimate relation between sound movements and other movements is recognized from the beginning, we have in principle the means of understanding how the various functions of language arose. The arms and hands, Wundt points out, are from the earliest stages of man's development the organs with which he grasps and controls things. These obviously original uses of the organs of prehension differ from analogous activities in nearly related animals only in grade, not in nature. Out of these primitive functions arise, by one of these gradual changes which in their results form important elements in progressive movement, the first forms of pantomime movement. The latter are nothing else than the grasping movements weakened to functions of indication. This development, Wundt also points out, appears in all stages of the child life, from the simplest to the most developed. The child also grasps at all objects which, because they are too far away, he cannot reach. Thereupon these movements pass involuntarily and immediately into pointing movements. After oft-repeated attempts to grasp the objects, the pointing movements become established of themselves.[1]

The triumph of Wundt's psychology of language, a linguist has recently said, is the inclusion of language in the field of expressive movements, and there seems to be no reason to doubt the importance of gesture in the development of the indicative and representative functions of primitive sounds. Its significance, in contrast to the earlier theories, is to be found in the fact that it helps to make intelligible the "meaning" or *Deutung* function in language. This function is derived from the merely biological functions of grasping and manipulating, but once it is developed it has already been inseparably united with the sound movements, conceivably merely emotive or imitative at the beginning. Through this association, the sounds themselves gradually take on the functions of indication which were primarily if not exclusively subserved by gesture. The earlier theories, we saw, were not able to explain the origin of non-significant sounds in language and the fundamental parts of speech. This the gesture theory to some extent at least does.

E

Human Speech and Animal Cries

The reflections of the latter paragraph lead us to consider the problem of the origin of language from animal cries, in other words, the question of its sub-human origin.

Traditionally speech was that which distinguished man from the lower animals. Whether it was looked upon as a special gift of God or as a creation conscious or unconscious of Reason, whether considered as a native human endowment or

[1] Wilhelm Wundt, *Völkerpsychologie*, Vol. I, p. 129 f.

as developed in experience, it was still conceived as the unique possession of man. With the step from Humboldt to Darwin, speech like every other human character became a part of nature; the general reductive procedure was applied to speech also. However "complicated" later, it is, in its essence and nature, the cries of the forest and mountains, and between these and its complicated forms there is in principle no difference. This assumption, so long taken for granted, is now undergoing revision at the hands of linguistic science itself, and it is important to see just what the situation is. The statement already quoted that language is a *purely human*, non-instinctive activity is a fair indication of the situation. It is important to see just what that statement means.

The question of an animal language is, of course, partly a matter of definition. If we define language at the beginning as any means of communication of living beings, we have by that definition already asserted the existence of animal language out of which the human develops. If, on the other hand, we define speech so as to include the notion of meaning, and the three meaning functions of language, emotive, indicative and representative or symbolic, the problem is quite clear.

The view that all the meaning functions of language are present explicitly or implicitly in animal cries is often maintained. This thesis is ably expounded and argued by Professor de Laguna. In animal cries of the proclamatory type all three functions are inherently present. The cry proclaims the presence of the object and is thus indicative; it expresses an emotional attitude, as in the warning cry; and finally, it has at least the potentiality of predication in that it proclaims something about the object or situation which it thus indicates.[1] The question here raised is obviously one of fact and not of theory. It is equally obvious that the question of fact is one upon which the animal psychologist is alone competent to pronounce. It must be admitted also that in so far as conclusions have been reached they are scarcely favourable to the above thesis.

All students of animal psychology agree that the great apes, for instance, have a considerable range of different sounds or cries and that they are ordinarily used in the expression of emotional attitudes. There is a difference of opinion as to

[1] *Op. cit.,* p. 28.

WHAT IS LANGUAGE?

whether these sounds are connected with particular objects or situations and so constitute what is called a *real* language, but the weight of opinion is that they are not. Thus B. W. Köhler insists that the phonetic expressions of animals, even of the higher apes, lack entirely the indicative and representative functions. "It may be taken as positively proved," he writes, "that their [the apes'] gamut of phonetics is entirely 'subjective' and can only express emotions, never designate or describe objects. But they have so many phonetic elements that are also common to human languages that their lack of articulate speech cannot be ascribed to secondary (glossolabial) limitations. Their gestures, too, of face and body, like their expressions in sounds, never designate or describe objects."[1] Again, in another article he speaks of the enormous manifold of *Ausdrucksbewegungen* through which the animals "understand each other," but there can be no talk of any sort of speech between them—of any *Zeichen und Darstellungsfunction* of specific sounds or movements.[2]

We may doubtless challenge the statement of Köhler that it is "positively proved" that these meaning functions are absent in the lower animals. Professor de Laguna deplores the absence of empirical evidence one way or another, an absence which she frankly admits. But we may surely say with Cassirer that the observations of recent animal psychology seem to widen rather than narrow the gulf between animal communication and human language. The most that we can say, perhaps, is that there are in animals functions analogous to those which characterize human language. In summarizing the situation he insists that of the three speech functions, the only one that is definitely present in animals is the expressive or emotive. Of the indicative function we may find analogies, but whatever element of indication may be present it is of the vaguest sort and refers only to the vaguest situations. Of the element of representation, or predication in any significant sense, there seems not the faintest trace. I am disposed to agree with Cassirer that this third meaning function is an absolutely *sine qua non* of any meaningful speech-notion, and that what is called animal

---
[1] *Mentality of Apes*, p. 317; also *Zur Psychologie des Schimpansen*, Psych. Forsch., Bd. I, Sections 27, 29.
[2] *Zur Psychologie des Schimpansen*, Psych. Forsch., Bd. I, Sections 27, 29.

speech "seems to be permanently held fast in a pre-linguistic stage."[1]

In any case this is the growing conviction of linguists, and what is called the *hiatus* between animal expression and human speech is more and more emphasized, leading, as we have seen, to the definition of speech as a "human, non-instinctive function." The hiatus is found precisely where Aristotle found it long ago. The step to human language is first made when the pure meaningful sound achieves supremacy over the affective stimulus-born sounds and this achievement has in it the character of a unique level of being. The notion of speech as an *Urphenomen* which is part of the new speech-notion in linguistics seems more and more confirmed by studies in animal psychology.

F

The Question of the Ursprache

From the earliest reflections on speech, when it was looked upon either as a divine gift or a human invention, the question of the nature of that original language was uppermost in men's minds. With the step from *Geist* to *Natur*, it naturally fell into the background, but the problem, in a different form, is becoming significant again.

For a philosophy of language the question of origins in this form is if anything more significant than the question of its sub-human origin, for it is upon views as to what human speech is in its original or primary form that many conclusions are based as to its intrinsic functions and limits. Speech was made to do so and so; it may not readily be invoked to do other things.

In the pre-Darwinian period the problem of the *Ursprache* revolved wholly about the question of the "logical" versus the "poetic" character of the primary language. For those to whom language was essentially *Geist* the problem was solely as to the aspect of *Geist* which is primary in language. Those who, in the spirit of Leibniz and the rationalists generally, looked upon sense and imagery as confused idea, thought of the *Ursprache* in essentially intellectualistic terms. For the anti-intellectualist tendency of the Romantics the *Ursprache* was "poetic" in

[1] *Op. cit.*, Vol. I, Chapter III, p. 127 f.

WHAT IS LANGUAGE?

character and the strictly logical aspects a later development. Closely bound up with this problem was that of the nature of myth and of its relation to language.

Herder in his famous work *Ueber den Ursprung der Sprache* had emphasized the primarily mythical nature of all words and speech forms—in other words, the origin of language in myth. The linguistics of the romantic period carried this theory further. Schelling, for example, saw in language a "verblichene Mythologie," which retained in abstract and formal distinctions that which mythology had apprehended in concrete and living differences. With the nineteenth century the opposite road of explanation was followed. Mythology was derived from language, in some cases considered a "disease of language." Max Müller and others followed this line, holding that by means of comparative mythology the derivation of myth from language could be shown.

This battle over the temporal priority of myth or language really is not so much a question of temporal priority as of the ideal relations between these two forms of symbolism, the mythical and the linguistic, and of the way in which each influences the development of the other. The question of actual priority cannot, of course, be empirically determined. That which seems undoubted, however, is that from the beginning language and myth stand in inseparable correlation, out of which they gradually developed as independent processes. Both are expressions of one fundamental tendency to symbol formation, namely, the principle of radical metaphor that lies at the heart of all symbolizing function.[1]

Since the Darwinian epoch the problem of the *Ursprache* has, as I have suggested, taken another form. It is no longer a question of the primacy of the rational or the poetic and mythical, but of the primacy of the "practical." Here again the question of actual priority cannot, of course, be empirically determined. The primitive languages open to our study are already "developed" in the sense that the fundamental groundwork of language is already present. They are also developed in the sense that the practical and the poetic are equally present, the question of the primacy of the one over the other being purely speculative, the determination of which can be

[1] Ernst Cassirer, *Sprache Und Mythos*, pp. 69 ff.

settled solely on *a priori* and philosophical grounds. This being the case, the question of the *Ursprache* is not so much one of temporal priority as of intrinsic character. In the words of G. Ipsen, *Ursprache* is not *Urstufe und Vergangenheit*, but, as it was really understood by Heracleitus and the Stoics, that which belongs to the phenomenological character of language as such, wherever found.[1]

That the *Ursprache* in this sense is primarily poetic is again maintained by many linguists. The notion has been revived by Jespersen[2] and notably by Vossler and others who have been influenced by Croce. On this point we may, perhaps, again agree with Ipsen when he says of the doctrine of Herder and the Romantics, that language is the *Urpoesie* of peoples, that while not true in any absolute sense, it is yet valid as a statement of one of the characters of all speech or language. The poetic is an intrinsic character of language as such, but not the only or, indeed, the final one. It is at once poetic, cognitive, and practical, and to call any one of these alone the character of the *Ursprache* is one-sided abstraction.

We shall not be far wrong, I think, if we take such a position as indicative of present-day linguistic conceptions. So far as our original question is concerned—namely, what language was made for, whether it was made solely "to serve the purposes of the familiar world, for the practical manipulation of physical objects, etc."—such a thesis represents rather a one-sided abstraction from the concrete totality of linguistic meanings. Far from being the result of unbiased phenomenological analysis it is rather an inference from unjustified metaphysical assumptions.[3]

G

Conclusion: Origin and Validity

In a review of a recent book on Human Speech the reviewer writes thus: "We can afford to be tolerant of theories of remote

[1] *Op. cit.*
[2] *Language: Its Nature, Development and Origin*, Chapter XXI. (Published by George Allen & Unwin Ltd.).
[3] A. H. Gardiner, *op. cit.*, pp. 21 and 37, attacks the exclusively expressive and aesthetic theory of speech of Croce. He rightly points out that without the "listener" there is no speech and that without communication there is no expression. But this does not disprove the fundamental character of the poetic in language. It merely denies its exclusive character.

origin, because they do not really matter. In the Book of Genesis speech is wisely taken for granted. Adam just simply gave names to the animals. The author of Genesis was right and so were the founders of the Société de Linguistique when in 1866 they banned speculations on the origin of language or the creation of ideal or universal languages."[1]

All this sounds well enough, and doubtless the Society was wise, from its positivist standpoint, in banning such speculations. But the simple fact is that these theories of origin matter tremendously and cannot really be banned. The philologist can hardly escape some working hypothesis regarding the genesis of speech. No more can the philosophy of language avoid being affected by concepts of origin in the evaluation of that which is derived.[2]

It is often maintained that origins do not affect validity, but notoriously they do and nowhere more clearly than in this sphere of language. It is, as we have seen, almost universally assumed that what speech was originally made for determines in some significant way what it is capable of doing now. It is therefore of no little significance to discover that the assumptions upon which current evaluations are based find little support in present-day linguistics. The possibility of developing the linguistic out of the non-linguistic, of human language out of animal cries, instead of coming nearer, is now felt to be more remote than ever. The notion of Speech as an *Urphenomen* as essentially human and non-instinctive, has fixed itself rather firmly in linguistic science. In similar fashion the behaviouristic and practical conception of the speech functions are recognized for what they are—as inferences from a naturalistic metaphysics rather than the results of a study of language in its intrinsic character and functions.

It is often said, as for instance by Professor de Laguna, that the historical fact that, "speaking and reasoning man did evolve by natural processes from anthropoid ancestors is not seriously disputed even by those whose deepest sympathies are opposed to such an admission. But so long as mystery surrounds the manner of that evolution the refuge of ignorance remains.

---

[1] *Human Speech: Some Observations, Experiments and Conclusions as to the Nature, Origin and Purpose and Possible Improvement of Human Speech*, Sir Richard Paget, London, Kegan Paul, Trench, Trübner and Company, 1930. Reviewed in *Journal of Philosophical Studies*, 1930.   [2] A. H. Gardiner, *op. cit.*, p. 19.

And the mystery is regarded by these transcendentalists as impenetrable."[1] I confess that to me such type of argument seems to be clearly a case of *ignoratio elenchi*. The issue here is not one of historical fact—although I for one find the phrases "historical fact" and "evolve by natural processes" both too ambiguous to be able to say whether the above proposition is or is not seriously disputed. In some interpretations it certainly is. No, the issue is not whether man actually evolved. The issue is precisely that with which we have already become familiar—namely, whether natural processes, in the sense conceived by the natural sciences, are applicable to the phenomenon of speech. This we have already seen denied by a large body of linguistic science.

As regards the transcendentalists, to whom "the mystery is impenetrable," it is not a refuge of ignorance. It is a result rather of increased knowledge of what language really is. The turning from *Natur* to *Geist*, characteristic of so much of present-day linguistic study, is not because the mystery of language is impenetrable, but rather because the mystery, yes, even the miracle of language, with the entire marvel of intelligible communication can be *understood* only on the basis of transcendental presuppositions. This we shall increasingly see in the following chapters. In any case, to revert to our primary question, historical origins may not affect values, but metaphysical concepts of ultimate origin certainly do. This the transcendentalists understand.

V

A

The Science of Language and the Notion of "Parts of Speech"

The third point at which problems of the philosophy of language and the conclusions of comparative linguistics touch each other most significantly is the question of the parts of speech. The reason for this is clear. With the postulate of "natural language" which dominated linguistic science until the evolutionary period, there went likewise the postulate of a universal grammar, of a grammar common to all languages, and with

[1] *Op. cit.*, p. 7.

WHAT IS LANGUAGE?

it the postulate of the potentiality of logical form in all language. A sort of pre-established harmony between the parts of speech and the parts or structure of reality was almost inevitably a part of this assumption. With the abandonment of this postulate of natural language and the substitution of the notion of development, there was likewise an abandonment of this latter assumption. With language conceived of as a part of nature, and not an expression of reason, the notion of universal and necessary parts of speech was abandoned. Colloquial speech is a part of the human organism and not less complicated than it. It is an ill-fitting garment made for other ends than the expression of reason and the representation of reality.

B

The Facts of Comparative Linguistics

The traditional notion assumed that analysis discloses certain parts of speech which are the *sine qua non* of the existence of speech as such, at least of developed language. Modern comparative studies of language make it quite clear, however, that the conventional classification of words into parts of speech corresponds only roughly, if at all, to the actual facts of language. This general conclusion was expressed by Steinthal in somewhat extreme form when he said, "A universal grammar seems no more conceivable than a universal plant or animal."

Even in any single given language, such correspondence is only a rough one. We imagine that all verbs are inherently connected with action as such, that a noun is the name of some definite object or personality that can be pictured by the mind, and that all qualities are necessarily expressed by words or groups of words to which we may appropriately apply the term adjective. As soon, however, as we test our vocabulary, we find that the parts of speech are far from corresponding to so simple an analysis of reality. Even in a given language the parts of speech do not represent fixed categories, but at best only a wavering approximation. They not only grade into one another, but are, to an astonishing degree, convertible into one another. Comparison of different languages only tends to strengthen this view. It shows that different languages and types of language have different schemes and that it is impossible to impose any one scheme, such as that worked out in the Aryan languages, on other types of language. For these reasons no logical scheme of the parts of speech, their number, nature, and necessary confines, is accepted by the linguist. The part of speech reflects not so much *a necessary intuitive analysis of reality as our ability to compose that reality into a variety of formal patterns.*[1]

Such is the general conclusion of a large part of modern linguistic science on the question of a universal grammar. And on this sceptical conclusion many inferences of logicians and philosophers have been more or less based. Language may be the expression and communication of our analysis of experience, but there is no sure road from that expression, from these formal patterns, to the analysis of reality itself. Language, as the clothing of thought, is indeed an ill-fitting garment, and it is not necessarily moulded on reality. A logic or a doctrine of categories which takes as its cue linguistic form—and this was the nature of Aristotelian logic, and of the doctrine of the categories, even in Kant—is not only not representative of reality, but leads to a false metaphysics. Of this general question of the philosophy of language we shall speak later; it involves questions which go beyond the province of linguistics as such. Here we are concerned solely with questions of linguistic fact.

On this point present-day students of language are not as sceptical as at first appears. In fact many, like Sapir, caution us against too sceptical an inference. They point out, first of all, that language, at least developed language, consists in a series of propositions. A natural and inherent character of speech is that there must be something to talk about and something must be said about the subject of discourse when once selected. This distinction is of such importance that, we are told, the vast majority of languages, if not all, have emphasized it by creating a sort of formal barrier between the two terms of a proposition. The subject of discourse is the noun. As the most common subject of discourse is either a person or a thing, the nouns cluster about concrete objects of that order. As the thing predicated of the object is generally an activity in the widest sense of the word, a passage from one moment of activity

[1] E. Sapir, *op. cit.*, Chapters IV and V.

WHAT IS LANGUAGE?

to another, the forms that have been set aside for the purpose of predicating, in other words the verbs, cluster about concepts of activity. "No language," we are told, "fails wholly to distinguish at least between noun and verb, although in some cases the distinction is an illusive one. It is, however, different with the other parts of speech. No one of them may be said to be imperatively required for the life of language, although they may greatly increase the fluidity and significance of that life."[1]

C

Reinstatement of the Doctrine of Parts of Speech

This notion of imperative or necessary parts of speech—necessary to the "life" of speech as such, and therefore the *sine qua non* of the "speech-notion"—is more or less characteristic of present-day linguistic science. We may therefore speak of the tendency to reinstatement of the doctrine of parts of speech. We shall discuss this tendency under two heads: (*a*) the parts of speech that are imperative; and (*b*) the nature of the imperative character of these "parts" and of their distinctions.

On the general thesis that there are universal and imperative parts of speech there is general agreement; on the question as to what particular parts are imperative, there is not. Sapir, we have seen, holds that only noun and verb are imperatively needed. Jespersen holds that there are five classes of "necessary and inescapable parts of speech"—noun, verb, adjective, particle, and pronoun.

In view of these facts it would seem, then, that the difference in opinion turns upon an ambiguity in the terms necessary and inescapable, an ambiguity that can only be dispelled by asking, necessary for what? It seems obvious that if we are looking for what is necessary for the *speech-notion* as such, for language in the simplest form that we can find it or conceive it, we shall have one answer to the question. If, on the other hand, we are looking for those distinctions that are inescapable in a developed language—in a language which has "developed" in the direction of increased differentiation and determinateness of meaning—we shall have another answer.

[1] Sapir, *op. cit.*, p. 125. So also A. H. Gardiner, *Speech and Language*, p. 269.

It has frequently been suggested that the earliest form of language must have been a series of self-significant signs which in sheer conjunction bore a natural "ad-significance." Thus Willis in his *Philosophy of Speech* suggests a form of speech of the following type. "God made heaven—earth—earth all dark —God say—come light—God see light—say good light—God put light there—dark there." Language at this stage has no grammar at all in the common sense of the term. In order to know the meaning of the whole it is necessary apparently only to know the meaning of each word. Whatever by-meaning these words carry is then natural and not connected by-meaning. It is apprehended as well by him to whom the language is foreign as by him to whom it is native. It is, accordingly, the implicit ad-significance which should be especially emphasized. The explicit development of the ad-significants, the particles and the substitutional signs such as pronouns, is necessary only in the sense of developed language with its increased differentiation and determination of meaning.[1]

The point I am making here is well brought out by Gardiner in his distinction between speech and language. According to his view there are only two parts of *speech*, but these are imperative and inevitable, namely, the subject and predicate. There must be something talked about and something said about it; otherwise there is no speech. The others are not necessary parts of speech but merely grammatical distinctions within language.

D

The Parts of Speech and the New Speech-Notion: the Intuitive Content of Language

Some conception of inescapable and necessary parts of speech, is, we may then say, part of the present speech-notion. It is now necessary to determine, if possible, what these conceptions mean.

The negative conclusions of comparative linguistics were expressed in the following way. The parts of speech reflect not so much a necessary intuitive analysis of reality as our ability to compose that reality into a variety of formal patterns.

[1] George Willis, *The Philosophy of Speech*, p. 103. (Published by George Allen and Unwin Ltd.).

Developed language is indeed the sounds of forest and mountain in highly *complicated* form, but the arrogant anthropoids that thus complicated these sounds should not suppose that these are anything but formal patterns, are in any sense an expression or intuition of reality. But just as there has been a tendency to return to the doctrine of necessary parts of speech, so there has been a tendency in many quarters to a return to the conception of these parts of speech as intuitional in character, as having, so to speak, intuitional content.

A well-known expression of this idea is, of course, that of Jespersen in his distinction between syntactical and "notional" or meaning categories. A comparative survey of the syntactical categories of various languages has led him to maintain "that beside or above or behind the syntactical categories which depend upon the structure of each language as it is actually found, there are certain extra-lingual categories which are independent of the more or less accidental facts of existing languages, though rarely expressed in them in a clear and unmistakable way . . . for want of a better common name for these extra-lingual categories I shall use the adjective notional and the substantive notion. The grammarian's task is to investigate the relation between the notional and linguistic categories."[1]

A somewhat similar point of view has recently been expressed by certain French linguists, C. Bally and F. Bruno.[2] Universal and necessary elements are found in linguistic fact (here there is variability), but in the *fact* as including meaning, not in the linguistic forms. M. Bruno, for instance, recognizes that linguistic science has been severed from its former dependence upon a logic of *a priori* categories. A table of grammatical categories or a set of parts of speech is assuredly not an affair of initial postulation, but a problem for solution. It is, nevertheless, a problem. In his own theory of language a classification is worked out, not of words, but of meanings which the symbols express. This is necessary because verbal elements abstracted from meaning lack constant values.

[1] *Philosophy of Grammar*, pp. 55 ff. and other places, especially pp. 237 ff. (Published by George Allen and Unwin Ltd.).
[2] F. Bruno, *La Pensée et la Langue*; C. Bally, *Le langage et la Vie*. A summary of the positions of these representative French linguists may be found in a "Survey of French Philosophy," by S. V. Keeling, in the *Journal of Philosophical Studies*, Vol. V, No. 17.

A like tendency can be seen in the views of Vossler.[1] All grammatical categories are, he tells us, experienced intuitively. For him also, behind language and the grammatical categories lies *die erlebte Rede* and in this speech, as lived or experienced, lie necessary meaning functions which are intuitive in character. That they are further conceived by him as "poetical as regards their psychic origin and spiritual value" is for the moment beside the point; we shall consider this aspect of his views in a later context[2]—the important point here is that his view also belongs to that general tendency to reinstate the notion of necessary parts of speech in a new form.

It need hardly be said that the presence of such tendencies constitutes no proof of a general reinstatement of the notion of necessary parts of speech. Certainly it is not meant as such. They do, however, constitute a warning against too sceptical and destructive inferences, and against the assumption that linguistic science has spoken finally and negatively on this question of fact. The notion of universal and necessary "parts of speech," properly understood, is not negatived by linguistic science, and conclusions for the philosophy of language cannot be based upon that assumption.

A reasonable view would seem to be that each part of speech represents in general some item or aspect of being, and that there is more or less exact parallelism between the structure of language and the nature of things and that all languages are confined to the same set of divisions. Linguistic science has not found definitions of the parts of speech that are sufficiently precise to fit all instances in actual usage. Indeed, it is hardly likely that this should be possible, for the character of language is historical and not abstractly logical. Nor has it discovered the same grammatical forms in all languages. But regardless of how words in their syntactical relations are classified, there is some general relation between their classification and the subject-matter to which they refer. This is, as we have seen, clear enough with regard to nouns, adjectives and verbs, and perhaps adverbs. With respect to prepositions, conjunctions, and articles it is not so clear. But prepositions, for the most part, represent relations and conjunctions, the intention of the speaker to consider two or more things together.

[1] Karl Vossler, *op. cit.*, p. 224. [2] Chapter IV, pp. 157 f.

The parts of speech, however selected, have something to do with the signification of the words, that is, with the things to which they refer. Just what this representation of items or aspects of being is or means, is a matter for later consideration.

We may then describe this view, however varied its forms, as the intuitive doctrine of the "parts of speech." This doctrine we shall develop more fully in Chapter IV, under the heading of "The Intuitive Meaning of Words and the Parts of Speech."[1] It is important here merely to make clear this tendency in present-day linguistics and to point out its significance. By the intuitive character of the parts of speech is here meant that *language is an indispensable part of perceptual knowledge, of the function of perceptual intuition itself.* The function of judgment, with the parts of speech necessary to predication, is part of the intuitive process. The parts of speech are therefore also intuitive and necessary. Otherwise expressed, it is the principle of the identity of intuition and expression. What is necessary to expression is therefore also necessary to intuition.

The significance of this tendency is twofold. In the first place, with the recognition of this tendency in present-day linguistic science, it is no longer possible to appeal to that science in support of the sceptical evaluation and criticism of natural language so common in present-day logic and philosophy. The tendency of the "new speech-notion" to reinstate the traditional conception of necessary parts of speech leaves the question open, at least so far as linguistic science is concerned. In the second place, this intuitive doctrine, as I have described it, affords at least a tentative basis for what I conceive to be a fundamental thesis of the philosophy of language, namely, the principle of the identity or inseparability of intuition and expression. This principle, fundamental to the understanding of the relation of language to cognition, will be developed in a later chapter. Here it is necessary merely to emphasize the support which such a principle finds in present-day linguistics.

---

[1] The most systematic development of this conception is to be found in the work of H. Ammann, *Die menschliche Rede*, to which more extended reference will be made later.

VI

GENERAL SUMMARY AND CONCLUSIONS

This chapter pretends to do no more than give in most general outlines what seems to the writer to be the situation in linguistic science on certain moot points of fundamental import for the philosophy of language—points, moreover, at which appeal to "fact" is constantly made in philosophical critiques or evaluations of language. In a field so changing and so uncertain, generalizations of this sort are doubtful things. That I have escaped either error or bias is doubtless too much to hope; the only excuse for such an attempt is that precisely such general statements as to what linguistic science "tells us" are constantly made, and upon them are based conclusions of far-reaching import for philosophy. It is important that these assumptions should be critically examined.

One thing we may say with assurance. The present state of linguistic science affords little ground for such dogmatic assertions about language as those with which the chapter opened. On all these fundamental issues, it is now clear, this science does not speak unambiguously. It has at least two voices—two different positions regarding the specific questions or issues about which our discussion has revolved—two different attitudes with regard to the nature of language which, with Vossler, we may describe as the positivistic and idealistic. This fact is in itself significant, and it will be well in conclusion to return briefly to this more general question.

With regard to specific issues, it may be said that there is a strong tendency in modern linguistics to deny, or at least to make doubtful, many of the assumptions regarding language which are made so dogmatically in current philosophical discussion. Language is not *merely* the sounds of the forest, not *merely* a succession of squeaks and grunts. It is not in principle animal cries. The hiatus between these cries and human speech is so great as to indicate that it is a purely human activity, an emergent, if we may make use of this conception, not in any sense reducible to prehuman behaviour. In sum, the notion of speech as a non-instinctive, voluntary, and purely human activity is increasing rather than decreasing, and with it has come the notion of an autonomous type of activity, not reducible to non-linguistic forms of communication. More specifically, the recent tendency in linguistic study has been to reinstate in new forms certain traditional conceptions, or at least to take a more cautious attitude towards them. The notion of an *Ursprache* with its own imperative and inescapable structure—no longer, to be sure, in an historical sense, if indeed it was actually ever so conceived—is being reinstated in new forms. The sceptical attitude towards the doctrine of necessary parts of speech is giving place to a more moderate view, according to which the actual historical variability and relativity of syntactical form is no longer taken to exclude the notion of categories or notions intrinsic to the notion of language as such.

Back of these specific points lie still more fundamental changes in our general attitude towards speech and its study. The reinstatement of so many older notions in a new form suggests that there has been something of the nature of a reaction in linguistic science itself, a revision of the premises of the science of no mean significance. This is, indeed, as we have seen, the thesis of Cassirer. The step from mind to nature has, he holds, been to a considerable extent retraced. In summarizing the later developments of linguistic science, he insists that, with all the extensions of knowledge of details, when considered from the standpoint of method, it has moved in a circle. The step from mind to nature consisted in abandoning the notion of language as a spiritual creation, an intelligible good, and in conceiving it as merely a part of nature. The step backward has consisted in the discovery that, thus viewed, it cannot be explained—much less understood.[1]

Now language is, indeed, as Vossler says, "embedded in the tissue of nature, so deeply and in so many ways, that the illusion of its being a piece of nature constantly arises anew," and, as he continues, "has as constantly to be dissipated." It is with the dissipation of this illusion that much of present-day philosophy of language is concerned. For our present purposes it

---

[1] Even in the sphere of sound changes (phonetics) the notion of natural law has broken down; and *a fortiori* in the sphere of semantics (Cassirer, *op. cit.*, Vol. I, pp. 118 ff.).

is sufficient to recognize the presence of this controversy within linguistic science itself, the opposition, namely, between positivism and idealism in linguistic science as described by Vossler in his book of that name. It is enough to indicate that, for many students of language at least, language is not a piece of nature, but rather an expression or embodiment of spirit, not the product of mechanical development but of creative activity. It is this which constitutes "idealism" in linguistic science and philosophy.[1]

It is at this point that the significance of this chapter for our ensuing studies appears. The essential feature of the idealistic, as opposed to the positivistic and naturalistic position, is, as Cassirer states it, the principle of "the primacy of meaning" in linguistic science. It is the impossibility of reducing meaning to a mere part of nature, when the term nature is used in any intelligible and unambiguous sense, which makes a purely naturalistic account of language impossible. This we shall find increasingly evident as we proceed to the study of the nature of linguistic meaning and the problem of the communication of meaning.

[1] In using these terms in linguistic science it is important to recognize that the contrast between positivism and idealism is primarily one of methodology rather than of epistemology and metaphysics. Vossler himself emphasizes this point when he writes (*Positivismus und Idealismus in der Sprachwissenschaft*, p. 1):

"Unter Positivismus und Idealismus will Ich nicht zwei verschiedene philosophische Systeme oder Gruppen von Systemen, sondern zunächst nur zwei Grundrichtungen unseres Erkenntnissvermögens wissen.... Unsere Scheidung in Positivismus und Idealismus hat mit der Zweiteilung des Erkenntnissvermögens in Sinlichkeit und Verstandt, Auschauung und Abstraction, Empirie und Metaphysik, nicht das Geringste zu thun. Sie bezieht sich nicht auf die Naturbeschaffenheit, sondern auf die Ziele und Wege unseres Erkennens. Positivismus und Idealismus sind nicht erkentnisstheoretische, sondern methodologische Begriffe."

This is undoubtedly true. Nevertheless, while the terms have, in the first instance, nothing to do with the theory of knowledge, it seems impossible that the methodological problem can be ultimately separated from the epistemological. In so far as language is inseparable from cognition, the nature of language which makes it necessary to use the "idealistic" rather than the positivistic or naturalistic method, cannot but have a bearing on the theory of knowledge itself.

CHAPTER III

LANGUAGE AS THE BEARER OF MEANING: WHAT IT IS TO UNDERSTAND

I

MEANING IN LINGUISTICS AND IN PHILOSOPHY

WHATEVER else language is, it is, in the first instance, meaningful communication between man and man. John Dewey, like many others, looks upon language as "the world's supreme wonder, because it changed dumb creatures, as we significantly call them, into thinking and knowing animals and *created the realm of meanings*" (italics mine). The study of this supreme wonder requires the study of the realm of meanings which it created and established. To be sure, this form of statement of the relation of language to meaning immediately raises issues of fundamental import for the philosophy of language. Language *created* the realm of meanings? Are there not rather pre-linguistic meanings also which language, so to speak, embodies and expresses? However this may be, the mere fact that it may be said with any show of truth at all that language and the realm of meaning are co-extensive indicates the central place of the problem of meaning in the philosophy of language.

Philosophical semantics is, accordingly, the name which may be given to the problems of this chapter. The point at which linguistics and philosophy chiefly come together is, as we have already seen, in connection with the division of linguistics known as semantics. The nature of linguistic meaning, the historical mutations of meaning, problems of translation, or of the conveyance of meaning from one linguistic medium to another—all these are problems of semantics, and at all these points problems of a philosophical nature arise. These problems include the nature of the meanings of words, of the meaning of things, and of their relations; and ultimately a general theory of meaning which has sometimes been characterized as the "meaning of meaning."

II

PRE-LINGUISTIC MEANING: "BEHAVIOURAL" MEANING

A

It is generally recognized that the question, What is Meaning? is pivotal in the philosophy of language. Words, both as things to be "understood" by the individual and as things by which understanding is conveyed from one individual to another, are things or entities that have meaning. But things that are not words also have meanings in a certain sense. Before investigating the meaning of words it will be useful first to determine what is to be understood by the "meaning of things."

It is true that if language first created the realm of meanings, then, strictly speaking, there is no meaning of things prior to and apart from language. Obviously in this implicit denial of pre-linguistic meaning we have a position which, on the face of it, at least, cannot be true. On the other hand, there is a sense in which the statement is true, that meaning, in one sense of the word at least, is created by language. Clearly, then, we are confronted with at least two "meanings of meaning," and one of the chief tasks of this chapter must be to clear up this ambiguity, to distinguish between the two senses of meaning, and to determine their relations. For our present purpose it will suffice to assume that there is pre-linguistic meaning, that there is a legitimate sense in which "things" have meaning. It is generally assumed that, genetically viewed, the meaning of "things" antedates the meaning of words. We shall accordingly start with this assumption, and our first problem is to determine the nature of this meaning.

B

The Simple Sign Situation: Animal Meanings

There is, then, in some sense pre-linguistic meaning. The "dumb animals" "sense" or apprehend meanings in some sense. The basal character of these meanings is well described by Bergson: "In the animal world the meanings of things are

LANGUAGE AS THE BEARER OF MEANING

largely instinctive and the signs of these meanings adherent to the things signified." This in contrast to human society, where, "on the contrary, all is mobile," where the sign is detachable from the thing signified and transferable to new objects. The character of this "instinctive" meaning, with its adherent signs, and the manner in which it is acquired, are then our first problem.

An oft-quoted illustration of such meaning is one afforded by Lloyd Morgan's experiments on newly hatched chicks. Such a chick, after picking indiscriminately at various caterpillars, comes upon the cinnabar caterpillar which has a bitter taste. After repeated impulsive movements of pecking, the tendency is finally inhibited. The markings of the caterpillar have become "signs" to the chick and the caterpillar is said to have "acquired meaning." This "simple sign situation" is taken as a type of all sign situations and the meaning thus acquired as the elemental form of all meaning.

For the psychologist the point of interest is how this meaning is acquired and what goes on in the animal's "mind" or organism (as one may prefer) when the meaning is acquired. From this point of view meaning may be said to be "our *name* for cues to adaptive movement." It is more or less identifiable with motor reaction or acquired tendencies to such reaction. Bergson has described such meanings as largely instinctive. In view of the dispute over instinct it will be well to employ another terminology. It will suffice for our purpose to describe these perceptual meanings of animals as *activistic*, by which is meant that the meaning is something in an act which is selected because it arouses an anticipatory reaction to its sequel. This perceptual meaning involves recognition but not revival of past experiences.

Thus do "things" acquire perceptual meaning and thus, when the meaning is acquired, whatever is the sign of the meaning is adherent to the thing signified. The power to intuit meanings in this sense is possessed by animals as well as by human beings. If all that is meant by intelligence is *reaction to adherent signs*, then animals have intelligence. It is indeed not certain that animals do not possess the beginnings at least of that mobility of signs which distinguish human language and other forms of symbolization. They seem, in some cases

[1] See Ogden and Richards, *The Meaning of Meaning*, pp. 52 ff.

at least, to be able to detach one aspect or part of a whole situation and make it stand for the whole. Thus there are forms of animal communication in which there is apparently the beginning of this mobility of signs. A bee, for instance, returns from the flowers which it has discovered to the hive. Here, through certain definite movements, a kind of dance, it invites its companions to a new flight. To each of them it gives a bit of the particular pollen which it has gathered, which serves as a means of orientation, as a *sign* through which it is directed to the source of the pollen. A degree of detachment of the sign is here in evidence, but if we seek to distinguish this kind of signification, and mutual understanding through signs, from linguistic communication among human beings, we find, as Bühler makes clear, that the signification and the communication which is bound up with it is confined to the *here* and the *now*, whereas the mobility of signs possible when once language, in even its simplest form, has entered in, is not limited by the "here and the now."[1]

There is, then, in the animal world the beginning of detachment and mobility of signs and of the process of symbolization that goes with it. But—and this is a point of importance for our study of meaning—this mobility has very definite limits. If, as our studies of the preceding chapter seem to indicate, the emotive function of speech is the only one definitely present, that the indicative function, if present at all, is of the vaguest and refers only to the vaguest situations, while the representative is not present at all, it seems likely that the hiatus between animal cries and human speech corresponds to a similar hiatus between human and animal meanings.

C

Human Perceptual Meaning. Intrinsic Meaning

In the animal world, then, meaning is largely "instinctive" and the signs of that meaning adherent to the things signified. In human society, on the contrary, all is mobile and signs are detachable. This characterization, while generally true, is not

[1] Karl Bühler, *Die Krise der Psychologie*, 1927, pp. 51 ff. For a discussion of this whole question, see Ernst Cassirer, *op. cit.*, Vol. III, pp. 385 ff.

absolutely so. Not all is mobile. Human, like animal meanings, are in the first instance adherent and the signs of the meaning adherent also. Some perhaps remain ultimately adherent and undetachable and, so far as language is concerned, inexpressible. In any case we shall begin our study of human meaning with those which quite obviously share the characters of animal meanings. Here it will be convenient to introduce a somewhat different terminology. We shall speak of the *intrinsic* and *extrinsic* meaning of things.

What is understood by intrinsic meaning may be illustrated in the following way. When I am thirsty I pick up a glass of water and drink it. When I am tired, seeing a chair, I sit down. In each case the meaning is an *integral* part of the datum: it is, so to speak, blended with it and is apparently as much a part of it as any of the sense qualities. Of course, the meanings were not always there. There was once a time when I did not know what water and chairs "were for." The meaning is then *acquired* in the genetic sense as are animal meanings. But we must not confuse the origin of meanings with the way they operate and with their status after they are acquired and established. Once meaning is acquired it is perhaps directly intuited. Meanings, once assigned as intrinsic qualities of objects, are then as immediately given in *intuition* as are the sense data.

Intrinsic human meaning, like the adherent meanings of the animal world, can be connected with tendencies to action. The primary meaning of the glass of water or the chair is *what they are for*. We may also say that meaning *here* is just our name for cues to adaptive movement. It might thus far be described as "just our way of saying that of all the ways that an individual or an organism has of reacting to an object, at one time he reacts in only one way. That way of reacting *is* the meaning which the object has for him."[1] But there are two things about this type of meaning that should be noted, which distinguish it from the adherent meaning of the animal world. In the first place, even this primary intrinsic meaning is variable to a degree not found in animal meanings. The primary meaning of the object chair is to sit upon. But in a certain context its meaning may be to use it for a weapon of

[1] R. B. Perry, *A General Theory of Value*, pp. 324 ff.

defence. Moreover, in addition to this greater variability of "practical" meaning there are differences in meaning attitudes which are not found, or at least not found in the same degree, in the realm of animal meaning.

D

Practical and Aesthetic Meaning

Of these ways of reacting the most important contrast is that of the practical and aesthetic. The practical meaning of a glass of water is to pick it up and drink it, or at least the arousal of an anticipatory reaction. But the meaning of the object is quite different if I look at it in the way an artist looks at it—let us say as an object in a still-life painting. The way of reacting is quite different and, on the theory of meaning thus far developed, the *meaning* is different also. The difference noted here is deep-lying and runs throughout the entire realm of perceptual meanings. On one theory of meaning, for instance Croce's, the aesthetic is the primary attitude and primary meaning, both the practical and the theoretical being developments out of it. At this stage of our study, this is the place neither to argue this question of primacy nor to analyse aesthetic meaning further, but merely to insist upon the fact of its primary and original character. This distinction between practical and aesthetic intrinsic meaning becomes of great importance in later connections, when we come to study the relation of the meaning of words to the meaning of things. The *vis poetica*, the intuitive expressiveness of words, consists in the power of language to apprehend and to embody this form of primary meaning. But the important point here is the recognition of this primary form of the meaning of things in determining our conception of pre-linguistic meaning.[1]

E

Extrinsic Meaning. Polarity

The character of intrinsic meanings is that they do not point beyond the datum of which they are the meaning. This is

[1] See Chapter X, p. 462 f.

true of both forms, practical and aesthetic. The character of extrinsic meaning, on the contrary, is that the very essence of the meaning lies in this pointing or reference. There are two types of this extrinsic meaning, namely perceptual and conceptual.

The simplest form of extrinsic meaning is that in which one perceptual object suggests or indicates another—is in fact a sign of the other. Thus clouds mean rain. A grimace means pain. It is quite common to subsume this type of meaning directly under the adherent or intrinsic meaning of things. That this is a false and dangerous over-simplification is evident on closer inspection. The clouds *do not* mean rain in the first or primary sense; they mean doing something: for instance, seeking shelter. The grimace does not mean pain; it means simply a certain motor or emotional attitude. For the clouds to mean *rain* or the grimace *pain* there must enter into the situation a certain individuation of both the sign and the thing signified, a certain polarity of indicator and indicated, which are not present on the level of intrinsic meaning. This polarity —of the sign and the thing signified—is the crucial point of this analysis. It is at this point that interpretation—or understanding—of the sign *as sign* first enters in. Until this element of polarity appears, "meaning" means only a cue to adaptive movement or to emotive reaction.

It may well be asked whether this element of polarity—and with it meaning in the sense of interpretation—can arise at all without the beginnings of language. My own view is that it cannot. For this form of meaning to arise at all there must be at least a minimum of individuation and ideal construction of the objects between which the meaning relation holds, and this is scarcely possible without language and its categories. In such case, language does create meanings in a certain sense. The reasons for this view will be developed presently. For the moment our interest is merely in distinguishing between meaning in the sense of a cue to action, and meaning as a relation between a sign and the thing signified. The former involves no consciousness of sign as sign—no interpretation or understanding; the latter does.

III

THEORIES OF PRE-LINGUISTIC MEANING; THE BEHAVIOURISTIC OR NATURALISTIC THEORY

A

From the foregoing it is evident that the problem of the meaning of "things" is in *some sense* prior to the problem of the meaning of words. What, then, is the nature of the meaning which language did *not* create? The answer to this question has been given by two theories which we may describe respectively as the behaviouristic and the realistic theories. Let us examine the behaviouristic theory first. This theory starts with the very simple and plausible notion that "meaning is simply our *name* for cues to adaptive movement or to behaviour." Starting with the simplest cases of animal meanings, it proceeds to consider them the type of all meaning situations or, otherwise expressed, to reduce all meaning situations to this simple form. For this purpose the meaning situation is conceived as a sign situation and a theory of perceptual signs is developed. The cinnabar caterpillar has, for instance, "acquired meaning" for the chick; that is, the sense datum (the stripes) is a sign. What, then, is the "meaning" of that sign? The answer is, "the residual trace" of a reaction or adaptation made by the organism to the stimulus. The sign is always a stimulus similar to some part of an original stimulus, sufficient to call up the residual trace, or tendency to adaptation. A corollary of the theory is that the meaning relation, the relation of "direction towards," is similar or identical to the relation of being "caused by."

The problem which this behaviouristic and causal theory of meaning sets is threefold. (*a*) Does it explain the meaning situation in its simplest form, that of animal meanings? (*b*) Does it explain all perceptual meaning situations, the cases of intrinsic and extrinsic human meanings described and analysed above? (*c*) Does it explain linguistic meaning? At this stage of our discussion we are concerned only with the first two questions.

This seems, at first sight, an adequate account of animal perceptual meanings, whatever its limitations may be when applied to all types of the meaning situation. And yet there

LANGUAGE AS THE BEARER OF MEANING

are serious difficulties even here. These difficulties arise from uncertainty as to what this simplest form of the meaning situation includes, in other words to depend upon our definition of meaning. If meaning be understood as "just our name for cues to adaptive movement" . . . that "the way of reacting *is* just the meaning which the object has for an organism," then the account would be adequate, for such an account is already implied in the definition. If, on the other hand, this simplest form of meaning is held to include *interpretation*, or understanding of the sign as sign, the situation is wholly different. On the latter assumption even animal perceptual meaning cannot be understood in this way.

The crucial question for the behaviourist theory is this: Does overt activity necessarily indicate meaning in the sense of interpretation of signs? Let us suppose that a dog comes for his food when the dinner-bell is rung. The bell has aroused an activity appropriate to the object and we assume that the bell *means* dinner to the dog. Yet we cannot be sure of that. The dog's act is not different from many other habitual acts. Are we to say that all habitual acts are acts of interpretation of signs, of understanding? The weakness of the behaviouristic theory of meaning, even in connection with the simplest meaning situations, is that it affords no criterion by means of which interpretation (understanding) can be distinguished from other habitual acts. The theory leads necessarily to the conclusion that any stimulus to which we react in an habitual way is a sign, and is identical with interpretation.[1] It is

[1] For a further development of the same point, see R. M. Eaton, *Symbolism and Truth*, p. 26. Ogden and Richards, in *The Meaning of Meaning*, who hold the behaviouristic theory of meaning, take the simple sign situation as the generic form of the meaning situation to which all forms of meaning, including linguistic, can be reduced. But they hold that "interpretation" *is* here present. They define interpretation in the following way: when a context has affected us in the past, the recurrence of merely a part of the context will cause us to react in the way we reacted before. That is, of course, the entire question at issue, whether causation and understanding or interpretation can be identified, in other words whether a causal theory of meaning is possible. This question we shall take up later. In the meantime it should be noted that this is precisely the point at which *Gestalt* psychology takes issue with Behaviourism, more especially in its principle of the "non-equivalence of stimulus and meaning." It is for this reason also that strict Behaviourism tends to eliminate meaning from psychology, while for *Gestalt* psychology it is the basal category. In any case it seems quite clear that a behaviouristic account of meaning is wholly inadequate if meaning includes the element of interpretation.

extremely doubtful, then, whether animal meaning, whatever it may be, involves interpretation in the sense of apprehension of sign as sign. Animals may *seem* to do so owing to associations, but appear to be debarred from crossing the line which so sharply distinguishes associative suggestion and conditioned reflexes from interpretation. This would be what we should expect if the line between animal expressions and genuine language is what we have seen it to be.[1]

Obviously no dogmatic statements are possible at this point, but in view of all the facts we seem justified in confining animal meaning to the behavioural type. Kant, it is well known, denied all awareness of meaning to animals. He did this on the basis of the identification of such awareness with interpretation and understanding. Animals have apprehension but not apperception, and cannot, therefore, make their representations universal.[2] In any case, we are justified in distinguishing clearly between behavioural and linguistic meaning. For, as we shall see presently, not only is it true that everything denoted by language at all is, in a sense and to a degree, already universalized, but also that until the element of language enters there is no apprehension of the universal. In so far as "understanding" involves the apprehension of the universal, it seems to be the correlative of language and linguistic expression.

B

Meaning as an "Observable Property": Realistic Theories

Our problem is that of the nature of the meaning of things, and of the sense in which it may be said that language did not create this realm of meanings. If the meaning of things cannot be said to be merely our name for cues to adaptive movements, perhaps it may be said to be a property of things of which we become aware and which we then express in language. This view of perceptual meaning has found expression in certain "realistic" theories of meaning, as they are called, which are of importance not only for the general problem

[1] Chapter II, p. 79.
[2] Norman Kemp Smith, *Commentary on Kant's Critique of Pure Reason*, pp. 47 ff.

of meaning, but, as we shall see, for the philosophy of language.

"Meaning," it is said by Keynes, "is something in the things of which we have direct acquaintance, something directly perceptible, like colour and sound, intrinsic to the things perceived." Or again, by B. Russell, "meaning is an observable property of observable entities." John Laird holds that meaning, at least in its primary significance, is "an object of direct perception."

A certain basis for this position is to be found, we have seen, in the facts of direct analysis. The meaning of an object, as in the case of the meaning of the water or of the chair, is, in one sense at least, an integral part of the datum. This meaning is, to be sure, acquired, but, as we have seen, we must not confuse the genetic question of the origin of meanings with the way they operate or their status when acquired and established. Nevertheless we must proceed with great care, for upon our analysis here depend consequences of the greatest importance for our entire theory.

It is true, of course, that in what we have called perceptual meaning the sign is adherent to the thing signified, and in that sense the meaning is an integral part of the datum. But everything turns upon the nature of the datum. It is assumed in the theory under consideration that "things" are *given*, and that their "meaning" is a property like sound or colour, whereas *thinghood itself* is a meaning, or, in the words of Kofka, it is "meaning that transforms sense data into things." We can, therefore, in a sense say that we intuit meaning, for it is precisely meaning that has constituted them things of perception. On the other hand, it is equally true that what we call things are to an incalculable degree "ideal constructions." Indeed things first become *things* to the degree in which they are the objects of human activity and therefore receive designations or names. Thus viewed, we indeed intuit meanings in a certain sense, but that is because language itself is intuitive and part of the very perceptual process itself.[1]

[1] The "Namenhunger" of the child, his passion for names, is of interest here. It is often described as a kind of survival of the "magic of names" of the primitive mind. What it really is, as indeed it is in primitive peoples, is the process of perceptualizing of the world, the process by which sense data are transformed into things.

This latter thesis—that language is part of the perceptual process itself, in other words the "identity of intuition and expression"—is basal in this entire study, more particularly when we come to the problems of *Language and Cognition*. For the moment let us call attention to a *petitio principii* which is necessarily involved in all "realistic" theories of meaning. It is assumed that "things" are given and have or acquire meaning when, as we have said, it is "meaning" that transforms sense data into things. The problem of meaning presents itself to the philosopher under a double aspect, the psychological and the epistemological. In the psychological treatment, as in any scientific method, the only possible standpoint is to start with the "things" or "objects" as already constructed, and then to ask how they acquire their "adherent" meaning and how this meaning becomes mobile through language. The *petitio principii* in this method is, however, obvious, as indeed, from the philosophical standpoint, all scientific method must be. The philosophical treatment of the problem starts out from an entirely different, indeed an opposite standpoint. It must study perception and perceptual meaning, not as determined from without, but as a constitutive element in cognition.[1] If it is really meaning that transforms sense data into things, it then becomes a problem whether language and linguistic meaning are not present in the first processes of the transformation. This is, I think, undoubtedly the case, as we shall seek to show in our chapter on language and cognition. In any event, the "realistic" theory of meaning is guilty of this fallacy of *petitio principii*. That the clouds mean rain is for this theory something observable and perceptible like a colour or sound. As a matter of fact, until both clouds and rain (that is, the sense data to which the name clouds is given and the sense data to which the name rain is given) are individuated through language and its categories, there is no relation of meaning between them. There is only meaning as cue to action. In other words meaning is not something that is perceived; it is understood. It is in this sense that language first created the realm of meaning.

[1] See on this point E. Cassirer, *op. cit.*, Vol. III, pp. 63 ff.

C

Summary and Conclusion

The results of the preceding analysis may be summarized in the following way: (1) There is a legitimate sense of the word meaning, in which "things" have meaning prior to language. Meaning in this sense is, however, merely *cue to action*; it is not to be interpreted as a relation of sign to thing signified. If the notion of meaning includes those of understanding or interpretation, a behaviouristic or causal theory of meaning is untenable. Moreover, if the meaning relation includes understanding or interpretation, the meaning situation must also include not only the two components, the sign and the thing signified, but a third component, the subject for whom or which it is a sign, in short an interpreter.[1] (2) In the second place, it has been part of our contention throughout that meaning, in the sense both of interpretation of signs and as attribute of objects, does not arise except as constituted by language. The realistic theory of meaning examined above begs the entire question at issue. An examination of language and of semantic meaning is then necessary even for an answer to the question: What is the meaning of *things*? On the general question, then, with which this discussion started, whether "language first created the realm of meanings," our answer must be, if the notion of meaning is to include that of understanding, in the affirmative. It is to the realm of meanings in this sense that we must now turn.

IV

LINGUISTIC MEANING, ITS NATURE AND DIFFERENTIA

A

In the animal world the meanings of things are largely instinctive and the signs of these meanings are adherent to the thing signified. In human society, on the contrary, all is mobile. So a language is required which makes it possible to be always passing from what is known to what is yet to be

[1] This will be developed more fully presently.

known. There must be a language whose signs—which cannot be infinite in number—are extensible to an infinity of things. This tendency of the sign to transfer itself from one object to another is characteristic of human language.[1]

In principle any kind of "things" or any sense data may become the material of language. There is gesture language and idiographic language, both of which are for the eye, but language in the sense of speech is made up of sounds. Ear language, as it is called, is from one point of view a series of sounds—of "squeaks and grunts," which have acquired meaning; this type of language, rather than the eye language has, it is assumed, developed precisely because of the possible greater range of sounds and their greater mobility and fluidity. It is, then, with the mobility of signs that linguistic meaning is primarily connected, and with this mobility may be related all the basal differences between the meaning of things and the meaning of words.

B

The Mobility of Linguistic Signs

Words are in the first instance sounds, and as sounds acquire meaning and become the bearers of meaning. It is, so to speak, the intrinsic meaning of the sound *buzz* that turns this sound into the word *buzz*, the inherent meaning of the sound *ache* that turns it into the word *ache*. The self-authenticating character of these sounds is their intrinsic perceptual meaning, and this type of meaning is very close to the adherent meanings already examined. But even here that which turns the sound into the word is precisely this beginning of mobility, this detachment or abstraction of sign from things signified. The doctrine of *Urwörte*—of primitive roots—has indeed largely disappeared from linguistic science, but some element of "self-authenticating" sounds seems necessary to any intelligible theory of language.[2] It is the detachment which turns the sound into a word, but to be detached it must have been adherent; an intuitive element always remains in language.

Sounds acquire meaning even in the animal world. It is

[1] H. Bergson, *Creative Evolution*, p. 158.   [2] See Chapter II, p. 75.

this fact, together with the fact of a limited communication through these cries, which lead us to speak of animal language. But even here the difference between animal cries and language is immediately apparent. Communication through cries is in principle not different from the instinctive communication of the bees, for instance, through the odour of the pollen. It is confined to the "here" and the "now." The cry is a cue to action which is not separable from the thing or situation signified. In the danger cry, for instance, the sound is primarily a cue to action, but it also has a reference, however vague, to a situation to which the sound points, or for which it "stands." None the less it is bound to this situation, to the "here" and the "now." If it includes implicitly indication and prediction, as is sometimes held, it is only in the vaguest way. It has nothing of the mobility which makes possible detachment from the here and now.[1]

It is apparent, then, that semantic meaning differs fundamentally from meaning as cue to reaction. Meaning in both cases is a relation, a relation between a sign and "something signified," but the relation in the two cases is different in important respects. We shall now proceed to make clear these differences by analysing the type of relation existing between the verbal sign and the thing signified.

C

The Triadic Character of Semantic Meaning. Communicability

The mobility of signs, the tendency of a sign to transfer itself from one object to another, is the characteristic of language. This phenomenon of transference forms the central fact of linguistic meaning, but before examining it, it is necessary to consider a characteristic of the verbal meaning situation which in a sense conditions this transference, namely, the *triadic* character of the meaning relation.

In the meaning situation described as meaning of "things" only a subject and an object are involved. Whatever theory we may hold of the simple sign situation, whether it involves understanding or interpretation or not, and therefore a sub-

[1] Chapter II, p. 77 f.

ject, there are still always two and only two terms to the meaning relation, namely the sign, or cue to action and that for which it is a cue. In the simplest linguistic situation, on the other hand, there are always involved, either explicitly or implicitly, more than one subject. Certain sounds *mean* the fire engine, but the word fire-engine implies at least two subjects; in other words, a "speech community."[1]

It is true of course that, superficially at least, there are many cases of language function where only a subject and an object seem to be involved. If I call out the word fire-engine, the meaning of the word implies the presence of a second subject, but I may think of a fire-engine in terms of words without any overt communication or intention of communication. This is undoubtedly true. But if we examine such a situation more closely, we shall find that I cannot really think of it *significantly* in terms of this word without implying that the word is significant for others also. This becomes even clearer when we pass from words that are names for relatively simple perceptual objects to those that are names for more complex situations. Words such as love and marriage have no single unambiguous reference. Marriage, for instance, means one thing in the mouth of an anthropologist, another in the mouth of a jurist, and still another in the mouth of a priest. It is impossible to think meaningfully of the object in terms of this word without implied reference to the universe of discourse, or the speech community, in which the word is used.

The position here maintained may be made clearer by making use of a distinction between the *process* of communication and a *state* of communication, between overt and latent communication.[2] Words, we have seen, are, from one point of view at least, "things" that have acquired meaning. This meaning has, however, been acquired *only in communication* and the communicability of this meaning is *part* of the meaning, irrespective of whether the actual process of communication is going on or not. The latent reference to other subjects of communication is as much a part of the meaning of the

---

[1] This conception of the language situation is, we have already seen, part of the new speech notion. So far as linguistic science is concerned, language has no reality except in the speech community. See Chapter II, p. 67.

[2] These terms are employed by Haserot, *The Logic of Being*, p. 5, who also insists that there is no linguistic meaning without the implication of communication.

word as its reference to objects. This is what we mean by saying that the meaning of a word does not exist apart from its context. The entire question of the nature of context will be discussed in a later chapter. Here it will be sufficient to insist that no theory of context can be constructed which does not involve the notion of communication either latent or overt.

Curiously enough, there are those who persist in thinking that verbal meaning is a dyadic relation. This view is, of course, inevitable on any theory that seeks to equate verbal meaning with the simple sign situation and to reduce all meaning to causal relations. It is possible to do this, however, only if we abstract language from "speech" or discourse and view it as a collection of entities to be related to other entities. If we do this we are no longer dealing with linguistic meaning but with something else—a pure abstraction.

D

Transference of Signs: Semantic Meaning as Transitive

Communication, whether overt or latent, is then the *sine qua non* of linguistic meaning. It is its triadic character, moreover, which conditions transference of signs and makes linguistic meaning transitive.

By transitive meaning I understand a relation between the sign and the thing signified such that the sign may be transferred from one entity to another and in that transference stand meaningfully for the second. One of the forms of distinction between relations in general is that between transitive and non-transitive. Some relations are such that if they hold between x and y and between y and z, then they hold also between x and z. In connection with the meaning of verbal signs the question is this. If a word x means y, are there relations between y and z such that x can mean z also? If such is the case, then the verbal meaning relation would be transitive. Such transitive relation manifests itself, we shall see, in the phenomenon of word transference.

It is, I think, in general the characteristic of sensible, non-linguistic signs to be non-transferable and for the meaning relation to be non-transitive. This is true, of course, of the intrinsic meaning of "things." It is the very character of the adherent perceptual sign to terminate in the thing signified. But it is also true, I think, of the extrinsic meaning. If one entity is the sign of a second entity and the latter a sign of a third, it does not at all follow that the first named is a sign of the third. The character of verbal meaning is, on the contrary, in general of the transitive type, and it is this character which underlies the fundamental mobility of linguistic signs. This is, of course, the essence of metaphor, which is a carrying over a word as an expressive sign for one object to another object related to the second in a definite way. The word kid is the name for the young of a certain animal, but it may also become an expressive sign for the human young, because of a certain relation between the young of the goat and the young of the man. It is in fact this transitive character of linguistic meaning which makes linguistic signs mobile in contrast to non-linguistic. Metaphor, as we shall see in a later chapter, is the primary law of speech construction and of the discovery and expression of meanings through language.

In speaking of transference of names we are of course applying an image from spatial motion, as indeed the whole notion of transitive relation is spatial in character. But here an important difference is to be noted in the things compared. When an object is transferred in space, the object quits its former position in process of assuming the second, but when a name is transferred from one thing to another, the name does not cease thereby to belong to the thing from which it was transferred. It is indeed possible to transfer signs from one meaning to another just as things are transferred in space. I can use X to signify 6 in one calculation and 7 in another and in the moment when it begins to signify 7 it ceases to signify 6. But that is not the way words are transferred in living speech. They signify the new objects not by losing but by conserving their former meanings.[1]

This double reference of verbal signs, like their triadic character, is a basal differentia of semantic meaning. The fact that a sign can intend one thing without ceasing to intend

---

[1] See in this connection Willis, *The Philosophy of Speech*, p. 57. (Published by George Allen and Unwin Ltd.).

another, that, indeed, the very condition of its being an *expressive* sign for the second is that it is also a sign for the first, is precisely what makes language an instrument of knowing. This "accumulated intension" of words is the fruitful source of ambiguity, but it is also the source of that analogous prediction, through which alone the symbolic power of language comes into being.

As there are those who deny the triadic character of linguistic meaning, so there are those who deny its transitive character. When they do so, however, it is because, as in the former case, they are viewing language no longer as speech but as sounds; no longer as words and sentences in discourse but as dead petrifacts, abstracted from that which gives them meaning, so that they may be treated as "things."

E

Linguistic Meaning as Non-Symmetrical

The uniqueness of linguistic meaning is seen in the triadic and transitive character of the meaning relations involved. But there is another aspect in which it is unique and from some viewpoints it is perhaps of even more importance. It may be described as the non-symmetrical character of the linguistic meaning relation.

In the perceptual meaning situation the position of sign and thing signified may be interchanged. Clouds mean rain, but rain also means clouds, although from the standpoint of behaviour the first is the more important relation. Similarly, the sound of the striking match means the flame, but the flame might also mean the sound, as is seen in cases in which, because of distance, light travels more rapidly than the sound. It has been maintained by Whitehead that the relation of the word to the thing is of the same symmetrical character. "Why do we say that the word 'tree'—spoken or written—is a symbol to us for trees? Both the word itself and trees themselves enter into experience on equal terms; and it would be just as sensible, viewing the question abstractly, for trees to symbolize the word tree as for the word to symbolize the trees." He continues by saying that this is certainly true and that human nature sometimes works that way, citing the poet, for whom he thinks the trees are the symbols and the words are the meaning.[1]

This, it seems to me, completely distorts the actual situation. Human nature simply does not work that way. The tree is not the sign or symbol for the word for the poet in the same way that the word is the sign or symbol for the tree. The latter, the word, is an expressive sign with all the characters of communicability and transference described, whereas the actual tree is at most a stimulus for association and imaginative description. The word tree is transferable, as when we speak of the tree of life, whereas the perceived tree is not thus transferable. The verbal sign is an expressive sign, and it is precisely for that reason that the relation must be non-symmetrical. This conception of the symmetrical character of the verbal meaning relation is obviously but a part of the general tendency to equate the verbal sign situation with the simple sign situation and to reduce the former to the latter—to view language not as words and sentences in discourse, but as entities.

F

Language and the Notion of "Expressive Signs"

The outstanding fact of the preceding analysis is, I think, the establishment of certain fundamental differences between the two notions, the meaning of things and the meaning of words. The triadic, transitive, and non-symmetrical character of linguistic meanings, with the element of mobility bound up with these characters, marks off the latter type of meaning from the former in a way that admits of no equating of the one with the other, or of reduction in any fashion of the latter to the former.

This is, of course, not to deny that the two notions of meaning have one very fundamental element in common, namely, the notion of sign and signification. Both the perceptual sign and the verbal sign are *signs*, but their relations to that which is signified differ fundamentally. The sound of the fire-engine and the word fire-engine are both signs. Both are bearers of meaning, but the word is a bearer of meaning

---

[1] A. N. Whitehead, *Symbolism, Its Meaning and Effect*, p. 12.

in quite a different way from that in which the sound is bearer. It is equally clear that the meanings of which they are bearers differ basally.

It will be well to bring out this difference more clearly. I shall do so by means of the following definition of semantic meaning. Meaning is the capacity of an expression to signify an aspect of reality. Here the significant term in the definition is *expression*. As Husserl insists, there is a fundamental difference between expression and sign. A word does not signify an entity in the way a happening or event, as for instance a cloud, signifies or means rain. In its signification is always involved *intentionality*. It is only *as an expression* that it indicates at all, only as it presupposes communication, either overt or latent, that it *signifies* in any sense whatsoever.

G

The Semantic Meaning-situation

The results of our analysis of linguistic meaning may be summarized in a statement of the components of the semantic meaning-situation.

Every meaning-situation, including the semantic, has two *prima facie* components, the sign and the thing signified—that which means and that which is meant. Meaning in its most elementary form is, then, this relation, our name for a unique relation not further analysable. Upon these *prima facie* components all analyses agree, but these components are not, it can be shown, the whole of the situation.

When we analyse more closely the first component, the sign, we find that there is always presupposed someone for whom it is a sign, someone for whom the meaning is. In so far as we are dealing with pre-linguistic meaning this one or X, for whom or for which the meaning is, may be left indefinite. All that we need to say is that a third component of some sort is needed to complete or round out the meaning relation. In the case of animal meaning we might substitute for the X in this relation organism or possibly even "thing," although there is something very awkward and artificial in such a notion. In the case of semantic meaning this is, however, impossible. The *X* must be either a speaker or a hearer. If our analysis has been correct, both must be present either explicitly or presupposed. Communicability is part of the meaning as such.

So much, then, for the analysis of the first of the *prima facie* components of the meaning-relation. Let us now look at the second, the *thing meant*. On the face of it, it would seem that the second component needs no further analysis; "what is meant" in the meaning-relation is just what it is, and has no further implicate. This is, however, not the case. Whereas the implicate of the first component is always the speech community for which the meaning is, the implicate of the second component is always some context, some "universe of discourse" in which the entity meant has its "being." Understanding of the meaning of a word is always determined by context of some kind, either the "context of situation" or in more developed discourse the more systematic context of "universe of discourse."[1] The study of the principle of context in detail is the problem of a later chapter. Here we shall insist merely that unless these implied components of the semantic meaning situation are left standing, this meaning becomes meaningless.[2]

V

SEMANTIC MEANING AND THE UNIVERSAL

There is, then, no semantic meaning situation which does not involve as necessary components both speaker and hearer.

[1] Chapter V, pp. 195 ff.

[2] This analysis of semantic meaning may be compared with a similar analysis of the meaning situation in general of G. Watts Cunningham in *On the Meaning Situation* in the volume *Contemporary Idealism in America*. According to him, "meaning becomes meaningless" unless three elements or components in the meaning situation are left standing—the sign, the thing signified, and the mind for which the meaning is. With this our analysis would be wholly in agreement. It is the difference between semantic meaning and other types of the meaning situation which Cunningham's analysis overlooks. The four types of meaning which he analyses, the perceptual, the conceptual, the emotive, and the evaluative, all have these three components, as he has abundantly shown. But these situations cannot be adequately analysed unless linguistic meaning is also included. For language enters into them all. Had he examined the semantic meaning situation he would have come to a somewhat different theory of meaning.

Words are signs, but they are expressive signs. As such they are characterized by *intentionality* and this intentionality implies communication, either overt or latent. So far as semantic meaning is concerned the correlatives, expression and understanding, constitute an *Urphenomen*. Language, as language, has no reality except in the speech community. This notion —of expression and expressive sign—cannot, of course, be completely developed except in connection with its correlative notion of understanding and interpretation. To this we shall presently turn. For the moment it is desirable to develop still another aspect of semantic meaning, namely, its relation to the universal.

There is a sense in which everything denoted by language is universalized. Whatever particular sign is named, the very act of naming, of speaking, transforms and universalizes it. To give the name "cold" to any particular experience not only takes it out of the realm of the merely individual and particular, but also takes it out of the realm of the subjective —objectifies it. But there are degrees or levels of universality. The primitive verbal sign situation is the sentence-word, e.g. "cold." The word is here still dependent upon the perceptual context or situation for its significance. The transition from this primitive form to the more independent and complete predication which *names* its object is as tep to a new level of universality.[1] A further step in this process is reached when speech turns back upon itself, so to speak, and transforms the original predicate into a subject of further discourse or uses the name to denote a class as such and not a particular member. It is then that the abstract universal emerges. With this highest level of universality speech has ceased to concern itself directly with primary things and meanings. Its reference to them is only indirect, and with this increased indirectness speech has acquired a virtual autonomy which includes in it functions quite other than those of the sensible sign, and which distingish linguistic meaning fundamentally from non-linguistic.

This notion of levels of universality becomes of importance in connection with problems of language and cognition; here we are concerned merely with the first level as present in *all*

---

[1] For further development of this point, see G. A. de Laguna, *Speech: Its Function and Development*, pp. 355 ff.

semantic meaning. In describing it we may make use with advantage of Lotze's term "first" or primary universal, to distinguish it from the secondary or abstract universal. This first universal appears, as we have seen, whenever any object is named. Nouns, verbs, adjectives, are all in a sense names and an element of universality inheres in them all. Lotze insists that this first universal is intuitive, is of a very different character from the ordinary class concepts of logic, and is indeed presupposed by them. Perception itself contains this universal. It is true, of course, that it is always a particular colour or tone that is perceived, always a particular *quale* or intensity. But this perception is always accompanied by the fact that every other colour or tone has an equal right to function as an example of the universal. The class concept such as colour or tone is not then, he further insists, constructed by repressing or eliminating the individual colour or tone phenomenon but rather by the recognition of a common element (in the individual phenomena themselves) already *intuited*.

This doctrine of the "double universal," as Cassirer calls it, is of great importance in the understanding of semantic meaning. Our problem here is the relation of the intuitive universal to language. We shall follow Cassirer rather closely at this point.[1]

Actually, we have seen, everything denoted by language is already universalized. Apart from purely formless interjections and emotive sounds, all forms of language contain in them this form of thought and of objectification. The universal is not the product of abstraction and *then* embodied in language. It is already present in the earliest forms of language and the later process of abstraction can take place only upon contents that are already thus universalized, already linguistically related. The primary universal receives its great significance, therefore, from the fact that it is the *sine qua non* of semantic meaning *as such*, is present, so to speak, in the first "precipitate" of language, and furnishes the basis for further more complex syntheses of logical thought. Here also lies the real secret of predication as a problem at once linguistic and logical. Predication, in the logical sense, is but the conceptual expression

[1] *Op. cit.*, Vol. I, pp. 249 ff. Also Vol. III, pp. 135 ff.

of relations already intuited. Earlier in this chapter we indicated how language is part of the perceptual process itself and developed the principle of "the identity of intuition and expression." We have now seen how the first or intuitive universal is present in the perceptual process.

The further consideration of the universal as a *sine qua non* of semantic meaning belongs to other contexts. We shall conclude our study here by indicating the relation of the universal to communication. Communication, either overt or latent, is, we have found, implied in all linguistic meaning. Communication, however, implies the universal. This fact has been expressed by Sapir in the following way:

"The elements of language, the symbols that are significant of experience, must be associated with delimited classes of experiences, rather than with the single experiences themselves. Only so is communication possible. For the single experience lodges in the individual consciousness and is strictly incommunicable. To be communicated it must needs be referred to a class that is tacitly accepted by the community as an identity."[1]

With this general statement of the relation of the universal to communication we may agree. But some further comment on the form of statement is in order—for it becomes of great importance in our later study of the nature and conditions of intelligible communication. It is entirely clear, first of all, that, just as the universal is the *sine qua non* of semantic meaning, so it is the *sine qua non* of communication. Strictly speaking, individual experiences cannot be communicated. It is equally clear that the universal must be at least *tacitly* accepted by the community. Mutual acknowledgment of the universal is the condition of communication. But it may well be questioned whether that which is thus accepted or acknowledged by the community is properly characterized as a *class*. If the preceding analysis is correct the class concept is a later development presupposing the intuitive universal already determined and embodied in language. It is this universal that, in the first instance, makes possible communication. It is indeed quite true to say that the formation of concepts and classes, and their tacit acknowledgment of identity, is the necessary con-

[1] *Op cit.*, p. 11.

dition of certain developed forms of communication—forms of communication corresponding to the levels of universality already distinguished. But for human communication, as distinguished from animal communication, confined as the latter is to perceptual signs and to the "here" and the "now," only the first level of universality is necessary.[1]

Semantic meaning is, then, conditioned by the presence of the universal on one of the levels of its development. It is in fact the presence of the universal which is not only the condition of communication, but of the other two characters which distinguish semantic from other meaning, namely, its transitive and non-reversible character. It is only by virtue of the presence of the first or "primary" universal that the transference of signs—and the double reference which is the outstanding character of the verbal sign—are possible. It is also for the same reason that linguistic meaning is non-symmetrical. The "word tree" and the "trees themselves" do not enter into experience on equal terms. It is only the word that can be an *expressive* sign and this for the reason that expression involves the beginning of the universal.

VI

LINGUISTIC MEANING. UNDERSTANDING (*Das Verstehen*)

A

The account of linguistic meaning given in the preceding pages may be tested and checked up, so to speak, by an examination of what is involved or presupposed in the understanding of words. To understand is to apprehend the meaning of whatever it is that is understood. To understand language is to apprehend the meaning of words as linguistic expressions or expressive signs. An investigation of what it is to understand language will throw light upon the nature of the meaning thus understood.

The entire problem of understanding (*Das Verstehen*) has bulked large in recent philosophical investigations. Ever since Dilthey enunciated his famous dictum in his debate with

[1] The conditions of "intelligible communication" will be considered more fully in Chapter VI.

Ebbinghaus—"things we describe, the soul we understand"—a special meaning has been given to the notion of understanding and the nature of this aspect of cognition has become a problem in all the more sophisticated epistemologies. The investigation of this notion has, accordingly, become the task of various types of philosophies and as a result of these investigations certain important distinctions and conclusions have emerged which we shall attempt to make clear.

In the first place, strictly speaking, it is only expressions, not things that are understood. It is true that we speak of understanding things. We say we understand a machine, or understand an event, or indeed we may talk of understanding the world. But this is true only in a derived sense. If we understand a machine it is because it is an expression of intelligence, speaks, as it were, a certain language. If we understand an event, in nature or still more in history, it is only in so far as it is an expression or embodiment of meaning. If we understand the world it is only in so far as it contains an element of expression, or is an ideal construction involving language and its categories. In sum, things we merely recognize; it is only expressive signs, language of some sort, that we understand.

There is much confusion of thought on this subject. Miss Stebbing has noted this confusion, and consideration of a passage from her *Logic* will help to make clear the point I wish to make.

"It is important to notice that in the strict sense of understanding with which we are here concerned—what we understand is always a symbol. . . . Only signs are understood and to understand a sign is to know what it signifies. Hence to understand a verbal symbol is to know what it refers to, i.e. to know the referend for which it stands. The word symbolizes the referend."

"People" (we are further informed) "sometimes talk vaguely about 'understanding the universe' or 'understanding life' or 'understanding a person.' In these phrases 'understand' is used loosely to signify knowing certain facts about, or having certain attitudes to, or capable of making certain responses to, or all these at once. But this is not a use of the word that is suitable to logic."[1]

Part of this statement we may accept. Strictly speaking, what we understand is always a sign or symbol. But, if our analysis

[1] L. S. Stebbing, *A Modern Introduction to Logic*, p. 14.

is valid, while *only* signs are understood, not *all* signs are understood. We have understanding only of expressive signs. The reaction in the simple sign situation is, as we have seen, not a case of understanding. On the other hand, it is not true that to understand a verbal symbol is merely to know what it refers to. A collection of meaningless sounds may be made a sign for an object. It has signification, and that signification may be *recognized*, but there is no understanding. We simply do not understand words when we merely know what they designate, as has already been pointed out. That is merely an arbitrary conception of understanding made necessary by a quite arbitrary view of logic. The second part of the statement we may also accept in so far as it maintains that there is understanding of things only in a very "loose sense" of understanding. Strictly speaking we understand only signs or symbols, and of these merely expressive signs. Understanding of the "universe" or of "life" does mean, strictly speaking, having certain attitudes towards them, or being capable of making certain responses to them, but such attitudes or responses are possible only in so far as the "universe" or "life" are expressions.

Be this as it may—and to this point we shall return presently—it is at least clear that the notion of *understanding* cannot be applied to the primitive sign situation. It is a misnomer to apply the terms understanding and interpretation to the element of mere recognition as cue to reaction, to those situations which are taken as typical in the behaviouristic theory of meaning. Recognitive meaning is not understanding or interpretation.

B

Understanding and Semantic Meaning

We may assume, then, that the understanding of anything presupposes that it has already become an element in an expression. Let us further assume that strictly speaking it is only words, not things, that are understood—that it is only in a derived sense that we may be said to understand things. What, then, is it to understand words?

LANGUAGE AS THE BEARER OF MEANING

Here again a second important distinction is in order. It is of the first importance to recognize that, strictly speaking, *single* words are not understood. They are, as Ammann says, known or not known. One cannot understand a word *in abstracto*. There are, indeed, single words that are understood, but they are sentence words. I say, indeed, I did not understand a man's name when it was spoken, or I did not understand the last word in a sentence, but closer analysis shows that what I mean is that I did not recognize it. But to know a word is not to know what it designates. It is important to insist upon this point. We do not understand words merely when we know what they designate. It is entirely possible to know what a word designates or indicates, without understanding it at all. The dual theory of linguistic meaning—indicative and emotive—reduces all understanding to knowing what a word designates and thus utterly fails to grasp the character of understanding. Single words, then, are not understood, but only recognized. When a child says "cold" he is understood, but that is because the word is a sentence-word, because the meaning is determined by a context of situation and when that context is made explicit the single word resolves itself into a sentence, such as I am cold, the ice is cold, etc. What, then, are the conditions of understanding of speech or of semantic meaning? Husserl has examined these conditions and finds them to consist of two, namely *Gestalt* and intention. Let us proceed to examine the first.

A man emits a series of "meaningless" words which we do not understand, which are unintelligible, but may become meaningful through arrangement. What distinguishes the first act of speaking from the second, the meaningless from the meaningful, the unintelligible from the intelligible? On the surface the difference is a matter of mere arrangement, of pattern. And in a sense that is true. This element of form or pattern is then, in the first instance, the condition of understanding. In a sense the meaningless combination of sounds is like any meaningless combination of sense data, and the non-understanding of the hearer like what is called psychic blindness in the case of perceptual meaning. In the case of the latter the visual apparatus is unimpaired but the sense data mediated through the apparatus are not able to come to a specific pattern or *Gestalt*, which, as we have seen, is also an element in the meaning of a thing.[1]

Understanding is then conditioned by apprehension of pattern (*Gestalt*). It is at this point that the relation of meaning and understanding to syntax appears. The minimum of such understanding may be seen in such pseudo phrases as "large brown on." The elements are recognized, but the wholes are without meaning. They present the semblance of wholes but they conform to no rules of syntax. They are not understood and are therefore called nonsense. The nature of syntactical sense and nonsense will be examined more fully in later contexts;[2] here the point is solely that syntax is a condition of understanding. This condition may be described as external speech form. Many linguists maintain, however, that for genuine understanding of language there must also be what they describe as "inner speech form." This notion, first introduced into linguistics by von Humboldt to distinguish the unique character of particular languages from the elements common to all languages, is now quite generally used to signify those peculiar patterns which distinguish the linguistic feeling of one people from another. The notion becomes of special importance in connection with the problem of translation and will be discussed more fully in that connection,[3] the main point being that the limitations to the translation of meaning from one language to another are explained, partly at least, in terms of inner speech form. In other words, one of the conditions of the understanding of any language is the apprehension of its inner speech forms. Understanding is then conditioned by apprehension of speech form both outer and inner. Without the former language is but a meaningless col-

---

[1] This phenomenon of verbal blindness has been studied by both psychologists and linguists and the facts have been brought together by Cassirer in Chapter VI of Vol. III, under the heading, *Zur Pathologie des Symbolbewusstseins*. These facts go far towards confirming the principle that language is part of the perceptual process itself. When in certain forms of aphasia the word is not recognized, or cannot be formed, the perceptual meaning is absent also. "The significance of speech for the construction (*Aufbau*) of the perceptual world" itself becomes obvious. It confirms the thesis of the correlation of speech structure and perceptual structure, and if the speech form does not come into being perceptual meaning is also lost. But something else appears equally clear, namely, that linguistic meaning is a matter of structure or *Gestalt* and that without this *Gestalt* meaning is absent.

[2] Chapter VII, p. 292 f.   [3] Chapter VI, p. 235 f.

lection of sounds. Without the latter it has meaning of a sort but lacks the meaning without which full and genuine understanding is not possible. But, according to Husserl, understanding involves more than this. The essence of semantic meaning is its intentionality, and understanding of the meaning involves the apprehension and acknowledgment of this intentionality. It is this notion of intentionality which is fundamental for the entire concept of understanding. It is necessary to examine it in more detail.

The intentionality of a linguistic expression always has reference to the secondary or implied components of the semantic meaning situation. These we have seen are two: (*a*) the speech community for which the meaning is, and (*b*) the universe of discourse in which the entity meant has its being. The conditions of understanding we shall then describe as the mutual acknowledgment of the universe of discourse and of the presuppositions which determine it.

In developing this notion I shall introduce a term of which considerable use will be made in the sequel, namely the scholastic notion of the *suppositio*. According to this notion, the meaning of a word, its intentionality, is determined by its supposition. Language is elliptical and in every use of language the context which is assumed or presupposed must be supplied. In the sentence "pope is derived from the Latin papa" there is one *suppositio*; in the sentence, "the Pope is old" another. Understanding of the statement involves the apprehension and acknowledgment of the supposition. The further application of this notion must wait upon the development of the principle of context in a later chapter.[1] Here we shall make use of it merely to bring out more clearly the nature of intentionality. The intentionality of words which distinguishes linguistic meaning from mere signification, includes not merely the *prima facie* relation between that which *means* and that which is *meant* but also a context or universe of discourse presupposed. That is the supposition, and this supposition, as part of the intentionality, must be apprehended and *acknowledged* if understanding is to be possible.

[1] Chapter V, pp. 200 ff.

C

Intentionality and Value

The supposition of a linguistic expression is part of its intentionality and the apprehension and acknowledgment of the supposition a condition of understanding. A second aspect of intentionality is a reference to values, and a condition of understanding the acknowledgment of values. Indeed we shall venture to say that the universe of discourse is partly determined by the mutual acknowledgment of purposes and values and the *suppositio* itself always contains a reference to them.

One of the moot problems of philosophy is whether "meaning" as such implies value. In the classification of theories of meaning given by Ogden and Richards, one type of theory holds that reference to values and their acknowledgment is a necessary presupposition of meaning; other theories maintain that it is not. The situation here is complicated and we must proceed with care. We may get the problem before us by examination of a passage from John Laird. "Meaning," he writes, "is an ambiguous concept. On one interpretation it presupposes value, on another it does not. Meaning is sometimes synonymous with intention. My meaning is what I intend to convey, to communicate, to some other person. Now intentions are of course intentions of minds, and these intentions presuppose values." But, it is held, "the 'facts' I intend to indicate have no necessary relation to the values implied and acknowledged in my intention. There is then a second meaning of meaning. When I say that such a perceived thing means so and so, this merely expresses a certain perceived state of the perceived facts, i.e. the way in which such fact or aspect of fact indicates something else in the facts. It is this second meaning of meaning that contains no implication of value."[1]

We may simplify our problem by noting the admission that wherever intentionality is involved meaning implies value: "intentions are, of course, the intentions of minds and these intentions imply values." This would mean that linguistic

[1] John Laird, *A Study in Realism*, p. 33.

meaning, which as we have seen, is always intentional, would necessarily imply value. This is, I think, beyond question. For intentionality, as a character of verbal meaning and as a condition of understanding, is, as our analysis has abundantly shown, inseparable from the "intentions of minds," both of speaker and hearer. It is precisely this that makes them expressive signs. What now shall we say of this "second meaning of meaning" which, according to Laird, "contains no implication of values"?

It is obvious that we have here in a different form the *realistic* theory of meaning considered in an earlier section of this chapter, as well as the theory that there is understanding of things apart from their relation to expression: in the terms of Laird, that "meaning, at least in its primary significance, is an object of direct perception." The difficulties in this theory of meaning have been already pointed out. We shall now consider it in the context of our discussion of understanding. If our analysis has been valid even here reference to value is presupposed. The mere perception of a relation between two perceived facts, e.g. the clouds and rain, does not constitute a case of understanding. Strictly speaking, the clouds do not mean rain and this "meaning of meaning" is a misnomer. There is no intentionality here. Except to mind, with purposes and values, there is no indication (because no expression) and therefore, of course, no understanding.

In commenting upon this passage elsewhere[1] I expressed myself as finding it exceedingly difficult to understand how the "facts which I indicate" can have any meaning to me unless they have reference to some purpose or value, practical or scientific, which leads me to indicate or point them out as facts. Nor can I convey the meaning of these facts to anyone who does not appreciate and acknowledge the same purposes and values which I have in mind in the indication. There is,

[1] This principle of the inseparability of understanding and value has been worked out more fully in *The Intelligible World*. It is also accepted and well expressed by A. N. Whitehead, especially in his lecture *Nature and Life*, p. 8. He is speaking of the Newtonian physics. "Newton's methodology of physics," he writes, "was an overwhelming success. But the forces which he introduced still left Nature without meaning and value. . . . He thus illustrated a great philosophic truth, that a dead Nature can give no reasons. All ultimate reasons are in terms of aim at value." The entire drift of his discussion is to insist upon the inseparability of intelligibility and value.

I am inclined to believe, no meaning of meaning that does not contain some implication of value. The second meaning of meaning, which as we have seen *is* secondary and derived, contains, it is true, no direct implication of value, but the implication is always there, to be analysed out.

VII

THEORIES OF LINGUISTIC MEANING: NATURALISTIC AND IDEALISTIC

A

The preceding study of the notions of "understanding" and "intentionality" substantiates our analysis of linguistic meaning and serves to make clear the fundamental distinctions between linguistic and non-linguistic meaning. Expression and understanding are strictly correlative terms; only expressions are "understood." The primary condition of an expression is that it is a *Gestalt*. But back of this coordination of sound complexes, this "formal" meaning, so to speak, lie further acts of understanding without which the understanding of language is impossible. It is the apprehension and acknowledgment of intentionality in the two aspects described, which marks off clearly the semantic from every other meaning situation.

With our present concepts of linguistic meaning we may now proceed to the consideration of theories of linguistic meaning. The fundamental ambiguity in the notion of meaning which made it possible to say that language first created the world of meanings and that it did not create it, formed the starting point of our entire study, and one of the chief tasks of this chapter was to clear up this ambiguity. This task has now been accomplished, with the result that the fundamental differences between pre-linguistic and linguistic meaning have been made clear. Our analysis of pre-linguistic meaning was followed by an examination of the theories of the nature of that meaning. In like manner our analysis of linguistic meaning leads naturally to a consideration of theories as to the nature of this type.

B

Behaviouristic (Naturalistic) Theories of Linguistic Meaning

The simplest theory of linguistic meaning is to conceive it as but a special case of the meaning of "things." The perceptual sign situation becomes the typical meaning situation and the meaning of words is reduced to this type. We have, then, what may be called the reductionist or behaviouristic theory of language and linguistic meaning. In the words of C. I. Lewis, "speech is only that part of behaviour which is most significant of meanings and most useful for communication."[1] In many quarters a behaviouristic conception of speech is held to be absolutely fundamental to the whole treatment of speech.[2]

In our earlier examination of the behaviouristic theory we described the problem which it sets as twofold. (*a*) Does it explain the meaning situation in its simplest form, that of animal meanings? (*b*) Does it explain linguistic or semantic meaning? The inability of the behaviouristic theory to explain even animal meaning, if in the concept of meaning is included the notion of understanding or interpretation of signs, would inevitably bring with it the conclusion that *a fortiori* it is unable to explain linguistic meaning. Nevertheless, since certain special problems are here involved, more especially those raised by our analysis of understanding, it is desirable to give a brief consideration to the theory.

The root notion of the entire naturalistic theory is the causal conception of meaning. Reductive behaviourism equates both the meaning of the thing and the meaning of the word with our way of reacting. The behaviour—which is the meaning—is itself the product of the environment. All meaning then—both the adherent meaning of things and the mobile meaning of words—is sufficiently accounted for by causal relations between the organism and the environment. The consequence for the philosophy of language is that all the meanings of words, both emotive and indicative, are reduced to causal reference and equated with it. The advantages of this causal theory are, it is held, very great. It gets rid, at one stroke, of the entire problem of representation, of correspondence in

---

[1] *Mind and the World Order*, p. 90.   [2] G. A. de Laguna, *op. cit.*, pp. 9 ff.

structure between the linguistic form and the structure of things. It makes such an assumption unnecessary and indeed highly improbable. For the entire notion of representation is substituted a simpler notion of indication, of "standing for," interpreted causally, and thus for a correspondence theory of truth a purely pragmatic conception may be substituted.[1]

This causal theory certainly has the merit of simplicity. It has also a certain plausibility; otherwise it would not have been formulated. In the simplest cases of animal meaning surely the sign is but a modification of the organism and may be viewed as the effect of the object acting on the organism. The relation of the sign to the thing signified is then merely the reverse of that relation. Even here, however, the plausibility is only apparent. The taste of the caterpillar or the sound of the bell are, to be sure, *caused by* the stimuli, but *unless* the notion of understanding, or interpretation of sign as sign be left out of the notion of meaning, the plausibility vanishes. A behaviouristic theory makes it impossible to distinguish between merely habitual actions and interpretation of meaning.

It is, however, when we come to linguistic meaning that the difficulties become insuperable. For here it is precisely *understanding* that is the *sine qua non* of such meaning. To be sure, even here there is a certain initial plausibility. Certainly, the sound rung out in the mating or danger cry, or the basal interjectional elements of speech, are effects of stimuli from the external environment on the organism. Surely they become signs for their causes and the meaning relation is a causal one. Again, whatever view we take as to the origin of "names," the sound which is taken as the sign of the perceptual object is *caused* by the environment and the meaning relation must ultimately be this relation. But this plausibility is not even apparent when the facts are actually examined. The sound does not become a linguistic fact at all until it is detached from its purely causal context, become mobile; and this detachment and mobility are not functions of the physical environment but of the speech community. In the second place, the linguistic sign acquires through this detachment and mobility, in addition to its direct reference or primary intention, an indirect reference or secondary intention. It is impossible to

[1] Ogden and Richards, *op. cit.*, p. 307.

equate this element of meaning with the causal relation. Here the principle of non-correspondence of stimulus and meaning applies with additional force. Applicable even in the sphere of perceptual meaning, it is *a fortiori* present in the case of verbal meaning.

The causal theory of meaning encounters an additional difficulty not so evident in the case of the meaning of things, for it must explain the element of intentionality which is the *sine qua non* of linguistic meaning. We "intend" or "think of things" in terms of words. A causal theory of linguistic meaning seems then to lead to the identification of intending with being caused by. Now this suggestion—that to say I am thinking of A is the same thing as to say my thought is being caused by A—is, it is admitted by upholders of this causal theory, a hard saying. In the words of Ogden and Richards, "it shocks every right-minded person." And it surely does, for it is very much like saying that wood is iron. But the natural incredulity with which we first meet this view disappears, we are told, when we interpret the phrase "being caused by" as merely forming part of a context. Colloquial speech compels us, we are told, to use certain forms of speech when we really do not mean what we say. We speak of cause when we actually mean context. Thus the meaning of the perceptual sign is the event that "caused it" or is in contextual relation with it. The sound of the striking of the match *means* the flame that results. So, in the last analysis, the meaning of the *word* match is its causal or contextual relation with the physical context of sound and flame. I do not think that our natural incredulity disappears by interpreting causality in terms of contextual relation. Context, on this view, is equated with the physical environment. The principle of non-equivalence of stimulus and meaning applies with even greater force to the notion of physical context than to the separate physical cause or stimulus. The entire physical concept of context will be subjected to critical examination in a later connection; here we are concerned merely to indicate the difficulties which inhere in the causal or naturalistic theory of linguistic meaning.

The behaviouristic theory of linguistic meaning involves, then, the equating of the meaning relation, intentionality, with the causal relation. When brought face to face with the actual facts of linguistic meaning, in its two aspects of expression and understanding, it loses all plausibility. If it fails to explain even the simplest case of perceptual sign situation, when that situation is conceived to include understanding or interpretation, *a fortiori* it is inapplicable to the sphere of verbal meaning where expression and understanding are the defining notions, in which the meaning relation is triadic, and in which meaning implies communication, either latent or overt.

C
Idealistic Theories of Linguistic Meaning

It may then be assumed that no merely naturalistic or behaviouristic account of linguistic meaning can do justice to its peculiar characters. The failure of purely naturalistic theories of language is recognized, we have seen, even in the field of linguistic science itself. It was precisely the principle of the "primacy of meaning" and the failure of the causal theory of meaning which led to the revision of the assumptions of linguistic science and to the development of the new speech notion. We have, as a consequence, the opposition between "positivism" and "idealism" in linguistic science itself. We may therefore quite justly speak of the idealistic theories of linguistic meaning as contrasted with naturalistic.

The essentials of the idealistic theory of language have already been stated in the preceding chapter. Negatively we found it to consist in a denial of the causal theory of meaning. The revision of the assumptions of linguistic science consists precisely in the denial of this equating of the meaning relation with the causal relation and the consequent application of the notion of natural law to language in the sense either of mechanics or biology. Positively it consists in the principle of the primacy of meaning and with it the primacy of *Geist* or spirit—of a spirit which lives in human discourse working as a totality. It is this that constitutes the sentence, the copula, the word, and the sound. It is this principle of totality, as over against the analytical principle of elements, which determines the methodology of this theory.

This is what the idealistic theory means in linguistics—as a

LANGUAGE AS THE BEARER OF MEANING

methodological principle. Let us now see what it means for a philosophy of language.

The essentials of the idealistic theory of meaning have already been brought out in our analysis of the semantic meaning situation and of the phenomenon of understanding. Here, too, the essential point is the denial that the *prima facie* components of the meaning relation are sufficient to constitute the meaning relation, that the causal theory based upon consideration of these components alone is adequate to account for linguistic meaning. Positively the idealistic theory develops the implications of this analysis. It insists that the implied components of the meaning situation are the necessary conditions of linguistic meaning and its understanding. The implicate of the first component, the sign, is always the speech community for which the meaning is, the implicate of the second component is always some universe of discourse in which the entity meant has its "being." When the significance of these implicates is realized, a behaviouristic or naturalistic theory of linguistic meaning is impossible.

The use of the term "idealistic" to describe the theory of linguistic meaning here developed is, of course, open to misunderstanding, yet there seems to be no other satisfactory term. We can therefore only attempt to avoid misunderstanding. The fact that in linguistics itself the term is used to contrast a theory of language with purely naturalistic and positivist theories justifies our use of it here. In linguistics it has no necessary epistemological implications but refers merely to methodological principles. Here, too, an idealistic theory of meaning is not a corollary of a theory of knowledge but rather a statement of the necessary conditions or presuppositions of meaning. The term idealism has had many meanings in the history of European thought, but surely one of its most significant uses is found in the contrast of naturalism and idealism. It is in this sense that it is here used. What necessary implications such a theory may have for knowledge will appear in our studies of language and cognition. The essentials of the idealistic theory of meaning itself will appear more fully in our study of the "normative problems of language" and in the "conditions of intelligible communication."

CHAPTER IV

THE PHENOMENOLOGY OF LINGUISTIC MEANING: THE PRIMARY FUNCTIONS OF LANGUAGE

I

A

ONE aspect of the philosophy of language is the phenomenological. Part of the answer to the question, what language is, is the phenomenological analysis of the meaning functions of language. Philosophy of language, in the sense of critique of language, is possible only upon the basis of the knowledge of what language is, and that is a phenomenological problem in the sense defined. It is for this reason that the study of language has passed from the physical and physiological through the psychological to the phenomenological.[1]

The fundamental character of the phenomenological approach is the apprehension of the nature of language in its uniqueness or "*absolute Besonderheit.*" It involves, as we have seen, the principle of the autonomy of language, its character as expressional, as intentional, and as non-instinctive communication. Negatively, it involves the irreducibility of linguistic to non-linguistic fact, of linguistic to non-linguistic meaning. Phenomenological analysis is to be clearly distinguished from both psychological and logical. For anyone who understands the phenomenological standpoint it is clear that such analysis is not concerned at all with what *goes on in our minds* when we use language with the intention of meaning something by it, but rather with what it is that we intend or mean. The difference between phenomenological and logical analysis is, however, not so clear. For our present purposes the *distinction* may be stated in the following way. Logical analysis is concerned solely with implicational or inferential meaning, and a logical analysis of language is concerned with words and sentences only in so far as they constitute the medium of such meanings. Phenomenological analysis, on the other hand, is concerned with the meaning functions of language in its primary character as speech or communication. Logic is discursive thinking, and, as such, presupposes discourse. It is possible

[1] Chapter II, p. 62.

THE PRIMARY FUNCTIONS OF LANGUAGE

indeed, to abstract logic from discourse, to examine "propositions" and their relations as though they were not embedded in communication, but in the last analysis "a proposition apart from discourse is nothing." Logical analysis presupposes phenomenological.[1]

The point may be made clearer by introducing a term from the German which has no satisfactory equivalent in English, namely, the notion of *die erlebte Rede*. We speak, indeed, of living, as opposed to dead languages, but the term living has a somewhat different meaning. The nearest approach to the idea that I wish to convey is Gardiner's distinction between speech and language which has already been commented upon. Speech is *erlebte Rede*; language is the petrifact which results from abstracting speech from the speech community in which alone it has reality, and from treating its "parts" as entities apart from the discourse in which they alone have both meaning and reality. *Erlebte Rede* involves, as part of its very nature, the two polar functions of expressing and understanding, and both functions are necessary for living speech. It is with *erlebte Rede* that phenomenological analysis has to do.

[1] In general, it may be said that it has been the great service of the phenomenological movement, associated with the name of Husserl, that it has again sharpened our sense for the fundamental differences in structural forms. In particular, the sharp separation of psychical acts from the objects "intended" in the acts led to a method of investigation which consistently distinguished meaning and psychical state and rescued philosophic thought from the "psychologism" and subjectivism into which it had been betrayed. The development of Husserl himself from the *Logische Untersuchungen* to the *Ideen der reinen Phänomenologie*, makes it entirely clear that the task of Phenomenology, as he conceives it, is not confined to the analysis of knowledge, but that it is concerned with the structure and essential character of very different realms of objects, according to what they mean, without reference to the question of their psychical conditions or the existence of their objects. The extension of this general point of view and method from the sphere of logic to ethics and art, from the world of "fact" to the world of values, has been one of the most fruitful movements of modern thought. Into this movement the present-day study of language has been drawn, not without noteworthy effects upon both linguistics and philosophy. The special points at which the phenomenological approach has thus affected linguistics are matters for consideration in special contexts: the point to be emphasized here is the general standpoint involved. To study "das Wesen der Sprache" in its unique character, without prejudice or presupposition, is considered the necessary prerequisite to any *Critique der Sprache* or to any consideration of problems of linguistic validity. The phenomenological method is followed throughout by H. Ammann, in *Die menschliche Rede*, and forms a large part of the methodology of the study of language in Ernst Cassirer's three-volume work, *Die Philosophie der Symbolischen Formen*.

B

The Primary Meaning Functions of Language

In the preceding chapter we were concerned with the problem of the nature of linguistic meaning in general. It became necessary, therefore, to investigate the entire notion of meaning: the meaning of "things," the meaning of "words," and the relations of the two. The results of that investigation may be summarized for our present purposes in the following way: Expression is the fundamental *differentia* of linguistic meanings. When this character of language is fully grasped, together with its implications, namely the corresponding notions of "understanding" and interpretation of expressions, the distinction between linguistic and non-linguistic meaning is so fundamental as to forbid the reduction of the former to the latter.

Within this general notion of linguistic meaning, three types of expression, or three meaning functions, may be distinguished. We may describe them as indicative expression, as emotive expression, and as representative or symbolic expression. These three meaning functions are present in some form wherever there is language and belong to the notion of language as such. They are present explicitly in all developed language and potentially or implicitly in the most primitive forms. Whether, as is sometimes maintained, they are present also in animal cries is, we have seen, a debateable question. Certainly the third function of representation (*Darstellung*) seems to be absent. But that they are the *sine qua non* of all human speech can scarcely be questioned. The reasons for this position need not be repeated *in extenso* here.[1] We may note, however, that a use of words that is merely emotive without any element of indication or representation, of reference or symbolization, is merely a series of squeaks and grunts and does not constitute language in any sense usable by the linguist. It is perhaps equally true to say that mere indicating or denoting without any element of expression or representation is not yet language, or has ceased to be language.[2]

This threefold conception of the meaning functions of language is generally accepted, although different terms are

[1] Chapter II, pp. 68 ff.   [2] Chapter II, pp. 66 ff.

often used to designate them.[1] An exception to this is the dual conception of meaning functions which has become popular in certain recent discussions of language. According to this view, language has two functions, the emotive or evocative and the indicative or denotative. The symbolic element in language is then identified with the indicative and denotive and all expressive elements lumped with the emotive. This dual view has important consequences for the philosophy of language and for our modern notions of symbolism, and will form a critical issue in much of the discussion to come. Here we shall content ourselves with pointing out that it is not in general the view of linguistics. Nor is it the result of a phenomenological analysis of language, but rather of certain prejudices regarding the origin and function of language, and is derived from a behaviouristic and causal theory of meaning.

The chief source of the errors of the dual theory is the confusion or the identification of the evocative with the emotive functions of language. It is true that we may speak of words evoking feelings or emotions, but they evoke other meanings than these. The evocation of intuitive, as distinct from emotive meaning, is one of the functions of language with which we shall be chiefly concerned.

II

THE FUNDAMENTAL MEANING FUNCTIONS OF LANGUAGE: THE NOTIONS OF DENOTATION AND CONNOTATION

A

These three types of meaning are primary and yet they are all in a sense but aspects of a more fundamental function which

[1] The dual theory of linguistic functions underlies all forms of logical positivism and is made the basis of its entire theory of linguistic validity. An interesting expression of the position is to be found in I. A. Richards' *Principles of Literary Criticism*, Chapter XXXIV, entitled "Two Uses of Language." His contention is that there are two wholly different uses of language, to indicate reference and to evoke feeling or emotion. To use language in its emotive function as though it were indicative, is to violate the principles of language. "Consider what failure for each use amounts to. For scientific language a difference in the reference is itself failure; the end has not been attained. But for emotive language the widest differences in reference are of no importance if the further effects in attitude and emotion are of the required kind." The entire question involved is, of course, a normative one of linguistic validity, and this is to be considered later. One difficulty with the position may, however, be pointed out even here. Attitudes are themselves

we shall call the *naming* function. The primordial elements of speech, the noun, the adjective, the verb, are all names. Language as such does not come into being until something is named. Even on the interjectional theory, language, strictly speaking, does not arise until the *ach*, as an emotional expression, passes over into the *ache*, or a name for that which is expressed. Even such a word as "naughty," when called out to a child, is a name for an aspect of behaviour which the child distinguishes by the name, although at the moment of utterance, for the one who speaks, it may be little more than an emotional expression. In the dual theory of linguistic meaning it is often characterized as wholly emotive, but it really includes both indication and connotation.

The fact that the primary function of words is naming has led to the idea that the meaning of a word (meaning *im strengsten Sinn*) is indication or designation. Now the capacity to designate or to signify is a necessary part of the meaning of a word, but, from some aspects at least, not the most important meaning of meaning. This has been expressed by the statement that words denote objects, but connote meanings. Objects are *what* we mean by words, but the *meaning* of the words is "something else again." Let us now see what this something else is.

B

Meaning as Connotation (Intention)

All the meaning functions of words, it is commonly held, can be expressed under these two terms, denotation and connotation. Thus under the rubric, meaning, in the last edition of the *Encyclopaedia Britannica*, all meaning is divided into these two types, as though all meaning functions of language could be subsumed under these two heads. To this classification there is, I think, no objection if the notion of connotation is broadly enough conceived, if in terms of our present discussion we view it from the phenomenological and not the exclusively logical point of view.

The term connotation (*connotare*) has had a long history in linguistic and logical discussion and has even undergone a

relations to objects or situations in the environment. If this reference is absolutely indeterminate or false, the attitude itself is no longer an attitude or is stultified.

complete alteration in its meaning since the days of Occam. The fixation of its meaning in modern logic is mainly due to J. S. Mill, who developed it in connection with his doctrine of terms.[1] "An ordinarily significant name, such as man," writes Mill, "signifies the subject directly, the attributes indirectly; it denotes the subject and implies or involves the predicates, or as we shall say henceforth, connotes the attributes." The fundamental notion in connotation is, then, indirect signification or reference, and it is this indirect reference to what is implied or involved which we have in mind when we speak of the "meaning" of a word.

In logic, then, connotation of a word is always indirect reference to *attributes*, to the characteristic or set of characteristics which are such as determine the objects to which the word can be correctly applied, and which are therefore sufficient to mark off these objects from other objects. Connotation in this sense is always conceptual meaning for the reason that such indirect reference always presupposes the formation of concepts; it is only with the concept that language and logic come together. But while conceptual connotation is always present in developed language functions, it does not exhaust those functions. There are other types of indirect reference which must be considered from the phenomenological point of view.

C

Connotation, Emotional and Intuitive

Linguists, as distinguished from logicians, have uniformly distinguished other forms of connotation of words than the conceptual. One of these is what is called "emotional connotation." Thus Erdmann[2] points out that besides the *Bedeutung* of words there is always *Nebenbedeutung*. Both are forms of connotation. The first is the indirect reference to the ideas with which the word is bound up as a sign; the second is also indirect reference, but to the feeling or emotion with which the word is bound up as an expression. This *Nebenbedeutung* is not referred to a particular emotion, but rather to an accumulated intension,

[1] For an historical note on this point, see H. W. B. Joseph, *An Introduction to Logic*, pp. 140 ff.
[2] Karl Otto Erdmann, *Die Bedeutung des Wortes*, Leipzig, 1925, Chapter IV.

sentiment, or mood, and it is because of this accumulated intension that the reference may properly be called a form of connotation. But Erdmann also distinguishes an intuitive or *anschauliche* connotation from both the conceptual and emotional. The intuitive character of poetic, as distinguished from scientific language is, of course, generally recognized without very careful determination of precisely wherein this intuitive character consists. Erdmann devotes an entire chapter to this analysis, and precisely such analysis is one of the chief tasks of the present study. It will suffice here to characterize it in the most general terms. Language does in some fashion *picture* reality: "conjure up" and make us relive objects, situations, characters in a way quite different from the conceptual descriptions of "science." This is an *evocation* which is quite different from the mere evocation of feelings, although feelings are involved.[1]

The task of this chapter is, then, phenomenological analysis of these three types of meaning or connotation and of their relations. The central theme, however, is that of the intuitive content or connotation of language, the study in fuller detail of the intuitive meaning or intrinsic expressiveness of words already considered in a preliminary way in the preceding chapter. I call this the central theme for the reason that many of the most fundamental problems of the philosophy of language and symbolism turn upon this question of the intuitive character of language. Defective phenomenological analysis at this point has led to the confusion of intuitive with emotional meaning, but no less frequently with conceptual meaning. On accurate analysis here depends the solution of the most fundamental problems of Language and Cognition.

[1] *Op cit.*, Chapter VI. The question may be raised as to the desirability of applying the term connotation in this way. For the purposes of logic connotation should, of course, be applied only to the concept, but for the purposes of phenomenology the broader use is justified. The reasons for this may be made clearer by a resort to an alternative term for connotation made use of in traditional logic, namely, *intention*. The intention of a word is commonly said to be all that we intend by it—what we intend by it, or what we mean by it, when predicated of any object. What we intend includes much more than the conceptual meaning of the word, and that which is included is precisely this intuitive meaning which we are here considering. For the purposes of logic this use of the alternative intention may be felt, in the words of Miss Stebbing, to be "an unfortunate intrusion of psychology into logic." It is not, however, an intrusion of psychology but of phenomenology, and the logical problems of language are not the phenomenological.

THE PRIMARY FUNCTIONS OF LANGUAGE

III

THE CONCEPTUAL CONNOTATION OF WORDS: MEANING AND THE UNIVERSAL

The central theme of this chapter is that of the intuitive connotation or intrinsic expressiveness of words. But in order to develop this theme properly it is necessary first to examine more fully the conceptual connotation of words. This involves the further study of the universal begun in the preceding chapter.

There is a sense, we have seen, in which everything denoted by language is already universalized. Whatever particular sign is named, the very act of naming or speaking universalizes it. But there are degrees or levels of universality. The concept and conceptual connotation we are now to examine is one of the later or higher levels.[1] Primitive languages often lack words for general concepts, both nouns and verbs. The Lapps, we are told, have no general term for snow but only words for different kinds or states of snow. The Klamath Indians have no general term for running but only for different kinds of running. In some languages of the North American Indians, Cassirer, quoting from Sayce, tells us, the activity of washing is represented by thirteen different verbs, according as the washing has to do with hands or face, etc., with clothes, utensils, etc.[2]

The interest of these facts for us lies in the picture they give us of a level of universality on which the word, whether noun or verb, cannot really be used without the intuition of the particular state or process with which it is still bound up. It represents a stage in mobility of signs, of detachment of the universal from the sensuous content which *it has determined and with which it is bound up.* In terms of Lotze's distinctions we may call it the intuitive universal, that which precedes and forms the basis for the concept or abstract universal. As primary universal it is the point of transition from the particular to the generic or abstract universal.

---

[1] Chapter III, pp. 116 ff.
[2] Cassirer has gathered together an extensive collection of such cases from primitive languages: *op. cit.*, Vol. I, pp. 257 ff.

The presence of the intuitive or primary universal in language is, as we have seen, the condition of predication. The secret of predication lies in the fact that the universal which is predicated as an attribute is already present intuitively in the most elementary linguistic expression and furnishes the basis for the further more complex analysis and synthesis of logical thought. The construction of concepts and the process of abstraction can take place only on such contents as are already linguistically determined and related.

Conceptual connotation, with which logic deals, is then indirect reference to predicates. With this aspect of connotation we shall be more fully concerned when we come to the problems of language and logic. Here we are primarily interested to distinguish between conceptual connotation or indirect reference to abstract universals, and indirect reference to the universal implicit in intuition itself. We may add, however, certain corollaries of this analysis which may be significant at this point.

The question of the "reality of universals" receives a certain kind of answer. They are real at least in the speech community, whatever other reality they may or may not have. They are the *sine qua non* of there being any linguistic meaning and therefore of any communication whatsoever. A word intends an object directly, but it always intends a universal indirectly, and these two intentions can never be separated. This situation may be put in the following way. We cannot look at a tall man, let us say, and give the result of our looking *in words*, without intuiting the seen man as a *man*. We cannot look at this man and give the result of our looking in words without intuiting him as *tall*. The universal is then not that which we see, but that through which we see. This is true even of the singular term. Thus in the expression "Nansen skates," Nansen is a grammatical proper noun and may therefore be supposed to stand for a particular and not a universal. But, as Stout points out, it is really a universal. Nansen perceived must be Nansen eating or Nansen sleeping or Nansen skating. The individual Nansen is a universal, as a connecting link of his own manifold and varying states, relations, qualities, and activities. We cannot *see* the individual Nansen except through this universal. These points will be considered more fully when we come to an

THE PRIMARY FUNCTIONS OF LANGUAGE

examination of the intuitive meanings of the parts of speech; here our only point is to distinguish the abstract universal from the intuitive, and with this distinction we may now turn to the entire problem of intuitive meaning or connotation.

IV

MEANING AS INTUITIVE CONTENT

A

An intuitive, *anschauliche*, character of language is generally recognized by all those who approach language from any but the most narrow logical standpoint. The language of poetry, as thus intuitive, is constantly contrasted with the abstract conceptual expressions of science. This contrast may, to be sure, be carried too far, for, as we shall see, many of the terms and symbols of science have this character and would indeed not convey meaning if they did not, but we may for the present allow the contrast to stand.[1]

It is recognized that poetry and science represent their objects in quite different ways. This difference has been expressed by Stein in his *A B C of Aesthetics* in the following way: The symbol of aesthetics differs from the symbol of science in this, that the scientific symbol, being merely a name, is external to the thing symbolized, whereas the aesthetic symbol is internal to the thing symbolized. The aesthetic symbol is not a label, but a sample; it is a partial representation which means more or less adequately the kind of thing it refers to. Leaving out of account the question whether scientific symbols are merely labels, and wholly external to the things symbolized, there is an important element of truth in this distinction.

B

The Intuitive as Intrinsic Expressiveness

This intuitive quality of language may best be expressed in terms of the notion of "intrinsic expressiveness." Words are not only extrinsically expressive in that they express a reference to

[1] See Chapter XI, pp. 457 ff.

an object external to the word, but they conjure up, so to speak —make us live in some degree—the object itself. In our study of pre-linguistic meaning we found it desirable to distinguish between intrinsic and extrinsic meaning. A similar distinction applies to *words* as expressive signs. The character of intrinsic meanings is that they do not point beyond the datum of which they are the meaning. The character of extrinsic meaning, on the contrary, is that the very essence of the meaning is this pointing or reference beyond the datum. It is commonly thought that the meaning of words is always and solely extrinsic and that this extrinsic reference is in the last analysis a matter of convention. It is doubtless true that the meaning of words may and does become wholly extrinsic. A word may be used to denote an object when we do not know the "meaning" of the word. But words also have intrinsic, intuitive meanings, the nature of which it is important to understand. Following Stout, we shall call this meaning *intrinsic expressiveness*.[1]

The onomatopoeic aspects of language are the primary forms of intrinsic expressiveness. It is this that makes them "self-authenticating" words. In his chapter on "Language and Conception," Professor Stout tells us that among the Botocudos in Brazil, *ouatou* stands for stream, *ouatou-ou-ou-ou* for the sea. He remarks that this phenomenon, which the philologists call reduplication, has often intrinsic expressiveness. It is this intrinsic expressiveness which I shall have in mind when I speak of the intuitive meanings of words. The *ouatou-ou-ou-ou* indicates the ocean, but there is more than indication here; there is intuitive representation. It is important to understand just what this intuitive representation is. In addition to the indication there is obviously an element of expressiveness. The combination of syllables which indicates the ocean evokes a meaning quite different from that evoked by the combination which stands for the stream. On superficial analysis it might easily be supposed that the meaning evoked is emotive and that, in addition to the indication, we have merely emotive meaning. This is, however, far from being the case. Emotive meaning is doubtless there and the intuitive is at first sight not easily separable from it. But it is separable, and to identify the in-

---

[1] G. F. Stout, *Manual of Psychology*, chapter on "Language and Conception," pp. 502 ff.

THE PRIMARY FUNCTIONS OF LANGUAGE 145

tuitive with the emotive constitutes, as we shall see, a serious defect in phenomenological analysis. In the present illustration the expression *ouatou-ou-ou-ou* not only indicates an object of perception, not only expresses an emotional attitude towards that object, but also, through the analogy of sound and syllable with the *Gestalt* or pattern of the object, gives us something intuitively of its nature.

This phenomenon of "reduplication," which is very common in primitive language, is worthy of further examination in this connection. On first view it appears to be determined wholly by the principle of imitation; the reduplication of the sound or syllable appears to involve merely the copying of the object or happening. Actually, however, it marks the beginning of analogical representation which, as we shall later see, is the fundamental principle of natural speech construction. The symbol is then, in the first instance, imitative and serves to conjure up the thing itself. Gradually, however, the *Gestalt* is detached from its primary material and becomes the means of intuitive representation of plurality and repetition and finally, in many cases, becomes the form of representation or expression of the fundamental intuitions, space, time, force, etc. In short, we find in this phenomenon one of the main points at which the representative, as distinguished from the merely indicative, function of language appears and at which the development of language, through the three stages of imitation, analogy, and symbol, most clearly appears.[1] It is, however, with its intuitive or intrinsically expressive character that we are here concerned.

C

Intrinsic Expressiveness on the Ideational Level

The phenomenon of reduplication may then be taken as the simplest form of the intuitive character of language. The symbol indicates objects, but it also evokes meanings. The meanings which it evokes are both emotive and intuitive, but the intuitive is clearly distinguishable from the emotive. This is intrinsic expressiveness on the perceptual level, although, as we have

[1] Cassirer, *op. cit.*, Vol. I, p. 143, has developed this point with many illustrations which cannot be treated in detail here.

seen, the form-quality may be transferred so as to represent non-perceptual relations. This intuitive representation may, however, be found also on the ideational level. Universals also have intrinsic expressiveness.

We may take as our illustration one which Stein uses to make clear his distinction between the aesthetic and the scientific symbol, and to mark the difference between the symbol which is external to the thing symbolized and that which is internal. It is the famous line of the poet Robert Herrick: "Gather ye rosebuds while ye may."

There is here undoubtedly a double meaning or connotation in the word rosebuds. Abstracted from the context in the line quoted, it refers to a certain class of objects. Its primary function is indication or direct reference to the members of this class. Indication is almost its sole function, although, as we have seen, it cannot really indicate or signify an object without expressing, through indirect reference, the qualities or predicates of the object. The same word in the present context has, however, an entirely different meaning function. Its indication is now changed. It does so by virtue of a connotation which can only be called intuitive.

The meaning function which first leaps to the eye is, of course, the emotive. The word occurs in an exhortation or command. That exhortation is the expression of an emotion and evokes emotion in the hearer. But while the meaning is partly emotive, it is no more exhausted in the expression of the emotion than is the Botocudos' expression for the sea. That it is not merely emotive is clearly seen in the fact that, while the indication has changed, indication is still a part, and an indispensable part, of its meaning. The meaning is therefore not merely conceptual nor yet merely emotive. The residual meaning is what I describe as intuitive. Let us analyse this intuitive meaning more carefully, for it is of far-reaching importance in the philosophy of language.

The distinguishing character of this meaning can best be seen at the point at which the primary indication passes over into the secondary, in other words, the point of *metaphorical transfer*. It is here that the intuitive character appears. The term "rosebuds" still stands, of course, for the objects to which the universal primarily refers: otherwise it would be meaningless in any context. But precisely in the process of transfer all the intuitive meanings present in the primary experience, and which were suppressed in the formation of the concept, spring into being again. It is indeed only this intuitive element which makes possible the transfer. All the freshness, bloom, grace, and charm which were present in the original intuition of the object are again evoked and it is this evocation that we call intuitive meaning.

There is, then, intrinsic expressiveness on the ideational no less than on the perceptual level, and the intuitive meaning thus expressed is as distinguishable from the conceptual and emotive on this level as it is on the perceptual. The illustration just examined is taken from poetry and it is, of course, precisely the function of poetry, taken in the broadest sense, to evoke just such meanings. But this intuitive element in language is present in all its uses, even the scientific. Many scientific symbols are, it is true, wholly external to the thing symbolized—their function is pure notation—but many are not. The latter are perhaps the most important, as we shall see, in so far as science includes understanding as well as manipulation and pure notation.

Karl Otto Erdmann has emphasized this intuitive aspect of linguistic meaning and illuminated the distinction with many examples. He also makes clear the differences of intuitive language from both conceptual and emotional. He is particularly concerned to make clear the distinction between the intuitive and emotive aspects of verbal meaning, and in making this distinction he quotes the famous lines from Faust:

> "Grau, teurer Freund, ist alle Theorie
> Und grün des Lebens goldener Baum."

The expressiveness of these lines has been rarely equalled and perhaps never surpassed. And yet from the standpoint of logical analysis of language they contain an apparent contradiction which should make them nonsense. The golden tree, which is also green, is sheer nonsense. But, as Erdmann rightly points out, there is no contradiction here, for in this poetic context the meanings of the terms green and gold are different. Green, he argues, in contrast to grey, has intuitive meaning, while the meaning of gold is almost exclusively emotive in character. We may agree that the apparent contradiction is not real, but the important point is the distinction between intuitive and emotive meaning. Gold, when applied to the tree of life, expresses only similarity of emotive attitude. The green, in contrast to grey, on the other hand, gives a real difference between life and theory which could also be expressed, although less adequately, in abstract conceptual terms. The latter is analogous predication, of which we shall have more to say later, the former merely emotive expression. This analysis of Erdmann's, which he carries out with many examples, seems to me not only sound, but to illustrate precisely the difference between careful phenomenological analysis and the careless inclusion of all non-indicative meaning under the term emotive.

D

Intuitive Meaning and Imagery

The distinction of intuitive meaning from both conceptual and emotive is, it may be assumed, reasonably clear. Is it possible to say more definitely what this intuitive meaning is? A very common procedure is to identify the intuitive meaning with imagery. Intuition, in the primary sense, as throughout Kant's entire treatment of experience and knowledge, is sense intuition. Whenever, therefore, it is used in any secondary sense, it is connected with sense images. Now it is entirely true that intuition is not possible without sense perception and imagery. But it does not at all follow that they are the same thing and that the latter includes the former.

This can be seen clearly enough in the case of intuition in so far as it is connected with sense-perception. The intuition of the melody as a *Gestalt* is impossible without the perception of the sense elements in which the form is grounded, but this perception is not the intuition of the melody. In a similar way the intuitive element or content bound up with words is connected with imagery and the processes of imagination. But these latter are the instruments of intuition, not the intuition itself. The same is true of the intuitive knowledge of other selves. This is not possible without certain processes of empathy or *Einfühlung*, but the latter are means of apprehension, not the apprehension itself.[1]

---

[1] Karl Jaspers, *Psychologie der Weltanschauungen*, pp. 64 ff.

The importance of this distinction between intuition and imagery (*Anschauung* and *Vorstellung*) for the phenomenology of linguistic forms is emphasized by H. Ammann.[1] Imagery is, by its very nature, subjective, whereas the intuitive content of words is by its very nature objective and communicable. Its objectivity is, to be sure, only in the speech community, however far that community may extend, but that is true also of all linguistic meaning.

This communicability of intuitive meaning is, it seems to me, the significant point. It rests upon the independent variability of this meaning and the subjective elements of the individual mind, both ideational and emotive. This distinction we shall find further confirmed when we come to examine value words, and the emotional intuition by which values as objective "entities" are apprehended. This notion of the communicability of intuitive meaning gives to language a power which goes far beyond the niggardly conception which thinks of it merely as an external tag, as merely denotative, and lumps all other meanings together as emotive. This intrinsic expressiveness of language assumes that language is so related to reality that it can conjure up that reality, make us live through the characters and qualities of things themselves. This assumption is, of course, open to question; it is possible that they are subjective projections and not genuine aspects of reality to which they refer. But this is the normative problem of linguistic validity and goes far beyond the phenomenological problem with which we are here concerned.

V

THE INTUITIVE MEANING OF WORDS AND THE PARTS OF SPEECH

Thus far we have been concerned merely to establish the fact that there is a form of connotation or "meaning" that cannot be subsumed under either the conceptual or emotional. But the significance of this fact, if thus established, is more far-reaching than at first appears. That words in their acquirement of reference should retain their intrinsic expressiveness, and, as symbols

[1] Hermann Ammann, *Die menschliche Rede*, Vol. I, Chapter 10.

be thus internal to the thing symbolized, is a fact that conditions many important meaning functions of language. But it might be held that this meaning is a sort of secondary *Nebenbedeutung*, left over from earlier stages of linguistic development, which survives in poetry but is not significant in connection with other uses of language. As a matter of fact—and this is really the most important part of our study—this intuitive meaning is inherent in all language functions, in the forms or "parts" of speech themselves. We may put it this way: We cannot use the parts of speech without indirect reference to intuitions: as parts of speech themselves, they have intuitive connotation. It is clear that if this position is sound it cannot but be one of the most important parts of our entire study. It will affect vitally our conceptions of the relations of language to logic and to cognition in general.

A
The Primordial Speech Forms

In our earlier study (Chapter II) of the position of linguistic science on the problem of the parts of speech, we found it necessary to note a tendency at present to reinstate the theory of distinct parts of speech in new forms, to insist that back of the formal patterns of grammar there are certain "notional" and meaning categories. Our conception of intuitive meaning may throw further light on the conception.

It is the special merit of Hermann Ammann to have brought out, and to have clearly distinguished, the intuitive meanings of the parts of speech from their grammatical forms. In presenting this phase of the question I acknowledge my indebtedness to his studies, although in no sense making him responsible for my own analysis.

The primordial and indispensable "parts of speech" are, as we have seen, the noun, the verb, and the adjective. On the question of the noun and the verb there is no dispute. Almost all languages make some division between the two parts of a sentence; the only question is as to the third. Assuming the three, however, we may ask what makes them thus indispensable. My answer is their intuitive content or mean-

THE PRIMARY FUNCTIONS OF LANGUAGE

ing. Let us attempt a phenomenological exposition of this meaning.

The intuitive content or meaning of the noun I shall describe, following Ammann, as ideal unity or individuality; that of the verb meaning as activity content; and finally that of the adjective as the *Erlebniss-Wert* of qualities and values. What is meant by these terms is the following. A noun not only indicates an object directly and attributes indirectly, but evokes also intuitively the individuality of the object to which it refers. The verb not only refers to an action, but it evokes intuitively the activity to which the reference is made. The adjective not only *refers* to the quality predicated of the object, but *evokes intuitively* that quality as it is immediately experienced.[1]

B

The Noun, Common and Proper

Language, we have said, is endless naming. All the parts of speech are really names for aspects of experience or reality, the verb and adjective no less than the noun or nominative proper. Let us begin, however, with the *name* of anything in the narrower sense. Grammar distinguishes between proper and common nouns.

The character of the intrinsic expressiveness of common nouns has already been brought out in our preceding analysis. Any common noun, by virtue of its being common, is a name for a *class* of objects; it refers indirectly, however, to the characteristic or set of characteristics which are such as to determine the objects to which the term can be correctly applied. But it refers also, we have seen, to the primary intuition of the individual object in all its concrete richness, and it is this concrete individuality that is brought out in the metaphorical transfer to other objects. The distinction between the

---

[1] *Die Menschliche Rede*, Vol. I, Chapters VI to XI; Vol. II, Chapter IV.
It is unfortunate that there is no English equivalent for this expressive word, *Erlebniss*, for it expresses something which, according to the view of language here presented, it is most important to emphasize. The nearest equivalent to *Erleben* is to experience, but this is too general a notion. *Erleben* is to experience something in a more *vital* way. We shall suggest, then, for *Erlebniss-Wert* the expression vital value of the adjective.

conceptual and intuitive connotation in our analysis of the word "rosebuds" can, I think, be extended to common nouns in general. Even such ordinary words as door and table and house have this intuitive character. When I speak of the door to the soul, the table of life, the house of God, this intuitive character comes out in full relief. This intuitive meaning of individuality which inheres in the use of every noun is different alike from emotive meaning and the conceptual meaning of class terms.

The question of the connotation of proper nouns serves to bring out the point with even greater clearness. It is not strange that great confusion has arisen concerning this question.

Mill, having defined connotation *merely* as indirect reference to attributes, naturally held that an ordinary proper name has no connotation, but merely indication. It is merely an "unmeaning mark" by means of which we may identify and refer to the object. Others, as for instance Bosanquet, insist that a proper name has a connotation, but not a fixed general connotation. It is attached to a unique individual and connotes whatever may be involved in his identity, or is instrumental in bringing it before the mind. The entire controversy arises from imperfect phenomenological analysis. In our discussion of conceptual connotation we made use of the expression "Nansen skates." Here the indirect reference is not merely to universals, but, as Stout properly says, to the unity and connecting identity of Nansen's varying and manifold states. It is this individuality or ideal unity which constitutes the intuitive connotation of every proper name. As in the case of common names, it is in the phenomenon of metaphorical transfer that this intrinsic expressiveness chiefly comes to light. When we speak of "a Caesar in the White House," or "a Daniel come to judgment," it is precisely this intuitive element that makes the transfer possible.

In connection with the discussion of the intuitive element in all *nominal* meaning, it is worth considering for a moment the character of pronominal meaning. In our study of the parts of speech from the linguistic point of view, we found that the pronoun belongs to the non-necessary, "non-imperative" parts of speech. Communication is possible without it. Genetically viewed, the use of the pronoun, both the personal and the impersonal, may be looked upon as the substitution of non-

THE PRIMARY FUNCTIONS OF LANGUAGE

significant sounds for gestures or pointing. It is a name only in the broad sense that it stands for something. Its speech function has been reduced almost wholly to indication. I say almost wholly, for a trace of intuitive connotation remains, namely, the element of individuality. When I substitute "he" or "she" for a proper noun—it, this, or that for a singular, they or those for a common noun—everything has been abstracted from except the "form of individuation" itself. The pronominal element in speech is of peculiar significance for the philosophy of language. According to the logical ideal of language which seeks *puri nomi* or pure notation, the "logical proper name" is a demonstrative symbol and the ideal language tends to become pronominal. It is at this point, as we shall see later, that logic and logical analysis (more especially in symbolic logic) and phenomenological analysis of language come into conflict. It is here also that the use of language becomes almost wholly pronominal and manipulative and ceases to be expressive and significant.[1]

C

The Intuitive Meaning of the Verb

Besides its indication, every noun of whatever kind has a double connotation, its conceptual and intuitive. This intuitive meaning is as much a condition of communication as is the conceptual. Nouns are the bearers of these intuitive meanings and it is only as such bearers that they are *expressive* signs. Other speech forms are also bearers of such intuitive meanings. Among the most important of these are the activity meanings, or intuitions of activity connected with the verb.

I say the wind blows, the rose blooms. I may, if I have elocutionary ability, by the very way in which I say "blows" or "blooms," conjure up before you the activity itself. You may *hear* the blowing and *see* the blooming. That you do this with your "imagination" has nothing to do with the point at issue, that point being that you do hear *not* the sounds, but the blowing; you do see, not the sense data of the rose, but the blooming. In other words, there is a direct intuition of activity

[1] The origin of non-significant parts of speech and their relation to significant has been discussed in Chapter II, p. 87 f.

and that intuitive meaning becomes part of the meaning which the word bears.

Now I may for certain purposes put these expressions in "logical form." The rose is blooming, the wind is blowing. I may go further and say, the class roses falls under the class blooming things, the class wind under blowing things. What have I done here? I have abstracted from all intuitive meaning and have left only conceptual meaning. It is with this conceptual meaning that the "logical" use of language is concerned, but the fact that logic thus abstracts from intuitive meaning no more proves that the meaning is not there than the fact that it abstracts from the intuitive meaning of the noun proves that it is not there. The entire question of the relation of logical to intuitive meaning is a problem of a later chapter.

This intuitive element in the verb is brought out clearly if we view the development of the verbal form genetically. It is apparently almost universally true that in the less developed languages of savages the intuitive element in the verbal form outweighs the conceptual. The Klamath Indian, we saw, has no single word for run, but a different word for the running of each animal. This is a specific case of the general law that words and phrases refer first to particular objects and acts, and only later to the class; but it also means that in the word for the different kind of running for each different animal, there is detached and embodied, in a form of intrinsic expressiveness, an aspect of the running that can only be intuitively *erlebt*. The point I am making may best be expressed by saying that the verb has a double function, that of intuition and that of conceptual predication. The first of these Hermann Paul has in mind when he points out that the speech form of the verb as such contains *ein Moment der Naturbelebung*: in the use of the verb as such there lies already *"ein gewisser Grad von Personifikation des Subjectes."* [1] Whether this intuition of activity is veridical, or whether it is a projection of the subject, a mythical *Beseelung* of the universe, is a question of linguistic validity, not of phenomenology. The predicative function of the verb is, on the other hand, a product of later analysis and presupposes the earlier function.

[1] *Principien der Sprachgeschichte*, p. 89. For a further discussion of this entire subject, see E. Cassirer, *op. cit.*, Vol. I, pp. 266 ff.

D

The Intuitive Meaning of the Adjective

The third type or form of intuitive meaning is that represented by the adjective, or by the part of speech that represents the qualities of things. The adjective is the speech form which brings out most clearly the element of intuitive meaning in language. The adjective, as the word indicates, is the speech form which *attaches* a quality to an object or entity, and to attach it presupposes that there has already been a *de*tachment from the immediate living experience of the object. It is this living experience, thus detached, that we are now to examine.

We may call it, following Ammann, the vital value of the adjective. What is here in mind may be brought out by an analysis of certain linguistic forms. Poetic diction has, it is generally recognized, the power, the *vis poetica*, of conjuring up the living reality itself. "Red blooms the rose," "wild blows the wind," writes the poet, and in this very arrangement or *Gestalt* he detaches from the object a vital quality which is, so to speak, a part of its very life. This intuitive meaning of the "red," and the "wild," can only be lived—*erlebt*. Phenomenologically the meaning here is very different from the conceptual meaning which the same terms, red and wild, may also have.

The difference of this form of meaning may be brought out in several ways—in the first place by genetic considerations. The first adjectival words which the child uses do not so much indicate abstract qualities and marks of things as *express* inner states.[1] The function arises only gradually and becomes ever stronger, finally gaining control over the speech function as a whole. At this early stage intuitive is closely bound up with emotive expressiveness, although even here they can be phenomenologically distinguished. In similar fashion, in the development of language as a whole, the adjective like the verb represents in the earlier stages of development intuitive rather than conceptual meaning. In the second place, the vital value of the adjective is but a special form of the primary or intuitive uni-

---

[1] Ernst Cassirer, *op. cit.*, Vol. III, p. 128.
See in this connection also Clara and William Stern, *Die Kindersprache*, Leipzig, 1907, pp. 35 ff. and pp. 224 ff.

versal which is present in all forms of language—already intuited in language itself and upon which all later conceptual abstraction and conceptual meaning are based.[1]

This distinction between the conceptual and intuitive connotation of adjectives is, I think, of special importance for the philosophy of language, more particularly in connection with problems of language and cognition. Some knowledge, perhaps all knowledge, is knowledge by description and the question as to what language describes and what linguistic descriptions can communicate is of great importance. In the theory of knowledge generally, this distinction is largely overlooked. In the logical and epistemological analysis of language, adjectives such as red or cold are ordinarily taken as illustrations, adjectives which represent the "primary and secondary" qualities of things. These can be equated more or less satisfactorily with simple sense data, although even here, as we have seen, there is an intuitive element which cannot be ignored. But there are other qualities, expressed by such adjectives as graceful, wild, etc., which cannot be equated with simple sense data. Here the notion of *Gestalt-qualität*, "form-quality," must be introduced and with it the notion of the *Erleben* of this *quale*. This point will be of special importance when we come to the phenomenological study of value qualities. It is true that in all these cases the intuitive meaning which is evoked by the adjective is closely related to emotive meaning, but if our analysis is valid they cannot be identified.

E

Intuitive Meaning and Metaphor

The intuitive meaning of words—and this is true of all the "parts of speech" considered—comes out most clearly when, through the inherent mobility of words, they become transferred metaphorically from one object or referend to another, and there follows what we shall later study under the term analogous predication. If I transfer a noun from one context to another, as in the case of the rosebuds of our illustration, it is precisely then that all the intuitive meaning comes to the

[1] See Chapter II, p. 118.

surface—it is then that the individuality, the ideal unity which is part of the meaning of the noun, comes to clearest consciousness. The same is true of the verb and the adjective. If I transfer the verb bloom from the flower to the woman, all the accumulated living meaning of the verb comes to the surface. If I say, "be still wild heart," all the lived meaning embodied in the term wild is then evoked.

The difference between such meaning and either conceptual or merely emotive is quite clear to anyone who cares to make the analysis. But the point that I wish to emphasize here, and one which later will become of increasing importance, is the fact that in this form of predication—analogical predication as it is technically called—we have a form of *judgment*, not merely expression of feeling. Whether they are *real* judgments or only apparent, in other words whether they give us real knowledge, is a normative problem of language to be considered later.[1] Here our problem is one merely of phenomenological analysis.

F

The Parts of Speech and The Categories

The preceding phenomenological analysis of the intuitive meanings of the parts of speech has made it clear, I think, that back of the formal patterns analysed out by grammar and logic lies an intuitive content, and that this intuitive content is always indirectly referred to and indirectly communicated in all natural use of language.

This conception of the grammatical categories is maintained by Vossler. All grammatical categories whatsoever are, he tells us, experienced and apprehended intuitively (*eingefühlt*), that is they are poetical as regards their spiritual value and psychic origin. He is commenting upon certain attempts of E. Lorck in *Die Erlebte Rede* to bring out this intuitive element in certain aspects of the verb. What I wish to emphasize here is that language as lived, in contrast with language as observed from the bystander's viewpoint which sees only formal patterns, has this intuitive content. It is a part of the meaning of all parts of

[1] See Chapter V, p. 170 f.

speech, and, as Vossler says, of grammatical categories in general.[1]

It is our contention that this element of intuitive meaning of the parts of speech cannot be subsumed under either rubric of conceptual or emotive meaning. So far as the emotive meaning is concerned, it is true that, as we dig deeper—to reach the roots of the grammatical categories—we do come, as Vossler says, closer and closer to the emotive meaning. The individuation which is connoted by our names for persons and things, the activity meaning connoted by the verb, and the vital value of the adjective, are all closely related to that personalization and empathy which are inseparable from those earlier stages in which speech and myth are one. But while genetically inseparable, they are phenomenologically distinguishable. The distinction between intuitive and conceptual meaning is equally clear. The intuitive individuation can be conceptually expressed in the notion of substance, the vital value of the adjective in terms of quality, the activity element in terms of causation, but these *are* conceptualizations and presuppose the intuitive.

The failure to realize the intuitive character of the categories was, I think, the basal error of the Kantian *Critique*, which in general suffers throughout from lack of a critical study of language. Kant, like Aristotle, was right, I think, in taking linguistic categories as the *Leitfaden* to the discovery of the categories of knowledge. For, however much we may think knowing to be prior to and independent of language, whatever we *know* must, if it is *expressed* at all, be expressed in language. If expressed knowledge is to be possible there cannot be any ultimate divorce between the categories of speech and of knowledge. On the other hand, Kant's sharp division of knowledge into *intuitus aut conceptus* and his confining of intuition to sense data, compelled him to think of the categories as conceptual. Kant was not wholly oblivious to the intuitive element in the categories, and his doctrines of "schematism" and "imagination" represent attempts to do justice to it. But the synthesis of the categories as conceptual and the matter of intuition as sensational, although the very heart of the doctrine of the categories, remained artificial and unconvincing.[2]

[1] Karl Vossler, *The Spirit of Language in Civilization*, New York, 1932, p. 224.
[2] This question will be further considered in Chapter VIII.

VI

EMOTIONAL INTUITION AND VALUE WORDS. TERTIARY QUALITIES

A

Our phenomenological study of linguistic meaning has up to this point maintained two positions. In the first place, there are three fundamental meaning functions of language: the indicative, the emotive, and the representative or symbolic. A twofold division into the emotive and indicative is the result of defective phenomenological analysis and of certain prejudices; it involves putting certain meanings under these rubrics which cannot be properly placed there. In the second place, we found occasion to distinguish within this third group a type of meaning called intuitive and to distinguish it from both conceptual and emotive meaning. With this we are brought to a class or type of words over which there has been much dispute in recent linguistic and philosophical discussions, namely, value words and their meanings. On the determination of the nature of their meaning turn many philosophical questions of far-reaching importance.

The nature of the problem involved may be stated most clearly by indicating the two opposing positions on this question. There are those who, following the two-fold division, insist that value words are merely emotive, merely expressive of emotion and have no indication. They stand for nothing. There are others who maintain that value words are not merely emotive, but have an indicative and representative function. They stand for entities which are emotionally intuited and, in thus standing for them, these value words represent and express intrinsically qualities of things which can only be intuited and intuited emotionally. The first position, following Scheler, we may characterize as value-nominalism, the second as value-realism.

The phenomenological problem here raised may be brought into direct relation to the preceding discussions in the following way. In our consideration of the intuitive meanings of the parts of speech, the third form examined was the adjective. In the adjective we believed to have analysed out and exposed an element of meaning which is neither conceptual nor emotive, but intuitive. The word red or wild may, as concepts, detach or abstract an aspect of reality, but they also always have an intuitive meaning which cannot be conceived but only lived. Now among these adjectival words is a special group which we may describe as *value* words. They contain the more concrete words, such as graceful, noble, sublime, and their opposites, and the more general words, such as good and beautiful, and their opposites. The qualities or entities to which the words refer—if they do refer—have frequently been described as tertiary qualities to distinguish them from the primary and secondary.

B

The Emotive Theory of Value Words. Value Nominalism

The purely emotive character of value words is rather widely held and indeed is implied in a certain type of value theory, more particularly such subjective psychological theories as those of Perry and Prall. In the field of the philosophy of language it has found expression in English writings chiefly in the works of Ogden and Richards, and in German writings in the so-called Vienna School, more particularly in the writings of Carnap. A moderate statement of this position is found in an article by R. B. Braithwaite.[1] Mr. Braithwaite maintains that at least many of the sentences in which such words occur are merely emotive, and taken as propositions are merely apparent propositions. Others, as, for instance, Carnap, hold that all value words are *Scheinwörte* and all the propositions which contain them *Scheinsätze*. The consequences drawn from this position are very important. All discourse about values is, in the strict sense of meaning, meaningless. A proposition, we are told, that expresses a value judgment cannot, in the nature of the case, be constructed, and that therefore all ethics and aesthetics, as normative disciplines, are really made up of meaningless propositions.[2]

[1] "Verbal Ambiguity and Philosophical Analysis," *Proceedings of the Aristotelean Society*, 1927-28.   [2] R. Carnap, *op. cit.*, p. 237.

C
The Thesis of Nominalistic Positivism

The paradoxical character of the above position—especially in its extreme form—is obvious. When a large part of human discourse is labelled meaningless and all ethics and aesthetics described as made up of meaningless propositions, second thoughts are in order. It seems more than likely that such a paradox could arise only from defective analysis, and from pre-existing prejudices. It is therefore necessary to examine this position more closely.

The thesis of value nominalism has been stated in two forms, that of Ogden and Richards and that of Carnap, both statements representing the same standpoint and both emphasizing the same consequences for the problem of language and cognition. According to Ogden and Richards, the word "good" (and this is true of all value words) stands for nothing whatever and has no symbolic use (symbolic in their terminology being equivalent to indicative). When we say "this is red" the addition of "is red" symbolizes an extension of our reference, namely, to some red thing. When we say, "this is good," we merely refer to *this* and the addition of "is good" makes no difference whatsoever to our reference. It has no symbolic function but is a purely emotive sign.[1] The same, according to their view, is true of the word beautiful. The statement of the position by Carnap is in principle the same, but adds a feature which is worth emphasizing for the purposes of our discussion. After developing the purely emotive character of value words, he concludes: Either one gives for the terms beautiful, good, etc., an empirical, perceptual denotation (*Kennzeichen*) or one does not. In the first case it is an ordinary factual judgment referring to a perceptually observed object. In the second case it is a *Scheinsatz* (an apparent proposition) and therefore meaningless. It is for this reason that, as we have seen, it is impossible in principle (*Überhaupt*) to construct a proposition expressing a value judgment, and such so-called sciences as ethics and aesthetics are either merely factual or made up of *Scheinsätze*.[2]

[1] Ogden and Richards, *The Meaning of Meaning*, p. 125.
[2] R. Carnap, *Die Uberwindung der Metaphysik*, etc., p. 237.

D

The Defective Analysis of Value Nominalism: The Argument of the Phenomenologist

The preceding thesis embodies the value nominalism which we have now to consider critically. To the careful student of language it appears to be an almost perfect example of defective phenomenological analysis, an analysis, in fact, which confuses the emotive and intuitive meanings of words in an unpardonable fashion. The phenomenologist makes this distinction. He finds, moreover, that these value words do stand for something, for objective essences no less a part of being than the *qualia* of perception, and finally constructs a doctrine of "emotional intuition" which plays an important rôle in his doctrine or theory of knowledge.[1] Let us consider these positions in order.

The defective analysis of the logical positivists appears in their failure to make distinctions at two important points. The first of these is the distinction between emotional meaning and value meaning, between verbal emotional expression and value language. The form of verbal emotional expression is the interjection, such as "Ah" or "Ach." It is perfectly possible to distinguish between the emotive meaning thus expressed and the meaning expressed in value predicates. Between an interjection such as "Ah" before a picture or landscape, and the assertions, this picture is beautiful or this is a good picture, there is a difference not merely of degree, but, phenomenologically speaking, of essence. The *ah* means nothing and intends nothing. It expresses merely an organic or emotional condition. Similarly in moral situations there is a complete difference between an expression of disgust, such as the German word *Pfui*, and the assertion, this is a disgusting act. In the latter forms of expression I am not merely reacting to the landscape or the act, but to a quality or meaning of the landscape or act, the beauty or charm of the former, the disgusting character of the latter. In other words, the value word is a name, and like other names, not only involves some element of universalization, but also detaches and

[1] For an excellent critique of the entire position of value nominalism and of the phenomenologist's argument, see Max Scheler, *Der Formalismus in der Ethik und die materielle Wert-Ethik*, Chapter III.

embodies some intuitive meaning. It is this meaning which is expressed in the judgment and which is evoked in the hearer.

But there is further defective analysis evident in the position of value nominalism. Not only can we distinguish, as we have seen, between the feeling attitude and the value meaning; we can also distinguish completely between *the qualities for which value words stand and our feelings towards those qualities*. Actions may be and are described as frivolous, daring, modest, proud, feverish, cowardly. That these words represent qualities detached and named, and not mere feelings (of like and dislike or of praise and blame) is evident from the following facts. Any one of these qualities may be apprehended by two or more persons at the same time, but reacted to by feeling in opposite ways. You may like the proud action, I may dislike it, but both of us acknowledge it to be proud. The quality remains the same. We both apprehend the same thing. *The independent variability of value quality and feeling seems to be clear evidence of a phenomenological difference*, a difference, moreover, which is not one of degree of objectification of feeling, but of essential character.

It is facts such as these that compel the distinction between emotive meaning and value meaning, and that show the untenability of value nominalism. But there is a further argument of a dialectal type which is not without its force in this connection. The nominalistic positivist must, as we have seen, label a large part of human discourse as meaningless. Now this, to the thoughtful philosopher, presents a most extraordinary situation. Quite apart from the general consideration that, in view of the analyses of linguistic meaning in the preceding chapter, it is doubtful whether one is justified in calling any linguistic expression meaningless, we are here presented with a special form of the difficulty. We say, this man is tall; we also say, this man is noble. We employ the same linguistic (and also logical) form in both cases. If the latter is merely an expression of feeling, why, asks Scheler, has it been disguised in the form of a proposition? How comes it that men, instead of expressing their desires and feelings directly, in linguistic forms appropriate to such expression, have put them in the form of judgments? It is, according to him, pure miracle, a miracle of distortion. Here value nominalism lacks all intelligibility. And who would, on second thought, not agree with him? It is only a mind clouded by prejudices and prepossessions that could propose such a theory.

The nominalist, to be sure, has an answer to this objection. He appeals to the imperfections of language, to a natural tendency of language to distort reality. But it is precisely here that the prejudices and the essential *petitio principii* involved in his position become evident. On such a view it would appear that almost the sole function of language is "to deceive the philosopher." But that is a wholly gratuitous assumption. It rests upon the prejudice that language was made only to deal with physical things and that when it is used for other ends it generates fictions and illusion. This is, however, an assumption we have already questioned. It begs the entire question of the nature and function of language and itself assumes a normative position. In any case, a position which makes such assumptions and turns a large part of man's discourse into the meaningless is one which, *prima facie* at least, lacks all intelligibility.

E

The Concept of Emotional Intuition. Value Realism

It seems, then, not only possible but necessary to distinguish between emotive meaning, or feeling attitude, and value meaning—between sounds as mere expressions of emotion and words as indicative of values. The meanings represented and expressed by value words belong to the class of intuitive meanings, as distinguished from both conceptual and emotive. This notion of value words as embodying intuitions of objects or entities of some sort, this "value realism," brings with it two problems—namely, what it is that is thus intuited, what it is to which the value words refer; and secondly, the nature of this intuition. We have, then, the problem of "values as essences" and the problem of the emotional intuition of these values or essences.

Some concept of emotional intuition is forced upon the value realist by the fact that, while phenomenological analysis can and must distinguish between the value apprehended and the feeling towards that value, yet the only way in which a value can be apprehended is through emotion and emotional intuition of the value. Were it possible by a violent abstraction to conceive of beings of a purely intellectual cast, minds in which the processes of nature and the actions of men were mirrored without any emotion, the qualities which we have called value qualities, even if they were present, would be wholly absent in so far as these beings were concerned. They would lack the conditions necessary to such apprehension, just as the absence of certain sense organs, with their sense intuition, would make impossible the apprehension of other aspects of reality. This dependence, in some fashion, of values upon emotion compels us, in case we disavow the idea that they are the mere expression of emotion, to postulate some sort of emotional intuition. The examination of the possibility of such a notion is therefore demanded.

In our examination of the notion of intuition in general, we enunciated the principle that the fact of the conditioning of one process by another does not justify their identification. We applied this principle in our distinction of intuition from imagery or of *Anschauung* from *Vorstellung*. The same principle is applicable here. The fact that the value qualities cannot be experienced other than emotionally does not mean that they themselves are these emotions, any more than the dependence of the intuition of the melody upon the sensations of the sounds means that the melody is identical with the sounds. This general principle has been shown to hold in the case of value qualities. The qualities expressed by the words daring, modest, proud, frivolous, can, to be sure, be only lived, or *erlebt*: they cannot be sensed. They can be lived only emotionally, but that emotional experience is quite different from, and an independently variable of, the feeling attitudes of liking and disliking. That there are difficulties in the notion of emotional intuition, as indeed there are in all notions of intuition, need not be denied. Value theory as such would have to consider the whole question of knowledge of values, including the relation of this emotional intuition to communicable and public knowledge: in other words, to verifiability. But the possibility—indeed, the actuality—of such intuition cannot be denied.[1]

[1] This problem is taken up in Chapter V, pp. 215 ff.

F

Value Words and Their Referends

It is now possible to distinguish between emotional intuition and emotional expression, although that they are intimately connected cannot, of course, be denied. The further problem then arises as to what is intuited and to what the value words which, according to our view, embody this intuition, refer. The notion of intuition without reference is, of course, meaningless.

Now it is, of course, as we have seen, precisely the contention of value nominalism, as represented by the logical positivists, that value words have no referends and are therefore "meaningless." This is, however, what we may describe as the extreme view. It seems to be recognized by some representatives of this view, at least in their more cautious moments, that this cannot be quite true. Ogden and Richards admit that it is probable that no use of language actually exists where there is not some element of reference or indication. So also Carnap. He does not deny categorically that there is any reference whatsoever; there is rather a disguised reference to a perceptually observed object, and then the value proposition is reducible to an ordinary factual judgment. Value words are then signs, but signs that merely point to a field of value-indifferent facts. The issue here seems to be reasonably clear. There must be some reference in value words, they must have some referends. Otherwise even the meaning which they do have, meaning even in the loose sense, would be impossible. But they cannot refer to that to which they *seem* to refer, namely, values. Value propositions are *Scheinsätze* because the predicates in those propositions refer to nothing. If the analysis of the preceding paragraphs is at all valid they do refer to something, and that not to observable entities of either a physical or psychological character, but to essences or universals. The entire doctrine of values as essences, like the conception of an emotional intuition of these essences, is full of difficulties. Here, too, a general theory of value would have to raise the question of the nature of these essences and their relation to other types of universals. Here our point is merely that analysis does disclose this reference of value words and indicates the direction

THE PRIMARY FUNCTIONS OF LANGUAGE

in which a theory of the nature of these referends must proceed.

VII

THE PHENOMENOLOGICAL AND THE NORMATIVE STANDPOINT. SUMMARY AND CONCLUSION

The preceding discussion of "value words" is, it must be pointed out, but a part of the general problem of this chapter, namely, the Phenomenology of Linguistic Meaning. As such it may seem to have been given an inordinate amount of attention in comparison with the other phases of our study. This is, however, not the case. The problem here discussed is crucial for two reasons. In the first place, it presents the main problem of this chapter, the existence of intuitive linguistic meaning, in its most critical and controversial phase. In the second place, it presents the problem of the relation of the phenomenological to the normative in the philosophy of language at a no less crucial point. Let us consider in conclusion the bearing of these two points on later discussions.

The question of the existence or non-existence of intuitive linguistic meaning is determinative for our position of several moot questions of the philosophy of language. As the recognition of only two types of meaning, the conceptual and the emotive, affects our entire view of the relation of language to cognition, so the establishment of meaning of the intuitive type will influence vitally our position on this question. The points at which this will chiefly appear are in connection with the relation of language to logic[1] and the different ways in which language may represent or express reality.[2] This will in turn affect our conception of the nature of symbols and our theory of symbolism. In this connection I will mention only the matter of logic and language. If the parts of speech have, as we have maintained, an intuitive content, then the question of the relation of logic to vocabulary and syntax cannot be unaffected by this fact. Logical analysis of language, whatever its function may turn out to be, cannot legislate these meanings out of existence.

[1] Chapter VII, pp. 285 ff.   [2] Chapter VIII, pp. 357 ff.

No less significant for a philosophy of language is our position with regard to value nominalism. That it can be shown to be the result of defective phenomenological analysis and, when thought out, lacks all intelligibility, was the main contention of our discussion. But there is another aspect to the situation which should be emphasized. Value nominalism is normative in character and the problem which it sets involves the entire normative problem of language.

First let us see that it is normative in character. It proposes to tell us what forms of linguistic expression are meaningful and what meaningless—how we ought to use language and how we ought not. It draws normative conclusions of far-reaching importance. Since a proposition containing a value judgment cannot, in the nature of the case, be constructed and, since the bodies of knowledge known as ethics and aesthetics contain such supposed propositions, such sciences are impossible. They are made up of pseudo-propositions. But it reaches these conclusions by a procedure that is itself normative, for it takes as its *criterion* or norm of meaning a specific use of language as the only valid use.

This view in itself presents an interesting problem for the philosophy of language, but the issue it raises is much more far-reaching. The condemnation of all normative science by a procedure that is itself normative involves a circle which seems to vitiate the entire line of reasoning. But it also suggests that any theory of the valid or invalid use of language must, by its very nature, be normative—every distinction between the meaningful and the unmeaning must rest upon a meaning norm. Thus we are led to an examination of the normative problem of language as such. With this the following chapter will be concerned. The studies of the present chapter have at least served to indicate the relation of phenomenological analysis to this problem.

CHAPTER V

THE NORMATIVE PROBLEM OF LANGUAGE: LINGUISTIC VALIDITY

I

A

WHATEVER else language is, it is in the first instance meaningful communication between man and man. Sounds have physical reality, but sounds are not speech. Meanings have a psychical reality in the individual organism, but the associations, the motor reactions, or what not, are not of themselves linguistic meaning. It is only through communication that language comes into being. It has no reality, as language, except in the speech community. This is a basal fact of linguistic science and it is out of this factual situation that the second main problem of a philosophy of language arises. We have formulated it in the following way: How shall we use language so as to communicate meaning rather than the unmeaning—truth rather than falsity? How shall we use it so as to convey that which is meaningful and true rather than the unmeaning and the untrue?[1] When the problem of the philosophy of language is stated in this way a new element is introduced which we may describe as the normative. The critical and evaluative element enters into the philosophy of language, as distinguished from the merely phenomenological.

The idea of a normative point of view in language may at first sight seem questionable. But it cannot be escaped if we once ask the foregoing questions. For the very questions themselves imply that we *ought* to use language in one way rather than another, and any kind of answer whatsoever implies that there are wrong ways and right ways. As a matter of fact, linguists and philosophers are constantly taking a normative point of view. We are told that we ought not to try to express certain things in language at all because by the very nature of language they are not expressible and our words do not

[1] Chapter I, pp. 36 ff.

communicate any meaning. In short, the normative point of view is implied in all discussions of language. We may call it the Problem of *Linguistic Validity*.

The use and abuse of words is then a topic in almost every kind of linguistic discussion. Hobbes's treatment of the normative problem is illuminating. According to him, we "abuse words" when "we use them metaphorically, that is in other senses than that they are ordained for, and thereby deceive others." The fact remains that we do deceive others and that we *ought* not. It is also a fact that to distinguish between the proper use and abuse of words, implies that we do know what they "are ordained for." In sum, Hobbes, like all of us, recognizes a normative point of view in language, however inconsistent it may be with the rest of his mechanical and materialistic philosophy.

We have already become familiar in the preceding chapter with one important phase of the normative problem of language—with the question of linguistic validity at one of its most crucial points. The task of this chapter is to consider the entire problem from a more general point of view.

B

The Notion of an Ideal Language

It seems scarcely necessary to say that when one speaks of the use and abuse of language, or asserts that words ought to be used in one way rather than another, such expressions are meaningless unless one has before him some idea of what language ought to be, some valid linguistic ideal.

Ideals of language are in general constructed from two points of view which we may describe as the cultural and the scientific or logical. In general the first represents the ideal of *expressiveness*, the latter the ideal of *pure notation*. We may begin our study by a description of the linguistic ideal which, while it embodies both standpoints, emphasizes the former. "An ideal language," writes Jespersen, "would always express the same thing by the same means and similar things by similar means; any irregularity or ambiguity would be banished; sound and sense would be in perfect harmony; any number of delicate shades of meaning would be expressed with equal ease; poetry

THE NORMATIVE PROBLEM OF LANGUAGE

and prose, beauty and truth, thinking and feeling would be equally provided for: the human spirit would have found a garment combining freedom and gracefulness, fitting it closely and yet allowing full play to any movement. "No language," he tells us, "has arrived at perfection, but from the beginning the tendency *has been one of progress towards this ideal*."[1]

A conception of an "ideal" language, such as the above, seeks to take account of *all* linguistic values. Other formulations of the ideal have been made from narrower and more limited points of view. Thus F. P. Ramsey in his *Foundations of Mathematics*, p. 283, tells us that "in a perfect language each thing would have its own name," so that "if in the sense of a sentence a certain object occurred, it would also be shown visibly by the occurrence in the sentence of the name of that object.... In a perfect language, then, all sentences or thoughts would be perfectly clear."

In contrast to the preceding ideal this "logical" ideal, if we may so call it, has a certain provincial character which results from ignoring all linguistic values except that of clearness, and proceeds upon the assumption that the only function of language, except that of evoking emotions, is one of indication or denotation. In any case it seems reasonably clear that this ideal of pure notation, according to which each thing would have its own name, is a narrow if not indeed a self-defeating ideal. It was Locke who doubted "whether a distinct name for every particular thing would be of any great use for the improvement of knowledge."[2] The carrying out of any such ideal would not only fail to improve knowledge but would even seem to be fatal to it. For it would eliminate the universal which, as present in all stages of language, not only makes possible name transference but the knowing of things together which is bound up with it.

C

The Relation of these Norms: the Proper Use of Words

An examination of these two ideals of language indicates both the nature of the normative problem itself and the two main

[1] *Language, Its Nature, Development and Origin*, p. 442. (Published by George Allen & Unwin Ltd.)
[2] Locke, Essay Bk., III, Chapter III, Sections 4–6. See also Cassirer, Vol. I, p. 76.

values or norms which struggle for supremacy. These we have described as the ideal of expressiveness and that of pure notation. The notion of the proper or valid use of words is determined by these two norms.

The capacity for indefinite expressiveness—or expressing any number of shades of meaning—is evidently required from the point of view of understanding and communication. It seems to be required from the noetic point of view also. A language is required which is fluid in such fashion that it makes it possible always to be passing from the known to the unknown. There must be a language whose signs, which cannot be infinite in number, are extended to an infinity of "things." This fluidity or mobility is then the first law of language. But this requirement is offset—and in a sense opposed—by another, namely, that of permanence or resistance to change. A language is also required, from the point of view both of communication and of knowledge, which shall not be thus indeterminate, but completely determinate in its references. Perdurability of meaning seems to be a condition of linguistic validity as of any other kind of validity.

The struggle for supremacy between these two ideals constitutes the very life of language. Obviously both are required from the standpoint of communication. No less obviously both are demanded from the noetic standpoint. The question may be raised as to which is primary. An interesting discussion of this question is that of H. Ammann in *Die Menschliche Rede*. "We could imagine," he writes, "a language that should remain unchanged for decades or indeed for centuries. Such a static condition of speech is by no means incompatible with the nature of speech. A constant change or becoming would, however, be completely incompatible with its essential character as a means or instrument of understanding."[1] It is clear, of course, that the latter statement is true. Absolute change is incompatible with the essential character of speech. On the other hand, it is equally clear that a static condition of speech would be equally incompatible, for communication of new nuances of meaning, new references, would be impossible. It is then simply a question of *primacy or priority*, and it seems clear that change or fluency must be given the "prior

[1] *Op cit.*, Vol. I, p. 44.

THE NORMATIVE PROBLEM OF LANGUAGE 173

rights." It is to be remembered, however, that words signify new objects *not* by losing but by conserving their former meanings or references. The fact that a sign may intend one thing without ceasing to intend another is precisely the condition of its being an *expressive* sign at all, and that which makes language an instrument of knowledge and communication.[1]

The normative problem of language is, then, that of the proper use of words—how we ought to use them so as to express the meaningful rather than the unmeaning, the true rather than the false. Closely connected with this notion is that of the "proper" meaning of words, namely, that meaning which they have, so to speak, by their own right, by virtue of primary as distinguished from acquired uses and meanings. This problem of "proper" meaning, or meaning "in the strict sense," is, we shall find, one of the fundamental problems of the philosophy of language.

We may now indicate the specific points at which these philosophical or normative problems arise in connection with language. They arise: (*a*) in connection with the mobility of language and consequent mutation of meanings. With the mobility of language there is mutation of meaning or reference; what are the conditions determining the validity of these acquired references? (*b*) They arise, secondly, in connection with the multiple meanings or references thus acquired and the consequent ambiguity or equivocation thus engendered. What are the conditions of meaningful discourse here? With this problem is involved the entire question of context. Finally, back of these questions lies, (*c*) the still more fundamental question of the criterion of the meaningful or the nature of linguistic validity as such. It is at this point that the question of the "empirical criterion of meaning" arises—namely, whether the criterion of the meaning of a word is its reference to sensuously observable entities, whether, in other words, the proper use of words involves our using them only when they have such reference.

[1] Chapter III, p. 112.

II

MUTATION OF MEANING: NAME TRANSFERENCE AND ANALOGOUS PREDICATION

The primary condition of language conveying the meaningful is, then, that it shall change, that the signs of which it makes use shall be not adherent but mobile. Fixity is an essential demand of intelligible language, but that fixity is, so to speak, parasitic on the mobility of language. Fixity, determinateness, has only a relative significance. This mobility of signs was expressed by our characterization of language as *endless naming*. Not only is every *part* of speech in reality a name, but the life of language consists precisely in naming an infinite number of objects or aspects of reality. It is out of the inexhaustible character of reality that the endless naming arises. This process of endless naming is carried on in two ways: (*a*) by the transference of names from one "thing" to another; (*b*) by the making of new names consciously. The first we shall describe as natural speech construction, the second as artificial or conventional speech construction.

A
Name Transference: Natural Speech Construction

Aristotle recognized this phenomenon of name transference and was among the first to attempt a study of its "laws." It will be well to take our departure from this early study. The name of anything, says Aristotle, is either its own name or one transferred to it from something else. Thus if I call a young goat a kid I am calling it by its own name, but if I call a young human a kid I am calling it by the name of something else. Now if one accepts any evolutionary or developmental view of language, all names must be viewed as thus transferred except those few which have a counterpart in nature, which are self-significant in the sense already defined. Even these must be viewed as transferred in a certain sense, namely, from the sound to the "cause" of the sound. Mobility is thus the first

THE NORMATIVE PROBLEM OF LANGUAGE 175

law of language. Linguistic meaning, in contrast to non-linguistic, is transitive in character. Aristotle also attempted a study of the laws of this transference. Names are, according to him, transferred in four ways: (*a*) the name of a species may be transferred to the genus; (*b*) the name of a genus may be transferred to the species; (*c*) the name of a species may be transferred to another species; (*d*) names are transferred according to analogy.[1]

Aristotle's account of name transference, while historically of the greatest importance, requires correction and supplementation at two points. In the first place, while all these four relations do constitute connections of thought which underlie the transference of names, no less important than these mentioned by Aristotle are the categorial relations of cause and effect, part and whole, substance and quality. In the second place, all those mentioned by Aristotle, as well as those which we have added, are logical or categorial. A complete account of mutation of meaning, through name transference, would include alogical connections.

But more important than either of these considerations is the fact that of the four ways of name transference distinguished by Aristotle, all are not of equal importance from the

---

[1] Aristotle's four laws may be illustrated as follows: The name of a species may be transferred to the genus. Thus the Latin name *felis*, a cat, has been transferred to the whole genus of which the cat is a species. Chattel meant formerly cattle, a species of movable property; it has since been transferred to movable property in general.

Secondly, the name of a genus is transferred to the species. Thus "fowl" in Old English was applied to the whole feathered race; it has since been transferred to one species. Poet in old Greek meant a maker, in general, but in classical Greek it meant one species of maker, namely, a maker of songs and dramas.

Thirdly, the name of one species is transferred to another species. Horse, for instance, has been transferred to a species of the genus domestic furniture. A few instances may be found in which a name has been transferred from one species to another of the same genus. Thus the Latin *nepos*, meaning a grandson or sister's son has been transferred in the form of nephew to a brother's son, that is, from one species of blood relationship to another.

Fourthly, names are transferred according to analogy. By this Aristotle means that when A is to B as C is to D, the name A can be used to indicate C. Thus, as the helmsman is to the ship, so the ruler is to the State, so that the Latin *gubernator*, a helmsman, is used in the form governor to indicate the ruler of a State. Or as salt is to food, so are wit and humour to literature, so that the name *sal* can be used to indicate these qualities in literature. By this species of metaphor or transference, Aristotle means precisely what we mean by "metaphor."

standpoint of the philosophy of language. In the first three we are concerned only with the conceptual content or meaning of a word. In the fourth, designated as metaphor proper, are included all those transferences of words involving the intuitive meanings of words as defined and developed in the preceding chapter. The fourth is not only different from the others; it also represents the primary and fundamental form of name transference, that form in connection with which the relation of language to knowledge is most significant. The development of language and linguistic consciousness is from copy to analogy, and from analogy to concept and symbol. It is this analogical stage that now demands our study.

B

Analogy as the Basal Principle of Name Transference: the Notion of Radical Metaphor

From the standpoint of the philosophy of language, then, it is the fourth principle of transference that is fundamental. Its fundamental character has been recognized by calling it "radical metaphor," by which it is meant to indicate that it is the root of all transfer of meanings and of natural speech construction.

It has been repeatedly pointed out that metaphor, in the sense here understood, must be clearly distinguished from metaphor in the conscious reflective activity of the poet. It is rather the unconscious activity that is creative in language itself. Of this radical metaphor Max Müller has said: "Man was compelled to speak metaphorically, not because he could not control his poetic phantasy, but rather more because he was compelled to strive to the uttermost to find expression for the ever-growing needs of his soul. It was completely impossible to grasp and hold the outer world, to know and to understand, to conceive and to name, without this fundamental metaphor, this universal mythology, if you will. Metaphor in this sense was much less the carrying over of a word from one concept to another as the creation or nearer determination of a new concept by means of an old name."[1]

[1] Quoted from Cassirer, *op. cit.*, Vol. II, p. 61.

Metaphor is, then, essentially discovery of new meanings and their fixation and determination by means of old names. What we ordinarily call metaphor, begotten by individual phantasy, is but a "little remainder" of what was formerly a universal and necessary element of natural speech construction. Nor shall we ever understand this radical metaphor, so closely connected with mythology, unless we understand also that what we call the elements of anthropomorphism and personification in mythology, far from being an arbitrary *Einfühlung* or "reading in" of subjective states, were actually necessary to the growth of reason and language themselves. The *Ursprache* is poetic in the sense that radical metaphor is the basal form of natural as distinguished from artificial speech construction.

The essence of radical metaphor is that it is intuitive and involves the intuitive meaning which we analysed out and described in the preceding chapter. This is seen especially in the *Erlebniss-Wert* of the adjective. The transfer of the coldness of ice to the coldness of a reception, the height of a tree or mountain to the height of nobility, the dirt of the streets to the dirt of the Yellow Press—in all such cases we recognize a certain natural affinity or likeness between the objects which makes the transference natural and even inevitable. In the preceding chapter we pointed out that it is precisely at these points of metaphor, or transfer, that the intuitive content of words comes most clearly to light. Roses can be carried over to all "fresh and pleasant things" precisely because of this intuitive element. Our point now is that *unless* there were this intuitive content the word could not be carried over. These transfers are frequently described as emotional, just as the meaning itself is called merely emotive, but an adequate phenomenological analysis makes it possible, as we have seen, to distinguish clearly between the emotive and intuitive meanings or connotations of the words.

The intuitive character of all such transfers raises the question of their validity, a question which leads directly to the problem of analogous predication to which we shall immediately turn. One point may, however, be noted in this connection.

The fact that there is this intuitive element makes these transfers in a sense self-authenticating. By this I mean that their justification lies primarily in the intuitive element in the transfer itself. The notion of self-authenticating elements we found necessary to any theory of language; no theory of linguistic meaning can be constructed which does not recognize verbal signs which are intrinsically expressive. Similarly, it is impossible to construct any theory of name transference which does not involve this notion of self-authentication. For such transference involves not merely the carrying over of a word from one object to another, by, let us say, some external association of ideas, but the predication, although analogously, of the name to the object. This predication is understandable only on the assumption that in that predication some aspect or quality of the object is intuited.

It is true that such transfers may often be conceptually justified, but such "verification" is always *ex post facto*. The transfer of the cold of the ice to the cold of a reception, of the name of the pilot of a ship, *gubernator*, to the ruler of a State, may be thus justified. It consists in arguing that when A is to B as C is to D, the name A can be used to indicate C. But such validation is significantly different from the self-authenticating process by which the transfer takes place. Arguments from analogy have a place in logic, and the nature and limits of such inference are problems important for logic, but they belong to another order of discourse.

C

Radical Metaphor and Analogous Predication

According to Hobbes, we abuse words when we use them metaphorically—that is in other senses than they are ordained for. It is, however, quite clear that if we do not use them metaphorically, we shall not use them at all. If there was any kind of ordaining, it was that they *should* be used metaphorically. But this metaphorical use brings with it one of the most fundamental problems of the philosophy of language, and of cognition generally, namely, that of analogous predication.

It is quite clear, first of all, that the metaphorical use of language does involve predication. When I say that my reception was cold, that the Press is yellow, I am not thereby merely

THE NORMATIVE PROBLEM OF LANGUAGE 179

expressing an emotion, but asserting a fact. I am predicating a quality, but I am predicating it analogously. When I say of a priest he is a physician of the soul, I am again not merely expressing an emotional attitude towards him: I am asserting a fact, but by means of an analogy. What is the nature of this type of predication? Is it a valid form of predication?

Both of these questions are of fundamental importance from the standpoint of the normative problem of language in answering our question how we shall use language in order to convey the meaningful rather than the unmeaning, the true rather than the false. Those who hold that we abuse words when we use them metaphorically would describe this as a case of equivocal predication, and since one ideal of language is to avoid equivocation and ambiguity, analogous predication is ambiguous and therefore not a valid form of predication. Thus univocal predication, the very condition of determinate meaning, would require that in all non-emotional uses of language, physician be kept for the primary reference or context, that the word cold be kept for the perceptual object of which it is the sign. Analogous predication is ambiguous predication. Closer examination shows, however, that this analysis does not represent the actual situation. When I say that a wise adviser is a physician of the soul, I am not predicating physician of such a man. When I predicate coldness of a reception or greenness of life, I am not predicating these terms of the reception and life. What then am I doing?

It seems quite clear what I am doing. I am bringing to light some aspect or character of the priest, of the reception, or of life, as the case may be, which could *not be determined and expressed except by such a transfer*. Metaphor is indeed "a nearer determination of a new concept by an old name." Analogous predication is then a genuine form of predication in so far as the communication of meaning is concerned. It is true, of course, that as analogy is a stage in the development of language and of the linguistic consciousness, so also analogous predication may, from some points of view, be but a stage in the development of conceptual judgment and predication. It is true also that there is still the question whether analogous predications are genuine propositions, assertions to which truth and falsity may be applied, a problem to be considered in the chapter on

Logic and Language. But neither of these problems affects the genuineness of this predication as unambiguous expression of meaning.[1]

These questions have, it is true, far-reaching importance for the entire problem of language and cognition, especially in so far as they are involved in the problem of symbolic knowledge, but they must be postponed until we examine the entire question of the relation of meaning to verifiability and the nature of verifiability itself. It will suffice here to point out that the truth of such predications rests upon the assumption that analogy is a genuine feature of "things," and that between different contexts and universes of discourse there exist such relations that a name can be transferred from one to another and still have reference, and that the name thus transferred can in some way represent the object to which it is transferred.

D
Natural and Conventional Speech Construction

All the forms of word transference described above I have characterized as natural speech construction. As this notion will be constantly used in the sequel it will be well to define it in the present context.

By natural is here understood, first of all, the opposite of arbitrary and conventional. In the making of arbitrary technical terms, for instance, one or more of these "laws" of name transference may be present, but they need not be. Convention, or *conscious* agreement for a purpose, is all that is necessary. For purposes of pure designation or notation it is even desirable that the sign shall have lost all its "meanings" except that of designation. With such signs, however, as we shall maintain later, we say nothing, we merely manipulate.

But by natural is here meant more than this, namely, self-authenticating transfer without which no natural speech construction takes place. All colloquial language—and indeed all

---

[1] See A. E. Taylor, *The Faith of a Moralist*, Vol. I, pp. 52 ff.
Taylor has expressed this situation in the following way: "It is simply not true that the alternatives univocal predication and equivocal predication form a complete disjunction." His entire treatment of this subject is worthy of careful study.

language, poetic or scientific, except in so far as it is arbitrarily manipulated to achieve certain ends—is of this character. In this sense it may be said that language is already *metaphysized*. The movement of language takes place along the line of certain fundamental relations which imply, as it were, a metaphysics. A common inherited scheme of intuitions and conceptions lies all around us and comes to us as naturally and unquestionably as the air we breathe. It is none the less imposed upon us—all the more surely and irresistibly because, being inherent in the very language we use, even to express the simplest meaning, it is already adopted and assimilated before we can so much as begin to question, and constitutes what we may call the "natural metaphysic of the human mind."

Whether natural speech construction, and the entire metaphysics it creates or involves, are valid, is precisely the issue of the philosophy of language. Logical analysis of language may conceivably find it necessary to condemn these natural tendencies as giving rise to a false metaphysics. A critical philosophy may find it necessary to condemn the natural metaphysic of the human mind which develops out of this natural speech construction. Kant, in the *Critique of Pure Reason*, was preoccupied with this problem; the "transcendental dialectic" was in this sense essentially a critique of language, the examination of the transcendental illusion, necessary and inevitable according to him, as growing out of the natural tendencies of reason which are bound up with language. All these are problems for later investigation. Here it is desirable merely to define these notions of which we shall make later use.

III

MUTATION OF MEANINGS AND THE "PROGRESS" OF LANGUAGE

A

The phenomena of name transference have now been considered. The notion of natural speech construction has also been defined and amplified. These facts may now be gathered together in a general "law" which may be described as the law of the development of language or of natural speech construction. This law has been formulated by Cassirer in the following way: The development of language is from copy (imitation) to analogy and from analogy to symbol. Before considering the nature of this law and its significance for the philosophy of language with its normative problems, it is desirable to consider briefly the general notion of "development" as applied in linguistics.

The underlying postulate of older conceptions of language was that of an *Ursprache*, or natural and universal language lying at the back of the particular languages. With the nineteenth-century historical way of thinking, this postulate received its death-blow and was replaced by another, namely, that of the development or progress of language. This postulate seems, in its turn, to have suffered eclipse, at least temporarily. The failure of comparative linguistics to discover any definite stages in the development of linguistic forms has led to the abandonment of the notion in many quarters. On the other hand, there are those who still maintain that there *has* been development or "progress" of language. Jespersen, for instance, distinguishes between "external" speech forms and the "inner" or meaning side of language, and maintains that there has been a parallel development in both aspects. We shall discuss this general question in Appendix I; here our sole interest is in the notion as it applies to the phenomena of the transfer of names and the consequent mutation in the meaning functions of language.

According to Cassirer, the development of language in this sense proceeds, as we have seen, through three main stages: (*a*) the imitative or copy stage; (*b*) the analogical; and (*c*) the symbolic. The characteristic of the first stage is that between the word, or verbal sign, and the "thing" to which it refers no real difference is made. The word *is* the thing. This initial stage is, however, broken up as soon as transfer of signs takes place. Here the relation is analogical. But this relation also gives way to the symbolic. The characteristic of this stage is that while the element of representation (*Darstellung*), which is the *sine qua non* of all linguistic meaning, still remains, the relation of similarity which conditions the representation becomes more and more partial and indefinite.

The stages of development, as here briefly sketched, constitute a mere scheme, but when this scheme is filled in with the rich content at Cassirer's disposal, it shows itself, as he has amply proved, not only as an important principle for the classification of the phenomena of language but as a principle of development in the *Aufbau der Sprache* which enables us to connect language with similar developments in other fields of culture such as science and art.[1] In so far as language itself is concerned, Cassirer is able to show by extensive comparative studies the presence of this tendency or the application of this law in connection not only with the parts of speech—the noun, the adjective, and the verb—but with special forms of the parts of speech, more particularly space and time words and the verb to be, both of which, as we shall see, have important implications for the philosophy of language.[2]

An important aspect of this law of development should be noted for its bearing on later discussions. It represents not merely a general description of the stages of the development of the meaning of words, but also of what I shall describe as the speech consciousness. There is not only a change or development of the meaning functions of words, but of our consciousness of that function. The function of language is not, as Cassirer repeatedly asserts, to copy reality, but to symbolize it. This law of the stages of development of meaning has two important aspects, one more general and one more specific, which require special consideration. This general tendency of language may be described as the upward movement of language or movement from the "physical" to the "spiritual." It occurs in connection with all types and aspects of words, but there is a specific application to space and time language which is not only significant for the philosophy of language in general but for the understanding of the entire symbolic function of language. Let us examine them in turn.

B

The Upward Movement of Language: From the "Physical" to the "Spiritual"

The notion of progress, when applied to language as well as to any other phase of culture, involves an element of evalua-

[1] *Op. cit.*, Vol. I, Chapter II, pp. 132 ff., 233 ff.
[2] *Op. cit.*, Vol. I, pp. 280 ff.

tion. If the "law" of change or development which we have just sketched is to be viewed as progress it can be only in the light of some ideal as to what language should be and do. The ideal of language, as we formulated it earlier in this chapter, includes both that of expressiveness and of pure notation. These two ideals struggle for supremacy—and this struggle is the very life of language—but if our argument there was valid, the primacy must be given to the ideal or norm of expressiveness. From this standpoint the tendencies of language as described by Cassirer may properly be called "upward."

I shall accordingly call this the upward movement of language and describe it further as movement from the physical to the spiritual. Both of these notions are taken from Willis's *The Philosophy of Speech*.[1] In its earlier stages the growth of language, according to him, is always upward. That is to say, from the species to the genus, from the effect to the cause, from the part to the whole, and finally from the physical to the spiritual. This can scarcely be otherwise, since mobility of signs —their detachment and transfer to an infinity of objects— is the first law of language. The mere process of naming involves, as we have seen, an element of universalization and the development of language includes the passage from lower to higher levels of universalization.[2]

Of these upward tendencies of language that described as movement from the physical to the spiritual demands special attention here. It describes the characteristic aspect of the metaphorical transfer of names which, as we have seen, is the basal form of name transference.

Examine closely any typical sentence taken from developed human discourse, such a sentence, for instance, as the following

---

[1] George Willis, *The Philosophy of Speech*, pp. 56 ff. According to him, in the later stages of the development of a language, the reverse processes are equally frequent. He maintains that since the Norman conquest the downward processes have predominated in the English language, presumably because foreign words have been taken for the more spiritual references. Thus he points out that *wean* (the German *gewohnen*) formerly meant to accustom. It is now applied almost solely to accustoming the child to do without the breast. Lust meant formerly desire in general; now it is applied only to the carnal aspect of sexual desire. This counter-movement does not mean that the general development of language has stopped. It means that the other meanings are taken by other words. (Published by George Allen & Unwin Ltd.)

[2] Chapter III, p. 117.

taken from Jespersen. "He *came* to *look upon* the *low ebb* of morals as an *outcome* of bad *taste*."[1] You will find that nearly every word is, in the terms of Jespersen, a "dead metaphor." All physical in origin, they have lost their physical reference and, with it, their character as metaphor. But you will also find that these same words have acquired a new reference, and this reference can be characterized only as reference to the spiritual, in contrast to the primary reference of the words to the physical. This, then, is the upward movement of language, from the physical to the spiritual. And it should be noted that if interpretation of meaning consisted in carrying back the meaning to the primary physical context, we should get nonsense or gibberish.[2]

C

Space-Time and Language

Closely connected with this first aspect of the natural development of language is a similar one in connection with space and time words. Just as all words have originally unquestionably a physical reference, so words for *relations* are primarily spatial in character. All such notions as "standing for," "referring to," "beyond our thought or knowledge," have a primary spatial meaning which is never completely lost. The outstanding case, however, is the relation expressed by the spatial words "in or within." One thinks of the many meanings of the word "in." I have *in* me a certain thought. That is *in* my power. Make for me a picture *in* the large. The truth lies *in* the following. All these cases are forms of radical metaphor as we have described it in preceding sections.

The primacy of space language is further seen in the case of our words for time. Bergson, and other thinkers following him, have maintained that all our words for time had formerly a spatial meaning and that the vulgar notion of time is simply

[1] *Language: Its Nature, Development and Origin*, p. 353. (Published by George Allen & Unwin Ltd.)
[2] A brilliant and amusing illustration of this fact is to be found in Anatole France's "The Language of Metaphysics," an essay in his *Garden of Epicurus*. There he takes a typical metaphysical "proposition," e.g. "The soul experiences God in so far as it participates in the absolute," and by reducing these words to their "original and undefaced image," turns them into gibberish. This is, of course, in principle the method of logical positivism in dealing with metaphysical words.

a copy of the notion of space. Of the fact itself there can be little question. The interchangeability of space and time words in primitive language, especially of space and time adverbs, is an almost universal aspect of primitive speech.[1]

Two considerations of importance for the philosophy of language seem to follow from the movement of language connected with space and time words. The first of these concerns the primacy of spatial language, the second space and time words as a whole. The primacy of space language has led to the view that all thought is essentially spatialized and that logic is a transfer of spatial notions to thought relations. Nor is this without an element of justification, as we shall see in our logical studies to come. The notion of "logical space," as developed by Wittgenstein and others, is either a doubtful analogy or it actually represents what it says, namely, that logic is actually spatialized. Be that as it may—and we shall consider this whole problem in connection with language and logic—it seems clear that Bergson is right in his main contention. Our intellect is primarily fitted to deal with space and moves most easily in this medium. Thus language itself becomes spatialized, and in so far as reality is represented by language, reality tends to be spatialized. Unless therefore this primary space language can become the symbol for non-spatial relations, be filled with "spiritual content," language must inevitably "distort reality."

A second consideration concerns the despatialization and detemporalization of our space-time language viewed as a whole. Here we are concerned with a special case of the analogous predication already studied. Concretely expressed, when we say that one thing stands for another, we are not actually saying that it is "standing" any more than when we say that a priest is a physician of the soul, that he is a physician. When we say that is in my power, the truth lies in the following, we are not saying that it is *in* my power, or that the truth is *in* anything. Univocal and equivocal predication are not a complete disjunction here any more than in the preceding cases. We have in fact come here upon the most important character and differentia of linguistic meaning, namely, its symbolic nature. All language goes through the stages of imitation,

---

[1] E. Cassirer, *op. cit.*, Vol. I, p. 168.

analogy, and symbolic relation, and space and time words are no exception to this general law. Cassirer sums up his exhaustive study of space and time language in the following words: "Again it is clear that the concepts of space, time, and number furnish the actual structural elements of objective experience as they build themselves up in language. But they can fulfil their task only because, according to their total structure, they keep in an ideal medium, precisely because while they constantly keep to the form of the sensuous experience, they progressively fill the sensuous with spiritual content and make it a *symbol* of the spiritual" (Vol. I, p. 208).

IV

THE PROGRESS OF LANGUAGE AND THE NORMATIVE PROBLEM

A

The upward movement of language in the two main forms described is, then, from the standpoint of "inner meaning," a fundamental "law" of language development and of natural speech construction. The normative problem at this point is obvious. It arises precisely in connection with the question of the validity of assertions or *Sätze* which arise out of this natural development or natural speech construction. Here, as elsewhere in the philosophy of language, there are in general only two main positions, the naturalistic and the idealistic.

According to the first, such movements from the physical to the spiritual, and from the spatio-temporal to the non-spatial and non-temporal, although "natural" in a purely psychological sense, are none the less in general without linguistic validity, and give rise to *Scheinsätze* or "apparent" propositions. They have meaning only in so far as they are *reducible* to primary propositions where reference to observable perceptual objects is possible. For the second view such assertions or propositions *have* meaning, for while they still retain the reference to the primary context or environment from which they have been derived, they have acquired a new reference—to entities and relations in a new context or universe of discourse. Both of these positions are *normative* in the sense defined; they propose to tell us what uses of language are valid and what are not, and they present to us the reasons for their evaluations, the norms expressed or implied which underlie them. Let us examine the naturalistic or positivist position first.

B

The Upward Movement and the Principle of Reduction

The naturalistic position is essentially *reductive*, as we have said. It was implicit in the empirical position from the very beginning, but received its first explicit statement at the hands of Bentham.[1] The underlying thesis of this position is the distinction between primary and derived propositions and the assertion that primary propositions are all physical, that is propositions about observable existents. By physical Bentham means those that predicate the existence of some state of things, either motional or quiescent, involving relations of bodies in space and time. All propositions are for him either physical or psychical, and the latter are derived from the former, that is, have physical propositions for their *Archetypes*. A second thesis is that the derived propositions, those developed through natural speech construction, are either wholly fictional or contain fictions. The way to expose and clarify these fictions is by what he describes as *paraphrases*, namely, the substitution of a real subject for the fictional subject in propositions. This is possible only by carrying back the derived propositions to their archetypes. Bentham held that the "best" archetypes to which fictions may be reduced are those that give space and time relations between bodies.

C

The Principle of Reduction and Conditioned Predication

Such in brief is the naturalistic position as represented by Bentham. It is in principle also the position of modern logical positivism regarding the primacy of physical language, a position which differs from that of Bentham in no important particulars.[2] The underlying assumption is a normative one—

[1] Bentham's *Theory of Fictions*, Kegan Paul, 1932. Also S. Buchanan, *Symbolic Distance*, Kegan Paul, 1932.   [2] R. Carnap, *The Unity of Science*, London, 1934.

namely, that of the *prior rights of the physical*—an assumption the validity of which we shall discuss in connection with the theory of contexts to be developed presently. For the moment we shall consider a certain consequence which follows from this position which we shall describe as the principle of *conditioned predication*.

As analogical predication is the necessary consequence of the natural tendencies of language, or natural speech construction, so another type of predication, conditioned predication, is the necessary consequence of the denial of the validity of these tendencies. When two references, the one to the primary, the other to the derived context, are associated or conjoined there will be a tendency under certain conditions for the one reference to be identified with the other and for the primary reference, the "archetype," to be considered the true reference. Consequently when two judgments or propositions are associated through their predication of concomitant properties there is the tendency for the predication of one property to become identified with the predication of the other, and for that property to be the defining term which belongs to the psychologically more primitive order.

This tendency is omnipresent in thought and is especially apparent in all discourse about ethical and social fact. In the case of Bentham himself, the outstanding example was his reduction of "obligation," as a fiction, to the spatio-temporal or physical archetypes from which the word was derived. A similar procedure characterizes the analysis of the notion of obligation in Nietzsche's *Genealogy of Morals*. But it is everywhere present and becomes the basis of all naturalistic method. Thus, when psychical states such as fear and anger are concomitant with physical states, the tendency is to take the physical states as identical with the psychological states that are concomitant. In the case of value predicates, such as good or beautiful, the tendency is to take the feeling or emotional as identical with the values with which they are associated—to identify the predication of value with that of the psychological character and for the term of the conditioning order to be the defining term.

This general tendency to conditioned predication is often characterized as the "genetic fallacy," and it is indeed a *petitio principii* in that, assuming the prior rights of the primitive—in the last analysis of the physical—it presupposes a criterion or norm, and on its own assumptions all norms should be meaningless. In any case—and that is all that is of importance here—the position is normative. To the examination of this norm or criterion, this doctrine of prior rights, we shall turn in the sequel. For the moment we shall examine a corollary of this principle, namely, the conception of empty or meaningless words which follows necessarily from this principle of reduction.

D

Acquirement and Loss of Meaning: "Meaningless Words"

The first normative problem of language appears, as we have seen, in connection with the mobility of language. With this mobility, or mutation of meaning, there are acquired new references. What are the conditions determining the validity of these acquired references?

Transference of names or of linguistic signs from one "object" to another is the first law of language. In the course of history words lose their old meanings and acquire new ones. Thus we have almost a complete change of meaning. It is often held that in many cases words may lose their old meanings without acquiring new. In that case we have *apparent* words, *Scheinwörte*, and that which they convey, if they convey anything at all, is, in the strict sense of the word, unmeaning.

This notion of "empty words"—of large regions of human discourse consisting of "empty verbalism"—has been the ultimate appeal of all anti-metaphysical tendencies of thought since thought began. We have already seen it applied to one large region of discourse, namely, ethics and value philosophy. We shall later see it applied also to religious and metaphysical discourse. We are for the present concerned with none of the specific applications of the thesis, but merely with the general standpoint and the assumptions underlying it.

First of all, let us see that it is a normative and not a factual problem. This may be shown in the following way. It is said that certain words have lost all meaning. But can a word used at all in discourse be said to have lost all meaning or reference?

THE NORMATIVE PROBLEM OF LANGUAGE

Can such a proposition itself be given an intelligible meaning?

It seems quite clear that as a mere statement of fact it cannot. Factually every word or sentence used in discourse has meaning by reason of its being so used. Not only have words, as words, reality *only* in the speech community, but in so far as they exist in the speech community they have reality. They have meaning by reason of the fact that communicability is part of the notion of linguistic meaning itself. When therefore words are said to have lost meaning the proposition itself has meaning only in some special sense, in a sense defined for a specific purpose and in a specific context. This is recognized implicitly, and often explicitly, even by those who maintain the positivist point of view. They do not maintain that words are still used in intelligible discourse without conveying any meaning, but only meaning, as they say, *in the strict sense*. This is, of course, a normative position and a norm or criterion is thus erected. This criterion we shall examine presently. Here we merely assert that the statement that words have lost all meaning is itself a meaningless proposition.

So much for a general answer to this question. This general answer may, however, be made more specific. When examined closely, this entire notion of meaningless words is seen to arise from a naïve and over-simple conception of reference. The statement that the meaning of a word is its reference or indication is, of course, in part true. But the view that all meaning is simple reference to an object involves certain misconceptions of the nature of this reference. In the first place, it neglects a more subtle type of reference which we described in an earlier chapter. Words, we found, still have meaning when the wholes of discourse in which they function, as wholes, refer to nothing. The denial of meaning to certain words and combinations of words arises from this oversight. In his analysis of the situation Eaton emphasized the notions of symbolic groups and complex intentions—and rightly from his standpoint—but this over-simple notion of reference arises from a still more fundamental error, namely, in the analysis of the meaning relation itself. In our analysis of the linguistic meaning situation we found that, beside the *prima facie* components, there were also certain implicates. In the case of the "thing meant" there is always implied a context or universe of discourse in which the entity meant has its "being." Without this implicate the entire meaning situation collapses.[1] The recognition of these facts leads us to a consideration of the second question raised by the normative problems of language, namely, that of context. To this we shall now turn.

V

THE NORMATIVE PROBLEM AND AMBIGUITY: THE PROBLEM OF DETERMINATE REFERENCE

A

All words then "stand for something"—have some reference, either determinate or indeterminate. The opposite of this can be maintained only by virtue of some very crude notion of "standing for" or by some equally crude notion of the "something" for which it stands. Some element of reference enters, for all civilized adults at least, into all uses of words, including that described as emotive and evocative. But this reference may be indirect and indeterminate.

Now this very indeterminateness is, as we have seen, the first law of language, as it is one of the conditions of meaningful communication. One of the ideals of language is that its signs shall be mobile enough "to express any number of meanings with equal ease." This is true no less from the noetic standpoint than from that of expression. For language to represent or symbolize reality, it must be fluid enough to express newly discovered aspects of being. To use language meaningfully, therefore, in one sense of the word at least, requires that it *shall* be used ambiguously, that words shall have many voices. This first law of language does not, however, exclude a second requirement, that meanings shall be made definite or determinate, that indirect and unlimited reference shall be made direct and limited. This demand for pure notation, *puri nomi*, is secondary and parasitic on the first, but it is a demand. It is here that the second normative problem

[1] Chapter III, p. 115.

THE NORMATIVE PROBLEM OF LANGUAGE

arises. It arises out of the second aspect of the ideal or purpose of language.

Traditional logic, in two of its main aspects or functions, is concerned with this problem of ambiguity, namely, its connection with the definition of terms and the logical analysis of propositions, the first having as its object the removal of ambiguity in words, the second the removal of grammatical and syntactical ambiguity in sentences and propositions. It is, to be sure, often assumed that all meaning is logical meaning and that all normative problems of language are logical problems. This is, however, as we shall see more fully later, not the case.[1] Logical meaning is but one aspect of meaning and the logical problem of ambiguity but part of a larger linguistic problem. It is with this more general problem that we are here concerned, the more special problem being reserved for a later context. Let us begin then by considering the range of ambiguity—the various kinds of ambiguity which the solution of our normative problem requires us to distinguish.

B

The Range of Ambiguity: Linguistic Ambiguity

Every linguistic expression is ambiguous. He who states this proposition gives with its very statement, as Erdmann says, an illustration of the fact. For the word ambiguous is itself an example of ambiguity. Let us begin then by distinguishing various meanings or kinds of ambiguity.

The first of these is ambiguity in the narrower sense of amphibole. Here we have two or more objects for the same word. This is simply the immediate and necessary result of the mobility of language where a limited number of signs must be used for an "infinity of objects."

To this simplest form of ambiguity we must add a type that grows not out of a multiplicity of objects to be named, but out of relations to be characterized. This ambiguity necessarily inheres in adjectives and adverbs, although it is present in nouns. The word "new" has different meanings in different contexts. A new stamp, a new planet, a new edition—in all

[1] Chapter VI, pp. 275 ff.

these cases new has a different meaning relative to the different times in the different contexts. The words "now" and "here" are also noteworthy examples. Now may mean the present moment or the present century. Here may mean a town or an entire country.

Finally, there is grammatical ambiguity. The expression "he plays the piano" may mean that he is playing it at this moment or that he has the capacity of playing it. Grammatical ambiguity inheres in all verbs, and it is for this reason that in the logical proposition the verb is turned into a class term which becomes the predicate of the substantive. This ambiguity also inheres in all connectives and especially in the connective "is," or copula.

C

Meta-linguistic Ambiguity

These are the types of ambiguity ordinarily distinguished. We may call them the more obvious forms of ambiguity. But there is another much less obvious form which seems to go beyond linguistic ambiguity in the ordinary sense. I shall call this meta-linguistic ambiguity.

The difference between this type of ambiguity and the linguistic may be made clear by the following illustrations. The word Socrates, we say, refers to the philosopher. But in one sentence it may stand for an "entity" presupposing a very different background or context from the word Socrates, with the same primary reference, in another sentence. Thus the same person Socrates in one context is an indivisible whole, while in another context "he may be divisible with respect to time and to different hypothetical states of things." Socrates in the mouth of a moralist means one thing; in the mouth of a physiologist it may mean something quite different. Again, let us suppose that we are using the word marriage. The word "means" one thing in the mouth of an anthropologist, another in the mouth of a priest, and still another in the mouth of a jurist. These meanings all presuppose very different and quite systematic contexts or universes of discourse, and the meaning we shall convey by the use of the word depends upon the

THE NORMATIVE PROBLEM OF LANGUAGE

acknowledgment of the presuppositions or suppositions which create these contexts or universes.

Meta-linguistic ambiguity may be distinguished from merely linguistic in the following way. In our study of the notion of understanding (*das Verstehen*) we saw that a word is never understood by itself, but only in an expression or a sentence. A single word may be known or recognized, but never understood. In the case of linguistic ambiguity the meaning of the word is understood only in the sentence in which it is employed. Thus the word "new" or the word "now" as employed in the preceding illustrations. In the case of meta-linguistic ambiguity the word can be understood only in a context which *goes beyond* the merely linguistic expression in which the word is found. The word marriage may be known but it cannot be understood unless the individual hearing the word shares in the *presuppositions* which, as we have seen, *constitute* the context or universe of discourse in which the word has its meaning.[1] Linguistic form is a condition of understanding, but so also is intentionality and its acknowledgment. Language has no reality except in the speech community, but the speech community is something more than the sharing of common linguistic forms. The point I am making is clear enough. There is meta-linguistic ambiguity and this type of ambiguity cannot be reduced to linguistic without a remainder. The word marriage in its different meanings may be thought of merely as the same word used for different objects or entities. Actually the reference is ultimately not to entities at all, but to universes of discourse.

VI

THE NOTION OF CONTEXT: THEORIES OF CONTEXT

A

Every meaning, we have said, presupposes some systematic context. In our analysis of the meaning situation in Chapter III, we found that, in addition to the two *prima facie* components, namely, that which *means*, the sign, and that which is *meant*, the thing signified, there are other components which must

[1] Chapter III, pp. 125 ff.

be present as presuppositions if the meaning situation is not to collapse. In so far as the *thing meant* is concerned, we found that it is never an isolated entity but always an entity as determined by some systematic context. In other words, the reference which constitutes the meaning relation is *prima facie* to an entity, but ultimately and in reality to a context. It is for this reason that the notion of context is the basal problem of philosophical semantics.

B

Types of Context: Linguistic Context

Our first problem is the examination of different types of context. I shall begin by distinguishing between linguistic and non-linguistic, or meta-linguistic context, corresponding with our two types of ambiguity. The point of this distinction lies in the fact that much ambiguity of the more obvious kind is the function of mere linguistic context and can be cleared up by defining that context. Still deeper forms of ambiguity go back to differences of universes of discourse lying behind the linguistic context.

The notion of linguistic context is simple enough. The ambiguities of a purely linguistic character may all be connected with the elliptical character of language. Single words, as we have seen, cannot be understood. When single words are understood it is only because they are sentence words. Thus in the classical illustration of Preyer, "stool" in the mouth of the child meant at different times four things: (*a*) Where is my stool?; (*b*) My stool is broken; (*c*) Lift me on my stool; (*d*) Here is my stool. The four meanings are all determined by the different contexts and the context here is, in the first instance, the sentence, in this case *understood*, in which the word occurs. In the terms of our earlier analysis it is a function of arrangement and involves, as we have seen, the principle of *Gestalt*. This, then, is linguistic context. But even here more than grammatical context is involved. Intentionality is involved, and this intentionality and its acknowledgment is part of the context in which the meaning subsists. The elliptical character of language involves more than mere ellipticality of *language*.

THE NORMATIVE PROBLEM OF LANGUAGE

Behind the linguistic context lie, then, other contexts which must be distinguished and characterized. The first of these we shall call the vital context. Malinowski describes it as the context of situation. Even in what we have described as linguistic context it is frequently the case that more than linguistic context is involved, and an understanding of the word involves the context of situation which arises out of vital contact between those communicating. Thus, in the case of the four meanings of the word stool it is the context of the situation in which they are embedded that, partly at least, gives them their determinate meanings. Nevertheless, it is still possible to distinguish between those ambiguities that arise merely out of the elliptical character of language and those which are more deeply grounded.

This type of context is, as Malinowski points out, absolutely necessary for the understanding of primitive language. It is necessary, so to speak, to penetrate behind the linguistic context to the vital context of situation in order to determine the meaning. "An utterance," writes Malinowski, "has no meaning except in a context of situation."[1]

C

Context as "Universe of Discourse"

An adequate and usable concept of context requires that the notion shall be widened out into that of the context of situation. Understanding of language requires that we go behind the merely linguistic form and the direct reference to the more indirect references expressed by the term situation. But an adequate notion of context demands a still further widening—to include what I shall describe as *universe of discourse*. By the introduction of this term I have in mind, in the first place, precisely that aspect of context which is characterized by the notion of universe as contrasted with situation. A situation, whether conceived of as physical or psychical, is relatively vague and undefined. A universe, as the term suggests, is a relatively

[1] Ogden and Richards, *The Meaning of Meaning*, Sup. I, pp. 299 ff. For further details on this point, see Chapter VI, section on translation, and Appendix II. It is in connection with the problem of translation—from primitive into cultural languages—that the notion of context of situation is developed. It may be more properly treated in that context.

articulated or systematized whole. It is, then, in the first instance, the character of systematized context that distinguishes the universe of discourse from the context of situation. Let us develop this point more fully.

The term universe of discourse was formed primarily for the purposes of logic, first, I believe, by De Morgan. The term also has reference, first of all, to the elliptical character of language. Thus the reference of such a proposition as "All voters are males" is *understood* to be limited to the time, the nation, etc., in short to the historical universe of discourse in which the proposition is made. The statement, "Some fairies are malevolent," presupposes limitation to a universe of discourse in which the existence of fairies is for the time being assumed. But something more than the elliptical character of language is involved. The term *universe* of discourse presupposes precisely what it says, namely, a universe or systematic context in which the propositions alone have meaning. Thus the proposition "Caesar is a prime number" is not only untrue but meaningless. The proposition "No virtues are triangular" is true, but in a sense also meaningless. The reason that both propositions are meaningless is that in both cases the subject and the predicate belong to such wholly different universes of discourse, types of context so unrelated, that they do not touch. The genus within which any attribute falls, or the subjects susceptible of some attribute within that genus, was called by De Morgan a "limited universe" or a universe of discourse.[1]

This, then, is the notion of context as "universe of discourse." As, recalling Malinowski's words, "an utterance has no meaning except in the context of situation," so a proposition has no meaning except in the context of a universe of discourse. Two further comments upon this notion are desirable.

In the first place, a universe of discourse is a limited universe, and it is this limited character which makes meaning as determinate reference possible. The determination of meaning is the passage from unlimited to limited reference and limited reference is possible only to a limited context or universe. In the second place, this limited universe is a universe of *discourse*. As language has reality only in the speech community so context, in the sense of universe of discourse, has reality only as

[1] *Formal Logic*, pp. 41, 55.

determined by communication. This second point is of major importance. For just as it is impossible to reduce linguistic context (in the narrow sense) to context of situation, so it is impossible to reduce context as universe of discourse to context of situation. A context of situation is but another name for environment. Context is equated with environment, in the first instance physical and secondarily psychological. It is this reduction of the notion of context to that of environment which is the essential feature of naturalistic and causal theories of context which we shall presently examine. Context as universe of discourse is not merely a psychological notion. There is a sense, of course, in which a universe of discourse is also a psychological context. The universe of human character in which the word virtue has meaning is a system of association of ideas. The word "virtue" itself, in its primitive meaning strength, refers to a physical context and only by word transference and analogous predication acquires its secondary reference. In contrast to the physical environment or context, this may be said to be psychological. The different meanings of marriage in the illustration used are acquired meanings, and the halo of acquired meaning may be described psychologically in terms of associations with past emotional experiences. The word marriage does evoke different associations in the mind of the priest from those in the mind of the anthropologist. But it is not these that make the two different *universes of discourse*. What is it, then, that makes the difference?

The primary difference is already indicated in the notion itself—namely, that it is a *universe*. It is its systematic character, its character as a relatively differentiated whole of meaning, that is here determinative. As such it has its own immanental meaning—its *Sinn*, as distinguished from the *Bedeutung*, or particular references of its components. It is, moreover, not merely a universe, but a universe of *discourse*. Semantic meaning, we have repeatedly seen, collapses when the implicate of communication, discourse, is withdrawn. Such a universe of discourse is both created and maintained by the mutual acknowledgment, on the part of communicating subjects, of certain presuppositions without which the universe in question has no being, and the particular references within it no meaning.

D

The Doctrine of the Suppositio or Presupposition: the Differentia of Universes of Discourse

We may make clearer our notion of the nature of this type of context by making use again of the technical scholastic term, the *suppositio* or supposition, already introduced in connection with our examination of the notions of intentionality and understanding.

The doctrine of the supposition which continued through many centuries is now practically forgotten. A philosophy of language would not wish to revive it in its old elaborated form, nor indeed to revive certain metaphysical implications in its scholastic use which would now be questionable. But the term itself is valuable and the fundamental notion underlying it one which must be retained if one wishes to form an adequate notion of linguistic meaning.

In the thirteenth century the scholastic logic added to the logic of Aristotle and his famous followers, Porphyry and Boethius, a new chapter, *de terminorum proprietatibus*, or the properties of words. The doctrine of *suppositio*, as here set forth, made use of the term to denote the various regular ways in which a name may in general be used to denote different objects. The notion thus expressed was that to understand the meaning of a word one must understand its supposition.[1]

The scholastics applied the conception largely for the purpose of removing ambiguities and developed the conception with characteristic mediaeval detail. Numerous distinctions were made and given names. There was, for instance, a *suppositio materialis* and a *suppositio formalis*, according as the word had reference to the sound or the sense. "Pope is derived from the Latin papa." "The Pope is an old man." In the first case the supposition is "material," in the second "formal." *Homo est animal*. Homo here stands for all men, and this is the *suppositio naturalis*. *Homo currit*. Here homo stands for some individual, and this is the *suppositio personalis*.

[1] For an account of the doctrine, see Prantl, *Geschichte der Logik*, Vol. II, Abscn. XV, Vol. III, XVII. There is a certain tendency to revive the notion of the *suppositio* in recent philosophy of language. Thus O. Erdmann, *Die Bedeutung des Wortes*, Leipzig, 1922, pp. 66 ff., A. H. Gardiner, *Speech and Language*, p. 32.

THE NORMATIVE PROBLEM OF LANGUAGE

It is not the scholastic uses of the notion, acute and valuable as these sometimes are, but rather the notion itself that we find significant here. And in making use of it we shall venture to give it a far wider significance than that contemplated by the scholastics. The essential of the notion is this: the meaning of the word is determined by its *suppositio*. To understand a word we must understand what it supposes. In our analysis of "understanding" we found that it is precisely the presence of that supposition which distinguishes linguistic expression from sign, linguistic meaning from the meaning of things. Understanding of a linguistic expression involves acknowledgment of the supposition. Not only is verbal meaning elliptical; the meta-linguistic which lies behind the merely verbal is also elliptical, and here, too, the supposition must be made explicit and acknowledged if intelligible communication is to be possible. Let us illustrate this point somewhat more fully.

If I say that "some fairies are malevolent," the utterance has meaning on a certain supposition. If the supposition (or assumption) is not accepted and acknowledged it is meaningless. Whether the utterance is true or false is another question involving other problems and turning, in the last analysis, upon the question of the relation of meaning to truth. Here we are concerned only with meaning. Similarly, the proposition, "marriage is a sacrament," depends for its meaning on the acknowledgment of a certain supposition—on a universe of discourse in which sacraments have reality. Whether such a proposition is true or false is again another question.

A universe of discourse is then conditioned by its supposition and that supposition is the assumption of the reality of the universe in which the discourse takes place. Mutual acknowledgment of that supposition is the condition of meaningful or intelligible discourse. The condition of the meaningfulness of an assertion or proposition is, then, *not* that certain entities about which the assertion is made exist, in the sense of being empirically verifiable, but that the universe of discourse in which these entities have their existence is mutually acknowledged. The condition of the meaningfulness of the assertion, "some fairies are malevolent," is not that fairies exist in the sense that their existence can be empirically verified, but that the universe of discourse in which fairies have their "existence" has being in some sense. When I say that "a griffin is a fabulous monster," I do not affirm that griffins exist, like pigs and cows. But my judgment, to have any meaning, implies the existence of a mass of fable in which griffins have their place as fables too. If there were no fables, I could not say that griffins were fabulous. But fables are an element in reality—i.e. in the totality of what is real—no less than pigs and cows.

There are two aspects of this doctrine of universe of discourse which must be specifically considered here. The first of these has to do with the question of the conditions of the meaning of words and of propositions which contain them. That a word may have a determinate reference, and therefore meaning, it is not necessary that there should be an "index proper," an object to be pointed to outside the context or universe of discourse. In general, it is true that there is such an index in the environment common to speaker and hearer, but it is not necessary. In principle it is sufficient for meaningfulness that there shall be mutual acknowledgment of the supposition on which the existence of the context rests. This was not adequately recognized by De Morgan and by the numerous upholders of the "empirical criterion" of meaning. Into this point we shall go more fully presently.

The second point has to do with the doctrine of different modes of being which seems to be implied. Some logicians accept this principle of different modes of being, different meanings of the ontological predicate as implied in the notion of the universe of discourse. Others maintain that it "leads to the fallacies of a false metaphysics" and therefore dismiss the concept of universes of discourse, thus asserting directly or by implication the existence of only one universe, namely, that of spatio-temporal existence. Into this question we shall go at some length later.[1] Here we wish merely to indicate the problem and to suggest certain considerations which arise out of our present analysis. The problem itself is evidently one of metaphysics—since the doctrine of universes of discourse is said to lead to the fallacies of a false metaphysics. Evidently it cannot be solved until the relations of language to logic and cognition have been explored. But even here it is possible to see that the denial itself involves a *petitio principii* since it pre-

[1] Chapter VII, p. 300 f.

THE NORMATIVE PROBLEM OF LANGUAGE

supposes the validity of a particular metaphysics. It gives a privileged position, prior rights, to one universe of discourse, namely, the physical—and that implies an already existing metaphysical prejudice.

E

Theories of Context: the Idealistic Theory

The theory developed in the preceding paragraphs may be described as the idealistic theory of contexts. The term is here used, as elsewhere in this discussion, to distinguish it from naturalistic and causal theories. As we were compelled to resort to this term in the development of our concept and theory of meaning, so here in developing that which is the correlative of meaning, namely context, the same terminology is necessary and desirable.

The naturalistic theory of context is already familiar to us from our studies of linguistic meaning. It is part of the causal theory of meaning.[1] The causal theory, although untenable even as a theory of the simple sign situation, encounters additional difficulties when applied to the meaning of words. The difficulty of identifying the intentional character of linguistic meaning with "being caused by" was, it was supposed, overcome if for "being caused by" we substitute the notion of "forming part of a context." Context is then defined as a set of entities (things or events) related in a certain way. Far from solving the problem of meaning, this theory of context makes it all the more difficult. For the causal theory is then merely transferred to the physical context or environment as a whole rather than to the particular object to which the word refers. The second notion becomes even more unintelligible than the first.

The idealistic theory of context, on the other hand, denies this identification of context with environment. It maintains that the universe of discourse or context is nothing that exists or subsists independently of discourse or communication, but is itself created and fixed by the mutual acknowledgment of communicating subjects. In every proposition the circumstances of its enunciation show that it refers to some collection

[1] Chapter III, p. 130 f.

of individuals or possibilities which cannot be adequately described or defined, but can only be indicated as something familiar and mutually acknowledged by both speaker and hearer. At one time it may be the physical universe of sense; at another, an "imaginary" world of some play or novel; at another, a world of validities or values, as in ethical discourse. In the second place—and this is the crucial point for this theory—it is this mutual acknowledgment, by speaker and hearer, that creates the context and therefore gives referential content to the word or term in question. That a word may have such reference, it is sufficient that there shall be this mutual acknowledgment of the supposition on which the context rests. The idealistic theory, moreover, points out that even when the context is the physical universe of sense, this world of sense does not itself become context except in so far as it also is mutually acknowleged as something familiar and *meant* by both speaker and hearer. Otherwise expressed, the physical environment itself becomes a context for meaning only in so far as it is presupposed: its very independence is itself an object of belief.

Thus far we have been concerned wholly with the question of a tenable theory of context as part of the general problem of meaning. All that we have been concerned to maintain is the fact that no notion of context is possible without the notions of communication and mutual acknowledgment. As language has no reality except in the speech community, so the context in which linguistic meaning alone can be determined has no reality apart from the speech community. Even the context of the physical universe of sense, to which many of our terms are referred (by pointing) for their meaning, *is made a context precisely by the beliefs and postulates of common sense* which have made of it a world. No one doubts that there is a physical environment independent of us, but that environment in so far as it is a context of discourse is itself largely "constructed." This fact does not, however, exclude the possibility that this context *should* have the privileged position in our determination of reference and meaning, or indeed the *exclusive* position. It is quite possible that we *ought* to call this reference alone meaning *im strengsten Sinn*, that this meaning alone is the *proper* meaning of words—that this alone is what they were "ordained

THE NORMATIVE PROBLEM OF LANGUAGE

for." With this we have the normative problem of "proper meaning."

VII

THE NORMATIVE PROBLEM OF "PROPER MEANING": THE QUESTION OF A PRIVILEGED CONTEXT

A

The notion of the proper meaning of a word is as old as meditation on language itself, and as new as the latest developments in the philosophy of language. It is, moreover, itself an illustration of the inherent mobility and all-pervasive ambiguity of words. The notion originated in the idea that each word had its *own* or proper meaning, God-given so to speak, which inhered in it as its *proprium* or property. In the words of Aristotle, a name of anything is its own name or a name transferred to it from something else. In the further development of the notion proper meaning was contrasted with metaphorical. Thus such names as king, father, light, are applied to God not *properly* but metaphorically. From this the transition was easy to the normative conception that the proper use in the sense described is also the proper use in the sense of the way they ought to be used.

This normative conception of "proper" meaning appears in modern form in the notion of the empirical criterion of meaning. According to this view, the proper meaning of a word, that which inheres so to speak in it as its proprium, is its primary reference to physical objects. All derived meanings and all secondary propositions containing these derived meanings are fictional. To determine the real or proper meaning these derived propositions must be reduced to their archetypes, and the "best" archetypes are the physical propositions where the reference is to the physical environment or context.

B

The Prior Rights of the Physical

The principle has been clearly enunciated by Professor Montague. The context in which he formulates it is in connection with the arguments for the existence of the soul.[1] We are told that it is possible that there may be a soul (in view of preceding arguments), but unless it is shown on other grounds to be not merely possible but also probable, the physiological scientist and the materialistic philosopher *have the right* (italics mine) and even the duty to disregard these arguments and the dualistic hypothesis. We are not interested so much in the context in which the formula is enunciated, as in the formula itself. "The materialistic theory is still very strong," we are told, because of "the prior rights enjoyed by the more nearly known over the less nearly known in all sound methodology." In other words, the prior rights of the physical context.

Here we are interested in two things: (1) the grounds for these prior rights, and (2) the view that their recognition is the basis of all sound methodology.

The grounds are to be found in the fact that the physical, and therefore the physical context, is more nearly known. Now the supposition that the physical is "more nearly known" may itself be open to question. It may be that, as Eddington insists, it is precisely the non-physical that is immediately known, whereas it is the external world of physics that is built up out of symbols.[2] But this is a secondary question and will not be raised here. The issue is whether the fact of nearness is a ground for assigning prior rights. Now to say that the physical is more nearly known is to say little more than that our bodies are in the same space with physical objects and that, owing to this contact, we know them first or have a primary interest in them. This is to argue from genetic priority to logical priority, a type of argument the fallaciousness of which has long been recognized and dignified by the term genetic fallacy. It is not different from the argument that because language was "first made" to deal with physical things, therefore physical propositions are the archetypes to which all others must be reduced. (Bentham.)

I see no reason therefore, except one of natural prejudice, why nearness should confer any prior rights. Still less do I see any reason for identifying this principle of prior rights with all sound methodology. To be sure, *if* the meaning of a

---

[1] *The Ingersoll Lecture, The Chances of Surviving Death*, p. 31.
[2] *Science and the Unseen World*, p. 82. (Published by George Allen & Unwin Ltd.).

proposition is the way in which it may be verified, and if verification is possible only in a physical context, then it *would* follow that the physical context must be given a privileged position in a sound methodology. Into this question of verifiability we shall go presently. Here I would merely suggest that if verification is possible in other than physical contexts, this principle of prior rights would be the very opposite of sound methodology. Methodology is determined by the material with which knowledge deals.

The denial of a privileged context in the sense of the prior rights of the physical, seems to involve the principle of linguistic relativity. In a sense this relativity is a fact. It is true that "in any group of symbol users there will arise a certain fixity of meaning, something which will be called the proper meaning or good use. This something tends to be spoken of as *the* meaning."[1] But the meaning depends in this case upon the suppositions of the symbol users. We thus seem forced back upon a purely "conventional" theory of proper meaning. It would seem that every meaning is in truth a stipulated meaning, every definition a postulate; therefore every affirmation of proper meaning a begging of the question, and every argument for one meaning rather than the other an *argumentum ad hominem*. The situation is, however, perhaps not as hopeless as it seems. Much depends upon the way in which we use the notion of "convention."

In the broader sense of convention—as mutual acknowledgment—every context depends upon convention and, since reference is never to the entity as such but to a context, the meaning of words is always conventional in this sense. But this is very different from convention in the arbitrary sense. The mutual acknowledgment on the part of communicating subjects of the suppositions which determine the universe of discourse in which the word has reference or meaning is not arbitrary, but necessary as the conditions of intelligible communication as such. The development of language—and the natural speech construction which is part of that development—"create," so to speak, these different contexts, but this creation is in no sense the work of individuals. In any case—and this is the point of importance here—the privileged character of

[1] Ogden and Richards, *op. cit.*, p. 206.

the physical context, and therefore the prior rights of the physical, is itself a convention, and any notion of "proper meaning" or meaning in the strict sense is a conventional meaning. This is the significance of the Kantian position which describes such assumption of prior rights as a "postulate of the empirical employment of the understanding"—not necessarily of other forms of employment of reason. This leads us to a critical consideration of the empirical criterion of meaning which is based on this assumption of prior rights and is therefore a "convention."

VIII

THE EMPIRICAL "CRITERION" OR NORM OF MEANING: MEANING AND VERIFIABILITY

A

The general problem of this chapter we described as the normative problem of language or the problem of *linguistic validity*. We formulated this problem in the following way: How shall we use language so as to express the meaningful rather than the unmeaning, the true rather than the false? Strictly speaking the linguistic problem as such is solely one of the meaningful and unmeaning. It is only because there is believed to be some necessary relation between meaning and truth, between meaning and verifiability, that the two are embodied in the same formula. That the problem as thus formulated is essentially a normative problem has been abundantly shown. We *ought*, to be sure, to express the meaningful rather than the unmeaning, but this "ought" itself has no meaning until we have some criterion of the meaningful.

The empirical criterion of meaning, namely that the meaning of any assertion is the way in which it may be verified, is itself a normative—not a factual—proposition. Any criterion is of course a norm or it is nothing.[1] The normative character of

---

[1] It is interesting to recall that, according to the logical positivists, all normative propositions are meaningless. They are merely expressions of feeling. In strict logic then, the empirical criterion is either a mere expression of feeling or meaningless, for it is a normative proposition and cannot be verified by its own criterion. We have therefore a circle which this positivism cannot easily avoid. We shall return to this point in the sequel. Here we wish merely to insist that the empirical criterion is normative in character.

this particular criterion can be seen by noting the assumptions that underlie it. It assumes the prior rights of the physical, for it is only in a physical context that verification in the sense of the criterion is possible. To enunciate this criterion is implicitly to assume certain valuations, and it is therefore of the character of a norm. Thus the final question of linguistic validity hinges upon this empirical criterion of meaning. It is necessary to examine it with care.

B

Meaning and Verification

The meaning of an assertion (*Aussage*), says Carnap, is "the way in which it may be verified."[1] In other words the meaning is the verification. A consequence of this is that all uses of language to which the question of truth or falsity is irrelevant (if there be such uses) are, *ipso facto*, meaningless.

Now I am not disposed to doubt this general statement of a necessary relation of meaning to truth, *if* it is properly understood. Everything depends upon the interpretation of the statement. It seems quite certain, for instance, that if there *were* an emotive use of language in which there were no reference whatsoever, in which the question of truth or falsity were wholly irrelevant, that use would, as we have seen, be merely a squeak or a grunt and have meaning, if at all, in a purely behaviouristic sense. As a matter of fact, those uses which are often described as merely emotive are actually not so. For they involve taking up an emotional attitude towards an object. This involves at least a minimum of reference, and in so far as any element of reference is present the question of truth and falsity is not wholly irrelevant.

Granted then the truth of this general statement, namely, that there is no meaning where the question of truth or falsity is wholly irrelevant, it is still possible that the relation of meaning to verifiability as here stated may be questioned. Much depends upon the interpretation of the notion of verification and verifiability. In one meaning of these terms it may be true, in another it may be wholly false. Let us then proceed with our examination.

[1] *Die Überwindung der Metaphysik*, etc.

Those who uphold this criterion of meaning are very definite in their assertions that the meaningful does not necessarily involve actual verification but merely verifiability. It need hardly be pointed out that the criterion of actual verification would rule out a large part of the meaningful propositions of science, and this even the positivists, despite their truncated view of science, are usually careful not to do. It is therefore merely *verifiability*, or the way in which it *may be* verified, which constitutes the criterion of meaning. But even this notion of verifiability must be scrutinized with care, for it contains an ambiguity which may lead to serious confusion.

Verifiability may mean two quite different things which must be carefully distinguished. On the one hand, it may mean a certain character of the content of one's assertion or hypothesis which makes it possible actually to satisfy the conditions of verification. On the other hand, it may mean merely a certain character of one's assertion or hypothesis which marks it off from the unverifiable, but which does not, however, involve necessarily the possibility of actual verification. Many logical positivists are careful to make it clear that they mean by verifiability only this latter. Thus Professor Schlicht holds that a verifiable proposition need not actually be verifiable in the sense that it can ever actually be an observable entity. He gives as an illustration, "There is a mountain ten thousand feet high on the other side of the moon." Such a proposition is meaningful, although physical and other difficulties may forever stand in the way of its actual verification.

C

Meaning Without Empirical Verifiability: Limiting Cases

It is verifiability in this latter sense alone, then, that can with any show of reason be made the criterion of meaning. Let us see, then, in what verifiability in this sense is held to consist, that which, although actual verification may be for ever impossible, yet makes the assertion in *principle* verifiable. This is clearly indicated in the illustration given above. It is the possibility of sense experience. The mountain on the other side of the moon may not be actually observable, but the fact that it is intrinsically observable makes the assertion meaningful.

Now we may, of course, accept without any demur the principle that wherever verifiability in this sense exists we have meaningful assertions. The question now is whether *only* such assertions are meaningful. This may, apparently at least, be denied. In his critical examination of this empirical criterion, Professor C. I. Lewis holds that there are limiting cases in which meaning may even outrun the possibility of verification altogether. Such is the conception of other selves. "In the nature of the case I cannot verify you as another centre of experience different from myself, and yet the meaningfulness of the supposition of other selves is unquestioned. There is nothing to which I can give more explicit empirical content than to the supposition of a consciousness like mine connected with a body like mine. The conception of other selves as metaphysical ultimates exemplifies the philosophic importance that may attach to a supposition which is nevertheless unverifiable on account of the limitations of knowing."[1]

It seems necessary to conclude, therefore, that while there is meaningful assertion wherever there is reference to empirically observable entities, there is also meaningful assertion where there is no such reference. The question now arises whether these facts contradict the preliminary position that the meaning of an assertion is connected with its verifiability. Obviously we are here faced with a definite alternative. Either we accept Professor Lewis's position or else maintain the view that there are other ways of verification. It is the latter alternative which seems to me to be demanded by the facts. I shall presently develop a theory of verification along these lines. Here I wish merely to indicate that it is not at all certain that the proposition that other selves exist is unverifiable in every sense.

Professor Lewis is sure that the supposition of other selves is meaningful. There is nothing to which I can give more explicit empirical content than to just this supposition. Now I am disposed to admit that without this empirical content the notion of another self would lack meaning. There is there-

[1] C. I. Lewis, "Experience and Meaning," *Philosophical Review*, Vol. VII, No. 2, p. 146.

fore some justification for the view that the condition of meaningfulness is not verifiability, but rather imaginability. If I can envisage—that is, give empirical content to—a notion, it is at least meaningful even if not true. On the other hand, I am equally disposed to think that such content alone does not make the supposition meaningful, and that what does make it meaningful here also is, in the last analysis, the way in which it may be verified. I am quite sure, therefore, that I can verify you as a centre of experience other than myself, and—what is more—that I am constantly verifying you as such a centre. To state my point baldly, the existence of another self is verified in the process of discourse itself. The reference to you in this discourse is indeed an indirect reference or co-implicate of experience, and is therefore only indirectly verifiable—but no less verifiable. Let us develop this point more fully.

Every assertion with the meaning of which we may be concerned is precisely what the terms indicate, an assertion. It is clear that it has no existence except as the expression of some mind. But it also has no existence except as it presupposes understanding by some other mind. Expression and understanding are strictly correlative and constitute, as we have seen, an *Urphenomen*. This is what we mean by saying that language has no reality except in the speech community. The abstraction of "propositions" from the matrix of communication, as is done in logic, may have a relative validity for certain purposes, but cannot be ultimately valid, as we shall see in our examination of the relations of logic to language.[1] The meaningfulness of any assertion, even in the empirical sense of meaning, depends upon the existence of other selves. The indirect reference to other selves is then constantly verified indirectly in meaningful discourse itself. This is the real reason why, as Lewis says, there is nothing to which I can give more explicit empirical content than to just this supposition. I doubt very much whether we could give any explicit empirical content at all to a supposition which itself is wholly outside the bounds of verifiability, but we shall consider this question more fully when we examine the entire problem of communication.[2] With one thing, however, we must take definite issue. "In the nature of the case," writes Professor Lewis, "I cannot verify you as a centre of

[1] Chapter VII, p. 269 f. [2] Chapter VI, p. 259 f.

THE NORMATIVE PROBLEM OF LANGUAGE

experience other than myself." Such a statement begs the entire question at issue.

D

Verification as Authentication: Ways of Verification

Our preceding analysis has forced us to the notion of different ways of verification. The fact of the meaningfulness of assertions about the existence of other selves does not necessarily affect the truth of the relation of meaning to verifiability. It simply raises the question of different ways of verification. Let us pursue this point further.

It has been repeatedly pointed out that the proposition that the meaning of an assertion is the way in which it may be verified, contains a circle and creates a predicament. For we cannot determine the verifiability of the assertion until we know what it means. What, then, does this predicament suggest? Not that meaning and verification are independent and unrelated, but rather that there are different ways of verification dependent upon the meaning of the assertions or the different universes of discourse in which they are made. It is true that when the universe of discourse in which the assertion is made is the "physical" context, verification does involve reference to an observable entity. On the other hand, it is equally clear that assertions are made in other universes of discourse in which no such reference is implied. It does not mean, however, that such assertions are either without meaning or unverifiable in every sense. We may say that such meanings are *authentic* even when they are not verifiable in the narrow sense of the empirical criterion.

I shall make use, then, of the term authentication to describe ways of verification not contemplated by the empirical criterion. We shall first define and justify the use of the term. From this we shall proceed to examples of such ways of verification, both direct and indirect, and finally seek to show that the notion may be generalized and extended to wider areas of meaning and meaningful discourse.

The notions of authentic and authentication are used constantly by all who recognize ways of knowing and ways of verifying other than those contemplated by the so-called empirical criterion. It is used most constantly and significantly, perhaps, in the sphere of art. We speak of literature as having the "authentic note." This expression may mean that we feel the sincerity of the writer, but it usually includes a great deal more. It means that, as we say, the writer has in some way managed to convey the "truth" of "man" or of "life." We also, therefore, speak naturally of authentic values. Now the question of the authentic in art, of aesthetic truth in general, is, of course, a large one into which we cannot go here. It will be a central problem of our later studies of the language of poetry and of aesthetic symbolism generally. It will be sufficient for our purpose to emphasize one point here. The authentic character of a work of art is not determined by the verifiability of its assertions in the sense of the empirical criterion. It is true that in every piece of literature—and indeed in every work of art—there are always specific references which are verifiable in the sense of empirical observation. Every picture, as we shall see, is in a sense a proposition. Realism in the photographic sense, whether physical or psychological, has references of this sort, but it is not these that give it the authentic note. That which makes a work of art authentic is the fact that it "shows forth," in its medium, certain qualities and values which are immediately recognized as authentic and acknowledged by the "observer." This is the process of authentication and such authentication takes place in communication itself. Again we may speak of the meaning (*Sinn*) of a work of art as a whole, as distinguished from the reference (*Bedeutung*) of the parts; it is this meaning also that is apprehended and authenticated in aesthetic communication. It is because verification in the sphere of the aesthetic is of this type—and cannot possibly be of the kind demanded by the empirical criterion—that art is often said merely to express or evoke emotion. But aesthetic meaning is not exhausted in the emotional. Some reference to reality is assumed both in the creation and appreciation of art, and, since this reference exists, the question of truth and falsity is not irrelevant.[1]

---

[1] The notions of the authentic and authentication in the sphere of art are developed more fully in Chapter X, pp. 485 ff.

E
Authentication, Direct and Indirect

This, then, is the notion of authentication, the use of which is, I think, justified by appeal to the aesthetic. But it is not confined to the aesthetic. As we shall see, it is everywhere present in human discourse, and is indeed—this is one of our main contentions—*presupposed in empirical verification itself*. Within this general notion of authentication we may distinguish direct and indirect. It is from a case of indirect authentication that we started, namely, the reality of other selves, and to this type we shall return, but it is important to understand first what direct authentication is—its nature and its range.

Direct verification, in the ordinary sense, consists in reference to an observable entity, and the primary instance is said to be "pointing." Verification in this sense is possible only in a physical context or universe of discourse, but there are similar or analogous types of authentication in other universes of discourse. In direct authentication we may speak of "showing forth" (*Aufweisen*) of some *quale* or relation. In developing this form of direct authentication, I shall purposely take my illustrations from the universe of ethical discourse and value propositions, for the reason that it is precisely assertions of this sort that, on the basis of the empirical criterion or norm, are said to be unverifiable and therefore meaningless. These illustrations are taken from a much more extensive and systematic treatment of the subject entitled *Value Propositions and Verifiability*.[1]

In the preceding chapter we have already made clear the difference between expression and evocation of emotion and value judgments or propositions. In the case of the former the question of truth and falsity is irrelevant; in the latter it is

---

[1] *The Journal of Philosophy*, Vol. XXXIV, No. 22 (October 28, 1937).
In this more extended study of authentication as a form of verification, the argument consists in showing (first) that there are value propositions and (secondly) that they can be verified or authenticated. In developing the second point the argument starts from the fact of valuational error. It is then shown that these errors can be corrected, and that such correction involves verification or authentication of true propositions. The argument as a whole involves a systematic study of the entire field of valuational error.

not. Assertions of value do not merely evoke emotion, but show forth some *quale* or relation which is intuited, and in that intuition acknowledged. It is this possibility of mutual intuition and communication which constitutes verifiability or authenticity. Let us take a specific example.

You and I may agree, we have seen, that an action is proud, although we may have opposite emotional reactions to it, but mutual agreement as to the quality of the action is quite possible independently of our liking or disliking. The situation here is, in principle, no different from the verification of any so-called ostensive proposition. In the case of the assertion, "this is red," the sense *quale* is shown forth, in the case of "this is proud" a value quality, but in essentials the process is the same. It may be said, of course, that the value judgment, this is proud, is really a judgment of fact, not different from the judgment, this is red. In a sense this is true, and, indeed, is precisely my point. But closer inspection shows a difference which is all-important. In order to call an act proud, whether correctly or incorrectly, I must apprehend the quality proud, and that can be done only by an "emotional intuition" which is quite different from sensuous observation. Still more, in order that you and I may agree that it is proud it is necessary that there shall be mutual recognition and acknowledgment of the value *quale*. It is here that the authentication takes place.[1]

Even clearer is the notion of direct authentication when it is applied to assertions in which the predicate "good" occurs. The assertion, for instance, that "the good is pleasure" is certainly a meaningful statement, one which is understood by speaker and hearer alike. Moreover, the question of truth and falsity is relevant and it is assumed that the assertion is verifiable in some way. Such, for instance, is the assumption underlying the famous statement of Sidgwick: "When I sit down in a cool hour and ask what it is that is good and valuable in itself I can find only a pleasurable state of consciousness." Now what is it that Sidgwick or anyone else finds? The pleasurable state of consciousness may be an observable entity, although whether it is or not involves the whole question of introspection as a form of observation. But whether pleasure is or is not an observable entity, certainly its identity with the

---

[1] Chapter IV, pp. 164 ff.

THE NORMATIVE PROBLEM OF LANGUAGE

notion of the good is not an observable entity. That is precisely the point of the insistence on the part of the logical positivist, namely, that any assertion containing the word good is an apparent proposition, because the predicate good refers to no sensuously observable entity, and in this he is surely right. If, therefore, the statement the good is pleasure is a meaningful proposition—and I think that can scarcely be denied—it must be true or false; if so it must be verifiable, and if verifiable it must be in some other way than by reference to an observable entity—in our terms, authenticated.

I do not say that this identification of the good with pleasure is the authentic meaning of "good." I think it can be "shown" that it is not—that precisely this identification is not acknowledged by those who understand the meaning of good. But this is not the point here. Assertions of this type may be authentic or not authentic even when they are not verifiable by reference to a sensuously observable entity.

This, then, is what I understand by direct authentication. It is a form of verification which takes place in communication—in the mutual acknowledgment of values and their relations on the part of communicating subjects. There is, however, also the indirect which, from some points of view, is even more significant for our present discussion. Let us first examine a case of indirect authentication and then consider the general significance of the notion for our present purposes.

Indirect authentication, like direct, takes place only in discourse, but whereas the direct consists in mutual acknowledgment of something that is "shown forth," indirect consists in the mutual acknowledgment of *the implications of that discourse*. Let us suppose, then, that a cynical sensualist asserts that the only goods are mastication and sex. In so far as this is a mere expression of feeling, nothing further can be said, for it is neither true nor false. But he does not mean it to be a mere expression of feeling, but rather a statement of objective matter of fact. As such it enters into the region of the verifiable. He assumes at least that his assertion is true and that, for some reason or other, a true assertion is "better" than a false one. Otherwise he would not make the assertion. Such, then, is his assertion, and by means of the implications of the assertion it can be shown indirectly that it is not true; in other words that it contains valuational error. For in the very assertion itself it is assumed—that is, if the assertion is to have any meaning—that truth is a value, a value other than the two he asserts to be the only values. Now it is important to note that the correction of his error does not consist in pointing out that others recognize other values, but that he himself actually does so. The indirect authentication of the value of truth does not again consist in verification by empirical observation of the psychological fact that he, as well as others, desires truth and desires to make true statements. It consists in the forced recognition or acknowledgment, in discourse, that *truth is a value*. How many other values are thus indirectly authenticated by this forced acknowledgment of truth as a value I shall not attempt to determine. Surely there are others. It is sufficient that this one may be thus indirectly authenticated.

Our example of indirect authentication, like the direct, has been taken from the universe of discourse constituted by value propositions, for it is here, as we have said, that the issue is clearest and most definitely joined. But the notion is applicable to all cases of meaningful propositions where the meaning does not consist in reference to a physical context. In this connection it is desirable to emphasize especially the process called indirect authentication. That such authentication is a veritable form of verification is, I think, clear. The forced recognition and acknowledgment in discourse that truth is a value, is as much a verification of that statement as the forced recognition that, if certain sense data are experienced, other objects, not immediately experienced, are real. It is no less clear that it is verification of this type which alone gives meaning to a large area of our most significant assertions. Such we shall see later are assertions of the metaphysical type which, on the basis of the empirical criterion, are said to be unverifiable and therefore meaningless.[1] Here I shall content myself with one of the most important of this type, namely, assertions about the existence of other selves.

We agreed with Professor Lewis that such assertions are among the most meaningful in all discourse. But we insisted that they do not "outrun verification," if verification be given an adequate interpretation. The existence of other selves is

[1] See Chapter XIII, p. 654 f. and pp. 671 ff.

indirectly authenticated by the very fact of discourse or communication itself. I can verify you as a centre of experience other than myself because, except on the assumption or hypothesis of other experiencing selves, my own experience, *which includes communication*, ceases to be experience or becomes meaningless. The reality of other selves is just as authentic as are the facts of communication themselves. It may be that there is no *real* but only apparent communication, that what we call communication is something else given that name. This is a question we shall take up in the next chapter. But granting that there is real communication, which is ordinarily assumed, the communicating selves are real and their existence verified in the communication.

We have contrasted the notion of verification by authentication with the empirical criterion as understood in the narrow sense. But this does not mean that authentication falls outside the realm of experience. The direct authentication of values is as much a part of experience as direct verification by reference to a sense datum. When a value is shown forth and acknowledged, this is no less a matter of experience than when a sense datum is pointed to and that pointing is understood. No less a part of experience, when experience is properly understood, is the indirect authentication. Just as propositions are indirectly verified when they are necessary to explain immediately observable facts, so propositions about values are indirectly authenticated when they are necessarily implied by experienced and acknowledged values. The limitation of the notion of experience to the sensuously observable is but a part of the false initial assumption of the prior rights of the physical.

F

The Empirical Criterion and Authentication

The account of verification by authentication, as here presented, is far from being adequate. Its deficiencies will, it is hoped, be supplied in later contexts.[1] Here our only object was to show (*a*) that there is genuine meaning where verifiability in the sense of reference to sensuously observable

[1] See especially Chapter VIII, pp. 383 ff.

entities is not possible; and (*b*) at the same time to retain the necessary relation of meaning to verifiability. Our sole object was to show that there is a form of verification through authentication—not to develop a complete theory.

Assuming, then, the general notion to be established, let us proceed to the last stage of our argument. The final proof of the thesis which underlies this entire discussion is to be found in an examination of the empirical criterion itself. Only that which is verifiable, it is said, is meaningful. But it is precisely the character of this criterion itself that it cannot be verified in the sense of its own formula. Either, then, the formula itself has no meaning, or, if it is held to be meaningful, it must be verifiable in some other way, in some such fashion as that which I have characterized as *authentication*. Now as a matter of fact it can be easily shown that the empirical criterion, as formulated by the positivists, is itself metempirical (or metaphysical) and on their own assumption should itself be meaningless nonsense. This fact, curiously enough, is actually recognized by Wittgenstein, the founder of the movement. The basal proposition that the meaning of a proposition consists in the method of its verification is, he admits, non-empirical, and therefore unsayable and nonsensical, in his technical use of the words. And it is at this point, among others, that the mystical element enters into his thinking.

In a recent paper entitled "A Demonstration that Metaphysics is Impossible," Mr. A. J. Ayer seeks to meet this difficulty.[1] He tries to show, unsuccessfully I think, that while this is true, we can still use the method without involving ourselves in a circle. In doing so, however, he brings out a hidden assumption of the entire position which has never been brought to light before, and which, when clearly seen, is of great significance. This is, to my mind, the first statement of the situation that is really frank and clear.

He attempts to meet this situation by maintaining that we may say all we need to, that we may use this criterion practically, without resort to the metempirical. How, then, does he attempt to do this? By frankly appealing to *"what people mean by meaning"*—by a purely psychological, not a logical procedure. Logically, he admits, the criterion is circular, but it is saved

[1] *Mind*, Vol. XLIII, pp. 335–345.

THE NORMATIVE PROBLEM OF LANGUAGE

from being vicious by this appeal to universal agreement as to what constitutes the meaningful and the meaningless. This, I think, is all the positivist can do, and that is why I think the recognition of the fact by Mr. Ayer is so significant. But where does it leave the positivist? It leaves him either in a wholly untenable if not ludicrous position, or else he is forced to the conception of verification other than that of the empirical criterion—in short, to our notion of authentication. The appeal is frankly to *what people mean by meaning*, and this is described as appeal to psychological matter of fact. This, however, is no criterion at all. For, in the first place, there is no universal agreement as to what constitutes the meaningful. People are, indeed, agreed as to the meaninglessness of certain statements such as virtue is triangular, Caesar is a prime number, but beyond these few simple cases, notoriously they are not. But in the second place—and this is the point I am concerned to make here—the appeal is really not to psychological fact but precisely to that mutual acknowledgment which is not psychological but epistemological. The criterion of the meaningful is found, then, within discourse or communication—not outside it. If the empirical criterion is itself to be meaningful, it must be verifiable in some sense. We must hold fast to the position that where truth and falsity are wholly irrelevant, there is no meaning. But it is not verifiable in the sense of the empirical criterion itself. Yet within limits at least it is meaningful.[1] Therefore, if it is verifiable, even to this limited extent, it is verifiable only within intelligible discourse, in other words, authenticated.

I think this situation is recognized—implicitly at least—by an increasing number of logical positivists. The present status of the empirical criterion is in the minds of many of its supporters that of a "convention." At first it was, supposedly, a self-evident matter of fact, and it was upon the assumption that it is such that large areas of meaningful discourse were

[1] I have used the expression within limits advisedly. Granted the universe of discourse which Kant described as the "empirical employment of the understanding," this criterion is authentic, for the postulate of that employment is precisely that reality *shall mean* the sensuously observable, and meaningful statements be only those that refer to such entities. But the universe is determined by this supposition or postulate, and such supposition or postulate can only be mutually acknowledged. Other universes of discourse have other postulates and condition other meanings.

declared meaningless. But the paradoxical character of such an assertion, when its implications were realized, required a modification of the position. The status of the criterion then became a "convention," namely, something mutually acknowledged by the logical positivists themselves—but not necessarily accepted as a statement of fact is accepted. In other words, it became normative. But what is the logic of this situation? Is it not clearly that, on their own assumptions, it is either meaningless (that is an expression of an attitude or a "demand" proposition), or it *has* meaning, and can therefore be authenticated in discourses? I think there is no other alternative.

IX

KNOWLEDGE AND COMMUNICATION: MEANING AND TRUTH

A

The object of this chapter was the consideration of the normative problem of language. This led us finally to an examination of the norm embodied in the so-called empirical criterion of meaning. The proof of the normative character of this criterion, and that in itself it has no meaning except as it is authenticated in meaningful discourse, constituted a demonstration of the main thesis of this section, namely—that meaning and verifiability are inseparable, but that there are other ways of verification than that contemplated by the empirical criterion, namely, authentication. The further development of this general thesis leads to far-reaching consequences for the entire theory of knowledge and the problem of the relation of cognition to language. These will be made clear in later contexts; here we shall content ourselves with considering one of them briefly, namely, the question of the relation of verification—*in any form*—to communication.

An essential part of this notion of authentication is that it takes place in the processes of communication themselves. The illustrations of such authentication, both direct and indirect, stressed this aspect. Moreover, the demonstration that the empirical criterion itself, in its narrow interpretation, presupposes such authentication, or is otherwise itself meaningless,

THE NORMATIVE PROBLEM OF LANGUAGE

suggests that the ultimate locus of all verification lies in communication and in the consequent mutual acknowledgment of the meanings and values which it presupposes. Otherwise expressed, confirmation through communication is not something added to verification but is the essential element in verification. All verification is essentially "public" in some sense of that word. This I believe to be true. The development of this point is an essential part of our entire thesis.

B

Verification and Communication

Scientific knowledge is often defined as knowledge that is verifiable *and* communicable. Two assumptions seem to underlie this definition, namely, that there is knowledge which is not verifiable, and secondly, that verifiability and communicability are separable. Both assumptions are highly questionable. That there is knowledge which is in no sense verifiable seems to rest upon the assumption that there is knowledge by "simple acquaintance" without any element of judgment and description. This I think can be shown to be impossible, as we shall attempt to do in a later chapter, *Language and Cognition*. Here, assuming that knowledge and verifiability are inseparable, we shall devote ourselves to the problem of the relation of verifiability to communicability.

It is frequently assumed that verifiability *and* communicability are two different things—in other words that a wholly solipsistic notion of verifiability can be maintained. At first sight the position seems unquestionable. I remember that the shade of a certain lamp is red. My memory may be true or false. I go to the shade itself, observe it, and my memory is verified or not as the case may be. Where, it may well be asked, is there the slightest element of communication involved in such a process? There is none if this is to be taken as the ideal case of verification. Verification is here wholly a solipsistic affair, and what we call confirmation is wholly extraneous to the intrinsic nature of the process. Suppose, however, I am colour-blind. My memory of the shade is "verified" in this sense even if the shade is not actually red. It would seem then that verification in any objective sense does not enter until the element of confirmation enters. Certainly in science a statement of fact or an experiment not reproducible by other scientists, would be ruled out of science *ab initio* as a fairy tale without significance.

The solipsistic character of verification is often argued from the facts of psychic experience. Thus "the statement, this pain is getting more severe, may represent what I know to be a fact quite apart from expression in any language (physical or behaviouristic terms) which can be publicly confirmed. For the import of assertions of this kind—referring to the psychic in its immediate, private aspect—the term significance has been proposed." Facts of this sort are called significant facts and their verification significant verification.[1]

Now, for one who, like the present writer, recognizes other ways of verification than that contemplated by the "empirical criterion" this notion should not be wholly unwelcome. It at least recognizes the basal idea in the notion of authentication, namely, that verification has meaning in other contexts than the physical. But it is necessary to proceed with care here. The statement, "this pain is getting more severe," may indeed represent what "I know to be a fact," but so, alas, may also the statement that the shade is red when it is not red—if I am colour-blind. That also is what I know to be a fact. It may also be added (in view of what we know of hypochondriacs) that the statement, this pain is getting more severe, may be as much an illusion as the colour-blind man's statement that the shade is red when it is not red. The difficulty in both cases is due, of course, to the ambiguity in the word know. When I say "I know" in these cases, it means no more than I "have" certain sensations. To have knowledge in any other sense, the experiences which I have must be expressible in sentences which can be confirmed by others.

It seems clear then that verifiability and communicability are inseparable, and that nothing enters into the sphere of knowledge except that which is intersubjectively public. It is often said that if we define knowledge as that which is communicable there is no escaping the logic of the physicalist position. But it does not at all follow that the only public

---

[1] Thus, Charles Hartshorne, *Beyond Humanism*, in his chapter, "Logical-Positivism and the Method of Philosophy."

THE NORMATIVE PROBLEM OF LANGUAGE

universe of discourse is the physical, and that the only language which has a public character is physical language. The entire drift of this chapter is in the direction of showing the contrary. Our study of the development of language, creating new universes of discourse; our disproof of the assumption of the prior rights of the physical context; and above all our demonstration of a public domain in which meanings and values are authenticated—all serve to disprove such a necessary consequence. This being insisted upon, let us proceed with our discussion of the relation of verification to communication.

The potentially public character of all genuine knowledge leads to the shifting of the emphasis from verification to confirmation. Indeed, it is said that some of the physicalists have given up the notion of verifiability for the weaker notion of confirmability. The emphasis upon confirmation is inevitable; the question is whether it is a weaker notion. To enter into the sphere of knowledge a proposition or assertion must be confirmed. What then is involved in the notion of confirmation? It is ordinarily said that statements are confirmed by facts or that an hypothesis is confirmed by the facts. But this is merely a naïve way of speaking. A necessary part of any fact is the language in which it is enunciated. A brute sense datum is not a fact in the sense of fact as used in science. Thus it is that sentences are confirmed by other sentences, the ultimate in knowledge always being sentences or propositions. Strictly speaking, then, mere sense data confirm nothing. This is implicitly recognized in another manner of speaking which is nearer to the actual situation in knowledge. We speak of one observer confirming another; one investigator confirming the findings of another. This is nearer to the true way of speaking. Facts do not confirm, but minds interpreting the facts confirm. But this interpretation is always a common, never a solipsistic process. Part of a fact is always the language in which it is enunciated. Language, however, has no reality, except in the speech community and propositions, as we shall see, no existence except in discourse;[1] communication, either overt or potential, is presupposed in all confirmation.[2]

[1] Chapter VI, p. 269 f.
[2] The "ideal" case of verification, it is often supposed, is that of direct pointing to an observable entity. It should, however, be wholly obvious that pointing, in

The locus of verification is then ultimately in confirmation. Far from weakening the notion of verifiability, or of knowledge in general, it is the only conception that gives it intelligibility. That communication or discourse is a necessary part of knowledge was seen by Plato long ago when he said that knowledge is judgment plus discourse. What he failed to see was that discourse is not merely a necessary *addendum* to judgment, but that it is only in discourse that the judgment has any "existence," and that therefore it is only in discourse that a judgment can ultimately be validated.

C

Meaning and Truth

This account of verification can be justified only by detailed analysis of the processes of verification in actual cases of knowledge, more especially in physical science. Such analysis we must reserve for later contexts.[1] Here we shall content ourselves with indicating certain important consequences of the main conclusions of this chapter.

The general theme of the chapter is the normative problem of language. This problem appeared at three points: (*a*) in connection with the mobility of language and consequent mutation of meanings; (*b*) the ambiguity of words and the problem of context; (*c*) the empirical criterion of meaning and the problem of a privileged context. The crucial positions of this chapter are: (*a*) the denial that there is any such thing as empty words—the principle that we cannot talk about anything that is not; (*b*) the contextual theory of meaning which results; and (*c*) the relation of meaning, as thus understood, to truth.

With regard to the first, the essential point is that the entire notion of empty or meaningless words rests upon an over-

---

whatever sense it is used, is itself a case of communication and involves a triadic relation. There is always some one who points, something pointed to, and some one to whom the object is pointed out. The act of pointing, and therefore whatever verification is achieved through it, is not complete until the pointing is acknowledged. This involves the mutual acknowledgment of common meanings. Back of verification in its simplest form is this process of confirmation.

[1] Chapter VII, pp. 383 ff.; Chapter XI, pp. 545 ff.

THE NORMATIVE PROBLEM OF LANGUAGE

simple, and therefore erroneous, conception of reference or meaning. While reference is the condition of the meaning of words, and of the propositions which contain them, this reference is ultimately to the context or universe of discourse. The condition of the meaningfulness of an assertion is not that certain entities about which the assertions are made "exist"—in the sense of being empirically observable—but that the universe of discourse in which these entities have their existence is mutually acknowledged. This leads to the second crucial position, namely, that, in so far as meaning alone is concerned, the physical context or universe of discourse has no prior rights, and therefore cannot be given a privileged position in a general theory of meaning. This leads to the third position which concerns the relation of meaning to truth.

Meaning and verification, we found, are inseparably related, but we cannot determine the way of verification of an assertion until we have determined its meaning. This fact seems to suggest that meaning is the ultimate notion, and that to distinguish the meaningful from the unmeaning among our assertions is ultimately to distinguish between the true and the false. In other words the true and the meaningful finally tend to coincide. The further fact that the locus of verification is in confirmation, and thus involves communication, seems again to suggest that truth is ultimately immanent in discourse; or, in other words, "the totality of intelligible discourse is the truth." Both of these statements, paradoxical as they at first seem, are, I believe, nevertheless true. All this is, however, the subject for later consideration and will form one of the main problems of the chapter on language and cognition. Here it is necessary only to insist again that communication is the basal fact in knowledge, as it is the sole and ultimate condition of meaning. Communication becomes thus a central problem of a philosophy of language. That it is central is seen in the fact that it is, in principle, not subject to purely empirical description or explanation, for it is presupposed in description and explanation themselves. What, then, is communication? What is its nature and what are the conditions of meaningful or intelligible communication? To the consideration of these problems we shall now turn.

CHAPTER VI

INTELLIGIBLE COMMUNICATION: ITS NATURE AND CONDITIONS

I

THE SPEECH COMMUNITY

WHATEVER else language is, it is, as we have said, meaningful communication between man and man. Language, as language, has no reality except in the speech community. This is one of the basal conceptions of linguistic science, part of the "new speech-notion" of which we spoke in an earlier connection (Chapter II). This position was further established by our analysis of linguistic meaning, in its aspects both as "expression" and "understanding." The triadic nature of linguistic meaning was established and elaborated in the proposition that linguistic meaning is present only where there is communication either overt or latent (Chapter III). A still further step was taken when we analysed the relation of meaning to truth or to "verification." It is quite true, we saw, that meaning and verification, intelligibility and truth, cannot be divorced. But we also insisted that just as there is no meaning except in the speech community, so there is no verification which does not involve communication. Even the notion of "pointing," which is taken as the primitive form and basal type of verification, is itself a case of communication.

Communication thus becomes a basal problem of any philosophy. Its basal character has, indeed, been recognized by all types of philosophic thought. For the idealist, as for instance Royce in his later stages (*The Problem of Christianity*), communication becomes a basal category. So also for the realist, as for instance Spaulding in his book, *A World of Chance*. For Pragmatism also the same is true, as witness the chapter on Communication in John Dewey's *Experience and Nature*.[1]

The basal character of communication—intelligible communication—is, accordingly, indisputable. But what that communication is—its nature and its limits, as well as the con-

[1] Published by George Allen & Unwin Ltd.

INTELLIGIBLE COMMUNICATION

ditions and presuppositions of such communication—are different questions. Expressed in Kantian terms, we h *quaestio facti* and the *quaestio juris*. The *quaestio facti* co the nature and range of communication; the *quaesti* concerns the question of what is involved in intelligible communication. How is intelligible communication *überhaupt* possible? In attempting to answer these questions we shall begin with the facts of communication, under the general heading, the nature of intelligible communication. We shall then proceed to the theories which attempt to explain or interpret it.

II

THE NATURE OF INTELLIGIBLE COMMUNICATION

A

Communication takes place in other ways and through other media than that of language, but intelligible communication, I shall maintain, is possible only through language. If language first created the world of meanings, it is only through language as a medium that these meanings can be communicated. It is true that meaning of a sort may be communicated through non-linguistic symbols, as in both science and art, and of this we shall have more to say in a later context, but it is out of language that these symbols have developed and to language they must ultimately return.

Communication by language is, to be sure, but one phase of a more general phenomenon. Naturalists make us familiar with marvels of communication between bees and ants, to say nothing of the higher vertebrates. Anthropologists find among primitives non-linguistic types of communication of extraordinary subtlety. But the fundamental characteristic of all such forms of communication is that they are bound up with the here and now. Karl Bühler has developed this point at considerable length, in contrasting animal communication with human, as extended by language. In the animal world the individual does enter into communication with others of his species through certain signs, but these signs always remain adherent to the thing signified and this non-mobility of signs for ever limits communication to the here and the now.[1]

This limitation of animal communication for ever marks it off from human. Even the case which comes closest to human language, namely, animal cries, shows the same limitations. Let us suppose that such cries, as for instance the warning cry, contain something more than the emotional element, namely, potential indication and predication; even these functions are never separable from the here and the now. The sign through which the communication is given, whether it be the bit of pollen which the bee gives to another member of the hive, as a means of orientation, or a cry of warning or mating, is always a *cue to behaviour*, and so far as we know, that is all that is communicated. The cooing of doves is a form of communication but, unless we are guilty of the psychologist's fallacy, all that it communicates is just this behavioural meaning. We may describe this as behavioural communication in contrast with intelligible.

There is this behavioural communication between human beings also. Linguistic communication is embedded in it and presupposes it. The "language" of eyes, of touch and of pantomime, above all of gesture, developed by means of empathy in the broad sense, acts both as vital context in which language gets part of its meaning and also as a means of enhancement of communication through language. But this form of human communication, in so far as it can be distinguished from linguistic, differs in no wise from animal communication. The gross but witty saying of Balzac, that "where we cannot understand each other with our heads, we can with our tails," expresses the point admirably. The erotic "language" of eyes and touch is made up of signs which have meaning, but unless supplemented by language, only behavioural meaning. Here also their meaning is their function as cues to behaviour. On this level human communication is also bound to the here and the now.

This, then, is what I shall describe as behavioural communication, whether found in animals or men. In contrast to this, intelligible communication is of a significantly different character. Here expression is not merely a cue to behaviour

[1] Chapter III, p. 97 f.

but has, as its correlate, understanding (*Das Verstehen*). Strictly speaking, behavioural communication involves no understanding, despite Balzac's doubtful use of the term. What understanding involves we shall presently see. One thing we may say with a degree of certainty at this point. Only language, in some sense and some form, is understood. Intelligible communication is always a speech transaction and involves language in some sense. It is only in this way that communication goes beyond the here and the now.

Intelligible communication, of course, presupposes behavioural. Communication, like language which is its medium, is, as Vossler says, deeply embedded in nature, and it is for this reason that the illusion constantly arises that they are of the same piece. But it is, as he further says, an illusion that must be constantly dispelled. As, to use the words of Sapir, "speech is a purely human, non-instinctive function," so also intelligible discourse, through language, although embedded in a wider area of behavioural intercourse and communication, is clearly distinguishable from it. Let us then turn to a closer analysis of linguistic communication.

B

The Nature of Intelligible Communication. Definition

Only linguistic communication is, then, intelligible in the sense defined. Let us now see wherein linguistic communication consists. In developing my thesis I shall start with a definition of communication by Ogden and Richards.

"A communication or language transaction," we are told, "is a use of symbols in such a way that acts of reference occur in the hearer which are similar in all relevant respects to those which are symbolized by them in the speaker."[1] We may accept this definition as a starting point. As all meaning involves reference, so all communication of meaning involves a similarity of reference in speaker and hearer. The real problem, however, is contained in the apparently harmless qualifying clause, "in all relevant respects." This is the "joker" in all such definitions.

[1] *Op. cit.*, p. 207.

It is immediately clear, of course, that there is no use of linguistic symbols in which the references are similar in all respects. The mere fact that, in addition to the primary reference or intention of any word, there are secondary indirect references, variable in speaker and hearer, makes it clear that if intelligible communication, or understanding, involved similar reference in all respects, communication in any sense and in any degree would be impossible. On the other hand, it is equally clear that, for a genuine speech transaction to take place, the indirect references, or second intentions, must be similar in some degree. It is, then, the notion of relevance that is crucial. Let us proceed to a further analysis of this notion.

It is precisely the character of all verbal signs that they have plural references. In the case of metaphorical language —and in a sense all language is metaphorical—there is a double reference, to two domains or universes of discourse. If the poet says, "Gather ye rosebuds while ye may," in order that the meaning may be conveyed, it is necessary not only that the primary reference be similar, but the secondary also. Again, if the speaker says, the sun rises and sets, and the hearer retorts, it does not rise and set, the two are, indeed, referring to the same thing or entity, but to different contexts or universes of discourse. They "speak different languages" and unless the one language be "translated" into the other, understanding or intelligible communication is impossible. We may say, then, that the similarity of reference which makes intelligible communication possible includes (*a*) similarity of referend, but also (*b*) similarity of context or of universe of discourse. Speaker and hearer cannot understand each other unless they recognize the same universe of discourse and mutually acknowledge the presuppositions which constitute or determine that universe.

We have here, I think, in principle, that which distinguishes intelligible from behavioural communication. In the case of the latter there is merely similarity of reference to objects; in the case of the former the reference is never merely to entities, but always ultimately to similar universes of discourse. All linguistic meaning is referential, but it is also systemic.[1]

[1] Chapter V, p. 201 f.

C

The Problem of "Understanding"

Returning, then, to our initial definition, a communication or language transaction is, indeed, a use of signs or symbols in such a way that acts of reference occur in the hearer that are similar in all relevant respects to those that are symbolized in the speaker, but when the notion of relevance is analysed, it is found to include not only similarity of references, but also similarity of suppositions which give these references their meaning. Every genuine language transaction involves mutual understanding or what we shall later designate as "mutuality of mind."

These notions may be further elucidated by reference to our previous analysis of "understanding." A language transaction always consists in the two correlative functions of expression and understanding. Until there is understanding no intelligible communication has taken place. I do not, of course, say that no communication has taken place. There is behavioural communication of the types described in which the expression is a cue to action. In purely behavioural communication there is, however, no understanding because there is no interpretation. The nature and conditions of understanding have been examined in an earlier context.[1] Our task here is to connect these results with our present study of communication and of the *mutual* understanding involved.

On one condition of mutual understanding, or intelligible communication, all linguists seem to be agreed, namely what Sapir calls "tacit recognition" of the universal. "For the simple experience is lodged in the individual consciousness and is, strictly speaking, incommunicable. To be communicated it must needs be referred to a class that is tacitly accepted by the community as an identity." The universal is present, we found, in the first precipitate of language and the acknowledgment of this, whether expressed or unexpressed, is the necessary condition of understanding.[2] But understanding, when adequately analysed, involves the tacit recognition or acknowledgment of more than this. There is, to be sure, the question of

[1] Chapter III, pp. 120 ff.   [2] Chapter III, p. 119 f.

"outer" and "inner" speech form—and of this we shall speak presently—but more fundamental still is the apprehension and tacit recognition of what Husserl calls intentionality.

Reference of a sign or symbol to an object or entity is not the sole condition of meaning. Meaning involves reference to a universe of discourse, and it is the mutual recognition of the presupposition (*suppositio*) that constitutes this universe which conditions the communication of this meaning. This supposition, moreover, when closely examined, is found to involve always a reference, direct or indirect, to values.[1] It is the tacit acknowledgment of these values which, as we shall see more fully later, ultimately conditions mutual understanding.

D

The Miracle of Language

The "miracle of language," as it is generally recognized by all who have given much study to it, is found precisely at this point. Language is *elliptical*; there is much more understood than is expressed. No account of communication can be given in terms of language considered as merely articulated sounds. It must include also that which is understood or presupposed. Communication, or conveyance of meaning, is not "transfer" of ideas from one mind to another (that is merely a figure of speech); the miracle of it is that, through the sounds, which alone can be conveyed in this sense, that which is merely "understood," in both speaker and hearer, can be mutually recognized and acknowledged. This mysterious fact any theory of communication must make intelligible.

In any case, communication is not the "simple and prosaic" thing sometimes supposed, or better it is simple only to those who do not realize what it includes. A language transaction is not simply a more complicated form of behavioural communication. Even the behavioural communication of animals has its element of mystery. Communication, even when limited to the here and the now, even when largely emotive, is a phenomenon which, while it may be described, is not wholly easy to understand, as we shall presently see. But linguistic

---

[1] Chapter III, p. 126 f.

or intelligible communication raises additional problems, precisely those indicated by its elliptical character. It is these which we must have chiefly in mind when we examine theories of communication.

III

INTELLIGIBLE COMMUNICATION AND THE PROBLEM OF TRANSLATION

A

One of the specific problems of linguistic communication is that of translation, and certain aspects of this problem must be considered if the real nature of intelligible communication is to be understood. "Merely listening to and understanding the speech of anyone is," as Vossler rightly maintains, "a translating of his meaning into mine."[1] Translation in this broad sense includes conveyance of meaning from one language, or one speech community, to another, and also from one universe of discourse to another within the same speech community. We shall use the notion in both these senses, this double use being sanctioned alike by usage and by the actual facts of communication.

The problem of translation is connected with that of communication in two ways: first with respect to the range and secondly with respect to the adequacy of communication. The possibility of the translation from one language to another—often languages very remote in both time and character—implies that the range of communication is very great, and this fact must be taken into account in our theories of communication. But even more than this extension or range is the adequacy with which meaning is conveyed. There are limits of translation—and just what these limits are is one of the important problems of a theory of translation—but meanings do get translated from one language to another with "astounding adequacy."

We shall then take up the problems of translation briefly from the standpoint of their bearing on communication (the details are more adequately discussed in Appendix II). We

[1] Karl Vossler, *The Spirit of Language and Civilization*, p. 181.

shall first examine translation from one language to another and secondly from one universe of discourse to another.

B

Translation from One Language to Another

The tendency to oversimplify the facts of communication in general appears again in connection with the problems of translation. Thus for Ogden and Richards, with their conception of communication as described above, translation also becomes, in principle at least, a simple matter, and they are disposed to make merry at the expense of such writers as Croce and Sapir who, to their minds, make of it much more of a problem than it really is. The issue here is in principle the same as that which arises in connection with the speech transaction in general, but in the case of translation the problem is complicated by the fact that where different languages are involved, the *media* of communication in question vary greatly both with respect to outer and inner speech form.

The position of Ogden and Richards is, as we have said, extremely simple. "Any purely symbolic use of words" (here symbolic is used in the purely denotative sense) "can be reproduced if in the two vocabularies similar symbolic distinctions have been developed. Otherwise paraphrases or new symbols will be required and the degree of possible correspondence is a matter which can be simply investigated." On the other hand, when "emotive functions" are involved "the less easy will be the blending of these two vocabularies." Here, as in the case of the speech transaction in general, the problem is simplified by the easy device of the dual classification of speech functions, the distinction between the translatable and untranslatable being thus accounted for.

For linguists in general, however, the situation is not quite so simple. There are problems here not even envisaged in the above account. The chief of these is the fact that in the case of literature, as distinguished from science, there are some forms, such for instance as a play of Shakespeare, which are translatable with scarcely any loss of meaning, while there are others, as for instance a lyric of Swinburne, which are as

INTELLIGIBLE COMMUNICATION

good as untranslatable. How account for this difference, not so much one of degree, as of fundamental character? To meet this situation linguists have formulated the hypothesis of two layers or levels of meaning in language—one, in the words of Sapir, "the latent content of language—our intuitive record of experience"—and the other "the particular comformation of given language—the specific how of our record of experience."[1] It is the former that is translatable, the latter thus is not. The same hypothesis is formulated by Vossler, although in slightly different terms. These differences, which are not of fundamental importance, will be discussed in the Appendix; here we are concerned merely with the doctrine of the two levels of meaning and its bearing on the general question of communication.

First of all, the theory seems necessary to account for the facts of translation if these facts are properly understood. Only so can we explain this extraordinary difference in the translatability of different forms of the literary art. This, I think, despite their differences in terminology, both Sapir and Vossler have shown. But, in the second place, this theory has important implications for our theory communication. It reinforces, I think, our conception of what is involved in the phenomenon of "understanding" in a speech transaction. In the case of translation understanding involves two things. In order to understand, in the intimate sense of those who share the same medium of expression, a feeling for the same "specific how" of our record of experience—the same inner form—is necessary; but for understanding in the more general sense it is the latent content of all language, or our intuitive record of experience, which is determinative. It is this "layer of meaning" which is significant for the understanding of the wider ranges of translation. It is this layer of meaning also that, as we shall see, is significant for our theory of communication.

Such attempts as the preceding to solve the problems of translation seem to many unduly complex and to involve the mysterious. Commenting on the theory, Ogden and Richards remark, "If we attempt to deal with the difficulties of translation in terms of the 'latent content' of the linguistic medium and of the non-linguistic layer in which intuition moves,

[1] *Op. cit.*, pp. 228 ff.

mysteries are inevitable."[1] Perhaps they are. Perhaps some element of mystery is not wholly escapable in dealing with the miracle of language and communication. It is better to leave an element of mystery than to be wholly inadequate. For Ogden and Richards there is no mystery in translation, or indeed in communication in any of its forms, apparently for the reason that they are not wholly aware of the problems really involved. This we shall see later, I think, in our examination of Richards's theory of communication. In any case it does not seem to me possible to characterize the line between the translatable and untranslatable except in terms of some such concepts and hypotheses as we have been considering.

C

Translation from One Universe of Discourse to Another

It is a well-known fact that while much that belongs to the special genius of a language is not transferable into an alien tongue, there is also often much that I cannot communicate to some of those who speak my own language. In fact it is frequently the case that there are meanings which I can convey linguistically to one of an alien tongue which I cannot convey to some of my fellow countrymen with whom I share a common speech. The man to whom I cannot communicate my meaning (because we do not share a common universe of discourse, the same assumptions and suppositions), does in very truth "speak another language," and translation of my meaning into his is a condition of understanding. The phrase is then not a mere figure of speech but a statement of brute fact. For language is, as we have seen, not the squeaks and grunts, nor the symbols on paper, nor again the syntax which makes up its structure; meaning is part of the speech-notion itself.[2] It is with translation in this second sense that we are now concerned.

A speech transaction within the same speech community admits of similarity or identity of reference in all these respects which we have considered in connection with translation in general, namely, in the "latent content" of all language. It

[1] *Op. cit.*, p. 228.   [2] Chapter II, p. 65 f.

also admits of similarity of reference with respect to what was described as the "inner speech form" of the particular language. To all Italians a *cavallo* is, as Vossler says, not only the quadruped which the Englishman calls horse, but it is also a *cavallo*, which to the Englishman it is not. But there is often something else involved—something that cannot be communicated if the hearer does not understand the "spiritual idiom" involved. Is it possible to make this notion of a spiritual idiom more definite?

The word love has its equivalent in all languages, although, as we are told, among certain primitive peoples there is no word for our "romantic" love. Again the English word love and the French word *amour* have the same primary reference, but for some purposes of discourse they are not similar in their references in all relevant respects. Within the same speech community, finally, the word may have different meanings. For one it may mean merely the biological urge and its consummation, for another it may mean something quite different. It is then that we say that people do not "understand each other" and that they do not "speak the same language." They speak an entirely different spiritual idiom. Here, obviously, we come upon the basal condition of all intelligible, as distinguished from behavioural, communication—namely, the mutual acknowledgment of the same universe of discourse and of its presuppositions. But the special problem here presented enables us to specify these presuppositions more definitely. In this case what is presupposed is the mutual acknowledgment of certain values. This mutual acknowledgment of values conditions all intelligible communication—all meaning ultimately goes back to values[1]—but it is especially obvious at this point. In order, however, that they be mutually apprehended and acknowledged, they must be *there*, and in some sense transcend the communicating minds. This, among other things, is the significance of certain of our earlier studies—namely, our contention that value words have objective references and that value nominalism cannot be maintained;[2] and, secondly, that there are value propositions which can be authenticated in discourse.[3]

There is, then, translation from one universe of discourse to another and mutual understanding involves such translation.

[1] Chapter III, p. 126 f.   [2] Chapter IV, pp. 162 ff.   [3] Chapter V, pp. 215 ff.

Marriage, as we have seen, means one thing in the mouth of a jurist, another in the mouth of a priest and still another in the mouth of an anthropologist. It is, however, possible for the one to understand the other. But the meaning understood does not consist merely in the similarity of reference—in the sense of reference to the same behavioural fact which is part of marriage in any sense of the word—but rather to the sharing, imaginatively at least, of the suppositions and values which determine the meaning.

D

Types of Intelligibility

At this point I should like to make a brief excursus into a related topic which grows directly out of the present one and which has considerable significance for the more philosophical considerations to come. It is the notion of different types of intelligibility. We have spoken of different spiritual idioms. Just as within two different languages there are different idioms, so within the same language there are different spiritual idioms corresponding to different universes of discourse. As communication involves passage from one idiom to another in the first case, so does it in the second case also. Such a spiritual idiom when it becomes systematized I call a "type of intelligibility." Thus, again by a figure of speech, we speak of the idiom of science or the idiom of poetry or religion. This is also no *mere* figure of speech, but, as I hold, a brute fact. These idioms represent different languages with different norms of intelligibility, and passage from one type to another, translation in the broad sense, is one of the fundamental problems of philosophical semantics.

This notion of types of intelligibility has received special attention in recent philosophical literature. It underlies the entire development of Cassirer's philosophy of different "symbolic forms," but it has also received a very interesting expression in C. Lloyd Morgan's recent Frey Lecture entitled *Science and Drama*. His main contention is that there are two radically different ways of describing and understanding the world: that of science, which broadly speaking consists in framing wider and wider generalizations based on observation and experiment; and secondly, that of drama which seeks to understand and describe in terms of the agencies and activities to which objects and events are due. His second contention is that, although radically different, the two ways are not antagonistic, but rather complementary. Finally, he holds that no adequate account of what happens in human life, the central home of action and drama, is possible if relations of the mental type and the dramatic way of rendering them are left out.[1]

Insistence upon the existence and necessity of these two types of intelligibility, without any determination of the primacy of one over the other, is the burden of Lloyd Morgan's contention. The primacy of the dramatic type is, on the other hand, argued by H. B. Alexander. In a suggestive article which in many respects parallels the position of Lloyd Morgan, he further insists upon the necessity of the dramatic categories in science. A cosmology is always action and has of necessity a dramatic character. "Upon drama, then, even our natural science has depended and does ultimately depend for its sense of rationality."[2]

For the purposes of the present discussion it is not necessary to determine the question of primacy, but merely the necessity of such a type for intelligibility as a whole. My own view is that, properly understood, the thesis of the primacy of the dramatic form must be maintained. It is part of my general thesis that all meaning is ultimately linguistic and that although science, in the interests of purer notation and manipulation, may break through the husk of language, its non-linguistic symbols must again be translated back into natural language if intelligibility is to be possible. Natural language is dramatic and all meaning expressed in language must ultimately be of this type.

This is, however, a problem for later chapters. In any case, the present discussion has made clear these large universes of discourse, these primal types of intelligibility. There are the different "languages" of science, of art and of religion—different symbolic forms as we shall later describe them—and

[1] *Op. cit.*, p. 21.
[2] H. B. Alexander, "Drama as a Cosmic Category," *The Philosophical Review*, March 1930.

one of the problems of philosophical semantics is the relation of these forms to each other and the possibility of translation—translation being used in this broader sense—from one such "language" or idiom to another. It is at this point that problems of metaphysics and of philosophical semantics are fundamentally related.

E

"Real Communication." Again the "Miracle of Language"

After this excursus we may return to the more general problem of the nature of intelligible communication to which our study of translation was intended to contribute—namely the problem of the range of communication and the related question of the adequacy of intelligible communication.

The impression of the "miracle of language" made upon us by an examination of all that is involved in a "speech transaction" is deepened by our consideration of the range of such transactions as exhibited by the facts of translation. It is true that there are limits to translation, but when these are duly weighed, it still remains the fact that both the range and the adequacy of translation are very great. This fact, no less than the miracle of any speech transaction as such, will, we shall find, necessarily have great weight in determining our theory of the conditions of communication.

The outstanding fact of linguistic communication is, then, its extraordinary depth and range. All language is elliptical, but the possibility of supplying that which is left out is, to all intents and purposes, unlimited. Despite this fact, there are views of language which stress the limits of communication rather than its range. "Does anyone believe," asks Maeterlinck, "that by means of language any *real* communication can pass from man to man?" It is the position expressed in the old saying: "*Spricht* die Seele, spricht die *Seele* nich mehr."

This idea of the limits of language as a medium of expression is very old. It is held, as in Plato's later theory, that the soul has direct insight into reality, but that this insight is not communicable in language.[1] It is the fashion to-day also to

[1] Chapter I, p. 54 f.

depreciate language and to speak of its inadequacy as compared with the non-verbal arts of painting and music. On this latter question we shall have something to say later; here we are interested merely in this notion of "real communication" which, it is maintained, is impossible through the medium of language.

The notion of real communication as here used is, of course, highly ambiguous. If by it is meant the communication of our individual sensations, our instinctive and emotional states, with all their privacy and darkness, then these can no more be communicated by language than can "life" itself; in so far as these are communicable at all it is only in the form of behavioural communication. If, however, we mean by real communication intelligible communication, involving expression and its correlate understanding—a form of communication which really communicates our meanings in the sense that we can mutually acknowledge the same presuppositions and values—then real communication is not only possible through language, but ultimately only through language. The question of what is meant by real communication is, however, important not only from the standpoint of the adequacy of communication through different *media*, but also from the standpoint of a theory of communication. If, as held by the view we have been considering, there is no real communication by means of language, what is then the situation? Is there then, perhaps, no real or direct communication at all, but only apparent communication—that is merely external and accidental similarity of reference; or is there such real communication, and if so, what is its nature? This question, as we shall see, plays a significant rôle in theories of communication. To an examination of these theories we shall now turn.

IV

THE CONDITIONS OF INTELLIGIBLE COMMUNICATION. THE BEHAVIOURISTIC OR NATURALISTIC ACCOUNT

A

The nature of communication both in its non-linguistic and linguistic, its behavioural and intelligible forms, is now before us. We have also examined the nature of linguistic communication or intelligible discourse. We may now ask what are the conditions of such discourse.

We have seen what the notion of conditions here means. It is the *quaestio juris* as contrasted with the *quaestio facti*—the problem, namely, of how intelligible communication, as we have come to understand it, is possible. What assumptions must be made in order to make this communication, this understanding, possible?

There are, generally speaking, only two possible answers to this question, namely the naturalistic or behaviouristic theory and the idealistic or transcendental theory. The first is undoubtedly the simplest and, *prima facie* at least, the most plausible account of communication. Let us examine it first and see how far it goes in its task of making intelligible communication itself intelligible.

This naturalistic theory is explicitly stated by I. A. Richards in Chapter XII of his book, *Principles of Literary Criticism*, entitled "A Theory of Communication." It is desirable to start with his version for he himself contrasts this theory with the "transcendental" theory in such a way as to bring out clearly the issues involved.

In the first place, we are told, "artificial mysteries are made out of this very simple and prosaic matter of communication. Transcendental considerations are brought in where they are unnecessary. All that really occurs is that under certain conditions separate minds have closely similar experiences." He starts, then, with the naturalistic assumption of the natural isolation and severance of minds, their experiences at best being, under the most favourable circumstances, merely similar. Communication then takes place when "one mind so acts upon its environment that another mind is influenced and in the other mind an experience occurs which is like the experience in the first mind and is caused by part of that experience. This is all there is to the prosaic matter of communication."

Now, communication may be prosaic enough—much of it doubtless is—but that it is as simple as all this we have already had occasion to doubt. One thing certainly is clear. It is simply not true that all that occurs in intelligible communication is that under certain circumstances separate minds have closely similar experiences. We have now only to examine the theory based upon this assumption to turn our doubts about its validity into certainties. This naturalistic or behaviouristic theory is stated much more adequately by C. I. Lewis in his *Mind and the World Order*. We shall therefore use his statement as the basis for our examination.

"The only conditions of communication," he tells us—and under communication he includes the entire range of linguistic and non-linguistic, behavioural and intelligible—"are the fact that we are creatures fundamentally alike and that we are confronted by a common reality." Negatively stated, there is nothing else of which we may say absolutely that "unless this much were common in what is given us, we could not understand each other at all." As speech itself is "only that part of behaviour which is most significant of meanings and most useful for communication," so linguistic communication is only that part of communication in general which is most significant, and the conditions of that communication are nothing more than the conditions of any other form.

B

The Limits of the Behaviouristic Theory

This simple answer is most natural and plausible. The law of parsimony would seem to counsel us to reduce the problem to its simplest terms and to seek only those conditions which are indispensable to the simplest form of communication. Nevertheless, whatever plausibility it has it gets, I think it can be shown from the exploitation of an ambiguity in the notion of similarity in both of its aspects. Let us then examine this view, separating for the moment the two conditions, namely, (*a*) similarity of organism ("creatures fundamentally alike") and (*b*) similarity of environment ("common reality").

The fact that the creatures concerned in communication are fundamentally alike does seem to explain behavioural communication without a remainder. The cooing of doves or the mating cry are forms of such communication and, unless we are guilty of the psychologist's fallacy, all that they communicate are cues to behaviour, and probably all that is required here is similarity of instinctive and emotive structure. But the situation is significantly different when we come to intelligible communication. In behavioural communication there is similarity of reference, but no sense of the "relevant respects" in which the similarity exists. It is this element of relevance—and the tacit or expressed recognition of this relevance, acknowledgment of the intensional element, of the universe of discourse and its presuppositions—that constitutes and conditions intelligible communication. This no mere external similarity of organism can explain. The likeness of the creatures communicating must go far beyond this conception.

We may conclude, then, that the notion of similarity of organism, of creatures fundamentally alike, is a wholly ambiguous notion. Taken in one of its possible meanings—its simplest—it cannot by any stretch of the imagination be made to explain any but the lowest levels of communication. Taken in a broader sense—so that it may be capable of application to higher levels of communication—it includes similarity of mental structure, a certain "mutuality of mind" to use a term also employed by Professor Lewis, an inclusion which as we shall see begs the entire question at issue. A similar ambiguity we shall find inherent in the second condition, namely a "common reality," or similarity of environment.

Communication in all its forms involves similarity of reference. Even behavioural communication, as in animal cries, involves reference, in the sense at least of indefinite reference to a context or situation. It is obvious, therefore, that this reference would be impossible unless the communicating organisms had a common reality. Now similarity of environment, in the sense of similarity of conditions of physical existence, may conceivably be sufficient to account for this element of reference in animal communication. But the common reality necessary to account for the similarity of reference in linguistic communication goes far beyond the physical environment. Such communication is not confined to the here and the now —to the context of situation—but extends to universes of discourse far beyond the merely physical context.

Here again, then, we may say that the notion of a common

reality is thoroughly ambiguous. Taken in one sense, the simplest, it can explain only the simplest cases of similarity of reference, namely the here and the now. Taken in a broader sense, so that it may be extended to include other forms of communication and reference, it assumes in the notion of common reality the very elements of community which it seeks to explain. Professor Lewis tacitly recognizes this fact in his admission that the reality is "largely constructed." This aspect of reality, however large it may be—in that it *is* constructed—implies not only mind, but an initial mutuality of mind, in other words the very communication which it is designed to explain.

C

Range of Communication on the Behaviouristic Theory

The basal issues involved in this question are so important as to warrant still further discussion. These issues are brought out clearly in a passage in which Professor Lewis puts his theory to the test of certain hypothetical cases. His thesis is that, on these simple assumptions, there would be the possibility of the indefinite extensibility of understanding and communication. Now it is just this thesis that I would challenge—not of course the "miracle of communication"—but its possibility on Professor Lewis's assumptions.

He points out, first of all, that, as an actual fact an initial community between like-minded individuals is capable of enormous expansion, and that the manner of that expansion is familiar. He supposes two men, speaking different languages but having a few words in common, to be chained to the opposite walls of a dark cell, so that the possibility of establishing common meanings by pointing and naming would be at a minimum. "With good luck in the initial common concepts and with a high order of intelligence, they would eventually establish a very large range of common notions." He cites the actual case of Helen Keller, in which a normal range of understanding has been developed from an original coincidence of merely kinaesthetic and contact sensations. He then passes to the illustration I have specifically in mind. Suppose there should be creatures on Mars of a high order of mentality. They might psychologically be rather different from ourselves and have senses and experience largely incomparable with our own. Yet if we could establish some initial common understanding (say if we should signal them by light flashes, — —, — —, — —, and they should eventually respond with — — — —, — — — —, — — — — —), then in spite of our differences from them, "it would be hard to set a limit beyond which it could with certainty be said that our common understanding could not go." He speaks of the indefinite extensibility of conceptual understanding.

Now it is just this thesis of indefinite extensibility of understanding that I would challenge. Not, I repeat, the fact—that is indeed the very character of linguistic communication—but the *possibility* of the fact on Professor Lewis's premises. Assuming merely a similarity of organism that consists solely in coincidence of kinaesthetic and contact sensations, and similarity of environment or common reality that is no more than light flashes, no such extension of communication is conceivable. Much more must be assumed—and actually much more *is* assumed in Lewis's statement of the situation—namely, "an initial community of like-minded persons, creatures of a high order of mentality." In these comparatively innocent phrases is concealed all that I am contending for. For what do these phrases mean? I do not know what like-minded individuals mean unless that they have like categories and acknowledge like values. I do not know what "a high order of mentality" means unless an order of mentality in which language, and the meanings it embodies, have already developed. In order that such an extension of conceptual understanding may be possible, it is not necessary, of course, that there should be languages of the same external form, but it is necessary as Jespersen says, that there shall be community of "notions" lying at the back of the linguistic or grammatical forms. It is not necessary that they shall have the "same sense of values" —the tremendous historical differences show this—but it is necessary that there shall be, however limited, a "commonwealth of objective values," mutually acknowledged.

D

Tacit Assumptions of the Behaviouristic Theory

The entire problem at issue here is clearly stated by Professor Lewis when he tells us (p. 96) that for our actual and most elaborate mutual understanding a simple foundation would be sufficient—"a relatively meagre mutuality of concepts, given human powers of discrimination, abstraction and relation and our human social habits, would be all that is necessary." He is not arguing, he continues, "that it is from such a meagre basis of initial mutuality that the community of understanding actually develops." He wishes only to point out the fact that, "given such a meagre mutuality, elaborate common understanding would develop, and that to argue straight from our common understanding to an equally extended coincidence of felt qualities or given experience, is unnecessary and fallacious."

With the actual extent of this initial mutuality I am not greatly concerned, but rather with the fact that such mutuality is postulated and what its postulation involves. The relatively meagre mutuality assumed by Professor Lewis seems to me a rather generous allowance, and one out of which almost any type of communication can be developed. It is, I repeat, with the notion of initial mutuality of mind itself that I am concerned. It includes, it seems to me obvious, much more than what was stated in the original premises. Not merely an external similarity of creatures, not merely a common external environment that acts causally upon the creatures in the same way. Mutuality of mind, if it means anything at all, means mutual acknowledgment of certain meanings and values and it is only upon the basis of such acknowledgment that any real communication, as distinguished from merely apparent, is possible at all.

Professor Lewis's interest in the problem of communication is primarily an epistemological one. He recognizes that knowledge is public and involves communication. Part of the problem of knowledge is then always the question of what is necessary for communication. On this point he takes issue with both the sensationalist and the rationalist, with the realist and the idealist, as to what is necessary for intelligible communication. The former insists that our common world is given to us in a common sensory experience; the latter insists upon the assumption of "an ideal and complete agreement in an immutable set of categories." Theories of both types, he holds, are based on "nothing more or less than beautiful myth" (p. 92). Elements of myth there may be in both these theories of community of mind, but the notion of community of mind itself is far from myth, for this notion in some form alone makes intelligible the element of communication necessary for knowledge. This is the essence of the transcendental theory to which we shall now turn.

V

CONDITIONS OF INTELLIGIBLE COMMUNICATION. THE TRANSCENDENTAL THEORY

A

Communication, I think we may now see from the foregoing, is scarcely the simple thing which the naturalistic theory envisages. It may be prosaic enough—much of it doubtless is—but that it is as described by Richards only a most naïve analysis could for a moment suppose. The mysteries made of this matter of communication are not at all artificial, but thoroughly genuine to anyone who takes the trouble to analyse what is really involved in a speech transaction. The miracle of language, as we have come to understand it, lies precisely in the fact that it is elliptical—that so much more is understood than is expressed. It is precisely the range of this mutual understanding, of this *a priori* mutuality of mind that necessitates some transcendental theory.

Let us then examine those theories which, according to Richards, bring in transcendental considerations when they are unnecessary. Our task will include three phrases, (*a*) the reasons for bringing in such considerations; (*b*) a statement of the transcendental theory; and (*c*) evidence for the theory.

B

The Reasons for the Transcendental Theory

First of all, those who reject the naturalistic theory, do so, according to Professor Richards, "because of some mystical, poetic conception of intermingling, penetration of minds, or even that particular minds are an illusory appearance of an underlying unity of mind." They reject the simpler theory and accept the more involved, "not on grounds of evidence, but on grounds of desire, due to the influence of the contrary opinion on their attitudes towards their fellows." We shall consider first this account of the motives for rejecting the naturalistic theory and then proceed to develop the real grounds of those theories which find transcendental consideration necessary.

The rejection of the naturalistic theory, it must now be evident, is not based wholly on grounds of desire, although it is not entirely clear why the presence of this desire for real communication with our fellows and oneness of a more internal kind should not be considered at least part of the evidence. Nor is the rejection due to mystical and poetic conceptions of intermingling or penetration of minds, although the transcendental conception has often been expressed poetically—and very beautifully at that—and there seems no good reason why in certain contexts it should not be so expressed. Indeed the omnipresence of this notion in all the higher ranges of poetry seems to me to be part of the evidence for its truth. No, the real reasons for its rejection are of quite another order. It is precisely the facts of communication, their character and their range, which, when examined closely, make such a theory wholly unintelligible.

But these are negative reasons. They are indeed part of the evidence but there are also positive reasons. It is admitted by Professor Richards that "if there were direct contact of mind with mind, if actual transference and participation did occur, we should of course be compelled to adopt the transcendental theory." "It does not occur," but he holds, "and no arguments that assume it have the least weight." Now, I am disposed to believe—and I think it can be shown—that just this "direct contact" and actual participation do occur (that is if the meaning of these terms is properly interpreted); but I do not think that it is this fact alone that compels us to adopt the transcendental theory. It is at best part of the evidence and, since it is felt to be compelling by many, we shall consider it briefly.

It is immediately clear that both of these terms, direct contact and participation, are figurative expressions taken from the physical universe of discourse. There is, of course, no contact in the literal sense and no mind becomes part of another mind in any spatial sense. Properly interpreted, the problem becomes this: is there any initial mutuality of mind, prior to and conditioning communication of meaning from mind to mind? In other words is there any *real* communication, as distinguished from merely "apparent" (that is merely similarity of references in two wholly separate minds)? If so, is there any evidence for it?

When the question is formulated in this way I think it will be seen to be in essence the same problem which we have in connection with "the knowledge of other mind." Is there any direct or immediate knowledge, or is what we call knowledge of other mind merely indirect or mediate knowledge by analogous inference or *Einfühlung* (empathy)? For real communication, in the sense in which we have defined it, presupposes this direct knowledge. The first type of theory holds that there is direct awareness or intuition of other minds, and that this awareness is a function of a oneness or mutuality of mind that transcends and is presupposed by experience. The latter, starting from the assumption of the natural isolation of minds, and their merely external similarity, attempts to account for what knowledge of other mind there actually is by processes of analogical inference or imaginative projection.

This latter theory is practicaly abandoned in either form. As for the first form, the most significant reason is the fact that analogical inference, one of the weakest types of inference, is made the basis for one of the strongest of all certitudes. This certitude is itself not generated by analogical inference; rather is it true that our inference by analogy, as to the *content* of other minds, actually presupposes this initial certitude and an initial mutuality of mind.

INTELLIGIBLE COMMUNICATION

This serious difficulty in the first form of the theory led to its abandonment and to the belief that the basis of this certainty must be sought in something deeper, namely, in the originality and immediacy of feeling. Yet, on examination, it becomes clear that this theory (of *Einfühlung*) is really in scarcely better position. It is true that it enables us to understand better those forms of pre-linguistic communication, before language and ideal construction, necessarily presupposed by the inference theory, have been developed. But this theory has the same fundamental weakness as the other—namely, that here again one of the strongest of certitudes is based upon nothing stronger than imaginative projection. A vicious circle is present in this form of the theory no less than in the first. It seeks to explain communication in terms which already presuppose its existence. It is one of the services of Scheler to have exposed the weakness of the *Einfühlung* theory no less than that of analogous inference.[1]

There are, then, reasons of fact for bringing in transcendental considerations. These are precisely the evidence for direct communication of mind with mind which, according to Richards, if it existed, would necessitate the transcendental theory. Let me state the situation in another way. There is real communication—not merely apparent, as on the theory of Richards and Lewis. In other words, it is not true that all there is in communication is the simple fact that separate minds have similar experiences. That would be no real communication at all but merely apparent. Now, the point I am here making is this. All the attempts to explain knowledge of other mind actually presuppose, as we have seen, this real communication.

In an interesting study of this problem by Karl Jaspers in his book entitled *Philosophie*, this point is argued with great force. He distinguishes between linguistic and what he calls existential or "eigentliche Kommunikation" and shows quite clearly that the former presupposes the latter. It is, he admits, always possible to deny real communication and to give it the status of illusion. It is also probable, as he further admits,

---

[1] Max Scheler, *Wesen und Formen der Sympathie*, Bonn 1923, pp. 282 ff. See also on this point Ernst Cassirer, *Die Philosophie der Symbolischen Formen*, Vol. III, pp. 101 ff.

that it is not possible to refute this denial logically. It may be maintained that man is after all ultimately himself and not another. Real sharing of meaning is impossible. The individual is a monad without windows. Such a denial cannot be refuted logically, for it starts with the metaphysical assumption of the severance of minds and therefore gets from its premises precisely what was included in them. But it can be refuted dialectically, for it can be shown that the very communication that is thus denied is assumed in the denial.[1]

The question of the nature and significance of evidence of this type will be considered presently. Here our only point has been this. If, it was said, there were direct contact of mind with mind—real or existential communication—then we should be compelled to adopt the transcendental theory. It does not, however, occur, therefore our arguments that assume it have not the least weight. We have shown that it does occur, and so we proceed to the consideration of the transcendental theory which, it is admitted, these facts make necessary.

C

Formulation of the Transcendental Theory: The Metaphysical Speech Community

We have seen the reasons, both negative and positive, which have given rise to the transcendental theory of the conditions of intelligible communication. Let us now proceed to a statement of it. The theory has, indeed, often been formulated in poetical and mystical terms. There is, for instance, a poem of Matthew Arnold's entitled *Isolation* in which the poet compares the souls of men to islands scattered in the main; at their invisible bases they are united into one vast continent, and in rare moments they become conscious of that deep-seated unity; but for the most part they are only sensible of the distance which divides them from one another, by reason of the "divine ordinance" which

"bade between their shores to be
The unplumbed, salt, estranging sea."

[1] Karl Jaspers, *Philosophie*, Berlin, 1932. An entire chapter in his second volume is devoted to the subject of *Kommunikation* and its relation to knowledge.

On the view here expressed, the isolation of minds is the surface phenomenon; the underlying unity is the more fundamental.

Poetical and mystical forms of statement are not to be dismissed lightly. Conceptions of intermingling and penetration, though figurative, are the only forms in which truth of this sort can be given concrete expression. If, then, we pass to more abstract forms it is because only in this form is the transcendental hypothesis or theory usable philosophically. The more abstract form substitutes for such notions the idea of an over-individual mind, of a transcendental self, or perhaps of a transcendental community of minds. The fundamental notion here is that of common experience—something shared by individual minds which makes possible intelligible communication. With this notion we are already familiar through Professor Lewis's criticism of it. This assumption or postulate of a common experience, whether in the form of common sensory experience or of an ideal or complete agreement in an immutable set of categories, is, we are told, nothing more than a "beautiful myth."

Now the essence of the transcendental theory is that we are dealing not with myth (although there may be mythical or figurative elements in our forms of statement) but rather with epistemological "fact" and "necessity." Few transcendentalists —certainly not Kant himself—would be disposed to think of the notion of the transcendental Self as more than a symbol for this underlying unity. But the unity thus symbolized is itself not a myth. It is a necessary condition of that universality, that mutuality of mind however small, without which knowledge and its communication are impossible. Whether for the unity thus symbolized we use the "myth" of an over-individual self or of an over-individual community is, from the present point of view, a matter of relative indifference. I do not much care in the present context whether one thinks of an all-embracing mind in which finite minds live and move and have their being, or as an over-individual society of minds. Important as these issues are in other contexts, they are not the significant thing here. What is significant is the *transcendental minimum*, or the minimum of "transcendental considerations," necessary for the understanding of intelligible communication. All the rest may well contain an element of figure or myth as, I am inclined to believe, it did for Kant—although even then it would be very significant myth.

It is interesting that Kant himself recognized, although dimly, the relation of his transcendentalism to the problem of communication. In a letter to Beck he is trying to make clear the ideas of the transcendental deduction of the categories. He writes: "We cannot perceive connection as given, but we must ourselves make it; we must do the relating if we are to represent something to ourselves as related (even space and time themselves). *It is solely in respect to this connection that we are able to communicate with each other . . ."*[1] (italics mine). He adds humorously, "I may say as I am writing, that I do not adequately understand myself." It is not strange that Kant, like many another wrestler with new thoughts, did not wholly understand himself, nor that later philosophers should understand him better than he did himself. Kant was dimly aware that communication and communicability are part of the very notion of knowledge itself and that the element of universality which alone makes possible communication involves the notion of mind or self that transcends both the object and the individual communicating subjects. He saw clearly that it was solely by virtue of the transcendental elements in knowledge that intelligible communication itself, when really understood, becomes possible. Surely that was a great thing to see, even if he saw it only dimly.

D

Criticisms of the Transcendental Theory. (Empiricism)

"Professed transcendentalists have as a whole," Professor Dewey tells us, "been more aware of the problems of communication than professed empiricists." I think that after our examination of naturalistic and empirical attempts to "explain" intelligible communication, we may see that he is right. Never-

[1] Letter to Beck, July 1, 1794, in the Kant manuscripts in the Royal Library in Berlin. Kant never worked out a theory of communication in its relation to knowledge, but it is clear from his discussion of the notion in the *Critique of Judgment* (in connection with the aesthetic and its objectivity) that objectivity and communicability were closely related in his mind.

theless, it may help to make clear our position if we permit him to show us just where in his opinion these problems lie.

"Thinkers," he writes, "may start with the naïve assumption of minds connected with separate individuals. But developments soon show the inadequacy of such "minds" to carry the burden of science and of objective institutions like the family and the State. The consequence was revealed to be *sceptically disintegrative*, malicious (italics mine). A transcendental, supra-empirical self, making human or finite selves the medium of manifestation, was the logical recourse. Such a conception is an inevitable conclusion when the value of liberation and utilization of individual capacity in science, art, and industry is a demonstrated empirical fact; and when at the same time individuality, instead of being conceived as historic, temporally relative and instrumental, is conceived of as original, eternal, and absolute. When concrete reconstructions of natural and social objects are thought of as a single constitutive act, they inevitably become supernatural and transcendent. When the movement terminates, as in the later philosophy of Josiah Royce, with a community of selves, the circle has returned to the empirical fact with which it might properly have started out; but the intervening insertion of a transcendental self remains as a plague. It isolates the community of selves from natural existence and in order to get nature again in connection with mind, is compelled to reduce it to a system of volitions, feelings, and thoughts."[1]

A transcendental supra-empirical unity of mind is, I think, clearly inevitable, as Professor Dewey admits, if we start with the assumption of separate selves. Mind, so conceived, is surely inadequate to carry the burden of human communication and all its works, both of science and of human institutions. But does Professor Dewey's substitute for such a unity of mind really solve the problem? Is it not rather, in fact, precisely when selves are conceived as merely historical, spatio-temporal, that the miracle of communication, as we have come to see it, becomes finally and wholly unintelligible? For if it is true, as Dewey argues, that, starting with the assumption of separate selves as original, eternal, and absolute, there is no real com-

[1] *Experience and Nature*, Chapter V, p. 168. Published by George Allen & Unwin Ltd.

munication but at best a mere similarity of reference, is it not even more obvious that, if we start with a purely historical and relative view of selves, real communication—that is, communication in any but a behavioural sense—is impossible? Such a conception also is inadequate to carry the burden of communication. This our examination of naturalistic theories has already abundantly shown. As a matter of fact, Professor Dewey actually starts with the assumption of *real* communication and does not try to explain it or make it intelligible. We are not surprised to find that, on the whole, he tends to make communication itself an ultimate category although he, of course, refuses to draw the transcendental and idealistic consequences involved.

It is precisely the drawing of these consequences that he criticizes in Royce in the latter part of the passage. "With the notion of a community of selves in Royce's later philosophy, the circle has returned," we are told, "to the empirical fact with which it might have started." *But that is precisely what it has not done.* Empirical facts of communication there are, indeed, and it is upon such facts, of course, that theories of communication must be based—but the community of selves as implied in these facts is itself not an empirical fact, verifiable in terms of the empirical criterion. It is, as we have seen, a transcendental requirement of intelligible communication. It is not, then, to a sociological notion of a community of selves that the circle has returned, but to a transcendental or metaphysical conception of community. Whether this also is verifiable, in its own way, we shall presently ask, but it is above all necessary to see that this community of selves is metaphysical.

In his *Spirit of Language in Civilization*, Karl Vossler makes use of the term metaphysical speech community. On his view —and it is the view here presented—it is impossible to understand speech or intelligible communication, in all its significance, without widening the notion of community and communication into a metaphysical conception. The linguist, as such, deals with what he calls empirical speech communities, some of them of very extensive range, but these empirical communities presuppose the metaphysical. The same requirement has been expressed by Husserl when he tells us that the "prerequisite" of linguistic communication, when properly understood, is "a transcendental monadism, a transcendental sociological phenomenology having reference to a manifest multiplicity of conscious subjects, communicating with each other."

E

The Question of Evidence

Whenever "transcendental considerations" are brought into any theory of knowledge, empirical and naturalistic thinkers always reply that for such there is no whit of evidence. Now I have already indicated why, to my mind, there is evidence for *real* communication in the sense of direct contact of mind with mind, or actual participation, if these terms are properly interpreted. But, as I also indicated, it is not this evidence alone, or indeed chiefly, that forces us to accept the transcendental theory. It is rather evidence of a more weighty character with which we are here concerned.

In order to recognize and weigh evidence we must know precisely what the theory is for which we are seeking evidence, and the kind of facts which would constitute evidence for the theory—in this case what the problems of intelligible communication really are. Of these problems the transcendentalists have had, as Dewey says, in the main a better understanding than the empiricists. They are, as we have seen, the problems set by intelligible communication, and it is these facts which when properly analysed seem to require the hypothesis of a transcendental mutuality of mind.

Now it is quite clear, first of all, what evidence for such an hypothesis or theory can *not* be. The supra-empirical unity implied in intelligible communication *is* supra-empirical and, therefore, by definition, not verifiable as an empirical fact by a direct application of the "empirical criterion." All that is directly observable are merely the facts of similarity of organism and of environment and these facts, as we have already shown, constitute merely apparent, not real, communication, and are wholly inadequate to account for intelligible communication in both its nature and its range. Indeed, even in the naturalistic theory itself something more was tacitly postulated, namely, the very antecedent mutuality of mind which was verbally denied.

Evidence for such a supra-empirical unity of mind must accordingly be indirect. Since this unity itself is not an object of sensible experience, but rather the presupposition of the possibility of any experience and its communication, we may call this *evidence for presuppositions*. With this notion we, of course, come to what has been the basal issue between pure empiricists and transcendentalists—an issue upon which it is difficult to come to an understanding—the issue namely whether the possibility of experience and of its communication are themselves facts which require to be interpreted or explained. If they are, as the transcendentalist always holds, then the evidence here must be of a special nature, the proof, as Lewis says, of a "peculiar kind." Let us examine this evidence.

The argument of the transcendentalist may be of a peculiar kind, but if so it is only because the facts upon which the argument is based are of a special order. Mind, conceived as wholly isolated separate selves, it finds, with Dewey, wholly inadequate to carry the burden of communication and all its works, both science and human institutions. But equally inadequate is mind when conceived in purely naturalistic terms of history and sociology. It is upon these considerations that the evidence rests. Such evidence is, to be sure, largely negative, but not wholly so. The force of the transcendental argument rests, in the last analysis, on certain positive considerations, namely the actual character of intelligible communication as we have seen it to be, more especially of understanding which is involved in such communication. If the character of these facts is acknowledged—if real communication, as contrasted with merely apparent—is recognized, then the "transcendental considerations" are necessitated for the understanding of these facts. This is evidence in any proper sense of the word.[1]

This entire question of evidence seems to be greatly misunderstood. It is a well understood principle that you cannot disprove a theory if you rule out *ab initio* the facts upon which

---

[1] This "kind of proof," this argument to presuppositions, will be discussed in more detail in the following chapter (p. 313). The question which it raises is important alike from the standpoint of logic and of metaphysics, and the conclusions reached have important bearings on all that follows.

the theory is based. This is, however, precisely what the naturalistic theory of communication does. It dismisses as irrelevant precisely those facts of communication upon which the transcendental theory is based. It assumes that the entire problem of communication is the scientific problem of the causal explanation of how communication develops. It forgets that this is no real explanation, for science itself presupposes the fact of communication, the very thing to be explained. Thus the naturalistic theory, starting with certain assumptions —namely, the natural isolation of minds, and the definition of communication as merely similarity of reference—rules out *ab initio* both the problem itself and the evidence which the transcendental theory finds most significant.

VI

COMMUNICATION AND KNOWLEDGE: THE PRIMACY OF LINGUISTIC COMMUNICATION

A

I began this study with the statement that language (and intelligible communication) are basal problems of any philosophy, a statement which the preceding discussions have, I think, amply demonstrated. The full significance of our conclusions will, however, be clearer if we develop briefly certain consequences or corollaries of the position here maintained. These we shall state briefly under the two heads: Communication and Knowledge, and (*b*) the Primacy of Linguistic Communication.

B

Knowledge and Communication

A necessary corollary of the positions developed in this argument is the inseparability of knowledge from communication. Plato's statement that knowledge is judgment plus discourse means that knowledge, in any full and significant sense of the word, has not eventuated until judgment is communicated and confirmed. In this he was undoubtedly right, his only oversight being that discourse is not something *added* to judgment, but is present, either overt or potential, in all judgment itself. It cannot, indeed, be said that that which cannot be expressed is not real, but it certainly can be said that that which cannot be expressed cannot be determined as true or false. Moreover, to determine whether it is true or false, it must be expressed and such expression involves discourse and confirmation.

This general position is, it is true, questioned by many philosophers. It is often maintained that communication—and confirmation by other mind—are not intrinsic to the knowledge function itself, but are, so to speak, merely an accidental *addendum*. Knowledge and verification, without which knowledge is scarcely conceivable, is essentially solipsistic. Confirmation has only a social value and adds nothing to knowledge itself. I confess that it is difficult for me to understand what this can mean. I see no objection, to be sure, to allowing the individual to speak, if he wishes, of his own incommunicable "truth," but I do see every objection to his saying that he can confirm or verify it without its being communicated. He may speak of a knowledge by "simple acquaintance," if he will—although I personally know of no case of knowledge without an element of description—but in the simple acquaintance he *knows* nothing; he simply *has* sense data or feelings. In other words a wholly solipsistic knowledge, still more verification, is for me an *Unding*.

On this point then, I hold, the logical positivist is wholly right, and the gradual shifting of emphasis in his theory from the notion of verification to confirmation is as sound as it is inevitable.[1] It is for this reason also, of course, that the problem of language becomes basal in any theory of knowledge. The only question is whether the theory of language and communication developed in logical positivism will bear the weight put upon it. Into this larger question of the nature of verification and confirmation I cannot go here. I will merely suggest that, once we find the locus of knowledge in confirmation (and therefore discourse), everything depends upon our *theory* of communication. For myself, I do not believe that a purely naturalistic or behaviouristic theory will bear the weight of knowledge when it is made to depend upon discourse. As Kant saw, it is solely by virtue of transcendental elements in

---

[1] Chapter V, p. 225 f.

INTELLIGIBLE COMMUNICATION

knowledge that intelligible communication is itself possible. We may likewise say that, in so far as knowledge in any full and significant sense implies discourse, the communicating subjects must be transcendent. They must transcend the empirical flux of experience, if confirmation of the experience is to be more than a form of behaviour. Communication itself cannot be naturalistically explained because it is already presupposed by the science which does the explaining.

C

Communication and Idealism and Realism

I pointed out at the beginning that the fundamental character of the problem of communication has been recognized by all types of philosophic thought, realistic, idealistic, and pragmatic. The latest philosophical work to make communication fundamental is E. G. Spaulding's *A World of Chance*. His essential point—and this is the only aspect of his very keen discussion that I have time to refer to—is that unless we postulate entities or essences *independent* of the knower, communication cannot be made intelligible. With this argument—that communication presupposes the mutual acknowledgment on the part of communicating minds of such objects—I am in entire agreement. The dialectic by means of which he shows the impossibility of communication on subjectivistic or pragmatic premises I find unanswerable and believe it to be the one fundamental argument for a necessary realistic ingredient in any philosophy. Spaulding does not find himself justified in extending this argument to cover values as having essential being independent of the subject. To my mind, however, a realism of values is as necessary a postulate of intelligible communication as a realism of non-value entities. Intelligible communication is, as our analysis has shown, as much conditioned by the mutual acknowledgment of values, upon which ultimately all meanings depend, as upon the mutual acknowledgment of "things."

"Realism" is then a necessary condition or presupposition of intelligible communication. But an equally necessary condition is an idealistic ingredient. For after all, transcendental selves, mutually acknowledging the independent entities, is as much a condition as the independent entities mutually acknowledged. This is the essential point of Husserl's transcendental monadology and it is the fundamental reason for the idealistic trend of his later writings. Now it was Royce, as we have seen, who, among American philosophers, saw most clearly this fact. It is true, as I have pointed out elsewhere, that it was a distinct disservice to philosophy when Royce, under the influence of the psychologism and sociologism of his time, overemphasized the sociological in his descriptions, and in so far tends to justify the statement of Dewey. But it is a mistake to exaggerate this aspect. For Royce the category of communication is fundamental in knowledge and there is no question that the community of minds he envisages is metaphysical and not merely sociological.

Knowledge, therefore, and the communication or discourse with which it is bound up, presuppose an element of both realism and idealism. No coherent theory of communication can be developed on subjectivist premises, and if idealism involves subjectivism, idealism must be abandoned. On the other hand, no coherent theory of communication can be developed without the notion of transcendent mind as well as transcendent objects. Any form of realism that denies this must be abandoned. I should further add, if both realistic and idealistic presuppositions are necessary for a valid or intelligible theory of communication, then since any philosophy presupposes such communication, no philosophy can ignore either element in its total structure. That is part at least of what I mean by saying, as I have in various contexts done, that a valid philosophy must be "beyond realism and idealism." It must be beyond the distinction or opposition, in the sense at least that it must include both. I would not go so far as S. Alexander and say that "no sane philosophy has ever been exclusively realistic or idealistic," but surely no adequate philosophy ever has.

D

The Primacy of Linguistic Communication

A further corollary of this general position we may describe as the primacy of language in all communication. All knowledge to be knowledge must, we have seen, be expressible. That which cannot be expressed cannot be said to be either true or false. All adequate expression, however, must, I shall maintain, be linguistic, for only linguistic communication is ultimately intelligible.

This primacy is challenged from two sources, both art and science. There are, it is maintained, media of expression, languages in the wider sense in both art and science, which afford more adequate means of communication than language in the sense of speech. Indeed, it is one of the characteristic tendencies of our modern "depreciation of the word" to hold that it is precisely the ideal of thought and its communication to break through the "husk of language" to non-linguistic forms of expression.

In the sphere of art it is often maintained that more can be communicated by non-linguistic symbols than by words. This is notoriously true of those theories of music which derive from Schopenhauer, for which music is the most metaphysical of the arts, in that it communicates directly the very will itself. But it is likewise maintained by many recent aesthetic theories (such as those of Dewey and Prall) of the arts in general. "Art," writes Prall, "is necessarily the nearest approach to anything like adequate communication."[1] "Our very need of the arts," he continues, "their unique functional value rests upon their expressing and thus communicating—what language cannot express directly in any case; for what language gives us directly is only words, conventional symbols, the meaning of which is found only in concrete non-verbal content." Language, he points out, "cannot name the feeling here given (in a Cézanne landscape), for language cannot reach in these regions of light, colour and volume, the specification that constitutes the quality of an actual determinate, individual picture."

Now, these statements may be accepted as true up to a point. There is that, doubtless, in the picture which language cannot express directly (although it may perhaps indirectly); but what is it that is expressed? It is real, doubtless, but very limited. It is, by the writer's own admission, simply the specifications of light, colour, etc., and "the vague feeling which

[1] *Aesthetic Analysis*, p. 183.

cannot be named." I am, of course, entirely willing to admit that in a landscape by Cézanne there is actually communicated much more than the light, colour, and the peculiar feeling—let us say the artist's way of envisaging reality. But when we ask what this is, that is what the picture "says," there is no way of answering it except in terms of language and the universals which condition linguistic communication.

The entire issue here evidently turns on the notion of *adequacy*. Communication, unless it is merely behavioural and emotional, must say something. Such communication is the more adequate, the more it can say, that is the more intelligible it is. Now, I am not denying, of course, that art is an important form of communication, but merely that it is not the most adequate or most intelligible form. The assertion that it is, as in the case of Prall's statement, really rests upon a certain assumption as to the nature of the real which is to be expressed, namely, that it is mere sense data—the specificity of light, colour, etc. But that is evidently a metaphysical assumption that begs the entire question at issue. Doubtless art can express these things better than language, but it is still a question *how much* of reality has really been expressed.

With regard to the challenge of science, the issue is perhaps even clearer. Here, again, it is doubtless true that by means of the *puri nomi*, the purer notation which the mathematical symbols make possible, whatever can be said by such symbols, can be said more clearly and accurately than by words. But it is still a question of *what* can thus be said. Mathematics, doubtless, "says something about everything," but it seems equally true that "it says very little about anything." Here, too, as in the case of art, the question is what it is that the mathematical formulas say. To this we are compelled to answer either that they say nothing, but merely manipulate; or else to tell what it is that they say in words. Here again it is not a question of denying that mathematical symbols are a form of intelligible communication, but merely that they can be the final and adequate form. Here again, as in the case of art, the assertion that non-linguistic symbols are more adequate than linguistic really rests upon a certain assumption as to the nature of the real to be expressed, namely, that it is ultimately a system of functional relations. But that again is evidently a metaphysical assumption which begs the entire question at issue. It may be that such relations, far from being the ultimate nature of the real, are merely its skeleton structure—or even an abstraction for certain specific purposes. In any case, until the mathematical language is interpreted, it "says nothing."

The real issue, then—in both cases—is what these non-linguistic symbols "say." For after all, all communication which is not merely emotive and behavioural, says something; intelligible communication cannot be divorced from language. It is possible, of course, to say that art says nothing, but merely evokes emotion. That is however, I think, an extreme position which cannot really be maintained. Again it is possible to say that mathematical symbols say nothing, but merely manipulate, that mathematics too is in a sense merely behavioural. But that also is difficult to maintain. It is much more reasonable to say that both say something but what it is that they really say can be ultimately expressed only in terms of language.[1]

[1] R. Honigswald formulates this principle in the following way: "dass adequatheit unter allen Zeichen nur dem Wort nachgerühmt werden kann . . . dass schlischlick jedlichen Zeichen die Beziehung auf das Wort als Bedingung zugrunde liegt." (*Grundlagen der Denkpsychologie*, p. 40.)

CHAPTER VII

LANGUAGE AND LOGIC: THE "LOGICAL ANALYSIS" OF LANGUAGE

I

A

"Philosophers," writes Mr. Russell, "as a rule believe themselves free from linguistic forms, but most of them seem to be mistaken in the belief." Now whether most philosophers do or do not believe themselves to be thus free, the assumption that they should be is a very common one, and when we seek the grounds for it we find it in the thesis that the "logical analysis" of language show these forms to be either inadequate for thought or actually erroneous, incurably infected with error. The nature and extent of this assumption may be seen in the fact that it is frequently held that by just such a logical analysis of language the fallacies of an erroneous metaphysics may be corrected, or that the whole of metaphysics be shown to be meaningless—an empty verbalism. The theme of the present chapter is, then, the logical analysis of language, more especially an examination of two assumptions which underlie this position, (*a*) the non-dependence of logic upon language, and (*b*) the primacy of logic in the determination of linguistic validity.

The problem to which we are thus led constitutes the third of the distinctly philosophical problems of language as outlined in the introductory chapter. As stated there, in the words of Mr. Russell, the question is this: "what relation the one set of facts—in the case of language the word and the sentence—must have to another set of facts—the term and the proposition—in order to be capable of standing significantly for them, or being a valid surrogate for them." Two comments upon this statement of the problem are in order.

In the first place, it is clear that the logical problem, as thus defined, is part of the normative problem of language as defined in Chapter V. The normative problem in general concerns the question, how we shall use language so as to express the meaningful rather than the unmeaning. As formulated here it asks the question how shall we use language, the word and the sentence, so that they shall express the *logically* meaningful rather than the unmeaning; in other words, be a valid surrogate for the term and the proposition. This does not necessarily mean that logic in its own nature is normative. It may be only secondarily and indirectly normative. It does, however, assume that in so far as language and linguistic meaning are concerned, logic is normative and that the logical ideal is primary.

In the second place, it is clear that in the very form of the statement certain theories of the nature of both logical fact and linguistic fact are already assumed and may, if they are accepted uncritically, beg the entire question at issue. More specifically, it assumes the complete separation of the word and the sentence from the term and the proposition. Now it may be that this assumption is justified and that the problem of language and logic as thus stated is properly formulated. On the other hand, such an assumption may be false. It may be that "a proposition apart from discourse is nothing," that, to the question, "do propositions exist?" in this sense of proposition, we may have to answer in the negative. In any case, everything depends upon the way in which the question is formulated, and it is clear that in this formulation the question is begged.

B

Sentences and Propositions

Both of these aspects are of great importance. For the moment we shall consider only the second. The assumption we are here considering is well expressed by G. E. Moore: "A proposition . . . does not itself contain words . . . it contains the entities indicated by words." This recalls Bolzano's notion of "sentences in themselves." Logic does not then deal with judgments—judgments are always expressions—but with the objective "sentences," or propositions, intended by these judgments or expressions. In this way it is believed that the human or anthropomorphic element involved in other views of logic is got rid of. The issue here involved is obviously of the greatest moment for the entire problem of the relation of logic to language. It is necessary to examine the position with some care.

It seems clear, in the first place, that when the terms proposition and sentence are used in this way they are given meanings wholly different from those in ordinary discourse. A proposition is a proposal and cannot be anything else without losing its character as a proposition. In other words, a proposition has no reality outside of discourse, that is, "expression" and "understanding" are necessary conditions for the existence (or subsistence) of a proposition. This would seem to be self-evident; why then this abstraction of "sentences in themselves" and hypostatization of the proposition as an "entity?"

The conception of logical propositions as entities arises from the fact that the "sentences" which refer to the "proposition" vary while the "proposition" is one. I am cold, *Ich bin kalt*, *je suis froid*, are sentences; that to which they refer is the proposition. Again, the same type of linguistic expression may have different logical meanings—have different referends. Socrates is a man, Socrates is mortal: the copula has a different meaning in the two sentences and to these differences correspond different "propositions." But this hypostatization of propositions is not at all a necessary consequence of these facts. The former class of sentences allows of translation, the latter of interpretation, and both translation and interpretation are functions of communication or discourse. We may therefore define a proposition as a class of sentences which have the same intensional significance for every one that understands them. It is this *common understanding* that makes the proposition, not something independent of all expression and understanding.[1]

It is, of course, possible that "propositional functions" may be abstracted from actual propositions, but propositional functions are always something less than actual propositions. Only actual propositions have existential import and only actual propositions are the subject matter of actual thinking. Such propositions cannot be separated from sentences; they have existence only in discourse. In any case—and that is the only point on which we are insisting here—the statement of the relation of language to logic which we are here criticizing is not necessitated by the facts which we have examined.

The doctrine that propositions are entities independent of discourse seems to be a metaphysical rather than a logical con-

[1] For a criticism of this doctrine, see G. Ryle, "Are there Propositions?" *Aristotelean Society Proceedings*, 1929–30.

ception. If we take the view that logic deals with such entities, then we should say that the subject matter of logic is not propositions but objective relations to which the propositions refer. Logic would then be the science of the "all-pervasive forms of everything that is." This is, as I understand it, the reason why some logicians, as for instance Professor Morris Cohen, would eliminate the notion of proposition from logic. In that case, however, logic tends to fuse with ontology, whether we conceive it phenomenologically or metaphysically.

II

WHAT IS LOGIC? PRELIMINARY DEFINITIONS

A

Traditionally, the problem of language and logic appears at three points: (a) in connection with the doctrine of terms; (b) the doctrine of propositions; (c) the doctrine of inference. An adequate development of all these themes, or chapters in logic, would obviously involve a treatise on logic. It is equally obvious that no such treatise is contemplated in this chapter. The consideration of these three points inevitably leads to certain debatable questions in modern logic. These we shall consider only in so far as they bear directly on our main problem. But these issues themselves, as well as the larger problems of language and logic, arise partly out of different conceptions of the nature and function of logic. The solution of our problem requires, therefore, certain preliminary conceptions, both of language and of logic, the two elements in the problem. We have already developed certain notions about language—certain conceptions of its nature and functions which we shall for the present assume. It is now necessary to establish certain preliminary notions of logic.

Logic is an extraordinarily difficult thing to define. As Peirce has said, "nearly a hundred different definitions have been given and dispute still rages over its first principles." The reason for these varying definitions is the fact that certain theoretical assumptions enter into the very definition of the subject matter as such. As I have shown elsewhere, the various logics, and therefore the various definitions of logic, given by these "logics," all involve certain philosophical and metaphysical assumptions.[1] It is clear that for the purposes of the present discussion all such definitions are question-begging. What is first of all required is that these assumptions shall be "put in brackets." It is necessary to begin with some notion of logic which shall represent the *minimum* of meaning acknowledged by anyone who uses the word logic. This I think can be found only in the definition of logic which connects it with reflective thinking.

B

Logic as the Science of Reflective Thinking. Traditional Notion

It will generally be conceded that the central problem of logic is right reasoning, the proper use of argument and the classification of arguments so that the good are placed in one division and the bad or fallacious in another. This is undoubtedly the popular understanding of logic and also, I think, the minimum which every logician must accept. This we may call the traditional notion, and from this notion emerges the traditional definition of logic as the science of reflective thinking. In accepting this traditional definition, however, several other notions are also implicitly accepted. It is right *reasoning* with which logic is primarily concerned—with inference and with the relations of implication upon which inference is based. Implication and implicational meaning are then the central notions in logic. In the second place, so defined, the notion of logic includes the further notion of logic as "the analysis and criticism of thought," and it is at this point that the notion of "logical analysis" with which we are concerned enters in. But—and this is most important—it is the analysis and criticism of thought only in so far as reasoning, inference, and implication are concerned. There are conceivably other aspects of thought and knowledge which logical analysis cannot touch. Finally the notion of right reasoning brings with it the notion of the normative; logic has a normative function—either direct or indirect. It is, in the words of Herbart, *die Moral des Denkens*.

[1] This position is argued at length in Chapter III of my *Intelligible World*. In general this chapter represents the position regarding the relation of logic to philosophy which underlies the discussion of the present problem.

C

Two Main Variants in the Definition of Logic

This is the minimum meaning of logic which all who use the notion must acknowledge. But from this point on, definitions vary widely. Let us examine two of the main tendencies. The first of these is in the direction of formalism. Logic is defined as the science of pure form. Logic, as so conceived, is quite different from the traditional conception as analysis and criticism of thought. The development of generalized logic from reflection upon the operations involved in reflective thinking has led to a science of pure form, or a general science of order, which has fused with mathematics.[1] It is not to be denied that the logician has the right to define logic in this way—for certain purposes—but as F. P. Ramsey has pointed out, "it really should be quite clear that those who say that mathematics is logic are not meaning by 'logic' at all the same thing as those who define logic as the analysis and criticism of thought."[2] Ramsey is, I think, unquestionably right on this point (his view is quoted with approval by Miss Stebbing), and our only recourse seems to be to recognize these two meanings of logic. Logic may be developed into a science of pure form, but when so developed it becomes logistic, another matter. The relation of logistic to logic is the problem of a later context. Here we need only point out the relation of language to logic is concerned with logic in its first meaning.

The second tendency is in the opposite direction—in the direction of the identification of logic with epistemology and philosophy. An illustration of this tendency is given in the definition of C. D. Broad: "Logic is simply the most fundamental part of critical philosophy, the part which deals with the most general beliefs which are the connective tissue of knowledge."[3] Here again those who define logic in this way should be equally clear that they are not meaning by logic the same thing as those who define logic as analysis and criticism of thought. This is not to deny that the development of logic leads into the problems of critical philosophy. It merely denies its identity

---

[1] L. S. Stebbing, *A Modern Introduction to Logic*, p. 476.
[2] F. P. Ramsey, *Proc. London Mathematical Assoc.*, Series 2, Vol. 25, Part 6, p. 353a.
[3] C. D. Broad, *Scientific Thought*, Introduction.

with such a philosophy. The "most general and pervasive of all concepts, and those fundamental beliefs which are the connective tissue of knowledge," of which Professor Broad speaks, belong to what I shall later describe as a *metalogical* sphere. The relation of the logical to the metalogical is defined in a later context.[1] Here we need only point out that "ordinary" logic, to use Kant's term, is not a "logic of truth," and that if we are to extend the notion to include the entire "connective tissue" of knowledge we shall have to call it philosophical logic to distinguish it from ordinary logic. In any case, the problems of language and knowledge are different from those of logic and language, and go far beyond them.

This is not the place to argue these questions—to determine whether these special definitions of logic are justified or not. It is, however, desirable in this context to point out that acceptance of either of these views of logic seems to have far-reaching consequences for the solution of our present problem. It would seem, for instance, that if logic is the science of pure form, its normative function would be distinctly limited. It must assume that terms have meaning and that propositions have sense; it could not determine that meaning and that sense. It could not pronounce upon either the meaningfulness or truth of language; that would be a *meta*-logical question. On this view, a proposal to overcome metaphysics by a logical analysis of language would be a contradiction in terms. On the other hand it seems equally clear that a logic identified with critical philosophy, if it should exercise this critique, could do so not because it is logic, but because it is philosophy. In other words, such a logic would itself be metalogical or metaphysical in character. The fundamental beliefs which are the connective tissue of knowledge are themselves not logically demonstrable. Nor are they empirically verifiable. The question of the epistemological value of logic has no solution *in* logic—logic cannot test itself[2]— and by the same token the epistemological value of language cannot be tested by logic. Here, too, a proposal to overcome metaphysics by a logical analysis of language would be really the attempt to overcome one metaphysics by another.

[1] Chapter VIII, pp. 330 ff.
[2] See on this point C. I. Lewis, "Logic and Pragmatism," in *Contemporary American Philosophy*, Vol. II, pp. 41 ff.

III

MEANING AND THE PROBLEM OF LANGUAGE AND LOGIC

A

It seems quite clear then, from our examination of these definitions and conceptions of logic, that we shall get little help from them towards the solution of our special problem. I propose therefore to approach the problem in a sense *de novo*. Going back to out initial definition of logic as the science of reflective thinking, and assuming the essential inseparability of thought and language—*die Worthaftigkeit des Denkens*—let us seek as our starting-point an element common to both language and logic and proceed from this point. This common element we shall find in the notion of *meaning*. The problem then is the relation of logical meaning to linguistic meaning. We have already developed certain basal notions regarding linguistic meaning. Let us now examine the notion of logical meaning.

B

Logic as a Science of Meaning

Logic has, indeed, often been defined as a science that deals with meanings—as the science of inference or of inferential meaning. As defined by A. E. Taylor, logic is the science of implicational meaning.[1] We shall presently examine more closely this notion of logic as concerned with *inferential or implicational meaning*. Here I wish to emphasize merely the notion of logic as a science of meaning and the general implications of such a definition.

There are two philosophers who have so defined logic whose statements on this question are worth consideration at this point. "It is evident," writes Husserl, "that logic must be knowledge of meanings as such, of their essential kinds and differences as well as of the laws purely grounded in them." It is evident, according to him, for the reason that "pure logic, wherever it deals with concepts, judgments, conclusions, has in fact to do exclusively with these ideal unities which we here

[1] A. E. Taylor, *The Faith of a Moralist*, Vol. I, Chapter II.

call meanings."[1] Rickert also defines logic as a science of meanings. Logic, he tells us, "deals neither with existents, physical or mental, nor with subsistent universals, but rather with the problem as to what values must be acknowledged in case any answers to the question, what is or is not, what is true or not true, shall have any meaning whatever."[2] The difference in philosophical point of view presupposed by these two statements should not hide from us the important common element.[3]

I think that we may accept this concept of logic as a science of meanings. We shall have to differentiate between logical meaning and other kinds of meanings. Logic, while a science of meanings, does not deal with all types of meanings. This we shall attempt presently to do. In the meantime an illustration will serve to make our point clear. A commonly accepted thesis of present-day logic is that the same verbal form may have different logical meanings, and that a fundamental source of error in traditional logic has been the failure to distinguish these meanings. If then we shall be able to formulate an adequate notion of logical meaning, we shall perhaps find the key to the solution of our general problem.

That the subject matter of logic is meanings may be seen from another angle. Logic is frequently defined as the science of symbols. For Bergson "it is the complete set of rules that must be followed in using symbols." For Mr. Russell, "Logic is concerned with the conditions of accurate symbolism." Now the relation of a sign or symbol to the thing symbolized, or for which it "stands," is a relation of meaning. This conception of logic as a science of symbols is an important one and with certain limitations may be accepted. It is true, as we shall see, that the problem of symbols and their meaning is one that transcends logic. We shall see also that the notion of symbol, as used in logistic or symbolic logic proper, applies only to substitutional symbols or signs, and that logistic itself is but a

---

[1] *Logische Untersuchungen*, II, 1, p. 916.
[2] *Der Gegenstand der Erkentniss*, fourth and fifth editions, 1921, Chapter IV, especially Sections 3, 4, 5.
[3] The differences, which are obvious, turn on the question as to whether meaning always presupposes values and their acknowledgment, a problem already considered in Chapter III. In Chapter III of *The Intelligible World* I have argued for a position similar to that of Rickert. Decision on this point is not necessary for our present purpose.

limited aspect of logic. Nevertheless the definition of logic as a science of symbols brings out an important aspect and indicates clearly that meaning is the central notion in logic.

C

The Concept of Logical Meaning: Its Differentia

Logic we may define then as a science of meanings. It is quite clear, however, that it does not include in its province all kinds of meanings. Evidently an entire range of meanings falls outside the logical. The intrinsic meanings of things, both practical and aesthetic, the intrinsic expressiveness of words, the entire field of emotive and intuitive meanings analysed and described in Chapter IV, are a-logical in character, and it is obviously the relation of these a-logical meanings to the logical that constitutes one of the most important problems of cognition and of the philosophy of language.

What, then, is the *differentia* of logical meaning?—for precisely that *differentia* is the important thing. Only *that* meaning can be properly called logical, I think, into which the element of implication and inference enters. Logic we have seen defined as the science of implicational or inferential meaning—and this definition, following as it does from the definition of logic as the science of reflective thinking, is, I think, determinative of the limits of logic and of logical meaning. "It is not the object of logic," writes De Morgan, "to determine whether conclusions are true or false; but whether what are asserted as conclusions are conclusions." This limitation of logical meaning is all important. For it follows—and I shall maintain this thesis throughout—that only those aspects of the meanings of words and sentences which are necessary for the relations of implication and for inference come properly within the province of logic and logical analysis. All other meanings are for logic irrelevant and beyond its competence.

To say that logic deals with implicational meaning is the same thing as saying that it is concerned with conceptual meaning. On the one hand, only concepts—not percepts—contain any implicit elements. It is true that perceptual meaning is already determined by language and anything that is named is to that degree universalized, but the intuitive universal, although the basis of the concept, is itself not conceptual. Implication and logical meaning begin only with the concept.[1] On the other hand, it is equally true that wherever there is conceptual meaning there is implicational meaning. The formation of the concept is itself always a function of judgment, and the explication of the concept constitutes an assertion or proposition.

Logic, then, is quite evidently engaged, at least primarily, with the kind of meaning described as conceptual. Any expression where the character of the logical appears has the concept or universal in it as subject or predicate or both—e.g. Socrates is mortal, man is a thinking animal. It is for this reason that, as Cassirer says, "the problem of the formation of concepts marks the point at which logic and the philosophy of language first touch each other, that point indeed at which they disclose their inseparable character." "All *logical analysis* of concepts," he adds, "seems to lead in the end to a point at which the examination of concepts passes over into that of words and names. From this point of view logic might be defined as the science or doctrine of the concept and its meaning."[2]

Any expression in which the character of the logical appears has the concept or universal in it as subject or predicate or both. But not every expression in which the universal appears has the character of the logical. The universal is present in some form wherever there is any linguistic expression whatever, but it is not necessarily of a logical character in the sense of our definition. From the point of view of language we may say, with Sapir, that thought is the highest latent or potential content of speech that is obtained by interpreting each of the elements in the flow of language as possessed of its fullest conceptual value. Logical form is potential in all speech, but only potential. It is only when this potential element is made explicit in inference that we have logical meaning.

Logical meaning, or the conceptual meaning demanded by logic, is then a very definite notion. The character of this meaning is that it must be precise and clear, or be potentially so, and must remain unaltered throughout any reasoning in which it occurs. But, as Lewis rightly says, "no other types of

[1] See Chapter III, pp. 116 ff.   [2] E. Cassirer, *op. cit.*, Vol. I, pp. 244 ff.

D

Logical Meaning and Denotation

It may be accepted then that wherever there is conceptual meaning there is logical meaning or potential logical meaning. Can we define logical meaning more accurately by relating it to specific functions of the concept? One view of logic does so by identifying logical meaning with the denotative function of the concept. Let us examine this theory of logical meaning. "To have meaning," it is said, "is a notion confusedly compounded of psychological and logical elements. *Words* all have meaning in the simple sense that they are symbols which stand for something other than themselves. . . . Thus meaning, in the sense that all words have meaning (psychological), is irrelevant to logic. But such concepts as *a man* have meaning in another sense; they are, so to speak, symbolic in their own logical nature because they have the property which I call denoting. . . . That is to say, when *a man* occurs in a proposition (e.g. I met a man in the street), the proposition is not about the concept *a man* but about something quite different, some actual biped denoted by the concept. Thus concepts of this kind have meaning in a non-psychological sense."[2] This definition of the "logical element" in the total notion of meaning is in every way of outstanding importance. It underlies, as we shall see, the entire conception of logical analysis of language which we are about to examine and the critique of logic upon language which is in consequence exercised. It is important to determine the truth of this notion.

Certainly not all logicians would agree that logical meaning is identical with denotation. Thus Frege tells us, "A word ordinarily stands for its indication. If we wish to speak of its meaning we must use inverted commas or some such device. The indication of a proper noun is the object which it indicates.

---

[1] C. I. Lewis, *Mind and the World Order*, pp. 68 ff.
[2] B. Russell, *Principles of Mathematics*, p. 47. (Published by George Allen & Unwin Ltd.)

The presentation which goes with it, he admits, is quite subjective (psychological). But, between the two lies the meaning which is not subjective and not objective. A proper noun expresses its meaning and indicates its indication." In other words objects are *what* we mean by concepts but the *meaning* of the concepts is something else again.[1] The question at issue is whether this "meaning" is part of the logical meaning of the concept. This meaning, which is other than indication and not identical with the psychological or subjective, is the universal which, as we have seen, as intuitive universal is not only present in the earliest levels of language and the condition of all communication, but is the basis of the conceptual universal and of all predication. Is it the condition of implicational meaning? This is equivalent to the question of whether a purely denotative logic is possible, or whether logical nominalism is possible. We shall consider this problem later and our answer will be in the negative. Here we shall simply assert that reference to the universal is as much an element in logical meaning as reference to the particular.

Reverting then to the illustration from which our analysis started, we may say that it is indeed true that when "a man" occurs in a proposition the proposition is about "some actual biped," some individual, but it is not clear that it is not also about the universal man for which the concept also stands. As we said in an earlier connection, we cannot look at a tall man and give the results of that looking in words without conceiving the tall man as *a man*. Nor can we do so without conceiving him as tall. In other words, the logical meaning includes the connotation as well as the denotation of the concept. In the second place, logical meaning is implicational meaning. Now there seems to be a correlation between the cognition of the implicative significance of a proposition and the validity of the proposition as correspondent with a designated item of being. A horse is one thing to an Eskimo, who has never seen one, and another to a farmer, and another to a biologist, and another to a biologist who is also a philosopher. As the connotation of a concept becomes more complete, the value of the reference of the propositions involving the concept becomes more adequate. In other words, the denotation of a concept (and

---

[1] See Ogden and Richards, *op. cit.*, pp. 273-74.

the correspondence of the proposition containing it) is not one thing and its connotation (and coherence with the whole of meaning) another thing. The notion that they differ arises from a lack of recognition of the fact that a proposition apart from discourse is nothing. Coherence or implication and correspondence or denotation are in true propositions identical. In sum, implicational meaning which is logical meaning does not well consort with a concept of logical meaning which defines it wholly in terms of denotation.

A further point is of importance in this connection. It concerns the question of the nature of the distinction between the "logical element" in the total meaning situation and the other elements. All meaning, other than logical, however logical meaning be conceived, is frequently, as in the passage quoted, included in the class psychological meaning. This is unfortunate from every angle; is, in fact, to do very much less than justice to the meaning notion. In an earlier context we distinguished between logical and psychological analysis of meaning, but we also distinguished phenomenological analysis from both, a distinction which will be of increasing importance throughout this chapter. Meaning in the non-logical sense is not identical with psychological meaning. We shall therefore speak of logical and extra-logical elements in meaning, leaving the extra-logical element to be later determined. With respect to language we shall speak of logical and metalogical meanings of words and sentences.

E

"Logical Analysis" of Language. Definition of Logical Analysis

With the above conception of logical meaning and of its relation to linguistic meaning before us, it is now possible to define more accurately the notion of logical analysis of language and to distinguish it from other forms of analysis, as, for instance, the phenomenological analysis of an earlier chapter. But first a word about the notion of logical analysis in general.

It is a quite common error to suppose that logical analysis is identical with "real" analysis, whereas they are two quite different things. Logical analysis is analysis of concepts, not of things. Moreover, if our position regarding logical meaning is correct, it is analysis of concepts only with reference to relations of implication and the reasoning or inference based upon these relations. Now logical analysis of *language* is no more an exhaustive *real* analysis of language as a totality—as discourse (or as medium for meaningful, intelligible communication)—than it is real analysis of anything else. It is, if our position has been sound, concerned with *the analysis of words and sentences only in so far as they occur as terms in propositions and as propositions in reasoning*, or only in so far as they support *logical* meaning. It follows that logical analysis cannot take the place of phenomenological analysis, which is concerned with language in its primary functions as speech and communication. Indeed, logical analysis presupposes phenomenological for, in the last analysis, a proposition apart from discourse is nothing. Nor can logical analysis legislate out of existence these other meanings. It simply means that there are other meanings. The validity of these other meanings is not a logical problem but, in our terms, metalogical. There are metalogical problems of language.

This limitation of logical analysis on the basis of a limitation of logical meaning is of great importance for our present problem and for the entire philosophy of language. It is true that wherever there is speech there is the universal and therefore potential logic and logical meaning. Logical form is so woven into our speech—and even into the play of our thoughts (which are not ultimately separable from expression and language)—that it is impossible to utter a phrase or indeed to recall to the mind past or future experience without throwing them into forms we call logical. Logic is therefore a condition, not only of intelligibility, but of intelligible expression. But this does not exclude the fact that speech has other meanings than the logical, and language other norms than those determined by the logical ideal of language. Logic is the necessary, but not the sufficient, condition of intelligibility. Logic is part of discourse, for it is concerned with discursive reasoning, but unless logic is defined so broadly as to make it identical with philosophy, intelligible discourse involves other meanings than the logical, and these no logical analysis can legislate out of existence.

IV

LINGUISTIC MEANING AND LOGICAL MEANING. THE "ILLOGICALITY" OF LANGUAGE

A

Meaning is, then, the point at which logic and language meet, the common notion which provides us with a standpoint from which we can understand the problems which arise in connection with the relations of logic and language.

The traditional view on this question is quite clear and definite. It may be stated thus. Language and thought are inseparable. Logical meaning is developed linguistic meaning. Its underlying assumption is the postulate of the potentiality of logical form in natural language. This traditional position was well expressed by John Stuart Mill in his St. Andrews address (1867), "Grammar is the most elementary part of logic. . . . The structure of every sentence is a lesson in logic." In the eighteenth century it was customary to talk of a philosophical or natural grammar which was supposed to be common to all languages, or a kind of common denominator to which all the particular grammars of individual languages could be reduced. The well-known exceptions in every language were called *idiotisms*. It was natural therefore to suppose that this universal grammar was a part of human reason and therefore the key to rational or logical discourse.

In recent decades this view has been questioned from all sides. On the linguistic side the tendency has been, as we have seen, to emphasize the diversity of human speech and to question the existence of any universal grammar. "A universal grammar seems," as Steinthal says, "no more conceivable than a universal plant or animal." Modern linguistics, while recognizing the general truth of the variability of language, yet tends to take a less sceptical position. We found it justifiable to say that while languages do display a variety of formal grammatical patterns, nevertheless when language is conceived as meaning, we find basal and inescapable forms or categories common to all languages and we may in a certain sense speak of universal parts of speech.[1]

[1] Chapter II, pp. 87 ff.

On the logical side the attack on the traditional view has been no less vigorous. In principle it denies the potentiality of logical form in natural language. The structure of every sentence is not "a lesson in logic," for the illogicality of grammar is its main thesis. Many verbal forms prove on analysis (logical analysis) to mean something quite other than at first appears. Many have no logical meaning at all. Apparent subjects of discourse are not always real subjects and many apparent propositions are not real propositions. In sum, that which we have described in a preceding chapter as the "natural tendencies of language" often lead to error and to the verbalism of a false metaphysics.

B

The "New Logic." The Illogicality of Language

The "new logic" deplores the tendencies of language as regards both vocabulary and syntax, the chief object of attack being, of course, the so-called subject-predicate logic with its substance-attribute metaphysic. The essentials of that attack are well stated in an article by Mr. Bertrand Russell entitled "Logical Atomism,"[1] and in presenting it we shall follow more or less his statement. But it is in principle the same attack, both in method and in assumptions and consequences, as that of Carnap and the entire Vienna School. By following out the lines of this critique, by examining both its premises and conclusions, it will be possible to see most clearly what the real problems of language and logic are and, as we shall hope, to form a valid theory of their relations.

There are, we saw, three main points at which problems of language arise; namely, (*a*) in connection with vocabulary and the doctrine of terms; (*b*) syntax and the doctrine of propositions (including the question of the existential import of propositions); and (*c*) the doctrine of inference and implicational meaning. At all three points the "new" logic finds reason to attack the "old" and in every case problems of language are involved. We shall proceed then in this order, beginning with the problem of vocabulary and the doctrine of terms.

[1] Bertrand Russell, "Logical Atomism," in *Contemporary British Philosophy*, First series.

V

VOCABULARY: THE DOCTRINE OF TERMS. THE FALLACIES OF VERBALISM

A

Modern logic or logistic deplores, then, all the natural tendencies of language, and, first of all, these tendencies as regards vocabulary. It turns its attention to the traditional doctrine of terms, more specifically to the subject of the proposition. The primal function of language is, as we have seen, *naming* (Chapter IV). But the naming of "things" is, it is held, permeated by an all-pervasive error. "We suppose, for instance, that there is a more or less persistent being called Socrates because the same name is applied to a series of occurrences which we are led to regard as the appearances of this one thing. Moreover, as language becomes more mobile and abstract, new entities enter into our thought—those represented by universals. Many of these abstract words at least do not stand for single entities, but the tendency of language is to assume that they do and logic *that trusts to language in any degree* (italics mine) is likely to lead to the verbalism of a false metaphysics."[1] The thesis embodied in this paragraph is a special case of the more general assertion of the divergence of linguistic and logical meaning. Natural language, when subjected to logical analysis, is seen to be permeated with two errors, inherent in the *naming function* as such, which we may describe as the fallacy of pseudosimplicity and the fallacy of verbalism, connected respectively with the singular and the universal terms. Let us consider them in order.

B

The Singular Term

The singular term used in the above illustration is a grammatical proper name (as distinguished from what is called a logical proper name).[2] In the use of this name it is supposed, or im-

[1] Bertrand Russell, *op. cit.*, pp. 367 ff. [2] See L. S. Stebbing, *op. cit.*, p. 25.

plied, that it refers to a more or less persistent being. This is part of its linguistic meaning, but not necessarily part of its logical meaning. Therefore, on the assumption of the primacy of logic over linguistic, logic may here exercise its right to a critical analysis of language. It is evident that in this clash of linguistic and logical meaning we have full justification for our approach to the problem of this chapter through the notion of meaning. The "fallacy" here involved we may describe as that of *pseudo-simplicity*. "Logical analysis" discloses this fallacy, for it shows that proper nouns and singular terms do not refer to simples but to complexes. What, then, shall we say to this?

In the first place, I think it may be said with certainty that logical analysis does not disclose a pseudo-simplicity, but only ambiguous simplicity. In one context "Socrates" is simple, in another not. In the practical context, moral and political, Socrates is a persistent being; in the physiological context he is not; he is a complex of elements. To describe it as pseudo-simplicity is to beg the entire question. It begs the question, for it assumes that only one of these meanings is the "proper" meaning, and that is possible only by giving prior rights to the physical.[1] The distinction made between ambiguous- and pseudo-simplicity indicates precisely the limits of the logical analysis of terms. Logical analysis can determine only the logical meaning of a term and that, we have seen, is limited to determining *whether it remains unaltered in any reasoning in which it may occur*. It is then with ambiguous simplicity that logic is alone concerned. On what grounds, then, can any type of simplicity be called false simplicity? Certainly not on logical grounds. Logic assumes that terms have meaning but cannot determine that meaning. The phenomenological analysis of meaning shows that the primordial parts of speech have an intuitive meaning—an intrinsic expressiveness—and that the intuitive meaning of the noun includes the meaning of ideal unity or individuality. This was especially evident in our discussion of the question of the connotation of proper nouns.[2] In other words, the linguistic meaning of Socrates includes the idea of simplicity in certain contexts, and logical analysis cannot legislate that meaning out of existence.

Let it be clearly understood that the question here is not

[1] Chapter IV, p. 205 f.   [2] Chapter IV, p. 151 f.

whether Socrates *is* or *is not* a persistent being. It may well be that in certain universes of discourse he is not, and that to this universe should be given the prior rights. The point is that this is a metalogical question and is wholly outside the province of logic.

C

Endless Naming: Universals

The second point at which this critique of the linguistic tendencies of vocabulary is exercised is in connection with the "new entities" which enter into our thought and are represented by universals or abstract concepts. "Many of these words, at least, do not stand for single entities, but the tendency of language is to assume that they do." On this tendency logic must exercise a drastic analysis and criticism.

The primordial elements of language are three categories of words—substantives, adjectives, and verbs. All these three parts of speech are in a sense *names*, names for aspects of reality. Moreover, as we have seen, in Chapter V, the very essence of language is endless naming, a continuous naming which takes place through name transference. It is, accordingly, the natural tendency of language to assume that its names refer to something. Part of their linguistic meaning *is* this reference. In the very use of these names in discourse it is implied that such reference is there. It is precisely this, however, against which logical analysis is supposed to raise its *caveat*, and the all-pervasive error it discloses is that of empty verbalism.

This problem has already been raised in other contexts, in connection both with the problem of the phenomenology of linguistic meaning and the normative problem of language. Here we are to consider it from the standpoint of logic—and its critique of natural language. This critique is exercised both on the universal as the subject of discourse and the predicate in discourse, both upon that which is talked about and that which is said about it. Let us consider them separately.

According to one of the main principles of our philosophy of language, there is no use of language which is not indicative. In the words of Plato, to be significant at all an utterance must always be directly or indirectly an assertion about what is. We cannot talk about what is not. Now we do talk continually about universals. In earlier studies we found that everything denoted by language is universalized. Even the primitive verbal situation, the sentence word, where the word is dependent upon the perceptual context, contains an element of universality. The transition from this primitive form to more independent and complete predication marks a step to a new level of universality. Finally a step is reached in the process when speech turns back on itself, so to speak, and transforms the original predicate into a subject of further discourse, or uses the noun to denote a class as such and not a particular member.[1] Substantives, adjectives, verbs may all be the subjects of discourse. This is possible for the reason that, as we have seen in our phenomenological analysis of language, all three have an *intuitive content*, and it is about this content that we are talking.[2] The scientist may speak of the "falling of a body," the poet may say "parting is such sweet sorrow," and in both cases alike the discourse is meaningful because their talk is about intuitive universals present in the first determinations of language. The condition of meaningful discourse is the assumption of their reality in some sense.

No less certainly do we use these universals as predicates in discourse *as though* these universals were entities. When we say all soldiers are brave, what do we mean? We mean linguistically (and also by Aristotelian logic, which exploits the natural tendencies of language), that there is a quality, bravery, which appears, so to speak, incarnate in each and every soldier, provided the statement is true. Soldiers are members of a class; they are alike and "bravery must shine out of them as the colour shines out of the rose." We also mean that these qualities, the redness of the rose or the bravery of the soldier, are objects of an intuition or *Erlebniss*. These are, as we have seen, intuitive meanings of our words, as contrasted with the conceptual meaning.[2] Now it is against these meanings that logic and "logical analysis" are supposed to raise their protest. When logically analysed, the universal, both as the subject of discourse and as predicate in discourse, is found to be a mere name for a collection of particulars. The "as ifs" which, so to speak, constitute the connective tissue of our discourse, are *really* "as

[1] Chapter III, p. 117 f.   [2] Chapter IV, p. 155 f.

ifs" in the sense of being fictional. What shall we say to this application of logical analysis?

As in our discussion of the preceding case, the proper name, it is all important that we shall be clear as to just what the problem here is. It is not the question of whether universals "exist" or, if so, in what sense they exist. That is a metalogical problem. It is here, as before, a question whether logical analysis can answer that question and therefore tell us how we ought to talk, or, otherwise expressed, tell us whether we should or should not trust language and its natural tendencies. Surely on any proper view of logical analysis and its function it cannot. So much follows directly from our general position regarding the relation of logical to linguistic meaning. Logical analysis cannot legislate the intuitive meanings of words out of existence. This general position is, however, greatly strengthened by a consideration of the consequences of such a critique of vocabulary as we have been considering. To these consequences we shall now turn.

D

Neo-nominalism. The Paralysis of Speech

The consequences of this critique of language in its aspect of naming or vocabulary are far-reaching. They lead, as has been apparent, to a thoroughgoing nominalism, not only with respect to the universal but also with regard to the individual. This nominalism we have described as Neo-nominalism,[1] and an examination of it is reserved for the next chapter to which it properly belongs.[2] Here we are interested in it only in so far as it concerns the relations of linguistic to logical meaning.

Now that such a critique should necessarily lead to nominalism is, of course, of itself no proof of the unjustifiable character of the critique. Nominalism, both of the universal and of the individual, may be a true doctrine of terms. Again, the question of nominalism as it bears on the problem of language is different in a sense from the problem of nominalism in logic itself. The question may indeed be raised whether a nominalistic logic is

---
[1] Chapter I, p. 35 f.   [2] Chapter VIII, pp. 366 ff.

possible, whether logic retains its significance on nominalistic presuppositions. If that question should be answered in the negative, the logical analysis of language which leads to nominalism would be self-defeating. This is a question we shall consider in a later context. Here the problem is solely the consequences of this critique for intelligible discourse. These we shall describe as the paralysis of speech.

These consequences have been stated admirably by Mr. Russell: "I say, I sit at my table. I *ought* not say that. What I ought to say is this: One of a certain string of events causally connected in the sort of way that makes the whole series what is *called* (italics mine) a 'person' has a certain spatial relation to one of another string of events causally connected with each other in a different way and having a spatial configuration of the sort denoted by the word 'table.' I do not say so, because life is too short; but that is what I should say if I were a true philosopher." We should be grateful to Mr. Russell not only for his insight into the consequences of this standpoint but for the candour with which he accepts them. The consequences are wholly apparent. In any such assertion as "I sit at my table," both singular and universal terms are merely names for strings or collections of atomic events. I *ought*, therefore, to use a language that corresponds to these facts. I cannot use such a language (life is too short). I must either be silent or speak falsely. If, however, I should try to speak truly, if I should say what a true philosopher would say, a language of such complication would be necessary as to paralyse all communication. This paralysis of speech, as I shall call it, is the necessary consequence of this nominalism. He who speaks at all—if he would speak intelligibly—must necessarily be a "realist."

The problem here raised belongs, to be sure, to the metalogical rather than the logical problems of language and will be considered more fully later; here it is merely a question of the application of logical analysis to vocabulary. The natural tendencies of vocabulary which are here criticized are, however, criticized precisely because trust in such tendencies is likely to lead to the verbalism of a false metaphysics, and this aspect of the question cannot, even in the present context, be wholly ignored.

These natural tendencies of vocabulary embody the postulate of the identity of the thing with itself as the condition of intelligible discourse. Out of this has arisen a "natural metaphysic" which, among other characters, has as a fundamental category that of substance. It is this substance-attribute metaphysic which is said to be erroneous. Now the question of the erroneous character of such a metaphysic cannot be determined by logic and logical analysis—that is precisely our main point—it is a metalogical problem; but it is possible to affirm that the integrity of the thing is the condition of intelligible discourse, and that to extrude this notion or category in every form is to paralyse speech and to stultify discourse. It is true that, when applied to the temporal (when it is schematized, to use Kant's term), it becomes the notion of the permanent amid the changing. It is true also that, when so applied, the notion of permanence varies greatly and by reason of this wide variation raises difficulties and problems. We speak of a sneeze, of a cloud or of a mountain and, by virtue of so speaking of them, postulate their integrity as things. A sneeze is doubtless a thing in a different way from that in which the mountain is a thing. In principle, however, there is no reason why there should not be many kinds of individuals and substances, and so far as the fundamental notion is concerned the period of duration seems irrelevant. Be this as it may, the point is that without this category embodied in natural language, experience cannot be intelligibly expressed and communicated. Kant would say that without it empirical knowledge is impossible. Since on our view, as we shall presently see,[1] knowledge and expression are inseparable, it is even more significant to say that without it intelligible expression and communication are impossible.

But the more general question, of which this is only a specific aspect, is the question of the function of logical analysis in determining valid linguistic meaning so far as concerns vocabulary. The denial of its competence here is but a special case of our general conception of the relation of logic to language. It may be said, of course, that the type of critique we have been here examining proceeds from a specific logical theory, namely, that of logical atomism, a theory which is in itself really metaphysical, and that our strictures do not

[1] Chapter VIII, pp. 347 ff.

necessarily apply to all forms of logical analysis. This is, however, I think, not the case.

VI

SYNTAX AND THE DOCTRINE OF PROPOSITIONS. THE ILLOGICALITY OF GRAMMAR

A

Modern logic deplores, then, the tendencies of language as regards vocabulary. But if the influence of these tendencies on logic and philosophy is vicious, even more deplorable is the influence of syntax.

Syntax has to do with linguistic form. The unit of syntax is the sentence. The word, as we have seen, has "reality" only in the sentence. Even where single words are used they are "sentence words" and their meaning is determined by their function in the sentence. Now the fundamental syntax form is the subject-predicate form. This springs out of the very nature of discourse; there must be something to talk about and something to say of it. On the assumption of traditional logic, that "grammar is the most elementary part of logic and that the structure of every sentence is a lesson in logic," it was held that syntactical form and logical form are in principle identical. To put a sentence into logical form was to put it into the subject-predicate form. Almost any proposition *can* be put into the form in which it has a subject and predicate and is connected by a copula. It was assumed that since this can be done, it should be done and, in fact, it was done—with disastrous consequences.[1]

[1] The problem of the relation of logical to syntactical meaning raises questions as important as they are difficult.

The difficulty arises out of uncertainty as to the relation of syntax to logic. On the one hand, it is precisely the divergence of logical and syntactical meaning which causes the modern logician to deplore the influence of syntax and to credit to its malign influence the development of an "erroneous metaphysic." On the other hand, "logical analysis" is said to show that certain propositions (pre-eminently metaphysical) are pseudo-sentences or contrary to the syntax of our language, syntax and logic apparently being taken here as identical. I shall not attempt here to argue the question thus raised, but merely state my own position, to be developed more fully later. Logic and syntax are, I should maintain, not identical. Syntax is the larger conception of which logic is a subordinate notion, just as discourse is the larger universe to which logic is subordinate. Syntax, as the word suggests, has to do with the rules for connecting words in meaningful communication; logic with the rules for connecting terms for the determination

LANGUAGE AND LOGIC

These consequences are two-fold: (1) the disguising and frequent distortion of the true *logical* meaning of the proposition, and (2) resulting in a false metaphysic, namely the substance--attribute metaphysic. It is with the first of these that we are primarily concerned.

It is obvious that we have here a second case of our general problem of the relation of logical to linguistic meaning. As in the case of problems of vocabulary, they are held to be divergent and, on the assumption of the primacy of logical meaning, logic may exercise its critique on language. This critique may be considered under the following heads: (*a*) the denial on the part of modern logic of the identity of logical form with the linguistic or subject-predicate form, and the consequent analysis of other types of propositions, especially relational. Closely connected with this is the question of the possible reduction of the syntactical subject-predicate form to the relational—in other words, the question of a relational logic. (*b*) The assertion that many propositions of the subject-predicate form are not *real*, but only *apparent*; in other words, the distinction between real and apparent propositions. Closely connected with this is the problem of the nature of descriptions. (*c*) Finally, there is the question of the existential import of propositions and the problem of the copula. Closely connected with this is the question of the competence of logical analysis to determine the existential import of propositions; in other words, to determine the relation of language to reality. Here again we are concerned with these special problems of logic only in so far as they bear upon our general problem of the relation of logic to language. There are many aspects important for the science of logic which we must ignore.

B

The Fundamental Error of Traditional Logic. Insufficient Analysis

The fundamental error of traditional logic, based upon the natural tendencies of language, is that it neglected every form of implicational meaning. As we shall see (Chapter XIII, p. 647 f.) syntactical meaning may be present when logical meaning is absent or at a minimum. It is true that wherever there is speech there is potential logical form, that it is impossible to utter a phrase without throwing it into forms we call logical, but syntactical and logical meaning may be clearly differentiated.

of proposition except the subject-predicate form. Its radical defect lay in insufficient analysis and therefore in oversimplification of propositions. Instead of one form there is really a plurality of forms. This over-simplification consists in the limitation of the propositional form to two constituents and to one form of combination. A more penetrating analysis discloses other types of propositions which cannot be reduced to this form.[1]

One of the first refinements of analysis was that instituted by Frege and Peano. "Socrates is wise" is of the subject-predicate form, but the proposition "Socrates is a philosopher," although of the same verbal form, has a different logical meaning. It is a class membership proposition. Analysis reveals further a second type of proposition which is different from the subject-predicate form, the so-called relational propositions. They are the type of propositions constitutive of mathematical science, as, for instance, "A is greater than B." Here we find by analysis that we have two terms, A and B, instead of the single subject term of the ordinary type. In the language of mathematical logic these two terms are the constituents and "greater than" is an expression of relation between them.

The assumption underlying this "logical analysis" and critique is again the divergence of linguistic and logical meaning —the difference between verbal form and logical meaning. Not every sentence expresses or supports a proposition,[2] and the linguistic meaning of the sentence *in discourse* and of the proposition *for discursive reasoning* may differ. Now there seems to be no reason to deny either the general fact of divergence or the truth of the refinements of analysis described above. The question is rather the significance of this divergence and the implications of this analysis. For the purpose of logic—for the purpose, namely, of determining implicational or inferential meaning—such analysis may be of the utmost importance. But the question still remains whether such analysis invalidates

---

[1] L. S. Stebbing, *op. cit.*, p. 159.

[2] The question of the *differentia* of sentence and proposition is here raised. It is commonly said that "a proposition is anything that is believed, disbelieved, doubted or supposed." Viewed merely grammatically there are perhaps sentences of which this character is not true. But as an element of real speech or discourse, every sentence has this character. The distinction between sentence and proposition tends thus to collapse. This question will be discussed in a later context.

the prelogical or metalogical meanings of language. This must of course in principle be denied *if* our general view of the relation of logic to language is sound. Logic, we have said, assumes that terms have *meaning* but cannot determine that meaning. We may now say that logic assumes that propositions have *sense*, but cannot determine that sense. Let us see what this general statement means in detail.

The primary "sense" of a proposition is that it is an assertion —an assertion about something, and this assertion predicates something of the subject. A proposition apart from discourse is nothing. From the standpoint of discourse the subject-predicate proposition is the basal form. The fact that for certain purposes of logic this "finer analysis" of propositions is both possible and desirable in no way conflicts with the fact that the primary sense of all propositions is that they are predication of something about something. The fact that when A is west of B and B is west of C, then A will be west of C, is interesting and important, but in no way conflicts with the fact that "west of B" is as much a predicate of A as "red" is a predicate of "rose." That the latter is a simple quality and the former a spatial relation does not affect their common similarity of inhering as predicates in a subject.[1] The question may indeed be raised whether even from the standpoint of logic itself, the Aristotelian logic is impugned by a more specific logic of relations. Our present point is merely that such logical analysis cannot impugn the primary linguistic meanings of discourse or legislate them out of existence.

The question just raised—namely whether even from the standpoint of logic itself, the subject-predicate logic is impugned by a more specific logic of relations—is itself one of far-reaching implications. It involves the question of the possible reduction of all propositions to the relational type and the development of what is called a relational logic. Relational propositions, it is held, are vastly more fundamental and important than those of the subject-predicate type. The propositions of mathematics

[1] In W. E. Johnson's *Logic* relations are treated as a special kind of adjective and are called transitive adjectives in distinction from ordinary adjectives which are intransitive. The adjectival nature of relations is, he holds, apt to be obscured by the inclusion under relative terms of what are merely substantives defined by relational characterization. All that holds universally of adjectives, including the relation of determinates to their determinable, holds of relations also. (Chapter XII.)

are all of the relational form, and it was precisely the failure to do justice to these that led to the critique of traditional logic. May not logic itself be turned into a logic of relations and fused with mathematics?

Now it is important to be quite clear regarding the nature of the problems as here presented. It is not a question of whether a specific logic of relations can be developed; that is a problem within the technical field of logic itself. The problem is rather whether such a logic is at all what we mean by logic when it is defined as the science of reflective thinking. That we have seen reason to doubt. But the problem is further whether the Aristotelian subject-predicate logic is thereby robbed of its intrinsic validity, and whether such a logic of relations has the status of priority. It is this that, on the basis of the principles we have been maintaining, must be denied. The subject-predicate logic deals with relations common to all forms of statement; the more specific logic of relations with relations peculiar to some forms of statement; the latter cannot take the place of or invalidate the former.

On this point Professor F. S. C. Northrop has made some suggestive comments.[1] According to him, there seems to be no good reason why the basal notions of the two logics should not be combined. All forms are not relations between relata. There are some forms which are attributes of individual substances. Roughly speaking, the law of the macrocosm is the subject-predicate form, that of the microcosm the relational. Expressed in other terms, thought and discourse about the microcosm may well be in terms of mathematical relations, in a "language" which extrudes the notion of substance and cause, but thought and discourse about the macrocosm must inevitably be in subject-predicate terms and in the categories which these imply. Now I see no good reason why such a combination of the two logics is not both possible and necessary. But from the standpoint of our present discussion it is not merely a question of the two logics living together, but rather of priority and fundamental character. On this point there seems to be no question. Priority must be given to the subject-predicate form.[2]

---

[1] F. S. C. Northrop, *Science and First Principles*, p. 235.

[2] See on this point W. P. Montague, *Ways of Knowing*, p. 84. Speaking of the attack on Aristotelian logic, he writes: "When a man writes an arithmetic he

LANGUAGE AND LOGIC

All intelligible communication must, in the last analysis, be in the form of "natural" language, language made, if you will, for the macrocosm. The general grounds on which this thesis rests have been already developed in the last sections of the preceding chapter on *Intelligible Communication* in which this conception of priority was argued. Here it is necessary merely to make a special application. A specific logic of relations may indeed be developed for microcosmic analysis, but mathematical formulas must again be translated into language before they say anything. They merely operate; they say nothing.[1]

All this becomes of crucial importance when we come to the problems of the language of science and scientific symbolism. The notions of a relational logic are carried over into science, with the result that all categories except those of functional relation tend to be extruded. With this has also come a notion of "scientific intelligibility" which holds that "intelligibility in science consists exclusively in necessary connections; the fact is no longer isolated and is therefore intelligible." Whether this is an adequate conception of intelligibility, even in science, is a problem for later consideration and will be taken up in Chapter XI. Here we are concerned merely to indicate the relation of the present logical problem to the epistemological questions of science.

C

Apparent Propositions. The Theory of Descriptions

The radical defect of traditional logic was insufficient analysis. This insufficient analysis led, as we have seen, to the failure to recognize different propositional forms—other forms than the subject-predicate relation—and consequently to the distortion

cannot be criticized for not writing an algebra. And when a man writes a treatise on the relations common to all forms of statement, he should hardly be blamed for not treating of relations peculiar to some forms of statement. . . . Whether or not Aristotelean *metaphysics* is properly chargeable with neglecting the types of external quantitative relationship which modern science finds fruitful, it does not seem to me that the Aristotelean *logic* is impugned either in its intrinsic validity or in its status of *logical priority* (italics mine) to any more specific logic of relations." This entire problem is treated more fully in my *Intelligible World*, Chapter III, Section 9.

[1] Chapter XI, p. 523 f.

K*

of the meaning of many propositions. But there was, according to this position, another consequence—namely, the treatment as propositions of many forms of words that are not really propositions. We are thus led to our second point, the assertion, on the part of modern logic, that many apparent propositions are not real propositions. With this notion of apparent propositions we come to the heart of the problem of logic and language. It is at this point that "logical analysis" proposes to tell us what is meaningful and what is meaningless, to determine what uses of language lead to an "erroneous metaphysics," and indeed to condemn in the name of such analysis certain uses of language *in toto*. Let us examine "logical analysis" at this point.

Traditional logic assumed that all propositions are of the subject-predicate form. One of the first refinements of analysis was to show that the same verbal form might conceal divergent logical meanings. Thus though "Socrates is wise" and "Socrates is a philosopher" have the same verbal form, they have different logical meaings. A second step is taken when certain distinctions are made among propositions from the standpoint of their simple or composite character. This point is not only crucial from the standpoint of the relation of logic to language, but has led to far-reaching consequences for the entire philosophy of language—the relation of language to reality.

Let us consider a group of propositions such as the following:

> This is yellow.
> All lions are yellow.
> Some carnations are yellow.
> The man in the moon is yellow.

Now propositions such as "this is yellow" or "this is large" are said to be simple propositions. The others are compound or composite and may be analysed into simple propositions. These are sometimes called atomic propositions.[1] The question of the existence of atomic propositions is itself of importance, involving one of the most difficult questions of the relation of language to knowledge, but that is not the question we are

[1] The problem of atomic propositions raises the entire question of knowledge by "simple acquaintance." It assumes that there are propositions which are not descriptive propositions and therefore lack the bi-polar character of subject and predicate. This question really belongs to another context and will be discussed in the next chapter.

concerned with here; it is the problem of apparent propositions.

Of the four propositions distinguished, the first three are said to be real propositions, the fourth is only apparently a proposition. The form of words, "the man in the moon is yellow," is apparently a proposition but not actually. It has the same propositional form but, when logically analysed, its form is found to disguise the reality. Actually it has no application, refers to nothing, and is therefore not a proposition. The man in the moon is a composite proposition. Analysed into simple propositions, it becomes "this is the man in the moon" and "this is yellow." But there is no entity for which the "this" in the first "proposition" stands. It is therefore not a real proposition and the compound proposition of which it is a part is a pseudo-proposition. The subject of a logical proposition must be an empirically verifiable existent. In other words, the form of words, "the man in the moon is yellow," says something linguistically, otherwise it would not be spoken; logically, it says nothing.[1]

The implications of this doctrine are obviously far-reaching. All such assertions as "Hamlet was mad," "a centaur is a fiction of the poets," etc., are pseudo-propositions. But on the basis of this analysis, many other apparent propositions become pseudo-propositions. "The soul is immortal," "God is just," "the world had a beginning"—in fact, all the types of metaphysical propositions dealt with by Kant in the transcendental dialectic are pseudo-propositions, and have no logical meaning. The question of pseudo-propositions involves, to be sure, the entire question of the meaning of the *copula* and of the existential import of propositions generally. Here we are interested in the question of what logical analysis has to say regarding this paradoxical situation, namely, of statements that have significance, but say nothing. To meet this situation a theory of logical description, as distinguished from proposition, has been developed, a theory of "descriptions that describe nothing." This notion is so important for our later studies that it must be examined with some care.

The notion of descriptive phrases is a familiar one. The syntactical distinction between a phrase and a sentence can be carried over into a logical distinction between a phrase and a

[1] For a statement of this position see L. S. Stebbing, *op. cit.*, pp. 139 ff.

proposition. Such descriptive phrases are a church in Rome, the author of *Faust*, the man in the moon. If now I say a church in Rome is large, the author of *Faust* is German, the man in the moon is yellow, I have in all three cases descriptions. In the first two cases these descriptions are also propositions. The third, however, is not. Wherein lies the difference? In the first case, to attribute any property to the author of *Faust*, that he is a German, is to assert also that he exists. In the second case, it is not so. To assert that the man in the moon is yellow, that Hamlet is mad, that the King of Utopia is kind, does not involve the assertion that any of them exist. Therefore they are descriptions that describe nothing. So much for the analysis; we now come to the issue involved. As a result of this analysis it is supposed by some logicians, following Russell, that descriptions may be used significantly when they describe nothing. Others would hold that if they describe nothing they are meaningless. They appear to have meaning, they are used in intelligible discourse, and yet if meaning is to be identified with reference, they should be meaningless.

It seems certain that the notion of descriptions that describe nothing cannot be maintained. Every description is a proposition. By the very fact that it is a description it asserts that some "thing" is so and so. An interpretation of the situation must therefore be possible which does not involve this paradox. Such an interpretation has already been prepared for by the discussions of Chapter V of the notions of presupposition and of universe of discourse.[1] The condition of the meaningfulness of an assertion or proposition is not, we found, that certain entities about which the assertion is made exist, in the sense of being empirically verifiable, but that the universe of discourse in which these entities have their existence is mutually acknowledged. When I say that a griffin is a fabulous monster, I do not affirm that griffins exist like pigs and cows, but my judgment, to have any meaning, implies the existence of a mass of fable in which griffins have their place as fables too. If there were no fables I could not say that griffins are fabulous. But fables are an element in reality—i.e., in the totality of what is real—no less than pigs and cows. Such descriptions as some fairies are malevolent, the man in the moon is yellow, are then

[1] Chapter V, p. 201 f.

LANGUAGE AND LOGIC

meaningful, not only syntactically but in the sense of reference. It is not necessary to say that they describe nothing because they have no reference. We have here rather that more subtle kind of reference of which we have previously spoken. These descriptions are "symbolic groups" which, while they refer to no particular entity, still *mean* through a complex intention, constructed from simpler intentions, when as a whole they refer to nothing. They still perform the function of reference which is the condition of meaning and are therefore really descriptive and significant.

We have been considering so-called pseudo-propositions which are not propositions because the subjects of the sentences "refer to nothing." There is also another type which may be held to be pseudo-propositions because of the nature of the predicate. These are propositions which predicate analogously or, as we shall later call them, symbol propositions. Thus if I say "Napoleon was a wolf," or "man is a reed but he is a thinking reed," such assertions, it may conceivably be held, are only apparent propositions. Genuine propositions arise only when these assertions are interpreted or reduced to propositions which have literal significance.

The doubtful character of such propositions does not lie in the subject but in the predicate. In every case the predicate has a dual reference, first to an object of sensible intuition, and secondly to an object not sensuously observable. From the logical point of view the issue turns on the further question, whether such double reference is ambiguous. We have already indicated reasons for holding that this is not so.[1] Analogous predication is a unique form of predication and symbol propositions genuine propositions. The nature of these propositions will be considered later when we examine the character of symbol sentences and their relation to literal sentences.[2] Here our interest is solely in asserting that metaphorical descriptions are true propositions to which, *as such*, the notions of truth and falsity are relevant.

This problem of descriptions has far-reaching implications for the entire philosophy of language and symbolism—implications which will appear in the sequel, more especially in the notion of knowledge by description, in the following chapter. Here we

[1] Chapter V, p. 178 f.   [2] Chapter IX, p. 432 f.

have been concerned merely with the logical question of pseudo-propositions and the existential import of descriptions. This raises the entire question of the existential import of propositions and the meaning of the copula. To this problem we shall now turn.

D

The Existential Import of Propositions. The Problem of the Copula

One of the basal forms of ambiguity is, we have seen, the grammatical (Chapter V). Modern logical analysis makes much of these ambiguities and especially of the ambiguity in the word "is" when used as a copula. Thus, as we have seen, Peano and Frege pointed out that the copula in the two propositions, All men are mortal and Socrates is a man, means two quite different things. In the first proposition the "is" signifies a relation between two different classes; in the second it represents the relation of an individual to a class, and these two relations are quite different. But there is also a second ambiguity in the word "is" to which logicians have called attention. While a proposition apparently asserts that the subject of the proposition is, or exists, it really does not, but simply asserts a relation between classes or between an individual and a class. The proposition, or apparent proposition, "a centaur is a fiction of the poets," directly denies, it is pointed out, that a centaur is or exists. It is maintained, then, that a judgment of the type A is B can never, by the mere fact that the subject and predicate are connected by the word "is," include the statement or the judgment that A is.

It would seem that the position here presented could be taken for granted, that there *is* this ambiguity in the word is, and that, when it is exposed, it becomes clear that the presence of the copula does not presuppose the existence or reality of that about which the statement is made. But this is not so clearly evident as at first appears. The natural tendencies of language, its genius so to speak, are directly contrary to this. The Platonic axiom, that for an assertion to be significant at all, it must always also be, directly or indirectly, an assertion about what is, seems to be a postulate of all discourse and all communication.

This view has been urged by many logicians and philosophers. Thus Überweg insisted that propositions such as "God is just," "the soul is immortal," "true friends are to be valued," must involve the statement that there are such things as God, a soul, true friends. To which Sigwart replies that "this is in so far true that the reality of the subject is generally presupposed by those who speak and hear such judgments; otherwise there would be no motive present for uttering them." In discussing this position, he admits that whenever "the thinking subject finds something present which is independent of the act of thought, whether it is in the material or spiritual world, Logic *will permit* the use of the word is, although not necessarily implying "existence" in the narrow sense. In other words, the use of the copula presupposes the reality of the subject of the assertion in some sense.[1] The word *permits* is here the significant word and it is with this notion that I wish to take my start. It involves the principle maintained throughout this discussion, that logical analysis of meaning cannot legislate the meanings for discourse out of existence. Let us now see why, according to many modern logicians, logic does not permit it. It is briefly that such use leads to absurd conclusions.[2] The traditional position argues that no significant assertion can be made unless there is something about which to make it, or, in the words of Professor G. E. Moore, "a thing cannot have a property unless it is there to have it. When I make a statement about the man in the moon or about unicorns, that statement implies that they have some property, if it is no more than the property of being thought about. Since they have some properties they must be there to have them, they must be 'existent' in some sense." To this the answer is immediately made: if, on this reasoning, we insist that there must be a unicorn or a man in the moon, in some sense, although they do not exist in the spatio-temporal sense, we are forced to conclude that there are non-existent individuals, which "seems to be an absurd conclusion."[3]

In considering this argument it should first of all be noted that the conclusion does not necessarily follow. There may be individuals of varying types. The assumption that individuals

---

[1] Christopher Sigwart, *Logic* (English translation), Vol. I, p. 95, especially note.
[2] For this traditional argument and the rejoinder, see Stebbing, *An Introduction to Modern Logic*, pp. 157 ff.   [3] *Op. cit.*, p. 159.

are necessarily spatio-temporal existents rests upon a theory of individuation which is metaphysical in nature. But we shall not press this point. The real issue concerns the question of the meaning of existence. The proposition, lions are hunted, assumes, it is argued, that lions exist. The property of being a lion and of being hunted both belong to something. But the proposition that unicorns are thought about does not assert that the property of being a unicorn and of being thought about belong to something. Consequently, although the proposition, lions are hunted, if it be true, does imply that lions exist, the proposition, I am thinking about unicorns, can be true without implying that unicorns exist. This is described as a confusion of real predicates with pseudo-predicates. I do not see that this type of analysis really meets the issue. Or rather it seems to beg the entire question at issue. For it assumes that existence means the same thing in the two cases; and still further that it *must* mean the same thing in the two cases; in other words, that existence is univocal. Now this is certainly a very questionable assumption. It is a serious error to assume that a word must be univocal or else ambiguous and equivocal. We have already seen that this is not so. In our study of analogous predication, which we had reason to maintain is a valid form of predication, there is a third possibility. When I say that my reception was cold I am manifestly not predicating cold in the sense that the ice is cold, but a relation exists between the ice and the reception such that name transference and analogical predication are self authenticating. Analogous predication is a special type but a valid one. A similar line of argument may be applied to the existential predicate. When I apply the predicate existence or being to Hamlet or a unicorn, to the soul or to freedom, I simply am not applying it in the primary spatio-temporal sense: I am applying it analogically.[1]

In fact, it is precisely here that we have an outstanding case of the development of language in the sense of the "inner development of meaning." By a comparative study of the copula in various languages, Cassirer has shown that there has been a uniform development in the direction of multiple mean-

[1] The questionableness of this assumption and the begging of the question involved have been made very clear, I think, by A. E. Taylor in his *The Faith of a Moralist*, Vol. I, pp. 51–55.

ings of the "is," particularly in the differentiation of the existential and the relational. But he also shows that there has been likewise development of multiple meanings of the "is" in its existential sense, and that these multiple meanings are a necessary aspect of the development of mind and language together. Language in general develops from the perceptual imitative stage, through the metaphorical and analogical, to the symbolic. In this general development the copula shares. The symbolic use of the existential predicate is part of the development of language and, as such, a necessary condition of intelligible discourse.[1] This is the point I would here emphasize—the necessity of the multiple meanings of "existence," which the traditional interpretation of the copula maintains.

This traditional view leads, however, it is pointed out, to a doctrine of different modes of being, connected with different universes of discourse. But this, it is maintained, leads to "an erroneous metaphysical doctrine," or to the errors of a false metaphysics. With this charge we obviously come to the nub of the question. Now it is unquestioned, I think, that such a doctrine does follow. It is possible also that such a doctrine constitutes an erroneous metaphysics. But it is equally clear to me that, if it is erroneous, its error cannot be shown by logic. In actual fact the critique exercised upon such a metaphysic is not one which arises out of "logical analysis," but out of another metaphysic. It assumes the "prior rights of the physical" and gives a privileged position to that universe of discourse. Such an assumption begs, as we have seen, the entire question at issue. In truth the question whether existence has multiple meanings—whether there are different modes of being, corresponding to different universes of discourse—is not a logical but a metalogical question.

E

The Wider Issue: The Stultification of Discourse

We formulated the issues of this discussion thus: Does logic *permit* the use of the copula with the implication or presupposition

[1] *Op. cit.*, Vol. I, Chapter V, p. 286. For a further important application, see Chapter XIV, pp. 709 ff.

of existence or reality? Some logicians hold that it does; some that it does not. But there is an even more fundamental issue involved in this question, namely whether logic has the right or power to decide this question at all. Our own view is that it has not.

The reasons for this position have already been stated and need not be laboured here. Logic *assumes* that terms have meaning and that propositions have sense, but cannot determine that meaning and that sense. But the meaning of terms includes their reference to reality and the sense of propositions includes their ontological import. That import is indeed a matter of interpretation, as we shall see in the following chapter, but it is not a matter of logical analysis. The denial of the referential meaning of terms means, as we have seen, paralysis of speech. Similarly the denial of the existential import of propositions means the stultification of discourse. Every proposition assumes the reality of the subject of discourse, otherwise it would not be uttered. To negate the very conditions of such utterance—of intelligible discourse—is to stultify all discourse.

There can be no question that all significant assertions assume the reality of the subjects of the assertion; otherwise they would not be made. Even Mr. Russell, despite his logical atomism, assumes this. When he says that "freedom may not be the highest good, but it is the highest political good," he means to make a significant assertion. In doing so he assumes that both the subject freedom and the predicate, highest good, are in some sense real; otherwise presumably he would not make the assertion. Now the denial of that assumption on the basis of a supposed logical analysis would be to make his own meanings meaningless and to stultify his larger discourse. The truth of the matter is that when he makes this assertion in his *Proposed Roads to Freedom* he is in a wholly different universe of discourse from that in which the logical analysis takes place. Either that universe of discourse is one of mere feeling or emotional expression or is one in which predicates of truth and falsity are relevant. If it is the former, then the above noble sentiment is but his own sentiment and does not interest us further. If it is the latter, then it is a statement about reality and interests us greatly. This is in principle the reply that must be made to all those forms of logical positivism which through "logical analysis" exclude all value propositions from meaningful discourse. Social and political "sciences" cannot be constructed without propositions such as these—that is, without propositions which contain non-physical notions. The assumption is made that such propositions can be "reduced" to propositions containing terms with reference to physical entities; in other words, to a "physical language." This was attempted by Bentham without conspicuous success. Does anyone really suppose that it can actually be done?

What is really assumed is that language is *in principle* misleading. That is, of course, abstractly possible, but we must remark here, as we have previously, that it seems "very curious that language should have grown up as if it were expressly designed to deceive philosophers." If statements containing value words, so we found ourselves justified in asking, are mere expressions of feeling, why should language disguise them by putting them in propositional forms? With equal right we may ask, if the "logical" meaning of an assertion in which the copula appears does not include the assumption or presupposition of "existence," why should its meaning in discourse always include it? Why the inevitable stultification of discourse that results? I can find no answer to this question except the natural one that logical analysis cannot legislate the "existential" meaning out of existence any more than it can any other meaning.

The issue here may be formulated in more technical terms. On the assumption that logic is the science of pure form it must, as we have seen, assume that terms have meaning and propositions sense; it cannot determine that meaning and that sense. The attempt is made in mathematical logic, as a science of pure form, to bring in the "individual" and "existence" as a variable, and thus make existence part of logical meaning in the sense that it can legislate regarding this meaning. This seems to me to be a mistake. In reality the meaning of existence is extralogical and always involves a metaphysic, whether expressed or unexpressed.[1]

Such considerations seem to dispose, in principle, at least, of

[1] For a fuller development of this point, see *The Intelligible World*, Chapter III, pp. 101 ff.

the underlying thesis of logical positivism, namely, that logical analysis enables us to distinguish apparent propositions from real propositions, and ultimately to exclude from discourse a large range of propositions as pseudo-propositions. This thesis, we now see, rests upon two untenable assumptions. The first of these is the major assumption as to the function of logical analysis, already considered. The second assumption, closely related to this, is that the criterion of meaning in logical analysis is the "empirical criterion." That this criterion is not logical but metalogical has already been shown in a preceding chapter. If susceptible of validation at all, it can only be on the basis of a prior metaphysics, namely, the assumption of the prior rights of the physical, an assumption that can never be demonstrated but only acknowledged. The assumption that the "syntax of our language," or that logic as logic, implies the prior rights of the physical, is a wholly gratuitous assumption.

VII

LANGUAGE AND REASONING. THE PROBLEM OF LOGISTIC

A

The final point at which problems of language and logic arise is in connection with the doctrine of inference. The special point at issue is the question of the function of language as a medium of reasoning or inference. The same type of critique which modern logic exercises upon language in connection with vocabulary and syntax it also brings to bear upon language as a medium of reasoning. Ordinary language, it is said, is only incompletely inferential. "If one follows merely the grammar of language he will not be led from true premises to true conclusions. Only some of his manipulations of words and sentences will be inferences."[1] It is for this reason primarily that symbolic logic or logistic has been developed. Such a logic alone is completely inferential. Inference may be defined as the development of implicational meaning, and in so far as language is an imperfect medium for such development it is subject to the critique of logic.

The divergence of linguistic and logical meaning evidently

[1] R. M. Eaton, *op. cit.*, p. 259.

appears here in its most serious form. Logic is the science of inferential meaning and, in so far as language is an imperfect medium for such meaning, its limitations are obvious. The problem as thus stated really presupposes a prior problem—whether, strictly speaking, there is any other medium than language. It may be imperfect, but it may also be the only medium we have. This involves the old and much-discussed question as to whether there is, or can be, thought without words. In considering this question we may start with a distinction commonly made between inference and implication.

Inference, it is said, is a psychological matter, at least partly, whereas implication is strictly logical. The development of implicational meaning which constitutes inference is a function of minds, whereas implication is conceived of as a relation between propositions, and to subsist independently of minds. Now without raising the question whether "psychological" is the proper term to apply to these "extra-logical" aspects of reasoning (that point has already been considered above), it seems clear at least that in reflective thinking, consciously active reasoning, there is an element which is not in implication thus abstractly conceived. That element is, I think, always bound up with linguistic meaning.

Inference develops the implicational meaning of propositions, and propositions in so far as they are the material of inference are judgments expressed in words. It is true that the distinction between inference and implication just made implies not only that implication is a relation between propositions which subsist independently of minds; it also implies that the propositions are entities outside discourse (sentences as such). But we have already seen that a proposition apart from discourse is nothing; it seems only reasonable to conclude that conscious reflective thinking—reasoning as distinct from mere calculation or operation—is nothing apart from discourse. This is, I think, true. Let us assume, for the sake of argument, that such a distinction between implication and inference is valid; even so inference, as distinct from implication, presupposes discourse. It involves communication, either overt or potential, and all intelligible communication is in the last analysis linguistic. This point may be made clearer by a further consideration of the nature of implication.

B

Implication—Material and Formal. The Extra-Logical Element in Inference

The fundamental principle of all inference is that what is implied in true premises is true. But the nature of the relation expressed by the word implied—in other words, the nature of implication—is a further question.

We may start with the well-known distinction between formal and material implication. In the universal proposition, all men are mortal, we have such a relation of formal implication between the concept man and the concept mortal. The true meaning, the meaning determined by logical analysis, can only be given without excess of defect in the form, "that X is a man implies that X is mortal." This again means, to state it more precisely, that "is mortal" is true of any subject of which "is man" is true. The form given above is what is called a propositional function, as distinguished from a genuine proposition. To make a genuine proposition out of this blank form it is necessary that we should replace the symbol X on both of its appearances by one and the same name or denoting phrase indicating one individual, *this*. Only when we have done this have we passed from asserting a relation between mere propositional functions to asserting a relation between propositions. And when we take this step, the relation is one of material implication and the propositions which figure in this material implication are seen to have existential import, whereas the propositional functions have not. For example, Socrates is a man materially implies Socrates is mortal, and this means that it is not the case that Socrates is a man and Socrates is not mortal.

Now just as a genuine proposition, as distinguished from a mere propositional function, presupposes the reality of the subjects of the assertion, otherwise the assertion would not be made, so genuine inference is always concerned with material implication. At this point two problems arise: (*a*) what is material implication and (*b*) how is it related to language? The fact that X is red implies, it is said, *materially* that X is a colour, the relation between redness and colour being material or factual and not merely formal. It is not the fact that X is red is true and X is a colour is false. What, then, is the nature of this material relation?[1]

Granted that the relation here is factual and not merely formal, one thing about its factual character becomes, I think, immediately clear. The factual relation does not subsist between two brute sense data, but between them as determined by language. Part of any "fact" is the language in which it is enunciated; it is not a fact until it is expressed. Language, we have seen, is part of the perceptual process as such; it is present in the first or primary universal and the class concept such as colour and red is but a development of this first precipitate of language, furnishing the basis for further more complex processes of conceptual thought.[2] It is therefore not true, as we have further seen, that a proposition contains entities, not words, for a proposition outside discourse is a "nothing."

It is, then, only within an actual "universe of discourse" that we have actual reasoning, for it is only in such a universe that material implication is found. Genuine propositions, as distinguished from propositional functions, subsist only in discourse. We may indeed disengage the blank form from the actual propositions and study this form for its own sake. It may also appear that genuine reasoning takes place in the blank forms—that reasoning is a *quasi mechanical* relation of these forms, the filling in of the blank forms with names or denoting phrases a secondary process *after* the reasoning has taken place. This is, however, not the fact. Actual reasoning is always concerned with genuine propositions and such propositions always involve linguistic meanings. Language, natural or artificial, is always the medium of reasoning.

The point I have been trying to make may be stated in another way. In his well-known book, *Implication and Linear Inference*, Bernard Bosanquet is engaged with the same general problem although not from the linguistic point of view. The general thesis of the book is that all real inference is within what

---

[1] It is not within the scope of our present purpose to discuss in detail the nature of implication, but to consider material as distinguished from formal implication only as it bears upon the problem of logic and language. The question, for instance, whether a further distinction between the relation of entailing and that of material implication is desirable, may be left among the technicalities of modern logic.   [2] See Chapter III, especially p. 118.

he calls a "connected system," and consists in reading off the implications of that system. In other words, implication is always material, not formal. This is the "natural procedure" over against which he sets the more artificial procedure of ordinary syllogistic logic (and the more modern logics which have resulted from the attacks on the syllogism), which he calls linear. The principle of the latter consists in affirming some principle of reasoning (mathematical), let us say "transitivity," which differs from that of the syllogism; but the conception remains linear.[1] That all *real* reasoning is within such a connected system, or universe of discourse, seems to me to be beyond question. And it is at this point that language as the medium of such reasoning becomes significant. By implication Bosanquet touches upon this aspect although he does not develop it. He points out how the *natural procedure* of real inference opens up the case *descriptively* and places the hearer within the system which is the development of the subject. The principle of context and contextual meaning becomes the basal condition of the insight which is of the essence of real inference.[2] As language is indispensable for judging, so it is indispensable for the development of the implications of the context in which the judgment takes place. The "linear inference" of which he speaks is really, as Bergson maintains, a spatialization of thought. Wittgenstein's conception of "logical space" represents perfectly this quasi-mechanical conception of inference.

This character of genuine inference, as distinguished from the quasi-mechanical conception, is in a way generally realized and is sometimes called the extra-logical factor in inference. We are told that from any set of premises an infinite number of valid inferences may be drawn. What is called the conclusion is a matter of selection which is determined by insight into its obviousness or by some purpose or interest. The direction of thought is always determined by an extra-logical factor. In other words, context and contextual meaning are the determinants of real inference. Whether we shall call this factor extra-logical or not is, of course, a matter of definition. The important point is that in actual inference non-formal elements are involved, and these elements are inseparable from language and linguistic context. We may, if we will, call this the

[1] *Op. cit.*, p. 31.   [2] *Op. cit.*, p. 113.

"psychological" element in inference, although the objection to such characterization has already been made clear. The assumption that all meaning not "logical" is psychological rests upon a faulty analysis of meaning. We shall therefore prefer to call these factors metalogical.

C

Implication and "Presupposition"

To return, then, to the main issue, language in some form is the only medium of real inference. It may be "imperfectly inferential," but this merely means that no *real* inference is perfect. It is possible to exercise a critique on language as a medium of inference, just as it is possible to criticize it from the point of view of vocabulary and syntax, but such a critique is valid only from the standpoint of the ideal of logic as pure form. It cannot affect the significance of language as the only medium of actual logical *discourse*. This fact will become more evident after our examination of symbolic logic and logistic. It is important, however, before proceeding to this question to consider a further point in connection with the problem of implication and inference.

It is, we have seen, necessary to distinguish between formal and material implication. It is now necessary to consider another meaning of implication connected with its material aspect. It is of special moment because it is precisely here that logic exercises its most drastic critique upon natural language and inference. Logic, we have seen, is concerned with implicational meaning. But implication may have two meanings. The first consists in the idea that certain things are true if they are implied in, or follow from, true premises. The second consists in holding that certain things are true if they are implied by or are the necessary presuppositions of some classes of more particular facts. It is the latter notion of implication which plays such a large rôle in epistemological and metaphysical reasoning and constitutes what is described as a "peculiar criterion of proof" in these fields. This second notion of implication—in the sense of presupposition—becomes of crucial importance when we come to the problems of language and metaphysics and of metaphysical reasoning, for reasoning of the metaphysical type is largely argument to presuppositions and involves this second notion of implication. The entire notion will be treated in more detail later;[1] here we are concerned with it merely in its logical aspect.

The issue in this context is entirely clear: whether, namely, implication in this second sense of presupposition is a valid form of implication. It is well stated by Professor Lewis. In discussing Kant's deduction of the categories he speaks of "a peculiar criterion of proof," and the nature of this proof consists in holding that certain things are true if they are the necessary "presuppositions" or implicates of some class of more particular facts, of science or of experience in general.[2] Such a form of implication he denies, and in consequence excludes this type of reasoning from discourse. Here, too, logical analysis exercises its critique upon natural language and natural discourse.

The meaning of presupposition here, he points out, is far from clear. In general, however, what is intended is the designation of certain principles as logically prior to what presupposes them, with the added thought that what is thus prior is necessarily implied and thereby proved to have the character of necessary truth—necessary, that is, if the facts of experience in general are taken for granted. Now this notion of implication contains a fallacy, he thinks, so simple that it is extraordinary that it should have ever gained currency. Correctly speaking, what is logically prior to a fact or proposition will imply that fact or proposition, but will not, in general, be implied by it.

[1] Chapter XIII, pp. 652 ff.
[2] *Mind and the World Order*, pp. 200 ff.
In general the strictures made upon this type of proof by Lewis are expressed by others who tend to identify thought with formal logic. Thus Professor Morris R. Cohen (*Contemporary American Philosophy*, Vol. I) writes: "renewed faith in formal logic showed me that since all proof rests upon assumption, it is vain for any philosophy to pretend to prove all material propositions. It must make indemonstrable assumptions in regard to existence, value and duty. This is particularly cogent against Kant's transcendental method, i.e. to attempt to prove certain propositions true because they explain how experience is possible. We cannot explain experience or anything else without assuming something, and it is downright logical fallacy to assert that because our assumptions explain something they are therefore demonstrably true. Obviously Kant does not and cannot offer any cogent proof that there may not be some other set of assumptions which will also explain the facts of experience."

Physics presupposes mathematics in the sense that it exhibits particular instances of general mathematical principles, while mathematics contains no necessary reference to physics. In the same sense all the special sciences presuppose logic. But if what is presupposed in this sense be regarded as thereby necessarily implied or proved necessary, the fallacy is easily detected. If I assert that two feet and two feet are four feet, I do not commit myself to the proposition that $2 + 2 = 4$. It is required only that this be true of linear measure. Gases under pressure or living organisms might—for all that is here in question—be governed by different laws. The particular fact does not require that there should be any general laws of mathematics.

There can be little doubt that this "fallacy," if it be such, has played an important part in the traditional conceptions of the *a priori*. There can be just as little doubt that this general way of thinking has played a large part in traditional conceptions of reasoning. Of this more later. Here we are concerned solely with the question whether this notion of implication is a valid one and whether reasoning based upon it is fallacious.

Now it seems quite clear that the notion of implication in this sense *may* be applied in an invalid way, although I am not sure that the fallacy is so simple and obvious, even in the cases given, as is assumed. I am not sure that when I assert that two feet and two feet are four feet I do not also assert that wherever number is applicable at all, the general relation expressed by the statement that $2 + 2 = 4$ does not also hold. Gases under pressure and living organisms might be governed by different laws, but then number, as here understood, would not be applicable. But that is not the point I wish to make. It is rather that the argument from the possibility or meaning of experience is not the type of implication assumed in this criticism. It is not an argument from particulars to universals but from the meaningfulness of experience to the presuppositions which alone make it meaningful. Such is really the essence of Kant's argument to which reference is made. The indirect proof by which he establishes the principles of the understanding is not from experience but from the possibility of experience. They have the peculiar property that they make possible the very experience which is their own ground of proof, and in experience itself they are always presupposed.[1]

It is, then, with this type of implication, this peculiar kind of proof, that we are here concerned. It is the type of proof employed in our argument from the nature of communication to the conditions or presuppositions which make it intelligible.[2] It seems clear that the concept of implication here involved is extra-logical, if logic be defined as the science of pure form. But to this fact there can be no objection when it is recognized that in all *real* inference there are extra-logical factors. It will suffice, then, for our present purposes to say that implication in this sense is extra-logical or metalogical—which does not, of course, mean that it is illogical. Logic is the science of discursive thought and, as such, cannot negate the conditions or presuppositions of intelligible discourse.

But our present problem is that of language and inference. Logic, as pure form, gives correctness—never truth. In so far as inference is related to truth as well as to correctness, there is always the extra-logical factor in inference, and this factor is inseparable from language. This will become apparent as we examine the ideal of logistic to which we shall now turn.

D

Symbolic Logic and Logistic

The statement that the medium of reasoning is in the last analysis language will of course be immediately challenged. The one field in which there is "strict implication" and in which "perfect" inference is achieved is mathematics, and it is precisely here that the medium is non-linguistic. It is precisely for this reason that algebraic logic or logistic was developed.

The ideal of logistic is to operate wholly with signs rather

---

[1] This type of proof is discussed by H. J. Paton in Vol. II of Kant's *Metaphysic of Experience*, pp. 103-107. The question can always be raised, he admits, whether such proof does not involve a vicious circle, although he thinks not. He makes it quite clear, however, that whether right or wrong the argument is not of the type assumed by the critics of the argument. The indirect proof from the possibility of experience is different from the proof of the facts of experience.

[2] Chap. VI, pp. 259 ff.

LANGUAGE AND LOGIC

than with words. Ordinary language is too clumsy to express the nice distinctions necessary for exact thought. Our language is so irreparably infected with error, the divergence between linguistic meaning and logical meaning is so great, that the ideal would be to abandon language entirely and substitute non-linguistic signs. Logic is concerned with the conditions of accurate symbolism. It is this idea of accurate symbolism that has led to the development of symbolic logic *eo nomine*. Symbolic logic is, then, that form of logic in which the combinations and relations of terms and propositions are all represented by *signs* in such a way that the rules of calculus can be substituted for actively conscious reasoning. An algebra of logic enables us to disengage from any subject-matter the formal element which gives apodeictic, necessary, force to reasoning. The ideal is to make logic purely formal and one of the exact sciences.

Ordinary logic has, from the beginning, substituted non-verbal signs for verbal symbols, as, for instance, the letters of the alphabet for terms, i.e. the significant elements of speech (Chapter II, p. 88). Symbolic logic goes further and adds signs for the non-significant elements, for combinations of terms, for functions of terms and for the statement of relations between them.[1] These signs are called "symbols," although strictly speaking they should perhaps not be so called. They are not symbols in the sense that words are symbols, nor indeed in the sense that the notions of symbol and symbolic are used in ordinary discourse. They are *substitutional signs*. The important point is that they are made in the interest of "pure notation" and do not represent the entities or relations for which they stand. They merely denote. This notion of substitutional symbols or signs is all-important and will be discussed more fully later.[2] Here the important point is to guard against the notion that when such signs are manipulated we are reasoning about real things. I have always felt that logistic should be conceived as a manipulation of signs.

Historically the movement originated in Leibniz, and the statement of the ideal which he had in mind may well be taken as our starting-point. That ideal was expressed in two proposals: (*a*) to substitute for human thoughts an "alphabet of human thoughts" and (*b*) to substitute for complicated

[1] Lewis, *Survey of Symbolic Logic*, p. 19. [2] Chapter IX, p. 407 f.

reasonings simple calculation. By this means philosophers would become accountants and the controversies of the sects would cease.[1] Modern logistic would scarcely state the ideal in so simple and naïve a fashion. It would scarcely ascribe to logistic the powers which, in the first flush of enthusiasm, Leibniz ascribed to his calculus, but in principle the ideal remains the same. We shall consider this point later when we raise the question of the significance of logistic.

Our problem, then, is this—whether we can, in Leibniz's words, substitute an alphabet of human thoughts for natural language, or, in other words, what we actually have when we have substituted non-verbal signs for verbal; and secondly, whether we can substitute calculation for ordinary reasoning, whether by so doing we actually have reasoning in the sense of actively conscious thought.

On the first question there has been a strong body of dissenting opinion. It is argued that an algebraic logic wholly independent of speech is unrealizable. For if such a symbolic did not take into account the thought content of language, to that extent it would not be a substitute for it. An alphabet of human thoughts would be just that—an alphabet and not the thoughts themselves. In the terms of our discussion the meaning of the terms which logic assumes and cannot itself determine is precisely what is left out in such a logic. But there seems to be a still deeper source of misunderstanding as to the possibility

[1] The idea underlying this whole way of thinking was expressed by Leibniz in his *De Scientia Universali seu Calculo Philosophico* (Latta, *Monad*, p. 85). It seemed to Leibniz that if all the complex and apparently disconnected ideas which make up our knowledge could be analysed into their simple elements, and if each of these elements could be represented by a definite sign, we should have a kind of "alphabet of human thoughts." By the combination of these signs, a system of true knowledge would be built up in which reality would be more and more adequately represented and symbolized. It seemed to him that such a synthetic "calculus" based upon a thorough analysis (as in the case of the mathematical calculus), would be the most effective instrument of knowledge that could be devised. "I feel," he says, "that controversies can never be finished, nor silence imposed upon the sects, unless we give up complicated reasonings in favour of simple *calculation*, words of vague and uncertain meaning in favour of fixed symbols or characters. It will then appear that every paralogism is nothing but an error of calculation. When controversies arise there will be no more necessity for disputation between two philosophers than between two accountants. Nothing will be needed but that they should take pen in hand, sit down with their counting tables, and (having summoned a friend, if they like), say to one another, 'Let us calculate.' "

of substitution of non-verbal signs for words. It seems to escape the recognition of some logicians that there are intrinsic limits to the possibilities of a universal symbolism. The symbols for primary indefinables have to be adequately apprehended before their combinations can be understood. In order to apprehend the symbols preliminary explanation is always implied. But this explanation is always in an idiom which is itself not impersonal, and a mere arbitrary sign, but intuitive and living—namely, language.

The ideal of logistic is to operate wholly with signs rather than words—in Leibniz's terms to substitute calculation for reasoning. The difficulty in substituting an alphabet of human thoughts for language simply appears in a new form when we seek to substitute calculations for reasoning. Calculation is no longer "actively conscious thought" because it does not bring the thought content to expression. It operates, but it says nothing. That is, until the results of the calculation are expressed in language, until the substitutional signs are replaced by words and phrases, nothing is said. The calculation does not replace the thinking, for the thinking, if it is *actual*, has already been done in the linguistic medium.

There seems to be another aspect to the limitations of symbolic logic. The limits to a universal symbolism, or the substitution of non-verbal signs for words, lay in the fact that the primary indefinables have to be apprehended before their combinations can be understood and, in order to apprehend them, explanation in terms of language is necessary. A similar situation arises in connection with the principles involved in inference. In any symbolic, completely inferential system, there must be some supreme principle or principles governing all the inferences and these obviously cannot be expressed in the symbolism itself. Thus every symbolically expressed demonstration depends upon the principle that what is implied in true premises is itself true. But neither this principle, nor the meaning of the terms implication or truth, can be expressed in the symbolism of any type of logistic. As Couturat says, it is necessary to define verbally both the primitive symbols and the primary formulas.[1] This fact means, apparently, that here

---

[1] See on this point, L. Couturat, *Les Principes des mathématiques*, p. 11. Also A. E. Taylor, *The Faith of a Moralist*, Vol. II, p. 73.

also logical meaning presupposes linguistic meaning. It presupposes it in a double fashion. On the one hand, it is apparent that logical meaning exists only within discourse. For this verbal defining which is necessary for any symbolic logic is a form of communication of meanings; and this communication of meaning, which is possible only in language, is the condition of the existence of the logistic itself. But it means also, I think, that no *real* thinking here is possible without language. We are really not thinking except as the symbols are defined. It is not that we actually think in the calculus and *then* interpret it. The meanings of the primitive symbols and of the primary principles are part of the thinking. The point here made is of great importance. It involves the distinction between thinking and operating already insisted upon. It is important here in connection with the problem of the relation of logic to language. It becomes of increasing importance when we come to the examination of the whole problem of the relation of language to symbolism, especially in science. So far as logic is concerned the point has been well stated by Husserl.

In a review of Schroeder's *Lectures on the Algebra of Logic*, while praising the work, he maintained that symbolic logic is not logic at all but only calculus.[1] Following Brentano, he claimed that natural language is indispensable for judging. Logic is concerned with the meaning of propositions which are judgments expressed in words. If symbolic logic claims to be able to work without using such meanings it differs fundamentally from logic, which is totally unable to function without using these meanings. It is quite possible that Husserl should not have said that symbolic logic is not logic. That is a matter of definition, and definitions of logic vary widely, as we have seen. It is true however that, as Ramsey admits, logic as conceived by logistic is not at all the same as logic when defined in terms of reflective thinking. Husserl is quite right in maintaining that reflective thinking "is not able to work without using meanings"—linguistic meanings. I repeat it is unimportant whether logistic be called logic or not, just as it was

[1] This review appears in the *Göttenische Gelehrte Anzeigen*, 1891. For a discussion of the review see *Journal of Philosophy*, etc., July 1934. Schroeder himself replied to Husserl, with the result that the latter modified his position somewhat. I am not here concerned with the debate, but with what I consider to be the essential truth of Husserl's first position.

unimportant whether we called the non-formal element in all inference extra-logical or not. The important thing is that actual thinking "is not able to work without linguistic meanings." Logistic merely operates and is in no sense a substitute for actively conscious reasoning. When the results of that operation are *interpreted* by a return to language, those results are valid only if they express, in formal fashion, the results of genuine reflective thinking.

E

The Function of Logistic

It is, of course, no part of our purpose to attempt any general evaluation of logistic. Nevertheless the preceding discussion of the relation of language to logic suggests certain questions as to the place and function of symbolic logic.

On this question the logicians themselves differ greatly. There are some who seem to assume that its applicability is practically unlimited and that it is a real surrogate for actual thinking. Others appear to hold that it is a mere play with symbols and that its applicability to the concrete reality of reflective thought is strictly limited. It seems, however, to be generally held that the logistic method is applicable wherever a body of facts or of theory approaches the completeness and systematic character which belongs to mathematical systems. By the use of this method, it is also sometimes held, the same assurance of correctness may also be secured for those portions which are not statable in terms of ordinary mathematics. Now this latter assumption seems to me to be quite doubtful, namely, that the same assurance of correctness can be secured outside the region of mathematics. But leaving that aside, it is certainly true that it is applicable only to mathematical systems and their analogues.[1] It is certainly inapplicable to that much larger range, both of fact and theory, in which most of human reasoning and discourse takes place. For the thoughts and meanings of this region in which organization of meaning and the connotation of terms is central, an alphabet of thoughts

[1] See on this question an article by F. A. Lindemann in the volume entitled *Mind* (London, 1927), in which the question of the limits of logistic is discussed.

is sheer illusion and calculation cannot be substituted for reasoning. Moreover, it is an assurance only of *correctness*, not of truth, that is secured, even in those non-mathematical regions where it is at all applicable. Truth is always a matter of the sense of terms and the meaning of propositions—in other words, their reference to reality—and this is a metalogical, not a logical question.

This latter point demands, I think, special emphasis. For it is often assumed that logistic is not merely an instrument of precision but also a method of knowledge. It is sometimes held that all sciences are merely applied logistic, logistic with the x's and the y's replaced by hydrogen or oxygen or any other entity for which we have names. But on examination of the systematic connections used by the logicians, for instance implication, we have reason to suspect that these connections have suffered an abstraction of such an extreme sort that the notions necessary in dealing with concrete propositions have been generalized away. In other words, as we have already seen, implicational meaning for actual science is always within a connected system and consists in reading the implications of that system. There is always the "intuitive" extra-logical factor in the concrete inferences of science. Even in mathematics, with which logistic is most closely connected, there seems to be some misunderstanding at least. It is here pre-eminently that logistic is to take the place of intuitive and other sources of knowledge. But it is not at all clear that even here this is possible. We have been told that, thanks to the progress of symbolic logic, especially as treated by Peano, the Kantian doctrine of the intuitive basis of mathematics has been disposed of. But the presence of intuitive theories of mathematics, although not in the Kantian form, makes this at least doubtful. In any case, it is not so outside mathematics. Even if it were possible to put the whole body of pure mathematics, including the primary indefinables and the primary principles of inference, into a stereotyped symbolism, all we should have achieved by this would be the construction of a purely abstract and formal pattern, inadequate to the description of the simplest piece of concrete fact. The world with which the physicist concerns himself is abstract enough, but even the physicist's world defies, as we shall abundantly see, all attempts to build it out of mathematical formulas. So long as the physicist remains in the region of these symbols, he merely operates, but "says nothing." It is only when he talks in the natural language of "intuition" that he says anything significant. Even in physics something slips through the meshes and this something is communicable, if communicable at all, only in natural language with its intuitible meanings.[1] This is *a fortiori* true of the macrocosm in which human beings live and move. When the suggestion is made, as for instance by Professor Whitehead, that aesthetic values may some time be expressible in symbolic logic one can only wonder what such values can here possibly mean.[2]

Leibniz, we saw, in the first flush of his enthusiasm ascribed powers to his calculus which he himself later disavowed. Apparently he became aware of the peculiar limitations and difficulties associated with the problem of adequate symbolic expression for the processes of real thinking. For him his calculus had appeared to be a calculus of realities. He later came to see that it was not. The difference between Leibniz and modern logistic appears at this point. He evidently regarded his set of primitive concepts as the necessary result of any proper analysis; modern logistic looks upon them as arbitrarily chosen. But if this latter position is taken, it is hard to see how the logical calculus can be a calculation of realities.

VIII

LOGICAL NOMINALISM: IS A NOMINALISTIC LOGIC POSSIBLE?

A

It is maintained by many that symbolic logic is inevitably nominalistic and that its limitations are to be found in the impossibility of its dealing with the intension or connotation of terms. On the other hand, it is maintained by others that a logistic of the logic of intension may be developed. On this question I am not competent to judge. One may, however, be pardoned the suspicion that in an intensional logistic the notion of intension, like the notion of implication with which it is so

---

[1] Chapter XI, p. 523 f.
[2] "Remarks," *Philosophical Review*, Vol. LXVI, No. 2, March 1937.

closely connected, has undergone an abstraction of so extreme a sort that the notion as it applies to concrete reasoning has been generalized away.[1] Be that as it may, the possibility of a nominalistic logic is assumed by many versions of modern logic, and an examination of this assumption is a necessary part of the general question of the relation of language to logic.

The consequence of the critique exercised by "logical analysis" on vocabulary and syntax was, as we have seen, a thoroughgoing nominalism—not only of the universal but of the individual. This leads inevitably to paralysis of speech and stultification of discourse. The problems raised by this all-pervasive nominalism are, however, not logical but metalogical in character and are reserved for a later context.[2] There is a problem, however, which is strictly logical, namely, whether inference and inferential meaning remain intact on nominalistic assumptions, whether nominalism of the universal does not also paralyse and stultify reasoning. Thus our question: Is a nominalistic logic possible? Or, does logic retain its significance on purely nominalistic presuppositions?

B

The Nature of Logical Nominalism. The Argument of the Nominalist

Logical nominalism is then to be distinguished from nominalism in general. W. E. Johnson makes this distinction and defines logical nominalism in the following way: "Nominalism," he tells us, "when applied as a special logical theory has a special meaning. In this sense it denotes the theory according to which the proposition is an indication of the names that have been arbitrarily chosen to denote things or classes of things and predicates merely what follows from the consistent use of these names. Propositions are thus used as mere formulae and repeated in thought when necessary without *demanding any consideration of their meaning* (italics mine). Consequently the only

---

[1] Leibniz, as is well known, lost his interest in his symbolic logic, and never mentioned his *De Arte Combinatoria* without apologizing for it. The probability is that he sensed the nominalism in it—the impossibility of dealing by means of such symbolism with the intension of terms. Whether later symbolisms are really able to do so I am unable to say.   [2] Chapter VIII, pp. 366 ff.

ultimate foundations or premises of knowledge are definitions, no other propositions of the nature of axioms being required."[1]

Logic is, then, merely the consistent use of names. Propositions are used as formulas without demanding any consideration of their meaning. It follows that to use propositions in reasoning no axiom or postulate of identity of meaning, such as is presupposed in ordinary intelligible discourse, is necessary. For logical meaning identity such as is represented by the universal is unnecessary. The notions of classes, of universals, and of identity are all fictions; only the individual is real. But, it is held, logic can proceed perfectly well on the basis of these fictions. The logical nominalist argues, in the first place, that they are fictions—that there is no empirical evidence for such identity; in other words, for universals. But even so it makes no difference to logic. The real issue, of course, is whether logic can proceed on the basis of such a theory of fictions. But a word may be said first on this question of evidence for universals. It is assumed in the argument that individuals are empirically given; for them there is ample evidence. And yet I think it can be shown that if universals are unreal individuals are also, that nominalism of the universal involve nominalism of the individual also. The very entrance of a "thing" on the stage of thought implies that it has a minimum of character and relations. But this is a metalogical, not a logical, question and will be considered in the following chapter.[2] Here the issue is wholly whether logic retains its significance on a nominalistic basis.

Evidently the question turns wholly on the meaning of the term significance. And this, in turn, goes back to the definitions of logic already discussed. If the significance of logic consists wholly in its formal character, then this significance can be retained, for logic is then precisely the manipulation of formulas without any consideration of their meaning. If, on the other hand, the significance of logic is that it is *die Moral des Denkens*—that it is the morality of discursive thinking, and as such within the context of intelligible discourse and communication—then its significance cannot be retained on nominalistic presuppositions.

[1] W. E. Johnson, *Logic*, Part I, p. xxix.
[2] Chapter VIII, p. 368 f. For a discussion of the question of evidence for universals see R. M. Eaton, *op. cit.*, pp. 85 ff.

The reasons for this are obvious. In this case logical meaning cannot negate linguistic meaning and retain its significance. The universal in some form is the *sine qua non* of all linguistic meaning. For language and discourse, the meaning of the universal and of qualitative identity is simply not exhausted in the negative notion of lack of discriminable difference. The universal is present in the first determinations of language and forms the basis of all predication and for the further logical processes of analysis and synthesis. The axiom or postulate of identity—of the universal—on the conceptual or logical level has its ground in this first or intuitive universal. This postulate of identity is the necessary condition of all communication or discourse. Discursive reasoning is but a part of discourse. For logic to turn the universal into a fiction is to paralyse speech and to stultify discourse. It must also paralyse thought, in so far at least as thought has any relevancy to concrete reflective thinking and to the discourse with which it is bound up. Logical nominalism is but a special case of the nominalism considered in preceding sections, and its consequences are the same.

IX

THE SIGNIFICANCE OF LOGIC. THE NORMATIVE PROBLEM

A

The question whether logic retains its significance on purely nominalistic presuppositions raises again the entire problem of what the significance of logic is. In other words, we are brought back to one of our initial questions: What is Logic? In taking up this final problem it is desirable to examine more fully an aspect of logic which was merely suggested in our earlier statement, namely, the notion of logic as normative.

The notion of logic as normative is a familiar one in the history of the subject. It is aptly expressed by Herbart in his characterization of logic as *die Moral des Denkens*. In other words, logic tells us how we *ought* to think. In so far as the problem of logic and language is concerned, logic is supposed to tell us how we ought to use language—how we ought to speak—how we should use language so as to express the meaningful rather than the unmeaning, the true rather than the false. It is this conception which, as we have seen, is assumed in the entire conception of the logical analysis of language. This question of the significance of logic involves then the problem of in what sense and to what degree logic is thus normative.

The notion of logic as normative has been modified in recent thought—especially by those who define logic as a science of pure form. According to this view, logic is a science of "facts"— only in this case the facts are of a special nature, namely, the all-pervasive forms of everything that is. Primarily, then, logic is a science of *what is*, not of what ought to be. It is only secondarily and indirectly that logic is normative.[1] Now there seems to be little question that logic is related to thought and to its expression much as morals are related to action. Just as in the moral sphere the ought or norm of action arises out of the cognition and acknowledgment of values which themselves have being, and is thus only secondarily and indirectly normative, so logic becomes normative or *die Moral des Denkens*, only when it becomes related to something extralogical or metalogical—only, that is, when the logical values of correctness, apodeictic certainty, perfect inference, etc., are acknowledged as values and related to values of an extra-logical character. It is only then that logic may acquire an "ought," only then that it can tell us how we ought to think, what we ought and ought not to say, how we should use language and how we should not use it. The normative character of the logical derives from the extra-logical or metalogical.

B

Summary and Conclusion: The Logical and the Metalogical

With this conception of logic as indirectly normative we may proceed to our final statement concerning the problem of the relation of language to logic. The main issue which has determined the entire course of this chapter is the question of

[1] For this distinction between the directly and indirectly normative I am indebted to Nicolai Hartmann (*Ethics*, Vol. I, Chapter 3), applied by him, however, only to ethics. For a somewhat similar view of the normative character of logic see Stebbing, *op. cit.*, Chapter XXIV, p. 474.

the relation of logical meaning to linguistic meaning; or, more specifically stated, whether logical meaning is normative for linguistic meaning. The assumption underlying the logical analysis of language we have been examining is that logical meaning is here determinative. We may call this the postulate of the primacy of logical meaning.

Now this postulate rests upon an important fact—one which, however interpreted, will scarcely be denied by anyone—the fact, namely, of the all-pervasive character of logical form in human discourse. Logical form is so woven into all our speech that it is impossible to utter a phrase, much less to form a sentence, without throwing it into logical form. Logic is not only the mould of thought but, in an important sense, the condition of all intelligible expression. It is, accordingly, easy to infer from this fact that the logical form may be disengaged from our speech and, when thus abstracted, be made the norm or criterion of the meaningfulness of all discourse—in other words, that the significance of logic as normative is absolute. This is, however, to draw unjustifiable conclusions from an undeniable fact. It does not at all follow that, because logical form is a necessary condition of intelligibility and intelligible expression, it is either the sole or the sufficient condition; that because it is indirectly a norm it is the only norm. Logic has its being in the more general field of discourse and communication—a proposition outside discourse is nothing. Logical analysis cannot legislate other meanings out of existence for the reason that logical meaning presupposes these very meanings for its own significance.[1]

This, then, is the main thesis of the chapter. This general principle has an especially important application in connection with the claim of logic to determine the existential or ontological import of propositions, and to show "the verbalism of false metaphysics." The unjustifiable character of such claims has been shown in specific contexts; here it remains merely to state our conclusions in general form. The normative function of logic is distinctly limited. It functions within a larger context of cognition which is concerned with metalogical problems of language and cannot legislate in this domain. This limitation

---

[1] For a fuller development of this entire position, see *The Intelligible World*, Chapter III.

may be seen within logic itself. Logic can give only correctness, never truth. Internal consistency and self-criticism are the only criteria of logic and these are not sufficient to determine its own truth. For the initial assumptions of logic are themselves logical in nature, and the "truth" of logic or of a logic must be independent of its initial assumptions. Thus logic can never test itself, or rather such test does not prove the truth of logic. The problem of the truth of logic lies beyond logic. It is a metalogical or epistemological problem.[1]

We are thus led to metalogical, as distinguished from purely logical, problems of language. The larger problem of the relation of language to cognition goes far beyond the problem of the relation of language to logic. Problems of knowledge cannot be separated from problems of language. Knowledge is "judgment plus discourse." Truth is the relation of a proposition to reality, but a proposition outside discourse is nothing. Knowledge, as we shall see, cannot be separated from expression. Verification, which is an essential part of knowledge, cannot be separated from confirmation within discourse and communication. It follows that the ultimate problems of knowledge are problems of language and expression and it is for this reason that, as we have said, problems of language are the last and deepest problems of the philosophic mind. To these problems we shall now turn.

[1] This point has been stated with great clearness by C. I. Lewis in his article, "Logic and Pragmatism," p. 41, in *Contemporary American Philosophy*, Vol. II.

CHAPTER VIII

LANGUAGE AND COGNITION: THE METALOGICAL PROBLEMS OF LANGUAGE

I

A

The preceding chapter on the relation of logic to language is but part of a larger problem of the relation of language to cognition. At various points in the preceding chapter we came upon problems of language which are outside the province of logic and logical analysis. Our way of stating this situation is to say that logic presupposes that terms have meaning and that propositions have sense, but it cannot determine that meaning and that sense. All that it can do is to determine the logical meaning or the meaning for logic, not the meaning or sense for discourse. The determination of this meaning and sense involves a standpoint which goes beyond logic.

To such problems we have already given the name metalogical, and there is ample historical justification for the term. From mediaeval times on, the term metalogic has been used to characterize a sphere transcending the logical. Kant and Hegel recognized, of course, both the field and the problems, and their enlargement of the field of logic was the result. The transcendental logic of Kant and the philosophical logic of Hegel are both concerned with the problem. So far as problems of language are concerned, the application of the term metalogical to the problems, already described, is also justified by usage. Carnap recognizes metalogical problems of language, as distinct from the logical, although he does not differentiate them very clearly. Such problems he defines in general as concerned with propositions about language or languages and their relation to things, or reality.[1]

B

The Field of Metalogical: Pre-logical and Post-logical

The field of the metalogical investigation of language is precisely determined by the limits of logical analysis. The starting-

[1] *Die Überwindung der Metaphysik*, etc.

point of the critique exercised by logic on language is the divergence of linguistic meaning from logical meaning. It is at these points of divergence that the field of the metalogical begins. Some of these problems we may describe as *pre-logical*.

Logic is concerned with reflective thought. But all that is reflected presupposes the spontaneous. However this spontaneous character of knowing and thinking may be conceived, it is bound up with language and its natural tendencies. The *Worthaftigkeit des Denkens* is a principle which cannot be successfully impugned. It is at this point that problems describable as pre-logical arise. They have to do with the relation of language to the most elementary forms of knowing—"perceptual" or "intuitive" knowledge—or with the relation of language to knowledge by "simple acquaintance" as distinguished from knowledge by description, if such knowledge there be. The entire problem of the relation of intuition to expression is involved, as is also the question of the categories and their relation to language.

But there are also what we may call post-logical problems of language and cognition. This same spontaneous character of thought manifests itself in another direction. Not only is language constitutive of reality in the sense described (language creates the realm of cognitive meanings); it also creates a world of post-logical meanings. By virtue of the close relations of language to thought, certain natural tendencies of language not only create new entities but generate reasonings about these entities. The general upward movement of language "from the physical to the spiritual," the transfer of names, analogical predication with the accompanying development of ontological predicates, creates an entire region or universe of discourse which is post-logical or metalogical in this sense. The classical form of this problem was presented by Kant in his transcendental dialectic. The problem there is indeed stated in the form of a "critique of reason" in its speculative use or aspect. Does *reasoning* about non-observable entities such as the soul, the cosmos, or total world, and God, give us truth or "*transcendentaler Schein*"? But the problem may just as well, and better perhaps, be stated in this way: Is discourse about such objects intelligible discourse or is it meaningless? It is for this reason that, as Mauthner says, Kant's *Critique of*

Reason is really a *Kritik der Sprache*. In any case, precisely these problems, and similar ones, appear from our standpoint as metalogical problems of language.

C

Language not "Moulded on Reality"

The metalogical problem, as here defined, constitutes the fourth of the problems of the philosophy of language outlined in the introductory chapter. The question, as there formulated, was this: What is the relation subsisting between thoughts, and the words and sentences which embody them, and that which they refer to and mean? More generally, it is the critical problem of the relation of language and linguistic forms to reality.

We have seen how this problem arises. Any experience which is more than a mere vague awareness is already constituted and categorized by language. Moreover, the natural tendencies of language, with the "natural speech construction" which results, create new objects and entities which become the subjects of discourse and supposedly the objects of knowledge. It is just here, as we saw, that the deepest problem of the philosophy of language arises. For the more energetically the human spirit builds its language—indeed all its forms and symbols—the more it thus *constructs* reality—the further it often seems to have departed from the original source of its being and from the immediate experience from which the constructions took their start. Has not the human spirit been caught in the toils of its own creations? Has not language woven a veil between us and immediate reality?[1] If so, language would not be *moulded on reality*; the divergence of language from reality would be the thesis of the metalogical—as distinguished from the logical—critique of language.

The general thesis of the logicians' critique of language is that if language is the mould of thought, it is an ill-fitting mould. In the words of Wittgenstein, "Language disguises thought; so that from the external form of the clothes one cannot infer the form of thought they clothe, because the

[1] Chapter I, p. 50.

LANGUAGE AND COGNITION

external form of the clothes is constructed with quite another object than to let the form of the body be recognized."[1] With this may be compared and contrasted the metalogical critique of which we have spoken. If language *disguises* thought, it *distorts* reality. In the words of Bergson or Whitehead our language is not moulded on reality, and consequently when reality is pressed into that mould, it is misrepresented or distorted. Here, too, "language being constructed for quite another object," namely, for purposes of practice, it is not moulded on reality and is therefore utterly unfitted to "represent" or to "express" it. On one view it distorts reality because it cuts out static states or phases from what is really a continuum of duration or events. On another view it distorts reality because, by its natural tendencies, it represents as integral that which is really a mere collection of entities or of events.[2]

The significant phrase is, then, "moulded on reality." It is assumed that the relation of language to reality should be that of a mould or copy. It is further assumed that a standpoint is possible from which this relation can be determined. As in the case of the critique of language by logic, it is assumed that a standpoint outside discourse can be found from which the irrational and ill-fitting character of language can be determined, so here it is assumed that cognition is independent of language and discourse, and that the relation of language to reality is an entirely external and artificial one.

In a sense it is the examination of these assumptions which constitutes the thread of discourse of this entire chapter. We shall attempt to show that this way of stating the problem of language and cognition is a false one, and that the assumptions underlying it are wholly unjustified. The development of what we believe to be the true conception of the relation of language to reality involves also a conception of the relation of language and linguistic meaning to truth. We have now no longer merely the problem meaning, nor merely the logical problem of rightness, but the problem of linguistic truth. In other words, the phenomenological problem of meanings and the logical problem of linguistic form pass over into the metalogical problem of knowledge.

[1] *Tractatus*, p. 63.   [2] See Appendix III.

II

PRELIMINARY NOTION OF "KNOWING." AMBIGUITIES IN THE IDEA

A

The general character of the metalogical problems of language is now before us, as well as a preliminary determination of the main points at which these problems arise. The problem of the cognitive value of language, or of linguistic validity, is the basal problem of a philosophy of language. But as it is the basal problem, so it is the most difficult—largely because of the uncertainties and ambiguities in our ideas of what it is to know.

We all assume that we understand what it is to know. But in reality knowing is very much like time, of which St. Augustine said, "If you do not ask me, I know what it is, but if you ask me, I cannot say." We have, to be sure, as John Dewey says, knowledge just as we have the measles, but when we ask what it is we thus have, we are no longer sure, and it is really very difficult to say.

We are all aware that when we use the word "know" we do not always use it in the same sense. Consequently when two people talk about knowledge they are often talking about quite different things and obviously cannot come to an understanding. If I say, with C. J. Keyser, that most knowledge is of the undefined, as for instance knowledge of love or knowledge of life, I obviously have a very different notion of knowledge from one who says that everything can be defined, and if I cannot define it I cannot know it.[1] If I hold that the soul is not an object of knowledge, because I cannot put the word soul in a proposition, "X is a soul," and point to X, I obviously have an entirely different notion of knowledge from one who says I have an immediate intuition of the existence of the soul.

It is well to recognize the different senses in which the word knowledge is used, and therefore the extent of the uncertainties and difficulties which result. It is well also to recognize that

---

[1] As when Wittgenstein says in the preface to the *Tractatus*, "What can be said at all can be said clearly."

this is a dialectical, not an empirical problem. By this I mean that the questions, what is knowledge and what it is to know, while "meaningful questions," are not meaningful in the sense of the "empirical criterion." It is a matter of mutual acknowledgment in discourse. All men, it is true, agree that knowledge is the apprehension of the real; all recognize that knowledge and truth are correlative conceptions; but there agreement ends and different meanings of knowledge begin. There is no empirical verification of any definition of either knowledge or truth. Their objects cannot be pointed to; the meanings can be merely acknowledged.

Recognizing then this situation, let us consider the chief ambiguities in the notion of knowledge. There are at least three which it is important to clear up as a preliminary to our study of cognition and language. They are concerned (*a*) with narrower and broader conceptions of knowledge, whether knowledge is confined to science and scientific method or not; (*b*) closely connected with this is the question of different ways of knowing; and (*c*) the different views of knowing involved in such distinctions as immediate and mediate knowledge, knowledge by simple acquaintance and knowledge by description. With this is also connected the problem whether there is knowledge by "dialectic" or interpretation.

B

Narrower and Broader Conceptions of Knowing

There are evidently, in view of the illustrations given, two fundamentally different conceptions of knowing, the one limited and narrow, the other broader and "more humane." With the narrower conception we are already familiar. It confines the notion of knowing to the domestic conception developed in science and scientific method. Knowing is identical with limited and directed reference. All so-called knowledge of the undefined, such as of love or of life, as in Keyser's illustration, is really not knowledge at all, but belongs to the field of emotion or emotive expression.[1]

---
[1] For a clear-cut statement of this position, see Ogden and Richards, *The Meaning of Meaning*, pp. 157 ff.

The acceptance of this narrower view would of course simplify the problem of language and cognition enormously, as indeed it has for those who accept it. It eliminates most of the metalogical problems of language by turning a large part of our words into *Scheinwörte* and of our propositions into *Scheinsätze*, and therefore most of our discourse into mere *flatus vocis*. Such a procedure is possible, however, only to one who deliberately cuts himself off from a large part of human intercourse in which the broader notion of knowledge is a necessary condition or presupposition. When the humanistically minded is outraged by the appropriation of "knowledge" to such narrow use, it is frequently replied that one "would gladly give him back his beloved word" if only he would provide some other word which will mark the distinction which it is necessary to make between knowledge in the "scientific" sense and these other humanistic uses of the word. That, however, it should be pointed out, is not the humanist's problem. The burden of proof, and therefore the providing of the new name, is the responsibility of those who have thus narrowed the use for their own purposes. The broader conception of knowledge is the necessary condition of intelligible human discourse.

One way of solving the difficulty and of retaining one's humanity, so to speak, is the way taken by John Dewey. We may arbitrarily reserve the word "knowing" for the scientific usage, and then maintain that knowing is only one of a number of possible "relations to reality," the others being the practical and emotive, such as the moral and the aesthetic. The difficulty with this solution is that there is no possibility of such relations to reality, without some element of assertion or judgment, either explicit or implicit. For a human being, however it may be with the lower animals, it is not possible to have any relation with reality which does not involve some cognitive element. It is not surprising, then, that in his actual use of the notion of knowing, Dewey vacillates, sometimes using the narrower meaning and at other times the broader and more humane. This vacillation is inevitable, as it was for Kant, for all who do not wish to limit their discourse arbitrarily to one universe.

C

Ways of Knowing

We shall assume then, tentatively at least, the broader conception of knowing. Part of this broader and more humane conception has always been the idea of different ways of knowing. This idea has historically taken many forms, the most significant and influential, perhaps, being that of Kant's distinction between the pure and the practical reason. In characterizing the latter, Kant vacillated between the two notions of faith and knowledge, but in the main there seems to be no question that the way of the practical reason was a way of knowing.

A modern form of this same general idea is that made popular for Anglo-American thought by A. N. Whitehead and his many followers, namely, that science with its method of abstraction is but one way of knowing. Whereas science and scientific method deal with the quantitative aspect of things, art and religion deal with qualities and values. This general position has been formulated by B. H. Streeter as the doctrine of *Bi-Representationism*.[1] It is not necessary at this point to discuss either the general question of the two contrasting ways of knowing, nor the details of the special form of it to which reference is here made. Both will receive due attention in the discussions to come. It is sufficient for our purpose here to point out that the broader conception of knowing inevitably brings with it the notion of different ways of knowing, and to emphasize the fact that an adequate treatment of the problem of language and cognition requires a consideration of these possibilities.

D

Knowledge by Acquaintance and Knowledge by Description

Whatever view of knowledge we may take, whether the broader or the narrower, whether there is but one way in which knowledge may present or represent its object or more than one

[1] B. H. Streeter, *Reality*, pp. 110 ff., 126 ff.

way, there is a third ambiguity in our notion of knowledge which permeates all conceptions, the ambiguity, namely, expressed by the contrast of mere acquaintance and description.

When we use the word know we do not always, as we have seen, use it in the same sense. For example, I may say "I know him," meaning that I am acquainted with him, or I may say I know that he is honest, meaning that I know that a certain description of him or proposition about him is true. This distinction between direct and indirect knowledge, between presentational immediacy and representation in idea, is of course very old; we shall make use of the modern statement of the difference, namely, that between mere acquaintance and description. This is perhaps the most striking fact in knowledge—that it seems to fall into these two divisions. In any case this dyadic conception of knowledge, as we may call it, sets one of the most fundamental problems of language and knowledge. Knowledge by description, precisely because it is description, involves language, or at least symbols developed out of language (and which as we have seen must ultimately be interpreted in linguistic discourse); but knowledge by mere acquaintance, if there be such, might conceivably be prior to and independent of language. This is one of the most fundamental problems of language and cognition, the solution of which has far-reaching consequences for the entire philosophy of language. The tendency in many contemporary schools of philosophy is to make a sharp distinction between these two kinds of knowledge, a distinction much sharper than an analysis of the factors of knowing will permit. In any case, this problem must be made the starting-point of our study.

E

Knowledge as Interpretation

The conception of knowing developed above may be described as the dyadic theory of knowing, because it insists upon the distinction between the *two* meanings of knowing and the two kinds of knowing—by direct acquaintance and by description—to which these two meanings correspond. This dyadic conception is to be distinguished, of course, from the theory of bi-representationism which refers to two ways or two types of description. Is there any other aspect of knowing not exhausted in these two? There are those, among whom the present writer is one, who hold that these two aspects of knowing must be supplemented by a third, which may be described as interpretation or dialectic.

A well-known form of this conception of knowing is that of Josiah Royce, which he described as the Triadic Theory. Royce put the position in the following graphic way: "Perception says it (knowledge) is not in me; conception says it is not in me; interpretation says it is nigh these, even in thy heart." By this Royce meant to say that the notion of knowing is not exhausted in that of perception or direct acquaintance nor in conception or description, for all description involves conception, but in a further process called interpretation. This meant in Royce's thought that all perception and conception involve elements of interpretation; but it also meant that there is a third level of knowing which so to speak transcends both perception and conception.[1]

This triadic notion of knowing with its conception of a third way of knowing—through interpretation—I believe to be not only true, but a conception of immense importance for the understanding of the relation of language to cognition. As we travel up the scale of knowledge—from presentation to representation—we come finally to a kind of knowledge in which the object conceived or meant is no longer *given* along with the symbols through which it is conceived. At the lower end of this scale we have direct acquaintance with objects in so far as such direct acquaintance is possible; this is cognition in which what is meant is grasped in perception, a union of sensation and conception. At the other end is pure thought—or approximation to such thought—knowledge which is meaningful or significant reference and nothing more. Here knowing must be interpretation. This conception of knowledge by interpretation has already been suggested in our discussions of the relation of meaning to verification in earlier contexts.[2]

---

[1] This well-known thesis of Josiah Royce is developed in his *The Problem of Christianity*. For further comments on this notion, see my book, *The Intelligible World*, p. 80 f.

[2] Chapter V, pp. 226 ff. Also Chapter VI, pp. 259 ff.

The notion of verification within communication involves precisely this knowledge by interpretation. I believe it to be the central problem of language and cognition. Be this as it may, we shall accept this triadic conception of knowing as the basis of our further investigations.

III

KNOWLEDGE BY MERE ACQUAINTANCE. THE FIRST METALOGICAL PROBLEM OF LANGUAGE

A

Metalogical problems of language we divided into two—the pre-logical and the post-logical. Logic, though concerned with meaning, does not include in its province all kinds of meanings —neither the adherent meanings of things nor all the mobile meanings of words. Logical meaning enters in only with conceptual meaning. Wherever there is conceptual meaning, wherever there is the conceptual form of knowledge, there is knowledge by description. But purely perceptual knowledge, knowledge by mere acquaintance, is a pre-logical problem, and the problem of language and knowing at this point a purely metalogical question.

Is there not, then, prior to all knowledge by description, knowledge by acquaintance, without any element of description, and therefore knowledge without any linguistic element? The problem here presented was already stated in a preliminary fashion in Chapter III, in our general discussion of language and meaning. As stated there the problem was, does language create the world of meanings, or does it find a world of pre-linguistic meanings which it embodies and expresses? There we saw that cognitive meaning, as distinguished from behavioural meaning, always contains an element of bi-polarity —of re-presentation—and this involves language.[1] This position, merely suggested as a corollary of our earlier analysis, we shall now seek to establish more fully.

The notion of knowledge by acquaintance is very ambiguous and includes cases of widely varying character. Awareness of sense data, such as the colour of a table or the sound of a

[1] Chapter III, p. 105 f.

motor, direct experience or *Erlebniss* of qualities and values, acquaintance with "things" or persons, or even direct acquaintance with such things as "life," time, etc.—all these are included under knowledge by acquaintance as distinguished from knowledge by description. Now, if we include all these under the notion there is clearly no absolute line between knowledge by acquaintance and knowledge by description. In the case of persons it seems more than probable that, in the strict sense of the word, there is no knowledge by mere acquaintance.[1] In our discussion of this point—knowledge of other selves—in earlier connections we found that while there is knowledge of other selves, this knowledge is not one of direct acquaintance but rather of interpretation—in the process of communication.[2] It seems reasonably certain, then, that the problem of knowledge by mere acquaintance, without language and description, revolves entirely about our analysis and interpretation of two cases, namely, (*a*) sensation and sense perception, and (*b*) non-sensuous intuition or *Erlebniss*. Let us take these up in order.

B

Language and Sense Perception. Sensuous Intuition

The argument for knowledge by mere acquaintance, without any element of representation or description, may be put in the following way. Surely re-presentation in any form requires and presupposes direct presentation. Surely there is cognition, knowledge in some form, before language arises. In our discussion of meaning, we started with the meaning of "things" as in a sense prior to the meaning of "words." Surely this pre-linguistic meaning is a case of knowledge, and therefore of knowledge without any element of description.

Bergson puts the case for this position excellently by stating a hypothetical situation. "Suppose," he writes, "language fallen into disuse, society (and communication) dissolved . . . the dampness of the ground will subsist none the less, capable of inscribing itself automatically in sensation and of sending

---

[1] Miss Stebbing says it is doubtful (*op. cit.*, p. 23). I should say it is more than doubtful. [2] Chapter V, p. 218 f. Also Chapter VI.

a vague idea to the deadened intellect. The intellect will still affirm in implicit terms. . . ." "And consequently," he adds, "neither distinct concepts, nor words . . . nor the desire of spreading the truth, nor that of bettering oneself, are of the essence of affirmation."[1]

This is, I repeat, excellently put—vividly and eloquently. There is no doubt also that something *would* be left if language were gone. But the question is, just what would be left? Could we call it knowing? Awareness of the dampness would still be there—the mere whatness of the sense datum and perhaps its otherness, although the latter is perhaps questionable. But what is it that the intellect, in Bergson's words, "will still affirm in implicit terms"? The only thing, I feel sure, would be something like "that is that." In order that anything else should be affirmed, language, supposed to have fallen into disuse, would have to come back. In other words, the only possible element of cognition which does not involve language and linguistic form is the tautology, "that is that." But even this tautology, affirmed merely implicitly, involves linguistic form.

We have asked the question: what would be left if language were gone? Our answer is nothing that is affirmed—even in "implicit terms." In other words, we "have" something, the sensation, but we "know" nothing. This distinction between having and knowing is one of real importance and one that is often overlooked. We may have a vague awareness that is not yet categorized by language, but knowledge does not arise until the intellect affirms, either explicitly or implicitly, and such affirmation is impossible without linguistic form. This is, of course, equivalent to saying that judgment is the elementary form of knowledge.

If, then, there is any such *pure awareness* as here postulated, it does not even give us presentational knowledge in any intelligible sense of the word; it is not an acquaintance with *objects*, not even with simple qualities. One cannot tell what this intuition gives him. Even if it is there it cannot be expressed. The expression "affirmation in implicit terms" represents the attempt to keep the notion of knowledge without the notion of linguistic form. The question may well be raised whether the notion of implicit terms is itself not a *contradictio in adjecto*;

---

[1] H. Bergson, *Creative Evolution* (English translation), p. 292.

LANGUAGE AND COGNITION

whether, indeed, affirmation in any intelligible sense is possible that is not explicit in the sense of duality between subject and predicate.

It is at this point that the question of atomic propositions, raised in the preceding chapter, can be properly considered. Propositions are the elements of knowledge, for only judgments or propositions can be true or false. An atomic proposition is one, I take it, which is closest to this knowledge by direct acquaintance and expresses or embodies that supposed knowledge. "This is green," or "this is damp," the case in Bergson's illustration, would be such a proposition. But that which is represented or expressed in this form of words is either not a proposition or it is not atomic. If it merely expresses the having of the greenness it is not a proposition; if it is an affirmation that this *is* green, it is not atomic, for it already contains the element of distinction and duality of which we have spoken. The entire notion of atomic propositions is a confused one, as shown by the illustrations used. It may mean merely a simple proposition as distinguished from compound propositions. In that case "Columbus was a sailor" is an atomic proposition, and all propositions which state single facts are atomic. But we may also call such a proposition a complex proposition and analyse it as follows: "There is an object which is Columbus" and "that object is a sailor." In this case the former proposition was not atomic. But even the simplest proposition analysis can reveal is not atomic in structure, for it contains that bi-polar character without which the most elemental form of knowledge is impossible.

That which is "implicitly affirmed" without language—if such an *Unding* is possible—reduces, we saw, to the tautology "that is that." Even here language and its categories are already present. But assuming that there is something that would remain were all language and communication dissolved, what is it that would remain? We may, perhaps, call it knowledge; that is, as we have seen, partly at least, a matter of definition. But as Eddington says, "if so it is not very significant." Very justly he maintains that there is no cognition in any significant sense which does not involve communication and some sort of language.

C

Language and Intuition (Erlebniss)

So far, then, as a hypothetical knowledge by mere acquaintance in the sphere of perceptual objects is concerned, there is good reason to believe that it is either non-existent or at least so insignificant as scarcely to merit the term knowledge. Let us now examine the second case, namely, that of non-sensuous intuition or *Erlebniss*.

There are those for whom the problem of knowledge is confined to the knowledge of things, or to that form of knowledge which is connected with sense-perception. Such a limitation is not possible for us who have taken that view of knowledge which is broader and, therefore, more humane. If we have accepted the position that there is knowledge vague and undefined, as knowledge of love and life, and that such knowledge is not perceptual but a matter of *Erlebniss*, it is incumbent upon us to examine this phase of knowledge also.[1]

That there is knowledge of this type is quite widely held. The objects of such *Erleben*, or non-sensuous intuition, are varied. They include (*a*) the emotional, non-sensuous intuition of values, or we may perhaps say, tertiary qualities; (*b*) the non-sensuous intuition of form and form qualities, as for instance of a melody; (*c*) the non-sensuous intuition of such indefinable and undefined objects as "love" or "life."

The problem has already been taken up in a preliminary way in Chapter IV in our discussion of the intuitive meanings of words, more especially our study of value words and the intuition of values through emotion. There we established the fact of such intuition and determined its nature by meeting the objections to the notion of non-sensuous intuition. It is not necessary to go over that ground again. Assuming the reality of such intuition we may proceed directly to the question of its relation to language.

I think we may say the same thing here as in the case of sense perception or sensuous intuition. Here again, if language were fallen into disuse and all communication were dissolved,

---

[1] The notions of *Erleben* and *Erlebniss* are defined and analysed in Chapter IV, pp. 135 and 151.

there would be no knowledge in the sense of *Erlebniss*. The argument for this positon would, of course, be the same, *mutatis mutandis*, as in the case of simple acquaintance by sensuous intuition. Without language, all that we could affirm, implicitly no less than explicitly, would be "that is that." But there is an additional element which enters into this situation that requires special consideration. This element is due to the fact that the very discovery and fixation of these objects is itself dependent upon language.

In our study of language development—the transfer of names through metaphor and the consequent analogical predication—we pointed out that this "figurative" use of language is not so much a fanciful expression for something otherwise known, as the means of apprehending and fixating new aspects and meanings. The natural movement of language, the upward movement as we described it, is from the physical to the spiritual. All words are physical in their origin and have a physical reference. It is through metaphorical transfer that they acquire their new references, their *second* intentions, but they acquire these new references because they become the vehicle for the intuition and description or expression of new entities. Moral qualities and values are expressible in this fashion alone. Nobility of character is what language designates as magnanimity, generosity, large-heartedness, high-mindedness, because there are no other words except such figurative expressions. But these very figurative expressions *are expressions* precisely because they are representative, or rather constitutive, of the intuitions themselves. Here intuition and expression are one, for the reason that the figurative expression itself is part of the apprehension or knowing. In a special sense, then, non-senuous intuition is bound up with language; intuition and expression are one. There is no knowledge of mere acquaintance which does not involve an element of description. It is indeed only in language that the objects of these intuitions can be "shown forth." They cannot be pointed to, they can only be acknowledged.

Knowing in its simplest forms, of both sensuous and non-sensuous intuition, is then inseparable from language. This inseparability holds, therefore, *a fortiori*, for the more doubtful forms of knowledge by direct acquaintance and intuition. We have already seen that this is so in the case of the supposed knowledge, by mere acquaintance, of persons. I know that there are other selves directly in the processes of communication, and their existence—as necessary presuppositions of intelligible communication—is verified in the process of communication. In this very process of communication itself language is involved, but even more when we pass from the mere "that" to the "what" (acquaintance involves knowledge of the what). There is no knowledge which does not involve an element of description and therefore of language. Let us now pass from this knowledge of selves to the notion of direct acquaintance (through *Erleben*) of "life," "flux of reality," etc.

Such intuition, as for example the Bergsonian, involves a notion of *pure awareness* even more immediate than the supposed forms of awareness we have been examining. It does not even give presentational knowledge in any meaningful sense of the term. It is not even an acquaintance with simple qualities. One cannot even begin to tell what this intuition gives him. He is unable to bring it under any concept or to make any statement about it. Here, more than in the former cases, all that can be said is "that is that"—the content of the intuition would be conceptualized only in the vague and general way as "something or other." Yet he must communicate the intuition; otherwise there is no verifiable knowledge in any possible sense of the word. It cannot be even pointed to. All that can be done is to "gesticulate in its direction with words and metaphors." As we shall see later, this is precisely what Bergson does—which means that, while no one can refute his statement that reality is other than as constituted by language, experience of that reality, except as vague awareness, must be so constituted. For either the words or metaphors with which the nature of this reality is communicated show forth or represent this reality, or they merely express emotional attitudes towards it.

I have emphasized this last point for a very definite reason. The thesis that language is not moulded on reality assumes, as we have seen, that we know reality and its nature directly by some sort of intuition independently of language and its categories. It is this assumption, in the form just examined, that underlies Bergson's critique of language, although it is assumed by other philosophies of language as well. We shall come to this point in its proper place. I wish merely to point out here that any intuition of reality, knowledge by mere acquaintance, without an element of description, is pure myth.

D

"Identity of Intuition and Expression." The Bi-polar Character of Knowledge

The conclusion of our preceding studies is, then, that knowing in any significant sense of the word is inseparable from language; that, in a very real sense, language *creates* the world of cognitive meanings, and that a knowledge by pure acquaintance, without any element or "description"—pure presentational immediacy—is, in the words of Cassirer, "a mythical phase of knowledge."

The classical expression of this relation of knowing to language is that of Croce in his thesis of the identity of intuition and expression, developed in his aesthetics. In this well-known work, which is entitled *Aesthetic or General Linguistic,* he maintains that intuition is impossible without expression. Developed mainly in connection with aesthetics, he extends it to the entire range of knowledge. So far as aesthetics is concerned, his thesis is that art is essentially expression. The artist does not first intuit or present his object to himself and then find linguistic or other forms with which to express it; the expression is rather a constitutive part of the intuition itself. More generally, one does not first possess an object in knowing and then express the nature of that object in terms of arbitrary and conventional signs, but the expression is a constitutive part of the knowing itself.

It is this thesis, then, that we wish to maintain. It is, viewed from every angle, the most important thesis, perhaps, of our entire philosophy of language. It is, to be sure, one which is constantly and emphatically denied; but only, I think, when the real meaning of the position is not understood. We have already maintained the principle of the inseparability of thought and language, the *Worthaftigkeit des Denkens* (Chapter VI). When this principle is denied the denial is founded upon certain equivocations and errors. It is undeniable that we can think with geometric figures, algebraic signs, and ideographic symbols—in short, without any words—but we forget that these are also languages, and that if we seek to communicate what we think we cannot do so without resorting at certain points to ordinary language.[1] But while we maintain the essentials of Croce's thesis we must be careful to avoid an error in his theory which not only vitiates much of his aesthetics but has baleful effects throughout his entire philosophy. Knowledge is indeed bound up with expression, but there is no expression without the correlative, understanding. Communicability is not an irrelevant *addendum* to aesthetic expression—it is the very heart of it. Still less is communicability irrelevant to knowledge in the narrower sense. Verifiability and communication are inseparable.[2]

Wherever, then, there is knowing, there is also expression. But expression always contains in it the beginning of re-presentation. Mere presentational immediacy without expression, and the beginning of re-presentation, lacks as yet the element of knowing. Let us take the simplest case of expression possible, namely, that *intrinsic expressiveness* of which we spoke when we were dealing with the different kinds of linguistic meaning.[3] When the Botocudos use the reduplication, ou-a-tou-ou-ou-ou, for the sea, this expresses their emotion towards the infinite sea, but it is also re-presentative of the sea; something of the nature of the structure is caught in the expression; the element of analogical re-presentation has already begun. It is only by virtue of this element of re-presentation that the expression of emotion passes over into knowledge and its communication. This general law holds for all knowledge, from the simplest and apparently most immediate to the most mediated and developed. There is no knowledge without expression. Expression is part of the knowing process; but there is no expression which does not involve the beginning of dualism between the expression and the expressed, and therefore an element of re-presentation and description.

This fundamental character of all knowing has been described

---

[1] B. Croce, *op. cit.*, p. 23.
[2] See in this connection Gardiner's comments on this point, *op. cit.*, p. 57.
[3] See Chapter IV, p. 143 f.

by Cassirer as the bi-polar nature of knowledge and is characterized by him as an *Urphenomen*. We understand now what is meant by the bi-polar character of all knowing; let us make clear what he means by calling it an *Urphenomen*. The doctrine of presentational immediacy, or knowledge by simple acquaintance, proceeds on the assumption that the original form of knowledge is one in which we merely have or possess the object. Such a hypothetical form of knowledge is for Cassirer a pure myth. What he calls *das reine Ausdrucksphenomen*, our "expression," is inseparable from the simplest intuition and is therefore an *Urphenomen*. But the element of re-presentation, what he calls *das Symbolische Grundverhältniss*, is equally original. It is the constitutive moment in all knowledge. Without this polarity, and therewith the reference of the presentation to the thing presented, the entire notion of knowledge collapses. It follows that the problems of knowledge and the problems of language are inseparable.[1]

E

The Identity of Intuition and Expression and Knowledge by Interpretation

An important corollary of the principle we have been developing is that all knowledge—even knowledge in its simplest form—involves an element of interpretation. This notion is indeed a commonplace in all theories of knowledge except those which hold to the doctrine of knowledge by simple acquaintance, but the significance of the notion is not always fully realized.

As ordinarily stated, the view maintains that all perception and perceptual knowledge contains an element of interpretation. By this is meant that such knowledge is not merely the *having* of sense data, but the sense data as interpreted by judgment. There is always an element of judgment in all perception—judgment being the elemental form of all knowledge. But more than this is really involved. Intuition is

[1] This thesis is the underlying theme of the entire *Philosophie der Symbolischen Formen*, but is especially clearly developed in Vol. III, Part I. A statement of it is found on pp. 143 ff.

inseparable from expression and knowledge includes interpretation of the expression. As Royce rightly says, mere perception says of knowledge, it is not in me. It is only in interpretation involving communication that knowledge has its being. All knowledge involves communication, either latent or overt. Or as Plato expressed it in the *Theaetetus*, "Knowledge is judgment plus discourse." It is this *plus* without which knowledge is not complete. Even the simplest case of perceptual knowledge, "it rains," "this is green," has no meaning until it is interpreted. Definition of terms and interpretation of propositions are part of the knowledge process. Such *interpretation* may be logical, logical in so far as implicational meaning is involved. But beyond the logical there is the metalogical, and this is part of the knowing process. This general statement holds, we shall see, for knowledge by description also. Here we are concerned merely to emphasize the element of interpretation in what is called knowledge by acquaintance.

F

Language and the Categories

A second corollary of the principle we have been developing is that the categories of knowledge are ultimately, and in the last analysis, categories of language in the philosophical sense of language. If intuition and expression are identical in the sense in which we have defined the notion, and if, further, expression must, in the last analysis, be linguistic, then the categories of intuition must also be categories of expression and these in turn of language. Otherwise expressed, *the only way to determine being or reality is in those forms in which statements about it are possible.*

This situation is grounded methodologically in the very nature of the relation of language to reality. Let us suppose, for instance, that the categories can be determined otherwise than through analysis of linguistic expression, whatever the means of that determination is supposed to be. Nevertheless the moment *statements* are made about being or reality (and there is no knowledge in the sense of public or verifiable knowledge until such statements are made) that moment the linguistic categories or forms must again come into play and must be determinative.

This is the heart of the category doctrine of both Aristotle and Kant. Both used the notional categories of language, as distinguished from the variable grammatical categories of different languages, as *Leitfaden* (Kant's term) to the categories. Kant, to be sure, made the mistake of taking the forms of logical judgments or propositions, thus limiting the field of the categories, as Hegel later saw. This is difficult to understand in view of Kant's conception of ordinary logic as purely formal and analytical, and his insistence upon the need of a transcendental logic or "logic of truth." Nevertheless, despite his mistakes, Kant saw clearly that whatever may be said of the "thing in itself," empirical reality must be constituted by the categories; that is, to determine the forms in which *statements* about reality are possible is at the same time to determine its constitutive elements. To take but one illustration, if no statement about reality is possible which does not have the form of subject and predicate, substance and attribute, then precisely such notions must be constitutive of reality in so far as it can be empirically intuited and *expressed*. For the expression cannot be separated from the intuition.

The problem of the categories is, then, in a very real sense the fundamental metalogical problem of language. Specific problems in this field belong to specific contexts and will receive attention when we come to the study of different "languages"—of science, poetry, etc.—and to the different symbolic forms. Here our sole point is to make clear the fact that, since knowledge involves expression and interpretation, the categories of knowledge must, in the last analysis, be those forms in which statements about reality are possible. This, I take it, is the meaning of Wittgenstein's statement that "the limits of my language are the limits of my world." With this, properly understood and interpreted, I should agree. It is true that by limiting language unduly the limits of the world may also be unduly narrowed. This certain so-called logical analyses of language may, as we have seen, do. But the statement is in principle sound.

IV

KNOWLEDGE BY DESCRIPTION. THE SECOND METALOGICAL PROBLEM OF LANGUAGE

A

The bi-polar conception of knowledge which we have developed involves the denial of any absolute distinction between knowledge by acquaintance and knowledge by description. There is, none the less, a place for a relative distinction between the two. An element of re-presentation is involved even in that form of knowledge which we call presentation, but this re-presentation may reach a degree of development which may properly be described as description in the specific sense in which the term is here used.

The notion of description has both a general and a more special meaning. It may mean the showing forth or representing of any "thing" or object, in any fashion whatsover—in short, representation as contrasted with direct presentation. It may however also mean a representation which is also a delineation. The more general notion of description involves no implication as to the mode or manner of the description. Even the showing forth of a state of feeling, as for instance in the emotional expression of a lyric poem, involves a description of that state. Many things can be shown forth which cannot be pointed to, and all such showing forth involves an element of description. Description in the narrower sense, or delineation, involves, on the other hand, not only the notion of a copy in some sense, but always, I think, the notion of a spatial copy. Description in the general sense includes at least three types of representation, namely (*a*) that of copying or imitation, (*b*) analogical representation, and (*c*) symbolic representation.

With this notion of description in its most general form, we may proceed to the specific question of "knowledge by description" and its relation to language. This is, as we have seen, a metalogical, not a logical problem. It is true that we became acquainted in the preceding chapter with the notion of a "logical description." We criticized the notion of descriptions that describe nothing, but our main point was that, in

# LANGUAGE AND COGNITION

the very nature of the case, the question of the truth of a description, of the relation of a description to reality, is not a logical question at all. It is to this second of the metalogical problems of language that we now direct our attention. Let us begin by attempting a more detailed analysis of the notion of description.

B

The Notions of Representation and of "Picture"

The entire notion of re-presentation and description has recently been subjected to examination in the logical studies of Wittgenstein and Ramsey. Any notion of re-presentation must have in it, it is held, the notion of picturing or of a picture. Wittgenstein starts out, as Ramsey says, with the difficult notions of a picture and of the "form of representation." A picture itself is a fact, the fact that its elements are combined with one another in a definite way. Whenever, then, we talk of a picture we have in mind some representing relation in virtue of which it is a picture. The representation of the picture lies precisely in the fact that it says that the objects are so combined as are the elements in the picture. This is the *sense* of the picture. What therefore the picture must have in common with the reality, in order to represent it after its fashion, is the *form*, "the form of representation."[1]

The best illustration of this "notion of a picture" is what we may call the *spatial picture*. Thus in a map, a patch of colour represents the height of a corresponding object above sea-level. Of the same general character is the *mechanical* model which the physicist constructs to picture or represent, let us say, the atom. Here, too, the likeness between the picture and that which is pictured can only extend to certain formal or spatial properties expressing structure, so that all we know is certain general characteristics of the thing described.

I think we may accept this analysis in so far as it finds the "sense of the picture" in the "form of representation." There

---

[1] See F. P. Ramsey, *The Foundations of Mathematics*, Appendix, pp. 270–86. In this critical notice of Ludwig Wittgenstein's *Tractatus Logico-Philosophicus* all the passages of this work relative to the notions of description and picture are examined.

are, however, two points at which it is necessary to take issue with the analysis as thus far developed. We shall question first the adequacy of the foregoing characterization of the "form of representation," and secondly the thesis that the notion of description or representation *must* contain in it the notion of a picture as thus defined. The sense of the picture is undoubtedly its "form of representation," but that form need not be either spatial or logical. An aesthetic or artistic description is a description, but the sense of the description may be very different from that of the spatial picture as above described. There are scientific descriptions and historical descriptions, but the latter differ widely in the form of representation from the former. In the second place, it is at least doubtful whether the notion of description must necessarily contain the notion of a picture. There are forms of symbolic representation which apparently abandon the notion of picturing entirely. Certain theories of the nature of the scientific concept, of the relation of the scientific symbol to the thing symbolized are, as we shall see, non-pictorial. In any case some descriptions are picturing, and it is with these that we are for the present concerned.

C

*The Spatial Picture and the Aesthetic Picture.
Bi-Representationism*

The ideal case of the notion of the picture in the above analysis is the spatial picture as illustrated by the map. The basal notion of form is always that of space so that, as we have seen, if we think of logic as pure form we are inevitably led to the analogical notion of "logical space." But this notion of the picture is not the only one, not the only form of representation. There is, in fact, a "form of representation" of a very different kind, namely the artist's picture. It is important that we should see wherein this difference lies. The city of Venice may, for instance, be pictured in two quite different ways. We may have a map of the city or we may have a picture, let us say one of Turner's. In both cases elements are combined in certain ways. In both cases the sense of the picture is to be found in the fact that the elements of the picture are combined as are the elements of reality. It seems quite evident that the sense of the picture in this second case is different from that in the case of the map. The "form of representation" is non-spatial, although it is related to the spatial in a certain way. Let us first seek to show the nature of this form of representation and then define its relation to the spatial.

Some kind of similarity is demanded of any picture in the aesthetic sense—from a statue similarity of form, from a drawing similarity of perspective projection, from a painting still further similarity of colours. But something else is required in addition to all these, without which it is not a picture in the aesthetic sense. In other words, these are *not* the sense of the picture. How to express this difference of "sense" is precisely the problem, and one not wholly easy. A rough way of doing so is to say that while the map, or the scientific picture in general, represents relations of quantity, the aesthetic picture expresses qualities and values. This difference is even more clearly shown in the case of portraiture. The sense of a portrait lies in the fact that the elements of composition, of light and shade, etc., are so combined as to represent certain qualities and values of the person. A "speaking likeness" is never a spatial copy, although the spatial form of representation is always there. This rough distinction we shall attempt to make more precise in a later context.[1] Our main point is that in the aesthetic picture the aesthetic "form of representation" is not spatial, although it is to some degree conditioned by the spatial. The spatial is the *necessary*, although not the *sufficient*, form of representation. Even this necessary spatial form may in the interests of aesthetic expression be greatly "distorted" as we shall see in our later studies of aesthetic distortion, but some common spatial form is necessary if there is to be any picture at all.

D

Bi-Representation. The "Sense" of a Picture

Even if the notion of representation be held to involve necessarily the notion of picturing or of a picture, an adequate notion of description or representation requires two notions

[1] Chapter X, pp. 471 ff.

of a picture. Reality is actually pictured in two quite different ways. In so far as the concept of cognition is concerned, the question is, to be sure, still an open one whether both kinds of picture, both forms of representation, give us *knowledge*, and also whether they give us knowledge in an equal degree. In any case it is quite clear that the "sense of the picture" is different in the two cases. It is also clear that the sense is not completely identical with the form of representation, but is conditioned by the *purpose* of the representation. What we demand of a picture, in order that it may have the "sense" of a picture, is always some kind of similarity, but that similarity may differ widely according to what the picture intends. This notion of the sense of a picture will be developed further after our study of the linguistic picture. Here we wish merely to emphasize the point that it is more than the form of representation.

This leads us to a further point which is necessary to make our notion of knowledge by description complete. We have already suggested that the notion of representation need not have in it the notion of a picture, that there are non-pictorial forms of representation—namely symbolic. It may be assumed that scientific concepts or symbols represent their objects and constitute knowledge by description. Yet the notion that these symbols *picture* reality is in many quarters abandoned. A well-known statement of the relation is that of Bertrand Russell, which likens it to the relation between the notes of a symphony and the symphony itself.[1] Between a piece of orchestral music as played and the same piece of music as printed in the score, there is a certain resemblance which may be described as a resemblance of structure. The resemblance is of such a sort that when you know the rules you can infer the music from the score or the score from the music. Of a similar character is the relation of our mathematical formulas to the relations in nature. Now, granting this to be a valid analogy, it seems clear that the notion of picturing does not exhaust the notion of representation and description. The mathematical formulas are certainly knowledge by description or they do not constitute knowledge at all. But equally clearly they do not picture

---

[1] Bertrand Russell, *The A.B.C. of Relativity*, London, 1925, pp. 226 ff. See on this general question B. H. Streeter, *op. cit.*, pp. 29 ff.

reality. This is an important distinction for science, but its importance extends much further, to the entire question of the relation of language to reality. The function of language is, as Cassirer says, ultimately not to picture reality but to symbolize it. With this we turn to the problem of language.

V

KNOWLEDGE BY DESCRIPTION AND LANGUAGE. LANGUAGE AS REPRESENTATIVE OF REALITY

A

The object of the foregoing analysis was to develop a notion of description or representation which could be applied to the solution of our metalogical problem of language and knowledge by description. Let us therefore transfer the results of our analysis to the sphere of language. It will be well to begin by again following Wittgenstein's procedure at this point.

Language, he maintains, in order to represent must also picture. And in order to be a picture, it must also represent the objective facts or state of affairs in much the same way as a spatial picture does. That is, the structure of the language, the combination of linguistic elements, must correspond to the actual structure or combination of elements in reality. Here too what the picture must have in common with the reality is the form, the "form of representation." This is the sense of the picture. Accordingly, the sense of a proposition is that the things meant by its elements (the words) are combined with one another in the same way as are the elements themselves, that is *logically*.

The question is, let us say, whether the subject-predicate proposition represents or misrepresents reality. That depends, according to this view, upon whether "things" are combined in the same way as the words in the proposition. Now, as to this particular question we have already expressed the view that this is the fundamental form of representation, in that it is the form in which alone statements are possible.[1] But this is not the question here. The problem is the more general one, namely, whether the linguistic "form of representation" is

[1] Chapter VII, p. 296 f.

in the last analysis *logical*. That it is, is the thesis we are considering. Language in order to describe must picture logically.

B

Logical and Poetical Picturing

The ideal linguistic picture is, therefore, the logical picture. It corresponds in principle to the spatial picture of our preceding analysis. But as there is also the aesthetic picture, the sense of which differs from that of the spatial picture, so also in the case of language we have aesthetic or poetic representation. As the aesthetic picture (painting, sculpture) is non-spatial so the poetic picture is a-logical. In making use of the notion of the poetic picture it must be understood that the term poetic is used in the widest sense of the word, in the sense, namely, in which it is used when it is maintained that the *Ursprache* is poetic.[1] The notion of the "language of poetry" will be made more definite in a later context[2]; here we may contrast it with the language of science in the broadest sense of the word.

For the purpose of our study it is necessary to distinguish two forms of this poetic representation. The first of these we shall describe as intuitive, the second as metaphorical (or analogical) representation. The first type is connected with the intrinsic expressiveness of words, and is therefore close to the immediate intuition or *Erlebniss* already discussed under the head of knowledge by acquaintance. The second type is one which is made possible by the transitive character of linguistic meaning, the transfer of words through metaphor which, as we have seen, is the most fundamental form of word transference.

In his account of bi-representationism in language Streeter makes use of a passage from Macbeth's soliloquy which illustrates this first type of poetic representation. It is the poet's "picture" of time in one aspect of its intuitive meaning:

> "To-morrow and to-morrow and to-morrow
> Creeps on this petty pace from day to day
> To the last syllable of recorded time
> And all our yesterdays have lighted fools
> The ways to dusty death."

[1] Chapter II, p. 80 f.   [2] Chapter X, p. 456 f.

The preceding passage describes or pictures something. It is not merely an expression of emotion, although such expression is there. It is an assertion of the futility of temporal existence and, as such, is a judgment claiming truth. Otherwise it would be meaningless. But there is more in it than this. It is a picture or representation of *time*—in a different way and for an entirely different purpose than any description that might be made by science—but still a picture. The picture therefore has its own *sense* and that sense is not at all the sense of a logical picture, any more than an artist's picture of Venice has the sense of a spatial map of Venice.

The above is, then, an illustration of an intuitive representation by a poet. In it there are, to be sure, metaphorical elements (*syllable* of recorded time; *dusty* death), but the intuitive predominates. Let us now look at metaphorical representation. I choose for my illustration here two lines from a poem of Robert Bridges:

"Man's happiness, his flaunting, honeyed flower of soul
Is his loving response to the wealth of nature."

To describe man's happiness as "flaunting, honeyed flower" of soul is to say something of it which conveys a meaning not expressible by any logical picture such as a psychological (scientific) picture might hope to achieve. Here, too, as in the case of the description of time, there is emotional expression, but much more is there. There is, too, as in the previous case, an *assertion*—in this case that man's happiness is a response to nature, and as assertion, claims truth. Otherwise it is meaningless. But it is also a pictorial representation of happiness.

Poetic representation, in the two aspects above described, constitutes, then, a special way of describing or picturing reality. The question of what it pictures and the truth of the picture—what poetry really says—constitute the problem of the special chapter on the Language of Poetry. We may perhaps content ourselves for the moment with a suggestion of Shelley in his *Defense of Poetry*. He is speaking of metaphor and of metaphorical language, but what he says holds true of poetic language in both its aspects. "It marks," he tells us, "the before unapprehended relations of things, bringing to light the real spiritual kinship, not observed by the eyes that see only material forms. These similitudes reveal the same footsteps of nature impressed upon the various subjects of the world, and hence they also lead through nature to the reality beyond them." We may, for the moment, ignore the metaphysical aspect of this account—although I also believe with Shelley that poetry is a *métaphysique figurée*, as Bergson says. Sufficient that it does mark the before unapprehended relations of things through similitudes—relations not exhausted in the logical description.

In calling the poetic picture a-logical I do not mean that it is illogical—although of course it may be—any more than that the non-spatial picture is without spatial elements. It has repeatedly been said that logical form is so woven into our speech, poetic as well as prosaic, that it is impossible to utter a phrase, still less to form a significant sentence, without such expressions involving logical form. Logical form is the condition of all intelligible communication, all communication which is not merely behavioural. Logical form is *there* and is one sense of the picture, but it is not *the* sense any more than spatial form is the sense of the picture of Venice. In truth, we have here a relation in many ways analogous to that between "levels of being." One level may condition another without the latter being identical with it or reducible to it.

C

The Two Senses of a Linguistic Picture and Interpretation

The doctrine of bi-representation which we have been developing maintains, then, that there are two fundamentally different ways in which language may "picture" or represent reality. It also maintains that there are two quite different senses of the picture. This difference was indicated in the case of the artist's picture. Let us now extend it to the linguistic picture and generalize the notion.

The sense of the picture is its "form of representation." But it is more than this. Every picture of whatever kind is in reality a proposition. A portrait is a proposition, for it asserts, either explicitly or implicitly, that it represents the person; and this assertion, though perhaps not verifiable in the empirical sense, is either true or false. The sense of a painting of Venice is, in the first instance, that this is Venice or it is like Venice. The sense of the line "Man's happiness, his flaunting, honeyed flower of soul," is that man's happiness is this or is like it. Every description, as we have seen, is a tacit proposition. There is no description of any kind that describes nothing. A description loses all sense or meaning if it is not a tacit proposition. But the moment this fact is realized, it also becomes clear that part of the sense of the picture is its interpretation. An aesthetic picture, no less than a spatial or logical picture, is true or false, but the meaning of truth and falsity is determined by the "universe of discourse" in which the statement or proposition is made. In other words, a description of man's happiness, such as that in the line quoted, is meaningless in one universe of discourse, but may have the deepest sense in another.

Considerations such as these become of great importance in our discussions of different languages and symbolisms in the chapters to come. Here the single point is that, while the sense of a picture is found in its form of representation, it is also only when that form is *interpreted* that the true sense of the picture is revealed. We have already shown that there is no knowledge by acquaintance (perception) that does not involve interpretation. Similarly there is no knowledge by description that does not involve the element of interpretation. Interpretation is part of the description. This leads us to the general question of knowledge by interpretation—the third problem of language and cognition.

VI

KNOWLEDGE BY INTERPRETATION. THE THIRD METALOGICAL PROBLEM

A

The triadic, as distinguished from the dyadic theory of knowing, holds that in a true account of knowing there must be a recognition of a type other than those of knowledge by acquaintance and knowledge by description, called knowledge by interpretation. In other words, there is an aspect of knowing describable neither in terms of presentational immediacy (perception) nor in terms of conceptual representation—to be known as interpretation.

The problem arises out of the fact that we have, or *seem* to have, knowledge of metempirical "objects," of objects that cannot be perceived and, since on the dyadic theory of knowledge concepts without percepts are empty, cannot be conceptually described. *Intuitus vel conceptus*—than these, according to Kant, in one of his epistemological moods, there is no other way of knowing. It follows according to Kant—again in one of his epistemological moods—that all this seeming knowledge is *transcendentaler Schein*—the product of reasoning which is not genuine reasoning, of syllogisms that are paralogisms. We are therefore faced with this dilemma: either much that seems knowledge is not knowledge, or else there is a third aspect to knowledge which is not exhausted in these two.

The way the problem arises in connection with language is also clear. Much of human discourse is about such objects. This discourse is meaningful to those who take part in it. Propositions such as "the soul is immortal," "God is a Spirit," "the world is will," are all meaningful in discourse, although there is no empirical object to which they refer. They are meaningful for the reason that, metalogically viewed, the "is" of predication presupposes ontological import, and to such presupposition logic, properly understood, is in no position to demur.[1] On the basis of the philosophy of language bound up with the dyadic theory of knowing, the words thus used are empty words (*Scheinwörte*), the sentences in which the words occur apparent propositions (*Scheinsätze*), and the entire discourse which contains them meaningless. Here, then, from the standpoint of the problem of cognition and language, we are faced with the same dilemma. Either much of discourse which seems intelligible is really unintelligible or else we must introduce a third concept of intelligibility. The two problems are really in essence the same—on the view of the inseparability of knowledge and language which underlies this whole treatment. It is for this reason that, as we have already said, the Kantian critique is really a critique of language.

[1] Chapter VII, p. 305 f.

B

The Solution of the Problem. The Element of Interpretation in All Knowing

This, then, is the problem. Is there any solution? I think there is, and I shall now indicate the direction in which it lies. I shall begin with certain conclusions of our preceding discussions, namely, that there is present in all knowing, both of acquaintance and description, a third element of interpretation. I shall, then, seek to show that, as a result of this, there appear certain cases of knowing which are knowledge by interpretation alone.

Our examination of knowledge by acquaintance showed us that all perception (whether sensuous or non-sensuous intuition) involves interpretation. Until this element of interpretation enters in there is no knowledge. Knowledge as simple presentational immediacy is a myth (in the most elemental form of knowledge there is an element of re-presentation). The principle of the inseparability of intuition and expression brings with it the further principle that knowledge includes the interpretation of the expression. Poincaré has said that all the scientist contributes to a fact is the language in which it is enunciated. But that is the whole point. There is no fact to be verified until it is stated, and verification involves mutual interpretation on the part of the verifiers before there can be confirmation. Even here, then, knowledge is not merely, in Plato's terms, right judgment *plus* discourse. Discourse is part of the right judgment. Knowledge in its simplest form involves interpretation and interpreters.

Even clearer is this third element in knowledge by description. Here there is the picture and the thing pictured, or the symbol and the thing symbolized. The sense of the picture is the form of representation which the thing and the thing pictured have in common. But the sense of the picture can itself be neither presented nor represented; it can merely be interpreted. The sense itself is metempirical and metalogical; it can be determined only by the mutual acknowledgment of communicating subjects. It is essentially a process of interpretation, of "coming to an understanding" in communication.

The question now is whether this interpretation of the sense of a picture or a description is *knowledge* or an aspect of knowledge. If it is not, what is it? For it is only when interpretation takes place that the other forms of knowledge have meaning.

Thus far knowledge by interpretation is merely the completion or conditioning of the other two forms of knowledge. We now come to knowledge by interpretation alone. All propositions about "meaning" and knowledge are themselves metalogical and metempirical and can by their very nature—*if they are knowledge*—be knowledge only by interpretation. This we have already seen in our discussion of the verification, or authentication, of the empirical criterion, a position accepted by Wittgenstein himself, although apparently not with all its implications.[1] It is on this point that we must put our chief emphasis, for in a sense our whole argument turns on it. It is the question of the "knowledge status" of propositions of this type. If they are not knowledge, then we have as the basis, or presupposition, of other elements of knowledge "propositions" which do not belong to knowledge. If, on the other hand, they do belong to the sphere of knowledge, they are such only by interpretation.

There comes, then, a point in knowledge where, *if it is to be knowledge at all*, it is knowledge by interpretation. It is sometimes maintained that this is not knowledge, but dialectic. Knowledge is given us in acquaintance and description and is extended by inference, inductive and deductive. Dialectic, on the other hand, determines not truth but meaning. This distinction cannot, if our analysis is valid, be maintained. The "dialectic" which determines the "meaning of meaning," the meaning of truth, the meaning of criteria of verification, must itself be knowledge, must contain in itself the possibility of verification or authentication; otherwise the entire structure of knowledge falls to the ground. It seems reasonably certain, therefore, that no intelligible theory of knowledge can be constructed which does not recognize interpretation and dialectic as part of the knowledge process. It seems certain that if this be true a tenable notion of truth must be one which includes the possibility of verification by such processes,

---

[1] Chapter V, p. 219.

and which does not limit it to the two forms alone recognized by the dyadic theory.

Our concern here has been merely to establish the necessity of the triadic conception of knowledge and of parts of knowledge which are solely knowledge by interpretation. But it is immediately clear that such a position, if true, has far-reaching consequences. One of these is the conceptions of truth and of verification which inevitably follow. In so far as there is knowledge by interpretation truth must, in the last analysis, be immanent in discourse; the totality of meaningful discourse must be the truth. To the development of this conception we shall turn presently. A second important consequence is the light such a view of knowledge throws upon the debatable field of metaphysical knowledge and the entire problem of metaphysical language. Metaphysics, we shall see, is pre-eminently this field of knowledge by interpretation. It is the language of maximum context, the language which alone makes intelligible our other languages. Here knowledge is knowledge by interpretation and the criterion of metaphysical truth is determined by that fact.

The dyadic theory of knowledge leads almost inevitably to negative views of metaphysics and to a criticism of metaphysical language as empty verbalism. Kant's doctrine of transcendental *Schein*, to which reference has been made, was the first great historic recognition of the problems involved, and positivism, both in its earlier and later forms, is a continuation of his negative line of thought. A recognition, however, of this third way of knowing opens up the possibility both of understanding metaphysical language and of validating the type of propositions expressed in this language. Kant himself never denied the meaningfulness of metaphysical propositions but merely their empirical verifiability. In fact it is one of Kant's main theses that metaphysics and metaphysical propositions are necessary for the regulation of empirical knowledge and for the interpretation of empirical propositions. Metaphysical knowledge is for him the determination and interpretation of the presuppositions or postulates necessary for reason in both its empirical and its practical employment. It is in terms such as these that we shall seek to deal with metaphysics and metaphysical propositions in later contexts. Metaphysics, we shall find, is precisely that activity which seeks to round out our experience and to make it intelligible. In this sphere intelligibility and truth are synonomous.

VII

LANGUAGE AND REALITY. REALISM AND NOMINALISM

A

The metalogical problems of language are now before us at the three main points outlined in our introductory section, namely (*a*) language and presentational immediacy or knowledge by acquaintance; (*b*) language and representation or knowledge by description; (*c*) language and dialectic or knowledge by interpretation. In every case the problem was that of the relation of language to reality, and in every case the answer to that problem was that reality and its expression in language are so closely related that the valid interpretation of language gives us reality.

It is clear that the basal question of this fourth problem has already been formulated in the historic opposition of Realism and Nominalism. The *nominalism* against which realism in its various forms contends is, as the term suggests, a doctrine of names or words. In its essence, and through all its historical forms, it holds that names or words as such are *flatus vocis*—empty sounds which stand for objects or entities only conventionally or arbitrarily. Realism, on the other hand, through all its varied historical forms, maintains that words, and language in general, are in some way constitutive of the real. Apart from vague awareness which has no cognitive value, the most elemental form of experience is already determined by language.

The question of realism and nominalism, we have maintained, is a metalogical, not a logical problem. There is, to be sure, such a thing as "logical nominalism," but it is concerned wholly with the problem as to whether a consistent logic can be developed if the universal presupposed in implication and inference has no real being—whether, in other words, a valid logic can be developed if the propositions in logic are merely indications, mere names arbitrarily chosen to denote "things" or classes of things. The metalogical problem is much broader. It is concerned with the more fundamental question whether knowing has any "sense" if words or names involved in the pre-logical processes of perception, intuition, and description are mere arbitrary signs, and if the names involved in the post-logical processes are merely empty verbalism.

The metalogical problem of realism and nominalism is, then, a problem of language and knowledge. In our studies of this relation we have maintained a realistic position throughout. As against the essentially nominalistic position of knowledge by pure acquaintance, we maintained the realistic position that intuition and expression are inseparable. As against the nominalistic position of descriptions that describe nothing, we affirmed a realistic position that wherever there is description there is objective reference. In opposition to the nominalistic position of empty words and mere verbalism, we maintained the realistic position that wherever there is intelligible discourse reference to reality, either direct or indirect, is presupposed. We have already examined in a tentative way the consequences of the denial of these positions in our account of the nominalistic consequences of the "logical analysis" of language. Let us now view these consequences from the metalogical point of view. In doing so it will be of advantage to define the notion of Neo-nominalism more adequately.

B

Traditional Nominalism and Neo-Nominalism

The opposition of realism and nominalism arose historically in connection with the concept and conceptual meaning. It was concerned with the restricted problem of the reality or ontological status of the universal. "Scholastic nominalism could not, however," as Mauthner has said, "have the last word because it still believed in the reality of individuals." Neo-nominalism is thoroughgoing in that it gives up this last remainder. There is now no substantive at all. All is flux, and words or names, as artificial tags imposed upon this flux, distort and misrepresent reality. By Neo-nominalism we understand, then, the extension of the nominalistic principle to the whole of language and to all its meanings.[1]

The nominalism of the individual was, to be sure, already involved in the nominalism of the universal. If universals are unreal, then individuals are also, and the distinction between individuals and universals falls to the ground. The very entrance of a "thing" on the stage of thought *implies*, as we have seen, that it has a *minimum* of character and relations. The simplest form of language, the mere naming of an object, involves an element of universalization. The universal is present in the most elementary form of perception and intuition, and denial of the reality of the universal is, *ipso facto*, denial of the individual, except as mere vague awareness. Neo-nominalism really denies the reality of both universal and individual and leaves only "events."

C

Critique of Metalogical Nominalism. Nominalism makes Nonsense of our Meanings

This is, then, the form of nominalism which we call metalogical and which must be examined from the metalogical point of view. We have already seen the consequences of this nominalism in what we have called the paralysis of speech and the stultification of discourse. All that is here necessary is to develop this line of thought more fully. The theme of our present critique may be expressed in a significant statement of John Dewey, to the effect that "nominalism makes nonsense of our meanings." The truth of this statement has already appeared at many points. It is now necessary merely to summarize these facts and to determine their significance.

Nominalism makes nonsense of our meanings at all three points at which problems of language and cognition arise. The crucial instance is, of course, to be found at that point

---

[1] Mauthner, *Kritik der Sprache*, Vol. III, p. 621. This narrower and broader interpretation of nominalism is quite generally recognized. Thus Vaihinger, for whom the real is the flux of sense data and all expression involves more or less of fiction, recognizes this broader use of nominalism (*The Philosophy of As-If*, p. 209). So also Cassirer, *op. cit.*, Vol. III, p. 238. "To the conceptual realism of the earlier form must be added a realism of perception. So also to the conceptual nominalism must be added a nominalism of perception."

at which all knowledge begins, namely, perceptual and intuitive meanings. It makes nonsense of our perceptual meanings, as is evidenced in the analysis of vocabulary which such nominalism exercises upon linguistic meaning.[1] Value nominalism makes nonsense of our value meanings, as has been shown in our examination of value words in Chapter IV.[2] It makes nonsense of our descriptions by the paradox of descriptions that describe nothing and pseudo-propositions that say nothing. It is, however, on the third level of knowledge (by interpretation) that the full consequence of such nominalism is plainly seen. The application of empty verbalism to all discourse about metempirical objects not only makes nonsense of a large range of our meanings but, in so far as propositions about metempirical objects condition our empirical meanings, makes nonsense of the latter also.

It seems quite clear, then, that a thoroughgoing nominalism such as we have been describing does make nonsense of a large part of our meanings. It is therefore not surprising that many who maintain this nominalistic position declare quite calmly that a large part of our meanings *is* nonsense and that a large part of our discourse is meaningless in the strict sense. But, it may be asked, *why not* make nonsense of our meanings? Why should we not come to recognize that a large part of our discourse is nonsense?

To such questions there is in a sense no answer. Certainly logic has no answer except in so far, perhaps, that it may show that nonsense is made of implicational meaning. But it is abstractly possible at least that logic itself is a fiction, as for instance in Vaihinger's view. Nor has a theory of knowledge any answer if knowledge is conceived as independent of language and expression. To one who holds that language is something external to knowledge—a mere conventional tag—there is no reason why a large part of our discourse should not be meaningless, or, as one writer elegantly puts it, "mere blah, blah." But for a theory of knowledge such as here developed there is an answer.

The necessary consequences of this nominalism are, as we have seen, paralysis of speech and stultification of all discourse. But if the relation of knowledge to language be as we have

---

[1] Chapter VI, pp. 289 ff.   [2] Chapter IV, pp. 164 ff.

maintained, then paralysis of speech and stultification of discourse mean the paralysis and stultification of knowledge also. The principle of the identity of intuition and expression—the inseparability of knowledge from communication—involves this consequence. He who speaks at all must, as Mauthner says, be a "realist," and until there is speech there is no communicable and verifiable knowledge. The very condition of intelligible discourse, and therefore of knowledge, is precisely the element of organization which is alone possible through the universal. Nominalism does make nonsense of our meanings and, in so far as it does this, it makes nonsense of knowledge also. The problem of this chapter is the relation of language to reality. The answer to that question is that language and reality are inseparable, and that the way to knowledge of reality is not by the denial of the meanings of language but by their development and interpretation.

VIII

LANGUAGE AND REALITY: "LANGUAGE NOT MOULDED ON REALITY"

A

With this critique of metalogical nominalism we may enter upon the most fundamental problem of language and cognition, namely, the issue raised by the thesis that language is not moulded on reality. In the introductory chapter it was pointed out that the typically modern tendencies in philosophy all revolve about a certain philosophy of language. This philosophy we found, moreover, to be connected with the Neo-nominalism there described in its more general and cultural aspects. There are three typical positions in recent philosophy which exemplify this philosophy of language. We may describe them as (*a*) Logical Atomism (represented by Bertrand Russell and others); (*b*) A-logical Intuitionism (represented by Bergson); and (*c*) The Philosophy of Events (as represented by Whitehead). In Appendix I we shall criticize these positions in detail. Here we shall merely state the positions briefly and bring to light the implicit assumptions underlying them.

The first of these positions, described as logical atomism, is already familiar to us from our studies of language and logic.

It assumes that fact, to which language must correspond, that reality on which language must be moulded, is a plurality of atomic elements. Obviously, ordinary language, which expresses and reflects organization, cannot correspond to fact and must be irreparably infected with error. It is also clear wherein that error consists. All those elements in language which correspond to organized and integrated elements in experience are fictions, and in true nominalistic fashion described as hypostatizations. Language, in both of its aspects—of vocabulary and syntax—thus misrepresents and distorts reality.

The second neo-nominalistic tendency in modern philosophy, that of Bergson, may be described as pure dynamism. For it, also, language is completely infected with error. Language, with its grammatical elements, was constructed merely to grasp the static. It developed merely for the practical purpose of grasping or apprehending those aspects of reality which are useful, which are necessary for manipulation. In order to manipulate we must turn movement or activity into static "things" or discontinuous states. But reality is not that. It is becoming, duration, continuity. Therefore language is not moulded on reality, and to know reality we must abandon language and the categories generated by language.

The third type of this philosophy of language is that of Whitehead—a peculiarly interesting form in that it combines elements of both the preceding theories. For him also, language is not moulded on reality. Like the preceding, he tells us that, while "language expresses a useful abstract" for practical purposes, "whenever we try to use it as a fundamental statement of the nature of things, it proves itself mistaken." Thus "philosophy must redesign language in the way that in the physical sciences pre-existing physical appliances are redesigned."[1] The assumption here also, as in the other two positions, is that we know *what* reality is independent of language, and know that language is not moulded on it.

The thesis, then, common to all these positions, in so far as the philosophy of language is concerned, may be expressed in the statement of Bergson that language is not moulded on reality. Underlying this common thesis are certain common assumptions which may be briefly stated as follows: (*a*) Lan-

[1] *Process and Reality*. For specific references, see Appendix III.

guage was made for practice and is thereby unfitted to express the nature of reality whatever that nature may be conceived to be. (b) In the second place—and in fact by reason of its practical character—it is something external to reality—a "mere tag." Reality is known independently of language. Intuition and expression are not identical or inseparable. Therefore, on the basis of some indirect intuition of reality, it is possible to exercise a metalogical critique on language. Let us examine these asumptions. In the more detailed examination of these positions (in the Appendix) our criticisms will be more specific; here we are concerned merely with the assumptions common to them all.

B

Critique of the Metalogical Assumptions Underlying these Theories

The first of the common assumptions is that language is made solely for practice, and that whenever we try to use it as a fundamental statement of the nature of things it proves itself mistaken. With this assumption we may deal briefly. Although constantly taken for granted, this assumption—of the purely practical character of the original language (*Ursprache*)—is not so much based on facts as it is an expression of the dogmatic evolutionary naturalism which dominated the cultural sciences of the last century. As far as linguistic science is concerned, there are many linguists of the first order who challenge this assumption.[1] But even if the assumption itself were unquestioned, the inferences drawn from it would not necessarily follow. To infer from the originally pragmatic character of language its present nature and function is indeed a rather flagrant case of the genetic fallacy. On the contrary, it has been the character of language, as of the intelligence with which it is bound up, to develop new functions which far transcend its original purposes. As a matter of fact language was not made for practice but for communication. The practical motive, while of course present from the beginning, is only one of several, all of which are subsumable under the more ultimate notion of communication.

[1] Chapter II, pp. 80 ff.

The second assumption is of a more fundamental character and demands more extended consideration. All three theories condemn natural language for not being moulded on reality, and thereby assume that it should be thus moulded on reality —in other words, that the relation of language to reality is that of a mould or *copy*, a copy of something antecedently given and wholly independent of language. This assumption is open to the most serious question. It involves a wholly false conception of the relation of language to cognition.

It must, of course, be admitted that the expression "moulded on reality" is figurative. It has its origin in that still more fatal analogy or figure which speaks of language as an extension of the tool-making function, and leads men to speak of redesigning language as we would redesign physical appliances. But allowing for the element of figure, it is nevertheless clear that the primitive notion of language as a copy is involved, and that the function of language is to copy or picture reality. This notion our entire preceding analysis of cognition and language has shown to be fallacious. The copy notion is but the first stage in the development of language and the linguistic consciousness, the later stages being analogy and symbol—so that we may rightly say, with Cassirer, that the function of language is to symbolize reality, not to copy it. But the fallacy of the assumption goes much deeper than this; for it includes the further assumption that the nature of reality is known independently of language and its categories, when as a matter of fact the truth is actually the reverse. Language, we have seen, is not an external tag or mould. It is rather a necessary condition of the experience of *objects* as such. Intuition and expression are inseparable. Anything that can become more than a diffused awareness has language as a constitutive element.

The entire notion of a language moulded on reality is, then, a gigantic *petitio principii*. It begs the very question that it is the problem of the philosophy of language to solve. That this is so is made manifest by the fact that the philosophies of language described, while agreed on the general proposition that language is not moulded on reality, differ widely as to the nature of the reality on which it is not moulded and on the points at which language diverges. For the first reality is atomistic, and all the organizing integrative elements in language, while useful for practice, are really fictions and distort reality. For the second, reality is the exact opposite. It is "duration," continuous flux, and those elements in language which cut out static states, analyse out atomic elements, misrepresent and distort it. For the third, reality is ultimately events, and language must be redesigned to express or represent this state of affairs. This divergence should in itself make us wary. It at least suggests that when language is criticized from such wholly opposite points of view there is something arbitrary—certainly limited—in the conceptions of reality from which the critique proceeds. It also suggests that the entire assumption upon which the critique proceeds—namely that language should be moulded on reality—is false.

C

The True Conception of the Relation of Language and Reality

There are in general only two ways of solving the problem of language and cognition. The first of these, the one we have been discussing, assumes a "reality" known independently of language and its categories, a hypothetical "pure experience" to be discovered by stripping off language. This way is closed to us, for the assumptions on which it is based are pure myth. The second way proposes an exactly opposite method and proceeds upon opposite assumptions. Instead, as in the first way, of attempting to get back of the forms of thought and language to a hypothetical "pure experience," it assumes that experience is never "pure" in this sense, and that intuition and expression are inseparable. It therefore proposes not to deny, but to complete and perfect the principles of expression and symbolism. It proceeds upon the assumption that the more richly and energetically the human spirit builds its languages and symbolisms, the nearer it comes, if not to the original source of its being, certainly to its ultimate meaning and reality. If the entire process of human culture consists in the creation of certain spiritual constructions, symbolic forms of various types, the way to truth and reality lies, not in negating these forms, but rather in seeking to understand them and in becoming more and more conscious of the formative principles embodied in these constructions. Negation of these forms, instead of enabling us to grasp the content and meaning of reality, serves only to destroy the spiritual form to which the content and meaning are necessarily bound.

Language is, as Hegel said, the "actuality of culture." It is only as culture actualizes itself in language and other symbolic forms related to language, that life emerges out of the sphere of the merely "natural," given existence; only so that it passes from mere biological process to the forms of intelligence and spirit. But more than this, it is only as the brute given thus actualizes or expresses itself in language that this given becomes, in any meaningful and intelligible sense, reality. Language which, as we have seen, is inseparable from thought and knowledge, is not moulded on reality. It is rather the mould in which reality as significant is first given. This is the *idealistic minimum* which must be present in any adequate philosophy of language.

IX

LANGUAGE AND TRUTH; TRUTH AS IMMANENT IN DISCOURSE

A

This, then, is the basal conception of the relation of language to reality which underlies the developments of this chapter. It is arrived at alike as the result of our analysis of the relation of language to cognition in its threefold aspect, and as the result of the criticism of opposing conceptions. The view here suggested in outline can, to be sure, justify itself only by a detailed application of this principle to the various types of language, poetic, scientific, religious, and metaphysical, and the various forms of symbolization in these respective fields. These constitute the problems and the task of the second part of this study. There are, however, certain general conceptions implied in this view—more especially the notion of truth as necessitated by our theory of the relation of language to cognition—which it will be well, in concluding this chapter, to make quite clear.

The problem of meaning and truth has already presented

itself to us in a preliminary way. In Chapter V, which dealt with the normative problem of language, we accepted the principle that the meaning of an assertion is inseparably connected with the way in which it may be verified and that, consequently, the problem of meaning is bound up with the problem of truth. The discussion of verifiability to which we were there led involved necessarily the general question of the nature of truth and of its relation to meaning, and the relation of both to language and linguistic expression. To these questions we must again turn our attention.

This is evidently the fundamental problem of this chapter on language and cognition. All men agree that knowledge and truth are correlative conceptions. If, accordingly, it is true, as has been maintained throughout this discussion, that there is no knowledge that does not involve expression and language, then the truth problem becomes in the last analysis a problem of the relation of expression to that which is expressed. It cannot be said that that which cannot be expressed is not real, but it is certainly true that that which cannot be expressed cannot be either true or false. The problem of truth involves, then, necessarily, the problem of language and of its relation to reality.

B

The Triadic Conception of Knowledge and the Truth Notion

We considered the problem of language and knowledge in connection with the three types of knowledge—by acquaintance, by description, and by interpretation. Strictly speaking, the notion of truth does not arise in connection with mere acquaintance. Presentational immediacy involves no element of truth or falsity; for such a notion to arise there must be the beginning of re-presentation. In the case of knowledge by description the notion of re-presentation is explicit and with it the notion of a picture. At this point the simplest and most primitive notion of truth arises—that of copy or correspondence. To be sure, the sense of the picture, and with it the truth or falsity of the picture, involve interpretation, as we have seen; but however differently the sense be interpreted, leading to nuances in our

LANGUAGE AND COGNITION

notion of truth, the element of representation, and with it of the "form of representation," is always there. In the case of knowledge by interpretation the truth problem also arises. The question of the truth or falsity of the representation or "picture" cannot be determined until such representation is interpreted, and there then arises the question of the truth of the interpretation. Truth thus becomes in a sense ultimately a question of interpretation. This is especially clear in specifically symbolic representation. It is the character of all symbols that they must be interpreted, and the truth or falsity of a symbol depends upon the truth or falsity of the interpretation. Thus a symbol may be literally false but symbolically true. It is clearly, then, in connection with knowledge by interpretation that the crucial problems of the truth of language arise.

C

The Nature of the Truth Relation: "Common Form of Representation"

If, as has been maintained, the element of truth or falsity does not arise until there is the beginning of re-presentation, the notion of copy or correspondence is at least the initial if not the final element in the truth notion. Now it has been held, as we have seen, that the notion of representation cannot be separated from the notion of a "picture" and that the sense of the picture is the form of representation, a form common to the picture and the pictured. Let us, then, start with this notion. It will be convenient to examine it in the form of a statement by A. N. Whitehead.[1]

Two objects, he tells us, may be said to have a truth relation when the examination of one of them discloses some factor which belongs to the nature of the other. A truth relation will be said to connect two objective contents when one and the same identical pattern can be abstracted from both of them. Mutual participation in a pattern is the essence of truth. The pattern may be only partial, there may be only partial coincidence. The two objects exhibit this partial pattern, though the omitted elements involve the differences which belong to

[1] *Adventures of Ideas*, Chapter XVI.

their diverse individualities. This is, according to Whitehead, "*the meaning of truth.*" On the basis of this definition he distinguishes between direct and indirect truth, direct truth being confined to propositions, indirect to sense perception and symbolic truth. We shall be interested in this distinction, but for the moment let us examine the definition.

I think we can see immediately that this is not a wholly true account of the truth relation. For one thing, the definition has too great an extension. Certainly not all objects that have this mutual participation in a pattern are in the truth relation. Two objects in nature, let us say the form of a tree and the form of the nervous system, may mutually participate in a pattern, but there is no truth relation between them, merely a relation of similarity. It is true that the pattern of the tree may be taken to *stand* for that of the nervous system—the former may be taken to represent the latter in discourse—but the question of truth or falsity arises only with the intention to make the one stand for the other, to make one the *expression* of the other. A picture, as we have seen, is always a tacit proposition and it is only as a proposition, or expression, that it is either true or false. The same considerations hold true in the case of an artificial construct, such as a model. The truth relation between a mechanical model of the atom and the atom does not consist in their similarity alone, but rather in the fact that because of such similarity, or supposed similarity, the model becomes an expression (for a certain purpose and from a certain standpoint) of the ideal construct we call the atom. In sum, the truth relation does not subsist between two objects, however they mutually participate in a pattern, but always between an object and an expression.

The point of this criticism is tacitly recognized by Whitehead in his further statement that only propositional truth is direct truth relation. That is that the truth relation, strictly speaking, exists only between assertions, judgments, propositions, and reality. Let us see, then, what is understood by propositional truth. A proposition is true, he tells us, when the nexus of events and the structure of the proposition exhibit the same pattern. The nexus and the pattern belong to different categories, he continues; there is no question of identification. In this statement we have in principle the "common form of representation" of Wittgenstein already examined. After our examination of that notion we can again see that this is not a true account of propositional truth. Here again, no more than in the case of the two objects just considered, is mere participation in the same pattern the essential of the truth relation. Here, too, we have merely similarity between the nexus of events and the structure of the proposition. It is only as the proposition *expresses an intention*, only as an expression of meaning, that the proposition is either true or false. It is for this reason that, as we have seen, the truth of a picture cannot be determined until the sense of the picture is determined, and the sense does not lie in the common form of representation alone. This statement holds equally good for the linguistic "picture." Here, too, the truth or falsity of the picture cannot be determined until we have determined the "sense" of the picture, and this sense does not lie in the common form of representation alone.

It follows from this that the truth relation is to be found in the last analysis not in the notion of correspondence, or coincidence of pattern, whether partial or complete, but in the notion of adequate expression. Let us develop this notion briefly.

The classical definition of truth contains this notion of adequacy, *adaequatio intellectus et rei*. Now it will not be denied, of course, that the truth relation is one between the mind (*intellectus*) and the thing. Truth is not a quality of things but of propositions, and a proposition outside discourse is a nothing. But this relation is not found between the object and an idea or image in the mind, but between the expression and the expressed. If, as we maintained, "intuition" and expression are identical or at least inseparable, then the only way to determine being or reality is in those forms in which statements about it are possible. Even though we think of the truth relation as one between the "idea" and the thing, such a relation can be determined, that is verified or confirmed, only when it is expressed. Truth, therefore, is, in the last analysis, adequate expression.

The consequences of this position are far-reaching. The truth of any expression, whether literal or symbolic, scientific or "poetic," is determined not merely by similarity between the form of the expression and the form of the expressed but by its adequacy as expression, and this can be determined only by processes of interpretation and communication. Thus in the case of the different kinds of representations or pictures, whether verbal or non-verbal, the criteria of truth are different, and in the last analysis matters of adequate expression. That these different "kinds" of truth must ultimately be made coherent and brought into a totality of intelligible discourse, does not alter one whit the fact that they are both forms of truth.

The facts established by the preceding analysis lead to consequences of considerable importance. The first of these is that the notion of truth is not satisfactorily expressed in terms of correspondence or of any modern adaptation of that conception, such as mutual participation in a pattern. The second is that propositional truth, which is the only direct truth relation, is a relation between an expression and that which is expressed. Now the only possible relation between an expression and that which is expressed is one of adequacy. This leads to the notion of truth as adequate expression. Let us develop this conception more fully.

D

Truth as Adequate Expression

The classical definition of truth, *adaequatio intellectus et rei*, conceives the truth relation as one between "mind" and "thing," and it cannot, of course, be denied that in the broadest sense the relation may be so defined. But the truth relation is not actually between an idea or image in the mind and the thing, but between propositions and that which they express. A proposition, as we have defined it, is a class of sentences which have the same intentional significance for every one who understands them. It is this common understanding which makes the proposition.[1] If, as we have maintained, intuition and expression are identical, or at least inseparable, then the only way to determine being or reality is in those forms in which statements about it are possible. Even though we think of the truth relation as one between "idea" and "thing,"

[1] Chapter VII, p. 270.

such a relation can be determined, that is verified or confirmed, only when it is expressed. Truth, then, is always a function of expression, and the relation between an expression and that which is expressed can be only one of adequacy. What, then, is adequacy in this context?

In answering this question the first point to emphasize is the nature of the relation between expression and that which is expressed. The primary element is, of course, that of reference. An expression that referred to nothing, if there be such, would not really be an expression, but rather a mere ejaculation; in this case truth and falsity are wholly irrelevant. Even a so-called emotional expression ordinarily contains an element of reference. Reference may, however, be direct or indirect—of a simple type or more subtle form. There may be direct reference to the object of discourse, but there may also be indirect reference—by implication—to the presuppositions of the discourse; both are equally part of the expression.

The relation between an expression and that which is expressed always contains, then, an element of reference, but it also contains more than mere reference. In our analysis of expression we found that an expression always contains an element of re-presentation. The necessary bi-polarity between expression and that which is expressed requires that between knowledge by simple acquaintance and by description no absolute line can be drawn, that simple presentational immediacy, in which there is no element of description and interpretation, is from the standpoint of knowledge pure myth. It is with this element of re-presentation that the notion of adequacy enters in.

The relation between the expression and that which is expressed, we have repeatedly seen, cannot be one of identity or even similarity, for the assertions or expressions belong to an entirely different category from the things which are expressed. There is, indeed, always a common form of representation or mutual participation in a pattern, but the nature and extent of the similarity is always determined by the intent of the expression or communication. The expression concerned may be a "picture" of either of the kinds described (a picture is always an implicit assertion or proposition), or it may be of the nature of symbolic representation; but before the question of truth or falsity can *even be raised*, it is necessary to determine the "sense" of the picture or symbol. Once this fact is realized it becomes clear that the only possible notion of truth is that of adequacy. A map is "true" when it represents certain spatial relations. A portrait is true when it represents the character of the sitter. A model of the atom is true when it represents the constitution of the atom. But in no case is the representation characterizable in any other terms than those of adequacy. But adequacy means different things in these different contexts. There is no such thing as adequacy as such, any more than efficiency as such; there is adequacy only with respect to the sense or intent of the expression.

It is sometimes said that certain "kinds" of truth or forms of the truth relation are "adequate for our type of consciousness," or that such truth "is conditioned by community of subjective form." It is our contention that, properly understood, this must be said of every kind of truth. By the very fact that truth in the primary sense is a relation between an expression and that which is expressed, it is impossible that there should be any truth relation that is not so conditioned. Expression and understanding are correlative terms. A proposition has no reality except in some universe of discourse. It is possible that for God there may be truth that is not so conditioned; for man it is not. This general truth does not, however, necessarily exclude the possibility that there are different degrees of this conditioning, or that the community of subjective form may be more universal in one case than another. There may be privileged universes of discourse. But it does exclude, and rightly, the possibility that any language, even that of "science," should be wholly unconditioned. To hold the opposite is to be subject to illusion.

It is also said that there is literal truth and symbolic truth of various kinds. Now, strictly speaking, there is no such thing as literal truth in any absolute sense, for there is no such thing as absolute correspondence between expression and that which is expressed. There can be no such thing as identity, or even complete similarity between expression and the state of affairs which it expresses, for they belong to wholly different categories. A "fact" is not a fact for knowledge until it is enunciated, and any expression in language contains some symbolic element. There is, to be sure, a relative distinction between the literal and the symbolic which is not only legitimate but of great significance in certain contexts—a distinction which will be made clear later[1]—but no absolute distinction is possible.

The view of the nature of truth here developed is necessitated by our critical examination of a modern statement of the correspondence notion. It is also really demanded as a condition of intelligible discourse. Earlier in this chapter we spoke of narrow conceptions of knowledge and of conceptions which are broader and more humane. The view of truth as adequate expression is the correlate of the more humane view of knowledge. The acceptance of narrower views of knowledge and truth simplifies the problem greatly. Such a procedure is possible, however, only to one who deliberately cuts himself off from a large part of human intercourse in which this broader notion of truth is a necessary condition or presupposition. The notion of different kinds of truth, scientific and poetic, literal and symbolic, is part of the humanistic position. That these different kinds of truth must ultimately be made "coherent" and brought into a totality of intelligible discourse is undoubtedly true. But this fact does not alter one whit the more fundamental fact that adequate expression is the ultimate meaning of truth. Coherence is but one of the conditions of adequate expression.

E

Truth and Verifiability. Perceptual Truth

The notion of truth here developed can, of course, justify itself only in the course of the detailed examination of the different languages and universes of discourse in which the adequacy of expression is determined. It has been possible here only to indicate in broad outlines the meaning to be given to the notion. One thing is, however, clear: that the truth problem cannot be solved apart from the problem of language and expression. Granted this, and the correlative notion that truth must then be adequate expression, it is immediately evident

[1] Chapter IX, pp. 432 ff.

that such a view involves necessarily certain modifications of our notions of verification and verifiability. Some study of these notions has already been made in connection with problems of meaning.[1] It is now desirable to carry this study further.

The conclusions of our earlier discussion may be summarized as follows: (a) Meaning and verifiability are inseparable if the notion of verification be properly understood; (b) Reference to an observable entity (the empirical criterion) is not the only way of verification. There is a universe of discourse in which this is the way and the sole way, but this universe is not the only universe, nor this the sole way; (c) There is verification by authentication, and we were able to show not only that a large number of meaningful propositions are verifiable in this way, but that the empirical criterion itself is a type of proposition which, if verifiable at all—and therefore meaningful—is verifiable only in this way; (d) Verification, in any way and in any form, involves confirmation, and confirmation is ultimately a matter of communication. With these conclusions assumed and the argument of that chapter in mind, we may carry our study of truth and verifiability a step further.

It is evident from our analysis of the truth notion that verification cannot consist in mere reference to an observable entity, for that which is verified is always an expression and, as an expression, includes, besides indication, representation in some form and description to some degree. It is equally evident that verification cannot ultimately consist merely in establishing a common pattern between an expression and a nexus of events. Mere coincidence, whether partial or complete, is not the "sense" of the truth notion. The meaning of truth is never reducible without a remainder to the copy theory in any form. Viewed from either approach, truth involves adequate expression, and verification of a proposition always involves determination of this adequacy—through interpretation.

This seems to be the general notion of verification to which we are forced by the entire drift of our analysis of the relation of language to cognition and of the corresponding notion of

[1] Chapter V, pp. 209 ff.

truth developed above. If the primary truth relation is propositional truth, and if a proposition is always an expression subsisting within discourse, verification can only be of this character. Nevertheless it will doubtless be maintained that there is one fact—and that a crucial one—on which this entire conception comes to grief, namely, *perceptual truth or the truth of sense perception*. Surely here there is truth in some other sense, and verification here is independent of interpretation and communication. This objection has already been raised in an earlier context and answered in principle,[1] but it is necessary to meet it more specifically. It is necessary to show that the truth relation here also is a case of relation between expression and that which is expressed, and that verification falls under our general notion.

Perceptual truth—together with verification by perception or observation—is ordinarily divided into direct and indirect. Let us examine them in order.

It is already clear that there is no purely perceptual truth if perceptual knowledge means knowledge by simple acquaintance. Verification of a simple ostensive proposition such as "this is green" is often supposed to consist in the mere awareness of the sense datum, but mere awareness, as such, verifies nothing; the mere sense datum as such is not a case of knowledge at all. Indeed, the very notion of an ostensive proposition (that is, purely ostensive) appears to be a contradiction in terms. It implies that there could be a sentence which consisted in purely demonstrative signs and at the same time be intelligible. This is, however, not even a logical possibility. A sentence which consisted of demonstrable signs alone would not even express a genuine proposition. It would be a mere ejaculation in no way characterizing that to which it is supposed to refer. This is the same thing as saying that there is no perception which does not include an element of description and interpretation.

The simplest case of perceptual knowledge is, then, an expression. This is in itself enough to do away with this misconception of direct verification. But an even more important consideration is the following. No proposition that enters into actual knowledge ever *really* refers directly to an immediate

[1] Chapter V, pp. 223 ff.

datum of sense experience. The simplest sentence in discourse (and this is pre-eminently true of that discourse which we call science), refers to other sentences. It is these, not the sense datum, which do the verifying.[1] It follows from this that the notion of direct verification is pure myth, all actual verification being in part indirect. It follows also that the verification which we call direct is always an interpretation in terms of pre-existing sentences or expressions.

The simplest case of perceptual truth is, then, a relation between an expression and that which is expressed. Verification, even the most direct, involves interpretation. The real character of perceptual truth becomes even clearer when we examine what is specifically described as indirect verification. As an illustration of such truth Whitehead gives the relation of contemporary experiences with happenings of the past, especially the remote past. There is a truth relation, it is said, between our present experiences of the light of the distant star and the star itself in which the light has actually died out, but it is an indirect relation. In this case the experience of the light is said to verify indirectly the existence of the remote star. Even more clearly than in the preceding case, it is not the brute datum, the light, which verifies; the verification takes place in the process of interpretation of the sense datum. The sentences or propositions about the distant star are the only adequate expression or interpretation of the experiences of the present light. It is this adequacy, involving as it does an entire context of relations, or universe of discourse, which constitutes the verification.

The importance of these considerations will become increasingly apparent when we come to the questions of the language and symbolisms of science. The nature of verification in this sphere becomes a problem as it becomes increasingly more indirect. Thus from certain observations we infer the deflection of light passing the sun or the displacement of the perihelion of Mercury, and see in these "facts" an indirect confirmation of Einstein's assertion that a non-Euclidian geometry prevails in the space of the universe. This, too, it

---

[1] See on this point A. D. Ritchie, "Errors of Logical Positivism," *Philosophy*, Vol. XII, No. 45, January 1937, an unusually keen and true account of verification in science.

is held, is a confirmation by observation. But the difference between this case and the confirmation of an ordinary empirical generalization lies in the fact that it is immensely more indirect and can be arrived at "only by the most complicated theoretical arguments." Now we are, of course, not denying that this may properly be called a confirmation or verification of a theory by an observation; we are interested in seeing wherein this verification consists. Purely theoretically, as has often been pointed out, the verification of an hypothesis by a single case might be an accident, a chance coincidence of events. It might be an accident that the displacement of the perihelion of Mercury given by the Einstein theory of gravitation is exactly 43 seconds of arc, and so just the same amount as that which the astronomers had inferred from their observations independently of the theory, or it might be only an accident that the spectral lines of glowing substances, so far as they have been observed, have exactly the regularity expressed by Bohr's formula. But the physicist does not believe that; indeed the absurdity seems so absurd that no one would seriously take it into consideration. This is undoubtedly true, but it is precisely this fact that shows that it is not the *isolated sense datum* which verifies the hypothesis, but the entire process of interpretation of the sense datum.

In the case of perceptual truth, then, verification, whether direct or indirect, is always a function of interpretation. Here, as little as in the case of propositional truth, is there any question either of identity or similarity, but only of adequacy. When a perceptual judgment or an hypothesis is said to be verified by observation, what this really means is that the judgment or hypothesis in question expresses adequately what is implied in the observational sentences.

This character of perceptual truth is indicated by the fact that all such truth is said to be merely probable. What the notion of probability in scientific method means must be left for a later context; what it means when applied here seems to be the following. There is the element of increase of confidence which comes from repeated observations which, as we say, confirm our perceptual judgment. But there is also another element equally important, namely, the degree to which the judgment or hypothesis in question fits into our accepted notions of rationality or intelligibility. The refusal of the physicist even to take into consideration the possibility that the single case might be an accident, because of its *absurdity*, means that his confirmation of an hypothesis takes place within a universe of discourse conditioned in its very character and constitution by mutually acknowledged assumptions as to rationality and intelligibility. It is here that the real *locus* of verification is found.

X

MEANING AND TRUTH: THEIR RELATIONS

A

This brief examination of verification will be carried further when we consider specifically the language and symbolism of science.[1] Here our sole purpose was to show that so-called perceptual truth is in no sense an exception to our general thesis that verification is, in the last analysis, a matter of communication and mutual interpretation of meaning. This is the significance of Royce's cryptic assertion when, speaking of truth, he writes, "perception says it is not in me; conception says it is not in me; interpretation says, it is nigh thee, even in thy heart." Truth is a function of adequate expression, and adequacy of expression can be determined only by interpretation.

Two consequences seem to follow from the preceding analysis of the notions of truth and verifiability. In the first place, it seems clear that truth is always a function of a relation of expression to that which is expressed. Some notion of correspondence between the expression and that which is expressed is the *primary* notion of truth. The correspondence or "copy" notion can never be wholly eliminated from the truth notion. But while it is the primary notion it is not the final one. The notion of correspondence must yield to the more general notion of *adequate* expression. In the second place, while the two notions of meaning and verifiability are inseparable, the notion of meaning seems ultimate; that is, verification itself seems ultimately to consist in the determination of adequacy

[1] Chapter XI, pp. 545 ff.

of expression of meaning and in the mutual acknowledgment of meaning on the part of communicating subjects. It is at this point that we may profitably carry further the reflections of the earlier discussion.

We have already called attention to the circular character of the relation between meaning and verifiability. The meaning of an assertion, it may properly be said, is the way in which it may be verified; but we cannot determine the way of verification until we have determined the sense of the proposition. The reason why the assertion that there are other selves cannot be verified by the "empirical criterion" is because it does not mean something that can be thus verified. Meaning is, then, in a sense "logically" prior to verification. But it is also logically more ultimate. That is, in the very fact that we have established the meaningfulness of the assertion of the existence of other selves, as the necessary presupposition of the meaningfulness of discourse about other things, we have in that very process verified it. This situation may be stated in the following way. All meaningful propositions, *qua* meaningful, are *ipso facto* true or contain elements of truth. To distinguish the meaningful from the unmeaning in discourse is inevitably to determine true propositions.[1]

This thesis, when thus baldly stated, is at first sight so paradoxical as to seem scarcely worth considering. Surely, it will be said, to establish the meaningfulness of the assertion that there are mountains on the other side of the moon does not establish its truth. And to this the only reply is, certainly it does not. In the universe of discourse in which this assertion is meaningful, part of the very meaning of truth itself is reference to a sensuously observable entity, and until the entity *is* observed the assertion is not verified; it is merely verifi*able*. And yet, if the hypothesis of mountains on the other side of the moon were the only hypothesis which would make meaningful or intelligible other facts, we should have to call it probably true, even if the mountains remained for ever inaccessible to sense observation. This is the situation with respect to many entities in science. In this respect, then, meaning is the ultimate notion.

In the universe of discourse in which propositions about

[1] Chapter V, pp. 222 ff.

mountains and moons are either true or false, part of the very meaning of truth is reference to observable entities. There are, however, other universes of discourse in which the meaning of truth does not include such reference. It is unnecessary to recall in detail the nature and extent of assertions or propositions of this type, as examined in our earlier study of authentication.[1] It is enough to remember that the assertion that there are other selves does not mean—never has and never will—reference to a sensuously observable entity. It means—and can only mean—that this assertion conditions the meaningfulness of assertions in any universe of discourse. Unless, then, there is real communication between real selves, all their discourse about mountains and moons is ultimately meaningless. The assertion that there are other selves is a meaningful proposition and, in this case at least, to say that it is meaningful is the same thing as to say that it is true.

Not only, then, is the notion of meaning more ultimate than that of truth, but the two notions tend—in the long run—to coincide. It must be observed that in this statement of the relation of meaning to truth it is only ultimately that the notions of truth and meaning (or intelligibility) coincide. It is quite clear that initially they do not. In the primary context of the physical universe the meaningfulness of an assertion is conditioned by reference to an observable entity, for the very presupposition of this universe of discourse is precisely that truth is reference to an observable entity, whether direct or indirect. In the terms of Kant, the postulate of the "empirical employment of the understanding" is just that existence (*das Wirckliche*) *shall* mean reference to the sensuously observable. It does not follow that this is the necessary postulate of every universe of discourse, or every employment of the reason.

Of this coincidence of truth and intelligibility we shall have more to say presently. For the moment let us consider this notion of truth in relation to other views of truth. This conception of the nature of truth and of its relation to meaning, although the only one ultimately intelligible, runs counter, of course, to certain of our natural prejudices. And yet it becomes necessary when we become aware of the difficulties in the other conceptions of truth. The various notions such as

[1] Chapter V, p. 201.

the correspondence, the coherence, and the pragmatic, are themselves criteria of truth, and presuppose the more ultimate notions of adequate expression and intelligibility which we have maintained. This may be shown in the following way.

It has long been recognized that no one of these theories can be proved by its own criterion. It is impossible to show that the notion of correspondence is true because it itself corresponds to a thing called truth. It is equally impossible to show that the coherence theory is true because it coheres with something else. It is impossible to show that the pragmatic theory is true because it works; indeed one of the most fundamental criticisms of it has always been that it itself is not pragmatic.[1] In sum, all these theories of truth, *if true*, are so in some other sense than that expressed by the criterion itself. If verifiable at all—and to the meaningful they must be verifiable in some sense—it can only be by mutual acknowledgment in discourse. They are truths only of interpretation. Here, at least, truth and meaning coincide and truth is immanent in discourse.

We have been examining the question of the "meaning of truth" as necessarily implied in our conceptions of the relation of language to cognition. We started with the analysis of the notion of truth made by Whitehead, and found ourselves compelled to modify it in ways which have become apparent. The problem of truth has thus shown itself to be an important part of the philosophy of language. And yet it is quite common to say that the question of the meaning of truth is itself a meaningless question; that "there is no problem of truth as it is ordinarily conceived."

This is the position of logical positivism, and it is only natural that, on its premises, this thesis should be maintained. If meaning is always reference to an observable entity then there is no meaning of truth, for there is no such referend for the word truth. Thus "to say that a proposition is true cannot

---

[1] Of the pragmatic theory it is sometimes said that it is "self-authenticating." If this statement means that it can be proved by its own criterion, it is false. If it means that it is the "meaning" of truth that must be acknowledged in meaningful discourse, it is certainly doubtful. But to say that it is self-authenticating, in the latter sense, is at least to recognize the truth of our thesis, namely, that a proposition about the nature of truth can itself not be empirically verified, but only authenticated in discourse.

be anything else than *to assert it*, and to say that it is false is just to assert its contradictory. And this indicates, it is held, that the terms true and false connote nothing, but function in the sentence simply as marks of assertion and denial. In that case there can be no sense in asking for an analysis of the truth notion."[1] This sounds plausible and yet clearly it will not do. For the terms true and false function in sentences in other ways than simply as marks of assertion and denial. No discourse in which distinctions between truth and falsity are intelligibly used is possible which does not imply mutual acknowledgment, on the part of those communicating, of some "meaning" of truth. The tacit assumption underlying most discourse is, of course, the primary notion of copy or correspondence in some form. If the notion is modified in discourse or dialectic, it is because it is found inadequate to describe the truth relation. It is for such reasons that, whether we like it or not, scientists and philosophers alike, to say nothing of ordinary folk, will continue to seek to determine the meaning of truth. Otherwise they cannot make themselves intelligible.

B

Truth as Immanent in Discourse: Veritas in Dicto

All meaningful propositions *qua* meaningful are, then, *ipso facto* true or contain elements of truth, references to reality. The process of discovering truth is ultimately simply the process of distinguishing those propositions which have meaning from those which have not. To distinguish the meaningful from the unmeaning in discourse is inevitably to determine true propositions.

This fact may be expressed in the thesis that the totality of intelligible discourse *is* the truth. Truth, *in the last analysis*, is immanent in discourse and not an external relation of discourse to reality. It is for this reason, however, that, as we have seen, the ultimate form of knowledge (and knowledge always implies truth) is knowledge by interpretation. The element of interpretation is present in knowledge by acquaintance and in knowledge by description. Part of that knowledge

---

[1] A. J. Ayer, *Language, Truth and Logic*, p. 122 f.

is always the determination of the sense of the presentation or representation, and sense and meaning can only be interpreted. But there are cases also of knowledge by interpretation alone, and here truth is wholly a matter of interpretation.

It is here that a limitation, introduced earlier in our discussion, becomes of the greatest importance. Truth and meaning tend in the long run to coincide, but only ultimately. In limited contexts or universes of discourse some notion of truth may be the primary concept, the notion upon which meaning itself depends. Such is the physical context, that universe of discourse in which the empirical criterion of truth is also the criterion or determinant of meaning. But in the maximum context this is not the case; the two notions must coincide. This we shall find of great importance in understanding that universe of discourse which we call metaphysics. Metaphysical discourse is concerned with the *omnitudo realitatis*, and therefore with maximum context. Here truth and intelligibility coincide; for in this context truth cannot be an external relation of discourse to reality—it can only be immanent in discourse itself.

The notion of maximum context as here employed requires further clarification, for it will be used repeatedly in discussions to come. According to our contextual theory of meaning, the condition of the meaningfulness of an assertion or proposition is not necessarily that certain entities about which the assertions are made "exist" in the sense of being empirically verifiable but rather that the universe of discourse in which these entities have their being be mutually acknowledged. The physical universe of discourse, conditioned as it is by acknowledgment of certain presuppositions, is not necessarily a privileged universe. It is a limited universe in which, it is true, the acknowledged condition of meaning is reference to a sensuously observable entity, but such reference is not necessarily the condition of meaning in other universes or contexts. In this, and other limited universes, there are, then, certain specific criteria of truth. But in the maximum context, which is that of metaphysics, no such limited criteria apply. Here truth and meaning coincide and the sole criterion of truth is intelligibility—a criterion which will be developed later.[1]

[1] Chapter XIII, pp. 673 ff.

By maximum context we understand, then, the universe of discourse in which the object of such discourse is the *omnitudo realitatis*. Whether meaningful propositions can be made about this object is a question to be considered later.[1] But if they can—and we shall attempt to show that they are possible—then truth in this context must be as we have described. It cannot be denied that this notion raises certain difficulties. This maximum context, or widest universe of discourse, must, after all, contain "contents" or entities; discourse cannot be abstracted from the objects about which the discourse takes place. Assertions are always assertions about something, and truth, even in the maximum context, must be the truth of "contents." In some fashion, then, the truth of the particular contents must be related to the truth of the whole, verification in specific contexts with the intelligibility which alone can constitute truth in the maximum context. This we shall attempt to do in a later chapter. For the moment, however, despite the difficulties in the notion, we shall still maintain that in this maximum context truth and meaning coincide.

Truth, then, in the last analysis, is immanent in discourse—the sum-total of intelligible discourse *is* the truth. *Veritas in dicto, non in re consistit.* If there is no knowing that does not involve expression (and ultimately linguistic expression), whether such knowledge be knowledge by acquaintance or knowledge by description, then it is only in language that the meaning of that knowledge can be elucidated and interpreted. The proposition *Veritas in dicto* is often interpreted as nominalism—and as used by Hobbes, with his theory of language, it could not be otherwise—but properly interpreted it need not be. For, as we have shown, it is precisely a nominalistic theory of language which makes it impossible that truth should be found in discourse. Nominalism not only paralyses speech but stultifies all discourse. It is precisely because names are not mere *nomina*, not mere conventional signs, that it is possible to maintain that if our discourse is ultimately intelligible it is also, in its totality, ultimately the truth. To say that truth is immanent in discourse, and at the same time to conceive the language of that discourse nominalistically, is to express a contradiction in terms.

[1] Chapter XIII, pp. 676 ff.

This theory of truth, I am well aware, will arouse the greatest opposition in many minds. And yet it seems to be the only one possible when all the relevant facts are taken into consideration. It may be said to be merely the "idealistic" theory in a new guise. In a sense it is idealistic—in the sense, namely, that our theories of meaning and of context were said to be idealistic as opposed to naturalistic. That such a view of language should have as its consequence an idealistic theory of truth in this sense was only to be expected. But it is not idealistic in any invidious sense, for, as we have already shown, the necessary presuppositions of any valid theory of communication are both realistic and idealistic.[1]

C

Symbolic Truth. The Problem of Symbolism

With this general conception of the nature of truth and of its relation to language, we may consider briefly the notion of symbolic truth, the third type of truth treated in Whitehead's scheme. This will at the same time serve to elucidate further the main notions of this section and afford a transition to the problems of the second part of our study, namely, *The Principles of Symbolism*.

It is, I think, only when we raise problems of symbolism and symbolic truth that the necessity of the foregoing conception of truth becomes fully evident. The notion of symbolic truth is one which arises immediately in connection with problems of language and cognition, for all language is symbolic in one sense of the word and some language is symbolic in the special sense of symbolic, as contrasted with "literal." What this contrast means we shall presently see; for the moment it is sufficient to recognize that it constitutes a well-recognized distinction within language itself, and the problem of the truth of the symbolic, as opposed to the literal use of language, becomes one of the main questions of an adequate theory of truth.

We may approach our problem by way of a consideration

[1] Chapter VI, pp. 263 ff.

of the notion of symbolic truth as defined by Whitehead in the context from which his discussion of truth was taken. According to him, all direct truth is propositional truth, but there are two forms of the indirect truth relation, perceptual and symbolic. In the case of symbolic truth the phenomena which stand for or refer to reality "throw no light by their own natures on the objects to which they refer except in the experiences of a set of specially conditioned recipients." Here the truth relation is indirect. There is a vague truth relation, but only by way of "community of subjective form." Such "symbols" give us truth but only indirectly. They do not therefore ultimately satisfy us, but demand reduction to the direct or literal truth of propositions.

Now I shall not be disposed to question this general notion of symbolic truth, namely, that it involves community of subjective form, but shall simply raise the question whether communication and community of subjective form are wholly absent from any truth relation. Still more am I disposed to question the statements that symbols throw no light by their own natures on the objects to which they refer, or that they demand reduction to direct or literal truth of propositions. But these are questions to be considered in the next chapter. Here our main point is that only a conception of truth as adequate expression can do justice to the notion of symbolic truth. A symbol is an expression, and the criterion of its truth, as in the case of all expressions, lies in its adequacy. But adequacy here, whatever it may mean in other forms of the truth relation, includes adequacy for our type of consciousness, as conditioned by community of subjective form. It is certainly clear that what ordinarily goes by the name of symbolic truth is thus conditioned. The truth of a symbol, whether in art, religion or science, is, seemingly at least, definitely conditioned by the nature of the symbolizers. That symbol propositions demand reduction to literal propositions —and that symbols "by their own natures, throw no light on the objects to which they refer" are, however, both highly doubtful statements—and indeed constitute the main issues in a theory of symbolism. In any case, the problem of symbolism and of symbolic truth grows directly out of the problems of the philosophy of language. The development of language is, as we have seen, from copy to analogy and from analogy to symbol. The "principles of symbolism," and the nature and interpretation of symbols, constitute fundamental problems of both language and knowledge. To these problems we shall now turn.

PART II

THE PRINCIPLES OF SYMBOLISM

CHAPTER IX

THE PRINCIPLES OF SYMBOLISM: THE GENERAL THEORY OF SYMBOLISM

I

THE problem of symbolism, like the problem of language, has, as we have seen, become fundamental in modern science and philosophy. The doctrine that all language is symbolic, the conception that logic is the science of accurate symbolism, combined with the notion that "science," no less than poetry, religion, and metaphysics, is in the last analysis a form of symbolism, all these distinctively modern ideas have served to bring the problem of symbolism into the forefront of philosophical discussion and to make a general theory of symbolism a necessary part of any adequate philosophy.[1]

The philosophy of language, as we have seen, leads directly into the philosophy of symbolism. The stages of the development of language itself—from imitation to analogy, and from analogy to symbol—point to the symbolic relation of language to reality as the ultimate problem. If the function of language is not to copy reality, but to symbolize it, it is necessary, in order to understand that function, to understand the principles of symbolism. But language, as we have also seen, is not the only symbolic form. In art, religion and in science itself, non-linguistic symbols are employed. In art, so some believe, more can be "said" by sound and colour, by tone and rhythm, than by word, music on this view being the most metaphysical of the arts. Symbolic rites in religion may, it is held, evoke and communicate meanings only inadequately expressible in words. In science itself non-verbal symbols, such as graphs and models and mathematical formulas, are often held to be a more adequate representation of the relations of things than any expression in words. The relation of non-linguistic to linguistic symbols becomes a basal problem of any philosophy of language.

Problems of symbolism also grow directly out of the problem

[1] Chapter I, pp. 46 ff.

of cognition. Knowing involves not only presentation but re-presentation. One form of representation is the symbolic. Immediately the problem arises of the nature of such symbolic representation and of its relation to other forms of description. Symbolic knowledge as distinguished from non-symbolic, symbolic as distinguished from "literal" truth—their nature and their significance—are problems of any general theory of knowledge.[1]

These, then, are the questions involved in the problem of symbolism. The answer to these questions constitutes a general theory of symbolism. Whether such a theory is possible—whether all the varied forms of symbolic representation can be brought under one general conception—remains to be seen. Such a theory is, however, the object of this chapter.

II

THE NOTION OF SYMBOLISM. DEFINITIONS

A

The first requisite of a general theory of symbolism is an adequate notion of the symbol and the symbolizing function. This notion must, as Cassirer rightly points out, be a broad one if it is to be adequate. "The philosophy of symbols and symbolic forms is not, as some suppose, concerned primarily and exclusively with scientific and exact concepts, but with *all* directions of the symbolizing function in its attempt to grasp and understand the world. It is necessary to study this function, not only in the realm of scientific concepts but in the non-scientific realms of poetry, art, religion, etc., not only on the level of the conceptual, but on the cognitive levels below the conceptual."[2] "We lose entirely our sense for the significance of this function when we think of the symbol concept only on the level of abstract thought. This function belongs not to a single level of the world picture, but holds throughout."[3]

The need of this warning is apparent when we realize that precisely this tendency to narrow the concept symbol has been

---

[1] Chapter VIII, p. 354 f. and p. 382 f.
[2] *Die Philosophie der Symbolischen Formen*, Vol. III, p. 16.   [3] *Ibid.*, p. 57.

THE PRINCIPLES OF SYMBOLISM

a conspicuous tendency of more recent philosophical thought. Under the influence of mathematics and "symbolic" logic, a notion of the symbolizing function has arisen which has introduced great confusion into the entire discussion, and has brought about an almost complete reversal of the traditional notion. This reversal appears at two points: (a) in the tendency to identify symbol with sign, and (b) the denial of the "intuitive" character of the symbol.

The traditional notion, formed largely in the non-scientific realms of poetry, art, and religion, applies the concept of symbol to non-literal forms of representation. A symbol is always a sign, but it is much more than a sign. Thus the definitions of symbol still given in the dictionaries: "A symbol is a representation of any moral or spiritual thing by the images or properties of natural things." The lion is the symbol of courage, the lamb the symbol of meekness or patience. In both artistic and religious uses the term is applied to uses of language, or other media of communication, whose object is *suggestion* or *insight* rather than direct or literal representation. If now an element of knowledge or truth, which is generally the case, is held to be conveyed by this symbolism, it is customary to speak of symbolic knowledge as contrasted with other kinds.

In contrast to this "traditional" conception there is a modern tendency to identify the symbolic function with the merely indicative or sign function. "A symbol," as Ogden and Richards, for instance, define it, "symbolizes an act of reference, that is, among its causes in the speaker, together no doubt with desires to record and communicate, and with attitudes towards hearers, are acts of referring. Thus a symbol becomes, when uttered, in virtue of being so caused, *a sign to a hearer of* an act of reference"[1] (italics mine). On this view, which divides the functions of language into two, the indicative and emotive, the symbolic function becomes identified with the sign function, and those aspects of the notion which were central in the traditional conception, namely, non-literal but intuitive representation, are denied part in the symbolic function as such, and identified with the emotive as distinct from the cognitive aspect.

[1] *The Meaning of Meaning*, p. 205.

Already in Kant's day this tendency was present, and in the *Critique of Judgment*[1] he speaks of it as a "sinnverkehrenden unrechten Gebrauch des Wortes Symbol." According to him, the symbolic form of representation is not opposed to the intuitive, but a sub-class under the intuitive. Kant is undoubtedly right in holding that this is the traditional meaning of symbol. Whatever justification there may be for the modern development, which in certain uses equates symbol with the merely indicative sign, there is no justification for narrowing the concept to this notion. In the discussion which follows we shall develop the thesis that a double conception of symbolism is necessary, and that the relation of the two types of symbol is one of the basal problems of a philosophy of symbolism. In developing our thesis we shall begin with an analysis of the relations of sign to symbol.

B

Preliminary Definitions. Sign and Symbol

"Any datum," it is said, "may be a symbol if it means something or operates as a sign." Such data, we are further told, include "conspicuous features of nature, monuments, written or spoken words, small images or familiar objects easily duplicated or distributed. Any of these is a symbol provided it directs expectation or interest to something other than itself. Symbolism is, then, the study of the part played in human affairs by all these signs and symbols, especially their influence on thought. Symbols direct and organize, record and communicate. For words, arrangements of words, images, gestures, and such representations as drawings or mimetic sounds we use the term symbols."[2]

Statements such as these will do well enough as a starting-point, but they are worthless for our purposes until we have made certain finer distinctions and sharpened our definitions.

Any datum, it is said, may be a symbol if it means something or operates as a sign. This statement may well be ques-

---

[1] *The Critique of Judgment*, translated by J. H. Bernard, 1914, Section 59, p. 248.
R. B. Perry, *A General Theory of Value*, p. 408 ff.

tioned on both points. It identifies the symbol relation with all meaning relations and identifies symbol with sign. It may well be that while the symbol relation is a meaning relation, it is a special type of such relation. It may well be that while all symbols are in a sense signs, not all signs are symbols.

In the first place, then, to identify the symbol relation with all relations of meaning is to make the symbol notion useless. It is precisely the nature of a symbol that it takes the primary and natural meaning of both objects and words and modifies them (in some cases we speak of "distortion") in certain ways so that they acquire a meaning relation of a different kind. All symbolic relations are meaning relations, but not all meaning relations symbolic. Again, the symbolic function cannot be identified with the function of "operating as a sign." The use of symbol as identical with sign also makes the symbol notion useless. There are many cases in which the term sign may be used in which the term symbol would be most inappropriate. Clouds are "signs" of rain, but not symbols. We feel it quite natural to say that a grimace is a sign of pain, a frown of anger, but we should feel it to be a violation of all linguistic feeling to call them symbols. From recent psychological literature I gather the following "gem": "My behaviour symbol relative to steaming foods may be a reacting of the salivary glands." To say that the reaction of my salivary glands is a sign of the presence of food is entirely appropriate, but to call it a symbol is a linguistic distortion which is not only in itself inexcusable, but bars the way to any proper use of the concept of symbol.

Obviously, then, symbols must be distinguished from "natural signs." Husserl has sharply emphasized this difference between the genuinely symbolic, the really *significative* sign, and the merely *designatory* sign. Meaning does not reside in all signs in the sense in which we, for example, think of the word as the bearer of meaning. In the domain of natural happenings and existences, for instance, a thing or happening can, as we have seen, become a sign of another as soon as it is bound to it by any constant empirical relation, especially that of cause and effect. In this fashion the smoke can become the sign of fire or the thunder of lightning. But that kind of signs does not *express* anything. "Das Bedeuten ist nich eine art des Zeichen-seins im Sinne der Anzeige."[1] Cassirer also warns against the danger of wiping out this distinction.[2] It arises, he also points out, whenever, instead of recognizing the symbolic relation as a primary and universal function, it is brought under the standpoint of scientific conceptions, especially that of causation. Everywhere there is the temptation to carry the purely symbolic relations back to causal relations and to explain the former through the latter. The naturalistic theory of symbols, which identifies them with signs, is but a special phase of the naturalistic theory of meaning in general which we have critically considered in an earlier connection.[3]

As symbols must be distinguished from natural signs, so the notion of symbol, in the historical sense at least, must be distinguished from certain forms of conventional signs. Certain kinds of substitutional signs have gradually come to be called symbols, but they are not, as we have maintained, *genuine* symbols. They are merely operational signs, in which no intuitive relation to the object for which they stand remains. I agree wtih Cassirer that, strictly speaking, these signs are not symbols. In all genuine symbolic relations, Cassirer tells us, some form of likeness is to be found. There are varied types of likeness. From a statue we demand only likeness of form, from a drawing only likeness of perspective projection, from a painting also likeness of colour. These differences in the likenesses in the copy of an object suggest also difference of likeness in the symbolic relation, and in difference of types of symbol. In the moral symbol there is one type of likeness, in the scientific another, in the religious still another, but all symbolic relations imply some type of likeness.[4] Some kind of likeness is implied also by the picture—namely "common form of representation," as described in the preceding chapter. A symbol is, however, not necessarily a picture. We shall in later contexts have to distinguish between symbol and picture. Here we are concerned merely to distinguish between symbol and sign, and here likeness of some sort is necessary.

---

[1] *Logische Untersuchungen*, II, pp. 23 ff.
[2] *Die Philosophie der Symbolischen Formen*, Vol. III, p. 375.
[3] Chapter III, pp. 129 ff.   [4] *Op. cit.*, p. 376.

C

The Relation of Sign to Symbol

No hard-and-fast line can be drawn between sign and symbol in ordinary discourse; otherwise we should not have the confusion that at present reigns. Signs may become symbols and symbols may, so to speak, degenerate into signs. Some distinction must, however, be made, otherwise the entire notion of symbolism becomes meaningless. All symbols, we may say, are signs, but not all signs symbols. We may assume, then, that symbol may be best defined as a special kind of sign. Signs may be conveniently divided into three classes according to the way they operate. We may characterize them as designative or indicative, expressive or significant, and substitutional.

A designatory sign is one by means of which we merely pay or draw attention to the thing to which it refers. In the case of such signs we normally do not pay attention to the sign itself, as for instance in the case of the sound in language, as distinguished from its meaning. An expressive or significant sign, on the other hand, calls to mind a certain idea, and the idea is attended to independently of the sign. Thus the Cross is a significant sign and its expressive character lies in the idea. It cannot express or signify except as attention is given to the sign itself. Finally, there are substitute signs, e.g. those used in logic and mathematics. Such a sign takes the place of what it stands for. It *merely* "stands for." Making use of a term later to be introduced, it is merely *pro*nominal.

According to our preceding analysis, the notion of symbol is not to be identified with every form of sign. We may eliminate all signs that are merely designatory, namely, all signs by which we merely pay attention to that to which they refer. There are left, then, the genuinely significant and the substitutional signs. Here our difficulties begin to appear. Stout, following the modern tendency, identifies the notion of symbol with the substitutional sign.[1]

---

[1] See his article on "Sign-making Function," in Baldwin's *Dictionary of Philosophy and Psychology*, Vol. II.

D

The Symbol and Intuition

This view of the nature of the genuine symbol and its distinction from "sign" may be described as the traditional, and is uniformly present in all post-Kantian theories of symbolism. It is well stated by Hegel, and comment upon his definition will serve to make our contention finally clear. "The sign is different from the symbol," he tells us, "for in the symbol the original characters (in essence and conception) of the more or less visible object are identical with the import which it bears as symbol; whereas in the sign, strictly so called, the natural attributes of the intuition and the connotation of which it is a sign, have nothing to do with each other. Intelligence, therefore, gives proof of wider choice and ampler authority in the use of intuitions when it treats them as designatory, rather than symbolic."[1]

It seems to me that in this passage the *primary* meaning of the symbol, as distinguished from sign, is clearly brought out. The *genuinely* symbolic is bound up with the intuitive and cannot be separated from it. In so far as the symbolic in language is concerned it is found precisely in the intuitive elements in language which we were at pains to analyse out in an earlier chapter. The symbolic, whether linguistic or non-linguistic, is characterized by this fact. "It is characteristic of all symbols," writes Höffding, that "images and ideas are taken from the narrower more intuitible relations and used as expressions for more universal and ideal relations which, because of their pervasiveness and ideality, cannot be directly expressed."[2]

Kant has stated this character of the genuinely symbolic by comparing and relating it to the concept. "All intuitions," he writes, "which we supply to concepts *a priori* . . . are either *schemata* or *symbols* of which the former contain direct, the latter indirect, presentations of the concept. The former do this demonstrably; the latter by means of an analogy (for which we avail ourselves even of empirical intuitions) in which

---

[1] Hegel, *Philosophy of Mind*, Wallace's translation, p. 76 f. (Section 458).
[2] H. Höffding, *The Philosophy of Religion*, p. 77.

the judgment exercises a double function; first applying the concept to the object of a sensible intuition, and then applying the mere rule of the reflection made upon that intuition to a quite different object of which the first is only a symbol."[1] We shall find this characterization of the symbol valuable at several points. Here we wish merely to emphasize the intuitive character of the genuine symbol and, more particularly, the kind of similarity which exists between the symbol and the thing symbolized, as Kant sees it. It is not similarity as in the case of the "picture." The "sense" of the symbol is not "the common form of representation," as it is in the case of the sense of the picture, but a similarity *in the way of reflecting on the two things*; a common rule of operation. An important aspect also is that the symbol is always a presentation, though indirect, of the concept. Were the conceptual element not present, there would be no judgment and, therefore, no knowledge.

E

The Double Conception of Symbol and Symbolism

The distinctions between sign and symbol here developed are of cardinal importance for the discussions to come. It may be said that the entire question is merely one of verbal definition and therefore wholly arbitrary. This is far from being the case. Quite apart from the violation of our linguistic sense, and the perversion of meaning involved in the modern tendency, metalogical questions of far-reaching import are involved. The identification of symbol with sign is part of the metalogical nominalism which identifies all cognitive meaning with mere indication or denotation.

The necessity of employing this double conception is apparent in the realm of science, no less than in the non-scientific domains of poetry, art, and religion. In science symbol is often used as identical with substitutional signs, and "sign"

[1] *The Critique of Judgment*, B. 248-9. Kant then goes on to illustrate his definition of the symbol by consideration of two symbolic representations of the State, the mechanical and the organic, by a machine and by a living body. He points out that between the State (an absolute State) and a machine there is no similarity (literal) but there is similarity "in the rules according to which we reflect upon these two things and their causality."

and symbol are used interchangeably. We speak of plus and minus signs, but we also speak of these signs as symbols of processes of addition and subtraction. But there is another meaning of symbol even in science. When scientific concepts such as atom and ether, are called symbols, they are never thought of as merely substitutional signs, as merely conventional. An intuitive element is always present in such symbols. This is even more patent in the sciences of life and mind. A notion such as "natural selection" in biology is essentially a symbolic concept in the "genuine" sense of the word. Taken from the sphere of voluntary selection, in the artificial breeding of animals, it is transferred analogically to the natural non-voluntary sphere. The notion of selection is "moulded," as we say, but it retains its meaning only in so far as the original "intuitive" element is retained. It is for this reason that, as we shall see in a later context, the language of these sciences can never be reduced to a "physical language."

F

Knowledge as a Whole as "Symbolic"

In any case it is clear that we must recognize these two uses of the notion of symbol and distinguish them carefully in any theory of symbolism. There is also, I believe, a third use of the notion which must also be distinguished. In the double notion just analysed the expressive sign or symbol and the substitutional sign are symbolic elements in two different senses within knowledge as a whole. There is also a concept of symbolism which speaks of knowledge itself as a form of symbolism.

This notion is of long standing. It was present in pre-Kantian thought but became of even greater importance in post-Kantian philosophy. Thus Lambert's *Organon* (Part II) contains a detailed discussion of this point. There we learn that "all discursive thinking is symbolic in two respects: first in so far as it operates with 'symbols' in the mathematical sense; and secondly in so far as all knowledge gained thereby forms but a kind of simile, image or counterpart of reality, but does not enable us to gain knowledge of reality itself, or at least not in adequate form." "A recognition of reality in an adequate form," he continues, "leads us to the concept of intuitive knowledge of intellectual perception."[1]

Now there is, to be sure, a sense in which knowledge itself may be said to be symbolic. The fact that there is no knowledge in which an element of representation does not occur—that presentational immediacy is not yet knowledge—involves of necessity that knowledge is a "kind of simile." The fact that there is no question of truth or falsity except with reference to that which can be expressed, that all expression involves language of some sort, and that in all language there are symbolic elements, means that there is no knowledge without a symbolic element. This "wider use" of the notion of the symbolic, as Cassirer calls it,[2] has fixed itself permanently in science and philosophy and has its justification. We shall ourselves make use of it as in succeeding chapters we develop our philosophy of symbolic forms. Nevertheless it must be clearly distinguished from the two concepts of symbolism already described. It is with these that we are concerned in the present context. Symbolic reference and symbolic knowledge, in this narrower sense, must then be distinguished from non-symbolic; otherwise the symbol notion becomes useless. The poetic, the scientific, and the religious symbol all require interpretation, and this interpretation must be in non-symbolic terms. This leads us to the problem of the symbolic in language.

III

SIGN AND SYMBOL IN LANGUAGE

It is quite common to-day to say that all words are symbols and that all uses of language are symbolic. Thus Miss Stebbing in her discussion of language writes: "a word is a special kind of sign called a symbol."[3] In similar fashion Ogden and Richards apply the term symbolic to all uses of language

---

[1] Quoted from Vaihinger, *The Philosophy of As-If*, p. 80.
[2] This wider use underlies the entire development of Vol. III of Cassirer's *Philosophie der Symbolischen Formen*. See in this connection especially the Introduction.
[3] *A Modern Introduction to Logic*, p. 13.

other than the emotive or evocative.[1] Whitehead likewise follows the same tendency. "The word symbolizes the thing. Language almost exclusively refers to presentational immediacy as interpreted by symbolic reference."[2]

This usage, the direct result of identifying symbolic meaning with every kind of meaning, and of symbol with sign, against which we have argued, is, however, quite contrary to earlier practice in discussions of language. Thus Locke in his third book describes words as "sensible *signs*" necessary for communication. He uses the term sign throughout, never the term symbol, thus showing a finer sense of discrimination than modern writers. It never occurs to him to use the term symbol, for to do so would be to make meaningless those special uses of language hitherto called symbolic. Just as to call all knowledge symbolic without qualification is to make the notion of symbol itself meaningless, so to call all language symbolic is to make unintelligible the distinctively symbolic uses of language.

That some uses of language are non-symbolic in any ordinary use of the term is evident on the slightest inspection. Words are often merely indicative or designatory signs in the sense that they are merely means by which we pay attention to that to which they refer. We do not ordinarily pay attention to the word itself. The word rose is a verbal sign for a certain object, and this object "by any other name would smell as sweet." But when I say "gather ye rosebuds while ye may," rosebuds is no longer merely an indicative sign; it becomes a symbol, in that there is not merely reference to the object, but a second reference depending upon the *meaning* of the sign to which we also now pay attention. Such reference is not merely conventional but grows out of natural speech construction.

In the second place, much of our arbitrary conventional speech construction is merely the manipulation of signs, and symbolic only in the secondary derived sense of substitutional signs. Just as many non-linguistic signs, such as those of mathematics, have been disjoined from the natural attributes of intuition and become merely substitutional, so also many words, especially those of a technical character. Intelligence

---

[1] *Op. cit.*, Chapter 10.   [2] *Process and Reality*, p. 263.

THE PRINCIPLES OF SYMBOLISM 413

does thereby "give proof of wider choice and ampler authority," but it is not functioning symbolically.

Finally, there is an important function of language which is clearly not symbolic in any intelligible sense. To the intent reader of a novel, for instance, the discourse of the writer who tells the tale becomes a transparent glass, so to speak, through which he follows and *sees* the events described. To his mind only the told is present; the telling is not in his consciousness at all. As it is here, so it is in any intensive *understanding* of language. The words cease to be either "signs" or "symbols." They become a relatively transparent medium for the communication of meaning. In our earlier discussions of communication this aspect of language, and the direct "contact" of mind with mind it involves, was emphasized.[1]

It is all-important that the distinction between symbolic and non-symbolic uses of language shall be maintained, just as it is important to distinguish between symbolic and non-symbolic knowledge. The symbolic function of language is found precisely at that point where the character of the symbol, as already defined, appears. As the symbol in general is the indirect representation of the concept through the intuition, so symbolic language is found where the intuitive elements of language function for the non-intuitive or conceptual. There is no symbolic element in language where the element of metaphor is not present.[2]

It is important also to emphasize the non-symbolic function of language as medium of communication. It is here, as we shall see later, that the solution of the problem of the interpretation of the symbol is to be found. The notion of the interpretation of the symbol presupposes that there is non-symbolic language in which it may be interpreted. It is true, as we shall see, that the notion of literal, non-symbolic sentences is but a limiting notion—all language is made up of

[1] Chapter VI, pp. 251 ff.
[2] A. H. Gardiner, in *Speech and Language*, agrees with my position on both counts, namely, in the distinction between sign and symbol and in the denial of the thesis that all language is symbolic. On page 101, note 1, he writes, "Symbols are a sub-class of signs in which some natural connection exists between the sign and the thing signified, e.g. the cross is a symbol of Christianity." He continues, "Among words, only those which are onomatopoeic are symbols." I agree that many uses of words are not symbolic, but I should extend the range to the metaphorical as well as onomatopoeic words.

"dead metaphors"—but it is precisely the fact that they have become dead that makes them no longer symbolic.

IV

CLASSIFICATION OF SYMBOLS

A

We have now clarified the notion of symbol, and determined the uses of the notion made necessary by its employment in different domains of thought and knowledge. Our next problem, namely, the consideration of the Principles of Symbolism, will be greatly facilitated if we attempt a preliminary and tentative classification of symbols.

Symbols may be conveniently divided into three classes, to which we shall give the following names: (*a*) extrinsic or arbitrary symbols; (*b*) intrinsic or descriptive symbols; (*c*) insight symbols. This classification is taken from a study of symbolism by H. Flanders Dunbar and is based, not only on a study of symbols themselves, but also upon a study of definitions of the symbol. In an appendix he shows that a comparative study of definitions reveals the fact that these distinctions are quite generally recognized.[1]

The first class is easily understandable. It includes many of the symbols of both art and science. The origins of such symbols are varied and have nothing to do with their function. They may arise by processes of mere association by contiguity, or they may be depotentialized intrinsic symbols. Many religious symbols are of the latter type. The significant thing is that they are mere tags, substitutional signs by means of which the object is attended to without attending to the "meaning." Their character as tags means that their function is primarily operational, whether they occur in science or any other domain of action and discourse.

[1] H. Flanders Dunbar, *Symbolism in Mediaeval Thought*, Yale University Press, 1929. The book is primarily a study of mediaeval symbolism and its "consummation" in the *Divine Comedy* of Dante, but it is valuable for the study of symbolism in general, especially in relation to the problem of symbolic knowledge. It is, of course, primarily of use in connection with the study of the poetic and the religious symbol, but it is also concerned with problems of the "philosophy of symbolism" as a whole.

THE PRINCIPLES OF SYMBOLISM

The nature of the intrinsic symbol is equally clear. Here the symbol is not a mere tag, but is in some way "internal to the thing symbolized." The symbols of art and religion are chiefly of this type and so, I think, are many of the symbols of science. In terms of the preceding discussion, "the original characters (in essence and conception) of the intuitible object are more or less identical with the import which it bears as symbol." The symbols of moral qualities, for example of the lion for courage, are intrinsic and descriptive in that, while the symbol is not identical with the thing symbolized, there is partial coincidence of such a character as to make analogous predication possible. It is symbols of this type that Kant has principally in mind in the description of the symbol given. Such a symbol represents, not by virtue of a common form of representation in the sense of delineation, but by virtue of a common "rule of reflection," as Kant phrases it.

Finally there is the "insight" symbol which is something else again. Such symbols are always intrinsic, that is, in some way and to some degree, internal to the thing symbolized; but the insight symbol, so to speak, goes deeper. The peculiar character of such symbols lies in the fact that they do not point to or lead to, but they lead *into*. They do not merely represent, through partial coincidence, characters and relations; they are, or at least are supposed to be, a vehicle or medium of insight. It is characteristic of both intrinsic and insight symbols that images or ideas are taken from narrower and more intuitible relations and used as expressions for more universal and ideal relations which, because of their pervasiveness and ideality, are not directly expressible. But while the merely intrinsic symbol only represents, the insight symbol makes us see.

B

The "Insight" Symbol—In Poetry and Religion

Since the question of insight or interpretative symbols is of such importance for a philosophy of symbolism, it will be well to develop the notion somewhat more fully. The essential of the notion, as Dunbar points out, is that this type of symbol does not merely describe and make more concrete, through images drawn from the data of sense, an object otherwise known (conceptually)—as does the merely descriptive symbol—but is given importance as a gateway into something beyond. Dunbar draws heavily on poets and religious writers alike in the search for terms in which to describe this symbolic form. The essential element in all the descriptions is the notion of an ideal or spiritual world, insight into which is given only through the sensuous.

Both poetry and religion are full of insight symbols. Dante's *Divine Comedy* is the epitome of the entire mediaeval notion of the insight symbol, but modern poetry makes use of the symbol in the same way. The entire symbolic period of Ibsen, from *The Wild Duck* on, uses the physical to give us insight into spiritual relations. Perhaps one of the best illustrations, however, is the symbol of the onion in *Peer Gynt*. The onion which, when one layer after another is removed, finally reveals nothing, is a symbol of the "Gyntish I"—which also is nothingness at the core. Insight into the nature of the social self is here given which no amount of conceptual description could afford. The very heart of religious language, as we shall see, is the insight symbol. The notion of God as father is not merely a descriptive symbol, but one by means of which we are given not only pictorial knowledge about, but actual insight into the nature of spiritual relations.

Fuller development of the notion of the insight symbol must be left to the special studies of symbolic forms in which they appear. Here we are concerned merely with classification. Nor is it intended by this classification to beg the question of the knowledge value of such symbols; this question is not yet raised. Here we have been concerned merely to name and describe a type of symbol everywhere recognized in all the historic philosophies of symbolism. It is only after we have examined the symbolic consciousness, in both its aesthetic and religious form, that the real nature of the insight symbol can be determined.[1]

---

[1] Chapter X, pp. 489 ff.

C

The Problem of the Scientific Symbol

Poetry and religion contain symbols of all three types. To what class or classes does the scientific symbol belong? To the arbitrary, the intrinsic, or the insight symbol? To this question, as we shall see more fully later, various answers have been given. There are those who hold that scientific symbols are purely arbitrary or conventional. Others hold that they are partly intrinsic in character, their intrinsic character being based upon a partial coincidence between the image or concept and the object symbolized, a coincidence of structural relations. These may be described as the purely operational and the descriptive theories. The notion of insight symbol seems to be foreign to the philosophy of science.

It is not our object to attempt an answer to this question here. The problem belongs to a later chapter on the *Language of Science and the Nature of Scientific Symbols*. The answer to the question turns wholly on the further question as to what the notion of science shall include. If science be identified with the mathematico-physical, and all propositions, in so far as they are to become scientific and verifiable, must be *reduced* to these, then there are no insight symbols in science, perhaps not even intrinsic. If, on the other hand, the sciences of life and mind have their own "languages" which are not reducible either to "physical" or mathematical language, then intrinsic, and probably insight symbols, are also part of the structure of their languages. In other words, science would disclose a "double symbolism," the function of its symbols being both to operate and to understand. As already said, the question of the nature of symbols in a specific sphere, such as that of science, and of their function in knowledge, can be answered only in the context of those symbols. Our problem here is the formulation of a general theory, one which will embrace all types of symbols. The symbolizing function is a general and fundamental function in all knowledge, and we are seeking conceptions of the symbol and principles of symbolism that will apply to this function in all its forms.

V

THE SYMBOLIZING FUNCTION. THE CONSCIOUS AND THE UNCONSCIOUS

A

From this study of the nature of symbols and their types, we may now turn to an examination of the symbolizing function and of the symbolic consciousness which goes with it. The point of approach here is the relation of the symbol to the conscious and unconscious processes of the mind. The *"verkehrter Gebrauch"* of the term symbol, of which we have spoken, also appears in connection with this point. "A sign *consciously* designed to stand for something will be called a symbol," writes Miss Stebbing,[1] and there are numerous writers who follow the same usage. Now many symbols, in the broadest use of the term, are thus consciously designed signs. In art and poetry, as well as in science and logic, we find such symbols, and their conscious and derivative nature is well understood. In art and poetry there are consciously designed symbols of the more allegorical type, but even these go back, in most cases, to an original symbolism which is not consciously designed. In science and logic also signs are consciously designed to stand for objects, but in so far as they are *merely* consciously designed, they are artifacts and purely substitutional. Most symbols, and these the more important and significant, are not consciously designed; they belong rather to what Nietzsche calls the natural or *"ursprünglicher Symbolismus"* of the human mind. This type of symbol is in large part unconsciously determined.

B

The Symbol as Used in Psychological Literature

In developing this point we may with advantage make use of the accounts of symbols and symbolization in psychological, and especially psycho-analytical, literature. The notion of symbol has here, it is well known, achieved a great, perhaps

[1] *Op. cit.*, p. 13.

an undue, importance. But the studies to which it has given rise are not without their value for a general philosophy of symbolism.

In the first place, as Jung points out, symbol for the psychologist is a very complex creation, arising from conscious and unconscious co-operation. For the psycho-analyst its chief function is that of effecting a transformation of the *libido*. Sexual symbols, for instance, in which natural sex images or signs are gradually transferred to non-sexual content, or in which that which is now no longer sexually understood is unconsciously taken as a surrogate for the sexual, are considered one of the chief if not the primal form of the symbolic function. In general, the tendency is to consider the symbolizing function as representative of the "inferior" functions, as a regression to the primitive, particularly to the "great natural mysteries." A feature of all such symbolism is a certain dual character, containing as it always does an instinctive, unconscious, and to that extent irrational character, and a more conscious, reflective and rational character. This dual character is, however, it is held, not without its important aspect. It enables symbols to exercise a reconciling function in the life of the spirit, of the conscious and unconscious life of men.

This account of symbol and symbolization, which is a *résumé* of many passages in Jung's *Psychological Types*,[1] need not be taken for more than it is—namely, as a very general account of the symbolizing function as viewed from the particular standpoint of psycho-analytical concepts and method. Nevertheless, this account of symbol formation may with due care be generalized—in the sense that any genuine symbol, in the primary sense, must be the result of the co-operation of conscious and unconscious factors. To be sure, the notion of the unconscious dare not be tied up with a special theory of "unconscious mind," but must be used in the broad way in which, as Ernst Troeltsch has clearly shown, it must be used in all social and historical science. It is, then, the unconscious factor that is, in the first instance, significant in all types of primary symbol formation. As in sex symbolism, natural sex images are gradually transferred to non-sexual content, or that which is no longer sexually understood is unconsciously taken

[1] C. G. Jung, *Psychological Types*. Also *Psychology of the Unconscious*.

as a surrogate for the sexual, so in general in all original symbolism. In the symbol, to repeat Hegel's definition, the original characters of the more or less visible object are identified with the import which it bears as symbol, and this identity is of unconscious origin. Natural speech construction is part of this unconscious symbolizing function.

C

The Symbolic Consciousness

It follows from this that, as Jung points out, a feature of all symbolism is its dual character. It embraces the real and the unreal, truth and fiction. The nature of the symbol as a function of the co-operation of the two factors, the conscious and the unconscious, necessitates this dual character. In symbol formation, as described by the psycho-analyst, two tendencies are at work, or two "instincts" in the terminology of Jung. The reality presupposed by the one differs from the reality of the other. To the other it would be quite unreal, or appearance, and vice versa. But this dual character is inherent in the nature of the symbol. If only real, it would not be a symbol, since it would then be a real phenomenon and therefore removed from the nature of the symbol. If altogether unreal, it would be empty imagining which, being related to nothing, would not be a symbol. Only that can be a symbol which embraces both.

Now this dual character, I shall maintain, belongs not only to symbol formation, but to the symbolic consciousness which results. This we shall find of great importance in our succeeding studies of the interpretation of symbols in the various fields of symbolic forms. By the term symbolic consciousness I mean something very definite—a unique type of consciousness which, while a form of the cognitive consciousness, differs significantly from the ordinary cognitive consciousness. The necessary postulate of any form of the cognitive consciousness is re-presentation of an object independent of the knower. The ordinary cognitive consciousness further assumes, tacitly at least, that this representation is in some sense a "copy" of the object, in other words that the re-presentation is in some sense literal. The symbolic consciousness, on the other hand, as part of the cognitive consciousness, shares the first postulate, but, so to speak, modifies the second. It is precisely the character of the symbolic consciousness to recognize that, if taken literally, the symbol is a fiction; it is when taken in another way (and this other way is precisely the symbolic way) that it has truth.[1] The symbolic consciousness is then always this dual consciousness, and such a dual consciousness is the *sine qua non* of both the aesthetic and the religious attitude in its developed forms. Without this dual element it becomes unaesthetic and irreligious. I think this holds also for science, for, as has been well said, the literalist in science is as much a nuisance as he is in religion.

VI

THE PRINCIPLES OF SYMBOLISM

A

With the development of the problem of symbolism in general in modern thought there has also come into increasing importance the study of what are called the Principles of Symbolism. By the principles of symbolism are understood in general those general truths concerning the nature and function of symbols, and the rôle they play in human thought and its communication, which must guide us in the interpretation and evaluation of symbols. They are the conditions under which symbols may be interpreted. The introduction of the notion of the conditions of interpretation suggests immediately what is the heart of a philosophy of symbolism, namely, the interpretation of symbols. To this problem of interpretation we shall presently turn, but a necessary preliminary is the development of the notion of the principles of symbolism.

The above constitutes a general definition of the "principles of symbolism," but what these principles are conceived to be is naturally determined to a large degree by the conception of the nature of symbols employed. Thus for those who identify symbol with sign, the principles of symbolism mean essentially

[1] This type of cognitive consciousness is developed in more detail in Chapter X, pp. 471 ff. and Chapter XII, pp. 591 ff.

the principles governing the determinate reference of signs; they tend to become identified with the canons of logic and to be predetermined by the theory of logic presupposed. This is the notion presupposed in the treatment of the subject by Ogden and Richards and R. M. Eaton. It is quite common to speak of "our ignorance of the principles of symbolism" and to mean by this the rules of "exact symbolism" as developed in logic; and to ascribe to this ignorance both the questions and the solutions of traditional philosophy. Metaphysics itself is just such an abuse of symbolism. However we may view the conclusions drawn from this notion of the principles of symbolism, we certainly cannot, after what has gone before, accept the notion itself. It is but a part of that narrow conception of symbolism against which Cassirer warned and means, as he says, a loss of all sense for symbolism.

It is quite clear, then, that, in the present context, the principles of symbolism must be understood as the general conditions under which symbols of all types, all symbolic forms, must be interpreted. It must include, in its proper place, the *special* conditions of exact symbolization. It is concerned with the principles underlying scientific concepts in so far as they are symbolic. But it must also include forms of symbolization that do not seek exactness, those forms which have developed in poetry, art, and religion. In short, the general principles of symbolism must be *general*; they must also be developed from the nature of the symbolizing function and the symbolic consciousness as such.

B

The First General Principle: Every Symbol Stands for Something

We may, then, without further preamble, state certain principles which follow more or less directly from our preceding analysis. The first principle, and perhaps the basal one, is that every symbol, *qua* symbol, stands for *something*. The statement, for example that of Eaton, that "a symbol may still be significant if it stands for nothing," is either wholly untrue or one of very limited truth in a special context. This principle was, to be sure, already implied in our discussion of the notion of apparent words in Chapter IV and of descriptions that describe nothing. But, apart from that, a symbol, on any theory of its nature, is a surrogate. Its very character demands that it shall not be the thing itself; but it also demands that it shall have a reference beyond itself. If the "symbol were wholly imaginary and fictional" it would, as Jung points out, be related to nothing real and thus not be a symbol. But a symbol may have a very indefinite reference, a preponderance of "unexpressed reference." Indeed this is precisely the character of the symbol in its primary and perhaps "proper" sense. "Interpretation" of symbols is the development of this unexpressed reference. A symbol, as symbol then, always stands for something. But this general principle does not exclude the possibility that there are symbols of an auxiliary and substitutional character which do not stand for anything. Certain substitute signs, which we may call symbols if we wish, are of this nature. It is entirely possible that signs may be used in an entirely operational or instrumental fashion which have no intrinsic meaning and are purely fictional in character. It becomes, then, one of the chief problems, especially in science, to interpret and evaluate these symbols.

C

The Second Principle: Every Symbol has a Dual Reference

It is frequently laid down as a basal principle of symbolism that every symbol has one and only one referend. The actual situation is precisely the reverse of this. The essential character of the primary symbol, as distinguished from mere sign, is that the original characters of the intuitible object are in a sense identical with the import that it bears as symbol. The symbol has, therefore, of necessity a dual reference, namely to the original object and to the object for which it now stands. When it loses its reference to the original object it ceases to be a symbol and becomes a mere sign, a depotentialized symbol. The close relation of symbol and symbolic construction to the metaphorical in language indicates the source of this character of the symbol. It is precisely the function of the symbol, partly "unconsciously," to relate two contexts or domains of discourse hitherto unrelated. Analogical predication is the very essence of the symbolic function, and the validity of symbolic knowledge depends upon the reality of the relation of the domains presupposed in such predication. All interpretation of symbols involves, as we shall see, this dual reference. It is, of course, this aspect which Kant has in mind when he speaks of "judgment exercising a double function, first applying the concept to the object of sensible intuition and then to a quite different object of which the first is only a symbol."

The truth of this general principle does not, of course, exclude the fact that any symbol may consciously be made to have one and only one meaning, and only one referend. It then becomes a symbol only in the narrower sense of conventional sign. In this type of symbolization the natural attributes of the intuition no longer have anything to do with the meaning. Intelligence in thus using the symbol as designatory rather than symbolic gives proof indeed of greater power and authority, but it is precisely the nature and validity of that authority which is the issue involved. In all spheres of the symbolizing function, but especially in science, the making of such symbols with a single reference, and therefore of "purer notation," is in evidence. The question is whether symbols of this type merely function in operations or whether they also really "say something."

D

The Third Principle: Every Symbol Contains both Truth and Fiction

It is, as we have seen, of the very nature of the symbol that it contains both truth and fiction, both the real and the unreal. This principle follows, in a sense, from the two preceding. We have already seen that a symbol must stand for something, otherwise it would not be a symbol. We have also seen that it cannot stand for anything in a wholly unambiguous way. If it did it would not be a symbol. A fictional element in every symbol is made necessary by the principle of dual reference. It is of the nature of the symbol that if either

THE PRINCIPLES OF SYMBOLISM

reference is taken exclusively it becomes unreal or else a mere substitutional sign.

A relation of two domains is involved in every symbolic function. If the symbol is taken *literally*, as we say, if, in other words, the reference to the primary domain is taken exclusively, the symbol is a fiction and *mis*represents. If it is taken wholly as a sign without any reference to the intuitive domain out of which it springs, it is again a fiction, in this case a merely conventional sign. The symbolic function, as distinguished from literal representation or description and from the merely conventional, is not only this dual reference but the combination of truth and fiction which arises out of it. This is as true in the region of scientific symbolism as in any other. It is, in fact, one of the main issues in modern, scientific epistemology, how much in our scientific concepts is truth and how much fiction.

E

The Fourth Principle: Of Dual Adequacy

This brings us to the final and, in a sense, most significant principle of symbolism, which we may describe as the principle of dual adequacy.

Adaequatio intellectus et rei is the primary notion of truth whatever special theories of truth we may develop in the course of interpretation. But the notion of adequacy itself has different meanings in different universes of discourse. The notion of adequacy as applied to the symbol has, like the symbol itself, a dual reference and meaning. A symbol may be adequate from the standpoint of representing the object *qua* object, or it may be adequate from the standpoint of expressing the object for our special type of consciousness. In the concept of symbol there is always this dual notion. This is entirely clear in all symbols of the aesthetic and religious type. When Hindu art symbolizes the infinity of divine activity by the figure of a god with innumerable arms and legs, an idea is expressed in sensuous form proper to the human type of consciousness. The symbol of God as Father is utterly contradictory and unintelligible unless this principle is recognized.

It is frequently supposed that this principle does not apply

o*

to scientific symbolisms, but this is wholly to misunderstand their nature, as we shall see more fully later. If there be any scientific knowledge that escapes this reference, and where adequacy of idea to thing is approximated to (and I do not here deny such knowledge), it is certainly not true in the realm of scientific symbols. The time has gone by when the mechanical concept of nature, for instance, can be held to be any more than a special kind of anthropomorphism. If it is in any sense an adequate form of representation, it also is adequate only for our type of consciousness and as determined by human purposes. To think otherwise is to be subject to illusion and this illusion, like some others, is not an "amiable" one.

F

Summary and Conclusion

These, then, are the general principles of symbolism which hold for all symbolic forms—aesthetic, religious, scientific, etc., and are presupposed in all interpretation of symbols and in the evaluation of the symbolic consciousness as a whole. These principles hold in general—however they may differ in detail—for all forms of the symbolic consciousness and for all types of symbols. But underlying these principles is a more general postulate to which, following the terminology of Jung, we shall give the name of the metaphysical presupposition of symbolism.

The "attitude of symbolism in general," he tells us, "consists in endowing an occurrence, an event in space and time, whether great or small, with a meaning to which greater value and significance is given than belongs to it in its pure actuality or existence." All symbolization and interpretation of symbols involves this assumption. The natural movement of both thought and language is to determine the as yet unknown by the known; the general movement of language is from the physical to the spiritual.[1] This is the affirmative element in all symbol formation and expresses itself in the first principle of symbolism. Every symbol stands for some object, and interpretation of the symbol is the determination of that object.

[1] Chapter V, pp. 180 ff.

THE PRINCIPLES OF SYMBOLISM

This affirmative element in all symbol formation we may describe as the postulate of the "prior rights of the affirmative," or the spontaneous element in all knowledge. The natural movement of language—and with it of all thought and knowledge—is from copy (imitation) to analogy and from analogy to the symbol. The underlying assumption of this movement is the prior rights of the affirmative element in the movement. Logic is concerned with reflected thought, but all that is reflected presupposes the spontaneous. The reflected cannot negate the spontaneous on which it rests; it can only clarify it and determine its true direction.[1]

Side by side with this affirmative there is also the negative principle, or "principle of negativity." Reflected thought cannot annul the spontaneous, but it can and does determine its direction. In all symbol formation there is an element of negation as of affirmation. It is this that the third principle of symbolism expresses. The object characterized by the symbol "is so," but it is also "not so." The insight of Hegel that all development of knowledge includes an element of negation—that knowledge cannot "proceed in a purely affirmative manner"—is pre-eminently true in symbolic knowledge. We shall see this element of negativity functioning in all types of symbol formation. The principle of aesthetic *distortion*, whereby the symbol is consciously made to vary from the actual in order that it may better represent the ideal, is one that has its counterpart in other spheres. Here negation of the symbol as copy is the very condition of its affirmation as symbol. This element of negativity in all knowledge was, perhaps, the most fundamental of all Hegel's insights. In so far as knowledge is representation and not presentational immediacy, in so far as all knowledge is expression and involves language, we must say of any predication that "it is so" and "it is not so." It is in this sense, of course, that all knowledge, short of the absolute, is symbolic. In any case, in all spheres of symbolism in the narrower sense the element of negativity is a basal element in the symbolic consciousness and in symbolic knowledge. This will become entirely clear in our study of the Interpretation of Symbols. To this we now turn.

[1] For a further development of this principle see *The Intelligible World*, Chapter III, especially pp. 121 ff.

VII

THE INTERPRETATION OF SYMBOLS AND SYMBOLISM

A

By the principles of symbolism we understand, as stated in our preliminary definition, the general truths concerning the nature and function of symbols, and the conditions under which symbols may be interpreted or evaluated. We may now turn to the question of interpretation.

Interpretation, as here used, includes a narrower and broader meaning. In the narrower sense it refers to the development of the meaning or reference of the symbol. In so far as the symbolic is contrasted with the literal, interpretation consists in distinguishing the *symbolic* from the *literal* meaning. In this sense interpretation involves what is called the *expansion* of the symbol, meaning by the term here the development of the unexpressed reference which is characteristic of the symbol as such. But interpretation in its broader sense involves much more than this. It eventuates in determining the existential or ontological import of the symbol—in determining not only what the symbol "says" but also what the reality is about which it speaks thus "symbolically." The general principles of symbolism demand that a symbol shall stand for something, that it shall have a dual reference, that it shall contain both truth and fiction, and that its adequacy shall be determined, not only from the standpoint of representation of the object, but of representation for our special type of consciousness. Interpretation involves the application of these principles.

There are various types of symbols and "symbolic forms"—the symbols of art, science, religion—and, as we shall see, even of metaphysics. Interpretation of each of these different types has its own special characters, and can be developed only in the domains or universes of discourse in which the symbols function, but it is possible to give a general account of interpretation and to formulate a general theory. This we shall attempt to do, leaving the special applications for later contexts.

B

Interpretation as "Expansion" of Symbols: Symbolic Meaning

Interpretation in the narrower sense may, we saw, be characterized as the *expansion* of a symbol. Let us see what is involved in this notion.

The term itself is, of course, a metaphor taken from the physical sphere. The basal idea is that the symbol is a contraction or condensation of meaning—of unexpressed reference—which may be expanded into expressed reference. The term is applicable to both of the fundamental types of symbols, the conventional symbol or substitutional sign and the intuitive symbol or expressive sign. Expansion of the former is exemplified in the interpretation of any mathematical or logical symbol and is, as we have seen, always verbal and of the nature of a definition.[1] It is, however, with the second type of symbol, symbol in the primary sense, that we are in the first instance concerned.

Intuitive symbols are both linguistic and non-linguistic. The character of all such symbols is that they are metaphors in the original sense of the word; they are objects or entities taken from the world of sensuous intuition and applied to non-intuitible objects. Non-linguistic symbols are of varying types and characters. They include, as our preliminary listing of symbols disclosed, objects of nature, images, conventional signs and tokens. One thing, however, they all have in common —their symbolic character consists precisely in the fact that they are concentrates of meaning, shorthand expressions for a manifold of ideas. These meanings or "ideas" may be embodied in other than verbal symbols, but the expansion or interpretation can never be in anything but words. This we shall find to hold true in the fields of art, science, and religion alike.

This fact we shall find of considerable significance for our entire theory of symbolic interpretation. A "behavioural expansion" of a symbol is sometimes set in contrast with the verbal.[2] A coin is a symbol of exchange, a flag a symbol of

---

[1] See in this connection Chapter VII, p. 319 f. (section on symbolic logic).
[2] See S. Buchanan, *Symbolic Distance*, p. 64 ff.

patriotism, a cross or other token a symbol of religion. Symbols of this kind are sometimes called effectual symbols because they are closely connected with action, and operate as signs of action in the broadest sense; in other words they are behavioural. Such symbols may, indeed, operate as signs for action, may also be effective in the communication of the primary emotional and volitional type, as described in an earlier context,[1] but the unexpressed reference remains unexpressed until verbal expansion and interpretation takes place. This is but a corollary of the general principle that intelligible communication can ultimately take place only in linguistic terms.[2]

We may take it, then, as certain that all expansion of symbols is ultimately verbal. Indeed we may go further and say that it is precisely this potentiality of expansion in verbal form that makes them symbols. The coin, the flag, the cross may be "tokens" about which emotional meaning gathers and which elicit emotive reactions, but it is only the unexpressed reference to ideas—which ideas may be expressed in language—that makes of them *symbols*. This situation may be stated in yet another way. In our discussion of the "meaning of truth" we saw that an object never stands for or represents another object except in so far as it is part of an expression.[3] Strictly speaking, only expressions, assertions, propositions are true or false. The symbol is a form of representation, although not pictorial in character. The "sense" of the symbol, no less than that of a picture, can be expressed only in language. Expansion of a symbol is the development of its "sense"; it can be only in verbal form.

Before developing this notion of expansion further it is desirable to take note of a misleading use of the notion. Ogden and Richards employ the concept, but they identify it with the interpretation of *any sign* and with *any* form of elucidation of meaning, a procedure which follows from their identification of symbol with sign. Ambiguous sign situations arise, we are told, out of the presence of contracted symbols. These need only to be interpreted, i.e. to be expanded, to become unambiguous. "Thus, 'this same stick which I see in the water is

---

[1] Chapter VI, p. 229 f. [2] Chapter VI, pp. 264 ff.
[3] Chapter VIII, pp. 337 ff.

both straight and bent.' Bad symbolization is indicated and we must expand the peccant symbol until we discover the ambiguous sign situation which caused the trouble."[1] Now it is important to note that this is not expansion of a symbol at all—in any proper meaning of the terms. The words stick, straight, bent, are not properly symbols. They are verbal signs for perceptual objects and characters. Nor is the elucidation of the meaning of these "signs," so that they become unambiguous, in any sense the expansion of a meaning already "condensed" in these signs. They are not symbols for the physical concepts substituted for them. Such ideal constructions as the laws of refraction are in no sense the expansion of the unexpressed reference of the percepts. Perception is in no sense a contraction or condensation of physical theory. Indeed, the relation is, if anything, the other way about. It is rather the physical concepts that are the symbols. The correction of our perception is not a correction of a "peccant symbol." It is simply the elucidation of the meaning of perceptual signs. To identify the interpretation of a symbol with the interpretation of perceptual signs is to confuse the notions of sign and symbol which we have found it necessary to distinguish, and to render the entire notion of symbols and their interpretation meaningless.

Expansion of a verbal symbol is, then, not identical with the interpretation of any verbal sign. This is equivalent to saying that such sentences as "this stick is bent" or "this stick is straight" are not "symbol sentences." We must therefore develop the notion of symbol sentences and their expansion.

A symbol sentence is always characterized by having a dual reference and therefore a double meaning. In it, in the words of Kant, "judgment expresses a double function, first applying the concept to the object of a sensible intuition, and then applying the mere rule of the reflection made upon it to quite a different object of which the first is only the symbol." Such a symbol sentence is the one used by Kant, namely, "the state is a living body." Another is the statement that "Napoleon was a wolf," or "Man is a reed, but he is a thinking reed." In all these cases the predicates—living body, wolf, reed—are taken from one intuitible domain and (ostensibly)

[1] *The Meaning of Meaning.*

applied to objects in a totally different domain—not directly intuitible by means of them. According to Kant, however—and he is right here—they are not *really* applied to the objects; it is only the common rule of reflection that is applied. If the former were done, we should have a literal sentence and, as such, it would be false; for there is no similarity, no common form of representation, in the strict sense, between Napoleon and the wolf, the State and a living body, or man and a reed. There is a similarity here neither for perception nor for conception, but only for interpretation. Such, then, is the symbol sentence, and the expansion of such a sentence involves the development of the rule of reflection. The sentence, Napoleon was a wolf, means that Napoleon was related to the people as a wolf is related to the sheep. Reflection on the context of wolf and sheep is carried over into the context of Napoleon and his people. To state the latter relation in terms appropriate to this context constitutes expansion of the symbol sentence. This characterization of expansion will hold good, I think, for any kind of symbol including the scientific. Scientific symbols are also, in the larger sense of the term, metaphors. The notion of natural selection, as used in biology, is a metaphor taken from the domain of artificial human selection and tranferred to nature. Expansion of the symbol consists in expressing the operations involved in the notion in terms appropriate to nature. In contrast to the metaphorical, these are "literal." The same will be found to hold for the outstanding physical constructs or symbols, such as electron, ether, etc., as we shall see more fully in a later chapter. Here we are concerned merely to give meaning to the terms "symbolic" and "literal."

C

Expansion of Symbol Sentences. Literal and Symbolic Meaning

Expansion of a symbol sentence is sometimes described as substituting for the metaphorical or symbol sentence, literal or non-metaphorical sentences. Symbol sentences are, then, condensed summaries of systems of literal sentences.[1] Now, there is no objection to describing the expansion of a symbol

---

[1] S. Buchanan, *op. cit.*, p. 28.

THE PRINCIPLES OF SYMBOLISM

sentence in this way if the term literal is used with care. The term literal is ambiguous; used in one way the statement is false, employed in another it has an important element of truth.

The term literal has at least two meanings. The primary meaning is "according to the letter." This may mean merely the opposite of figurative, and the rendering of symbol sentences into literal sentences is equivalent to the expression of the figurative in non-figurative fashion. But literal has also another meaning, namely, primitive meaning. To interpret a symbol sentence literally would, then, be to interpret it according to the primary or original meaning of the words. If literal be taken in this second sense, then to say that expansion of a symbol sentence is the substitution of a literal sentence is wholly false. For the symbolic meaning is precisely not the literal meaning. So interpreted, the symbol sentences, Napoleon is a wolf, and the State is a living body, are false. But if literal be taken in the first sense, then the above statement is, up to a point, a true account of the expansion of a symbol sentence. Every interpretation of a symbol does just this: substitutes for the metaphorical or symbol sentence literal or non-metaphorical sentences. To be sure, as we shall note presently, there are no strictly literal sentences; the notion is merely a limiting concept. In a sense, then, symbol sentences may be viewed as condensed summaries of literal sentences. By literal sentences, however, is here meant sentences appropriate to the universe of discourse of the subjects of the symbol sentences. I shall first illustrate this point and then indicate its significance.

The essential character of every symbol is that it is a metaphor—in the case of the verbal symbol a word transference from one universe of discourse to another. In the symbol sentence, Napoleon was a wolf, the term wolf is transferred from the context of wolves and sheep to the context of Napoleon and his subjects. In the symbol sentence, the State is a living body, the concept of living body is transferred from the biological universe of discourse to the social and political. If now we wish to determine what the symbol *means*, or what the symbol sentence really *says*, we can do so only in terms (sentences or propositions) appropriate to the universe of Napoleon and his subjects; or, in the second case, sentences or propositions appropriate to non-biological or volitional relations of the State and its members. Such sentences would be literal in the sense of our definition.

This notion of literal may be made clearer in another way. It is, as we have seen, the general character of all symbols that images and ideas are taken from narrower and more intuitible relations and used as expressions for more universal and ideal relations which, because of their very pervasiveness and ideality, cannot be adequately expressed directly. If, then, we seek to expand this unexpressed reference we can do so only in terms of the ideal or universal relations which the symbol expresses indirectly. The language of the expansion of a symbol is therefore always more abstract and less metaphorical than the language of the symbol. Thus if we wish to expand the symbol of the onion in *Peer Gynt*, we say that it *means* that in the moral universe of Peer Gynt the individual is nothing without the layers of relations which make up his character as an individual or person. If we wish to expand a religious symbol such as God is the "maker" of heaven and earth, or the "Father Almighty," we can do so only in terms appropriate to the concept of God and these are always more abstract and metaphysical.

The facts here described bring to light a situation which may be described as the paradox of symbolism and of the symbolic consciousness. Every symbol demands interpretation, and this involves the expansion as above described. Only so can the symbol ultimately be understood; and only so also can its truth or falsity be determined. On the other hand, thus to expand the symbol tends to defeat its end as a symbol. It is precisely because the more universal and ideal relations cannot be adequately expressed directly that they are indirectly expressed by means of the more intuitible. To pass from the intuitible to the non-intuitible is to negate the function and meaning of the symbol. This paradox pervades, as we shall see, all regions of the symbolic, the aesthetic, religious, and even the scientific. Is it possible to resolve this paradox?

We have here one of the most difficult problems in connection with language and cognition, as indeed in the entire theory of knowledge. We are apparently faced with a dilemma. If we are to interpret the "sense" of the symbol we must expand it, and this must be in terms of literal sentences. If, on the other hand, we thus expand it we lose the "sense" or value of the symbol *as symbol*. The solution of this paradox seems to me to lie in an adequate theory of interpretation of the symbol. It does not consist in substituting *literal* for symbol sentences, in other words substituting "blunt" truth for symbolic truth, but rather in deepening and enriching the meaning of the symbol. The symbol consciousness, as we have seen, is a unique form of the cognitive consciousness, symbolic truth, while indirect, a unique form of the truth relation. The function of the symbol is, in Kantian terms, to supply intuition to the concept. It remains symbol only in so far as the intuitive element is retained. This will become clear when we consider the notion of symbolic truth.

There are two further comments which should be made in connection with this notion of the "literal" and "symbolic." The first concerns the relative character of the distinction; the second the notion of literal which connects it with the *primary* or original meaning of a word.

As has already been indicated, the distinction between literal and symbolic is in an important sense only relative. When we describe expansion of a symbol as substitution of literal and non-metaphorical sentences for metaphorical and symbolic sentences what is really meant is that, with reference to the symbol sentences to be expanded, the language in which the expansion takes place is less symbolic and approaches the literal in the sense of our definition. This is immediately apparent from the nature of language itself which, even in its most abstract form, is a collection of "dead metaphors." It is actually impossible to find any use of language which is wholly non-symbolic. No language is even approximately free from the symbolic element except the artificial language of "symbolic" logic, and that language as we have seen is really not a language but a collection of substitutional signs. Or, if we wish to call it a language, it is wholly pronominal, one in which all the elements are *pro*-nouns.[1] It is true that, as we have seen, there are non-symbolic aspects to language. Words may be merely indicative signs, and language as a medium of discourse may be an almost completely transparent medium. Language may thus approach the non-symbolic as a limit,

[1] Chapter VII, p. 316.

but in actual interpretation the distinction between symbolic and literal is only relative.

This leads to the second point, namely the notion of "literal" which equates it with the original and primary meaning of a word. According to this view, a literal sentence is one which refers to a sensuously observable entity. On Bentham's theory of language, already examined, it is only when sentences are carried back to their original reference that they have any *literal* significance. Otherwise they are fictions. Applying this notion of literal and literal significance to the language of morals and religion—in short to all sentences which have non-sensuous reference and are therefore symbolic—all such language is pronounced meaningless. The assumption underlying this procedure is that if language has no literal significance in this sense it has no significance at all. Thus from one point of view the entire position rests upon an exploitation of the ambiguity in the notion of literal.

VIII

INTERPRETATION OF SYMBOLISM: SYMBOLIC KNOWLEDGE

A

Expansion of symbols we have defined as the first stage in interpretation, but this stage always involves interpretation in a second and broader sense. In ordinary use interpretation often means merely expansion. Thus to interpret the symbols of a poet, such as those of a Dante or an Ibsen, means first of all to express their meaning in literal and non-symbolic language. But expansion always involves, either explicitly or implicitly, interpretation as the determination of the knowledge value or ontological import of the symbol.

Theoretically, the expansion of a symbol might take place without involving any implication as to its ontological import. Not only might the symbols of the poet be "enjoyed," those of the scientist understood, without raising any question of their reference to reality, but they might be interpreted in the narrower sense of expansion, even if they were wholly fictions. As descriptions are sometimes held to have meaning when they describe nothing, so it might be held that a symbol

THE PRINCIPLES OF SYMBOLISM

is still a symbol when it stands for nothing. Actually, however, this is not the case. An attitude such as that described is wholly repugnant to the symbolic consciousness which, as we have seen, is always characterized by a dual character—always includes the real and the unreal, both truth and fiction. In the second place, and for this very reason, no sharp line can be drawn between interpretation in the first and in the second sense. Expansion of a symbol is always development of its unexpressed *reference*, and this means determination of its ontological import.

Although true of all symbols this is, of course, especially true of the scientific symbol. A scientific concept in physics, such as the ether or the electron, is a symbol in the sense of our definition, in that it takes images from the immediately intuitible world and, after "moulding" them, applies them to non-intuitible relations. Interpretation of such symbols always includes ultimately the determination of the question whether they refer to actual entities, or are merely useful fictions, "phantoms," or "just a dummy" in Eddington's phrase. The distinction between the two stages of interpretation marks a relative difference, but actually the two are always interwoven.

It is, then, with interpretation in this second sense that we are now concerned. Here the question is not merely the expansion of the meaning or unexpressed reference of the symbol, but also the determination of the truth or validity of the symbol. Truth and falsity, as we have seen, are properly applicable only to propositions. Even in the case of a "picture," such picture may be viewed as a tacit proposition. It tacitly asserts that it *so* represents that truth and falsity are applicable in some sense. Now a symbol is, as we have seen, not a picture; it is a form of re-presentation, but it is not a pictorial representation. A symbol is also a tacit proposition and a symbol sentence is also a proposition, but of a special kind. In pursuing our problem of the interpretation of symbols we must first examine the nature of symbol propositions.

B

The Notion of Symbol Propositions

Symbol sentences have the propositional form, but they may be only apparent or pseudo-propositions. Such statements as

Napoleon was a wolf, all flesh is grass, man is a reed, but he is a thinking reed, are statements or assertions about Napoleon, about flesh, and about man. As such, they not only lay claim to being meaningful, but to have truth (symbolic truth); but these claims may be wholly illusory and the propositional form only apparent.

This is, as we have seen, the position of those who hold that metaphorical or symbolic sentences are simply cases of ambiguity and that, when the ambiguity is resolved, the symbol proposition becomes a pseudo-proposition. What remains to the symbol sentence is then merely a meaningless group of words or, at most, an expression of emotion. But this certainly they are not. To Pascal, the enunciator of the sentence: Man is a reed, but a thinking reed, the sentence was both meaningful and true. His readers not only understand the meaning of the assertion, but for them also it expresses a truth which their own experience "confirms." It is an authentic symbol. The statement that the State is an organism (a living body), that the ether is a perfect jelly, or that the electron takes up the whole of space, are equally symbol propositions in this sense. Are these, then, pseudo-propositions?

Sentences may be pseudo-propositions for two reasons—because of some character of either subject or predicate. The statements, the man in the moon is yellow, Hamlet was mad, the soul is immortal, may have meaning in discourse, but may be held to have no "logical" meaning because the subject of the sentence has no reference to an empirically observable entity. Certain symbol sentences in all the regions of symbolism may be held to be pseudo-propositions for this reason. Symbolic propositions about God may be descriptions that describe nothing because there is no God. Symbolic propositions about the ether (or conceivably about the electron, for, as we shall see, the electron is a pseudo-sensible symbol)[1] may be pseudo-propositions because there is no ether or no electron (in the sense of physical existence). Metaphysical sentences are in the main held to be of this type. In general, however, symbol sentences are about real objects—about Napoleon, about man, about the State—about subjects for which there are direct

---

[1] Chapter XI, p. 547.

THE PRINCIPLES OF SYMBOLISM

empirical references. The difficulty in this case is with the predicate.

This difficulty arises, it is clear, from that which is precisely the unique character of the symbol sentence, namely, the ambiguity in the predicate. In every case the predicate has a dual reference, first to the object of sensible intuition and secondly to the non-intuitible. In other words, the judgment expressed in the "proposition" exercises a dual function, and it is just this function that is in question. The question is whether a sentence, when it expresses the exercise of this dual function—when the predicate has this dual reference—can be called a proposition.

There is no question, of course, that such a sentence is a proposition in the sense of our definition. A proposition we defined as a class of sentences which have the same intensional significance for everyone that understands them. It is the common understanding that makes the proposition.[1] The symbol sentence fulfils this requirement. Analogous predication is a unique form no less understandable than univocal predication. When I say Napoleon was a wolf there is as surely the same intensional significance for all those that understand the sentence as in the case of the sentence, Napoleon was a soldier. Moreover, there is something in Napoleon to which the predicate wolf refers as certainly as something to which the predicate soldier refers. It is, indeed, as we have seen, precisely the statement of what this referend is, in terms of literal sentences, that constitutes the expansion of the symbol sentence. But the unexpanded sentence is nevertheless, as such, still a proposition.

There is, however, a further question, namely, whether the notions of truth and falsity are applicable to such sentences, whether a sentence which exercises this dual function can be true or false. Here, again, there is no question that these notions are applicable when the symbol sentence is taken literally. It is precisely the character of symbol propositions that, when taken literally, they are always false. But it is of their very essence that they are not to be taken literally. There is also no question that the notions of truth and falsity are applicable when these sentences are expanded or translated

[1] Chapter VII, p. 270.

into non-symbolic or literal sentences, i.e. literal in the second sense. But that is not the question. In what sense, if any, can they be conceivably true or false when taken symbolically, when, in other words, they retain their *dual* reference?

Certain notions of truth are evidently not applicable. Any merely copy theory, however subtle and refined, will fail to apply for the reason that such notions, even when expressed in terms of "common form of representation," or participation in a common pattern, express relations which can hold only between an idea and a single referend. If, however, the notion of truth can, as we have contended, be expressed only in terms of adequate expression, the notions of truth and falsity may conceivably be applicable. Let us develop our conception along these lines.

C

The Notion of Symbolic Truth: Dual Adequacy

Every truth relation must have in it some element of similarity, of common form of representation. In the case of the symbol, however, the similarity between the symbol and the thing symbolized is not, as in the case of the picture, similarity of pattern but in the "way of reflection." When the similarity between symbol and thing symbolized is interpreted as though it were a picture, it is taken literally and always involves an element of fiction. It is only when the similarity is taken in the second sense that we have symbolic truth.

This concept of way or "rule" of reflection is, to be sure, susceptible of different interpretations in different regions of symbolism. In the sphere of the scientific symbol rule of reflection *may* be interpreted as rule of operation; and if we should adopt a purely operational view of scientific symbols the truth of such symbols would be in the success of our operations quite independently of the question of the existence or non-existence of objects to which the symbols referred. On the other hand, in other regions of symbolism, such as those of art and religion, the object is not at all to operate or predict, but to understand. It is the function of the "insight" symbols in these regions to give us insight, by means of sensuous intuition, into relations which otherwise could not be ade-

THE PRINCIPLES OF SYMBOLISM 441

quately apprehended or expressed. The statement of this distinction does not by any means prejudge the question as to the nature of scientific symbols. It may be that science, taken in its full length and breadth, discloses a "double symbolism" in which the functions both of operation and understanding are included. It merely asserts a distinction which any adequate theory of symbolism must recognize.

A symbol is true, then, if between the symbol and the thing symbolized there is a common form of representation sufficient for the purposes of reflection, whether the "rule of reflection" be interpreted as operation in the narrow sense or as understanding in the sense of penetration or insight. But while the notion of symbolic truth thus falls under our general notion of truth as adequate expression, adequacy in the case of a symbol must be distinguished clearly from adequacy in the case of a picture, in any of the senses of picture developed in the preceding chapter.

In developing this point let us revert, first of all, to our discussion of the general principles of symbolism. There we found that an essential principle was that of dual adequacy. As a symbol always has a dual reference, so it also demands a dual adequacy. In the case of adequacy of expression of a symbol or symbol proposition, adequacy includes not only a "common form of representation," but also adequacy for our type of consciousness. Without this second aspect the expression is in certain respects inadequate, for something of the experience which it seeks to express remains incommunicable. The notion of dual adequacy has already been defined in a general way. It remains to develop one point specifically which is fundamental to the whole notion of symbol and symbolic truth, namely, that symbolic knowledge and truth are conditioned by community of subjective form.[1]

It is entirely possible to have a "common form of representation" which abstracts wholly from the subjective and concrete, whether this be conceived as sense or feeling, and such form is adequate for certain purposes. Thus a "language" which strives after pure notion (*puri nomi*), as in the case of signs or substitutional symbols in the sense of our definition, may be adequate for the expression of certain structure or

[1] Chapter VIII, pp. 395 ff.

functional relations—and for certain purposes this may be all that we desire—but such a form of representation is not adequate for the expression of the experience itself. In addition to this type of community of form there must be community of subjective form. Only when this second aspect of community of form is present is communication of meaning, in the full sense, possible. It is for this reason that it is impossible to "dispense with symbolism" without also dispensing with large areas of meaning and their communication.

This notion of adequacy for our type of consciousness is clear enough in the case of symbols in the aesthetic and religious realms. The reason for this, as we shall see later, is that that which is symbolized or symbolically expressed always contains or includes values or valuational content, and values, however objective or transcendent they may be, are, as experienced, always conditioned by subjective form.[1] The real issue arises in connection with symbols in the sphere of science. Here, however, the situation is in principle the same. We may, indeed, operate with mathematical signs (with "symbols" in the substitutional sense), but equations and the operations they involve must always be interpreted and, when interpreted, they must always be expressed in terms which are adequate for our sensible consciousness. The sensible and pseudo-sensible symbols in physics, of which we shall speak later, are always conditioned by community of subjective form.[2]

D

Symbol Propositions and Verifiability

The entire issue of symbolic truth comes to a head with the question of the verifiability of symbol propositions. It is indubitable that such propositions have meaning. It is equally indubitable that they communicate knowledge of a sort. It is, however, equally certain that the notions both of meaning and of knowledge are inseparable from those of verification and verifiability. We have, therefore, the problem of the way, if any, in which a symbol proposition may be verified.

Now, it is obvious that this is a question that can be answered

[1] Chapter X, pp. 481 ff.   [2] Chapter XI, p. 552.

here only in the most general form. The facts of our earlier analysis—namely, the need for a double notion of symbolism, the different types of symbols in different regions of symbolism, and finally the still unsolved problem of the nature of scientific symbols—make it impossible to do more than suggest certain very general notions and principles. All detailed analysis of the processes of verification must be left to specific contexts. With this in mind we may proceed with our analysis.

Now, a symbol proposition certainly cannot be verified directly in the sense of the empirical criterion as narrowly defined. It is true that it is thus verifiable when taken literally, but when so taken it is always false. Another possibility is that the symbol proposition may be expanded into non-symbolic literal propositions, in the second sense of literal, and these may be verified directly or indirectly like any non-symbolic proposition. Thus the proposition, the State is an organism, although when taken literally leads to inferences about the State which are not only untrue but absurd, may yet be expanded into certain abstract or non-symbolic propositions which are verifiable in the sense that any such propositions are verifiable. This is what proof or disproof of the organic theory of the State would mean. It is, then, obviously, only when expanded or interpreted that a symbol proposition can be *shown* to be true or false. This we shall find to be true in all the specific regions of symbolism, aesthetic, scientific, religious. And yet there are serious difficulties in this notion. In this case it is apparently not the symbol proposition, as such, that is verified, but literal or non-symbolic propositions into which it is translated. The question arises whether there are symbolic propositions at all in the sense of our previous definition. If they cannot be verified *as* symbol propositions can they be propositions at all; can there be any such thing as symbolic truth?

This, surely, is a real difficulty. We seem to be presented with a dilemma, and this dilemma is seen to be but a special case of the paradox of the symbolic consciousness already described. Is there any solution to this dilemma?

It seems to me that there is, and that the way to this solution lies in making a distinction between two notions, namely, the truth *of* a symbol and *symbolic truth*. This distinction may at first sight seem merely verbal, but it is not really so. The truth *of* a symbol can be determined only by expanding its unexpressed reference, and this can be done only in relatively non-symbolic terms. Symbolic truth, on the other hand, has reference to the validity or authenticity of the symbol as a way of expressing the non-symbolic for our common type of consciousness. We constantly make this distinction, I think, although we may not always state it in precisely this fashion. We constantly speak of "good" symbols and, what is even more to the point here, of "authentic" symbols. By such expressions we always mean that the symbol expresses adequately for our type of consciousness that which could not be fully expressed in "literal" sentences. That which constitutes a "good" symbol may, of course, vary greatly in different regions of symbolism, depending upon the particular way or rule of reflection involved. The authenticity of a symbol may and does vary with the nature of the specific symbolic form. But the notions of good and authentic always involve adequacy for our type of consciousness and community of subjective form.

With this distinction between the truth of a symbol and symbolic truth we may proceed to develop our notion of verification. The determination of the truth of a symbol is always indirect. It involves the translation of the sentence in which the symbol occurs into literal sentences, and it is these that are verified. In the case of scientific symbols, unless the sentences containing them can in some way be translated into sentences which refer to sense data, they cannot be verified. In principle the same is true of all symbolic forms. Symbolic truth, or the authenticity of the symbol, is, however, another matter. Here adequacy for our type of consciousness is involved; here it is community of subjective form that determines the authenticity. We may thus speak of the authentication of a symbol, although such authentication is part of the larger notion of verification.

This notion of authentication of a symbol—which must of course be demonstrated in detail for various forms of symbols—is an important notion for our entire theory. The authenticity of a symbol being dependent upon community of subjective form, such authenticity can be determined only in the

THE PRINCIPLES OF SYMBOLISM 445

processes of communication themselves. In the most general sense it is, of course, true that all verification is ultimately conditioned by communication; verification is not ultimately separable from confirmation and confirmation is a form of communication.[1] But this is a special case of this general principle. For in this case what is confirmed is the adequacy of the symbol *as symbol,* and this is determined by the fact that in the symbol the symbolizers are able to communicate common meanings and references. Much of what is called aesthetic and religious "truth" is of this character.

Such, then, is our theory of verification or authentication of a symbol in its general form. The dilemma presented by the symbolic consciousness is thus, in principle at least, solved. Truth, we have seen, is ultimately adequate expression, and adequacy in the case of symbols is always dual adequacy in the sense described. This notion can justify itself, of course, only as we see it applied in the various regions of symbolism yet to be examined. There will, to be sure, be significant differences in application in the case of different types of symbols. Between aesthetic and scientific symbols there are, as we have seen, such important differences that verification in these fields must show corresponding differences, but the notion itself is applicable to all. Symbols in all fields have this character of community of subjective form, the principle of dual adequacy is characteristic of all, and symbolic truth is in principle the same for every type. The application of the principle to aesthetic and religious symbols would probably be generally admitted, but it is precisely the contention of our general theory that it is true of scientific symbols also, a position which we shall later attempt to justify.[2]

Symbolic truth—in all fields—is, then, conditioned by community of subjective form. It follows, as we are told, that such truth is only an indirect relation. What we want is direct or "blunt" truth. In Whitehead's words, the symbol is merely a surrogate for something else and what we want is that something—not the substitute. In other words, the ideal would be to dispense with symbolism or to have wholly non-symbolic truth. This, it seems to me, is a fundamentally mistaken notion. In the first place, such an ideal is really impossible

[1] Chapter V, pp. 223 ff.   [2] Chapter XI, p. 551.

in view of the very nature of language and expression. If there were such a thing as wholly non-symbolic truth, it could not be expressed. This is not to deny that there is a non-symbolic element in knowledge, but merely to assert that the symbolic and non-symbolic are never completely separable. But there is a second, even more important, reason. "Blunt" truth is a pure abstraction; it is realizable only by abstracting from all the allusiveness, the unexpected reference, which it is precisely the function of the symbol to embody and conserve. In dissolving the community of subjective form we should also dissolve the conditions of communication of meaning and adequate expression of reality. To dispense with symbolism, were it possible, would be to dispense with truth when truth is adequately understood.

It seems to me equally untrue to say that, because symbolic truth is indirect, symbols in their own nature (i.e. before dissolved into literal sentences) "throw no light on the objects to which they refer." The assumption underlying this position is, as we have already seen, the nominalistic view that language is wholly external to that which it expresses, a view the untenability of which we have already shown.[1] If it is true, as we have argued throughout, that it is only through language and its development (from copy to analogy and from analogy to symbol) that new objects of reference are discovered and fixated, then it is also true that it is only through these symbols that the nature of the objects can be adequately expressed. Because symbols involve adequacy for our type of consciousness, it does not at all follow that they say nothing of reality itself. That is to beg the whole question at issue. Symbols would throw no light on the subjects to which they refer only if symbols were *merely* community of subjective form. Symbolic truth is conditioned by community of subjective form but not exhausted in that form.

It is now possible to relate the conceptions of symbolic knowledge and truth to the general theory of knowledge developed in the preceding chapter. In our examination of the relations of language to cognition we found it necessary to maintain a triadic theory of knowledge. The ordinary dyadic theory which divides knowledge into perceptual and

[1] Chapter VIII, pp. 372 ff.

THE PRINCIPLES OF SYMBOLISM

conceptual—into knowledge by acquaintance and knowledge by description—cannot do justice to the facts of knowledge. Not only is there a third aspect to all knowledge, that of interpretation, in both perceptual and conceptual knowledge, but there is also an aspect of knowledge which is essentially knowledge by interpretation. It is to this latter type of knowledge that symbolic knowledge belongs. It is precisely because symbolic knowledge cannot be reduced to either the perceptual or the conceptual mode that it has always shown itself refractory to all ordinary theories of knowledge. It is only when we recognize that no theory of knowledge is adequate which does not include this third moment of interpretation—and that interpretation of the symbol is itself a form of knowledge—that we can form any adequate conception or theory of symbolism. To the consideration of the outstanding theories of symbolism we shall now turn.

IX

THEORIES OF SYMBOLISM AND OF SYMBOLIC INTERPRETATION

A

There are in the main but two basal theories of symbolism, which may be described as the naturalistic and idealistic, or transcendental, the terms being here used in the sense previously defined.[1] As there are but two basal theories of language and of linguistic meaning, so it follows that, in the case of the problems of symbolism which grow directly out of the problems of language, there are only two fundamental answers to these problems.

The first, or naturalistic, may be described in the following way. It seeks to explain the symbol in terms of the reality not meant by the symbol itself. It is essentially genetic and regressive, or reductive, in method. The symbol, if it stands for anything, stands for or symbolizes something other than it consciously intends. This theory is in principle connected with the causal theory of meaning and reference already examined in an earlier connection.[2] In its extreme forms it tends to turn the symbol into fiction or illusion. The transcendental

[1] Chapter III, pp. 132 ff. [2] Chapter III, pp. 129 ff.

theory, on the other hand, seeks always to interpret the symbol in terms of the reality meant. It is properly called transcendental because the true reference of the symbol is held to be not to "causes" but to objects. In contrast to the first theory, which is negative, this theory is positive in character. It assumes the prior rights of the positive, as described—that existences in space and time have a reference or significance beyond that which belongs to them in their pure actuality or existence. Its method is, therefore, not genetic and regressive, but prospective and progressive. It does not "resolve" the symbol into the non-symbolic, but develops and interprets it.

B

The Naturalistic Theory

The naturalistic theory of symbolism is obviously but a special case of the naturalistic or causal theory of meanings considered in Chapter III. Its regressive or reductive method of interpretation is, again, but as pecial case of the normative principle of the prior rights of physical propositions and of the physical context. In so far as it is this, we need not repeat our criticism of these positions here. The difficulties apply, however, with even greater force to the type of meaning described as symbolic. In this case the regressive or reductive method resolves the symbol into a fiction and makes it say what it does not really intend to say.

An illustration of the application of this theory will bring out the points at issue, namely, the difference between resolving a symbol (on the naturalistic theory) and interpreting it. Mr. Carveth Read in his book, *Natural and Social Morals*, develops a purely naturalistic theory of morals, and becomes eloquent in defence of the realism which such a theory presents. "Unless," he writes, "somehow the natures that can endure ideas propagate themselves in sufficient numbers, every practical enlightenment must be succeeded by reaction in the direction of illusions, old and new." Among such illusions he would reckon romantic love and religion. They are *symbolisms*, he holds, and their utility, such as it is, consists in presenting indirectly truths which are far better apprehended directly.

THE PRINCIPLES OF SYMBOLISM 449

"Understanding *resolves* (italics mine) all such symbolisms into the relations of men and women who act and suffer; and unflinchingly to set this bare reality before the mind's eye, to love it and to live for it, is what I mean by the capacity to endure ideas."

This is, to be sure, but one application of a general theory to a special field, but it brings out the point at issue clearly. In examining this view critically it is not necessary to deny the desirability of the capacity to endure ideas, no matter how bare the ideas may be—this has its value also—but rather to raise the question whether in this theory the function of symbols is rightly apprehended. In the first place, it is not at all clear that interpretation of these "symbolisms" consists in resolving them into the bare relations of men and women in their biological nature. This is not what the symbols mean. Indeed, it is the very nature of these symbols to deny the possibility of so reducing them. One function of symbolism here is precisely the negation of this reductionism. Symbols, it is rightly seen, present truths indirectly, but it is not at all clear that such truths are better apprehended directly: The "bare" relations are just as the word says, *bare*, that is, stripped of all the accumulated intension which it is precisely the function of the symbols to retain. In the second place, and this is perhaps the most significant aspect of the theory, it turns the symbols into illusions—fruitful illusions perhaps—but still illusions. Now it is true, of course, that one of the principles of symbolism is that a symbol contains both truth and fiction. The naturalistic theory resolves it wholly into fiction, and thereby violates one of the fundamental principles of symbolism. The essential character of all purely regressive theories is the ultimate dissolution of symbols in all regions of symbolism, aesthetic, religious, and scientific.

C

The Transcendental Theory

The naturalistic theory seeks always to interpret the symbol in terms of a reality not meant by the symbol itself. It assumes always that the user of the symbol is in error as to what he really means. Instead of recognizing the symbolic function as primary and universal and as a part of knowledge, it attempts, as Cassirer says, "to bring it under the standpoint of scientific conceptions, especially that of causation." Everywhere the procedure is regressive and reductive, resolving the symbolic relations into causal and "explaining" the former through the latter. In contrast to this, the transcendental theory always interprets the symbol in terms of the object meant by the symbol. It assumes that the symbol user knows, although imperfectly perhaps, what he means. Interpretation is not causal explanation, but the development of the meaning or reference.

The underlying assumption of this second theory is none other than the basal postulate of the symbolic consciousness as such. The transcendental theory merely formulates this postulate. The attitude of symbolism consists, as we have seen, in endowing an occurrence in space and time, whether great or small, with a meaning to which greater value or significance is given than belong to it in its pure actuality or existence. The essential character of all symbolism, in its primary form, is that images or ideas are taken from narrower and more intuitible relations and used as *expressions* for more ideal and universal relations which, because of their very pervasiveness and ideality, cannot be either directly intuited or expressed. The transcendental theory merely confirms and formulates this attitude. This theory is, of course, nothing more or less than the traditional or classical theory of symbolism from Plato on. Expressed in many ways, it has one underlying notion, namely, that the phenomenal world is an expression of a noumenal or intelligible world and, because of this relation, the phenomenal may be taken to represent or stand as a symbol for the noumenal. This is not the place to develop either the Platonic form of the theory or the various forms in which it has been stated throughout the story of European philosophy. This belongs to other contexts. It is sufficient for our present purpose to indicate the historical background of the theory.

As the naturalistic theory of symbols is but a special case of the naturalistic theory of meaning, so the idealistic or transcendental theory is also a special case of the general theory developed in earlier contexts. The arguments there developed may therefore be applied *mutatis mutandis* in this connection. There is, however, one aspect of the general argument that should be emphasized here. In the preceding chapter we spoke of the general relation of language to reality and pointed out that there are in general only two ways of solving the problem of language and cognition. The first assumes a reality known independently of language and its categories, a hypothetical pure experience to be discovered by stripping off language. The second assumes that experience is never pure in this sense and that, since intuition and expression are inseparable, the true path to reality consists, not in denying but in perfecting and completing the principles of expression and *symbolism*. This latter, the idealistic, proceeds upon the assumption that the more richly and energetically the human spirit builds its languages and symbolisms, the nearer it comes, if not to the original *source* of its being, certainly to its ultimate meaning and reality. This we described as the idealistic minimum necessary to any adequate philosophy of language;[1] it is also the idealistic minimum necessary for any adequate theory of symbolism. Negation, dissolving of symbolic forms, instead of enabling us to grasp the content and meaning of reality, serves only to destroy the spiritual form to which the content and meaning are necessarily bound.

D

Whitehead's Theory of Symbolism

The examination of these two fundamental theories of symbols may be further illuminated by the consideration of a theory developed in Whitehead's *Symbolism, Its Meaning and Effect*, and in certain parts of *Process and Reality*. It is made quite clear in *Symbolism, Its Meaning and Effect* that the author seeks to develop a broad and liberal theory of symbolism. "The imperative impulse to symbolism suggests," he holds, "that the notion of an idle masquerade is the wrong way of thought about the symbolic elements in life" (p. 62). "We enjoy the symbol, but we also penetrate to the meaning. The symbols do not create their meaning; the meaning is the form of actual

[1] Chapter VIII, p. 374.

effective beings reacting upon us, exists for us in its own right. But the symbols discover this meaning for us" (pp. 56–57). Impressed with the function of symbols in life, he often tends to a largely pragmatic evaluation of the symbol, but in principle it is quite clear that for him there are "insight symbols," symbols that discover for us meanings, or "presences" in nature which, while "unmanageable, vague, and ill defined, are things with an inner life, with their own richness of content, with the destiny of the world hidden in their natures," and these are "what we want to know."

A broad conception of symbol, and a liberal view of symbolic knowledge, are then clearly the motives and objectives of the work. But in the carrying out of this objective, the theory of symbolism developed is of quite another character, and one which does not seem consistent with the objective. In the first place, he develops a realistic basis of symbolism which, when closely scrutinized, differs little in principle from all naturalistic theories. "There are," he tells us, "no components of experience that are only symbols or only meanings. The more usual symbolic reference is from the less primitive component to the more primitive as meaning." This statement, he adds, "is the foundation of a thoroughgoing realism. It does away with any mysterious element in our experience which is merely meant and thereby beyond the veil of direct perception. It proclaims the principle that symbolic reference holds between two components in a complex experience, each intrinsically capable of direct recognition. Any lack of such conscious analytical recognition is the default of the defect in mentality on the part of a comparatively low grade percipient."[1]

The presuppositions of this theory of symbolism are reasonably clear. Symbolic reference is from the less primitive to the more primitive as the meaning of the symbol. This "realistic" theory turns out to be a disguised naturalistic theory. As in all naturalistic theories, prior rights are given to the "literal" in the sense of the primitive. We are not at all surprised to find, therefore, that in the latter part of the book, when the symbols of art and religion are discussed, no clear and consistent theory of their nature and function is possible. We expected a theory of symbols which would indeed

[1] *Op. cit.*, p. 10.

THE PRINCIPLES OF SYMBOLISM

show that they are more than "an idle masquerade." We find instead that their function is little more than emotive and vaguely pragmatic, and the brave promise held forth at the beginning—of the "insight symbol" as a way of knowing—comes to nothing. We feel that the book has merely scratched the surface of the problem of symbolism. It is more than possible that I have not understood Whitehead here. If so, I feel justified in laying that misunderstanding to an ambiguity and uncertainty inherent in his own view. It seems to me that in his theory of symbols, as in his general theory of language, he attempts to combine two strains which are really incompatible, namely, the naturalistic and the transcendental or idealistic. In another context I had occasion to point out the difficulties inherent in his theory of language.[1] Language is for him external to reality and therefore has only pragmatic value and significance, and yet as he uses language for the expression of his metaphysical conceptions, another theory of language is really implied. The same difficulties inhere in his theory of symbolism. The notion of "an idle masquerade" may be "the wrong way of thought about the symbolic elements in life," but I cannot see that he has shown convincingly what is the right way of thinking about them.

X

THE PHILOSOPHY OF SYMBOLIC FORMS AND THE THEORY OF "LANGUAGES"

A

The present chapter has dealt merely with the question of a general theory of symbolism, including the nature of symbols, the principles of their interpretation, and the general theory of symbolism and symbolic knowledge. This is, however, merely preliminary to the application of these principles and this theory to the interpretation of symbolism in the varied fields of art, science, religion, and metaphysics. This further study we may, borrowing a term from Cassirer, describe as the Philosophy of Symbolic Forms.

This term, as is evident, implies that there are different forms or types of symbols which, while all belonging to one

[1] Chapter XIII, p. 372. Also Appendix III.

general field of symbolism, yet have different functions and different ways of expressing reality. In other words, there are different universes of discourse—let us say the poetic, the scientific, the religious, and perhaps the metaphysical—and these universes have different symbolic forms. This notion of symbolic form is of such significance as to justify further definition and development at this point.

In an earlier connection we took up the question of languages as distinct from language—different universes of discourse or contexts in which communication takes place. Among other things we distinguished between Science and Drama, between the scientific and the dramatic ways of rendering reality.[1] These constitute, in our present nomenclature, different symbolic forms. They symbolize reality in different ways. Interpretation of symbols involves, then, not merely the expansion of the particular symbol—in poetry, religion, science, as the case may be—and the determination of its validity as symbol, but also the interpretation of the general symbolic form in which the symbol occurs, and the evaluation of that form as a way of rendering reality. The point I have in mind may be made clearer by the use of a distinction which will play an inportant rôle in the chapters to come. We have the problem of what the symbol "says"—in other words, the development of the meaning of the symbol; but we have also the problem of what the particular symbolic form says implicitly. What does the dramatic form, as used in art and religion, say implicitly about the reality it renders in that form? What does the scientific symbolic form have to say implicitly about the reality which it thus, in its own way, represents or symbolizes? What, further, is the relation of these symbolic forms to each other? These are the problems of the philosophy of symbolic forms. As thus formulated, they raise again the problem already stated, namely whether all knowledge is symbolic or whether the knowledge thus given us in these symbolic forms presupposes a form of non-symbolic knowledge. This problem may be stated in another way. The different languages (idioms) and symbolic forms belong to certain universes or contexts. The ideal of knowledge and of its communication is to strive towards a maximum context, towards

[1] Chapter VI, p. 240 f.

THE PRINCIPLES OF SYMBOLISM

one universe of discourse into which all symbolic forms may be translated. "Metaphysics" is traditionally the discipline which seeks this unity. We may in the present connection describe it as the science of maximum context. The language of metaphysics is, as we shall see, a special form of language determined by this fact. Is metaphysics also a special form of symbolism, a specific symbolic form, or is it the science which, by its very nature, seeks to transcend all symbolic forms—or in Bergson's words, seeks to dispense with symbolism? Is metaphysics, if it exists at all, a form of non-symbolic knowledge? The philosophy of symbolic forms as thus described is, then, at once the culmination of the philosophy of language and, in a sense, the root problem of philosophy itself. As parts of philosophy we have the philosophy of art, the philosophy of religion, and the philosophy of science. Each of these fields of philosophy has its own unique problems, but the one problem common to them all is in each case the understanding and evaluation of its own symbolic form.

CHAPTER X

THE LANGUAGE OF POETRY AND ITS SYMBOLIC FORM

I

A

A POPULAR division of symbolism is that which places the symbols of art, poetry, and religion on one side and those of science on the other. The former evoke feelings, the latter refer to objects. Needless to say, we cannot adopt this simple and popular division. It over-simplifies the problem and begs all the important questions at issue. It assumes, in the first place, a distinction between art and science which, at least in this extreme form, does not actually exist. More and more science itself tends to deny the absoluteness of this distinction and to insist upon a kinship between the artistic and scientific imagination. It assumes, in the second place, that art and similar functions, because they evoke feelings, do not give us "truth"—an assumption which involves a definition of truth which again begs the whole question. We shall accordingly follow a method which does not thus beg important questions. We shall start with a purely phenomenological study of the two contrasting forms of symbolism, the poetic (aesthetic) and the scientific, which, although they are not unrelated, have important differences which may be clearly defined. We shall then proceed to the symbolisms of religion and metaphysics.

B

The Poetic Symbolic Form: Definition of Poetry

We shall begin our study of symbolic forms with the poetic or, more generally, the aesthetic symbol. There are significant reasons for this procedure. In the first place, there is reason to believe that the aesthetic form of expression and representation is an original, if not the primary form. Certainly, of the two forms of language and of symbolism, the poetic and the scientific, the former is the original and the latter the derived.

THE LANGUAGE OF POETRY

The language of poetry is generally recognized as primary. Both the reasons for this view and the meaning of it have already been given and need not be repeated here.[1] To be sure, the classical lines:

> "Thus nature drove us; warbling rose
> Man's voice in verse before he spoke in prose,"

are, when taken literally, false. They do not, however, mean that man spoke first in *numbers*, but rather—and in this sense they are essentially true—that the speech of everyday life had in it that which later developed into "verse." Nature drove man to communicate, but the first apprehension of things— and the forms in which it was communicated—have the essentially poetic character.

The larger conception of poetry here indicated is generally acknowledged. Even the dictionary definitions, although they define poetry first of all as metrical composition, invariably add as a secondary meaning, "imaginative composition whether in prose or verse." It is in this sense that Coleridge in his *Biographia Literaria* insisted that the true antithesis of poetry is not prose but science. S. Alexander is entirely right in accepting this as the fundamental antithesis and is equally sound in maintaining that the contrast runs throughout all the arts.[2] Language is but one medium of aesthetic expression, and the characters which make language "poetic" are in principle the same as those which make the other media aesthetic.

Poetry, then, instead of being a special kind of language is rather an aspect of all language that is *alive*. Croce has expressed this truth in the following words: "Man speaks at each moment like the poet, because, like the poet, he gives expression to his impressions and feelings. It does not matter that this is done in the tone of ordinary conversation or familiarity, for there is not the slightest distinction between this and the other forms that are called prose, prose poetry, narrative, epic, dialogue, drama, lyric, or song. And if the ordinary man will not mind being regarded as a poet, which he is because of his humanity, the poet may not take it amiss that he is coupled with ordinary humanity; for this relation alone

---

[1] Chapter II, p. 80.
[2] S. Alexander, *Beauty and Other Forms of Value*, Chapter VI.

explains the power of poetry on all human minds in the narrow and in the highest sense. If poetry were a special language, 'a language of the gods,' human beings would not be able to understand it."[1]

If poetry is not a special language—"of the gods"—neither is it a special language of the "poets," although that special language, like the technical language of science, will have its own interest for us in the sequel. The poetry of which we are speaking is not the "poet's meaning of poetry," as something *consciously* made: it is rather something inherent in all natural language as such, the unconscious natural speech construction already described as "fundamental metaphor." Poetry and poetic language, in this broader sense, are present in the entire "mythical" construction of the universe and are part of the language of religion and metaphysics—perhaps, as we shall see, of the language of "science" itself. We shall presently characterize the language of poetry more definitely. For the moment it will suffice to emphasize one point. Just as mythology is but "a little remainder" of a general stage in the development of our thought, so what we ordinarily call poetry is a little remainder of what was formerly universal.

II

POETRY AND THE AESTHETIC IN GENERAL: AESTHETIC MEANING AND SIGNIFICANCE

A

Poetry is but one form of art, language but one medium of aesthetic expression. Forms, colours, tones, rhythms are all non-linguistic forms of expression. It will be well, then, to consider briefly the aesthetic and aesthetic expression in general before passing to the language of poetry. This we may best accomplish by considering the notions of aesthetic meaning or significance.

In an earlier context we distinguished aesthetic meaning from practical and cognitive as a primary mode of the meaning of "things."[2] We may now develop this point more fully.

---

[1] B. Croce, *Foundations of Aesthetics*. For his general position on this question, see *Aesthetic as Science of Expression*, Chapter III.   [2] Chapter III, p. 100.

A definition of aesthetic experience by L. A. Reid will bring out clearly the points I wish to make. "When," he writes, "an object of perception—whether actual or imaginal perception or both—is contemplated 'imaginatively,' that is so that it appears in its very qualities and forms to embody valuable meaning, and when that embodied meaning is enjoyed intrinsically, for its own sake, and not for its practical, or cognitive, or existential implications, then the contemplation is aesthetic contemplation and the total complex before the mind we may call an aesthetic object."[1]

I have chosen this definition for a double reason. In the first place it distinguishes the aesthetic meaning from the practical and the cognitive and finds the *differentia* in intrinsic enjoyment. In the second place, an aesthetic object embodies valuable meanings. It is the embodied meanings that are "enjoyed." These meanings are not the aesthetic meaning, but the non-aesthetic element in the aesthetic experience. As embodied meanings, they have a reference beyond themselves—practical, cognitive, moral, implications. It is these references that make them valuable meanings.

B

Aesthetic Meaning and Significance

The primary character of the aesthetic experience is that it is intrinsic rather than extrinsic meaning. Since Kant and Schopenhauer, this notion of "intrinsic enjoyment" has been expressed in terms of disinterested or desireless contemplation. As a means of distinguishing aesthetic from practical meaning this *differentia* is of great importance.

In the thinking of both Kant and Schopenhauer—and of their numerous successors—this notion of desireless contemplation has a cognitive and philosophical significance. For them art is revelatory in character, and the "contemplation," freed from desire and practical interest, is a source of insight into the nature of reality. Into this aspect of the problem we shall go later; here our interest is in the aesthetic as intrinsic

[1] L. A. Reid, *A Study in Aesthetics*, p. 43. Published by George Allen & Unwin Ltd.

enjoyment—and enjoyment not for its practical, cognitive, or existential implications. From this point of view, we may speak of the aesthetic consciousness as a mode of intuition. The aesthetic is, then, a mode of intuition in which, as in all forms of intuition, the subject "takes possession" of its object, but it takes possession and "enjoys" it in a special way. The aesthetic mode has often been described as a unique state of *attention*, a state of equilibrium in which enhanced activity is combined with a fundamental repose. This psychological rendering of the "desireless contemplation" of the philosopher is, I believe, a true account. I think further that, as I have shown at length in my *Valuation*, it is this equilibrium which affords the conditions for the apprehension and appreciation of the object for its own sake—in other words, intrinsic enjoyment.[1]

The autonomous character of the aesthetic attitude and of aesthetic meaning must, then, be held fast to. Aesthetic meaning must be distinguished alike from the practical and the cognitive. To be aesthetic the object must be enjoyed for its own sake and not for its practical, cognitive, or existential implications. But *the implications are still there*. Without these implications there would be no meaning, for meaning is always reference. Without these implications the object would not be enjoyed—even for its own sake. It is therefore the rôle of these implications to which we must give our attention.

[1] This account of the aesthetic attitude is accepted by Ogden and Richards in their *Foundations of Aesthetics*, p. 89. "A more solid and satisfactory adaptation of this theory of equilibrium to the modern psychology of appreciation may be found in W. M. Urban's *Valuation* (p. 219), where it appears as 'the concept of the widened ground of diffused stimulation, the *balance* of impulses, so that no one shall constitute an illusion-disturbing moment and lead to readjustment in a new value-movement; the consequent *response* of emotion in the object and the *expansion* of feeling which goes with it. The ordering, rearrangement of content characteristic of the aesthetic experience is, therefore, in the service of the deepening, or enhancement of that fundamental mode of worth experience which is appreciatively described as immanental reference.' And, again, in primitive dances the object of desire, whether martial, erotic, or religious, is 'distanced,' and the fundamental conation becomes dispositional. This rhythm, usually of the form of advance and retreat, of affirmation and arrest of expression, produces an equilibrium of impulses, which prevents the fundamental tendency from breaking forth into overt action." It is true that in accepting the truth of this analysis of the aesthetic experience, Ogden and Richards take exception to the notion of "illusion-disturbing moments," but the doctrine of aesthetic illusion is unnecessary in this account.

C

Aesthetic Embodiment of Non-Aesthetic Meaning

The aesthetic object embodies valuable meanings. We must now examine the nature of these meanings and the character of the embodiment.

Aesthetic objects are both perceptual and ideational. Let us, then, begin with perceptual objects. The meaning of a chair is that it is something to sit upon, of a glass of water that it is something to drink. This "meaning" is intrinsic in the sense that it is part of the object; it is meaning that transforms sense data into "things."[1] However the meaning of an object is acquired genetically, when once acquired it is part of the object. This meaning is non-aesthetic, but both of these objects may have what may properly be called aesthetic meaning. Both chair and glass of water may find a place in a picture of still life. What now has happened and what change in meaning has taken place? In answering this question we must proceed with care. One answer is that the artist is concerned only with the appearance of things. The aesthetic meaning of a perceptual object abstracts, so to speak, from its thinghood, both as a practical and a cognitive category. This I believe to be a fundamental misinterpretation of the situation. If the chair is no longer recognizable as something in which to sit or the glass of water as something to drink, if, in other words, they have no longer these practical and cognitive meanings, the aesthetic meaning is thereby diminished if not destroyed. Aesthetic meaning is completely destroyed in those cases, not infrequent in modern art, where the aesthetic intuition embodies no non-aesthetic meaning. The aesthetic intuition is autonomous, but it is always an intuition of the non-aesthetic.

The aesthetic object may be ideational as well as perceptual. Non-linguistic arts, no less than the linguistic, may be expressive of ideas, both moral and theoretical. Here, too, non-aesthetic meanings may, as Croce says, become part of the aesthetic intuition. Thus in his lyric, *The Passing Strange*, John Masefield

[1] Chapter III, p. 105.

expresses intuitively the evolutionary process in the following words:

> "Out of the earth to rest and range
> Perpetual in perpetual change
> The Unknown passing through the Strange."

The ideas here aesthetically embodied are all ideas of high generality—philosophical ideas. The cognitive implications are of large significance. The poem in question contains not merely an emotional attitude towards the evolutionary notion, but both explicitly and implicitly assertions, propositions which claim truth. What the value of such insights, such assertions, may be for discursive knowledge, is a problem for later consideration; here the sole point is the fact of the aesthetic embodiment of non-aesthetic ideas, and the further fact that, without this non-aesthetic meaning, the aesthetic meaning is lost.

This aesthetic *embodiment* is merely another term for aesthetic expression. The general principle of the inseparability of intuition and expression holds with special force for the aesthetic intuition. Here it means that form and content, or content and medium, are inseparable. The artist does not first intuit his object and then find the appropriate medium. It is rather in and through his medium that he intuits the object. The "languages" of the arts are then all intuitive languages. Since our interest is primarily in poetry as a symbolic expression of reality, we shall turn directly to the medium of poetic expression—the language of poetry.

III

THE LANGUAGE OF POETRY. THE "VIS POETICA"

A

In a sense all art is expression and therefore a kind of "language." Non-linguistic media of communication, it is often said, may convey meanings which language cannot. Things may be "said" with music that words cannot say. Nevertheless, as was pointed out, when we attempt to tell what music says, we must resort to language.[1] In a very real sense, words are the only ultimately adequate medium of communication. In any case it is with language that we are here primarily concerned. Now, all linguistic embodiment or expression of aesthetic meaning is the language of poetry in the sense of our definition; it is therefore with this language that we are here concerned. Our ultimate problem is the study of poetic symbols and symbolism, but the study of poetic language is required as a background. A beginning of such a study has already been made in our discussion of the poetic "picture." There we distinguished between two forms of poetic re-presentation, described respectively as intuitive and metaphorical or analogical.[2] For our present purpose a further development of this distinction is desirable.

We are already familiar with the conception of the dual function of language. According to this view, language has two uses, the evocative and the indicative: it evokes feeling or emotion and indicates objects. Poetic language, it is held, is a development of the former, scientific a development of the latter. Now the primary function of poetic language *is* evocative. The *vis poetica* lies first of all in the power of language to evoke feeling. But it evokes much more than feeling, namely, intuitive meanings as distinguished from emotive. In our phenomenological investigations of the meanings of words we distinguished intuitive meanings from both emotional and conceptual meaning. The basal elements of language, the noun, the verb, the adjective, have intuitive as well as denotative and emotive meanings. It is these intuitive meanings which poetic language, in the first instance, exploits. Sentences such as "red blooms the rose," "wild blows the wind," tell us something. They also evoke emotion. But they do much more than this. They conjure up, so to speak, a living reality. He who hears such words is placed in a living landscape where winds are blowing and flowers blooming. The "life" of things is caught in the very forms of expression.[3] This intuitive re-presentation is then the primary form of poetic re-presentation. Merely psychologically expressed, it is a function of imagination. The *vis poetica* of language, out of which con-

---

[1] Chapter VI, pp. 264 ff.   [2] Chapter VIII, p. 358 f.
[3] Chapter IV, p. 153 f.

scious poetry develops, consists in its power to evoke images, but the images are the means of the intuition, not the intuition itself; the intuition is bound up with imagination and imagery but, as we have seen, is not identical with it.[1]

We may say, then, that poetic language is a form of re-presentation or picturing. Our general thesis, that intuition and expression are inseparable and that all expression contains the beginning of re-presentation, holds here. Poetic language is a form of description, and since there is no such thing as a description that describes "nothing," there always arises the question of the truth of the description. In other words poetry "says something," even in its primary intuitive form; the question is as to what it says and whether it speaks truly.

This becomes even clearer when we come to the second form of poetic re-presentation, the analogical and metaphorical. The reason why the *Ursprache* is described as poetic is because it is intuitive in the sense described, and secondly because it is characterized by "fundamental metaphor" in the sense in which this term has been defined. In a sense metaphor is but an extension of the intuitive character of language, as has been pointed out.[2] Metaphor also has the *vis poetica*, the power of conjuring up the living reality in the way in which "literal" and abstract propositions have not. When the poet tells us to "gather rosebuds while ye may," we may indeed say that he conjures up all "sweet and pleasant things," but what he really conjures up is not expressed in these abstract terms. When we are told that "man's happiness is his flaunting honeyed flower of soul," the words in which that happiness is thus described conjure up its real quality in a way that descriptions of the moralist or the psychologist can never achieve. The *vis poetica* is the power to make these things "real and alive in language."

B

Dramatic Language

A special aspect of the language of poetry may be described as its dramatic form. In the realm of aesthetic discussion it is

[1] Chapter IV, p. 148.   [2] Chapter IV, p. 145 f.

distinguished specifically from the lyrical. The former is concerned with the expression and evocation of feeling or emotion directly, the latter more indirectly through the re-presentation of "action." In its primary meaning the dramatic is concerned with representation of human action, although non-human action, both of the gods and of nature, may be included in so far as the latter are *anthropomorphized*. We shall use it also, in a secondary or derived sense, to describe all language which is the language of action.

In a sense all forms of the language of poetry contain dramatic elements. Whether we talk of wind or roses, objects of perception, or objects of ideation, such as time or evolution, in so far as we talk about them "poetically" we speak in terms of action. "Time *creeps* on from day to day"; life, as seen by the poet, emerges from "the earth to rest and range"; it is "the unknown *passing* through the strange." Dramatic language is concerned always with "relations of the mental type" and these relations are always "activistic."

Without dramatic language, as Lloyd Morgan points out, "no adequate account of what happens in human life is possible."[1] But dramatic language extends to the description of the non-human also. The "symbolic form" in which reality is represented or pictured by poetry is always dramatic. It is at this point, as we shall see, that the question of symbolism in its larger form—namely, in what way and to what extent poetry is symbolic of reality—raises a problem which it is one of the chief tasks of this chapter to attempt to solve.

It is the function of poets, so Vossler tells us, "to remove the things of this world out of their practical, empirical, and natural reality, in order to make them live again in the realm of art and make them real and active in language."[2] It is, indeed, the function of the poet to make things "real and active in language." It is, however, a question whether in order to do this he "removes them out of this world"; or whether by making things real and alive he does not rather throw light upon this very world. It is true that the poet makes us see them other than in the contexts of the practical, the material, and the "natural," but it is possible that the special context in which he makes us see them is itself a sym-

---

[1] Chapter VI, p. 240 f.   [2] *Op. cit.*, Chapter IX, p. 233.

bolic form no less fundamental than that of the scientific and "material."

IV

THE POETIC SYMBOL; AS A FORM OF THE AESTHETIC SYMBOL IN GENERAL

A

With this account of the language of poetry, and its preliminary distinction from the language of science, we may turn to the specific problem of the poetic symbol. It will be of advantage first to examine the notion of the aesthetic symbol in general of which the poetic is a special form, as it is found in present-day literature on aesthetics. We may start with a definition.

"A symbol in aesthetics," according to Tufts, "is an object which, apart from its own immediate significance, suggests also another, especially a more ideal content, which it cannot perfectly embody."[1] This, of course, the aesthetic symbol is, but it is also the characteristic of all symbols of the primary kind (as distinguished from substitutional symbols or mere signs); it is therefore necessary to differentiate the aesthetic symbol more definitely within the larger group. This difference is obviously determined by the unique character of aesthetic intuition and expression. The aesthetic symbol is always some object of intuition, perceptual or imaginal, which suggests or embodies an ideal content. But the purpose of the suggestion or embodiment is not primarily cognitive as in the case of the scientific symbol—to enable us to manipulate objects or to "express a complex of facts compendiously" —but rather for the *enjoyment* of the embodied meaning. The aesthetic symbol is therefore essentially an insight symbol in the sense of the definitions of the preceding chapter. This does not mean that art does not also employ merely descriptive symbols, but that the primary function is insight and the "enjoyment" of that insight. The aesthetic symbol thus has, or claims to have, a noetic character and value. This is the classical or traditional view of the aesthetic symbol, which has always emphasized its revelatory character. The general tendency in modern aesthetics, however, has been in the

[1] Article on "Symbol (and Symbolic)," Baldwin's *Dictionary of Philosophy*, Vol. II.

direction of reaction against the classical conception, charging it, in Croce's terms, with the "intellectualist fallacy." We shall examine this reaction and attempt to evaluate its significance.

B

The Aesthetic Symbol and "Intuition"; The "Intellectualist Error"

The classical view of the aesthetic symbol emphasized its cognitive and existential implications—in other words, its revelatory character. The general tendency in modern aesthetics has been in the direction of reaction against the classical conception in favour of what we may, speaking broadly, call an intuitionist view. This reaction has taken two main forms, according as the emphasis is put on the emotive or the cognitive side of the intuition. The first form is well represented by R. M. Waerner in his study, *Das Aesthetische Symbol*, the second by Croce in his well-known work on aesthetics. Let us examine these two views briefly and attempt to evaluate this position as a whole.

Croce's statement of the problem brings out the issue clearly. "Symbol," he writes, "has sometimes been given as the essence of art. Now, if the symbol be considered as inseparable from the aesthetic intuition it is a synonym for the aesthetic intuition itself which always has an ideal character. In this case all art is symbolic because all art has an ideal character. But if the symbol is conceived as separable—if the symbol can be conceived as on one side and on the other the thing symbolized, we fall back again upon the intellectualist error; the so-called symbol is the exposition of an abstract concept, an allegory; it is science, or art aping science."[1]

We may well sympathize with Croce's desire to avoid the intellectualist error—the view too often present in classical aesthetics—which would make of the symbol merely a substitute for or exposition of an abstract concept. We may sympathize also with his insistence on the inseparability of the symbol from intuition. The symbol is rooted in the intuition itself and is not merely a surrogate for the abstract concept.

[1] *Op. cit.*, p. 34.

On the other hand, to make, as Croce does, the aesthetic symbol merely a synonym for the aesthetic intuition itself is to make impossible any distinction between aesthetic expression as a whole and specifically symbolic expression and representation. There is, to be sure, a broader use of the notion of symbolization in which all art may perhaps be said to be symbolic of reality—just as science, as a special symbolic form, represents or symbolizes reality in its own way—but this is not the notion we are now considering. Symbolic expression and representation must, then, be distinguished from intuition. The symbol, while not a mere surrogate for the abstract concept, nevertheless, by its very nature, embodies an ideal content, a non-aesthetic meaning which cannot be expressed in any other way.

The issue becomes even clearer when we examine that form of the "intuitionist theory" which puts the emphasis on the emotive or feeling side of the aesthetic intuition. In the work referred to, Waerner distinguishes between the classical or intellectual notion of the aesthetic symbol and the modern, which emphasizes the emotive or feeling side. He connects the aesthetic symbol with the processes of *Einfühlung* or empathy which he conceives of as a kind of intuition. This emphasis on the feeling or emotional side of art is, as the development of his thesis shows, also a reaction against the older, classical conception of symbol with its tendency to make it an "exposition of an abstract concept," and thus make of art a lower form of knowledge or science. Instead of this he develops what he calls the modern notion. The essential character of the symbol, according to his view, is the fusion of the object and feeling content in an inseparable unity.

Millet's famous picture the Angelus is, according to Waerner, a symbol in the modern sense because in it picture and feeling content are fused in such an inseparable unity. The peasants standing in the potato field at sunset, at the close of a laborious day—and bowing at the sound of the Angelus bell—this is the picture. But we penetrate beneath the sensuous, grasp a spiritual content and combine these, form and content, into a spiritual whole. Waerner then proceeds to interpret or expand the symbol. As we look at the picture we first feel, he says, what goes on in the soul of the young man and the young woman, the belief in God, the Father of all mankind who has protected them through the day, comforted them during the heavy labour . . . who loves them and from whom they look for further help and happiness. Then, however, this personal element in the feeling, bound up with the two peasants, widens into one which is much deeper and embraces the whole of mankind.

There are two aspects of this theory which create difficulties —difficulties brought to light by this very illustration. In the first place, this account tends to identify the aesthetic symbol with the aesthetic "picture"; in other words, to make no real distinction between aesthetic intuition as a whole and that form of it which is "symbolic"—a tendency which, as we said, is also present in Croce's account. But to make all art symbolic is, as we have said, to make the whole notion of the symbol meaningless. An even greater difficulty inheres in the emphasis on feeling. Precisely in the illustration taken by Waerner we see the limitations of any purely emotive theory of art and aesthetics. Picture and feeling content are indeed fused in an inseparable unity—that is characteristic of the aesthetic mode in general—but there is a noetic element also. We "penetrate beneath the sensuous and grasp a spiritual content."

It seems clear, then, that the essentials of the classical conception of the aesthetic symbol must be retained. The symbol, although it has its roots in intuition, is not identical with intuition, although related to *Einfühlung*, it is not identical with it. A symbol is always a form of re-presentation, not of presentation. Some duality between the intuition and the concept, between the idea and the intuition which stands for it, is necessary for the symbolic relation to exist. The distinction between the object in its immediate and "proper" significance and that which it suggests (the ideal content), must be maintained. All this will become clearer when we consider the nature of the *poetic* symbol as a special case of the aesthetic, and even more when we examine the element of distortion in the aesthetic symbol. For the present we shall simply insist that this notion of the symbol does not involve the intellectualist's fallacy. That fallacy, I conceive, lies in viewing the aesthetic symbol, and the aesthetic in general, as a mere stage of, or imperfect substitute for, scientific and philosophical knowledge. That is precisely what it is not, for the very essence of this view is that the symbol contains an unexpressed reference which the abstract concept cannot express.

C

The Poetic Symbol as a Form of the Aesthetic Symbol

The conception of the aesthetic symbol here developed applies to all forms of art, non-linguistic and linguistic alike. But it is especially significant when applied to the linguistic. It is with the poetic symbol that we are chiefly and ultimately concerned. It is therefore important to determine the place and function of the poetic symbol in the language of poetry as a whole.

The language of poetry, we have seen, is evocative in that it evokes feeling and emotion, but it also evokes intuitive meanings. Since all expression involves re-presentation in some form and to some degree, the language of poetry is always representative and descriptive. The poetic symbol is a form of this representation. Can we now distinguish it from other forms? The general law of language development is, as we have seen, from copy to analogy (metaphor) and from metaphor to symbol.[1] It is the point at which metaphor passes into symbol that interests us, for it is at this point that the essential character of the poetic symbol should disclose itself.

The simplest solution of our problem would be to *equate* symbol with metaphor. The symbol sentences made use of in the preceding chapter are all also metaphorical sentences. All flesh is grass, man is a reed but he is a thinking reed—in sentences such as these the predicates, grass and reed, are applied analogically to the subjects, flesh and man, on the basis of certain similarities, namely, the perishableness of the grass and the frailness of the reed. All poetic symbols are, then, metaphors and arise out of metaphor. But a symbol is more than a metaphor. *The metaphor becomes a symbol when by means of it we embody an ideal content not otherwise expressible.* The difference between *mere* metaphor and metaphor become a symbol may, I think, be expressed in this way. We often

[1] Chapter V, p. 181 f.

speak metaphorically and figuratively when we do not speak symbolically. In the former case, we use metaphor to *illustrate* ideas or assertions which are expressible wholly in abstract or non-figurative terms. The metaphor is a symbol when it *alone* expresses or embodies our ideal meaning. In other words, it is only as the metaphor is part of the intuition itself and functions in the intuition, that it is a symbol. Thus it is that the "fundamental metaphor," embodied in myth and language, is the source of all the great and lasting poetic symbolisms, while much of the more recondite symbolisms—that "little remainder" which we call poetry in the narrower sense—is often merely over-intellectualized figure. It is this which Croce has in mind when he speaks of the "intellectualist error."

The point I am making may be still further brought out by means of the distinction between metaphor and simile. The difference lies in the fact that in the case of simile we say one thing is *like* another, in the case of metaphor, *is* another. Metaphor has been defined as similitude reduced to a single word, or as a word expressing similitude without the signs of comparison. To say that a man is like a fox is a simile, to say that he is a fox is a metaphor. The *is* expresses a certain identity of intuition and idea, and the development of this constitutes the symbol. A symbol is never a mere similitude, although it grows out of similarity or likeness; the intellectual development of similitude is allegory. An identity of intuition and idea is always implied in the symbol, but not complete identity, for to be a symbol it must contain both truth and fiction.[1]

D

The Aesthetic Symbol and Aesthetic Distortion

The essential character of the aesthetic symbol is that while it has its roots in intuition it is not identical with it. The essential character of the poetic symbol is that while it has its roots in metaphor—the verbal form of intuition—it is not identical with it. In the more general case of the aesthetic and in the special case of the poetic symbol alike, the intuition becomes

[1] Chapter IX, p. 424.

symbol when it stands for something which is ideal and not immediately intuited. This character is brought out clearly by the consideration of the phenomenon known as aesthetic distortion.

The phenomenon here under consideration is so general in all forms of art as to be given this special name. It consists in so *moulding* the immediately given intuition or phenomenon—so distorting it, so to speak—as to express an intuition, a meaning, not otherwise expressible. We shall first describe the phenomenon and then connect it with the symbol and the symbolic consciousness.

Let us start with distortion in the non-linguistic, pictorial, arts. This distortion may take many forms. An outstanding case is the over-emphasis or under-emphasis of the lines of the human form (over-emphasis of the curves and masses, of breasts and buttocks, on the part of the "primitives" and more self-consciously by modern primitives such as Matisse); or the under-emphasis of the same curves and masses (by the pre-Raphaelite painters and their more sophisticated modern followers). It seems more than likely that when the natural primitives over-emphasized buttocks or breasts to express physical fertility, it was wholly unsophisticated—the distortion was part of the intuition itself. For the modern "primitives" it is thoroughly self-conscious and sophisticated. It is also possible that when the early Christian artist under-emphasized the lines of the female body it was done more or less unconsciously. For the modern pre-Raphaelites it is thoroughly self-conscious and sophisticated. In either case, however, it is in the interest of expressionism. For a "literal" copy is substituted a variant which, precisely by its variation, suggests or symbolizes an idea other than itself, namely, spirituality or physical fecundity, as the case may be. I have used the word symbolize, for it is precisely at this point that we see the essence of the aesthetic symbol. I have insisted that the symbol is not to be identified with the intuition although it has its roots in the intuition. In the case under consideration the immediately given intuition is moulded *in the very process of intuition* in such fashion as to make the intuition a symbol for the non-intuited.

The true inwardness of the phenomenon of distortion is

THE LANGUAGE OF POETRY

brought out in an illuminating way by Van Gogh. "Tell Seurat," he wrote, "that I should despair if my figures were correct. Tell him that if you take a photograph of a man digging in my opinion he is sure to look as if he were not digging. Tell him that I think Michaelangelo's figures magnificent, even though the legs are certainly too long and the hips and pelvis bones a little too broad. . . . Tell him that it is my most fervent desire to know how one can achieve such *deviations from reality* (italics mine), such inaccuracies and such transfigurations that come about by chance. Well, yes, if you like, they are lies; but they are more valuable than the real values."[1] The distortion is, then, a deviation from the real—in the sense of *literal copy* of the real. As such these deviations are lies, if you like. The fictional element is present and recognized as fictional. But these deviations, these lies, are more valuable than the real values. It is this last phrase that especially demands our attention, and contains the whole essence of the aesthetic symbol. What, then, does valuable here mean? It means for Van Gogh—and it must mean the same for every artist—that precisely by these deviations certain aspects of reality are apprehended and expressed which could not be otherwise shown forth. It presupposes a distinction—between objects as merely perceived and as apprehended by the artist in aesthetic intuition—which is of fundamental importance for the philosophy of art.

The same phenomenon of distortion appears also in linguistic art. But here it is of even more significance for the reason that, seeking as it does to express or represent reality in words, "poetry" is brought into relation to logic and science, and the "deviations from reality," the element of error and fiction, are expressible in logical terms.

Every metaphor represents a distortion of reality in a certain sense, in that it involves the transfer of a name from an object to which it belongs to one in which in reality it does not belong. To call a young human a kid is to distort the human as much as to change the proportions of his leg. To call a woman a bitch is to distort the human as much as to overemphasize her buttocks. An extreme case of such aesthetic distortion is the symbol sentence, "Man is a reed, but a

[1] *The Letters of o Post Impressionist*, p. 23.

thinking reed." To say that man is a reed is to place him in a class so remote from him as to make the proposition a biological grotesque. Yet it is by precisely such deviations from the real that certain aspects of reality, otherwise inexpressible, are actually expressed. It is, however, in poetry in the narrower sense that the function of such aesthetic distortion comes out most clearly. An interesting case is found in certain lines from a poem of T. S. Eliot, "Morning at the Window":[1]

> "They are rattling breakfast plates in basement kitchens.
> And along the trampled edges of the street
> I am aware of the *damp souls* of the housemaids
> *Sprouting* despondently at area gates."

The distortion is here so extreme as perhaps to appear to some a poetic lapse, and yet it seems to me that, although it verges on the grotesque, it is expressive or revelatory to an extraordinary degree.

The true inwardness of this phenomenon of aesthetic distortion in poetry has also been well brought out by Ezra Pound. The poetic use of language "takes words ordinarily having conventional objective meanings, and by forcing them into a new and independent structure objectifies fresh meanings. . . . The function of the artist is precisely the formulation of what has not found its way into language, i.e. any language, verbal, plastic or musical."[2] Fresh meanings—in Van Gogh's phrase, new values more valuable than the real values. It is at this point also that there appears an aspect of poetry of great significance for the philosopher—namely, what we may describe as its immense irrelevance. In one of his essays, Gilbert Chesterton speaks of "the abrupt and abysmal irrelevancies in Dante's poetry and, indeed, in all great poetry." "Instead of saying that Beatrice looked beautiful Dante says that he felt like Glaucus when he ate the grass that made him sea fellow of the gods. . . . This summoning of remote symbols," he continues, "this calling of spirits from the vasty deep, like the sea green Glaucus, does suggest something involved in the theology of the matter. It suggests that *all*

---

[1] T. S. Eliot, *Collected Poems*, 1909–35.
[2] Article in *The Criterion*, April 1930.

beautiful images are shadows of the one real beauty and can be, in a sense, shifted or interchanged for its service. It prevents *mere* fixed idolatry of one shadow in one mirror as if it were the origin of all. Beatrice is to be loved because she is beautiful; but she is beautiful because there is behind her a many-sided mystery of beauty, to be seen also in the grass and the sea and even in the dead gods."[1] Now, I am not at all disposed to question "the theology of the matter"—indeed in principle I accept it—but that is not the point I wish to make here. It is rather the mere fact of the remoteness, the irrelevancy of the poetic symbol, whereby fresh meanings and new values are revealed and objectified. It is precisely through such aesthetic distortion that the revelatory character of art is served. This distortion may indeed be so great, this relevance so abysmal, as to become grotesque. Such, I think, are certain lines from the poem, *Tulips and Chimneys*, by E. E. Cummings:

> ". . . the Cambridge ladies do not care, above
> Cambridge if sometimes in its box of
> sky, lavender and cornerless, the
> moon rattles like a fragment of angry candy."[2]

There is perhaps a thrill in the association of "rattles" with "moon" and "angry" with "candy," but it is useless as a guide to insight. The distortion here is not the expression of an insight so keen that ordinary language will not embody it, and the words must lose their normal meanings in order to suggest it. On the contrary, far from revealing values "more valuable than the real values," it obscures the real values themselves. Taken solemnly, as it is doubtless meant to be, it sounds like a kind of sophisticated baby talk.

E

The Aesthetic Symbol and the Scientific Symbol

The problems which we have been considering come to a head in recent discussions of the relation of the aesthetic

[1] G. K. Chesterton, *All is Grist, A Book of Essays*, "Essay on Dante and Beatrice."
[2] Quoted from R. P. Blackmur, E. E. Cummings's Language, *Hound and Horn*, Winter, 1931.

symbol to the scientific symbol. The general recognition that many at least of our scientific "concepts" are, as the saying is, "symbols"—not pictures—of reality, has led to the attempt to distinguish between the aesthetic and the scientific symbol and to determine their relations. A very common view is that expressed by Stein in his *A B C of Aesthetics*. The symbol of science, we are told, is different from the symbol in aesthetics in the following way. The scientific symbol is merely a *name* and is "external" to that which it symbolizes; it is a mere label. The aesthetic symbol, on the other hand, is not a label but a sample. It is internal to the thing symbolized; it is a partial representation which means more or less adequately the thing to which it refers. As an illustration of the aesthetic symbol he uses one of which we have been making use, namely, "rosebuds" in the line of Herrick. As illustrative of the scientific symbol he takes the mathematical symbolism of modern physics. The former is internal, or in Coleridge's terms, "con-substantial" with the thing symbolized, the latter is external and its function is wholly that of prediction and manipulation. In his view science, by its very nature, tends towards nominalism. This is an extreme statement of a widespread theory. It is, indeed, as we shall find, a question whether this nominalistic view of science can be consistently carried out—whether, in other words, a view of science can be developed which denies that its symbols are, in any sense and in any degree, internal to the thing symbolized. These are problems for later investigation; for the present we may take this contrast as a working basis and modify it later as it becomes necessary.

V

THE LANGUAGE OF POETRY AND "POETIC TRUTH"

A

Thus far we have been concerned with two main problems, namely, the nature of the language of poetry and the nature of the poetic symbol as part of that language. Following the scheme of the preceding chapter, our next task would be that of interpretation of poetry and poetic symbolism; in other words, the determination of what poetry "says." Such interpretation would include, as we have seen, interpretation in the narrower sense of expansion, and secondly the determination of the existential or ontological import of the symbol. Unfortunately there stands in the way of this task a widespread view which holds that poetry (and the aesthetic in general) says nothing. It merely evokes feeling and communicates emotion.

This general position has been well expressed in the well-known works of Ogden and Richards. I quote from *The Meaning of Meaning*. "Poetry, we are told, seems about to return to the conditions of its greatness by abandoning the obsession of knowledge and symbolic truth. It is not necessary to know what things are in order to take up fitting attitudes towards them and the peculiarity of the greatest attitudes which art can evoke is their extraordinary width."[1] We may overlook for the moment the historic falsity of the statement that the conditions of poetry's greatness was the absence of this obsession. The traditional view that poetry is revelatory— in its extreme form that it is actually "truer than history"— can I think be actually shown to be the assumption of the greatest poets and artists. We may also waive the question whether in order to take up fitting attitudes towards things it is not necessary to know something of the things. We shall go to the very heart of the question, which is, I think, this: whether poetry can abandon this "obsession" and remain anything but a sort of "important nonsense." To this question there can be, to my mind, no answer except an unqualified no. Certainly no poet has ever given any other answer. Nor can any aesthetic theory, however sophisticated, when once the question is properly formulated and really understood.

That "knowledge" is applicable in some sense to the aesthetic is, and must be, admitted by all theories, even the most "emotional." The notion of truth when applied in this sphere often means simply sincerity of feeling and expression. But even sincere expression is revelatory of something; the person in whom a corresponding attitude is evoked has, by that very evocation, apprehended and "understood" something to which can hardly be denied the name of knowledge. All art is thus "an objectification, qualitative in character, of the spirit of

[1] *The Meaning of Meaning*, p. 271.

man." All art is *at least* this, but much of it goes farther. It claims truth in another sense—in the sense, namely, that it re-presents, whether in picture or symbol, something in the objective realm of being as well as in the inner nature of man. This has been made sufficiently clear in our studies in Chapter VII and the conception of bi-representation developed there. The sense of the aesthetic picture whether linguistic or non-linguistic always includes the notion of knowledge in this sense. A picture of whatever kind, to have the "sense" of a picture, must be an implicit assertion or proposition. Even in such non-linguistic arts as music and pure design, where the element of assertion is apparently absent, it is, I should hold, only apparently so. All expression involves the beginning of re-presentation, and some reference to reality is always present. In any case, the novel, the drama, and the lyric poem—all forms of poetry—make sufficiently definite assertions, not only about feelings, but about the human beings that have them and about the "life" of these human beings. They also make assertions about nature and the cosmos.

B

The Special Problem in Linguistic Art (Poetry)

The issue is, therefore, definitely joined in the case of linguistic art. That issue is perfectly clear. Either poetry contains assertions which are real propositions or it is nonsense. The issue may be stated in the form of a dilemma. Either these apparent assertions of poetry are real assertions or they are not, that is, mere expressions of feeling. If they are the former, then part of their understanding is their acceptance as true or false, and the notion of truth is applicable to poetry. If on the other hand they are the latter, then they "say nothing"—they are the expression of a nonsense, however pleasant that nonsense may be.

There are many who maintain the view we are criticizing but do not accept this alternative, who hold that the poet is neither talking nonsense nor making an assertion which must be accepted as true or false. The question of truth and falsity does not enter. The position is clearly presented by L. S. Stebbing. When, we are told, Shelley says:

> "Life, like a dome of many-coloured glass,
> Stains the white radiance of Eternity,
> Until death tramples it to fragments,"

he is neither talking nonsense nor making an assertion that must be accepted as true or false. The question of truth and falsity does not enter.[1] In examining this position it must be noted first of all that Shelley himself *thinks* that he is making an assertion whether he is deluded or not. He is saying something about life which he believes to be significant. He also believes it to be true; otherwise he would not say it. This I should venture to generalize for all poets and indeed for all artists, at least whom I should call the titans. It may be said, of course, that Shelley misunderstood his function as a poet (and similarly Beethoven his as a musician), but that is a position difficult to maintain; it is as gratuitous as to say that the scientist simply does not understand his function as a scientist if he does not take the operational and pragmatic point of view.[2] So far as Shelley is concerned, then, his assertion is a real and not apparent one. Life does something. It "stains the white radiance of Eternity." Now, it is quite possible to say that this is nonsense, that such predicates are meaningless when applied to life, just as it would be nonsense to say that virtue is triangular; the domains are too far apart to be joined by any significant relation; the "immense irrelevancy" of poetry is here extended beyond all conscience.

---

[1] *Op. cit.*, p. 17.

[2] There is, of course, no question as to what Shelley himself believed. He held the so-called "romantic" theory of poetry which is essentially revelatory. For him a poem, as he expressed it in *The Defense of Poetry*, is "the very image of life, expressing an eternal truth." This view is, I am convinced, the working theory not only of all the great poets, but of all the great artists, painters, sculptors and musicians. In this connection an interesting book by John W. Beatty, *The Relation of Art to Nature*, New York, 1922, is instructive. As a student of the fine arts (he is director of the Fine Arts of the Carnegie Institute), he has made a study of the writings of the great artists, and maintains the thesis that the masters of painting and sculpture, both ancient and modern, have uniformly worked on the assumption of the revelatory character of art, that the object of art is the truth of nature and of character. He quotes from a long array of the greatest artists, the modern names including Corot, Millet, Whistler, Abbott, Thayer, Winslow Homer, La Farge, and Rodin.

This position I am prepared to understand, although it is one that I should not care to take. The "silliness of poetry" is something hard to disprove to a literal mind or to a modern logician. But Professor Stebbing explicitly states that this line of Shelley is not silly. She explicitly says that "he is saying something significant." This I cannot understand, for how can he be saying anything significant about life if what he says is not a true character of it?

The dilemma becomes even more cogent when we turn from the speaker, the poet, to the hearer, to the enjoyer of the poetry. Shelley, we are told, is not making a statement that must be accepted by the hearer as either true or false. The question of truth and falsity does not enter. Now, there is an element of truth in this statement which must be separated from the larger element of error. I may indeed "enjoy" these lines of Shelley merely for the music of his words, the beauty of his imagery. There is, I suppose, also a minimum of meaning present if I merely *assume* for the moment the truth of the assertion, the assumption to be dropped the next moment. But it is equally true that I am *not* enjoying or understanding the *poet's* meaning—for part of his meaning is precisely the assertions, the non-aesthetic meaning embodied in the aesthetic. It has been said that even the artist, in the moment of creation, knows nothing of truth or falsity, or of minds other than his own. But that is just the point. The artist in the moment of creation is not the whole artist, any more than the lover in the love trance is the whole lover. The whole artist includes what he *intends* in his creative act and what he thinks the product of that creative act to be. In both of these moments he is concerned with truth and falsity. The dilemma so far as the hearer is concerned is, then, this. If the hearer is enjoying the poet's utterances without any reference to their truth or falsity, he is not enjoying the poet's meaning but something else. If, on the other hand, he is really *understanding* the poet, that understanding does involve communication of meaning in which questions of truth and falsity are relevant.

The view we have been criticizing is in a sense merely a special case of the more general thesis which we had occasion to examine in the chapter on Language and Logic, the thesis, namely, involved in the notion of descriptions that are signifi-

THE LANGUAGE OF POETRY

cant and yet describe nothing. Applied here, it means that the poet's description, such as that of Shelley, is significant although it describes nothing. On the general question of the possibility of this notion we have already decided negatively, and our argument need not be repeated here.[1] One point may, however, be added. It is true that when the poet says that "life stains the white radiance of Eternity," he is describing nothing *literally*, for the *life* to which the words "stains the white radiance of Eternity" is applied does not physically exist. The assertion has therefore no literal significance. If it has significance at all it is of another kind, namely, symbolic. In an interesting passage, Peirce quotes the lines:

> "Full many a gem of purest ray serene
> The dark unfathomed caves of ocean bear;
> Full many a flower is born to blush unseen
> And waste its sweetness on the desert air."

Of them he says: "But that there are gems at the bottom of the sea, flowers in the untravelled desert, etc., are propositions which, like that about a diamond being hard when it is not pressed, concerns much more the arrangement of our language than the meaning of our ideas."[2] This is precisely the point at issue. Literally these lines have no significance. If not nonsense, what is their significance?

C

The Revelatory Theory of Art and the Insight Symbol

Aesthetic theory is in a quandary to-day. It is not too much to say that the majority of philosophers feel the difficulties in the purely emotive theory of art, but find equal difficulties in formulating any satisfactory revelatory theory. Professor Reid's thinking at this point affords a good illustration of the situation. He takes definite issue with the position of Mr. Richards. He finds it altogether too narrow. Mr. Richards, he tells us, is so engaged in refuting the "pointer" or "mirror" theory of art that he tends to go to the other extreme. The logical outcome of his view is that art has no meaning at all.

---

[1] Chapter VII, p. 300 f.   [2] *Chance, Love and Logic*, p. 58.

Professor Reid therefore presents what may be called an intermediate theory. He begins by recognizing that one function of art is to evoke emotions, but he holds that it also embodies a meaning and a reality which, as he says, "transcends the body and in a sense certainly lies beyond it, although it is fused with it. Art is therefore revelatory and the term truth is applicable to it."[1]

Professor Reid's amplification of this thesis is so close to that which I have been developing that I shall make use of it as a starting-point. Art, he tells us, "is a special revelation of reality whose nature and structure is determined by the principle of value appreciation. Art is revelatory. The term truth is applicable to it." There are values which are very light though charming, as in *A Midsummer Night's Dream*. These values are real enough, but the expressions true or real do not seem appropriate, rather such terms as lovely or charming. On the other hand, the poet may reveal a vista of values in connection with which the terms real and true, which before were inappropriate, are now felt to be fitting. This great art does. With Professor Reid's position up to this point I am in complete accord. That the element of "value appreciation" is fundamental I agree. We get "aspects of reality which reveal values to the artist" and "the term truth is applicable to these upon revelations." But the adequacy of the formulation depends the answers to two questions on both of which, unfortunately, Professor Reid is rather vague. Is the reality revealed merely the value appreciations of the artist, or do his appreciations reveal values in the structure of the object? Are the revelations of art assertions about the object, or are they merely expressions of the appreciations of the artist?

Taking up the first question, there is one sense in which the revelatory character of art cannot be denied. "All art is an objectification, qualitative in character, of the inner spirit of man", and, in so far as it is this, it is a revelation of the artist's appreciation of values. In the field of poetry it is the lyric preeminently that objectifies this spirit. But the novel, the drama —even the picture and the symphony—are revelatory in this first sense. The way the novelist or dramatist—even the painter and the musician—envisage their material may be revelatory

[1] *Op. cit.*, Chapter X ("Art, Truth and Reality"), p. 207.

of emotional and other attitudes towards life and, in so far as these attitudes are evoked in us, there has been revealed to us something of the inner spirit of man which is "truth" about it, and which may be taken as part of our intuition and understanding of the world. In this sense the notion of aesthetic truth cannot be denied without making meaningless a large part of our converse which we know to be meaningful and intelligible. But this is far from an adequate revelatory theory of art. Such a theory must view art as a special revelation of *reality* as determined by values. Without the artist's "appreciation of values" there could be no appreciation and therefore no revelation of this reality. But it is because the "nature and structure" of reality is determined by values, and not merely by the artist's appreciation of them, that truth in any significant sense is applicable to art. The view here developed involves an objective theory of values. Such a theory cannot be argued here, although it is, I should maintain, the only theory which makes art intelligible. A sufficient indication of such a theory has, however, been sketched in Chapter IV, in which the arguments against value nominalism and the subjective character of value terms have been presented.[1] The important point for our present purpose is that, as has been shown, the artist's consciousness implies this objectivity.

Closely related to this first question is the second, namely, whether art, as revelatory, "says something" about reality. Here, too, in attempting to maintain his intermediate position, Professor Reid is unfortunately vague. It is true that he explicitly denies that there are assertions in a work of art. He distinguishes between the "perspected" reality of a work of art and the "asserted" reality of propositions. Art, he tells us, "is not true as propositions are true, but like the knowledge of which propositions are the expression, art is a revelation." Though art may contain propositions and imply knowledge, its aim is not this, but the appreciation of value. I do not believe that this position can be consistently maintained. Every work of art, we have already seen, is a "tacit proposition"; only as such has it any meaning. It always "says something." What a particular work of art actually says and

[1] For a more extended development of the objective theory, see my *Intelligible World*, especially Chapter IV.

what poetry, as symbolic form, says implicitly, are questions later to be considered. Here the issue is merely whether the distinction between perspected and asserted can be maintained. On this point it seems to me there can be no question. I should be disposed to insist, and were it necessary to argue the point, that even in those forms of art in which the element of representation is at a minimum, as in certain modern developments of the graphic arts and in music, there is always implicit assertion. The slender, elongated metal object which its creator, Branchusi, calls *Bird in Flight*, does not say, even implicitly, that this is a representation of an actual bird in flight, but it does say, or else it means nothing, such is the *movement* of flight; and the question is relevant, *does* it express that movement or not? Stravinski's *Fire Bird*, besides being a series of tones, expresses something. The writer of the music says that it expresses the life of our age of steel and noise as Bach expressed the sense of life for his age, and the expression implies an assertion which may be true or false. But it is not necessary to argue the point here, for we are concerned primarily with the art of poetry, and here there can be no question. Perspected truth cannot be separated from asserted truth. Intuition is inseparable from expression and wherever there is expression, aesthetic no less than any other kind, it contains the element of bi-polarity, of expression and that which is expressed. True even for the non-linguistic arts, it is *a fortiori* true for that art whose medium of expression is words.[1] This position is, of course, all important for what follows. Poetry, both as containing explicit assertions and symbolic representations and also as a general symbolic form, or way of rendering reality, *says something*. It is what it says and the truth of what it says that is of interest to philosophy.

This general notion of the revelatory character of art may be applied specifically to the poetic symbol. When thus applied, we get what has been characterized as the *insight* symbol. In our general classification of symbols it was possible to do no more than suggest its general character as distinguished from the merely substitutional and descriptive. This general character may now be made more specific. The insight symbol,

[1] Chapter VIII, pp. 347 ff.

we found, does not merely *describe*, through images drawn from sense, an object otherwise known (conceptually), but finds its importance as a gateway into a "spiritual" world. We may now characterize more satisfactorily this spiritual world. It is in fact precisely the world the structure of which is determined by value appreciation. Actually, any of the illustrations of poetic symbols used in other contexts will show this to be true. Images from the narrower world of sensuous intuition are taken, not merely to picture, but to give us insight into, to enable us to intuit a non-sensuous world of value relations. The enlarged buttocks of the primitives or the damp sprouting souls of housemaids are in the first instance perspected reality, art determined by value appreciations, but they also contain implicit assertions. These symbols "say something," and what they say may be not only "more valuable than the real values," to use Van Gogh's terms, but more true than the literal truth.

D

Insight and Verification. The Notion of Authentication

A revelatory theory of poetry, one which holds that the term truth is applicable to it, must of necessity develop a theory of verification in this sphere. I have already indicated the lines on which such a theory must be developed in an earlier study of the notion of *authentication*.[1] It is necessary to bring out these lines somewhat more clearly.

It was pointed out that the terms authentic and authentication were taken from the aesthetic sphere and widened into a general theory of non-empirical verification (empirical here meaning sense experience). The term authentic is a peculiarly apt synonym for true in the aesthetic sphere. We speak of literature having the authentic note. This expression may mean simply that we feel the sincerity of the writer, but ordinarily it includes a great deal more. It means that, as we say, the writer has in some way managed to convey the "truth" of man, of life, and in some cases, of nature as a whole. If the poem or the novel has, then, this authentic note it

[1] Chapter V, pp. 213 ff.

must be a note which, so to speak, "sounds" in ourselves and which is in some way verified either directly or indirectly.

There is, to be sure, to a limited degree, verification in the sense of the empirical criterion. Realism, in the photographic sense, whether physical or psychological, has references of this character and an adequate theory of aesthetic truth will not ignore this element. But this is a minor element and, as is well known, a "picture" may be true in this sense and essentially false as a "revelation" of reality. Art, as a revelation of reality determined by value appreciation, can be verified or authenticated only by value appreciation. Thus a portrait which is, as we say, a "speaking likeness" speaks because the artist has, through his value appreciation, apprehended a value character of the one portrayed; the sitter has unconsciously spoken to him. If *I* find it a speaking likeness also, it is for the same reason. The same is true in principle for the authentication of a poetic symbol. If I find Shelley's lines good poetry—that "life *does* stain the white radiance of Eternity"—it is because I find it an authentic symbol for actual relations in life, as determined by value appreciation. It is true that a symbol may be expanded into "literal," non-symbolic propositions and verified in other ways, but it is then no longer authentication of the symbol. The symbol rosebuds may conjure up "all sweet and pleasant things," but what it really conjures up is not expressible in these abstract terms. Verification of the non-symbolic rendering of the symbol is not authentication of the symbol.[1]

The point is that, since art is a revelation of reality as determined by value appreciation, this "revelation" can be authenticated only by value appreciation. Let us make this clear by illustrations from the several arts. Branchusi's *Bird in Flight* or *Bird in Space* expresses in a wholly "abstract" symbolic way the appreciation of the artist of the flight. If that is conveyed or communicated to the observer, it is an authentic expression of the object in question. Eliot's statements that "the damp souls of the housemaids sprout despondently at area gates" is a wholly symbolic way of expressing a value appreciation of the poet. If that appreciation or insight is conveyed or

---

[1] Chapter IX, pp. 442 ff. This is a special case of the general principles of authentication of symbols discussed in that chapter.

communicated to the reader, it is an authentic expression of the object of the description and is adequately shown forth.

It is implied in these statements that the authentication or verification of an artistic expression or symbol is conditioned by communication, and this raises the entire question of art and communication. It is obvious, of course, that on the basis of our general position a work of art does not come into being until it is communicated. As language has no reality except in the speech community, so the special "languages" of the arts have no reality except in the aesthetic community. Contrary to Croce's view, I should maintain that "expression" has no meaning without its correlative "understanding." In any case there is no authentication of it as a work of art except through communication. There is no purely solipsistic verification, and to this general rule "art as expression" is no exception.

VI

THE INTERPRETATION OF POETRY. WHAT POETRY SAYS

A

Poetry, like any form of aesthetic experience, may be enjoyed intrinsically and not primarily for its cognitive and existential implications. But poetry is also to be interpreted, and precisely that interpretation is in a sense part of the enjoyment. It is true that there is an aspect of poetry, and of its enjoyment, which may consciously abstract from interpretation, because we abstract from the implications (to this aspect we have done full justice); but the implications are still there, and until they are made explicit the full aesthetic meaning is not realized.

Interpretation of poetry is the determination of what poetry says. This assumes that in addition to what the poet says "superficially" or on the face of his poem, he is also saying something which can only be brought out by interpretation. One of the essential functions of the teaching of literature is its interpretation. It is quite common to speak of the "philosophy" of a poem or of a novel, and this philosophy is brought out by interpretation. Now a character of such interpretation is that it is always carried out in non-poetic terms or in *less* poetic terms than those of the thing to be interpreted. In general, as we saw in the preceding chapter, interpretation is the rendering of "symbol sentences" into literal or non-symbolic, although the distinction is always relative.[1]

This leads us to a further necessary distinction, namely, between what poetry says *explicitly* and what it says *implicitly*. Poetry means what it says, but it does not always say all that it means. There is always a great deal of unexpressed reference. What poetry says explicitly is always in its first intention fiction—at the best silly, at the worst, as in the minds of naturalistic literalists, dangerous lies. It tells us that "flesh is grass," that "men are reeds," that "housemaids' souls are damp and sprout." This silliness of poetry may become very dangerous as when, for instance, a Nietzsche is taken literally. When, however, we seek to determine what the poet is saying implicitly, we find not only that in order to express adequately what he really means we must say it in language of greater generality and abstraction, but must recognize that what he says implicitly is not wholly identical with what is explicitly said. To say what is really meant by the assertion that "housemaids' souls are damp and sprout," we must translate the predicates damp and sprout into terms appropriate to the context in which souls have their being. We should not, indeed, find these terms unless the terms taken from the physical context pointed the way (that is where the poet is a discoverer of new qualities and relations); but it is only in these latter terms that we can express what the poet really says.

These considerations may now be applied to the problem of the interpretation of the poetic symbol. In the preceding chapter we enunciated certain principles of symbolism which apply to all regions of symbolism. We also divided the general process of interpretation into interpretation in the narrower sense, or expansion of the symbol, and interpretation in the broader sense, as development of the existential or ontological implications of the symbol. The former, the expansion of a symbol, is the determination of what the symbol says explicitly, or the development of the unexpressed references of the symbol; the latter is the determination of what poetry as symbolic form says implicitly. The former is only a part of the inter-

[1] Chapter IX, p. 432.

pretation of the poem (or work of art); interpretation is not complete until the first stage develops into the second.

This distinction is of great importance. Its importance may best be seen by anticipating an application of the same distinction to science in the following chapter. Science also says many things explicitly, and the determination of the meaning of its concepts and symbols is the determination of what it explicitly says. But even more important is what science, as a symbolic form, as a way of rendering reality, says implicitly about the nature of reality. This is the philosophy of science. It is the relation of these two symbolic forms, of poetry and of science, which is of interest to the philosopher.

B

Interpretation of the Poetic Symbol. Expansion of the Symbol

Expansion of any symbol we characterized as development of its unexpressed reference. In the case of the poetic symbol it is, according to the view of the aesthetic and the aesthetic symbol already maintained, the development of its unexpressed value references. Art is a special revelation of reality whose nature and structure are determined by the principle of value appreciation; the unexpressed reference of the symbol is always to these values and expansion of the symbol is the explicit development of them.

This can be shown by the examination of any poetic symbol. For our purposes two great symbolists, one ancient and one wholly modern, are of special significance, namely, Dante and Ibsen. One might take any of the outstanding symbols of the *Divine Comedy*, the symbol of Beatrice herself, the physical symbols by means of which Dante's spiritual journey in the *Divine Comedy* is pictured, or the cosmic symbols by means of which spiritual things and relations are suggested. The interpretation of any of them would constitute proof of our thesis. This has, however, been so frequently done, and the principles underlying this symbolism are so generally understood, that I shall turn forthwith to the modern symbolist, Ibsen.[1]

[1] For a study of Dante's symbolism, see H. F. Dunbar, *op. cit.*, Chapter II (*Symbolism Basic in the Divina Commedia*).

Ibsen is an outstanding example of the use of the poetic symbol in order to give insight into "spiritual reality," in order to embody an ideal content not otherwise expressible. In the poetic period of *Brand* and *Peer Gynt*—and still more in the deliberately symbolic period of his latest works, such as *The Wild Duck, The Master Builder, John Gabriel Borkman,* and *When We Dead Awaken*—we have symbolism at its highest. The latter have been described as the chamber music of the soul. Ibsen uses symbolism to express the interior life of his characters, but also to express certain characters of nature of which the human is a part. It is, however, with the former that we are at present chiefly concerned. In the Ibsen symbolism we have, moreover, an excellent illustration, and indeed proof, of the inseparability of the symbol from the aesthetic intuition. Whether we take such a symbol as that of the onion in *Peer Gynt*, of the climbing and falling from the tower in *The Master Builder*, or that of the wild duck in the play of that name—in every case the symbol is not merely a surrogate for a concept, but rather the way in which the ideal content is apprehended and expressed.

The interpretation of any one of these symbols would be an illustration of the expansion of a symbol. Let us take the symbol of the onion in *Peer Gynt*. Peer Gynt is an egoist whose maxim of life is "Peer, to thyself be enough." After a life in which the following of this maxim has ended only in his losing himself, Peer comes back to his native land an empty and a broken man. In his hunger he strips off peel after peel of an onion, to get at the core. Each peel symbolizes in Ibsen's thought a layer of social content or relations, and when the last is removed there is nothing left. That is the "Gyntish I." In this image or symbol Ibsen *suggests* the social nature of the self; the expansion of this symbol, the development of the unexpressed reference, is precisely the statement, in terms appropriate to the universe of discourse, of these value relations. The expansion of any other of the Ibsen symbols, let us say the climbing and falling from the tower in *The Master Builder*, would illustrate the same principle.

In all these cases the symbol is the means of apprehending and expressing certain value relations not otherwise expressible, and their expansion shows this to be so. The apprehension and appreciation—for the apprehension is possible only by the appreciation of values—involve the element of feeling and emotion. It is this aspect of the situation which leads to the emotive theory of the aesthetic symbol—to the theory which says, with Vaihinger, that "the aesthetic symbols or fictions serve the purpose of awakening within us certain uplifting or otherwise important feelings." This the aesthetic symbol always does. It evokes feeling for the reason that values cannot be appreciated except through feeling. An "emotional intuition" of values is as much a corollary of an objective theory of values as sense intuition is a corollary of an objective theory of sense qualities.[1] But to say that this is the essential function of the symbol is to misapprehend and to misrepresent the entire situation. The essential function of the symbol—and this the expansion of any symbol shows—is to give us insight into, or knowledge of, certain aspects of reality. We may, if we will, call this "perspected" in contrast to "asserted" reality—although, as I have already shown, assertions are always implicit—nevertheless, it still remains true that when the symbol is expanded, the insight given by the symbol finds expression in assertions which have significance for discursive knowledge.

The view I am presenting here has already received classic expression in Kant's famous theory in his *Critique of Judgment*.[2] There he develops his notion of "Beauty as the Symbol of Morality." It may well be that the use of the term "morality" here is unfortunate because of its narrow connotation. It may well be also that "beauty," in all the various meanings of that difficult term, cannot be pressed into this narrow moralistic mould. Finally, it is quite probable that Kant's attempt to interpret the entire realm of the aesthetic as a transcendental reconciliation of the theoretical and the practical (moral), is a "metaphysics of taste" that it is difficult to maintain. Yet when all this is admitted, it still remains true that beauty *in the sphere of the human* is a symbol of the moral; the aesthetic as symbolic form implies the moral with its presuppositions and postulates, as we shall attempt to show. It also remains true that the function of these symbols is not merely to evoke emotions, however important and uplifting,

---

[1] Chapter IV, pp. 164 ff.   [2] *Critique of Judgment*, Section 59.

but to give us knowledge. In sum, poetry tells us something about man, both explicitly and implicitly, and when we seek to interpret what it says—when we seek the philosophy of poetry—we find it to be moral, or better, "value" philosophy. This will become clearer when we seek to develop what poetry says *implicitly*. To this task we shall now turn.

VII

THE PHILOSOPHY OF POETRY: WHAT POETRY REALLY SAYS

A

The complete interpretation of a poetic symbol leads ultimately to the interpretation of poetry itself as a mode of apprehending reality. To determine the existential or ontological implications of a symbol is to determine the ontological implications of the language of which the symbol is a part. Otherwise expressed, the language of poetry "says something" about reality. Interpretation of that language as a whole is to determine what it really says.

The question as to what poetry says has, as we have seen, a double aspect; it involves the distinction between what it says explicitly and what it says implicitly. On the one hand, poetry says many things explicitly about reality—about both man and nature. Speaking as it does a different language, what it says is different from what science says—what the two languages say being often, on the surface at least, in contradiction. There is, in the second place, the question of what poetry *as poetry*, as a special symbolic form, in contrast with science as symbolic form, says implicitly.

This distinction is of importance for a further reason. To the question what poetry says, the answer may be given that poetry as such says nothing specific. It is the individual poet that speaks—not "poetry"—and each poet envisages man and the world in a different way. What the poets say explicitly is, moreover, very varied; for reality, as determined by value appreciation, varies as the values vary. This is doubtless in a sense true. The three philosophical poets, Lucretius, Dante, and Goethe, envisage life and the world differently; even more is this true of Dante and Ibsen, although the differences may easily be exaggerated. Yet while this is true, all are poets, and the fact that they speak in the poetic rather than the scientific idiom implies that they share a common view of the reality thus rendered. This is what is meant when we speak of the poet *as poet* and raise the question what poetry *as poetry* says.

With this we come, of course, to what may be called the philosophy of poetry, and this in turn is but part, although from our point of view the most important part, of a philosophy of art. The philosophy of art may be defined as follows: it investigates the nature of the aesthetic consciousness and the significance of its expressions or pronouncements for our view of reality. Using our own special terms, we may say that the philosophy of art investigates art as symbolic form, and the significance of it as a way of expressing and symbolizing reality. All art speaks, but poetry speaks in the language of words. What is it that poetry says and what is the significance of its "assertions"?

B

What Poetry Says About Man

Art in general, and poetry in particular, is primarily a revelation of man, "an objectification, qualitative in character, of the inner spirit of man." This it is both directly and indirectly —directly in the lyrical, narrative, and dramatic expression and representation, indirectly in the way in which it envisages and pictures nature. All art is a special revelation of reality whose nature and structure are determined by the principle of value appreciation. Indirectly all art is revelatory of man.

I think it would be generally agreed, except by those influenced by purely modern prejudices, that what the novelist and dramatist say about man and human life is a truer objectification of their nature, and therefore more representative and more revealing, than representation of these objects in the universals and "symbols" of science. Without begging any of the questions which can be solved only by the considerations of the next chapter (namely, the nature of scientific language and symbolism in the sciences of life and mind), we may at least say that, while the humanistic sciences (psychology and sociology) may doubtless describe man more accurately for certain purposes, it is only the poet that can "objectify" his inner meanings and values. This general statement may be made more specific by reverting to the thesis of Lloyd Morgan. With him we should agree that no adequate account of what happens in human life, the central home of action and drama, is possible if "relations of the mental type"—and the dramatic way of rendering them—are left out. Poetry, then, whether as intuitive, metaphorical, or dramatic language, always says certain things explicitly about man and about human life. What it says explicitly is manifold and varied and often contradictory; but in so far as it is authentic, all explicit assertions have one common character—they are assertions about *persons*. This may seem to be the veriest platitude, but it is, properly understood, of the utmost significance. For science, rightly understood, never speaks of persons and has no interest in them as such. Indeed it has no interest in the individual as such, but only as an exemplification of a universal. "Scientific" psychology is always psychology without a soul. Poetry, as poetry, always speaks of "souls," even when paradoxically, as in naturalistic poetry, it denies their existence. By this I mean that even the naturalistic dramatist, let us say, in so far as he is a dramatist, must treat the characters of the play *as though* they were persons even if he thinks they are not. Now, what is a person? The one differentia of a person that is significant is, that he alone of all the parts of nature has consciousness of values and of the "ought" or obligation inseparable from the awareness of values. In him at least, whether it is or is not true of other parts of nature, purpose, finality, "axiological determination" is the fundamental character and the deepest "law."[1] To have this character is to be a "soul," and poetry, in contrast to science, always speaks about souls.

For the poet, then, the individual is always the centre and bearer of values, and his function, as poet, is to reveal them. In his account of motivation he may often use the language of science—of psychology and sociology—but he does so at his peril, for the language of the latter fights against the former.

---

[1] For a complete development of this notion, see N. Hartmann, *Ethics*, Vol. I, Chapter XIX.

The psychological novelist or dramatist is not psychological in the sense of science, for both the implications and the symbolism of science are, as we shall see, different from those of poetry.

But the language of poetry is even more significant ontologically in what it says implicitly and indirectly about man and human life. It says many things, but one thing it always says, namely, that human life and man are unique, free, and self-determining parts of nature. The dramatic mode of representation always implies this; it is the necessary presupposition of all drama, and in so far as the poet employs the dramatic way of rendering life, he always says this implicitly.

This is true of all drama, but it is pre-eminently true of tragedy. A naturalistic view of man—one which makes of him merely a part of nature—cannot rise to tragedy. The death of a tree or of a dog cannot be tragic. It is only that unique part of nature which is the bearer of values, and of the obligation which arises from them, that can be the subject of tragedy. The "tragic sense of life" is possible only on the supposition of the transcendence of nature, and the tragic *catharsis* is possible only when the drama expresses that transcendence. Naturalistic drama can only "depress" us. We have, then, what a recent writer has called "the dilemma of modern tragedy."[1] If the modern dramatist writes on the basis of naturalistic assumptions he cannot achieve the tragic; if, on the other hand, he writes on the basis of the transcendental assumptions of classical tragedy, he is not "realistic" in the modern sense. He must choose between the two. This dilemma runs throughout the whole of the modern drama and, as this writer further points out, is especially patent in Eugene O'Neill, whose vacillations, in both objective and method, are due to a fundamental indecision. In any case, the drama is possible only on humanistic rather than scientific postulates, and in so far as the dramatic mode is used in rendering life, the humanistic view of man is assumed and postulated. The significance of these facts is far reaching. They mean, in the first place, that the poet, in so far as he is a poet and speaks

[1] This essay, entitled "The Dilemma of Modern Tragedy," is by Allen Reynolds Thompson and is found in *Humanism and America*, edited by Norman Foerster.

the language of poetry, cannot say anything explicitly about man without implying a great deal more than is explicitly expressed. They mean, in the second place, that when this "more" is examined, when the implications are fully developed, they are always of a specific kind and imply a specific metaphysics. But of this more presently.

C

What Poetry Says About Nature

Poetry is primarily revelatory of the life and spirit of man. But that same life and spirit are parts of nature in the sense of reality as a whole. It cannot be directly revelatory of man without being indirectly revelatory of the nature of which he is a part. Now, poetry has much to say about nature. In so far as it speaks directly—*in its own form*—in so far as it speaks explicitly, it can only speak in one way; it must speak a dramatic language. It must speak in terms of relations of the mental type and these relations must be rendered in the dramatic way. In other words, it must *personalize* nature; the poetic form must be the anthropomorphic.

The anthropomorphic form is the only possible way of rendering the anthropic, the only form which gives intrinsic intelligibility in connection with man. When man is symbolized in non-human terms, all intrinsic understanding vanishes and we achieve only instrumental intelligibility. It is, however, quite another question when the anthropomorphic form is applied to the non-human, when we speak of "nature" in dramatic terms. Here poetry may be wholly out of place; here we may have nothing but the "pathetic fallacy," nothing but a misrepresentation and falsification of nature. In order to reach any conclusions on this point we must again distinguish what poetry says explicitly from what it says implicitly, and seek, as we did in the case of man, to interpret its implications.

It is immediately clear what poetry does and *must* say about nature explicitly. For the poet the river runs, the brook ripples and even sings, the mountains rear their heads, the sea roars. Even where metaphors are not used, where merely

THE LANGUAGE OF POETRY

the intuitive language of poetry is employed, this language conjures up a living universe. The first book of Wordsworth's *Prelude*, Whitehead tells us, "is pervaded with the haunting presences of nature...." "Of course," he continues, "Wordsworth is a poet, writing a poem and is not concerned with dry philosophical statements. But it would hardly be possible to express more clearly the feeling of nature as exhibiting entwined prehensive unities, each suffused with modal presences of the others."[1] Now, it is not here the question whether Whitehead has found the "right words" in which to say what poetry says symbolically; the significant point is that something like this Wordsworth does say, at least implicitly. What is true of Wordsworth's *Prelude* is true of all poetic rendering of nature—by the very condition of its symbolic form. Let us see whether we can state explicitly its implicit assertions.

Professor F. S. C. Northrop puts it in the following way. "Art in all its forms," he tells us, "*asserts implicitly* (italics mine) the reality of the experienced qualities of things. The painter on his canvas, the musician in his tone poem and the poet in his language, all deal with these aspects of things as *realities*.... The poet hears the rippling brook and, unlike the physicist, he does not abstract the atoms and sound waves and forms of the running water. Instead he tries to catch the whole of that elemental fact in its unity.... In this he is correct, for the ripple is the physical made determinate by the molecules and waves, and there can be no physical factor in the object except as it is constituted by the experiencing subject." It is, then, this partly that poetry strives to express, but it expresses a good deal more. "Poetry at its best," we are further told, "always suggests something grounded far beyond the ripple and the man, so far indeed that it must have its basis in the ultimate eternal nature of things. And in this also the artist is correct, for that which the poet or painter catches and the physicist misses, is the bare indeterminate experienced quality which the psychical contributes, and this has its roots neither in observed nature nor in man, but in the ultimate atomic elements out of which both are constituted."[2]

This passage is of great interest. That the poet or painter

[1] *Science and the Modern World*, p. 121 f.
[2] *Science and First Principles*, p. 267.

catches something which the scientist misses is a view common to many scientists who, through self-critical considerations, have come to recognize that their own symbols and symbolic form constitute but one way of rendering reality among others. It is also a view more and more adopted by philosophers.[1] But what is it that poetry catches which science misses? It is first of all the immediately experienced quality of things. But it catches more than this. Implicitly at least "it refers to something metaphysical, something in the eternal nature of things." Whether that something is expressible in the terms of physics, as Northrop suggests, may be left undetermined until we consider science and its symbolic form. If, however, the physicist misses it, we may wonder how it is expressible in his terms. My own view, which will be developed in the following chapter, is that physics, by reason of the very nature of its language and its symbolism, cannot express it, and if it is expressible at all, being metaphysical, it can only be expressed in metaphysical language. Be that as it may, the point here is that in rendering nature in its symbolic form the poet does catch something which the physicist misses.

VIII

POETRY AS "COVERT METAPHYSICS." THE PARADOX OF LITERATURE

All this poetry—and in their own way and to their own degree, the arts in general—say implicitly. It is only upon these assumptions that the poetic type of communication is at all possible.

---

[1] E. G. Spaulding also expresses this view in his *A World of Chance*. On page 20 he writes: "Poetry and, in particular, lyric poetry, is, in my opinion, not only the expression of what the poet thinks and feels, i.e. of insights that are much finer and more delicate than those of the average mortal, but it is also the means of the poet's communicating, or endeavouring to communicate, to other minds those meanings that are present to him. According to the theory of this chapter, then, those meanings are not the poet's invention—they are not the products of his imagination; rather they are *objective realities* in the world, to observe or discover which only the poet is a sufficiently sensitive instrument." This is a note appended to a chapter on the *Communication of Minds* and the theory of communication there developed has, the writer holds, a very definite bearing on the interpretation of the nature of literature, especially of poetry.

It is only in such a context, and with such implicit assumptions, that poetry can live. They are the "suppositions" which make its universe of discourse possible. If we should really become mechanistic, poetry would die. As, in Whitehead's view, it was the poets who kept alive this insight during the reign of mechanistic science, so also we may say that, had that reign really been as absolute as it seemed, there would have been no poetry to keep it alive. It is these suppositions of the poetic universe of discourse which constitute its metaphysics. It is in this sense that poetry is, in Coleridge's phrase, "covert metaphysics" and that all art is, in the terms of Bergson, *une métaphysique figurée*. What is more, it can only be one type of metaphysic, namely, a metaphysic that corresponds to and is expressible in dramatic language. Such a metaphysic must be, in *some* sense of that much abused word, spiritualistic. Now it may be, of course, that when this "hidden" metaphysic is uncovered, the figurative metaphysic stated in abstract terms, the abstract statements may vary. The metaphysics implied by poetry as interpreted by a Bergson or a Whitehead may differ in important respects, but one thing they have in common: they are both spiritualistic. This is seen alike in their negations and their affirmations. Poetry by its very nature negates as ultimate a materialistic and mechanistic view of reality. This it must do, for poetry, to remain poetry, implies these negations. But poetry, by its very nature, also makes certain affirmations, as we have seen—affirmations about both nature and man. These, too, imply a spiritualistic metaphysic in some sense, and these, too, any interpretation of poetry, however varied, must share. The reality which poetry expresses and symbolizes must be a reality of which values are an essential part, and this is what I mean by a spiritualistic metaphysic.

This metaphysical character of poetry raises two fundamental questions, and with the consideration of these our study of this fundamental symbolic form may properly close.

In the first place, whatever is hidden seeks the light, whatever is expressed in figure, in lower forms of generality, strives towards expressions of highest generality. Is it not the ideal of poetry to become explicit metaphysic, of figure and symbol to become plain science? Is there anything expressed symbolically which may not better be expressed literally? With this question we are brought to what has been called the "paradox of literature." And it is a paradox in the toils of which all the greater creative minds find themselves more or less caught. Poetry says what it means but it does not say *all* that it means; in attempting to say this "all" it often ceases to be poetry. The "metaphysical poets" *eo nomine*, just as the philosophical novelist and the dramatist, are always on the point of killing the goose that lays the golden egg. This is evidently a problem which, from the artist's point of view, can be solved only *in ambulando*; it is only his genius and tact which can discover the *via media*, the way between the horns of the dilemma. But from the philosopher's point of view a more reasoned and intelligible answer may be given to this question. The transition to metaphysics is inevitable, but the poet, as poet, is not the one to make it. He does well to speak in figure, to keep to his own symbolic form. For precisely in that symbolic form an aspect of reality is given which cannot be adequately expressed otherwise. It is not true that whatever is expressed symbolically can be better expressed literally. For there *is* no literal expression, but only another kind of symbol. It is not true that we should seek the blunt truth, for the so-called blunt truth has a way of becoming an untruth. It is for this very reason also that poetry, while covert metaphysics, may at the same time be "very intelligible poetry and very wild philosophy," as Coleridge said.[1] The insight into nature which poetry gives might presumably be translated into the abstract terms of a very crude and even ridiculous panpsychism. Moreover the metaphysic implicit in the poetic way of seeing and rendering things may, unless corrected by the metaphysic implicit in other symbolic forms, as for instance that of science, give us a distorted view of reality. But when all is said and done, it remains true that poetry is covert metaphysics, and it is only when its implications, critically interpreted and adequately expressed, become part of philosophy that an adequate view of the world can be achieved.

This leads us to our second problem, namely, the transition to metaphysics which the philosopher and not the poet himself may make. The problem has already been raised by

[1] Quoted from A. E. Powell, *The Romantic Theory of Poetry*, p. 86.

THE LANGUAGE OF POETRY

implication in our discussion of poetic (or aesthetic) truth. There we saw that propositions which claim truth indubitably occur in poetry. As Professor Reid holds, "out of the processes of poetry may arise propositions which have their value for discursive knowledge." These propositions (used, it is true, in a non-aesthetic way) give us at least the "breath and finer spirit of some knowledge." According to him, these pronouncements only give food for philosophical reflection. All poetry can do is present a *prima facie* case for knowledge.

This statement of the situation is, I think, properly understood, a fair one. What it means in our terms is that it is not the explicit statements of poetry that have this value—although these also may have their symbolic truth—but the implicit assertions, both positive and negative. These implications as to what reality is and what it is not, constitute the food of philosophy. Even more than this, however, the very symbolic form of poetry itself—a special form in which meaning is apprehended and communicated—has, as we have seen, certain presuppositions which are philosophically significant. From this way of envisaging reality and expressing it the philosopher, and even the scientist, may learn much. But the point must be held fast that out of the processes of poetry arise *propositions* which thus have their value for discursive thought; otherwise the above statement is misleading, if not false.

What this value is we have partly shown. Poetry is covert metaphysics, and it is this hidden metaphysics—involving both man and nature—which is significant. The full nature of these propositions—and their ultimate value for knowledge—can be shown only after we have studied other forms of symbolism such as science and religion. It is only after we have determined what they really say, implicitly as well as explicitly—what they also say by virtue of their own essential symbolic form—that we can properly evaluate the deliverances of poetry.[1] This is, of course, pre-eminently true of science. What

[1] An interesting attempt to deal with the problems of this chapter is found in *Scepticism and Poetry*, by D. G. James (George Allen & Unwin Ltd., 1937). The subtitle is, "An Essay on The Poetic Imagination." As an answer to the recent attempt "to transfer interest from the theory of the imagination to a theory of emotional and volitional response to poetry," it is very welcome. But when it comes to the fundamental issues as to what poetry says, and the truth of what it

the language of science really is, and in what way it "symbolizes" reality—what science really says, both explicitly and implicitly—are problems of moment not only for the philosophy of science itself, but for the philosophy of symbolic forms, which for us constitutes the main problem of philosophy as such. To these problems we shall now turn.

says, the writer shows himself to be in the same fundamental confusion which characterizes all recent aesthetics.

It is true that for James, as for Coleridge, imagination is the "prime condition of all knowledge whatsoever," and Kant's view that "the productive imagination is the fundamental faculty of the human soul, present in sensibility and understanding alike," is made the basis of his entire position; but when it comes to the question of the knowledge value of the poetic imagination, the position taken seems to the present writer to be vague and contradictory. Apparently, the imagination gives us knowledge and it does not. The revelation theory, we are told, "is a useless and impossible doctrine, for we do not know the ultimate truth of the universe" (p. 67). On the other hand, we are also constantly told that imagination gives us "an imaginative prehension of reality," inner and outer, and the term truth is even applied to these prehensions. "The imagination may be compared to Adam's dream—he awoke and found it truth" (p. 192). What is lacking, of course, is that which also fails in most writings on these questions—an analysis of truth and, even more, of the relation of truth to communication. Despite these fundamental difficulties in the book, it has much to offer in the way of detailed studies, especially the treatment of the *Imaginative Use of Language* in Chapter III.

CHAPTER XI

SCIENCE AND SYMBOLISM: SYMBOLISM AS A SCIENTIFIC PRINCIPLE

I

A

THE recognition of the symbolic element in science—and, in extreme cases, the notion of the whole of science as a kind of symbolism—is perhaps the chief mark of the modern self-critical attitude of science and of our sophisticated era in general. Even Kant was enlightened enough to say that "what is ordinarily thought of as examples of the pure understanding (in science) is to be reckoned mostly as examples of symbolic knowledge." More specifically still, we have such statements as that of Vaihinger, that "scientific symbol or fiction is but a special chapter in the symbolizing activity of man."[1] These are, of course, the sayings of philosophers, but they can be matched by equally emphatic assertions on the part of the greatest men of science, the names of Clerk-Maxwell and Poincaré being particularly associated with this point of view.

It is especially the mathematical or physical sciences that first became conscious of the symbolic character of their fundamental concepts and developed the notion of symbolism as a scientific principle most clearly. In his *Principien der Mechanik*, for instance, Hertz, to whom we chiefly owe this revolution in thought, describes the ideal of physical science as the prediction of future happenings. The procedure that makes this possible consists in the fact that we make for ourselves *innere Scheinbilder* or *Symbole* for the outer objects, pictures or symbols of such a character that the necessary relations of the pictures are in constant relations to the necessary relations of the pictured objects.[2] Perhaps the most enlightening illustration of the notion of scientific symbol is its application to mechanism and mechanical models. Thus Clerk-Maxwell calls the whole idea of

[1] *The Philosophy of As-If*, 1925.
[2] Heinrich Hertz in the above-mentioned book, published in 1894, is probably the first to turn the copy theory of physical knowledge into a symbol theory. The latter becomes especially the object of investigation by Pierre Duhem, *La théorie physique, son objet et sa structure*, Paris, 1906, for whom the relation of the scientific concept or symbol to sensuous experience is a fundamental problem.

"lines of force" a symbolism, and the most recent physical science has come to think of the entire notion of mechanism as a gigantic metaphor, the carrying over symbolically of the mechanical models of man to the workings of nature.

Many thoughtful scientists agree, then, with Kant that much of science at least must be reckoned as examples of symbolic knowledge. The questions at issue concern largely the nature and range of that symbolism. On these points positions vary widely. There are those who hold that only a part of science is symbolic; others that the whole of science is a form of symbolism. Many, for instance, would regard the persistent particles of mathematical physics as symbolic constructions or "fictions" enabling us to express compendiously very complicated assemblages of fact, but the knowledge of these "facts" is non-symbolic. Others would hold that these assemblages of fact are themselves constructions. Only the flow of immediate experience is non-symbolic; all the rest is symbolism. On still another point there is wide variation in opinion. Our conception of the nature of the scientific symbol depends upon our conception of the nature of science. It is in the mathematical or physical sciences, as we have seen, that the notion of scientific symbolism first developed. Is all science, in the last analysis, physical science? If so, the notion of the scientific symbol is identical with the notion of the symbol developed in this sphere. If, on the other hand, there are sciences of "life and mind" not reducible to the physical, then we shall have the concept of a "double symbolism" in science. It is necessary therefore to consider briefly, in a tentative way at least, the notion of science.

B

Science as a Symbolic Form. Definition of Science

Science, it is said, is any verifiable and communicable knowledge. As such it is presumably to be distinguished from other kinds of knowledge—such, for instance, as that given in art and religion. But serious difficulties immediately arise. There are many things in the non-scientific spheres which are communicable and so far forth verifiable, which, however, cannot be expressed in the scientific form. One may, indeed, make verifiability the criterion of science, in the narrow sense of the "empirical criterion," but even that does not define science satisfactorily. For there are parts of science—not only mathematics but parts of physical science itself—in which, as we shall see, their verifiability consists ultimately in their being "self-authenticating symbolic systems."[1]

It is frequently proposed to define science more narrowly—in terms of method. The method of science, it is said, is, broadly speaking, that of framing wider and wider generalizations based upon observation and experiment. But such a definition also has its difficulties. It applies only to what are called the generalizing sciences. It excludes history, for instance, which does not seek generalizations at all, but which deals solely with "one-time happenings." It includes with difficulty also the humanistic sciences (*Geisteswissenschaften*), in which observation in the sense of physical observation does not exist. Now, to be sure, both history and the humanistic sciences may be excluded from science, except in so far as they are found reducible to the physical, but such procedure merely begs all the questions at issue. Still less can the criterion of science be that its methods are quantitative, since, apart from the fact that there are regions of science where mathematics cannot be applied, there are aspects of mathematics also which are not concerned with quantity but rather with order.

It is hopeless to attempt to define science in any way which is not question-begging, or will satisfy even the scientists themselves. It is the most ambiguous concept in the modern world. Instead, therefore, of attempting to do so, I shall deliberately beg the question and confine the notion of science, as here used, to a single type or form. We shall take as our starting-point natural or physical science, examine the ideal or ideal form towards which it has constantly and consistently striven, and define science in terms of that form. This form is the mathematical or, perhaps better, mathematical-logical. This usage is in a sense justified. Ever since the days of Galileo the attempt has been made to bring all science under this single form—or, at least, to make this form *normative* for science. The ideal was confirmed by Kant in his *Critique of Pure Reason* and has, as an ideal, become part of modern culture. This ideal has not yet been reached, but it marks the

[1] See p. 549.

direction in which the sciences are moving. "If," as it has been said, "all the arts aspire towards the condition of music, all the sciences aspire toward the condition of mathematics." When, therefore, we speak of science as "symbolic form" we understand by that phrase the mathematical-logical way of representing or symbolizing reality. There may be limits to natural science and limits to the application of this symbolic form, but in so far as *science* seeks to represent reality it strives towards this form.

There are undoubtedly objections to this definition. Are there not, it will be asked, even within the natural sciences themselves, forms of science in which the ideal is other than mathematical? This is undoubtedly true and this fact—of a "double symbolism" within science—itself makes the problem difficult. Again, have we not the right to speak of a science of ethics, or indeed of theology, as many theologians do? Can we not speak of value sciences and their methods? In a sense, yes, but this is again a matter of definition. If science be just another name for all kinds of knowledge, this is true. But then there seems to be no point in speaking of the relation of science to religion or indeed to poetry and metaphysics, and that is precisely the kind of problem I wish to consider. It is, then, with science as one ideal, or symbolic form, among others that we are here concerned and, thus viewed, science can, I think, be defined only in this way.

We may connect this conception of science with our doctrine of bi-representationism developed in an earlier chapter.[1] There are, as we have seen, two ways of representing or expressing the world of our experiences, two ways of "picturing" reality. One seeks to retain and express qualities and values; the other abstracts from these and seeks to express only quantitative and logical relations. In other words, man speaks a double language which may be described as dramatic and scientific.

II

THE LANGUAGE OF SCIENCE

A

We may accordingly with advantage begin our study of scientific symbols and symbolism by inquiring into the nature

[1] Chapter VIII, pp. 354 ff.

SCIENCE AND SYMBOLISM

of this *scientific* language as distinguished from other types of language. As in the case of the study of the poetic symbol, so here the best procedure is to relate the symbol as a part of language to the totality of the form of language in question. A contrast of the language of science with the language of poetry will serve best to bring out the differences between the two types of symbol.

Poincaré has said that all that a scientist creates in a fact is the language in which he enunciates it. But that little "all" is in reality a very great deal—indeed, almost all of the fact. If the scientist enunciates the "fact" in the language of ordinary speech, he has already assumed the categories of that language. In naming a fact (in giving a name, let us say, to a chemical element) he assumes the category of substance (of intuitive individuality) already implied in naming. In like manner, when he enunciates the fact that "acid turns blue litmus paper red," in the very enunciation the verb and the adjective both carry with them intuitive meanings and categorical notions implied in these parts of speech. In fine, the simplest enunciation of a fact is a construction of the fact; there is present, *in the fact itself*, the entire subject-predicate apparatus of language. The language in which the scientist enunciates the fact contains a hidden metaphysic without which the fact is not a fact.

Science, then, *is* language. But, as we are told, it is "language well made." In investigating this notion of a well-made language we shall get at the heart of scientific language and ultimately of the scientific symbol.

First let us note that the notion of well made has absolutely no meaning except in relation to some notion of purpose or function. Poetic language also is extremely well made for its purpose. That it is made to evoke feelings is true, and the more subtle nuances of imagery and rhythm fulfil this function. But if our previous studies are valid the *vis poetica* also evokes the living reality as directly intuited. Now it is a commonplace that the ideal of scientific language is the opposite of all this. Its object is not to evoke feelings but to denote objects; not to conjure up a living reality but to analyse and describe entities; not allusiveness, but definiteness and exactness. On these negations all would more or less agree. It is comparatively easy to say what scientific language is not; it is not so easy to say what it is and what it is for. The reason for this lies in the fact that, as we have seen, the notion of science is itself ambiguous. If our notion of science is determined by the mathematical ideal and its procedures are made normative for science, then the nature and function of scientific language is one thing. If, on the other hand, we include within science historical knowledge and knowledge of life and mind, the nature of scientific language will be quite another thing. This ambiguity in the notion of science extends to the notion of its objective or purpose and, therefore, to the nature of the language which it employs. There are those for whom the object of science is merely to *control* and not to *understand*. There are others who maintain that its purpose is both to control and to understand,[1] but even in that case there is great uncertainty as to what understanding in the case of science is—in other words, what constitutes intelligibility.

The point is really of great importance. If the object of science is, in the words of Hertz, to predict or to control, the ideal language of science becomes that of pure notation, without any other meaning, or, in the words of Galileo, *puri nomi*. Following this ideal, the "language" of science will tend to break through speech altogether and to represent or express its objects in terms of graphs and equations. We have then manufactured languages, languages "well made" for certain purposes. It is through these languages that the scientist takes possession of his objects and operates with them. Indeed, a point is often reached where relations are expressible only in these non-linguistic forms and when expressed in language are *mis*-represented. The problem then arises where understanding in the sense of scientific intelligibility lies—in the graphs and equations or in the words. It remains true, however, that words called these equations into being and words are necessary for their interpretation. It seems that, as N. Bohr says, "in the last analysis we are compelled to express our thoughts in a word painting which we use in unanalysed fashion."[2]

[1] Science, according to Julian Huxley and N. da C. Andrade in *More Simple Science*, 1936, "always has two sides to it. On the one side it gives us knowledge and understanding of what was previously unknown or mysterious or misunderstood; on the other hand, it increases our control over nature and the forces at work in nature."

[2] On this entire question of the indispensable character of "verbal expressions" and of the "fundamental concepts of classical physics," see Bohr's *Atomic Theory and The Description of Nature*, 1934, pp. 16 and 94.

B

Science and "Common Sense." Pre-Scientific Language

The question of the relation of scientific language to natural language is closely related to the problem of science and common sense, so much in the foreground in present-day discussion.

The position of the science of the nineteenth century, well represented by T. H. Huxley, was that science is "organized," or, as sometimes stated, "glorified" common sense. Huxley, the popularizer of science, naturally believed that it is organized common sense, otherwise it could not be popularized, but the basis of this identification was deeper than this: to wit, the assumption that the language of science is nothing but the ordinary language of common sense refined and made accurate for certain special purposes. It is a truism to say that our contact with the objective world is based directly or indirectly upon our sense perceptions, and that to be intelligibly transmitted from one person to another such data must be common to many individuals. It is equally a truism that to be thus transmitted, there must be words, names, linguistic categories common to these individuals.[1] The conception of science as organized common sense involves necessarily that the language of science, if it is to communicate common perceptions, must be in principle the same as the language of common sense.

As an actual fact, however, nothing is clearer than that science, at least in its later developments, far from conforming to this assumption, violates it at every turn. When the physicist speaks of air, water, wind, heat, movement, or of space and time, he connects with these words meanings which are in no sense the same as in pre-scientific language. Even more is this true of the invented words, such as energy, entropy, etc., for which there is no correlate in common sense and which cannot be expressed in its language without misrepresentation of their meanings. Finally—and this is perhaps the most important point of all—the break of science with common sense and its language is in the realms of modern physics complete. The analysis of matter in the last century has, as Mr. H. G. Wells

[1] Chapter VI, pp. 248 ff., the conditions of intelligible communication.

says, "reached a point where it has in any human sense ceased to be wonderful. It is simply incomprehensible. Every statement is a paradox; every formula an outrage on common sense. . . . In the deeps or heights of physics—for one word is as good as another where all direction is lost—I find my mind sinking down at last, exhausted of effort in much the mood of Albrecht Dürer's Melancholia."[1] This is not merely the impatience of the layman in science; it expresses also the mature conviction of many specialists in physics—namely, that the break between science and common sense is complete—in our terms, that there is no longer any possibility of translation of the manufactured languages of science into the natural language of common sense. The recognition of this fact has given rise to what is quite commonly called the "crisis of modern physics." The significance of this crisis for a general philosophy of science we shall consider later.[2] Here it is of interest for us merely as confirming the conception of the language of science which we have been developing. The assumption of the nineteenth century, that scientific intelligibility, or comprehensibility, is the same as the intelligibility of common sense, has been shown by later developments to be wholly untrue.

C

Scientific Language and Dramatic Language

Science *is* language well made. It is not the language of common sense, however glorified. Indeed, in its full development it tends to break through all natural language and to become an artificial language—a language made for very definite and specific purposes.

As the opposite of poetry is not prose, but science, so the contrast of languages is between the poetic and the scientific. If we connect the poetic with the dramatic, as in the preceding chapter, we may say that the ideal of scientific language is to be *un*dramatic, and that when science takes on the dramatic form of expression, we have to that extent a mixing of linguistic idioms and of symbolic forms.

By this character of scientific language is meant that it seeks

---

[1] *The World of William Clissold*, p. 53.   [2] P. 540 f.

to extrude all the intuitive elements of language—the element of individuality in the noun, the activity meanings of the verb and the vital values of the adjective. In more philosophical terms, it tends to extrude the notions of substance and activity (causality) and to substitute the notion of functional relations. Finally, as it tends to exclude all qualities, so this language of science is well made only when it also eliminates all values and value terms. For this ideal of science all such language is pre-scientific and anthropomorphic in character.

From this standpoint, the extrusion of teleology and teleological categories from science is seen to be the exclusion of the dramatic from the language of science, for teleology is essentially dramatic. And it is precisely at this point that the ambiguity of the notion of science and the mixed character of its language becomes most evident. In certain domains—of life and of mind—it seems impossible to express relations significantly except in these terms. Teleology is therefore often described as a *heuristic* principle in science, especially in the sciences of life and mind. By this is meant that, unless we envisage the processes of life and mind *as though* they were directed towards ends, we can neither apprehend them nor adequately express them. The idea of "evolution by natural selection through struggle for existence, leading to the survival of the fit," is an essentially dramatic idea, involving "purpose" of some kind and can actually be expressed *only in dramatic language*. I venture to suggest also—the point to be developed more fully later—that it is impossible to express more general cosmological propositions in any other than the dramatic form. The notion of the universe as "running down," or "building up," are propositions of this type. The notion of the degradation of energy is a teleology even if it is a magnificent dysteleology. The merely mathematical formulas "say nothing"; it is only when translated into dramatic language that they say anything significant for our world view. This question of the nature of scientific language is of the utmost importance. Science is "language well made," and the question what this language is and what it is made for is fundamental. On this depends the entire question of what "science says." If the language of science is, in its ideal form, merely mathematical, then what it says is doubtless very important but also very limited. If, on the other hand, the language of science also includes the dramatic element, if, in other terms, it also apprehends and expresses "qualities and values," then what it says is meaningful in a quite different way, and scientific intelligibility is of another order. In this latter case, what "science says" is not only vastly more far-reaching, but of a wholly different significance for human life and thought.

III

THE SCIENTIFIC SYMBOL: ITS NATURE AND FUNCTION

A

With this preliminary account of the language of science we may hope to come to some understanding of the nature of the symbolic function connected with it. The tendency of science to break through natural language, to create a non-linguistic idiom, whether for the possession or manipulation of its objects, brings us directly to our problem, for it is precisely in the ideal of a *purer notation* that for many the true nature of the scientific symbol, as distinguished from other types, appears.

The symbol in science, we are told, is different from the symbol in aesthetics. The latter is, so to speak, a sample and is internal to the thing symbolized, whereas the scientific symbol is merely a label and external to the thing symbolized. Symbol in science really means nothing more than a name and a label. It is for this reason that science tends to become nominalistic in its theory of language. The ideal of science, then, would be to become wholly "symbolic."[1] This is, indeed, one theory of the scientific symbol and the one perhaps intrinsic to the mathematical-physical sciences. On the view of science which identifies the scientific symbolic form with the mathematical-logical method, this theory has become the dominant, if not the only, orthodox conception. In terms of our discussions of an earlier chapter, scientific symbols are wholly extrinsic and substitutional. Intrinsic symbols, whether descriptive or insight symbols, are wholly foreign to scientific symbolism. We shall not accept this view forthwith, but rather examine empirically the notion of symbolism as it has developed in modern natural

[1] Chapter X, pp. 475 ff.

science. Let us then begin with the question of the relation of the scientific symbol to intuition.

B

The Scientific Symbol and Intuition. The Question of Intrinsic Symbols

In developing this notion of the scientific symbol we may begin with a definition by Höffding in which he seeks to distinguish the symbolism of natural science from that of religion and poetry. "The symbolism of natural science," he writes, "sheds light on a complex material phenomenon by means of a simple material phenomenon."[1] This characterization of the scientific symbol is a special application of the more general concept of the symbol. It is characteristic of all symbols that images and ideas are taken from narrower and more intuitible relations and used as expressions for more ideal relations which, because of their pervasiveness and ideality, cannot be directly expressed. Natural science is full of symbols in this sense. Thus when Clerk-Maxwell says that the whole idea of "lines of force" is symbolism, what he means is that the simple intuitible geometric lines are taken to stand for non-intuitible "forces." It is symbols of this sort which Kant has in mind when he contrasts symbolic knowledge with knowledge of the understanding, or non-symbolic. Again, spatial models of the atom or the ether represent the non-intuitible by images taken from narrower, more intuitible relations. It is symbols of this sort which Vaihinger has in mind when he identifies symbol with fiction, and speaks of the scientific symbol as but a special chapter in the symbolizing activity of man. Scientific symbols of this sort are then directly connected with sensuous intuition. The problem immediately arises whether such symbols are in any sense *internal* to the thing symbolized; in other words, whether they are intrinsic and give us insight into the nature of the thing symbolized. Such was the view of the science of the nineteenth century, for which to *understand* a phenomenon or event was to make a model of it. But there is not only the question of whether such symbols shed light on the complex material phenomenon,

[1] *Ob. cit.* p. 97.

but *what* light they shed; not only whether they are in some sense internal to the thing symbolized, but in what sense they are internal. Now it is precisely this question, as we shall see presently, that constitutes the crux of the problem of scientific symbolism. It is part of our present scientific consciousness to recognize the "fictional" character of such symbols; that they are "factitious" concepts—made and constructed for certain purposes; in other words, are taken from the realm of the sensible and intuitible and applied to the non-sensible and non-intuitible. In this process they must be *moulded*. This process of moulding or construction is brought out clearly by the element of *distortion* present in all such scientific symbols. To this aspect of the symbol we may now turn.

C

Distortion and the Scientific Symbol. The "Moulding" of the Intuition

There is, as we have seen, no possible type of symbol which does not contain some element of "fiction" (of the *factitious*, to use Descartes' terms), and which does not in some way and to some degree "distort" reality. In the case of the aesthetic symbol the artist seeks to achieve deviations from reality in order, paradoxically, to represent reality better or to penetrate more deeply into it. In the case of the scientific symbol the scientist also deviates from the intuitive, phenomenal reality—in this case, however, to *explain* and ultimately to control reality and predict happenings. In the case of science we call such distortion "moulding of an hypothesis."

A significant illustration of this principle of distortion is found in the physiological conceptions of the seventeenth and eighteenth centuries. "The human body," writes La Mettrie, "is a machine that winds its own springs. . . . If these springs," he continues, "differ among themselves, these differences consist only in their position and in their degrees of strength and never in their nature; wherefore the soul is but a principle of motion or material and sensible part of the brain which can be regarded, without fear of error(!), as the mainspring of the whole machine, having a visible influence on the

SCIENCE AND SYMBOLISM

parts."[1] The kinship of such a case of distortion with aesthetic distortion is immediately evident. A machine that winds its own springs is as much a fiction as a thinking reed. Or, again, the symbol of the ether as a "perfect jelly"—as an imponderable substance which has the qualities of a physical, intuitible object, but is perfect in the sense of being frictionless—is a perfect illustration of the moulding or distortion of the intuition in order that it may stand for or represent the non-intuitible.[2] In common with the aesthetic the scientific symbol deviates from intuited reality, but whereas the aesthetic has its eye largely on the qualitative aspects of things, the scientific is preoccupied almost wholly with the quantitative. Whereas the former seeks insight into values and value relations, the latter does not care whether reality is made more meaningful and intelligible or not, if only by its means objects may be controlled or operated with.

Both the relation of the scientific symbol to intuition (and the moulding or distortion of intuition involved) come out admirably in contemporary concepts of the physical world. "If," writes Jeans, "we must have a model of the physical world the electron and proton must be represented by the simplest things known to us, tiny hard spheres. The model works well for a time and then suddenly breaks in our hands. . . . A hard sphere always has a definite position in space; the electron apparently has not. A hard sphere takes up a very definite amount of room; an electron—well, perhaps the best answer is that it takes up the whole of space." The atom thus has to give place to something else, namely, the electron, which is no longer an object of "imaginative sense," but only a symbol. For the electron is not to be conceived of as a correlate of the senses that give us most conviction of certainty—sight and touch—and is definable by no sense at all that we possess in distinction from other senses.[3]

The preceding illustration is significant for two reasons. In the first place it brings out clearly the nature of the intuitive or intrinsic symbol. If we must have a model! Yes; we must have

---
[1] La Mettrie, *Man a Machine* (English translation by G. C. Bussey), p. 93.
[2] See Chapter IX, p. 417.
[3] *The Universe Around Us*, pp. 133-4. See for comments upon this passage Thomas Whittaker, *Prolegomena to a New Metaphysic*, p. 46.

one if we are to "understand" in a certain way. But such a model is always partly fictional. It is for this reason that, in the end, it suddenly "breaks in our hands." It sheds light, but only a partial light. In the end we must pass over into non-intuitible concepts and these can be expressed only mathematically. It is this, as we shall see presently, that has happened in modern physics. But that is not the point which we wish to emphasize at the moment. It is rather that scientific concepts of the type we have been considering are symbols in the sense that they are intuitively interpretable. It is at the point where they "break in our hands" that this character ceases and symbolism in another sense enters in. This point is where we pass from the intermediate world to the world of the infinitely great and the infinitely little. Not only do our concepts become more and more symbolic, but the nature of the symbol and of the symbolic relation changes in character. This aspect of scientific symbolism will be developed more fully in a later connection. Here we are concerned wholly with the moulding of the intuition to represent symbolically the scientific concept.

D

The Scientific Symbol and the Scientific Concept. (Theories of "Principle" and Theories of "Construction")

Clear thinking with regard to scientific symbolism is impossible until we have considered the relation of the symbol to the concept. There is much confusion on this point. One tendency in present-day thought uses the notions of symbol and concept interchangeably and thus makes all scientific knowledge symbolic. Another view tends to confine the notion of symbol to only one type of scientific concept and thus speaks of non-symbolic scientific knowledge.

Scientific concepts are clearly divisible into two kinds, those which deal with things or entities and those which deal with relations. The concepts of atom, electron, ether, etc., refer to supersensible entities; concepts like those of gravitation and entropy to relations and to rules of procedure. Einstein has the same distinction in mind when he distinguishes between theories of principle and theories of construction. To the latter belong the theories of ether and electrons, etc.; his own theory of relativity is a theory of principle. Now the importance of this distinction lies in the fact that only theories of construction are concerned with symbols in the sense of intuition; the latter are concerned with non-intuitible relations. If, then, the latter type of concepts be described as symbolic it can only be in a different sense of symbol. It is this different sense which Cassirer has in mind when he describes the entire tendency of science as the movement from theories of construction to theories of principle, or, as he states it, from schematism to symbolism. In his terminology "schematism" describes the sensuous schemes or models by which it is sought to represent or "picture" reality; "symbolism" refers to the mathematical rules or formulas by which relations rather than things are represented. The entire development of modern science is from substance to function; and understanding, in the scientific sense, or scientific intelligibility, consists solely in mathematical-logical relations.[1] The question of the relation of symbol to concept in science may then perhaps be answered in the following way. The sensuous schemes or models with which we seek to picture the non-intuitible are symbols of relations expressible conceptually in mathematical terms. The mathematical formulas (and the theories of principle which they express) are symbolic of reality in another and more fundamental sense. Science itself is a symbolic form—not a picture or representation of reality but a symbolization of it. The sense in which this latter statement is true will appear if we consider the historical development of the symbol concept in science. To this we shall now turn.

IV

DEVELOPMENT OF THE CONCEPT OF THE SYMBOL IN PHYSICAL SCIENCE. MATHEMATICAL SYMBOLISM

A

The history of scientific concepts makes it entirely clear that physical science began with a literal or copy theory of such con-

[1] *Op. cit.*, Vol. III, p. 545.

cepts. The outstanding notions of early Greek science—those of the atom, the psyche, energy, etc.—all involve the analogical transfer of an image from the domain of perception into that of the imperceptible; and in all cases there was included the further notion that the image constitutes a copy or picture of the thing for which it stands. This character of the scientific concept continues far into the later history of science and is part of the symbolic notion as it functions to-day. Modern physical science, beginning roughly with Galileo, changed the character of the concepts but not the fundamental epistemological position. It stripped off the secondary qualities of things, leaving only the primary qualities of extension and motion, and extruded all symbols of an "anthropomorphic" character. It developed what we call the mechanical conception of the physical world. But this was simply to change the metaphor, so to speak. Here, too, images were taken from the perceptible domain and projected into the imperceptible, and with this procedure the *literal* view of the scientific concept was implied.

Until recently, then, this was the almost universal view of the scientific concept. The Newtonian world view, with its terrestrial and celestial mechanics, was accepted as the most perfect illustration of scientific language and as the ideal to which all types of scientific language should conform. Theoretical physics from the beginning had been a synthesis of phenomena in terms of mechanics. The physical properties of heat, sound, and light were expressed by the same mathematical formulas which express the motions of a wave in fluids. To distinguish them there were assigned different *names* to the substance involved, as a molecule of air, a corpuscle of light or ether, but whatever names might be given them, however they might be distinguished, there was assigned to all of them the common attribute of mass and inertia which is the only essential coefficient in a mechanical equation. With this scientific world picture there went a definite conception of the nature of that picture. To know or to *understand* a physical happening in nature was equivalent to the ability to make a mechanical physical model or picture of it. "Do we understand a phenomenon of nature or do we not?" asks Sir William Thomson. "The question," he replies, "appears to me to turn on another question—whether we can construct a mechanical model which represents the happening in all its parts."[1] The important point here is the phrase "represents the happening in all its parts"—a clear expression of the copy notion of the scientific concept as distinguished from the symbolic. Scientific understanding or intelligibility was bound up with this notion.

The great change in the notion of the scientific concept came with modern electro-dynamics. The same thinker who first made possible, through his discoveries, the new electro-dynamic world pictures also revolutionized the theory of the scientific concept. With him the copy theory was definitely abandoned. The ideal of science is no longer to picture but to predict, and the procedure which makes prediction possible is that we make for ourselves *innere Scheinbilder* or *Symbole* of such a character that the necessary relations of the pictures or concepts correspond to necessary relations in the objects. The function of the scientific concept is no longer to picture reality but to symbolize it. There are two aspects of this revolution which must be emphasized. The first of these is the changed rôle of the mechanical model in scientific knowledge and understanding; the second is the development of the symbolic consciousness in science, or of the notion of symbolism as a scientific principle.

To understand a phenomenon in nature is, in the first place, no longer dependent upon our ability to construct a mechanical model of it. The electro-dynamic theory of the field abandons the intuitible model entirely. More than this, the mechanical models themselves are reduced to the rôle of "dummies," to use Eddington's phrase. "Our electrons, however we may like to talk about them, are merely phantoms, just a dummy." It is not the mechanical models that are required for understanding, but the mathematical formulas in which these dummies function. Just *what is* understood by these formulas, what the mathematical equations "say," is another question to be considered later; the point here is that *with modern science mathematics tends to become the fundamental symbolism.*

It is in connection with the phenomena of light that this fundamental change is particularly in evidence. The corpuscular theory of Newton, according to which light consists in very

---

[1] *Lectures on Molecular Dynamics and the Wave Theory of Light*, Baltimore, 1884, p. 131. Cited by Duhem, *La théorie physique*, etc., p. 112, as illustrative of the earlier position. See also Cassirer's discussion, *op. cit.*, Vol. III, p. 537.

small particles, proved untenable and gave way to the undulatory theory. of Huyghens based upon an analogy taken from perceptible phenomena, and giving rise to the construct of the ether as the substance which has these waves. Contradictions arose in the predicates of this hypothetical ether which could not be eliminated. Physics was led ever more deeply into paradoxes, and all *ad hoc* hypotheses invented to solve the difficulties only served to lead more deeply into the morass. Finally there came the electro-dynamic theory of the field. The characteristic here is that the reality which is designated as the "field" is no longer a complex of physical "things" but an expression for a system of relations. But the important thing for us is that the notion of the intuitible is completely abandoned and the entire notion of the scientific concept is changed.[1] This change, which we may take as an outstanding illustration of the movement from "schematism" to "symbol," illustrates also the change in the modern symbolic consciousness of science. The symbol symbolizes not things but relations. This will become clearer when we examine the development of the "language" of mathematics in science.

B

Mathematical Symbolism: The "Language" of Mathematics

So far as *physical* science is concerned, understanding of a phenomenon of nature is no longer held to be dependent upon intuition and intuitive symbols. It is the mathematical formulas in which the "dummies" function through which nature is understood. In order to grasp the full significance of this notion and its bearing upon the general philosophy of symbolism, it is necessary to consider briefly the nature of mathematics and mathematical symbolism. There can be little doubt that the development and refinement of scientific language is coincident with the development of the language of mathematics.

First of all let us consider the sense in which mathematics *is* a language. At the beginning the equation is but a form

[1] For an excellent presentation of this development in detail see Cassirer, *op. cit.*, Vol. III, pp. 542 ff.

of the syllogism. The difference may be expressed in this way. Speech contains symbols that *mean* something as well as *designate* something—in our terms, expressive as well as designatory signs.[1] Mathematics is a language in signs or symbols which, *in themselves*, mean nothing.

Mathematical symbols may be divided for our purposes into three groups: (*a*) Signs of constant or fixed meaning such as, for instance, numbers 2, 7, 15. (*b*) Secondly, signs as representing elementary arithmetical operations ($+$, $-$, $=$, $\div$). (*c*) Thirdly, signs of systematic universality, this last expressed by letters $A + B = B + A$. In principle, the above and similar formulas make possible the abandonment of language. It required, of course, a logical calculus before relations of implication could be expressed by signs, but with the above symbols the main steps were taken. This is the decisive step, namely, when it became possible to express entire mathematical statements without language. A completely word-free logical calculus became possible with signs which in themselves mean nothing. In the older mathematics (of Gauss, for instance) intuition still remained, but in the later formalistic mathematics we have merely manipulation of signs. It is, however, precisely this "symbolic"—and not the intuitive mathematics—which forms the basis of modern physics.[2]

It is at this point, then, that we see the revolution in thought, the transformation of the symbolic consciousness of modern science. Modern physics has not only transformed our basal physical conceptions, but also transformed our conception of the relation of these concepts or symbols to reality. These fundamental concepts or symbols are not capable of, nor need they be susceptible of, intuitive realization, and of expression in the natural language of intuition. Its symbols are in this sense intrinsically impenetrable and unintelligible. Their intelligibility is wholly instrumental.

In a sense physics has always to a degree worked with such *impenetrable* hypotheses. Even the classical Newtonian physics made use of the hypothesis of *actio ad distans*, which seemed to

---

[1] Chapter IX, p. 407.

[2] For an excellent discussion of mathematical symbolism from the standpoint of the philosopher, see Oscar Becker, "Das Symbolische in der Mathematik," *Blätter für Deutsche Philosophie*, Band I, Heft 4.

some of Newton's contemporaries, for instance Huyghens, unintelligible. Nevertheless, in the classical physics the theoretical construction follows the natural process into its geometrically intuited details. The fundamental mechanical concepts of force, inertia, etc., purport to be generalizations of concretely intuited phenomena. Since the middle of the eighteenth century, however, the picture has gradually changed. The physics of the field, of the nineteenth and twentieth centuries (from Faraday and Maxwell to the Relativity theory), presents in increasing degree self-authenticating formal systems which are not any longer in their details intuitively interpretable. This reaches its culmination in the completely unintuitible character of the Quantum theory, where even the relatively most intuitive theory of Schroedinger already operates with oscillation signs in many-dimensional space.

The significance of this development is to be found at two points, namely, the completely unintuitible character of the concepts and symbols in the later physics and the development of self-authenticating formal systems which are no longer intuitibly interpretable in their details. If the concepts of physics are thus completely unintuitible it follows of necessity that the language of physics cannot be translated into the language of common sense. In that case, science is in a dilemma. If it remains in the region of unintuitible mathematical concepts or symbols, it can operate but it can "say" nothing. If the scientist attempts to communicate his conceptions in ordinary intuitible language, he inevitably says what he does not mean, either too little or too much. He even runs a grave risk of saying what is "untrue." This dilemma is so real that it has even given rise to the notion of a crisis in modern physics, and its significance becomes of the utmost importance when we come to the question of what science and its symbolic form "really says." But in the second place, if scientific systems are no longer intuitibly interpretable in their details, but become self-authenticating formal systems, it is evident that the empirical criterion of verifiability is not the ultimate notion of verifiability in science. Science in its ultimate reaches also passes beyond the observable and intuitive, and verification must include the notion of self-authentication, an authentication which takes place in mathematical discourse itself. This does not mean that science does not start from the intuitible or that it does not return to the intuitible in certain details, but it does mean that it is the self-authenticating character of the formal systems themselves which constitutes a large part of the notion of verification in science. This means that not only has the notion of the symbol changed in modern science but, to a degree, and in a very significant way, the notion of verifiability also.

It is, however, the first point which I wish to emphasize here, namely, the dilemma in which science finds itself. If it works with completely unintuitible concepts it merely *operates*, but *says* nothing. This situation may be stated in another way. The language of mathematics is, as Vossler says, *pronominal*, that is, it speaks, if it speaks at all, only in pronouns, only in substitutional symbols. With such symbols the ideal of pure notation is achieved, but the notation is *so pure* that science is no longer talking about the objects from which it started—about the "real" world—but about a world of its own in which the things talked about are no longer the things known by intuition but determined by definition. In other words, on this view it becomes difficult to determine what it is that science is talking about and what it actually says, a question which is of extreme importance for the "philosophy of science."

V

SYMBOL IN THE SCIENCES OF LIFE AND MIND. THE PRINCIPLE OF DOUBLE SYMBOLISM

A

The conception of science as an elaborate symbolism—in the sense of a system of signs or labels for relations—has been developed largely in the exact sciences of mathematics and mathematical physics. If we should base our theory of scientific symbolism on the physical sciences alone, the nature of that theory would be more or less predetermined. It is, however, when we come to the sciences of life and mind that the problem becomes more complicated and the solution more difficult.

There is, to be sure, one fairly easy way of solving it. We may maintain that the ideal of science is the mathematical-logical and look upon all those aspects of life and mind not expressible in this symbolic form as more or less pseudo-science. We may, for instance, as Sir James Jeans seems to hold, maintain that the universe is *exhaustively* analysable in terms of pure mathematics, and only in so far as that analysis is carried out have we science. But such a solution is too simple; in fact, it seems to be the very reverse of the truth. To say that the concepts of the mathematical physical sciences are those which are most suitable for the purposes of the biologist and physiologist is to fly in the face of the most obvious facts. Living organisms and conscious minds are, to be sure, a part of nature, but the concepts of nature by means of which their *character as living and conscious* is investigated and expressed are certainly not mathematical-physical.[1] It is at this point that the problem, already raised in our discussion of the definition of science, becomes pressing. There are two possible solutions. Either we may identify science, as symbolic form, with the mathematical-logical method and exclude from science, and its form, all language and symbols of other types; or we may broaden the notion of science and include in its language and symbols those of a non-mathematical "dramatic" kind. In any case all rendition of reality involves a double symbolism; it is a secondary question whether we shall call both forms scientific. Let us proceed, then, to a consideration of this double symbolism.

B

The Concepts of the Living and the Mental

The history of science presents us with a paradoxical situation which has often been commented upon. Whereas, as we have seen, knowledge of the physical world proceeded by means of metaphors or "symbols" taken from the living and mental, knowledge of the latter proceeded by means of symbols taken from the bodily and physical.[2] The manner in which the first

---

[1] See on this question C. E. M. Joad, *Philosophical Aspects of Modern Science*, p. 65. (Published by George Allen & Unwin Ltd.).
[2] This paradoxical situation is described by Kemp Smith, *Prolegomena to an Idealist Theory of Knowledge*, pp. 126-27.

concepts of physical science were formed has already been indicated; it was the final extrusion of these dramatic or anthropomorphic notions which constituted the "triumph" of modern physical science. In the case of the knowledge of life and mind, knowledge proceeded by the transfer of physical concepts (such as psyche, breath) from the physical to the living and mental. It has not yet been realized that the triumph of modern psychical science might possibly be the extrusion of the physical mythology from this region. The situation does seem paradoxical, but in reality it is not. The primary way of apprehending and expressing the living and the mental is the dramatic. The pre-scientific or mythical consciousness knows only this type of category and this form of symbol. But there developed also in the pre-scientific consciousness another function and with it another language—the function, namely, of manipulation and control, and the language necessary for this function. This "physical" language with its spatial character was made to manipulate the bodily object, but with the perfection of this instrument it was only a matter of time when it should be transferred analogically to the living and the mental also. Thus developed a *dual language* and a *double symbolism*, and it is the presence of this double symbolism in science which makes of science an ambiguous symbolic form.

C

The Double Symbolism in the Science of the "Living"

This double symbolism in the science of the "living" is recognized by Bergson and considered by him as significant for a general theory of knowledge. He notes it specifically in connection with theories of instinct. "A very significant fact," he tells us, "is the swing to and fro of scientific theories of instinct —between likening it to an intelligence lapsed and reducing it to a pure mechanism. Each of these theories of explanation triumphs in its criticism of the other, the first when it shows us that instinct cannot be a mere reflex, the other when it declares that instinct is something different from intelligence, even fallen into unconsciousness. What can this mean but that there are *two symbolisms* (italics mine), equally acceptable in certain respects and in other respects equally inadequate to their objects?" He then continues: "the concrete explanation, no longer scientific but metaphysical, must be sought along quite another path, not in the direction of intelligence, but in that of sympathy."[1]

We are concerned here neither with the question of an adequate explanation of instinct, nor yet again with Bergson's inference that the explanation must ultimately be found in a metaphysical concept of sympathy, but solely with the fact of a double symbolism and its significance. Of the fact itself, I think there can be no doubt. Not only in the case of the specific phenomenon of instinct, but throughout the entire range of biological and mental descriptions, this principle of the double symbolism reigns. In biology it is the source of that perennial conflict of point of view and of method so inadequately expressed in the opposition between mechanism and vitalism. For a large number of biologists it is impossible to express the truth of life and mind except in terms of a non-physical and non-mathematical symbolism. "The very nomenclature of biology," J. S. Haldane writes, "embodies the conception that life, in whatever form it may occur, occurs as a specific whole in which the parts and actions are essentially related to one another and cannot be isolated without destroying their nature."[2] In the same context he makes it clear that the very essence of these wholes is to be self-regulative. All this is, of course, a form of teleology, although not the kind of teleology which necessitates a *conscious* agent adapting a means to a consciously desired end. The important point, however, for our present purpose is that only by such nomenclature—by means of a teleological symbolism—can the nature of the living be expressed.

This question of the nomenclature of biology, and the character of its symbolism, is so important as to require further

[1] *Creative Evolution* (English translation), p. 175.
[2] *The Sciences and Philosophy* (*Gifford Lectures*), p. 92. It is interesting that Professor Haldane's son, J. B. S. Haldane, while recognizing that life and mind cannot be reduced to the physical, and recognizing that aspects of these forms of reality cannot be expressed in the symbolism of natural science, denies that science can work with any other symbols than the mathematical-physical. See in this connection his recent book, *The Causes of Evolution*. J. S. Haldane's *The Philosophical Basis of Biology* also goes into the problems of biological knowledge. Also Joseph Needham, *Order and Life*, especially Chapter I.

comment. The Darwinian formula of evolution, "Natural selection, acting on chance variations, through the struggle for existence, leading to the survival of the fit," is an excellent example of the symbolisms of biology. First of all it is clear that the notion *is* essentially symbolic in character. It is formed by taking the human notion of selection (artificial selection) and "moulding it" to apply to "nature." "Struggle" for existence and "survival" are essentially dramatic terms which symbolize processes in which there is no struggle in the primary sense of effort to realize ends; survival of the fit, it is said, does not really refer to fitness in any value sense but is only a symbol for non-value relations. What now does this symbol symbolize? On the view that the essence of science is the mathematical-logical method, this dramatic form of rendering the facts is really fictional in character; the ideal would be a rendering of the facts in a purely physical or mathematical language. But let us see, then, what follows. All that makes the *living*, in the sense of immediate intuitive experience, is eliminated; this *ideal* language could not really express it at all. But even more follows. It is only as expressed in this dramatic language that the theory of evolution says very much. Stripped of this "verbiage" evolution becomes, as Lloyd Morgan sees, merely a *name* for a succession of events and really says nothing more. It is true, as Bergson and many others have pointed out, that there are parts of biology in which a physical-chemical language is spoken—and only by such symbols can the living process be manipulated, in so far as it is manipulatible at all—but there are also other parts (namely, those in which we are concerned with a unique *series* of events which constitute a history) where another language and a different symbolism are demanded. If it is true, as Bergson maintains, that "embryogenists and naturalists believe much less readily in the physico-chemical character of vital actions than do the physiologists, it is partly due to the fact that when they speak a purely physical language the essential quality of the vital escapes their symbols."[1]

The general view that the organic is characterized by a collection of distinctive and irreducible "vital" properties constitutes a strong current in present-day biology. With it goes, however, the further consequence, only dimly realized at

[1] H. Bergson, *Creative Evolution* (English translation), p. 36.

present, that it has its own language and its own distinctive symbols. This situation is affirmed by Professor George Birkhoff in an article contained in the volume, *Science and the New World*, when he says each science represents a distinct level and "each level is a natural one in the sense that it possesses its own special fundamental intuitive language which is largely if not completely independent of that used on the other levels." The only rational view, he holds, is "to regard these levels as having co-ordinate reality." The issue between the mechanists and the Neo-vitalists in biology is then, from one important point of view, an issue between two types of language and two forms of symbols. What the opponent of the mechanist is really saying is that the level of the living possesses its own "intuitive language" which, if not "completely independent of that" of the physical level, certainly cannot be translated into physical language. Biology has its own nomenclature because only by the use of that nomenclature can the nature of the living be expressed.

D

The Double Symbolism in the Domain of the Mental

What is true of the living is *a fortiori* true of what we call the mental or the conscious. This, as Lloyd Morgan pointed out convincingly, can be expressed only in dramatic language. Mind or consciousness is the centre of drama because it is the centre of values. In this sense the "soul" is, as Dilthey said, to be "understood" and not primarily to be described like things. The only intelligible language here is the dramatic, and the only adequate symbolism the type of symbol which grows out of that language. If biology has its special nomenclature which embodies a certain conception of life, so psychology has its nomenclature which embodies a certain conception of mind. If the former embodies the conception of a specific whole in which all the parts are necessarily related, the latter embodies the notion of consciousness as a centre of meanings and values. But here, again, we have the problem of psychology as a science. If we insist that science cannot work with any language except the physical or with any symbols except the mathematical-logical, then we must conclude that the mental cannot be "expressed."

The issue here presented in the form of problems of language and symbolism will be readily recognized as the basal philosophical problem in psychology to-day. Corresponding to the issue of mechanism versus Neo-vitalism in biology, is the issue between behaviouristic and all non-behaviouristic psychologies of whatever kind. From the standpoint of science and its methodology, behaviourism is essentially the assertion that there is no scientific language except the physical and no scientific symbol except the mathematical-physical. What the opponent of behaviourism is really saying is that the level of the mental possesses its own intuitive language, which, if not wholly independent of the physical, cannot be translated into physical language. Psychology has its own nomenclature because only by the use of that nomenclature can the nature of the mental be expressed.[1] This is what the anti-behaviourist means when he says that even the arguments designed to make consciousness superfluous presuppose that we know what consciousness is, and that we have language in terms of which that knowledge may be expressed. If, as Laird says, anyone who denies this is beyond the pale of argument, what is really meant is that the denial places the one who denies outside the realm of intelligible discourse.[2]

The importance of this problem of a double symbolism in science is two-fold. There is, of course, first the very significant question whether the real nature of the living and the mental can be expressed in any other than dramatic nomenclature, whether, in other words, these aspects of reality can be expressed at all in "physical" or mathematical language and their symbolic forms. But there is a second, and in a sense much more

[1] In thus contrasting behaviouristic with non-behaviouristic psychologies, I am aware that there are those who call themselves behaviourists, such as McDougall, who do not profess this extreme form. Quite apart from the question whether anything is gained by the use of the term behaviourism when it does not involve this principle, certainly behaviourism, from a metalogical standpoint, means this. It is bound up with the notion of "physical language"—with the idea that only propositions which refer to sensuously observable entities are empirically verifiable and, therefore, that only such propositions can enter into science.

[2] For a fuller discussion of this entire subject, see my study of the conditions of intelligibility and intelligible discourse, *The Intelligible World*, Chapter V, especially Section IV, one of those conditions being the keeping of the categories of the living and the mental intact.

important question—namely, whether both symbolisms belong to the language of science. It is not a question of there being two languages and a double symbolism. That is merely a matter of fact. Nor is there any question of both being necessary for any adequate rendering of reality. That also is a matter of fact. The issue is merely whether both symbolisms are part of the language of science. Whatever answer be given to this question, the implications are far-reaching and have an important bearing upon the question of "what science says." If science has but one symbolic form, the mathematical-logical, then obviously it says very much less and speaks much less significantly than if it has the double symbolism. The more its language is developed the less it really says. If, on the other hand, science uses also dramatic language and the symbols which develop from that language, then it says very much more and speaks much more significantly from the standpoint of the philosophy of life. To these problems we shall return in the sequel. For the moment, however, we must turn to the question of the interpretation of the scientific symbol. Having examined the nature of scientific symbols we must pass to the principles and theories of their interpretation.

VI

INTERPRETATION OF THE SCIENTIFIC SYMBOL: MEANING OF INTERPRETATION IN SCIENCE

A

The notion of symbolism as a scientific principle has already been defined as the recognition, on the part of the modern scientific consciousness, that, paraphrasing Kant's statement, scientific concepts, formerly reckoned as copies or models of reality, are now to be reckoned mostly as symbols, and that scientific knowledge is, in large part, at least, symbolic knowledge. The establishment of this principle brings with it immediately the problem of the interpretation of these symbols; in other words, the determination of what the scientific symbol *says*.

It has been our contention all along that the scientific symbol is but "a special chapter in the symbolizing activity of man," and that, consequently, the principles of symbolism, as developed for symbols in general, apply in principle to scientific symbols also. This is true, but as we have also pointed out, true only in the most general way. The fundamental differences between the aesthetic or poetic symbol, on the one hand, and the scientific, on the other, mean necessarily differences in the nature and methods of interpretation.

It is customary to distinguish between two meanings of interpretation in science. The first is a limited technical meaning. A question of interpretation in this sense arises whenever we have the problem of what a scientific concept or construct means, that is, whether it stands for or refers to some existent, although unintuitible, object or entity, or whether it is merely a dummy functioning in a mathematical equation. In view of the fact that such physical concepts or formulas represent operations or formal logical properties, it is a real problem in the philosophy of science how far we may go in the "free rendering" of such concepts; in other words, how far we may substitute for these non-intuitible concepts intuitible entities— whether, and in what sense, the atom, the electron, or the quanta *exist*. This we may describe as the expansion or elucidation of the scientific symbol-concept. But there is also a second meaning to interpretation in science. To the limited more technical meaning must be added a more general philosophical significance. Interpretation involves the bringing back of the concepts or formulas of science to the immediate experience from which they started and the determination of the degree to which these concepts express or represent the reality experienced; but in so doing we inevitably interpret and evaluate the scientific as a *way* of expressing or representing the reality. This may be described as the interpretation of science as symbolic form, as a way of rendering reality. Another way of expressing the same thing is to say that interpretation in this second sense is the determination of the ontological import of the symbolism.

B

Expansion of the Scientific Symbol

We have said that interpretation in the first sense is not easily separable from interpretation in the second sense. This is peculiarly true in the case of the scientific symbol, for the reason that the expansion of the meaning of a symbol is bound up with the question of theories of scientific symbolism. If, for instance, we hold the operational theory, that the scientific concept is synonymous with the corresponding set of operations, then the expansion of that symbol will be precisely these operations. The discussion of this problem will then involve the entire question of the theories of the scientific symbol. To these theories we shall presently turn. It is necessary, however, to comment briefly upon the scientific procedures out of which these theories have grown.

It is characteristic of all types of symbols that in the case of the symbol concept "the judgment exercises a double function, first applying the concept to the object of sensible intuition and then applying the mere rule of reflection upon that intuition to a quite different object of which the first is only the symbol." The similarity between the symbol and the thing symbolized is therefore similarity in the way of reflecting upon the two things; in other words, a common rule of operation.[1] This general character of expansion of symbols applies also to the expansion of the scientific symbol. In the case of the scientific symbol, however, the notion of a rule of operation has a specialized meaning, namely, that expressed by the phrases, prediction of future happenings, control of phenomena, or whatever the objective of science may be defined to be. There are, speaking generally, two theories of the expansion of a scientific symbol, namely, the operational and the modified copy theory, the latter being also describable as the partial representative theory. Let us examine them in turn.

C

The Operational Theory of the Scientific Symbol

The operational theory begins with the analysis of the basal physical concepts, such, for instance, as length, weight, etc. Such concepts, says Bridgman, are "synonymous with their corresponding set of operations."[2] The concept length, for instance, involves as much as, and nothing more than, the set

---

[1] Chapter IX, p. 408.   [2] *The Logic of Modern Physics*, p. 5.

of operations by which the length is determined. The significant thing here is the *as much as* and *nothing more than*; there is nothing more to the scientific concept than the operations or actions for which it stands. Let us apply this notion to the constructions of physics or the symbol concepts in the proper sense. As "length" is a sign for certain operations, so the persistent particles of physical science or any other such ideal construct are in similar fashion merely synonymous with more complicated sets of operations. The meanings of such symbols are the mathematical operations; in any other sense they are "just dummies."

It must be admitted that both the present procedures of physical science and the character of the symbols with which it has been operating make the theory exceedingly plausible. A succession of hypotheses, both unintuitible and contradictory —which are nevertheless fruitful—has not only led to the abandonment of the copy theory, but to an overwhelming impression that the symbol does not *represent* in any fashion whatsoever. Further, as the hypotheses of modern physics *have* become increasingly impenetrable and its constructs, when translated into ordinary intuitible language, ever more disconcerting, the essence of science seems to be merely prediction and control. All "this inhuman hypothesis, this knowledge at odds with the knower, seems, nevertheless, to leave behind an increasing store of facts. It is these that are science; all the rest is moonshine."[1]

---

[1] Bridgman's argument against the literal character of mechanism, found on page 49, illustrates the point at issue. "An examination of specific proposed mechanisms," he tells us, "will show that most mechanisms are more complicated than the simple physical phenomenon which they are invented to explain, in that they have more independently variable attributes than the phenomenon has yet been proved to have. An example is afforded by the mechanical models invented to facilitate the study of the properties of simple inductive electrical circuits. The great number of such models is sufficient indication of their possible infinite number (Poincaré). But if the mechanism has more independently variable attributes than the original phenomenon, it is obvious that the question is without meaning whether the mechanism is the real one or not, for in the mechanism there must be simple motions or combinations of motions which have no counterpart in features of the original phenomenon as yet discovered. Obviously, then, the operations do not exist by which we may set up a one to one correspondence between the properties of a mechanism and the natural phenomenon and the question of reality has no meaning." He concludes that such a mechanism is a useful tool of thought, but is to be regarded no more seriously than is any mnemonic device or any other artifice by which a man forces his mind to give him better service.

The purely operational theory is, then, extremely plausible, and yet it faces insuperable difficulties. I need hardly point out that at best it is applicable only to physical science and to the mathematical physical type of symbol. If science should contain the principle of "double symbolism" it would be to that extent inapplicable. Expansion of a symbol of the second type is not an operation but an understanding. But even in the sphere of physical science there are difficulties. The significant thing in this theory is that the scientific concept or symbol involves a set of operations or measurements, but only this and *nothing more*. Now it must be quite clear that, if our scientific symbols are synonymous with their corresponding set of operations, then they merely operate and *say nothing*. All the significant statements of science about nature and the cosmos rest, for ever, upon the assumption that its concepts represent reality in some sense and to some degree. It is one thing to say, with Planck, that "for physical science reality is the *measurable*"; it is quite another thing to say that it is synonymous with the *measurements*. Finally—and this point is not without its significance—the operational theory is not that generally held even by physicists, for the interpretation of whose symbols the operational theory was mainly developed. The double criterion of the validity of a scientific hypothesis insisted upon by Einstein—namely, that it should enable us not merely to control, but also to understand the phenomenon in question—is quite widely demanded by physicists (among others Planck), and means, quite definitely, that the scientific concept or symbol is something more than merely the corresponding set of operations. In other words, the demand for "understanding," or the demand for intelligibility, is not completely satisfied by this theory. To be sure, there is still the question of what understanding means in science, and that is a very debatable question, but it certainly includes more than operation. Even though the copy theory be abandoned, some element of representation seems necessarily involved in any notion of understanding, and any satisfactory theory of the interpretation of the scientific symbol must include it.[1]

[1] In his *The Quest for Certainty*, Chapter V, John Dewey identifies science and scientific method completely with the operational theory, basing this identification largely upon the account of scientific concepts given by Bridgman. To the

D

The Relational Theory: Partial Representation

The difficulties which we have found in the operational theory of the scientific symbol are not unlike those which inhere in the purely emotive theory of the poetic symbol. As it is unintelligible to speak of taking up proper emotional attitudes towards objects unless the symbol gives us some knowledge of the nature of the object, so it seems unintelligible to say that we can operate intelligently with certain signs without their being in any way expressive of the intrinsic nature of the objects on which we operate. It is this difficulty which, in part, at least, gives rise to the second theory which I have described as the relational theory.

This interpretation of the scientific symbol is, on the whole, the most generally accepted in modern science and philosophy. It has already been stated in our discussion of symbolic representation as distinguished from the notion of a picture. According to this view scientific concepts or symbols are related to reality as the notes of the symphony to the symphony itself. There is resemblance here, but it is a resemblance of structure, or of relations; a resemblance such that when you know the rules you can infer the music from the score and the score from the music.[1] The symbol is *like* the thing symbolized, but only in certain limited respects. We naturally represent the world pictorially, that is, we imagine that what goes on is more or less like what we see. But in point of fact, this likeness can only extend to certain formal logical properties, so that all we know is certain *general* characteristics of its changes.

This view is, I repeat, the commonly accepted theory. According to Cassirer, it represents the essential scientific standpoint to-day. Using the three stages of the development of the theory of light, already quoted, as an illustration, he concludes

fact, which he recognizes explicitly, that science generally is still under the dominance of a representative theory of the scientific concept, he can reply only by suggesting that the scientists themselves do not understand their own method and its implications. That, of course, is *possible*; but surely the only source of information we have of the scientific consciousness and of the meaning of its procedures is the scientists themselves. (Published by George Allen & Unwin Ltd.).

[1] Chapter VII, p. 356.

that "physics has finally abandoned the reality of description and representation in order to enter upon a realm of greater abstraction. The schematism or symbolism of pictures has given place to a symbolism of principles. Physics is concerned no longer immediately with the actual, but is concerned with its structure and its formal characters. The tendency to unification has conquered the tendency to intuitive representation. The synthesis which is possible through pure concepts of law and relation has shown itself more valuable than the apprehension in terms of objects and things. Order and relation have, then, become the basal concepts of physics."[1]

Now there can be little question, I think, that this second theory of the scientific symbol is much nearer to the actual working assumptions of science. It is just as little doubtful that it is a more adequate theory. It abandons the copy theory—no longer tenable—of the model which "represents the happening in all its parts," for one of partial representation. We can predict and control because the necessary relations in the symbols are in constant relation to the relations in the pictured or symbolized objects. But this theory has its own difficulties. No more than the operational theory does it apply satisfactorily if we include in science the symbolisms applicable to life and mind. The languages of the biological and mental "sciences" do not strive merely towards a "symbolism of relations," but towards one of things and activities. But even more important is the following consideration. According to this view, science in its *ideal form* is, as Cassirer says, no longer concerned with the actual but only with its structure and formal characters.

The position I am characterizing is often stated in the following way: "Intelligibility in science consists exclusively in necessary connections. The fact is no longer isolated and it is therefore intelligible."[2] In other words, the essence of science, as symbolic form, is to represent reality only as a relational structure with abstraction from the concrete wholes of intuition. Now, that this gives intelligibility of a certain sort cannot be denied. The operational theory also has a certain concept of intelligibility (in so far as we can operate with a

---

[1] *Die Philosophie der Symbolischen Formen*, Vol. III, p. 545.
[2] L. S. Stebbing, *op. cit.*, p. 392.

concept it has instrumental intelligibility). But it must be quite clear that mere "lucidity of relations," no more than a system of operations, constitutes the understanding or intelligibility which science is ordinarily supposed to give. We may state this fact in the following way. All significant statements about nature and the cosmos rest upon the assumption that their concepts represent more than merely logical structure—are not merely a symbolism of relations but a symbolism of things in relations. In sum—and this is the conclusion I would draw from the entire discussion—granted the double criterion of a scientific theory or symbol, that it should enable us not only to control but to understand the phenomenon, the type of understanding or intelligibility afforded by this second theory is of a very limited character, and not at all the kind that science is ordinarily supposed to give.

We may express this in terms of our question as to what science "says." According to the operational theory, science, strictly speaking, says nothing about the cosmos; it merely operates. According to the present theory, science says something, but in reality it says very little. The well-known saying that mathematics says something about everything but ery little about anything, is applicable to this entire mathematical-logical concept of science and scientific intelligibility. It gives us a "picture" or symbolic representation of a complex of relations, but the important thing is that in such a representation there are no longer any things to talk about; they are all dissolved into relations. Even such ultimate units as survive are not independent reals, but can be described merely as essences that become real only by entering into relations. Surely this mathematical physical structure is not the world itself. It is only, as one physicist puts it, an intermediate sphere between the world and our perception. Surely it presents only that aspect of the world to which the mathematician has access, and understanding of this sphere does not mean understanding of the cosmos. The view that "our knowledge of the external world must always consist of numbers," that our picture of the universe must necessarily be in mathematical form, is one which, as we shall see, cannot be intelligibly maintained.

VII

SYMBOLISM AS A SCIENTIFIC PRINCIPLE: SCIENCE AS SYMBOLIC FORM

A

We have now examined two outstanding theories of the scientific symbol. Both have their difficulties, but both agree—and that is the significant thing for our purposes—that what we call scientific knowledge is largely symbolic. This leads us to the discussion of interpretation in the second sense, namely, the evaluation of science as symbolic form, or "symbolism as a scientific principle."

The significant thing is that scientific knowledge is in large part symbolic knowledge. What, then, does this fact mean? It means, as we are told over and over again—by a Jeans and an Eddington, a Weyl and a Planck—that to an incalculable degree our concepts of the physical world are constructions and the knowledge which they give symbolic. Some draw the inference, as does for instance Weyl, that "science concedes to idealism that this its objective world is not given but only propounded (like a problem to be solved) and that it can be constructed only by symbols."[1] For myself I draw the same consequences as does Weyl, but these are not necessary for the present argument. All that is necessary is the acceptance of symbolism as a scientific principle, namely, that the objective world can be known only symbolically. Otherwise expressed, this means that science is a symbolic form, like other symbolic forms—one way of apprehending and expressing the world in contrast to other ways of apprehending and expressing it.

It is immediately clear that in this conception of science notions of far-reaching import are involved. The fact that the objective world of science is constructed and not given raises immediately the question of what is *given* and what is *constructed* symbolically—in other words, the distinction between symbolic and non-symbolic knowledge in science. The further fact that physical science gives us a "construction" of the "world" or of the "universe," even though it be only of the world or universe

[1] *Mind and Nature*, 1933, p. 38 f.

as seen from the angle of physical science, raises the question of the knowledge of "physical wholes" or, as we shall phrase it, the significance of "cosmological propositions." Both of these questions we shall examine immediately. Here our sole concern is with the general notion of symbolism as a scientific principle.

This notion includes two ideas, both of which are of importance for the philosophy of science and for metaphysics. In the first place, the scientific way of representing things is symbolic and not literal, or, at least, in large part symbolic. But there follows from this a second notion, namely, that science, as such, is itself a symbolic form which does not exclude other symbolic forms. Modern critical science has come to recognize that its symbols, like the symbols of any region of experience, are constructions for a special purpose—in this case primarily "to deduce, as from models, what will happen in the outer world." As such, they correspond to the standpoint of science and have no ultimate meaning outside that standpoint. Art and religion are equally symbolic forms, equally ways of representing the world when viewed as the *omnitudo realitatis*. None of these forms are direct reproductions of realistically given facts. All share in a common fundamental character, namely, that there dwells in them a common spiritual power which makes of them media of genuine communication and interpretation of experience.[1]

B

Science and the "Wholes of Physics." Cosmological Propositions

It is customary to speak of the "world picture" which physical science gives. This notion of a world picture includes in it the idea of a world, as a whole, which science "pictures" or about which science *says* something. This aspect of science we may call cosmological, and we may speak of the cosmological propositions of science. We must now consider the character of such propositions and their relation to symbolism as a scientific principle.

In his recent presidential address Jeans discusses the question of the relation of scientific concepts to the "wholes of physics."

[1] Ernst Cassirer, *op. cit.*, Vol. III, *Einleitung*. This general position is, however, maintained throughout the work.

He points out that "it is a reasonable requirement that a man should represent each bit of territory in its proper shape and its relatively proper size—that is literally." The ideal would be the map as a spatial picture. But he points out that "this apparently reasonable requirement can be fulfilled only when the map is of a very small part of the globe, as, for instance, the County of Surrey. The larger the whole the more symbolic the representation." It turns out, then, according to him, "that the Newtonian mechanics, like the map of Surrey, good as far as it goes, is not adequate for picturing the wholes with which physics is concerned. The inconceivably great and the inconceivably small are both beyond its ken."[1] The Newtonian world view is then, even from the standpoint of physics, not a literal but a symbolic representation of the "whole" of physics. Moreover—and this is no less an important part of the position—the larger the whole the more symbolic the representation. This is true even of the whole of physics known as the universe; it becomes doubly true when for the universe in the sense of physics, we substitute universe in the sense of the philosopher—as the sum total of reality—the *omnitudo realitatis*.

Let us consider, then, the "whole" of physics. Here it is the inconceivably great and the inconceivably small that are beyond our ken and can be expressed, if at all, only symbolically and never literally. The discoveries of modern physics, we are told, have not only given new content to our existing framework of concepts, but have placed that framework itself in question and remade it. Even our concepts themselves have been revealed as appropriate to moderate dimensions only. The recognition of this fact constitutes, as Reichenbach says, the Copernican crisis of our time.[2] This crisis expresses itself not only in the fact that the basic concepts of science must themselves be changed (as in the change of our notions of space and time in the theory of relativity), but in the still more significant fact, to which we have already referred—the difficulty of translating these concepts, which are really expressible only mathematically, into the language of common sense and of ordinary communication,

---

[1] Sir James H. Jeans, *The New World Picture of Modern Physics*, British Association for the Advancement of Science, Aberdeen, 1934. Printed in *Nature*, 1934.

[2] H. Reichenbach, *Atom and Cosmos*, 1933, p. 28. Also Section IV in its entirety. (Published by George Allen & Unwin Ltd.).

which is essentially the language of this world of moderate dimensions. With this aspect of the crisis we are not immediately concerned, but rather with its significance for a theory of scientific symbolism. This crisis has made it clear, not only that the existing framework of concepts is symbolic, but that any framework which replaces it is again a symbolism, although a more adequate one. Cosmological propositions are always symbolic.

This seems to be the place to consider this whole question of "physical universes." As is well known, there is an infinite number of possible universes. Einstein's original one, now abandoned, was full of matter and static. At the other end was de Sitter's, which was empty. Finally, there is the universe of Abbé Lemaitre, which contains matter (stars) and which is dynamic. In other words, it is expanding, expanding like a soap-bubble. Our concern here is neither with the question as to which of these universes is most satisfactory to the physical astronomer—they seem to come and go—nor, for the moment at least, with the question as to how the "truth" of one conception rather than another is determined, but merely with their epistemological status as world pictures. About this there can scarcely be any doubt. They are, as Jeans says, not literal pictures, but symbols. More than this, since they involve cosmological propositions—propositions about illimitable wholes which, by their very nature, are metempirical—their truth cannot, strictly speaking, be empirically verified. It is true that we speak of one "picture" being more probable than another, but probability here means something significantly different from probability when applied to an empirical generalization.[1] We may be persuaded that one of these universes may be more reasonable than another, that one picture makes the world, as a physical universe, more intelligible than another, but there is no verifiability in any strict sense of the term. It is perhaps going too far to call these pictures cosmic myths, as do some scientists, but they are certainly purely symbolic. All this will become of importance when we consider the question of what science, in its cosmic aspects, *says*, when, in other words, we seek to interpret its symbolism. The important point here is that these world pictures are symbols.

[1] Chapter VIII, p. 387.

C

Symbolic and Non-Symbolic Knowledge in Science

The notions just developed—namely, that our knowledge of the objective world is in large part, if not wholly, symbolic, and that the knowledge of the cosmos is wholly symbolic—leads to two further questions which must be briefly discussed. The first of these is the problem of the non-symbolic element in our scientific knowledge—its nature and its extent. The second is the problem of symbolic truth in this sphere or, in other words, the validity of our symbolic constructions. This involves the entire question of verification in science. Let us consider them in order.

It need scarcely be reiterated that the whole notion of symbolic knowledge becomes meaningless unless there is assumed some form of non-symbolic knowledge with which it is contrasted. Our discussion of the notions of the literal and symbolic significance of sentences and propositions in an earlier context has made that clear.[1] We have, therefore, the problem of literal or non-symbolic knowledge in science. This problem is a difficult one, as is immediately evident when we observe the confused and ambiguous notions of scientists themselves on this point. In the address already referred to, Jeans has something to say on this point, and a consideration of his views will serve both to show this confusion and to make clear the point at issue.

"Our knowledge of the external world must always consist of numbers and our picture of the universe—the synthesis of our knowledge—must necessarily be mathematical in form. All the concrete details of the picture, the apples, the pears, the bananas, the ether, the atoms, the electrons, are mere clothing with which we drape our mathematical symbols—they do not belong to nature, but to the parables with which we seek to make nature comprehensible." The "ether, the atoms, the electrons" are, then, on this view, symbols or parables with which we seek to make nature comprehensible. But what are they symbols of? What are the truths of which they are the parables? Apparently of the mathematical relations which are asserted to be the real knowledge of the external world. This would then be non-

---

[1] Chapter IX, pp. 432 ff.

symbolic knowledge. But no! These parables are the drapery of the "mathematical symbols." When a statement such as this is thought out all scientific knowledge is dissolved into symbolism and the distinction between symbolic and non-symbolic knowledge vanishes. There is, it need not be insisted, a real difficulty here. It may indeed be true that, as Weyl says, our objective world is a construction and can only be constructed by symbols, but there must be something to be constructed. What is this "something," and is this something describable as knowledge?

The problem here evidently involves the further question of what propositions in science have *literal* significance. Is there any literal knowledge in science, and if so, what is it? It would seem that the answer to this question would be obvious. The ordinary factual propositions of science, the judgments of perception of quantitative and causal relations, empirical generalizations, it would ordinarily be maintained, have literal significance and give literal knowledge, whereas the conceptual structures in terms of which they are interpreted, themselves not sensuously intuitible, are symbolic. This was apparently Kant's answer, or at least the answer implied when he distinguished between examples of knowledge of the pure understanding and examples of symbolic knowledge in science. Apparently also it was the necessary implication of the Newtonian world view which constituted the background of Kant's thought.

This answer, although apparently obvious, contains difficulties; at least it is not satisfactory to modern science. It is precisely the denial of literal significance to what Newton and Kant thought of as literal which constitutes one of its chief tendencies. Even the categories, such as substance and cause, which seem necessary to the expression of empirical matter of fact, are extruded as "anthropomorphic" and are, if significant at all, significant only as symbol. What, then, is left as the wholly non-symbolic element in scientific knowledge? Apparently only the sense data themselves or the flux of sensation.[1] In other words, the "objective world" of science "is not given but only

---

[1] One of the most consistent expressions of this view is that of Vaihinger, *op. cit.*, p. 29. All knowledge which goes beyond simple succession and coexistence is symbolic. Even the categories are fictions (Chapter XXXVI).

propounded and can be constructed only by symbols." This is also, apparently, the view which underlies the statement of Jeans, already quoted, namely, that both the "numbers" and the "parables" are symbols, although of different kinds, the only non-symbolic element being the immediately given sense data.

The difficulties inherent in this position are evident, for, paradoxically enough, the only literal or non-symbolic element in scientific knowledge is then precisely that which is not knowledge at all, namely, the mere sense datum. The source of the difficulty seems to lie in the ambiguity of the word literal and the only solution to consist in recognizing the relative character of the distinction between the literal and the symbolic. It is true that part of a "fact" is the language in which it is enunciated; a fact is not a fact for science until it is expressed, and all expression involves symbolic elements. But these enunciated facts may be literal relative to the further constructions of science, namely, the theories of construction, the atoms and electrons, etc.—what Jeans calls the "fables." It is in this sense that those sentences in science are called literal which are more or less directly referable to sensuously observable entities—entities which have already, of course, been constructed by language; while sentences are symbolic when, in order to be verified, they must first be translated into the so-called literal sentences.

In view of this situation, the ordinary distinction between literal and symbolic knowledge seems, after all, to be in principle sound. In the world of moderate dimensions our propositions may be said to be literal in an intelligible sense; it is when we come to the world of the infinitely great and infinitely small that our constructions are clearly symbolic. The distinction between the literal and symbolic in science seems to be connected with the directness or indirectness of the verification of its propositions, as we shall presently see. In any case, the assumption of the literal significance of scientific propositions *as such*, in contrast to other types of sentences, is wholly uncritical and ignores all the problems involved.

This entire question of symbolic and non-symbolic knowledge in science evidently has far-reaching implications for a philosophy of science. Some of the implications are apparent in the statement of Jeans with which we started. In the first place, if our knowledge of the external world consists exclusively in numbers, and if our mathematical formulas are themselves symbols, then science gives us *nothing but* symbolic knowledge. But there are further difficulties. For really when one considers it, our knowledge cannot be exclusively in numbers, for numbers of themselves say nothing. This is tacitly admitted by Jeans himself, for it is the parables (non-mathematical symbols) which are necessary to make nature "comprehensible." Is not comprehensibility a part of knowledge? One might with justice say that it is only in the parables that anything intelligible is really said. The mathematical formula must be interpreted, otherwise it is meaningless. This is pre-eminently true of the cosmological propositions of science. Cosmological discourse can never be merely mathematical. There is a great gap between the mathematics of the law of increasing entropy and the proposition that the universe is running down, but it is only in the latter dramatic and "fabulous" form that anything significant is really said.

D

Symbolic Truth: The Notion of Verification in Science

Science, it is said, is verifiable and communicable knowledge. Verifiable means here, moreover, verifiable in the sense of the empirical criterion. The assertions of science which have literal significance have this significance precisely because they have reference to entities which are immediately observable or intuitible. The factual assertions, such as that acid turns litmus paper red, are verifiable directly, and other assertions, in so far as they are part of the body of science, verifiable indirectly. This notion of verifiability works reasonably well for the ordinary generalizations of science. From these generalizations may be predicted consequences which can be confirmed by just such observable happenings or facts. But the development of the symbolisms of modern physics has radically changed the situation in certain respects. In the first place, verification in many cases has become increasingly more and more indirect—that is, "between the given facts and the principle lie the most complicated theoretical arguments." In the second place, the constructs or symbols with which modern physics works are no longer intuitible in their details and consequently verification by intuition or experience—if it is still in force—takes on a different meaning. If, as for modern critical science, a large part of its knowledge is symbolic, what is the criterion of the "truth" of its symbols?

The problem of verification in science has already been examined in a previous context.[1] There we saw that the notion of verification by observation of sense data, whether conceived as direct or indirect, is quite generally misconceived. It is often supposed that the sentences or propositions of science have literal significance because they refer either directly or indirectly to immediately given data of sense experience and are verified by these data. This notion we saw to be a myth. No sentence or proposition which enters into the discourse of the natural sciences describes or refers directly to an immediate datum of sense experience. The simplest sentence in such discourse refers to other sentences and it is these, not the sense data, that do the verifying. This is even more the case in what is called indirect verification. There, as we found, it is not the "fact" that confirms the theory (that is merely a manner of speaking), but rather the total context in which the fact or observation finds its place. The assumptions underlying verification—and without which it is impossible—are themselves not empirically verifiable. It is for this reason also that no proposition in science, however "literal," is ever completely verifiable.

With these considerations in mind we may now approach the problem of symbolic truth in science, or the verification of symbolic as contrasted with literal propositions—more especially the cosmological propositions, which are always symbolic. It is clear that this verification, if there be such, is always indirect. On the basis of earlier conceptions of the scientific symbol, verification by direct reference to sensible intuition might conceivably be possible; according to modern views, no such direct reference is possible. This is true whichever of the two outstanding theories of the scientific symbol we may hold.

Verification of a scientific symbol is, then, always indirect, but we do not always realize how indirect it is. "Between the given facts and the principle lie," we say, "the most complicated

[1] Chapter VIII, pp. 383 ff.

theoretical arguments," but the nature of these arguments is not always realized. The development of modern physics, we found, "presents to an increasing degree self-authenticating formal systems which are no longer intuitible in their details."[1] Now this means, if it means anything, that verification in modern physics consists no longer wholly, if indeed primarily, in reference to intuitible entities, but rather in the inner consistency of formal mathematical systems. This view, which Cassirer accepts, does not, he is careful to point out, signify that science abandons sense experience. Science starts from observable objects and is not content until it deduces from its concepts or theories objects and events which can be observed. Without this connection with sense, however remote, there is no verification. But in so far as these formal structures, as structures, are themselves not referable to sense, their truth is not determinable by the empirical criterion, but consists in their self-authenticating character.[2]

This, then, is the general character of the indirect verification of a scientific symbol. It is necessary to apply it now to different types of symbol. We have already distinguished between theories of construction and theories of principle, and found the ordinary symbols of physics to fall under the former. Let us develop this point more fully. H. Margenau, a physicist, distinguishes between three classes of constructs or symbols in physics, namely, (a) the "sensible" or *anschaulich* of which the physical models are examples; (b) the "pseudo-sensible," which includes atoms and electrons and many similar entities; (c) a class which he describes as "abstract," which are "wholly insensible." Quantum mechanics actually replaces the electron and any other physical system by an abstract construct of this sort.[3]

---

[1] P. 522.

[2] *Op. cit.*, Vol. II, pp. 522 ff. See also on this point, Pierre Duhem, *Le théorie physique, son objet et sa structure*. Paris, 1906, pp. 245 ff. and 269 ff.

[3] H. Margenau, "Methodology of Modern Physics," *Philosophy of Science*, Vol. II, Nos. 1 and 2 (January and April, 1935). This is an important study of the philosophical problems set by the developments of modern physics.

Professor Margenau recognizes symbolism as a scientific principle in physics and the problem of the "ontological status" of its symbolic constructs. He adopts the partial correspondence theory of symbols; the constructs of physics correspond with the perceptible world, but the correspondence is not a one to one correspondence. The world of physics has, he holds, retained its connection with the

It is plain that such pseudo-sensible symbols as the atom, molecule, or electron do not satisfy the requirement of the empirical criterion of verifiability. For they neither stand for sense content, nor are they explicitly definable in terms that stand for sense contents. For this reason some physicists of a positivistic tendency have been ready to exclude them from science as illegitimate. This situation is, however, supposed to be overcome by indirection, namely, by giving a rule for translating the sentences in which they occur into sentences which refer to sense contents. In other words, if it is possible to indicate how the propositions which it "helps to express" may be empirically verified, then the propositions in which the symbol occurs are indirectly verified. Now we have, of course, no intention of denying that by such a process, supposing it to be possible, such pseudo-sensible symbols may be said to be "verified." It is simply a question of what verification here means. As shorthand expressions for propositions about sense data they may be pragmatically useful, but this does not necessarily involve the proof, even indirectly, of their existence. Their "value," as Professor Margenau insists, bears absolutely no relation to their mode of existence.

Indirect verification of the pseudo-sensible symbols does not, therefore, involve the demonstration of their existence in the sense that the words atom, electron, etc., can be shown to refer to sensuously observable entities. But there is a third class of symbols, namely, the abstract constructions, which raise still further questions. Quantum mechanics, we are told, replaces the electron and any other physical system by an abstract construct. Formerly the electron was presumably round, of definite size and mass, and it carried a certain charge. Now it is described by certain mathematical symbols called Hamiltonian momentum operators and others. These symbols "are placed in corre-

perceptible world but that connection has now been placed on a statistical footing.

He finds it necessary to distinguish three classes of physical constructs or symbols, the sensible, the pseudo-sensible and the wholly abstract. "If the physicist were to restrict himself exclusively to the use of sensible and pseudo-sensible constructs his dream of an ultimate system of explanation would never come true." In his section on the ontological status of these constructs he insists (p. 165) as his main point, "that physical constructs cannot be said either to exist or not exist; their ontological status has to be fixed in accordance with a more elaborate analysis of the meaning of existence. In particular, *the value of a construct* bears absolutely no relation to its mode of existence." (Italics mine.)

spondence with nature much in the same way as the previous sensible and pseudo-sensible constructs, and the resulting system of explanation is just as satisfactory and proper to the physicist as any other." It is the legitimacy of these symbols and the way in which they are verified that constitutes the epistemological or methodological question here. Evidently verification here is even more indirect than in the preceding cases. Between the "facts" and the construct lie the most complicated theoretical arguments, and these arguments are mathematical. The question now becomes this: whether the symbols employed in these mathematical formulas represent existential data or whether they are to be taken as merely expressions of the "mathematical sense functions of consciousness," to use the terms of a modern physicist? In other words, what is the "meaning" of the mathematical symbols called Hamiltonian momentum operators? Professor Margenau replies that "this question is no more embarrassing than that as to the meaning of imperceptibly small particles, neither construct being part of nature although both are essentials of the physical universe." Although not any more embarrassing to the physicist, there is still a difference in status here which is significant for the present discussion.

We may, perhaps, admit that in principle there is no fundamental difference between the verification of the two types of symbols in the methodology of the physicist. Both equally are not parts of the spatio-temporal world, although both are essential to the physical universe. But it does not seem—to the present writer, at least—that verification is quite the same thing in the two cases—that, in other words, the sentences in which the abstract concepts occur can be translated into sentences which have reference to sense contents in quite the same way as the sentences which contain the sensible and pseudo-sensible symbols. Verification of the abstract symbol seems to lie more definitely in the mathematical processes themselves. I must explicitly disavow competence in this field—a field, however, in which there seems to be some uncertainty among the physicists themselves, who appear, to the layman at least, to be far from clear on these points[1]—but if our analysis thus far is sound, it

[1] It is difficult to find out what is the real situation in physical science in respect to this matter of verification. Thus in the recent book, *The Evolution of Physics*,

would at least seem that in connection with these abstract symbols the *locus* of verification is more and more shifted to the sphere of mathematical intelligibility, that more and more verification tends to become the self-authentication of formal mathematical systems. In science also, truth and intelligibility tend to coincide, although the coincidence is never complete.

This does not mean, we must repeat, that the relation to sense experience is cut, but merely that the relation becomes more and more tenuous and indirect. This indirect relation brings us to the question of probability in scientific verification.

The world of physics, we are told, retains its connection with the perceptible world, but that connection has now been placed on a statistical footing. The physicist has, of course, well-established technical methods for determining the correlation between his constructs and the world of "fact," and with these we are not primarily concerned. Our interest is in the connection of the notions of probability and verifiability. In this context probability means probability in the mathematical sense, and has no connection with that "feeling of confidence" which repetition of observations affords in the sphere of perception. But this very fact means that the *locus* of verification is shifted to the sphere of mathematical intelligibility. Moreover, the fundamental element in all notions of probability—namely, the

---

by Albert Einstein and Leopold Infeld, the question is left very vague. It is true that the book is specifically written for the layman and therefore cannot be expected to be explicit on such matters. Nevertheless, even the layman may wish for light on so crucial a point.

In discussing Newton's law of inertia, on page 88, the authors observe: "We have seen that this law of inertia cannot be derived directly from experiment, but only by *speculative* thinking consistent with observation. The idealized experiment can never be actually performed, although it leads to *profound understanding* of real experiments." (Italics mine.) Do the authors regard such speculation as a mode of verification? If not, do they consider the law of inertia and similar laws as conventions or assumptions rather than laws and hypotheses? And what are we to understand by this profound understanding? Is that a form of verification? Similar questions arise when we come to the abstract symbols, the quanta which we have been considering. We are told that these are "new and free inventions," that not properties but probabilities are described, but we are not told either what is the status of these new inventions or wherein their verification consists. So far as anything is specifically said on this question, it would seem that here again the real *locus* of verification lies in the speculative significance of our constructions and in the profound understanding which they afford. "A fundamental belief in the ability of our theoretical constructions to grasp the reality of the world underlies all science," we are told, and that "the satisfaction of this demand is the fundamental motive of all scientific creation" (pp. 310 ff.).

SCIENCE AND SYMBOLISM

degree to which the hypothesis in question fits into our accepted notions of rationality or intelligibility—is involved. The refusal of the scientist, even to take into consideration the possibility that the single case which is crucial in his verification might be an accident because of its absurdity, signifies that the confirmation of an hypothesis takes place within a universe of discourse conditioned in its very character and constitution by mutually acknowledged assumptions as to rationality and intelligibility. Even in physical science truth and intelligibility tend to coincide.[1]

These views of the scientific symbol and of its verifiability have significance not only for the philosophy of science, but even more for our entire theory of symbolism. In an earlier context we distinguished between the truth of a symbol and symbolic truth. The truth of the symbol, "the value of a scientific construct for explanation," bears no relation to its mode of existence. Verification of propositions in which these symbols occur does not involve demonstration of the existence of any referends of the symbols in the sense of any specific mode of existence. On the other hand, these symbols or constructs are necessary for comprehensibility and intelligibility. As constructs, they share in the character of all symbols, namely, that they are conditioned by community of subjective form and are "true" for our type of consciousness. The pseudo-sensible symbols—the atoms and electrons "with which we drape our mathematical symbols"—do not belong to nature but to the "parables with which we seek to make nature comprehensible." This comprehensibility or intelligibility is in principle as much determined by community of subjective form as is the intelligibility of any other type of symbol.

These considerations become of special significance when we examine the cosmological propositions of science. It is commonly supposed that between these and the ordinary empirical generalizations of science there is a difference merely of degree and not, so to speak, of kind. This is, I think, a misunderstanding. It is not only true of physical wholes, that the greater the whole the more symbolic the representation, but it is also true that the symbolic representation of the physical universe as a totality is related to it in a different way—and, if in any sense

[1] See Chapter VIII, p. 386 f.

verifiable, verifiable only indirectly through mathematical trains of thought. By the very fact that such propositions are about metempirical wholes, that the "world picture" is a picture of a physical whole, which by its very nature is not intuitible, no verification in the ordinary sense is possible. Conceivably, the statement that there is a mountain on the other side of the moon could be thus verified; *conceivably* also statements about atoms and electrons might be so verified; but by no possible stretch of the epistemological imagination can any proposition about the universe be verified in this way. Between the empirical facts of the dissipation of energy and their verification, and the statement that the universe is running down, and *its* verification, there is a difference, not only of degree but of character, which cannot be bridged.

In sum, the symbolisms of science, no less than the symbolisms of any other region of human experience, are ideal constructions and, like the others, conditioned by community of subjective form. The "world pictures" of science are pictures, symbolic representations of that which can be known only symbolically. It is true that we say that one picture is more probable than another, but if the notion of probability is used here it is a different conception of probability from that applied to our ordinary generalizations. The notion of probability cannot be formed in this context except with reference to our form of consciousness. If truth is applicable to our cosmological propositions, or world pictures at all, it is symbolic truth in the sense of our earlier discussions.[1] Science, in so far as it is cosmological in character, is a metaphysic—a *métaphysique figurée*, a symbolic form which has value and significance solely from the standpoint of its own purposes and presuppositions. The two questions raised in this section—namely, regarding the non-symbolic or literal elements in scientific knowledge and the truth or verifiability of the symbolic representations in science—have a profound bearing upon the philosophy of science or the interpretation and evaluation of science as symbolic form. It is to this final question that the studies of this chapter have all been leading up. Let us attempt some answer to this question.

[1] Chapter IX, pp. 440 ff.

VIII

THE PHILOSOPHY OF SCIENCE: WHAT SCIENCE REALLY "SAYS"

A

A common expression is "science tells us," so and so. It tells us, or is supposed to tell us, certain facts about individual happenings or events, about certain "laws" which "govern" the happenings or events, and certain things about the world or cosmos, for instance that it evolves or is running down, etc. But what it really tells us depends very much upon what we think science is. If we take the operational view of science it tells us very little; it merely operates. If we take the mathematical-logical view, it tells us something—namely, that the world is a complex of relations, but that is far indeed from the things which it is supposed to tell us. Thus we have the problem of what science says, or more specifically, what it *really* says. It is generally recognized that popularizations of science say a great deal more than real science would dare to say and often constitute a veritable misrepresentation of the actual situation. Bertrand Russell has described this situation vividly and even goes so far as to say that the more science develops the less it actually says.[1] This is pre-eminently true in the physical sciences, in which it becomes increasingly difficult to translate the unintuitible hypotheses and symbols with which it works into intuitible language. In any case, science cannot be taken at its *face value*. What it says *superficially* is not always what it says fundamentally.

B

The Higher Criticism of Science

We come, then, to what is known as the *philosophy of science*. The philosophy of science may, I think, be adequately defined in the following way. It investigates the nature of the "scientific" "way of knowing" and evaluates its pronouncements upon the cosmos and upon the place of life and mind in the cosmos.

---

[1] *The Outlook of Science*, p. 74 f. (Published in Great Britain by George Allen & Unwin Ltd. under the title of *Scientific Outlook*).

I think it requires no argument to demonstrate that the problems of a philosophy of science are recognized even by science itself. Quite apart from the existence of innumerable books on the subject, from the pens of leading scientists, the presence of the self-critical element in modern science constitutes an acknowledgment of this field. This "higher criticism of science" means precisely that the pronouncements of science are not to be taken at their face value; the mere recognition of symbolism as a scientific principle proves this. It is important as a preliminary step to determine just what this means. The evaluation of the pronouncements of science is impossible until we determine just what science really says.

It is now generally recognized that science cannot be taken at its face value. In the beginning of the nineteenth century it was assumed without question that science is the discovery of the laws of nature, that it is the determination of the structure actually existing in the world of intuitible facts. A generation ago this opinion began to collapse, not owing to the attacks of those hostile to science, if such persons actually existed, but owing to reflections upon their own work by scientists themselves, who began to form the view that science is essentially hypothesis and, as we have seen, deals not with intuitible reals but with formal systems of relations. Finally, and most important of all, is the recognition of what was long maintained in principle by many philosophers—that science as a method, as a symbolic form or way of rendering reality, does so only by far-reaching abstractions made for its own purposes. The result of these beliefs is the growing realization that what science really says about reality—when it is understood—is vastly different from what it appears to say. That is to say, so long as science was taken literally, when a scientific concept was held to be a copy, corresponding in all its parts with reality, what science said had a different significance from what it has when it is taken symbolically. In short, the recognition of symbolism as a scientific principle affects vitally our interpretation, not only of specific scientific concepts, but of science itself—as symbolic form.

The problem of the philosophy of science is therefore a continuation of the problem of interpretation in its second and broader sense, for it involves the question of the ontological import of scientific concepts and symbols, or the import for philosophy of the scientific "world picture." In this sense it corresponds, therefore, to the problem of what poetry really says, or the significance of poetry as symbolic form. In following out this problem it will then be useful, as in the former case, to distinguish between what science says explicitly and what it says implicitly.

C

What Science Says Explicitly

Science says a great variety of things explicitly. It tells us that gold is a metal and that its specific gravity is so and so. It tells us that acid turns blue litmus paper red, that oxygen and hydrogen in certain proportions (H_2O) become water. These are statements of "fact" and are representative of like statements in all the different sciences. A second class of explicit assertions are empirical generalizations of wider generality. Even statements of fact in the sense of the preceding illustrations are empirical generalizations, for the reason that no statement of fact is possible which does not include the universal in one of the stages of its development. But the tendency of science is to ever wider and wider generalizations, to the determination of formulas applicable to "everything that happens"—in other words, to become cosmological in character. This third class, as we have already pointed out, differs significantly from the other two types, and since it is these that have the most bearing upon the problems of the philosophy of science, it is with these that we are chiefly concerned.

All explicit statements of science are of the three preceding types. For the purpose of simplification we may reduce them to two: assertions of the nature of empirical generalizations and assertions about unique wholes and ultimately about the cosmos as the whole of reality. The question then is, whether these assertions say what they seem to say.

The self-criticism of science of which we have spoken is inclined to say that in both these types of statements, science does not really say what it actually means. In the first type it actually says that the acid *turns* the blue litmus paper red, that the elements oxygen and hydrogen, mixed in certain proportions, *become* water. Modern science tends to become critical of this mode of statement. We ought not to speak thus, says Duhem. What is actually given is the presence of the elements of oxygen and hydrogen separately and then the water. In other words, science does not *really* say anything about substances and activities but only about functional relations. The consequences of this are far-reaching. The nominalism towards which science strives expresses itself in a nominalistic conception of the fundamental notions of science. Thus energy becomes in Duhem's view merely a *name* for functional relations expressed in mathematical equations. That this is the inmost drive of modern science we have seen in our examination of both of the outstanding theories of the scientific symbol. It is commonly assumed that "causal" explanation, in its literal sense, is confined to the earlier stages of science. It is even more generally assumed that the type of explanation which uses the substance notion is equally primitive and unsatisfactory. Intelligibility in science consists exclusively in necessary connections and these are of the mathematical-logical type. Well and good! But it must be immediately clear that what science says, on this view, is very different from what it says when it uses the categories of natural language and of common sense. It no longer tells us much that it was supposed to tell us.

This situation may be put in two ways. If the scientist puts the results of his analysis and of his mathematical symbolism into ordinary language he not only inevitably says very much more than his mathematical language means, but he actually falsifies what it says. If, however, he remains in the realm of his mathematical formulas, he actually does not say at all those things which are felt to have such significance for our view of life and the world. Science, then, really gives us no worldpicture, no *Weltanschauung*. It operates and says nothing, or else very little. In other words, science seems to carry on a system of double bookkeeping, just as it speaks two languages. But it cannot have it both ways. It cannot have all the values of exactness and rigour which come from the abstraction from all "anthropomorphic" categories, and at the same time have all the meaningfulness and philosophical significance which comes with the use of them. It cannot serve God *and* Mammon, leaving it for science to decide, of course, which from its point of view is God and which Mammon. This is true everywhere in

SCIENCE AND SYMBOLISM

science, but nowhere more so than in connection with its cosmological propositions. Here the question of what they really say is of special importance.

D

Cosmological Propositions

A large part of science—and that the most interesting and significant—consists in propositions of this type. All the special sciences claim to make propositions about wholes which themselves can never be known in the sense of the empirical criterion of verifiability.

This is true in both the historical and the generalizing sciences. We cannot talk history without talking about peoples as wholes, about cultures, and epochs; and, as Troeltsch, in his *Historismus*, has made clear, we cannot have history without discourse about these metempirical wholes. It is a commonplace of present-day methodology of history that one of the conditions of historical judgments or propositions is the assumption of a *completed series of events*, although in the nature of the case no such completed series is empirically given. And this is true of natural history no less than human. No theory of evolution can be constructed which does not contain such propositions. The fundamental problems of biology are all metaphysical in this sense.

But there are also the *generalizing* sciences, and it is with these that we are chiefly concerned. They also make propositions about metempirical wholes. Their method, they hold, enables them to infer from a part or a limited number of parts, that which holds for all parts and therefore for the whole. Physics, for instance, has to do with the limitless and to that extent inexhaustible world of bodies. It claims to develop concepts which hold for every part of the world and therefore, to that extent, for the whole. This is even more evident in that part of physics which is historical—that part which claims to say something meaningful about the running down or the building up of the physical universe. The second law of thermodynamics which, as Bergson rightly says, is the most metaphysical of all scientific laws, is so precisely because it is an historical proposition and, when applied to the physical *cosmos*, becomes a statement about a limitless metempirical whole. It is of the utmost importance to be quite clear on this point. It is customary to say that metaphysics is impossible because the world-whole is endless and cannot be known in its entirety. But this in itself proves nothing, for the same is true of the partial totalities of the particular sciences in regard to which no such question is ordinarily raised. In principle the partial totalities of science are metempirical also. But it is precisely cosmological propositions, assertions about these wholes, which are the really significant thing for the interpretation of science in the larger sense.

The point I am making receives special illumination from the consideration of the cosmological proposition to which I have just referred, namely, that the physical universe is "running down." As is well known, this proposition, accepted as "probable" by many physicists, is also felt to be one of the most significant (in its implications) of all the cosmological propositions—not only the most metaphysical for the reasons given, but as having maximum significance for life and values. In other words, science here says a great deal, and says it so certainly, in the minds of many, that upon this foundation we must build our entire conception of life and its meaning. The point that I am raising is first of all, whether science really does say this. If it does, there is then the further question of the significance of its assertions on this point.

Now it may be contended with a show of reason that science does not really say this at all. What it does say explicitly—and what alone is in any sense empirically verifiable—is that the second law of thermodynamics holds for finite conservative systems with which we may experiment. Its extension to the "whole of physics," or to the universe in the physical sense, is neither explicitly stated by science nor even necessarily implicit in its statements. The warning given by Lotze long ago against "crediting as a prophetic announcement with regard to the future those ingenious calculations which draw conclusions as to the final state of the world from our experimental knowledge of the economy of heat," is still repeated by many physicists themselves. It may well be, then, that the extension of this notion to the universe as a whole is illegitimate. But this is not the point I wish to emphasize in this connection. It is rather that, even if these ingenious calculations may be extended to the physical whole of the universe, there is still a great gap between what the mathematical formula "says" and what the dramatic language (from this standpoint, "fable") of the running down of the universe says. The former is mathematical language while the latter is historical and dramatic. Which language is it that science speaks, the former or the latter? If merely the former, it says one thing; if the latter, quite another; but they are *not* the same language, as is so often assumed.[1]

But to return to our main point, cosmological propositions, such as that the universe is running down, are metaphysical propositions, not only because they are historical in character, but because they are propositions about a metempirical whole which cannot be verified in the strict sense. This is true even when we speak of the cosmos in the abstract and arbitrary sense of the "universe" of physics. But it is even more so when by universe we mean the *omnitudo realitatis*. But it is only as such a metaphysical proposition that it has the significance for our world-picture which it is supposed to have. If it is not that, it has an entirely different significance. Here too, then, science is presented with an alternative. Either it contains cosmological propositions and is metaphysical—and then it says a great deal —or it does not contain them, because they are metaphysical propositions, and then it says very much less than it is supposed to say. More specifically, if such terms as running down or building up are simply anthropomorphisms, or "fables" with which we deck mathematical equations, then they are significant only as myth. Now from the standpoint of this discussion there is no objection to calling them myth if we define myth as all assertions which trench on the metempirical and metaphysical—although the wisdom of using the term in that way may be questioned. The important thing is to recognize that only when science becomes thus "mythical" does it say the significant things which it is supposed to say.

It is at this point, also, that the entire issue between scientific and dramatic language comes to a head. It is the cosmo-

---

[1] In another context, *The Intelligible World*, Chapter XII, I have discussed in detail the metaphysical nature of this law and the whole problem of its relation to philosophy. Here the problem is treated from the standpoint of the "language of science."

logical propositions that have always been significant. It is these which we have largely in mind when we speak of what "science says," what in other words it says about the world—its nature and its origin, and the place of life and mind in it. But a cosmology is always action and has of necessity a dramatic character; it is only in dramatic categories that cosmological meaning can be expressed. H. B. Alexander is, then, wholly right when he insists that even our natural science has always depended, and ultimately must depend, upon drama for its sense of rationality.[1] In other words, if science uses dramatic language and its symbols, it says something and speaks intelligibly; if it does not, it says nothing—it merely operates. It does not much matter, for our present purposes, what our philosophy of science at this point is. The important thing is to recognize that the significance of these cosmological propositions arises solely from the dramatic language in which they are stated. If, therefore, we extrude from scientific language all dramatic categories as anthropomorphic, we must be equally ready to recognize that science does not speak to man as man, but only to him as a mathematician and logician. If science speaks a double language we must recognize that fact. We cannot pass uncritically and recklessly from one concept of understanding or intelligibility to another. These general conclusions which hold for the explicit assertions of science, of both the factual and cosmological types, become all the more apparent when we turn to the implicit assertions of science, to what it appears to say implicitly.

E

What Science Says Implicitly

It is in what science appears to say implicitly that we are in a sense chiefly interested. We are, to be sure, interested in operating and predicting—in manipulating things for practical purposes. To know that acid turns blue litmus paper red is to give us a test for acid with which we may always operate; to know the mathematical equations for the stresses and strains of materials is to know facts from which we may make

---
[1] Chapter VI, p. 240 f.

predictions of tremendous importance. We are interested also in the great descriptive generalizations of science such as the laws of gravitation or of evolution, those conceptions which put the "fact" in a system of necessary relations and in so far make it "intelligible." But what we are chiefly interested in, after all, is the things these generalizations and cosmological propositions seem to say implicitly about the world—about its nature, its ultimate origin and perhaps even its destiny. It is accordingly the "picture of reality," as Reichenbach phrases it, which science gives, the ontological import of science, which claims our final interest.[1]

What science says on these matters is never said explicitly, but is only found implicit in its other assertions. The "science" of the nineteenth century was supposed to say that reality is ultimately material, that it is through and through determined and that it is mechanistic in structure. Now, it is important to realize that, if it did say these things, it did not say them explicitly. If it said them at all it was only because they were thought to be implicit in its statements of matters of fact, of general laws and cosmological propositions. If science now says something different on these points, it also says it only implicitly.

We may illustrate the point we have been making by considering one of the moot points of modern physics, namely, the Heisenberg principle of indeterminancy. Prior to the developments of recent physics it was assumed that one of the most certain things which science says is that everything is determined, in other words, the principle of determinancy. While uncritical scientists might have assumed that this was one of the explicit statements of science, more critical thinkers recognized that it was an implicate or postulate of science. Itself not empirically verifiable, it was rather the tacit assumption underlying all verification. Although only probable, whatever probability here means, it was so highly probable that it could be included among those things that science says. It is now maintained, by many scientists at least, that science does not say this either explicitly or implicitly; that if its implications are read aright it says rather that reality, in so far at least as its microscopic character is concerned, is characterized by a

[1] *Op. cit.*, pp. 288 ff.

fundamental indeterminancy. Many at least say, therefore, that science tells us now that "nature is simply not completely determined," meaning by nature the whole of reality as conceived by the physicist. It is a statement, therefore, with metaphysical significance.

An examination of this situation discloses the fact that the distinction between explicit and implicit assertions is here of fundamental importance. All that the Heisenberg principle says explicitly—and many physicists are loud in insisting on this point—is a principle of "inaccuracy." It merely tells us that it is not possible by observation to compute the changes in an electron. Heisenberg succeeded in showing that it is not possible accurately to predict such changes. He showed that one may choose *either* to determine the place of a flying electron *or* to ascertain its speed with precision, but that there can be no experiment which will fix location and velocity at once, and with the maximum accuracy. This peculiar coupling of inaccuracies is, then, the Heisenberg principle of uncertainty. Position and velocity are so linked together that only one of the two can be exactly fixed; the more exact the determination of the one, the less exact is that of the other. We may content ourselves with a moderate degree of accuracy for each, but it always turns out that the product of the two inaccuracies remains constant.

But what does this principle of inaccuracy mean? First of all it may be repeated that the only explicit statement of science is just this principle of *inaccuracy*. It is an operational principle, a statement about measurements, a generalization of the type already considered. The debate is as to what it says implicitly. By some it is held that we have here an implicit statement about an ultimate property of nature. Nature is simply not determined in all its parts. The decision in favour of the statistical nature of measurement here is a decision in favour of the nature of physical reality. The principle of inaccuracy may be turned into a metaphysical principle of indeterminancy. On the other hand, there are those who deny that the principle says this either explicitly or implicitly. Into this debate we shall not enter. Of interest to us is merely to point out the fact that, unless the Heisenberg principle does say this implicitly, it tells us very little which is of significance for a philosophy of science. Moreover, if it does say this implicitly it says something which is not empirically verifiable and is metaphysical in its implications. It is a gross epistemological misunderstanding to suppose that the facts of the "principle of inaccuracy" verify a "principle of indeterminancy."

The conclusions which emerge from the examination of this one principle of science may be generalized, I think, for all the supposed implicit assertions of science. The principle of determinism, no less than the so-called principle of indeterminism, is not an explicit statement of science, but rather a notion implicit in the methodology of science. The mechanistic world picture which the science of the nineteenth century was supposed to give was not an explicit assertion such as the law of gravitation, not an explicit part of the world picture, but rather a notion implicit in its methodology, namely, in its exclusion of teleological categories and principles and in its concept of understanding or intelligibility bound up with the notion of a mechanical model. Such implicit assertions are all metempirical and metaphysical and, as such, not empirically verifiable. They are, indeed, precisely as implicit assertions, that which makes the language of science significant in the larger sense, but they are significant only because they are metaphysical.

IX

SCIENCE AND METAPHYSICS. THE ONTOLOGICAL IMPORT OF SCIENCE

A

The question of what science really says, explicitly and implicitly, is, as we said, the problem of the philosophy of science. More particularly, what science says implicitly in its cosmological propositions leads us directly into the metaphysics of science. When the positivist and phenomenalist speak of the anti-metaphysical attitude of natural science they should be more circumspect and should first tell us what science, or rather what conception of science, is anti-metaphysical.

Now, it is fairly obvious that, on one view of its nature, the anti-metaphysical attitude can be consistently maintained. If science be truncated and confined to its explicit assertions of the type of empirical generalizations, then what science says may, with a show of reason at least, be said to be non-metaphysical. Or, if all that a scientific concept means is a sum of operations, then also it says nothing metaphysical, for, as we have seen, in reality it says nothing. But the moment science makes cosmological propositions or implicit assertions of the type we have been examining, it trenches on the metaphysical. This is really too obvious to require extended consideration. Propositions about wholes or about the structure of reality as a whole are always metempirical propositions. Logically it helps nothing to say here that such extension of concepts to the metempirical is probable, for probability means here only reasonableness. The fact remains that the subjects of such propositions are metempirical and never the objects of observation.

B

Science as Covert Metaphysics

Poetry, as we have seen, is covert metaphysics. Science—at least in its full untruncated form—is no less so. As we cannot talk poetry without talking metaphysics, so we cannot make ourselves ultimately intelligible in science without talking a metaphysical language. If art and poetry constitute a *métaphysique figurée*, no less does science, only the figures are very different in the two cases. The difference has, I suppose, become fully clear through our consideration of the two types of symbolism, or, as we have expressed it, the two types of symbolic form. The metaphysics implicit in poetic symbolism is, as we have seen, of a very definite character. Whether the poet speaks of man or of the cosmos, of nature or of human nature, the very fact that he speaks the language of poetry at all means that what he sees and what he expresses is reality *as determined by value appreciation*, and presupposes that the values and qualities of persons and things are part of their nature. The metaphysics of scientific symbolism is also of a very definite character. Whether the scientist speaks of man or the cosmos, of nature or human nature, by the very fact that he speaks the language of science is implied that he has excluded *ab initio* the qualities and values of things, and that the values and qualities of things and persons are not part of their nature. To be sure, the actual procedure of science discloses, as we have seen, a double symbolism and, to that extent, science speaks ambiguously. But in so far as it strives towards its ideal symbolic form, it implies this negative metaphysics.

No wit is reasonably clear what this covert metaphysics is and what the figures or symbols are in which it is expressed. It is a negative metaphysics—one of exclusion—and the figures it uses are closely related to this character of its implicit metaphysics. The opposite of "poetry," in the philosophical sense in which we have used the term, is not prose but science; and it is in the nature of this opposition that we find the key to the solution of our problem. Poetry (and pre-eminently poetry in the dramatic form) simply cannot be written except upon the basis of certain assumptions or presuppositions, and when these are examined they are found to contain an implicit metaphysics. The same is true of science. Science, too, simply cannot be prosecuted except upon the basis of certain assumptions or presuppositions and these also, when examined, are found to contain an implicit metaphysics. For one thing, science does not *find* the world *wert-frei*. Unless it excludes *ab initio* all values and their presuppositions, it simply cannot get under way at all. Unless it abstracts from the qualities which the poet retains it cannot realize the ideals of intelligibility which determine its very existence. It is for this reason that the *métaphysique figurée* of science is always in some sense mechanical. It may abandon the mechanical models of the older physics in certain regions of its researches, but the mathematical models which it substitutes are from the philosophical point of view still mechanical. It is for this reason also that it is an error to suppose that because mechanism in the older sense has "broken down," mechanism in its intrinsic character has been abandoned. The dehumanization of nature —in the sense of elimination of ends and values—means its mechanization. This is inherent in the very nature of its symbolic form.

In evaluating this situation the scientist often moralizes in the following fashion. "We may regret this dehumanization of nature. We may say that it takes the soul out of nature and thus makes it lifeless and uninteresting. But these are all notions to which the scientist pays no attention, because they judge scientific research by criteria which are taken from another sphere—of the poet and artist—and therefore have significance for this sphere only." He will often add that "such a rejection does not mean that we would deny the value of the artist's world; it means simply that we decline to bring the artist's concepts into a sphere in which they do not belong. The artist's way of comprehending nature carries its own value with it; but for that reason it cannot do the work of science—the foretelling of future events." This attitude is what he means by the anti-metaphysical tendency in science.[1] The confused thinking in such generous sentiments—for they are little more than sentiments—is obvious. It is quite clear, of course, that the scientist, as scientist, has a perfect right to pay no attention to such notions. But if this rejection does not mean the denial of the "value of the artist's world," if the artist's way of comprehending nature carries its own value with it, then by that very fact, since the artist does "comprehend," this way of comprehending must be taken into account in forming our world picture. If, on the other hand, this rejection does mean the denial of these notions for knowledge and comprehension, then this denial must rise from some antecedent, *a priori*, concept of the nature of reality. In either case—and this is the point to be emphasized—a metaphysics is implicitly involved. On neither interpretation of this ambiguous attitude can science be described as anti-metaphysical.

C

Science and the Nature of Reality

Science, then, is implicitly metaphysical. However it may struggle against it, this is the logic of its own activity. In order to round out our phenomenal experiences and to make them intelligible, it extends its statements symbolically to the transphenomenal and metempirical. In so doing it makes statements, either explicitly or implicitly, about the ultimate nature

---

[1] H. Reichenbach, *op. cit.*, p. 286.

of reality. Questions of this sort are for the positivist and phenomentalist meaningless questions. And yet it must be clear that this cannot be the case—at least for one who speaks at all about the world picture which science gives us. It is inevitable that science should say something about the world, at least implicitly, and it is important to know if possible what it really says. Despite the positions of such scientists as Mach and Hertz and the philosophical positions built upon their positivism, the question of the nature of reality cannot be excluded, even from the standpoint of science itself. The world cannot consist in functional relations alone; there must be something to be related. It cannot consist in operations alone; there must be something to operate upon. It cannot consist in constructions alone; there must be that which is constructed—and this something cannot be merely sense data. We have the score that represents the melody, but what is the melody? The grin, but there cannot be a grin without the cat.

The metaphysical questions raised by science are, then, not meaningless. Science may not indeed say anything explicitly on these questions, but it does so implicitly. An important question of this type is the question of realism and idealism. This is specifically asserted by the positivist to be a meaningless question, although the fact that it is not really meaningless is demonstrated by the contrasting interpretations of physics by the physicists themselves. The problem may be stated in this form. Is science implicitly realistic or idealistic? Does science say anything implicitly on this point?

On this point Weyl is, I think, right when he says that science does say something implicitly; and he is right also, I think, in his account of what it does say, namely, that it is both realistic and idealistic. "Science," he tells us, "proceeds realistically when it builds up an objective world in accordance with the demand . . . that the objective configuration is to contain all the factors necessary to account for the subjective appearances; no diversity in experience that is not founded on a corresponding objective diversity." On the other hand, science "concedes to idealism that this its objective world is not given but only propounded like a problem to be solved and that it can be constructed only by symbols." Thus, as Weyl says, the *Weltanschauliche* contrast of realism and idealism is reflected within science by two non-contradictory methodological principles. In other words, modern science—in its very methodology and in its very symbolic form—implicitly contains both principles.

There is no question of the realistic ingredient in science. Science and scientific method are implicitly realistic and any adequate philosophy of science must do full justice to this element. There is a genuine sense in which subjective idealisms and phenomenalisms are in contradiction to the implicit assertions of science and its method. The feeling of the "ordinary consciousness" that this is so is a well-grounded feeling. It is accordingly with the "concession to idealism" that we are chiefly concerned. This, I believe, is as truly implicit in science as the realistic.[1]

The thesis that "the objective world is not given" and that "it can only be constructed by symbols"—that the world picture which science gives us is a construction—is implied in everything which science does and says, and this implicit assertion is of far-reaching significance. It means, when properly interpreted, that science is a symbolic form among other symbolic forms. It means, as we have already said, that its symbols, like the symbols of any region of experience, are constructions for a special purpose. As such, they correspond to the standpoint of science and have no ultimate meaning outside that standpoint. There are other ways of representing or "comprehending" reality. None of these forms, even that of science, are direct reproductions of facts. They are all constructions and interpretations. When this "concession to idealism" is admitted, consequences of far-reaching importance

---

[1] Since writing this chapter Professor L. S. Stebbing's *Philosophy and the Physicists* has come into my hands. With some of the positions of this book I am, as will be seen from the preceding pages, in sympathy. My own discussion of Jeans's theory of symbols indicates my sense of his confusion of thought on this point, as well as that of many other physicists. But with other positions I cannot agree. The underlying assumption in Miss Stebbing's book seems to be that "intelligibility in science consists exclusively in necessary connections." If this is all science is, then it is true, of course, that science has no metaphysical implications, either idealistic or realistic, but it is difficult to accept this limitation. It is true that she has shown that the idealistic inferences of some physicists are scarcely justified by their methodology, but I am convinced, with Weyl, that the methodology of physical science is implicitly both realistic and idealistic.

follow. Science—in so far as it is such a construction, such a symbolic form—is subject to interpretation and such interpretation constitutes the philosophy of science. This interpretation can, however, mean only that, since the scientific concepts *are* constructs, their significance can be determined only with reference to the purpose of the construction. Whether that purpose be limited to mere operation, to mere correlation of phenomena, or is held to include understanding in some more significant sense, the question of the ontological status of these constructs cannot be separated from the question of the ends or values presupposed in the construction.

It is at this point that the special problems of the "double symbolism" in science and of the dramatic character of cosmological propositions enter. In both cases, obviously, more than mere correlation of phenomena is sought. As we pass from the physical to the living and the mental, a different language and a different symbolism are necessary if we are to express or represent the reality with which we are concerned. When we pass, even in physical science, to propositions about the cosmos a different language and a different symbolism are involved. In both these cases we trench more and more upon the language of other symbolic forms. Whether this means that in these cases we do not have science in the proper sense of the word, or whether we must broaden our notion of science to include them, is not the issue here. Our only point is that the constructs of science *are* symbols and that they cannot be understood or evaluated except in terms of the purpose or objective of the construction.

This much, then, the necessary "concession to idealism" inevitably implies. But it implies something more. Not only is there a philosophy of science in the above sense, but this philosophy of science, or of the scientific symbolic form, must be related to the interpretation of other symbolic forms. The symbols of science, no less than those of the other fields, are conditioned by subjective form and, in so far as their symbolic truth is concerned, are conditioned by our form of consciousness. They are "parables" in terms of which we seek to understand. There are other problems, other symbols such as those of art and religion, with other purposes and objectives. It is not until this character of science is fully realized that any fruitful philosophy of science, or indeed any adequate philosophy in the more general sense of the word, is possible.

D

Science and Other Symbolic Forms

Philosophy, I shall then maintain, is ultimately an interpretation of these symbolic forms. Two of these symbolic forms we have now already examined. There remains a third, namely, religion and its symbolism, which we shall examine in the following chapter. Before doing so, however, it is necessary to reconsider briefly the question with which this chapter opened, namely, the definition of science.

It is evident that in thus contrasting science, as symbolic form, with other forms such as those of poetry and religion, science must be taken in the limited sense of our initial definition. There is a sense in which one may speak of a science of ethics or of theology, in the sense, namely, that these constitute *scientia* or knowledge. One may even speak of metaphysics as a science, as when Bergson speaks of metaphysics as "the science which claims to dispense with symbolism." But in modern thought, science, in a narrower sense, is contrasted with all these. Indeed, unless science be given this narrower meaning there is no point in speaking of the relations of science to religion or to metaphysics. Science is, as we have said, one of the most ambiguous notions in the modern world —and we can scarcely escape this ambiguity—but we can at least avoid its most disastrous consequences. The only way to overcome the question-begging character of so much of modern thought is by a philosophy of symbolic forms as we have defined it.

CHAPTER XII

RELIGIOUS SYMBOLS AND THE PROBLEM OF RELIGIOUS KNOWLEDGE

I

RELIGIOUS symbols constitute the crux of any general theory of symbolism. It is possible, perhaps, for a poet to think of his symbols as merely means of evoking feeling, although actually he rarely does, but this is not possible for the religionist. It is conceivable that a critical scientist might take a purely operational view of his symbols, or think of his concepts as merely a shorthand language for the control of phenomena, but it is not possible to think of religious ideas in this way. It is true that the attempt is often made to do these things. But it may be safely said that to do so is to denature religion. What really happens is that a state of sophistication is created that cannot long endure, or else the truly religious man—in moments of actual religious experience such as worship—really abandons his sophisticated attitude.

Religion, like science with which it is so often contrasted, is a difficult notion to define. It is highly ambiguous and we constantly find ourselves in the predicament of not knowing precisely what it is that we are talking about. Instead, therefore, of starting with a definition we shall begin with the phenomena of religion themselves, with these phenomena, moreover, in the form of expression, namely, the *language* of religion. By the study of this language, in contrast to the languages of poetry and science, we may hope to place it in a system of languages and from this proceed to a study of the nature and significance of religious symbolism.

II

THE LANGUAGE OF RELIGION. NUMINOUS POETRY

A

The close relation of the language of religion to that of poetry has long been recognized. It has even led to a complete identification of religion and poetry in many minds. This identification has been aptly expressed by Mr. Santayana in his famous statement in *Religion and Poetry*. According to him, they are "identical in essence and differ merely in the way in which they are attached to practical affairs. Poetry is called religion when it intervenes in life and religion poetry when it merely supervenes upon life." Without raising, for the moment, the question of the adequacy of this statement of the relation, we may accept it as a starting-point for our analysis.

Certainly there is great similarity, if not "identity of essence," in religion and poetry. This is seen in a certain community of language. The cry of the psalmist, "All flesh is grass," is equally poetic and religious. The simile, "as the flower of the field, so it flourisheth," is both poetic figure and religious insight. Finally, the highly dramatic "the wind bloweth over it and it is gone, and the place thereof shall know it no more" is a highly poetic way of stating a fact of tremendous religious import. It is immediately clear what it is that constitutes the similarity. Both are, in the first instance at least, highly emotive forms of language, and both have the characters of intuitive and metaphorical representation which we found to be intrinsic to poetic language. The *vis poetica* is present in all genuine religious language, only in the case of religious language it is heightened and deepened in a peculiar way. It is, so to speak, poetry transposed to another scale.

B

The Lyrical and the Dramatic in Religion

We have been considering phrases and sentences which are both religious and poetic. Let us now consider the language wholes in which these phrases and sentences are found. We may describe them respectively as the lyrical and dramatic modes.

By lyrical language in religion I understand the form of hymn or psalm or prayer—any form in which the worshipper or devotee addresses the object of his devotion. As it appears in the literature of religion, it includes the Hebrew psalms, the Vedic hymns, the hymnology of the various religions, from the hymns to Dionysus in the Dionysian mysteries to the *Veni Creator Spiritus* and *Ave Maria* of Christian devotion. Prayer includes magical incantations, "empty repetitions," and the exalted dignity of the Stoic prayer to Zeus or the so-called high priestly prayer of Jesus. The emotive element in religion is here at its highest. Exaltation and depression, love and hate, the entire gamut of human emotions find expression in the language of devotion. But all these emotions have a peculiar tone-quality which has been described as the sense of the "holy." This quality varies all the way from the grovelling awe of the primitive to the "Holy, Holy, Holy" of the *Sanctus*, but it is the same religious mode (or sentiment) which in all cases informs and permeates them. The hymns of religion are, as a well-known Christian hymn expresses it, "songs of love and praise." They are expressions of love, but of "love *divine*, all loves excelling." They are expressions of praise, but of that peculiar praise, as in the *Gloria in excelsis*, which ascribes glory to God in the highest—to that plenitude of reality which in philosophy can be called by no other name than the *ens perfectissimum*.

The language of religion is, then, evocative. But it is also invocative. It evokes feelings but it also invokes objects. Invocation of spirits, of saints and angels, and of the Godhead itself, is of the very essence of religion, and distinguishes its language from that of poetry. Poetry itself may invoke objects but when it does so it is a "little remainder" of religion—as invocation of the muses—or it tends to pass over into religion. There is no invocation of inanimate objects or of abstract qualities. Invocation of the dynamo, as in Eugene O'Neill's play of that name is, as rightly seen, the expression of a disordered mind, and invocation of an abstract quality of "deity" would be equally so. The notions of a religion of science or a religion of humanity are similarly contradictions in terms. Invocation involves not only the existence of higher powers, but also, by the very fact of invocation, something of the nature of these powers. They are powers that "make for righteousness," for the enhancement and conservation of human values. Not only does invocation involve intervention in life, but the story or account of these powers that thus intervene—since they are personal or quasi-personal—can only be in dramatic form.

The second fundamental type of religious language is accordingly the dramatic. By the dramatic mode I understand primarily all that element in religion which goes under the name of myth. Dramatic language is not, as we have seen, primarily the language of emotion, although emotion is always present, but rather of will and action. The myth is the fundamental form, but the entire mode may be described more accurately as the historical element in religion.

It is needless to say that in using the term myth we are employing it in a purely phenomenological sense without any implications as to truth or falsity; this aspect of the problem will be considered later. As used here, we could speak equally well of the myths of science as of the myths of religion. For the dramatic and anthropomorphic way of rendering the events of nature is, from the mathematical-logical point of view, mythical in this technical sense.[1] The mythical is often conceived of as a primitive way of "explaining" natural happenings and human events. This is wholly to misunderstand the mythical consciousness. What is sought in myth is not explanation in any later derived "scientific" sense. The myth is in no sense a primitive substitute for science. What is sought is rather the intrinsic intelligibility which dramatic language alone can express. The creation of myths among peoples denotes a real spiritual life, however undeveloped or developed that life may be. Myth is the original phenomena of the spiritual world expressed in terms of the natural. Living knowledge is always mythical in character.

So far as myth is concerned, dramatic language appears at two main points, the myths of creation and the myths of divine transactions with men. They correspond respectively to the cosmic and historical elements in religion of which we shall speak more particularly later. The cosmic myths, in presenting dramatically the origin and destiny of the "world" and of mankind, make intelligible, in their way, our life and the universe in which our life is lived. The myths of divine transactions with men, and the entire notion of providence

[1] If the ideal science is the logico-mathematical, as defined in the preceding chapter, then all except the statement of functional relations becomes pre-scientific, or in Jeans's words, "fables." These fables may be necessary for a certain kind of understanding, but from the point of view of strict science they are mythical.

which has developed out of them, make intelligible in their way historical process which would otherwise be "sound and fury signifying nothing."

C

The Language of Theology

The primary forms of the language of religion are, then, the lyrical and the dramatic. But there is an aspect to all religious language not exhausted in these two. We may call it theological language.

The religious hymn, psalm or ode invokes objects, but it also ascribes predicates or qualities to those objects: "Holy, Holy, Holy, Lord God *Almighty*." Religious myth and drama picture—and as we shall see, in developed religions "symbolize" —the activities of these objects; but they also assert, either explicitly or implicitly, certain relations of the divine object or objects to the world and to human life. It is these assertions —together with the development of their implications and relations, the one to the other—that constitute theology.

The primary form of such language is the creed. All creeds are both lyrical and dramatic, but they also contain assertions or "propositions" which are factual as well as emotional, and which are existential in their import. The Christian creeds, for instance, more especially the Nicene, contain linguistic modes which are clearly figurative and "poetic" (and in interpretation are viewed as "symbolic"), but they also contain elements which, for the believer at least, contain literal and non-symbolic truth. To call God "father almighty" and "maker" of heaven and earth is to use dramatic language, but in this language are rendered relations which are metaphysical in character. The Christian creed is said to suffer from the injection of Greek metaphysics, but if it did not use a metaphysical language it would be *mere* poetry.

The creed, and the "dogmatic theology" developed from it, never lose, therefore, the character of poetry. To do so would be to lose the dramatic form of expression, and with it the expression of *living* experience and reality. To lose the *vis poetica* is at the same time to lose the *vis religiosa*. It follows, therefore, that even theology—that part of religion which treats systematically of the Deity, his nature and attributes—retains this character. For credal belief God exists and he has certain attributes and characters; for theology the question is the grounds for that belief and for the ascription of those characters. For credal belief "God became man"; for theology the question is why, God became man. Thus in the two classics of theology, the *Proslogium* and the *Cur Deus Homo* of Anselm, the thinking never loses the dramatic character of religious language. And this is true of all theology.[1] Theology is, as the name indicates, discourse about God, and no talk of God could ever be in the purely mathematical-logical form. To the question, then, whether the language of theology is also poetic language we can only answer in the following way: theological language, like metaphysical language with which it is necessarily connected, contains elements which are not poetic, but its basal elements still remain dramatic; otherwise theology would lose its touch with religion.[2]

D

The Notion of "Numinous" Poetry

Our examination of the language of religion has disclosed certain marked similarities between poetry and religion, but also certain significant differences. It is the differences upon which we now wish to fix our gaze. We may distinguish the language of poetry from that of religion by describing the latter as numinous poetry.

In his book, *The Idea of the Holy*, Rudolf Otto has a chapter on what he describes as numinous poetry. The well-known thesis of this book is that the religious consciousness is a unique form of consciousness characterized by a sense of the numinous which he describes as the *mysterium tremendum*, the wholly other,

---

[1] The truth of this assertion is amply demonstrated in the important volume by A. O. Lovejoy, *The Great Chain of Being*. In developing the history of this "Idea," and of the metaphysical notions of plentitude and continuity bound up with it, he makes use of many passages from Western theology. An examination of these passages, which space will not allow me to quote here, would serve to disclose this character of theological language.

[2] The nature of metaphysical language will be developed in Chapter XIII.

the Holy or Sacred. The holy is for him an *a priori* category, not analysable or reducible to other categories, whether existential or moral. He quite rightly finds this element present in all religious poetry—as that which distinguishes it from other poetry—and gives illustrations from various religions. The religious hymn, ode or lyric shows this element especially, but it is also present in the religious dramatic and epic forms.[1]

This conception of Otto's may, I think, be welcomed for two reasons. In the first place, for what may be described as its phenomenological significance. If we examine the religious consciousness for its own intrinsic quality—one that cannot be reduced to any other mode, such as the moral, the aesthetic or the scientific—such quality can be no better expressed than in this "sense of the holy." In the second place, it not only emphasizes the uniqueness of the religious consciousness, but also what we may call its "religious realism." The notion of religion which identifies it *in essence* with poetry is a form of nominalism. The "names" or words for deity and the divine objects have no transcendent reference but are merely the means of evoking emotions and of referring to human values. It is part of the purely humanistic conception of religion. We shall consider the question of religious realism later after we have examined the entire field of religious symbolism. Here we wish merely to emphasize the realism of this conception of religion.

This view—that the language of religion, while sharing with poetry its fundamental character, is *numinous* poetry—brings with it the notion of the uniqueness of the religious experience and of the object of that experience. This has been expressed by many philosophers of religion as the religious *a priori*. For Otto the holy is an *a priori* category. By this is meant both that the religious experience is unique and irreducible to any other form, such as the moral or aesthetic, and also that this unique quality of experience corresponds with or refers to a unique object. This doctrine of religious intuition

---

[1] Rudolf Otto, *The Idea of the Holy* (translation), Oxford University Press, 1923. The notion of numinous poetry is developed by Otto in Appendix II, in which illustrations are taken from Hindu, Jewish, and Christian hymns and liturgy, but important aspects of the phenomenon are treated in Chapter IX on *Means of Expression of the Numinous*. Here the non-linguistic media of expression—of art, more especially music—are studied with insight and understanding.

constitutes the essence of "religious realism," of which more will be said later.

This conception of numinous poetry enables us to see the truth in the notion of the language of religion as the language of poetry. It also enables us to connect religion with our discussions of poetry as symbolic form in a preceding chapter. It was the essential contention of that chapter that the poet catches something about both nature and man which the scientist misses, that there is such a thing as poetic truth and that poetry, as symbolic form, expresses an aspect of nature, both human and physical, which cannot be expressed in any other way. In so far as religion is poetry—and in a very real way it is—it shares in the implications of what poetry says. The description of religion as poetry in no wise militates against the former's ontological character and implications. But if our contentions are sound the religionist also catches something which both the poet and the scientist miss, and that something it renders in its unique language and in its special symbolic form. It is here, then, that we see the fallacy —or at least inadequacy—of that differentia of religion from poetry with which we started, namely, that poetry and religion, though identical in essence, differ in their relations to life. Poetry which is in no sense religious may intervene in life and constantly does so. It is not mere intervention in life that constitutes the differentia of religion, but rather the unique character of the intervention. The *vis religiosa*, that power which makes the language of religion intervene so mightily in life, is the sense of the Holy, of the "wholly other," which it expresses and communicates. In its earlier forms it is not, as Otto points out, identical either with the moral or the rational. Indeed the numinous may be connected with both the irrational and the non-moral and with that which is later found immoral. But he also recognizes that which is a fact, namely, that with the development of religion these notions tend to approach each other and to coalesce. The holy tends to become identical with the perfect. It is through this connection of poetry with the moral that it intervenes in life, and as it intervenes becomes less and less identical with poetry. It remains to a degree like it in form of expression, but differs more and more in essence. It is this essence which becomes of the utmost significance when we come to the problem of the nature of the religious symbol.

E

Religious Language and Communication

That the language of religion communicates something which is not expressible in any other type of language is, of course, a commonplace to all religiously-minded people. As Lavinia says in Shaw's *Androcles and the Lion*, "Religion is such a great thing that when I meet really religious people we are friends at once, no matter what name we give to the divine will that made us and moves us." It is precisely the numinous character of the language which we have been describing that performs this miracle of communication. Religious people "understand" each other no matter what names they give to the divine will that *made* them and *moves* them; they speak a common language. Communication of the religious or numinous experience is possible with the widest possible variety of religious ideas and names, as Scheler very clearly points out.[1] This is not merely because they share a common emotion, but because the "names" have a common reference. What this reference is and the nature of the object of the reference is the problem of the philosophy of religion, as we shall see when we come to the theories of religious symbolism; but the fact of communication and the possibility of translation from one language to another are outstanding facts of the phenomenology of religion.

Religion has been defined by Whitehead as "that which a man does with his solitude"—and this definition has, of course, its truth—but it is not in solitude that the truth of religion is known any more than the truth of any other type of propositions. There is no merely solipsitic verification in religion any more than in any other field of human experience. Intuition involves expression and communication. On the other hand, it is equally merely a partial truth to say that the essence of religion is communion—meaning by communion, communication with our fellows. The essence of religion can be found only in both aspects, and the common

[1] *Formalismus in der Ethik und die materielle Wert-Ethik*, p. 205.

element which binds them both together is the numinous. This is sensed in solitude and verified in communion as the one Being in whom we all live and move and have our being.

III

THE RELIGIOUS SYMBOL: ITS NATURE AND FUNCTION

A

With this account of the language of religion as a background we are now in a position to understand the nature and function of the religious symbol. We have, moreover, at our command an understanding of both the poetic and the scientific symbols; we should be able now to define the religious symbol and to place it in a general theory of symbolism and symbolic function.

The religious symbol shares of course in the general characters of all symbols. Images are taken from the narrower and more intuitible relations and used as expressions for more universal and ideal relations which, because of their pervasiveness and ideality, cannot be directly expressed. In like manner the general "principles of symbolism" hold also, *mutatis mutandis*, for religious symbols. But there is a fundamental difference which affects vitally both the function and the interpretation of the religious symbol, which must be made clear.

Höffding has sought for that difference and finds it, in the first instance, in the regions of intuition from which the symbol is taken. These he describes as "the great fundamental relations of nature and human nature—light and darkness, power and weakness, life and death, spirit and matter, good and evil, love and hate, etc."[1] This is undoubtedly a relative difference between religious symbols and those of ordinary poetry and science. It is indeed by means of these fundamental oppositions and contrasts—this *ursprünglicher Symbolismus*—that the deepest insights of religion are expressed, but this distinction of material does not go to the heart of the difference. This is to be found rather in the objects or referends of the symbols. The significant point at which the religious symbol differs from every other type is that that for which it *stands* always transcends the intuitive and the perceptible. Speaking of the religious

[1] *Philosophy of Religion*, pp. 70 ff.

symbol, Recejac says, "not all the images in which thought clothes itself properly bear the name of symbols, if we contrast them with the representations by which the absolute shines out in consciousness." We shall consider presently the precise meaning to be given to this word "absolute" and in what sense it stands for an object. For the moment we shall merely take it as the *differentia* of the religious consciousness and the religious symbol.

The point I am making may be brought out more clearly by relating religion and its symbolism to metaphysics and metaphysical symbolism. Here, again, we may make use of the analysis of Höffding. Höffding holds that the symbolism of religion, "considered epistemologically and not psychologically," differs from the metaphysical symbol only in that its figures are more concrete, richer in colour and more toned with emotion—are, in short, similar to the poetic symbol. In principle they are metaphysical in character. How, then, is the metaphysical symbol to be characterized? It differs from the scientific, for instance, "in that it seeks to shed light on existence in its *totality* (italics mine) or in its innermost essence, by figures that are taken from the phenomenal, from single aspects of existence as it appears in our experience."[1] The scientific symbol seeks also to shed light upon more complex relations of existence by figures taken from the more simple and intuitible, but, while more complex, the referend is still phenomenal.

The religious symbol is, then, in its essence—and epistemologically—metaphysical in character, although psychologically it is more akin to poetry. The reason why the religious symbol, even in its most developed forms, never loses the characters of poetry is, as we have seen, that religious language must be lyrical and dramatic or it is nothing. Even where, as in theology, this language approaches the logical character of science and the abstractness of metaphysics, it must still retain its poetic elements. God may be a logician or even a mathematician, but his relation to the universe and to man can never be merely a logical or a mathematical one, and those relations can never be expressed in a merely mathematical or logical form. It is for this reason that theology, which seeks to syste-

[1] *Op. cit.*, p. 77.

matize these relations must, in its reasoning, as well as in its descriptions, be dramatic in character; otherwise it could not communicate its meanings.

B

The Religious Symbol and the Principle of Distortion

This fundamental *differentia* of the religious symbol comes out clearly in the specific character of the element of distortion in connection with this type of symbol. All types of symbol have this element—the scientific no less than the aesthetic; a symbol that did not contain this element would not be a symbol. It is the uniqueness of the religious symbol in this respect that demands our attention.

Up to a point the procedure in the case of the religious symbol is similar to that in the other types. Religious symbolism also takes material from the realm of the sensuous and intuitive (from both the non-human and human parts of nature) and so *moulds* it that it may stand for or represent the non-intuitible. But the difference, which goes back to that which is represented, shows itself also in the character of the moulding or distortion. The religious symbol distorts the intuition not, like the aesthetic, to suggest "greater values" of the intuitional or phenomenal; nor like the scientific, to operate with or represent phenomenal relations; but to suggest and represent the infinite and the transphenomenal. The religious symbol is always supernatural in all the possible meanings of this word. An extreme, but in a sense typical, illustration of such distortion is that already used in a preceding chapter. When Hindu religious art symbolizes the infinity of divine activity by the figure of a god with innumerable arms and legs we have a distortion of nature in order to express that excessivity which is a necessary character of the infinitely other. Such distortion, like that of art discussed in the preceding chapter, is a fiction, but it is never felt as such, either by artist or worshipper, for it is apprehended *as a symbol and not as a literal picture,* and expresses "values more real than the real values."

Both the fact of distortion itself and the peculiar nature of the distortion were clearly recognized by Hegel in his philosophy of religion. In his doctrine of the religious symbol the dialectical movement which he sought to establish between the Oriental, the Greek, and the Christian religions undoubtedly led to the forcing of the varied and manifold expressions of the religious imagination into a narrow procrustean bed, but it also served, as theory often does, to disclose significant facts.

The "fantastic shapes," which, as Hegel said, "attracted the imagination of the Orientals," were for him a distortion for the expression of the infinite. More particularly, the zoomorphism of these religions is a case in point. The body of a lion with the head of a man and the wings and feathers of a bird represents, in the first instance doubtless, an attempt to render abstract attributes in sensuous form. In like manner it seems probable, as the result of recent studies, that the figure of the Sphinx is an attempt to combine the ideas of royalty (power) and wisdom. But there is more to it than this. Studies in animal symbolism, which we have called zoomorphism, make it increasingly clear that the deeper significance of animal symbolism lies in the fact that the more than human (super-human) character of its objects is expressed in the sub-human direction. These forms do not correspond to the idea, but it is precisely this *Unangemessenheit* which suggests the excessivity of the object, that is, the object which the symbol does not reach. To the Greek mind—at least the more rational side of the Greek mind—this type of distortion was, according to Hegel, more or less repugnant. It is true that more recent views of Greek religion emphasize the dark and Dionysiac side of life and its closer relation with the "Oriental." Nevertheless, on the whole, it is rather the *human* body that serves as symbol of the Divine. It "appears to them," as Hegel says, "as a nobler symbolism than that of the barbarians who discover in animal shapes the image of the divine." But here, also, there is distortion in a wider sense, a moulding of the intuition in the direction of the "ideal." The point to be emphasized here is that the symbolic expression of the noumenal on the higher levels, where grandeur and sublimity replace mere terror and dread, also involves a moulding of the intuition and the phenomenal. Here, then, as in the case of the artistic and poetic symbol, we have in the words of Van Gogh deviations from reality, lies if you like, but something more valuable than the real values. In the case of the religious symbol, however, the values thus achieved and expressed have, as we have seen, that numinous quality which transposes the language of religion to another scale.

We may speak of an "immanental law" of this symbol-making as it extends in both directions. It is the idea of the *mysterium tremendum*, of the infinitely holy working in and moulding the intuition. It may work *below* the human, creating the fantastic shapes of which Hegel spoke, or it may work *beyond* the human, creating the ideal shapes of the more developed ethical religions. This idea is, however, a unique value. It is not a predicate of an already given God-idea but rather the inmost essence of that idea. It is, so to speak, the kernel around which the pictures and the symbols crystallize. In other words, it is, if we use the term with care, the "quality of deity." Or speaking still more philosophically, here essence and existence are one. The point we are making is of great importance, and will be of determining significance when we come to the question of the referend of the religious symbol and the more general question of the nature of religious knowledge. We shall maintain a form of "religious realism," as against the religious nominalism which says that the religious symbols merely express emotions and refer to nothing. But it is of the utmost importance to characterize this realism properly and to determine adequately what the reference of the religious symbol really is.

It is at this point also that we must call attention to the unique rôle which the element of negativity plays in all religious symbolism. The element of negation is present in all symbolization and is, as we have seen, a basal moment in the symbolic consciousness. For Shelley the nightingale is a bird and he is not a bird. For La Mettrie the body is a machine and it is not really a machine. And so on throughout the whole realm of symbols, aesthetic and scientific. The consciousness of disparity between the representation and the thing represented is always part of the symbolic consciousness. But in the religious consciousness the element of negativity plays a unique and determining rôle. Since it is the excessive, the infinite, the *mysterium tremendum*, that is always symbolized, the consciousness that the symbol both is and is not a re-presentation of the thing for which it stands is the very essence of the religious consciousness as such. It is this, as we shall see, that for ever distinguishes the religious consciousness from the mythical; it is this also that determines uniquely the nature of *interpretation* of the religious symbol to which we shall presently turn. The "shapes" taken from the sensible world may symbolize the noumenal but never are the noumenal. The myths may represent dramatically the noumenal world but they are never literal pictures of that world. The essence of the religious symbol in all its forms is that it both is and is not the truth about the object symbolized.

C

Classification of Religious Symbols

A large part of the language of religion—in the broader sense of medium of communication—consists of non-linguistic signs, although these are always related to language and ultimately interpretable only in language. It is customary, therefore, to distinguish between "symbolism of act" and "symbolism of thought." It is with the symbolism of act that we are at first concerned.

It is part of the activistic and pragmatic tendencies of our time that, like language, religion is subsumed under the practical rather than the theoretical activities of man. From this point of view the primacy is given to cult and ritual, which are conceived to be both more permanent and significant than the more unstable intellectual elements that gather around them. The essential of such symbolism of act is a "showing forth." Certain acts from the physical life of man, such as washing, the breaking of bread, the common meal, are taken as signs or symbols of something taking place in a more mysterious, transcendent, spiritual world. In consonance with the activistic and emotive views of religion these have been called "behavioural" symbols, and we might conceivably speak of a behavioural expansion or interpretation of the symbol. We have seen, however, that there is no behavioural expansion of symbols, and this general principle holds for religious symbols also. All expansion of symbols is ultimately verbal.[1] Of the central and supreme Christian sacrament, for instance, the Holy Communion, it has been said: "It is a simple piece of symbolism to express a number of spiritual ideas too great for ordinary language. It shows forth directly, so to speak, something which words could express only weakly and indirectly." True as this seems at first sight to be, it really contains a paradox which, as we have seen, is present in all forms of symbolism. The symbol expresses something too great for words; yet if we ask what these things are that are too great for words we find that they are "spiritual ideas." If we then ask what these ideas are, we must either be silent or seek to give them verbal expression. This paradox we found present in all regions of symbolism. Thus in science, as we have seen, the mind breaks through the husk of language to a purer notation which will enable it better to take possession of its objects and their relations. If, however, we ask what these symbols mean, we must either be silent or express this meaning in words. The conclusion of all this is, then, that the language of religion must ultimately be the language of theology and the symbols of religion are primarily religious concepts. From this point of view we may suggest the following classification which will prove useful in the discussions to come.

The main forms of religious symbols we shall describe as (a) symbols of divine objects, and (b) symbols of sacred acts. The first general group with which we are primarily concerned may be divided into (a) symbols of deity or God; (b) symbols of divine attributes; (c) symbols of divine transactions or acts. The first may be called primary religious symbolism, the second and third secondary symbolism. The third group consists in taking natural and historical happenings as symbols of divine activity.

IV

THE MATERIAL OF RELIGIOUS SYMBOLISM: THE PROBLEM OF THE "MYTH"

A

It is characteristic of all types of symbolization that images or ideas are taken from the narrower, more intuitible fields of

[1] Chapter IX, p. 430.

experience and used for expressions of more universal and ideal relations which, precisely because of their pervasiveness and universality, cannot be expressed directly. Religious symbols are also taken from these intuitible domains, but they differ from those of art and science in the depth and range of the experience. As Höffding says, religious symbols are taken from "all accessible" spheres of human experience, but chiefly from certain great and fundamental relations of nature and human nature, already described. It is in the myth that these relations are dramatically portrayed, and therefore from the myth that the material of religious symbolism is chiefly taken.

In taking up this fundamental relation of religion to myth it is necessary to go into the question of the myth, until now only suggested. As defined in the dictionaries, and as ordinarily understood, a myth is "a story, the spontaneous product of unreflective and uncritical consciousness in which the forces of nature are represented in personal or quasi-personal forms and as performing supernatural and superhuman functions." With this definition has ordinarily gone a dyslogistic meaning of myth which practically identifies it with fiction. This is, however, neither the classical nor the most modern conception of the myth; it is rather the product of the intellectualism of the Enlightenment. Both the use and the evaluation of the myth by Plato are too well known to require comment, and the notion of the myth as a way of rendering reality is a commonplace of the classical tradition. On the other hand, for the most critical modern minds, the term myth has again become a neutral term. What this statement means is that it is not conceived as a sort of pseudo-science of the childhood of the race, but rather as a unique way of apprehending the world with its own character and presuppositions. It is indeed the character of the myth that it represents forces in personal and quasi-personal forms and as performing supernatural and superhuman functions. But—and this is the important point— the forces are not the "forces of nature" in the scientific sense at all; they are the forces of *reality* before reality has been transformed by the formation of a concept of nature as opposed to supernature. Reality is represented in forms which we now, in contrast to the symbolism of science, call "anthropomorphic," but these forms are not "projections" into nature but rather the primary way of apprehending nature in so far as it is immediately given. Living knowledge is always mythological in character in this sense. This is something which we must grasp quite clearly if we are to have any understanding whatsoever of what myth really is.[1] In any case—and this is all that we are really concerned with here—when the philosopher connects religion with myth it is this conception of myth that he employs. Religious thinkers and philosophies of religion increasingly employ the notion of myth in this sense and it may be therefore called, in Cassirer's terms, the critical view of myth.[2]

B

Religion and Myth: Their Relations

The mythical origin of most of the primary symbols of religious expression is historically beyond question. Even the most spiritual symbols of the most moralized religions have their source in the womb of the unconscious out of which the myth and its symbols have been born. The most exalted idiom of theology, no less than the language of purest devotion, makes use of this treasury of the ages. The chief sources of religious symbolism are, then, the great nature or cosmic myths and the historical or hero myths. Let us then start with this distinction between nature and human nature.

For the purposes of simplification (we are interested here only in illustration of a principle) we may single out two great classes of nature myths, the sun myths and the life

---

[1] The best recent treatment of the myth from this point of view is to be found in Cassirer's *Sprache und Mythos*, which constitutes the second volume of his *Philosophie der Symbolischen Formen*. It is true that the use of the notion of myth in this neutral sense creates difficulties because of the dyslogistic associations of the past and the prejudices of nineteenth-century science, but these misunderstandings must be risked. No other use is possible from the standpoint of a critical philosophy.

[2] One of the latest works to employ the notion in this sense is that of the well-known orthodox theologian, Nicholas Berdyaev, entitled *Freedom and the Spirit*, New York, 1935. See especially Chapter III, entitled "Symbol, Myth, Dogma." On page 70 he writes: "It is high time that we stopped identifying myth with invention, with the illusions of primitive mentality, and with anything, in fact, that is essentially opposed to reality. For that is the sense which we give to the words 'myth' and 'mythology' in ordinary conversation. But behind the myth are concealed the greatest realities, the original phenomena of the spiritual life."

myths. Our justification for so doing is found in two considerations: (a) their practical omnipresence in all mythology and religion, and (b) their contribution to the spiritual symbolism of all developed religions.

The wide diffusion of the worship of the sun and of sun myths has been questioned, as for instance by Frazer,[1] but it is probable that the solar implications of many myths have been obscured by the luxuriant overgrowth of lesser images. In any case, the worship flourishes in all nations that have achieved a certain degree of civilization and certainly enters into the symbolism of all the higher religions, the point in which we are mainly interested. The sun with its powerful rays, its warmth and light, its life-giving qualities, becomes a natural symbol for the creating and eliciting power. Moreover, the contrasts bound up with it, light and darkness, power and weakness, life and death, spirit and matter, good and evil, become a natural vehicle for the expression and embodiment of moral and other value contrasts as they develop in the life of man.

As the sun is the most appealing and significant centre for the mythical organization of external cosmic experience, so the life functions, more particularly the sexual, afford the most powerful centre for the organization of internal experiences. Hunger and self-preservation may be more fundamental drives or instincts, but sex, "the burning glass of the will," as Schopenhauer called it, is that which focuses and organizes our inner experiences. There is reason to believe that the worship of fertility, and the sex symbolism which goes with it, are indigenous to all agricultural and grazing peoples. The agriculturist, in order to live, must give life; and his highest ideal, his value of all values, is fertility—fertility of plant and animal, and of the human family itself. His deity becomes the Life-Giver—the life-giver in both male and female form.[2]

---

[1] *Worship of Nature*, Vol. I, p. 441.

[2] In primitive religions of certain types the sexual act may be connected with the general productive and reproductive processes of nature, and not only represent in some fashion these forces and processes, but also, in some magical way, affect and control them. Thus ritual acts of a sexual character are born. Lifted out of their merely human context, they are given a transcendent reference and, like other acts, such as washing and the common meal, become dramatic representations of a supernatural world.

Whether, as in some types of social organization, the relation of motherhood is singled out and the symbol of the Great Mother is dominant, or in other forms the notion of fatherhood is supreme, is immaterial; both become natural and appropriate symbols in which to envisage the *mysterium tremendum* from which our being comes, as well as the "infinitely holy" to which love and devotion aspire.

Nature myths are paralleled by those taken from human nature and the latter often fuse with the former. As the cosmic myths are the significant centres for the mythical organization of external cosmic experience, and the life myths for *internal* volitional experiences, so the hero is the significant centre about which historical and racial experience is organized. The great Aryan myth of Prometheus represents or symbolizes in a sensible manner, and on the natural plane, certain events of the spiritual life of man, of his destiny and of his relations to nature. The same may be said of the Dionysiac myth. The myth of the fall of Adam and Eve, a fundamental one for the Christian consciousness, expresses the greatest of all realities in the spiritual world. The separation of man and of the world from God is one of the original phenomena of the spiritual life, but the spiritual happening is symbolized in the natural and sensible world.

Perhaps the most significant of the historical myths are those which deal with incarnations. It is unnecessary to emphasize the prevalence of this notion in the great positive religions. The language of devotion represents man's approach to God; the dramatic language of the stories of incarnation represents God's approach to man. We should be ignoring one half of the picture of religion if we omitted those aspects in which the divine is supposed to enter into the human scene. Apparitions, voices, commands, through the sacred book or the sacred law, culminating in the consummation of an actual incarnation of deity itself, the presence of God with man! The *real presence*—in the spatio-temporal process—of that which transcends space and time is the essence of religion, in its highest no less than its lowest forms.

The significance of the foregoing paragraphs obviously does not lie in their value as an account of mythology. As such they are not only sketchy but wholly inadequate, although in this over-simplification I have, I hope, avoided saying anything untrue. Their significance lies wholly in showing how myth provides the material of religious symbolism. The myth, with its *ursprünglicher Symbolismus*, provides a fund of imagery which can be more or less consciously and religiously used as representation of Deity (*imago Dei*). Light (as in the Creed: God of God, *light of light*); love (as in the hymn, "Love Divine, all loves excelling"); fatherhood, motherhood—these are not in any sense arbitrary symbols, but intrinsic in the sense of our definition. Both their original character and their presence in all the higher and more spiritual religions give to these symbols the character of "adequacy" for our type of intuition. Here, too, in the myth we see that which makes of the mythical material the natural source of the *imago Dei*, namely, the numinous quality of that material. The sun, with its unearthly radiance, becomes easily a symbol for another light "that never was on land or sea," that light which "lighteneth every man that cometh into the world." Sex love, its heights and its depths—its horrible darkness and its blinding light—is never wholly alien to that creative love of which Plato, no less than Christian theologians and philosophers, discourse. The primitive worshipper and the mystical saint are brothers under their skins and find it natural to use a common imagery and a common speech.

C

The Relation of Myth (and Cult) to Religion

It is clearly impossible to make any study of religious symbols without the study of their relation to myth and cult. There is no positive religion without these elements. The further we follow the content of the religious consciousness to its beginnings, the more it is found impossible to separate it from the mythical consciousness. If one does attempt to separate the belief content of religion from the mythical language, one has then no longer religion in its actual historical and objective nature, but merely a shadow picture, and an empty abstraction. Nevertheless—and this is a point often overlooked—despite this inseparable interweaving of the content of myth and religion, *they are far from being identical*. Neither the form nor the spirit of the two is the same.

The peculiar character of the religious form of consciousness shows itself precisely in a changed attitude towards the mythical picture of the world. It cannot do without this world, for it is in the mythical consciousness that the immediate intuition of the meaningfulness of the world is given. It cannot abandon this world without abandoning the meaning also. Nor can the religious consciousness express its deepest insights without using the language of the myth, the story and the parable, as not only Plato, but the religious geniuses of all times and all peoples have discovered. Yet in the religious consciousness the myth acquires a new meaning; it becomes symbolic. Religion *completes* the process of development which myth as such cannot. It makes use of the sensuous pictures and signs but at the same time knows them to be such. The religious consciousness as such *always* draws the distinction between mere existence and meaning.[1]

Every religion (in the historical sense) comes to a point in its development where this distinction is made, and until it does so it cannot be called religion in the phenomenological sense. This is *symbolism as a religious principle*, and it is a fact of the utmost importance when we come to the interpretation of religion and the problem of what it is that religion says. It is precisely this consciousness, in all developed religion—that it is using the mythical to symbolize the non-mythical, the phenomenal to symbolize the noumenal—which determines all valid interpretation of religion, all determination of what religion really "says."

D

The Notion of the "Indispensable Myth"

Ever since Forberg and Lange there has grown up the notion of the indispensable myth. With an examination of this notion we may conclude our study of the phenomenology of religion and religious symbolism and turn to its interpretation and evaluation.

[1] See in this connection Cassirer, *op. cit.*, Vol. II, p. 294.

In the first place, then, myth is indispensable in religion for the reason that, as we have seen, it is wholly impossible to separate myth and religion. If we attempt to do so we have left merely a shadow picture and an empty abstraction. Myth is indispensable for the reason that it is only from the language of myth that the symbols of religion can be formed and only in such language that its real insights can be expressed. This we may, if we will, call its psychological indispensability. But the necessity of the myth, and of language formed in myth, goes deeper than this. It is indispensable from the epistemological point of view. The essential point here is that the myth is a primary and unique way of apprehending reality. It intuits and embodies qualities and values of things which elude the language and symbolism of science, these being made for wholly other purposes. It was this aspect of myth which Schelling emphasized in his philosophical evaluation of myth.[1] Finally myth is indispensable from the standpoint of expression and intelligibility. Myth is dramatic language and only dramatic language is ultimately intelligible. It is for this reason that Plato found the myth indispensable. As we have seen in a preceding chapter, it was precisely the recognition on the part of Plato that cosmologically significant propositions could not be expressed in mathematical-logical language, which led him to resort to the dramatic language of myth. It was not that this language is an imperfect prescientific form, to be abandoned for the mathematical-logical; it was rather a clear recognition of the essential limitations of the latter.

This thesis of the "indispensable myth," and our interpretation of the conception, raises one of the most fundamental problems of language and religion. Can we express truth in terms that we know are not true? We have only to recognize that the question is wrongly stated, and to put it in its proper form, in order to get an immediate answer. We can, of course, express truth in terms which we know are not *literally* true, but not in terms that are wholly untrue. It is quite possible to say with Plato that something like this must be true. Of the myth we may say: because it is not to be taken literally it does not follow that it is not to be taken seriously. Because

[1] *Lectures on the Philosophy of Mythology.*

the language of theology does not have literal significance, it does not follow, as the logical positivist is wont to contend, that it has no significance at all.

V

INTERPRETATION OF RELIGIOUS SYMBOLISM

A

We have insisted, and repeatedly shown, that interpretation, in the sense of expansion of a symbol, passes over directly into interpretation in the broader sense—that determination of what the *special* symbol "says" is inevitably bound up with the question of what the symbolic form as a whole says about reality. This is, of course, pre-eminently true in the sphere of religion and the religious symbol. Interpretation of a religious symbol is bound up with theories of religious symbolism.

The point requires special comment in the case of the religious symbol, however, for the reason that, as has just been shown, the historical source of the material of religious symbolism is to be found largely in the sphere of myth. The identification of religion with myth is inevitable in many minds and theories of interpretation are coloured by that fact. It is therefore necessary to preface our study of theories of religious symbolism by certain special comments. In our earlier study of the General Theory of Symbolism, we found that theories of symbolism fall into two main groups which we described as naturalistic and idealistic. The naturalistic theory is regressive in character. For it, interpretation of a symbol consists in carrying back the symbol to its origins; it is a form of reductionism—the reduction of the higher to the lower, of the more developed to the less developed. It seeks to interpret the symbol in terms of a reality *not meant by the symbol*. This is, of course, the principle and method underlying all application of psycho-analytical principles to the religious symbol. Not without its value, this method is, as Jung himself has shown, a wholly inadequate account of the significance of the religious symbol.[1] Interpretation of a symbol is, indeed, development of its unexpressed reference, but that

[1] Chapter IX, p. 420.

reference includes not only what it *has* meant but what it means now.

Closely connected with this is another point which requires special emphasis in the sphere of religious symbolism. It is a peculiar prejudice of present-day naturalism that, whereas scientific symbols are never interpreted genetically, religious symbols constantly are. Science and its symbols have had their history no less than religion. Chemistry had its beginnings in alchemy and astronomy in astrology. It never occurs to us, however, to evaluate science and its deliverances in terms of its origins. We always take science in its latest and most developed form. A really objective view of religion would do likewise. There is not a basal scientific concept which is not "mythical" in origin and primary import, but these pre-scientific meanings have long been shed. So also is it with the religious symbol.[1]

The principles underlying the expansion and interpretation of religious symbolism could be worked out equally well on the developed levels of any great cultural religion. Ideally, in fact, an adequate philosophy of religion would draw its material from all the developed religions. Such comparative studies are here manifestly impossible. Moreover, it is the symbolism of the Christian religion which is bound up with the other symbolic forms of European thought and culture and it is from this, therefore, that both the method and the theory of interpretation can be most significantly drawn.

B

Expansion of the Religious Symbol: The Classical Theory

In view of the preceding we are prepared to find that, as is actually the case, the entire notion of symbols and their interpretation (in the sense of expansion) was first worked out in the sphere of religion. The clear distinction between myth

[1] It is quite possible to connect the "light of light" of the Nicene creed with sun worship. But it is also possible to expand the basal scientific symbols, such, for instance, as atom and energy, in the same fashion. On the general question of theories of interpretation of symbols, we have argued in a preceding connection for the interpretation of symbol in terms of what is meant, not in terms of what it does not mean.

and religion and the recognition of the mythical as a symbolic, not a literal rendering of reality, forced the problem upon the religious consciousness in a sense not realized by the poetic and scientific consciousness. It was Christian thought which developed the principles of symbolism—and the theory of the expansion of symbols—for the Western world. But both principle and method had their roots in Hellenic thought and may therefore be properly characterized as representative of developed religion in general. There is a continuous tradition from Plato and Philo through Origen and Clement, Augustine and Neo-Platonism, up to its complete statement in mediaeval times. In its completed form, it constituted the so-called *Fourfold Method* of symbolic interpretation. According to this view, religious assertions are symbol-sentences or propositions, the meaning of which must be expanded or interpreted. There are four stages in this interpretation, or four meanings of the symbol, all of which have their "truth," the literal, the allegorical, the tropical or tropological, and the anagogical; and the development of these meanings constitutes a progressive interpretation. This notion was applied primarily to the statements of scripture, more particularly the parables and miracles, but it had a universal significance.[1] This we may describe as *symbolism as a religious principle*.

It became an established principle that every fact or event, in the realm of nature or of scriptural record, might be conceived as conveying, besides its *literal* meaning, these three symbolic interpretations, all three being of the nature of insight symbolism—that is, giving us insight into meanings or references not immediately present in the literal form. The interpretation called allegorical, as the term suggests, had reference primarily to truths of humanity as a whole; the story is an allegory of human life. The interpretation called tropological applied specifically to the moral lesson which might be learned from an event—the assumption of purpose, of teleological meaning, in nature and history being an underlying postulate of all symbolism. The final truth was that of the *anagoge*—ultimate truth belonging neither to time nor

---

[1] For the history of the development of this method and an account of its application in detail, see H. Flanders Dunbar, *Symbolism in Mediaeval Thought*, especially Chapters IV and V.

space—such knowledge as had been the norm of all knowledge since the formulation of Plato's doctrine of absolute ideas. Anagogical meaning was essentially metaphysical in character and ultimately religious and metaphysical truth coincide. These four meanings were sought especially in two sources of external revelation, nature and scripture—the spatial and the historical or temporal world. The phenomenal world is the "body" of the noumenal, the sensuous world an image of the intelligible world. It is because the absolute "Good" expresses its nature in creation, that that which is created may become the symbol of the uncreated.[1]

This instrument of thought, like so many of the mediaeval instruments (for instance the doctrine of the *suppositio*), became itself over-elaborated, mechanized, and literalized. It led not only to complexities and obscurities, but also to serious falsifications. Applied to nature, it begot many mediaeval works of pseudo-science, such as the lapidaries and bestiaries. Applied to scripture, it begot absurdities of interpretation which have become the sport of sceptics and rationalists. It is, as Kant said, wonderful what little minds can do with big issues. But in its highest form it was the source of the richest fruits of mediaeval thought and culture, Dante's *Divine Comedy* being in a sense its epitome.

The significance of this fourfold method is that it is the doctrine of the expansion of the religious symbol that was developed *within religion by the religious consciousness itself*. Two aspects of this doctrine are of especial importance for the understanding both of the principle itself and of theories of religious symbolism developed in later times.

The first of these is that the *literal* rendering of a religious assertion or proposition is not its inner or essential truth. The essential of the religious consciousness is not, as we have seen, identical with the mythical which is always literal. The religious consciousness, phenomenologically speaking, is not achieved until its symbolic character is realized. But—and this is an extremely important part of the entire conception

---

[1] It is because of the "analogy of being" between the Creator and the created "that the invisible things of God are known by the things that are made." It is on this analogy of being and on the identity of the *ens perfectissimum* and the *ens realissimum* that the entire principle of symbolism rested.

and method—the literal, though transcended, is not negated. The primary conception of truth as of language is the "copy" notion, and it cannot be completely abandoned without destroying the notion of truth itself. All intuition involves expression, and the notion of expression cannot be formed without including the notion of re-presentation in some form.[1] In this sense the religious consciousness is incurably literal— or better, perhaps, has a literal element in it. This fact appears at two significant points later to be discussed, namely, the place of the "historical element" in religion and the "dilemma" in religious knowledge created by the symbolic principle.

The second aspect of importance is the nature and relative significance of the last two stages of interpretation, the tropic and the anagogic. The tropological interpretation of the symbol was always an important aspect both of Christian practice and theory. The moral significance of the symbol—its meaning for life, both individual and social—has always been stressed. Whether religion is poetry or not, poetry becomes religion only when it intervenes in life and its intervention is possible only through relation to the practical and moral. This has led in modern times to a purely moral interpretation of the religious symbol and a purely moral theory of the nature of religious knowledge. But for the classical theory the ultimate stage is the anagogic, which is not only beyond the phenomenal, but beyond the moral in the narrow human sense: literally, "a leading up to," an elevation of mind to things "above." The things above for this classical theory are, of course, the denizens of the "intelligible world," perfect truth, perfect beauty, and perfect goodness, which, for Christian theology, constitute the essential nature of Deity himself. Thus for Dante, "the bread of angels," on which the soul feeds, is both the Eucharist and the knowledge or wisdom of theology and philosophy.[2]

C

Theology: Symbolism as a Theological Principle

Apart from the religious "signs" or symbol-acts—the effectual symbols, as they are called—religious symbols fall into three

[1] Chapter VIII, pp. 352 ff.   [2] See on this point Dunbar, *op. cit.*, p. 314.

groups: symbols of divine objects, divine attributes and divine acts. These three classes of objects constitute the subject-matter of theology. Theology is, in the first instance, talk or discourse about God, about His existence, His nature or attributes, and His acts. In so far as any or all of these objects are interpreted symbolically, we have symbolism as a theological principle. It is accordingly with symbolism as a theological principle that we are here chiefly concerned. And it may be said at the outset that there is no type of theology which does not, in some sense and to some degree, recognize the symbolic character of its language and use symbolism as a theological principle. The classical theology of Christendom looks upon both the attributes and activities of God as in some sense symbolic representations.

There are, as is well known, two types of theology, the positive and negative, and both of these are theories of religious symbolism. They bring out in clear relief the essential principles of symbolism. The essential of the negative theology is that God really cannot be named. The application of any names or attributes to the Deity falsifies Him. He, the infinite and the infinitely Holy, spurns all phenomenological categories, whether "physical" or "moral." All that we can truly *say* is *that* He is, not *what* He is. With this theory is naturally associated that negative mysticism which makes being and non-being identical. The positive theology, on the other hand, believes that God can be named, that predicates may be applied to Him *per analogiam*—that analogical predication which we have considered in other contexts is a true form of predication, even when applied to the noumenal or metempirical.

The importance of these considerations is twofold. In the first place, both theories contain by implication the fundamental problems of religous knowledge—both symbolic and non-symbolic—to which we shall presently turn. For both imply some non-symbolic knowledge of God. If, according to the negative theology, we assert that God cannot be named, in order to be able to do so we must know not only that He is but also what He is, at least to the extent that we may be able to say, *that* He is *not, that* He is *not*. On the other hand, if with the positive theology we assert that God is this or that, but that our predicates are applicable only analogically or symbolically, we must again know non-symbolically that He is, and also something of His nature. In the second place—and this is of more immediate import—symbolism as a theological principle implies an anagogical and not merely a moral theory. Even a negative theology asserts by implication the anagogic character of the religious symbol. Even if, so to speak, our symbols are merely a ladder by which we reach the infinite, to be kicked away as false in the blinding light of the direct vision, they are still a ladder. For the positive theology, on the other hand, the final or anagogical stage of interpretation is essential, for the philosophical basis of the positive theology is precisely that relation between God and His creation, between the noumenal and phenomenal, the infinite and the finite, which underlies the fourfold method. In considering modern theories of religious symbolism we must therefore view them from this standpoint of the traditional or classical theory.[1]

D

The Moral Theory of Religious Symbolism
(Symbolo-Fideism)

We may divide theories of religious symbolism into two main types, the moral and the metaphysical. The naturalistic theory, according to our view, is not a theory of religious symbolism at all, for in principle it denies that there are such symbols. The purely naturalistic view, with its regressive method, maintains that the religious symbol stands for nothing and is merely an expression of emotion. At the mythical stage of human development it may have stood for something, falsely of course, but with the development of knowledge it stands for nothing. According to both the moral and metaphysical theories, the symbol stands for something and both are therefore theories of symbolism. Besides these two outstanding types there are, to be sure, others which must be more or less considered. There is the theory of Humanism which, while naturalistic in its presuppositions, is moral in its significance. There is also the Pragmatic theory, as for instance that of Le Roy

[1] The classical theory, as developed by St. Thomas in the *Summa*, is presented in detail in Appendix IV.

which holds that the religious symbols have a transcendent reference but are primarily moral in import.

The moral theory attaches itself to one of the stages of the classical theory. It is, accordingly, even from this point of view, not untrue, but at most inadequate. Its essential character is its denial of the *sensus anagogicus* to the symbol. This theory, as developed in modern times, is naturally connected primarily with Kant for whom, it is ordinarily held, although unjustly I believe, that the religious symbol has only moral meaning and import. However that may be, the moral theory in the Kantian form has given rise to a modern theory of religious symbolism which has become clearly defined and has established itself firmly within the borders of both Catholic modernism and Protestant liberalism. Sabatier, and Symbolofideism in general, and the Humanism of Feuerbach are illustrations of this view.

It is not our purpose here to enter into an extended critique of this theory from the standpoint of the philosophy of religion. That has been done many times.[1] What I wish to emphasize here is its inadequacy as an account of the language of religion, of religion as symbolic form, and of a theory of expansion of the religious symbol. In the first place, then, I should wish to point out that the language of religion is no more *merely* moral language than it is merely poetic. The moral theory fails entirely to explain its numinous character. If, as it has been said—and rightly—this theory is a profound misrepresentation of the religious consciousness, and "is possible only because it ignores the postulate of the transcendent life, which is of the very essence of religion," it is also true that it is a profound misrepresentation of religious language. Morality has its own language and its own terms and, as mere morality, does not require religious symbols. Moral truth requires symbol only when it trenches on the transcendent and metaphysical. This is brought out clearly in Feuerbach's own interpretation of the element in religion which gives the numinous character to the language of religion. The essential of man as religious is that he is aware of his finite limits. For both Kant and Hegel he who recognizes a limit is already in reflection beyond

---

[1] For an excellent statement of this criticism see Charles A. Bennett, *The Dilemma of Religious Knowledge* (1931), Chapters III and IV.

it, and this sense of the "beyond," of the infinite, is for both the source of religion, for it implies that man is part of infinite being. For Feuerbach—and for the moral theory in general—the sense of the infinite implies no such thing. It implies merely that man is part of humanity and the stirrings of the so-called infinite in him are merely the stirrings of humanity. That this is an inadequate account of religion a mere realization of the numinous quality of religious language is enough to make clear. Kant himself, although because of the ambiguity of his language at many points he is unfortunately the modern father of this theory, did not himself really hold it. In reality he held a metaphysical theory of the religious symbol, as the entire tenor of his *Critique of Practical Reason* makes clear, no less than a careful reading of his *Critique of Judgment*. He specifically held that phenomenal categories could be applied to the noumenal symbolically.

An important passage in the *Critique of Judgment* brings out this point clearly. It is a "General Remark on the Application of the Categories to God." "The alleged contradiction," Kant writes, "between the possibility of a Theology asserted here (in the preceding paragraphs) and that which the Critique of the speculative reason said of the Categories, viz. that they can only produce knowledge when applied to objects of sense, but in no way when applied to the supersensible—vanishes if we see that they are here used for a *cognition* (italics mine) of God, not in a theoretical point of view (in accordance with what His own nature, inscrutable to us, may be), but simply as a practical. In order then at this opportunity to make an end of the misinterpretation of that very necessary doctrine of the Critique. . . . I add here the following elucidation."[1] The rest of the passage, in which the possibility of a theology is maintained, is too long to quote *in extenso*. It must suffice to summarize his main points. Kant points out, first of all, that it is true that if I apply a phenomenal category to a supersensible being, namely God, I must so mould, or in our terms "distort" it, as to make of it no longer that category, *literally*. Thus if I think of him as *first mover*, I must abstract from all spatial and temporal elements involved in the notion of motion, and the notion can therefore no longer give us knowledge in

[1] *The Critique of Judgment* (translation by J. H. Bernard), Sections 89 and 90.

the sense of empirical science. Nevertheless the categories are applicable to God. We cannot, of course, operate with them for operation involves space and time, but we can understand with them. He holds, then, that "a cognition of God and of His Being (Theology) is possible by means of the properties and determinations of his causality merely thought in him according to analogy, which has all requisite reality in a practical reference though only in respect of this." For Kant, then, phenomenal categories do give us knowledge of God—not merely of moral fact—but it is analogical or symbolic knowledge. That the symbols function in a practical or moral context in no wise excludes the fact that their reference is beyond the human and the moral. In fact it is precisely this reference which, for Kant, alone enables them to function morally. If symbolic knowledge is all that is requisite in a practical reference, it is none the less *knowledge* that is requisite.

Returning, then, after this excursus into Kant, to the main point of our study, we may repeat that a purely moral theory of the religious symbol is untenable. It is only in so far as religious symbols are more than moral in their reference that they can function morally. With this we are led to a consideration of the anagogic or metaphysical theory. But we shall do well before formulating this theory to examine briefly certain naturalistic or humanistic theories which, while historically derived from Kant, are nevertheless at variance with the fundamental contentions of the Kantian theory.

E

Humanistic and Pragmatic Theories

Humanistic and pragmatic theories of religion may be looked upon as the final stage of the process of the truncation of the classical principle of religious symbolism which gave rise to the moral theory. In principle these recent theories differ in no important respects from the humanistic theory of Feuerbach which contains all the leading conceptions. What is new is the carrying over of the operational theory of the scientific symbol into that of religion, and the use of the special ideas which have resulted from anthropological studies such as those of Durkheim and the psychological studies of the psychoanalysts.

Here again it is not my purpose to consider humanism critically from the standpoint of the philosophy of religion, but merely to examine it as a theory of religious symbolism. As such, it has all the difficulties of the moral theory, with the additional defect that it also misrepresents the moral consciousness of which the religious is supposed to be symbolic. The essential character of these theories is that they interpret the symbol in terms of what is not meant by the symbol. Its apparent meaning is its reference to over-individual social values; its real meaning is to be found in the *causes*, environmental and social, which have produced the images and symbols. On this theory, then, the religious symbol becomes doubly illusory. It is illusory, in the first place, because, although apparently referring to the superhuman, it actually refers only to human values; it is illusory in the second place because, while apparently referring to values, in reality it refers to physical causes. Humanistic theories inevitably become, then, theories of fruitful illusion. The symbols of the "religious imagination" are really fictions, although useful fictions. They become, in a phrase already used, behavioural symbols; the question is then not one of symbolic truth but of symbolic effectiveness.

The virtual atheism implied by Humanism is much more intelligible when it becomes an explicit atheism—as it inevitably tends to do. From the standpoint of the philosophy of language and symbolism, it would be much more intelligible to see in the language of religion a purely emotive language and one which, strictly speaking, is meaningless. The symbols of religion originally had an empirical reference, although a false reference, and therefore had a literal significance. They no longer have this literal significance; therefore they have no significance whatsoever. The humanistic theory, however, still accords to them a significance which, properly speaking, they should not have. Such a theory not only stultifies all human discourse, but ultimately reduces itself, *as theory*, to absurdity.

In this connection the theory of religious symbolism developed by the French philosopher Le Roy is of special interest. In his well-known book, *What is a Dogma?* he formulates a theory which at first sight seems to be wholly moral and pragmatic but which, on closer examination, turns out to be really anagogic and metaphysical in its implications. As such, it will serve both to bring out the element of truth in humanistic and pragmatic positions and also as a transition to the anagogic theory. Le Roy examines the various dogmas of Christianity, such as the personality of God, and concludes that they are symbols whose primary and most important meaning lies in their significance for practice. Such symbols are significant, he holds, much more for their negations than for their affirmations. When we are told to think of God as a person, the primary significance lies in the implication that we should not think of Him as impersonal. The Christian consciousness has discovered the practical consequences which have followed from thinking of God as impersonal and the dogma tells us not to think of Him so. This is the primary significance of the symbol; but Le Roy is careful to insist that it is only because the symbol is more than moral (metaphysical) in its reference, that it has this moral significance. A careful examination of this theory shows that it is really not a theory of the nature of the religious symbol—here the theory is metaphysical—but rather a theory of the verification of the symbol as symbol. Symbolic truth is for Le Roy also conditioned by our form of consciousness; the truth or falsity of the symbol can therefore also be determined only within our experience.

F

The Metaphysical Theory of the Religious Symbol; The Sensus Anagogicus

The classical theory of the religious symbol holds that the literal, allegorical, and moral meanings culminate in and presuppose the anagogic or metaphysical. The ultimate reference of the symbol is neither to objects in nature nor to merely human and moral values, but to some trans-phenomenal co-implicate of these values. The anagogic interpretation develops this latter reference and implication.

The *sensus anagogicus* of the symbol is, according to the classical theory, the "sense" which it has by virtue of the relation of the phenomenal to the intelligible world. It is because the absolute "Good" expresses itself in the created world that that which is created may become the symbol of the uncreated. This holds pre-eminently for the human notions of the good, which may therefore become symbols of the noumenal. This position has been well expressed in modern form by E. Brunner in his excellent study of religious knowledge.[1] In his discussion of the religious symbol he distinguishes between primary and secondary religious symbolism. The secondary symbols correspond to the divine attributes and activities, the primary to God or Deity, the subject of the attributes and activities. Expansion of the meaning of the secondary symbols shows their reference to be, as the moral theory maintains, to "the highest and deepest" in human experience—in other words, and in modern terminology, to values. But the unique character of the primary religious symbol, God, is found precisely in the fact that it stands for, or refers to, not these values as such, but the metempirical or transcendental implicate of these values—in Brunner's terms, "the over-world latent or implied in the moral consciousness." Thus, while both the names for God Himself and for His attributes and activities have a symbolic element, there is an element in all religious knowledge which is non-symbolic, namely, the direct knowledge or intuition of this reference to an "over-world." The question of the existence of such direct, intuitive knowledge we shall leave for consideration under the topic of religious realism. It is, of course, the problem of the religious *a priori*, already raised in our study of religious language. Here we are concerned merely with the question of whether the religious symbol has this reference, this *sensus anagogicus*. On this point there can be no question. Until the religious symbol is given its *sensus anagogicus*, until it is metaphysically interpreted, its character as religious symbol is misrepresented. The numinous character of religious language is already an expression of this "sense" and its implied noumenal reference. Unless this reference is retained in our interpretation of religious language, this language loses its *vis religiosa* and the religious symbol its religious character.

[1] E. Brunner, *Das Symbolische in der religiösen Erkentniss*, especially pp. 49 ff.

VI

THE PROBLEM OF RELIGIOUS KNOWLEDGE; THE OBJECT OR REFEREND OF THE RELIGIOUS SYMBOL

A

Any theory of religious symbolism must be a theory of religious cognition. It is true, as we have seen, that there is a type of theory which denies that the religious symbol gives knowledge at all. For this theory religion is emotion and religious symbols have merely emotive significance. On this view, however, the symbol stands for nothing and is therefore not really a symbol at all. There are, as we have seen, two classes of religious symbols, the names for the objects of religion and for the predicates applied to these objects. The moral and humanistic theories we have been examining hold that the latter have referends, namely, human and social values; the former have not. For them the name of God stands for no object, but it still has a pragmatic meaning. We shall call this position religious *nominalism* in contrast to religious *realism*.

Religious nominalism has received repeated statement throughout our modern naturalistic era. I choose as my illustration a presentation taken from Ludwig Feuerbach's *The Essence of Christianity*. "If," he writes, "the predicates of God are an anthropomorphism, if love, goodness, personality are human attributes, so also is the subject which you suppose here, the existence of God, the belief that there is a God, an anthropomorphism, a presupposition purely human. Yet he alone is the true atheist to whom the predicates of the divine being, e.g. love, wisdom, justice are nothing, not he to whom the subject of these predicates is nothing. And in no wise is the negation of the subject necessarily also the negation of the predicates considered in themselves. These have an intrinsic, independent reality; they force their recognition upon man by their very nature. The idea of God is dependent on the idea of justice, of goodness, of wisdom . . . but the converse does not hold. Religion, however, knows nothing of anthropomorphism; to it they are not anthropomorphisms

... they are pronounced to be images only by the understanding which reflects on religion."[1]

The essential of all forms of religious nominalism is expressed in this passage. It is that the existence of God, the belief that there is a God, is itself an anthropomorphism, a supposition purely human. It is an attempt to retain the religious symbols and their values without the object which alone gives them significance as values. Religious nominalism is *empty* symbolism. Being thus empty it tends to the stultification of all religion.[2] The only alternative to such stultification is the thorough atheism as represented in the next stage of development of Feuerbach himself as expressed in his completely naturalistic and cynical *Lectures on the Essence of Religion* (1851). In the earlier stage there is still conviction of the divine predicates, of the "quality of Deity," with of course the denial of the bearer of the attributes. In the latter stage the predicates, the values themselves go also. Nominalism is, indeed, the most terrible of all heresies. Religion must be *realistic* or it is nothing.

B
Religious Realism

Religious realism, defined in its broadest sense, is an epistemological theory which asserts that religion gives us knowledge, both of the divine attributes and of the subject of the attributes. It insists that assertions about the nature of God are real assertions and that theological descriptions are not "descriptions which describe nothing." In this sense all genuine religion is realistic. But there is also a special meaning to the term religious realism which must receive our attention, namely, the view that there is an immediate non-symbolic knowledge of the divine or Deity, distinct from any other type of knowledge.

In our discussion of numinous poetry we had occasion to point out that this conception implied a theory of religious realism. The view that the religious is an *a priori* category not reducible to other categories, either ontological or axio-

---

[1] *The Essence of Christianity*, 1841, pp. 17 ff.
[2] The extreme form of such stultification is well expressed in the witty characterization of the belief of such a nominalist, of whom it was said that for him "there is no God but the Blessed Virgin is His mother."

logical, implies that religious experience has its unique object and that propositions embodying that experience have a unique reference. Now some form of religious realism in this sense is necessitated by any adequate theory of religious symbolism and by any satisfactory philosophy of religion. The difficulty is to state the theory satisfactorily.

There is one form of religious realism which, by associating itself with ordinary empiricism, plays directly into the hands of the positivist and the humanist. We have, it is held, a unique experience of the divine being or entity, God. But an object, to be experienced in the sense of empiricism, must be an observable entity and God to be experienced must be such an observable entity. With this form of religious realism criticism makes short work. Religious words, the "names of the gods," had it is true an empirical meaning (in this sense) originally, for they referred to observable entities such as the light, the thunder, the fire, etc. But they have ceased to have meaning, for they no longer refer to anything observable. It is for this reason that, for the positivist, religious sentences have no *literal* significance and are therefore only expressions of emotion.[1]

Somewhat more tenable is that form of religious realism which speaks not of an entity which is the object of religious experience, not *the* Deity, but the "quality of Deity"—a quality, namely, which pervades as a presence the phenomena of experience. This notion of an emergent quality of deity, maintained by S. Alexander and others, in some way experienced as other qualities, is an attractive and fascinating one. It affords a sort of empirical and realistic way of explaining the "numinous" character of religious experience and language. But such a notion has its difficulties also. There is no "sense," in the strict meaning of sense experience, by which such a quality could be intuited. Moreover, the notion of God as a quality, still more as an emergent, is one which it is diffi-

---

[1] In the attempt to make religion purely empirical, awareness of God is likened to perception of a physical object—"perception in a complex"—the only difference being that the data are not sensuous. Much more understandable is the step taken by Professor Wieman when he maintains that the data are as sensuous as those of science. In his article, "Can Religion Become Empirical?" (in the volume *The Nature of Religious Experience*), Professor J. S. Bixler remarks that "the resort to empiricism in religion has raised as many problems as it has solved." Surely he is right.

cult to make intelligible to the religious consciousness. Nevertheless, it is possible to make use of this notion if we are careful to avoid the implications which a too literal conception of quality seems to involve.

There is, then, a sense in which we may speak of a numinous quality of experience and in which we may call it the quality of Deity. What, then, is this quality? Much depends upon our answer to this question. It is, I think, not a unique datum of experience, but rather a unique dimension which many data of experience may have. In the terminology of value theory the "holy" is not a separate value but a dimension of the other values. This unique dimension may be experienced in connection with all types of intrinsic values, sensuous, aesthetic, moral. Though not exclusively connected with the moral it is, however, only in connection with the moral that the full religious quality is felt. It is only when the infinitely other fuses with the infinitely good that the full quality of deity is experienced. The referend of the primary religious symbolism is not, as we saw, the moral values as such, but rather the met-empirical or transcendental co-implicate of these values. It is this that gives them their religious dimension. This dimension, I should maintain, is as much a part of the experience of these values, is as much *intuited*, as the values themselves.

The essential of man as religious is that he is aware of his finite limits. He who recognizes a limit is already in reflection beyond it, and this sense of the beyond, of the infinite, is the source of religion. The finite implies the infinite, the relative the absolute. Thus we experience degrees of good, as the moral argument for the existence of God asserts, and from this we argue to the "existence" of the infinitely good, to the *ens perfectissimum* implied in it. But this is not a purely empirical argument, for if the sense for the perfect—and "the lust for the perfect" which goes with it—were not a part of our experience we could never argue to it. Man's sense of imperfection is, as Emerson says, that "fine innuendo by means of which he makes his immortal claim." Without the "sense" for the quality of perfection the sense of imperfection would have no meaning. This is the essence of all true religious realism.

The "infinitely holy" is, then, *a priori* in our experience. This idea, this unique value predicate, is not a predicate or "quality" of an already given God-experience, God-idea or object; it is its inmost kernel around which all pictures and symbols crystallize. This "intuition" of the infinite and perfect, as a necessary co-implicate of all experience and all intelligible discourse, we shall consider in a later context.[1] Here our sole point is that it is both the source and the referend of religious symbolism. It is the source in the sense that it determines and moulds (through its unique principles of distortion already studied), the empirical content of the symbol. It is the object or referend in that for complete reflection the *ens perfectissimum* is the *ens realissimum*; the notions of value and being are found inseparable.

This is the great, the inexpugnable, element of truth in the historical ontologism of Christian theology and in the ontological argument. The *ens perfectissimum* is God. Perfection is not a predicate of Deity but the essence of Deity itself. It is quite generally held that Hume and Kant once for all disposed of the ontological argument, but it should be realized that, if they did, it was only on the assumption that there is no other employment of the reason except the empirical. As a matter of fact, the really significant contribution of Kant was to show finally that there are no *purely* empirical proofs for the existence of God, as Hume inconsistently believed; that these so-called proofs really presuppose the ontological proof—or better expressed, perhaps, in the words of Gilson, it is the *initial datum* of the empirical or inductive proof.[2] What Kant did not see is that the moral argument also presupposes it. This is clearly seen in the nature of the argument from degrees of good by St. Thomas, out of which Kant's moral argument developed. There has been much dispute among Thomistic scholars as to whether this moral argument is not a form of the ontological. I should not wish to say that it is a *form* of the ontological, but, using, Gilson's terms again, I should say

---

[1] Chapter XIII, p. 635.
[2] *The Spirit of Mediaeval Philosophy*, p. 60. The entire discussion of this chapter is worthy of careful study. The point I wish to raise here is merely this: what really is the difference between saying, with Kant, that the empirical or inductive proof presupposes the ontological, and saying that the latter is the initial datum of the empirical? The point at issue is whether, were there no such initial datum, however we get it, there could be, by any empirical argument, proof for anything other than a finite being. I think not.

that the ontological is the *initial datum* of this as of all other proofs.[1]

The recognition of this inexpugnable element of truth in historical ontologism does not, however, mean either that the moral argument, or the argument from values, is not the primary basis of religious knowledge, nor that the empirical arguments are in any sense superfluous. In calling it the *initial datum* it is meant merely to emphasize the element of religious realism inseparable from any adequate theory of religious knowledge, and to bring into clear relief that which seems to me to be the necessary metaphysical basis of the classical theory of religious symbolism.

C

Religious Knowledge and Verifiability

The problem of religious knowledge, as of all forms of knowledge, reduces to the question of verifiability, and the question of verifiability reduces to the question of experience. Now, there *is* religious experience in some sense of the word and this experience is communicable. The question is whether it is verifiable, or rather whether the assertions in which this experience is expressed are verifiable.

We may simplify the problem by admitting forthwith that there is no verification of religious propositions in the sense of the empirical criterion as narrowly defined. This follows, in the first place, from our denial of religious realism in either of the forms described. It follows also from the fact that, by their very nature, no metempirical propositions, such as those of religion, are empirically verifiable—a statement which is as

---

[1] Thomistic scholars differ, as is well known, on this point. Some maintain that unlike the others, the argument from degrees is conceptual in appearance and in some way ontological, in other words, a concession to ontologism. Others, while admitting that the sources of the proof point to this—namely, St. Augustine's text, praising the Platonists for their recognition of a supreme principle in view of degrees of beauty, etc.—yet insist that we must not conclude from this that it is ontological in character and that it can be brought back to the properly Thomist point of view of moderate realism. (See Gilson on the *Quinque Viae* of St. Thomas, *Thomisme*, 83, Quatrième Preuve.) It seems to me, however, that the argument from degrees presupposes also, as initial datum, that we know, by "the light of reason," of an *ens perfectissimum*, a being than which a greater cannot be conceived. Otherwise we should never know that there are degrees, or rise from the finite to the infinite.

much true for such propositions in science as in religion. The symbolic sentences of religion and theology are propositions about the metempirical and, like all such propositions, have no literal significance in the sense of reference to empirically observable entities. It is obvious that if they have truth they cannot be verified in that way.

In attempting to answer this question, then, it is necessary to be quite clear as to what symbolic truth in religion would be, and wherein verification and confirmation conceivably could consist. Verification here would consist in the authentication of our symbols as valid expressions, for our type of consciousness, of the numinous quality of experience and its corresponding reference. It seems clear then that, while the reference of the religious symbol is beyond our human moral and value experience, its authentication can take place only within that experience. This is the element of truth in all moral theories of the religious symbol. It is only as they express the "highest and deepest" in human experience that they can be authenticated *as symbols*; a critique of all revelation must, as Fichte saw, in this sense, be moral. On the other hand, it is no less true that verification of the "existence" of the object to which the symbol refers must be metaphysical in character and verifiability here depends upon the possibility of verification in the metaphysical context. This is the significance of our distinction between symbolic truth and the truth of a symbol as developed earlier. The former is truth for our type of consciousness, the latter is the truth of the symbol sentences when translated into "literal" or abstract propositions.

The position here maintained may be made clearer by considering a position which is very popular in the experience philosophies of the present. It may be stated in the following way: "The intuitions of faith are called true not because their necessary correspondence to truth can be demonstrated, but because a man dwelling on these intuitions is conscious of a certain moral transformation, of a certain warmth and energy of life. To the religious man religion is inwardly justified. God has no need of natural or logical witnesses." This view represents such a complete confusion of truth and error that it is difficult to disentangle the two elements. There can be little question that one phase of this statement expresses.

although inadequately, something of fundamental importance. To the religious man religion is inwardly justified or authenticated, although that authentication cannot, if the views maintained throughout this study are valid, be wholly solipsistic. Religion, as we have seen, is "such a great thing" and religious experience such a genuine experience, that religious people understand each other, no matter how varied the symbols in which their experience is expressed. Religion, too, is verifiable and communicable knowledge. This much, then, is true. But the second part of the statement is wholly untrue, namely, that "God has no need of natural and logical witness."

This situation may be expressed in two ways. We may say that the authenticity of a symbol as embodying or expressing our experience of God, or of the numinous quality in experience, can be determined only within that experience, but the question of the *existence* of God, of the object of that experience—and our right to extend *per analogiam* our phenomenal categories to Him—can be determined only by evidence which involves both natural and logical witnesses. Or, we may say, God is not only the *ens perfectissimum*, but the *ens realissimum*. Value and being are inseparable. Values as such have significance, but in order to have significance in the religious context, they must also have cosmic significance. The witnesses for God in this aspect of His nature can only be natural and logical witnesses.[1]

---

[1] Since the completion of the manuscript of this book, the recent Gifford Lectures by Edwyn Bevan, entitled *Symbolism and Belief*, have been published by George Allen & Unwin Ltd. (1938).

In general the theme of symbolism in religion is treated with a wealth of detail not possible in this chapter. Attention may be called especially to the discussion of the distinction between literal and symbolic in Lecture XI, to the relation between symbolism and analogy in Lecture XIII, in which the scholastic position is discussed, and finally to the discussion of the cognitive element in religion in the last two chapters, *Rationalism and Mysticism* and *The Justification of Belief*. With this part of the work I do not find myself wholly in sympathy. Much less than justice appears to be done to the "rational" element in religion. A somewhat narrow view of reason coupled with a possibly too literal view of the "theistic proofs" seem to make the grounds for rational belief less cogent than they really are. That ultimate reasons are in some way bound up with value seems to be recognized, but value is conceived much more subjectively and psychologically than it need be. Despite these limitations, the book as a whole seems to me to be an important study of religious symbolism, and in general a valuable contribution to this much neglected chapter in the philosophy of religion. Had it been possible for me to make use of it earlier, it would have doubtless affected my presentation of the subject in significant respects.

RELIGIOUS SYMBOLS

It is for these reasons that, despite its reluctance to do so, religion must in a certain sense "pass over" into metaphysics. As we found in our examination of the language of religion, despite the fact that to retain its character it must remain poetry, it must, nevertheless, in theology become also metaphysical, so now it appears that notwithstanding the fact that religion, as experience, can only be "inwardly justified" the significance of that experience can be interpreted only metaphysically. With this we come to our last task, namely, the interpretation of religion as symbolic form. This we shall consider under the heading, the philosophy of religion.

VII

THE PHILOSOPHY OF RELIGION; WHAT RELIGION "SAYS"

A

The late Pope is reported to have said: "Those who speak of the incompatibility of science and religion either make science say that which it never said or make religion say that which it never taught." For myself, I believe that to be in principle true, but for such a statement even to have any meaning, still less to be true, clearly some interpretation of both science and religion must be presupposed. It is assumed that both science and religion are made to say things which they really do not when their nature is properly understood. To determine what they really say is interpretation, and such interpretation is philosophy of science and philosophy of religion respectively.

As a matter of fact, many of the things which science says explicitly contradict things which religion says explicitly. Such contradictions are too numerous and too well known even to need mention. But as in the case of both poetry and science, so in religion, we often have explicit statements which are quite different from what religion says implicitly. Moreover, while there is great variation in the explicit assertions of various positive religions—on the levels of the mythical and historical —there is a singular unanimity on the higher and more developed levels of the ethical religions, or in what they say implicitly. It is accordingly with what religion really says, more particularly with what it says as symbolic form, that we are ultimately concerned.

The task here described is the specific problem of the philosophy of religion. "The philosophy of religion," according to a definition of Pringle-Pattison, "investigates the nature of the religious consciousness and the value of its pronouncements upon human life and man's relation to the ground of things." From the standpoint of our present discussion we may restate this definition in the following way: The philosophy of religion investigates the nature of religion as a symbolic form and the validity of its symbols as a representation of reality. It seeks, therefore, to determine the meaning and the validity of what religion says both explicitly and implicitly.

B

What Religion Says Explicitly

The things religion says explicitly are very varied in the different positive religions but, like the explicit statements of science, they may be classified under certain types. It is possible for us to treat them only as types and in so doing contrast them with the explicit assertions of science.

The latter included three types: statements of fact, statements of laws (empirical generalizations), and cosmological statements. All these demand, as we have seen, interpretation, for the reason that all are, as assertions, expressed in language and as such are already "constructed."[1] When interpreted by science itself, they are held to mean something quite other than what they explicitly assert, and this difference in meaning we found to be all important. This is true of all types, but is especially important in the case of the cosmological propositions. In religion also we find three main types of propositions, but as we should naturally expect, they do not correspond completely with the scientific. These, following a generally accepted classification, may be described as the historical, the cosmological and the metaphysical. Otherwise stated, and brought into conformity with our classification of religious symbols, they are propositions about the being of God, or the

[1] Chapter XI, p. 555 f.

divine (metaphysical); propositions about the relation of God to the world (cosmological); and propositions about divine transactions or acts in time (historical).

C

The Historical Element in Religion

Special consideration must be given to the class of historical propositions or to what is called the "historical element in religion." This is necessary for two reasons: (*a*) because it is the historical propositions of religion that come into most notable conflict with the factual statements of science, and (*b*) because it is the symbolization of acts that presents the crux of a philosophy of religious symbolism.

According to the classical principles of interpretation, events in nature and history and the recorded events of sacred scriptures have their literal meaning, although their full meaning and their real truth cannot be known until we pass to the higher stages of interpretation. The latter part of this statement the philosophy of religion understands; it is the retention of the literal meaning which creates the difficulty.

Here, as in the case of the "factual" propositions of science, the higher criticism of religion insists that what these propositions say superficially is not what they really say. This follows of necessity by reason of the fundamental difference between the mythical and religious consciousness already made clear. The mythical consciousness, as mythical, is literal and must be. The religious consciousness, as religious, consists precisely in the recognition of the fact that, while the poetical and mythical is a necessary form of expression (without it the *vis religiosa* is lost), it is nevertheless symbolic. It seems quite clear, therefore, that the historical element in religion, while necessary if religion is to remain religion, is different for religion from what it is for science. For both it is factual. For science (history) the fact has no numinous quality; for religion it has. As a fact in space and time it is therefore for religion *revelatory* of non-spatial and non-temporal relations and values—as indeed the entire spatio-temporal world is a revelation of the "intelligible world."

The point I am making may be made clearer by considering the questions which have arisen in connection with the problem of the nature and interpretation of the Christian creeds, more particularly the Nicene. These contain, as is generally recognized, all three types of propositions, those which have to do with the timeless being and nature of God ("before all worlds"), those which have to do with relations to the cosmos and those which are the statements of "historical fact." The issue here raised is discussed with admirable clearness and candour by A. E. Taylor in his chapter on Religion and the Historical.[1] He points out that attempts to divest religion of attachments to historical persons and events is an attempt to manufacture the supreme reality out of mere "universals," or to make an "is" out of a mere "ought," and ends in degrading religion into a mere theosophy. The "historical" element in religion is an essential part of its nature. But he also rightly sees that no hard and fast line can be drawn between the "symbolical" and the historical as is often done in the interpretation of the creeds. Such a distinction can only be regarded as one of degree. The fundamental difficulty, as he rightly sees, in any such absolute division lies in the nature of language itself. "I think," he writes, "it actually impossible to describe *any* real event in language wholly non-symbolic. No language, if I may be pardoned the merely apparent 'bull,' is even approximately free from the symbolic except the artificial language of 'symbolic logic,' and that language is impotent to describe the simplest and most familiar event." Here we have, indeed, the crux of the matter. All language, and *a fortiori* dramatic language in which alone religion can speak, is symbolic.

This fact, however, does not exclude the other fact, that real events take place in time which have the numinous quality of deity, and these constitute the historical element in religion. And that, in rendering these real events and their quality in language, only that language can be used which was made to describe the phenomenal—with the inevitable consequence that the language must be symbolic. It is for this reason that, as we have seen, the language of religion must be numinous poetry. It is for this reason also that in

[1] *The Faith of a Moralist*, Vol. II, Chapter IV, pp. 141 ff.

Christian theology the creed as a whole is called a **symbol**, and is recognized as a symbolic form in which the non-symbolic is expressed. That which religion really says can only be determined by the interpretation of the symbol.

D

Cosmological Propositions

It is, however, with the cosmological propositions of religion that the philosophy of religion must be especially concerned, just as in science it is these around which the main issues of a philosophy of science turn. The cosmological propositions are fundamentally of two kinds, assertions about the creation of the world and assertions about its end or destiny.

The cosmic myths from which religion gets its language and its symbolism are fundamental elements in every positive religion, and cosmological propositions basal in every religions view of the world. When, as in the Christian creed, it is asserted that God is "the maker of heaven and earth and of all things visible and invisible," something of tremendous significance has been said, although it is said symbolically. God, if there be a God, is not a "maker" in any literal sense. Maker is a purely phenomenal notion and, like the notion of prime mover of which Kant wrote, is inseparable from "spatial and temporal elements," and therefore cannot be applied in an empirical or literal sense. In like manner, when in the same creed belief in a "last judgment" is expressed, something of immense import has also been said, although symbolically. It is precisely such propositions about "first and last things" which have basal significance for religion. What, then, is this significance?

When these explicit cosmological propositions of religion are interpreted—and they must be interpreted—what they are really found to say may be summed up in the statement: *the cosmic significance of values.* It is only in so far as the cosmological propositions of science deny this that they are of any significance for religion. If, for instance, a statement or formulation of cosmic evolution comes into conflict with the meaning of the doctrine of creation at this point, it is then, and only then, that they have any significance for each other. A formulation of cosmic evolution which derives values from the non-valuable is of course inimical to religion. Similarly a doctrine of cosmic devolution—of a running down of the universe—which includes, so to speak, the dissipation of values, as well as the dissipation of energy, is inimical to religion. But, as we have seen, all depends here upon the interpretation of the cosmological propositions of science, as well as of those of religion—in other words, on what science also really says. As already pointed out in the preceding chapter, the cosmological propositions of science and of religion come into conflict only when both speak the same language, namely, the dramatic. If science speaks merely a mathematical-logical language the two are not in the same universe of discourse. Cosmological propositions in both science and religion are metaphysical propositions, and it is only in the universe of discourse of metaphysics that they have significance.

All this may be summarized in the following general statement. The exploration of the external world by science leads, not to concrete reality but, in the words of Eddington, "to a shadow world of symbols beneath which these methods are not adapted to penetrating." The exploration of the world of the religious consciousness and its symbols leads to another world outlook than the scientific one. We may the more boldly insist that there is this other outlook, continues Eddington, because in practice a more transcendental outlook is universally admitted.[1] The problem is, then, not so much whether there is this other outlook; that is a mere matter of fact. It is not a question whether it is meaningful. There is, as we have seen, a language of religion and a type of symbols by means of which this outlook and its meaning are communicated. The question is rather of the relation of these two languages and symbolic forms.

So far as the conflict between these two outlooks and these two symbolic forms is concerned, one consideration is of prime importance. There is not—and in principle cannot be—any conflict between science in its ideal symbolic form, the mathematical-logical, and the dramatic form of religion, for they do not speak the same language. God may be a mathematician, although He is, if He is God, a great deal more, but the godly

---

[1] *Science and the Unseen World*, p. 82. (Published by George Allen & Unwin Ltd.) Also in other writings.

never speak a mathematical language, because, as such, it literally says nothing about any of the things which to them are real. It is only when science also speaks a dramatic language that it comes into conflict with religion. If I say that the world was not created but that it evolved, there are implications for religion, but that is because I am dramatizing nature. If I say that the universe is running down, that has implications for religion in that the mathematical formulas which it so freely renders have been dramatized, but when thus dramatized they not only come into conflict with religion but also with another part of science, namely, biology, as Duhem has pointed out. These are facts the full significance of which are rarely appreciated. Put into more philosophical terminology, it is only when I speak a scientific language which retains in its structure elements of meaning and value that anything which science says is significant for religion. If I exclude these *ab initio*, I can by no possible stretch of the imagination say anything which is in the least significant for any but the exclusively scientific point of view.

E

What Religion Says Implicitly: Metaphysical Propositions

It is generally recognized that what religion tells us implicitly is of more fundamental significance than what it tells us explicitly, and that when the philosopher wishes to determine the "truth" of religion it is to what it implicitly says that he instinctively turns. The religious consciousness, while perfectly clear that it cannot abandon the concrete terms, so rich in colour, that belong to its poetical and mythical aspects, is also perfectly clear that this is not what it really says. When it says what it really means it passes on to ideas which can be expressed only in terms of greater generality and abstractness. In the explicit assertions of religion, both historical and cosmological, there are contained certain implications which, when made explicit through interpretation, constitute the most significant elements in religion. In this respect religion is not different from science. It is also what science says implicitly that is most significant for our view of life and the world.

Of the things which religion, as symbolic form, says implicitly the most immediately significant is what it says negatively. It is a true insight of Le Roy's that the dogmas and symbols of religion are in a sense more significant for what they tell us not to believe than for what they positively affirm. When, then, we turn to religion as a whole, as symbolic form, its first significance is its implicit denials. By its use of the language of poetry, without which as we have seen religious experience cannot be expressed, it, together with poetry, denies the adequacy of science as symbolic form, to express reality—the "fullness of being." By that very fact also it accepts in principle all that poetry, as symbolic form, has to say about man and nature. The implicit presuppositions of the universe of discourse in which poetry alone can have its being are also shared by religion. It would perhaps be too much to say that if poetry should die religion would also perish from the earth, but we may at least say that so long as religion survives poetry will also. But religion is *numinous* poetry and, as such, catches and communicates something which ordinary poetry does not. It is this which is significant. Whether expressed in a merely negative theology (which tells us what ultimate reality is not) or in a more positive theology (which, while telling us what this reality is, nevertheless tells us that it is more than this), in either case it is this *more* which constitutes the significant implication of every word that religion utters. What is it, then, that religion says implicitly yet positively?

Many attempts have been made in the philosophy of religion to express in the terms of the highest generality—in metaphysical language—what it is that religion, *as religion*, says. In one form or another they all say the same thing. They all assert implicitly that values have cosmic significance, that value and reality are inseparable—the identity of the *summum bonum* or *ens perfectissimum* with the *ens realissimum*. This is not only the essence of the European tradition but, I think, also of all developed religion.

In developing my point I shall take my start from a modern attempt to express this implicit content of religion, namely, that of Höffding. Religion he defines as the belief in the conservation of values. By a comparative study of religion he makes it quite clear, I think, that all religions, from the most

RELIGIOUS SYMBOLS

primitive and relatively amoral to the most developed and ethical, have this belief as their common element. In other words, what they all say implicitly is that human values have in some way cosmic significance. Now I am not concerned here either with the arguments by which he shows, or seeks to show, the compatibility of this belief with the cosmic propositions of science, nor with the metaphysics which his philosophy involves, but merely with the question of the truth of this account of the implicit content of religion. This, I think, is beyond question. Whatever specific historical propositions a positive religion may contain, whatever cosmological propositions about the "beginning" or "end" of all things it may embody, when these are interpreted they are seen to be symbolic statements of this notion.

To be sure, the notion of the conservation of values carries with it the idea of time and temporal process. The "laying up of treasures in Heaven," however literally or figuratively the notion may be envisaged, seems to imply the idea of a future time. The conception that there "neither moth nor rust doth corrupt," however literally or figuratively this notion may be envisaged, seems to imply continuance in time, or eternity in the temporal sense. This, too, is doubtless all it can mean for the religious consciousness in so far as it speaks a wholly historical or cosmological language. But this notion of conservation of values means more than this; it is an expression *in the time form*—and therefore, to that extent symbolically—for a timeless and metaphysical relation of the "good" or value to being. Values not only have cosmic significance but ultimate metaphysical or ontological significance. It is this *metaphysical* assertion which constitutes the essence of what all religion says implicitly.

Religion contains, then, implicitly an assertion about the ultimate nature of reality—about the *omnitudo realitatis*, about "the fullness of being," to make use of an expression of traditional philosophy. It is, when thought out in all its implications, precisely that ontologism which, as we have seen, is both the presupposition and the postulate of the classical theory of religious symbolism. It is the metaphysical assertion that the *ens realissimum*, being in all its fullness, is identical with, or at least inseparable from, the *ens perfectissimum*. It is for this reason that it may be truly said, in the words of Brightman, that "the idea of God *symbolizes* a unity or harmony between existence and value." In other words, when the "primary symbol," God, is interpreted, its implicit content is a metaphysical statement of this sort. We can put this truth in still another way. Religion *says* many things; it includes historical, cosmological, and metaphysical statements. Many of its explicit statements are "mythical," in the neutral and technical use of the word myth, and symbolic in the sense that the "things that are unseen" are expressed in the terms of the "things that are seen," but what it really says, in so far as its ultimate metaphysical content is concerned, can be expressed only in propositions of this type.

VIII

RELIGION AND METAPHYSICS: THE ONTOLOGICAL IMPORT OF RELIGION

Both poetry and science are covert metaphysics. So also is religion, but religion is pre-eminently so. Not only is the very language of religion numinous and loses all meaning when the metempirical reference is lost, but, as we have seen, the religious symbol differs only psychologically, not epistemologically, from the metaphysical symbol.

It follows from this that in religion, more than in other symbolic forms of human culture, the drive to uncover the hidden metaphysics is irresistible. Translation from the implicit symbolic to the explicit metaphysical is, then, inherent in religion itself. This translation is, to be sure, always made only in the teeth of very definite resistance—a resistance felt also by poetry and science. It is only unwillingly that any of these symbolic forms realize their own immanental logic. But religion is even more unwilling, for it senses, even more than art or science, the possibility of its own death—the loss of the *vis religiosa*. In all religion there is accordingly always a drive towards metaphysics and a counter-drive away from it. Every move towards interpretation of religion is followed by "fits of literalism."

This drive and counter-drive—this contradiction at the heart of all symbolic forms—we have described as the paradox of symbolism.[1] It presents a dilemma to every form of consciousness, but one which is peculiarly insistent in what we may describe as the *Dilemma of Religion*. That religious knowledge must be in part symbolic we can see, but what we want is the "blunt truth," not reality seen through a glass darkly. But literal or "blunt" truth has the unhappy fashion of becoming untrue. The fallacy of misplaced literalism is, if anything, even more disastrous in religion than in science.

This dilemma may be stated in another way, which brings out its insistence even more clearly. "Religion," writes Bennett, "cannot do without the supernatural, yet it cannot do with it; for it refuses to be completely rationalized." The term "supernatural" has indeed many meanings, but when it is taken in its proper sense it is evident that religion cannot do without it. When the humanist tells us that "until the supernatural is eliminated from the minds of men we shall not be able to comprehend religion," we can only answer that to "comprehend it" in this sense would be to dissolve it into something else. The dilemma remains in all its stubbornness. It is usually supposed that there are only two ways of meeting this dilemma, both of which involve the dissolving of religion into something else. The first of these is the familiar one of dissolving it into poetry. On the assumption that there is no significance except literal significance and no truth but literal truth, an easy solution of the problem consists in reducing the language of religion to purely emotive language and in denying that it really says anything at all. It is not surprising that this solution has attracted many who seek short cuts to the solution of difficult problems; one of the easiest ways of solving problems is to deny that there is any problem at all (and unfortunately when a man says that he sees no problem it is a little difficult to show him that it is there). The difficulty with this solution is, as we have already seen, that it goes counter to all the facts. Religion is neither identical in essence with poetry nor does it say nothing. It says a great deal, and what it says, whether true or false, is highly significant.

The second way of meeting the dilemma is to dissolve

[1] Chapter IX, p. 434.

religion wholly into philosophy or metaphysics, a solution advocated by certain forms of metaphysical idealism. According to this view religion must, in the words of Croce, "allow itself to be dissolved into philosophy."[1] Religion is in principle mythology, in the broad sense of the term, and as such its fate is to be but the vestibule to metaphysics. It is true that Croce recognizes in religion a puzzling something which is more than philosophy, namely worship; nevertheless its fortune, whether good or bad, is to be thus dissolved. This solution obviously does greater justice to the facts of religion which, whatever else it is, is metaphysical. At first sight, indeed, it seems the only one possible. And yet it also cannot be right. For thus to dissolve religion into philosophy would be also to denature it. It is true that when thus dissolved it would still say much that religion implicitly says, but the peculiar numinous quality of religious experience and the "quality of deity" found in the objects of this experience would remain unexpressed.

Is there, then, a third possibility, another way of solving the dilemma? I think there is. This possibility may be expressed by saying that religion is not to be *dissolved*—into either poetry or philosophy—but to be *interpreted*. Such interpretation involves translation of the language of religion into the language of metaphysics, but a translation which retains the meaning of religion. The important thing is that the essential of all genuine translation is the retention of the nuances of meaning of that which is translated. The one thing it does not do is to *dissolve* that meaning into something else. Applied to our present problem, this means that what religion says implicitly—and that is its most significant part—must be made explicit, and that can be done only by translation into metaphysical terms of higher generality. But if it is to be interpreted and not dissolved, metaphysics must find language adequate for the expression and interpretation of the meaning of religion. First of all, I should insist that this is precisely what classical theology has always actually done. Thus St. Thomas writes: "Love which works good to all things, pre-existing overflowingly in the Good . . . moved itself to creation, as befits the superabundance by which all things are generated. . . . The

[1] B. Croce, *The Conduct of Life*, authorized translation, 1924, Chapter XXI.

Good by being extends its goodness to all things. For as our sun, not by choosing or taking thought but by merely being, enlightens all things, so the Good . . . by its mere existence sends forth upon all things the beams of its goodness."[1] Here, as Professor Lovejoy writes, "the phraseology of the primitive Christian conception of the loving Father in Heaven has been converted into an expression of the dialectic of emanationism." I should prefer to say, into the terms of metaphysics. The important point, however, is that it is converted or translated, not dissolved—the *vis religiosa* is retained.

But this is not only what classical theology has actually done; it is what it must do, because it speaks implicitly a metaphysical language. It is true that in thus attempting to translate the language of religion into that of metaphysics the "dilemma of religion," of which we have spoken, can never be completely resolved. Certain differences between the language of religion and the language of metaphysics remain which give rise to internal conflicts of thought. Nevertheless, it is incumbent upon philosophy to find language adequate for the expression of all forms of experience.

The crucial instance of this dilemma is to be found precisely in the central notion of all religion, namely, the God notion itself. So far as European religious thought is concerned, as has been frequently pointed out, "two antithetic ideas have been constantly conjoined," the God of religion and the Absolute of philosophy. The situation began with Plato. In the *Republic* the ground and source of all being is the idea of the Good itself, and it was therefore held by many interpreters that the Creator who figures in the *Timaeus* is simply a poetic interpretation of that idea. More probable is the view that two originally distinct strains in Plato's thought are here fused, the religious and the metaphysical, and that the fusion was never wholly satisfactory. In any case the entire tendency in the succeeding European tradition was to perpetuate this fusion. The concept of self-sufficing Perfection inherent in the metaphysical notion of the Good was, without losing any of its original implications, converted into the concept of a self-transcending fecundity of creativeness. A time-

---

[1] *De div. nom.*, IV, 1; *ibid.*, col. 695. Quoted from A. C. Lovejoy, *The Great Chain of Being*, p. 68.

less and incorporeal One became the logical ground, as well as the dynamic source, of a temporal and material universe. The proposition that, as it was later phrased in the Middle Ages, *omne bonum est diffusivum sui*, makes its appearance as an axiom of metaphysics. With this was introduced into European philosophy and theology a combination of ideas that for centuries was to give rise to many of the most characteristic internal conflicts. Anyone acquainted with European thought will know that this conflict has been one of the chief driving-forces in its development. These two notions have never been satisfactorily fused, nor has it been possible to "dissolve" the one into the other. And yet it remains true that the two languages—of religion and metaphysics—despite the conflict, live on together. "The soul possesses God in so far as it participates in the absolute"; so a well-known philosophical assertion expresses this situation. The virtual identity of the two notions is, I think, both psychologically and philosophically true, but neither can be wholly dissolved into the other.

It is probable, then, that this dilemma can never be completely resolved—that the language of religion can never be translated into that of metaphysics without leaving a remainder. None the less, it is a task which the philosophy of religion cannot escape, for it is the only possible way of solving its fundamental problem. Nor can metaphysics itself escape the task of an adequate interpretation of religion. For religion is one context in which meaningful discourse is carried on, one symbolic form, or way of representing and communicating our experience of reality. Metaphysics, whatever else it is, is concerned with maximum context; it is the language of languages, and in this language the language of religion must find a place. The problem of the language of metaphysics becomes, then, for religion, as for the other symbolic forms, science and art, an inescapable problem. Until we know what the language of metaphysics is—what its nature and functions really are—our philosophy of language and of symbolic forms is wholly incomplete. To this question we must now turn.

CHAPTER XIII

THE LANGUAGE OF METAPHYSICS: SYMBOLISM AS A METAPHYSICAL PRINCIPLE

I

THE problems of the philosophy of language culminate in the problem of the language of metaphysics; those of the theory of symbols in the problem of symbolism and metaphysics. The issues raised by these ultimate questions may be seen in two characteristic positions of present-day philosophy, namely, the denial of the possibility of all metaphysics on the basis of the logical analysis of language, and, secondly, the view of Bergson that metaphysics is "the science which claims to dispense with symbols."[1] The former looks upon metaphysics as a form of poetry, although a "sorry sort of poetry," and denies to it, as it does to poetry, any meaning but emotive. The latter, while recognizing a form of "knowledge" which may fairly be called metaphysical, denies that this knowledge can be expressed in the language or symbols of either common sense or science.

Neither of these positions is, of course, wholly new. If they were they would not be as significant as they really are. Neopositivism is in principle not different from any of the basal forms of positivism. The Bergsonian view is in principle not different from any of the classical forms of mysticism from Neoplatonism on.[2] What is new in both—and it is this that gives them their significance in the present context—is the fact that they are immensely more sophisticated than the earlier forms, and that this sophistication arises from the fact that both see that a critique of metaphysics is in the last analysis a critique of language.

The relation of these problems to the foregoing may be seen in the fact that the various languages and symbolic forms always pass over into metaphysics or require metaphysical language for their ultimate interpretation. In addition to what they say explicitly they also contain implicit assertions, and

[1] *An Introduction to Metaphysics* (authorized translation, 1912), p. 9.
[2] Chapter I, p. 35 f.

these assertions, when made explicit, are always metaphysical in character. In other words, metaphysical language is the language of maximum context. The meaningfulness of the other languages always depends upon the meaningfulness of metaphysical language. It follows from these considerations that the language of metaphysics is the central problem of a philosophy of language.

This is implicitly recognized even by those who deny the meaningfulness of metaphysical language or that metaphysics has any special content. They frequently make a distinction between metaphysics and philosophy and, while denying the former, give an important place to the latter. For them also the language of metaphysics becomes a basal problem. According to this view, the function of philosophy, to put it in Ramsey's frivolous form, is "to cure headaches and not to answer questions." More technically, its function is the clarification or elucidation of meaning; it is a system of definitions and elucidation of meaning of words. The essential point is that philosophy has no special content, no specific propositions of its own which might be called metaphysical as distinct from those of science. I do not think that this position can be carried out—that statements such as these can be really made intelligible. In the first place, science itself, as we have seen, contains metaphysical elements. In so far as it contains cosmological propositions it trenches on the metaphysical, and while these are necessary to "round out" science, they are of a different type from the factual and general propositions of science.[1] In the second place—and this is even more significant—this very elucidation of meaning, which is supposed to be the characteristic of philosophy as distinguished from metaphysics, itself involves metaphysics. There is a significant difference between merely logical and philosophical elucidation of meaning. The sense of a proposition which, as we have seen, logic must assume and can never itself determine, involves always a reference to reality, and elucidation of this reference is always metaphysical or implies a metaphysics. The theory of meaning which denies meaning to metaphysical propositions is itself a metaphysics, as has been repeatedly shown. There is, then, we shall maintain, no hard-and-fast line to be drawn

[1] Chapter XI, pp. 557 ff.

between philosophy and metaphysics. There is also, we shall further maintain, a special content to philosophy which can only be described as metaphysical. What this content is we shall see in detail when we come to the examination of the language of metaphysics. A necessary preliminary, however, is some attempt at a definition of metaphysics.

II

THE SUBJECT-MATTER OF METAPHYSICS: DEFINITIONS

A

It is related of a metaphysical society in England that it was compelled to disband because its members could not agree on the preliminary question of what metaphysics is. It is understandable that this was a source of endless mirth to the profane, but surely the mirth was premature. For this is precisely the predicament in which we all find ourselves whenever we try to talk about any of the interesting and fundamental things. Science finds itself in the same predicament, as we have seen, in the attempt to define it, and it has been said with a show of truth that mathematics is the science in which we do not know what we are talking about. The fact is that the things we know best are, if not indefinable, at least the hardest to define. I shall therefore not start with a definition, but rather with a description or characterization. To the question, What is metaphysics? I shall answer with Kant, that it is a *Naturanlage* and I shall add, also with him, that, should civilization and even science itself perish, metaphysics would still remain.

I think it is well to begin with this conception—that we should recognize that, like the prose of the famous play, everyone is talking metaphysics without knowing it. In Bernard Shaw's *Man and Superman* Don Juan is trying to get over to the man and the woman, and to the perverse Devil himself, his understanding of life and of the universe in which that life is lived. "Life," he cries, "is driving at its darling, brains, at its object and organ by which it can attain, not only self-consciousness, but self-understanding." "This is metaphysics, Juan," retorts the Senior Commander, and he was right in his retort. Juan is here talking metaphysics, as we all do whenever we use such terms as life, the world, the universe, and whenever we attribute to them qualities or activities, or ascribe to them ultimate origins or ends. In all such talk we are trenching on the metaphysical and are using metaphysical language.

The first characteristic of metaphysics, then, is that it makes assertions or propositions about metempirical "entities" which themselves are not directly experienced but are, in some fashion, the co-implicates of experience. In this sense science itself is metaphysical, as are, indeed, all the fundamental symbolic forms, such as poetry and religion. A further character appears in the fact that these metempirical entities are "wholes." In the case of the sciences, both historical and generalizing, the assertions are about partial wholes, whereas in metaphysics proper the assertions are also about the totality of totalities, the *omnitudo realitatis*. The partial totalities are, however, as we have seen, no less metempirical than the totality of metaphysics; if propositions about the latter are meaningless, so are propositions about the former. The cosmological propositions of science all trench on the metaphysical, and if metaphysics is impossible, so also is science except in a very truncated form.[1]

It is desirable in the present context to develop this point a little more fully. A definition of Whitehead's will be helpful. "By metaphysics," he writes, "I understand the science which seeks to discover the general ideas or principles which are indispensably relevant to the analysis of everything that happens."[2] *Everything* is the significant notion here. But "everything" may be taken in two senses. In the first or collective sense, metaphysics deals with the ideas and relations that apply to all aspects of being. In this sense we have the definition of Hartmann when he tells us that "metaphysics deals with the widest categorial connections possible."[3] But it may also be taken in a totalitarian sense. In this case metaphysics is the science which deals with the ideas applicable to reality as a whole.

The distinction here made is of considerable importance. It is held by many philosophers that while metaphysics deals

---

[1] Chapter XI, p. 563 f.   [2] *Religion in the Making*, p. 84.
[3] *Ethics*, Vol. III, p. 140.

with "everything" in the former sense, it does not speak about the whole in the second meaning of the term, or at most deals with totality only as "a loose connection." But I think it is clear that we cannot speak of everything in the former without also including the latter sense. If I say that the world is a mere collection or a plurality I am thereby also predicating of it a character as a *whole* which has wide-reaching consequences for both theory and practice. The world or universe is one, as James admitted, in the sense that it is one subject of discourse. And indeed we cannot talk intelligibly without our discourse including propositions about the whole. As well ask a man to whistle and smile at the same time as to be a physicist and not speak about the universe in the sense of a physical whole, or to be a philosopher without talking about the whole in the sense of the *omnitudo realitatis*. I have argued this point at length in another connection.[1] Here I shall take as my illustration a recent instance.

A philosophical work has appeared entitled *A World of Chance*, the main thesis of which is that "chance or contingency runs through and through the entire universe." "By this universe," the writer continues, "I mean *the entire realm of fact* and this realm I find very extensive."[2] Now it is one thing to say that we find contingency or chance in things; it is quite another thing to say that chance and contingency run throughout the *entire* world of fact. To say that this is a "world of chance," that chance is a *fundamental character* of the world as a whole, is to say something, not about a collection of things but about a unique whole which is more than a collection. And since the subject of this assertion can itself never be an object of experience, the assertion can never be verified by any accumulation of evidence with respect to the elements of the collection. It is assertions of this type which are essentially metaphysical.

B

Metaphysics and the Co-implicates of Experience

The first characteristic of metaphysics is that it makes assertions about metempirical entities. Included in these entities or

[1] *The Intelligible World*, pp. 51 ff.   [2] E. G. Spaulding, *A World of Chance*.

objects are metempirical wholes, partial and total. The important thing here is that unless such assertions are made we cannot make intelligible assertions about experience itself or about the experienced parts of the wholes. The significance of this is chiefly apparent in the cosmological propositions of science which are all of this nature and without which, as we have seen, science really "says" very little.[1] Kant saw this point clearly when he ascribed to the metaphysical "ideas," especially to the idea of the cosmos, at least a regulative function in knowledge—regulative in the sense that "the empirical employment of the understanding," the knowledge of science, is dependent upon them for its very life and significance. The "existence" of metempirical entities about which significant propositions can be made is, then, the necessary presupposition or co-implication of intelligible discourse. I have stated this fact in a summary fashion in my *Intelligible World*. "There are three well-nigh invariable beliefs, certain necessary presuppositions of intelligible communication, namely, that I exist and others like me, inhabiting a world. Of these presuppositions there is not, nor will there ever be, any empirical proof or disproof. Not being the result of experience, but implied in experience, they are intangible to its vicissitudes. They are not the *outcome* of experience and its communication, but its co-implicates."[2]

The sense in which these are the co-implicates of experience, and in which they are the necessary presuppositions of any intelligible communication (communication or expression and experience not being ultimately separable), has been made

[1] Chapter XI, p. 556 f.
[2] Chapter II.
In his *Philosophy and Logical Syntax*, p. 15, Carnap writes: "I will call metaphysical all those propositions which claim to represent knowledge about something which is over or beyond all experience, e.g. about the real essence of things, about things in themselves, the absolute and such like. I do not include in metaphysics those theories—sometimes called metaphysical—whose object is to arrange the most general propositions of the various regions of scientific knowledge in a well ordered system; such theories belong actually to the field of empirical science, not of philosophy, however daring they may be." I do not believe that this distinction can be satisfactorily maintained. The notion of a system of science is not separable from the notion of a whole of reality and wherever the latter notion enters we have metaphysics. Either one has pure empiricism and with it mere knowledge of parts, or one has knowledge of wholes and with it metempirical presuppositions. This was made plain in Chapter X.

clear in other contexts.[1] That a world in some sense other than and independent of communicating minds is necessary to make such communication possible is a way of stating the minimum of realism necessary to any theory of communication; but an equally necessary condition and therefore co-implicate of experience is the reality of other minds.

In the formula presented above we spoke of them as well-nigh invariable *beliefs* of which there is not and, in the nature of the case, never will be any *empirical* proof or disproof. They are not the outcome but the co-implicates of experience. In reality they are beliefs only in the sense that they are not verifiable by the empirical criterion in the narrow sense of the definition; actually, as necessary co-implicates of experience and necessary presuppositions of communicaton, they are part of experience and verifiable in communication itself.[2] They constitute, therefore, what I shall describe as the element of non-symbolic knowledge of a metempirical or metaphysical sort. To be sure, as we shall see, statements about these implicates are always symbolic in character. The subjects of metaphysical discourse are metempirical, the predicates always taken from domains of experience (or phenomena). This we shall see is the essential character of metaphysical sentences or propositions. It is precisely the extension of phenomenal categories to the noumenal or metempirical which constitutes the problem of metaphysical knowledge and it is here that the problem of the metaphysical symbol arises.

C

The "Infinite" as Co-implicate; The Limited and the Limitless

These, then, are necessary co-implicates of intelligible discourse. No language of any kind, whether poetic, scientific or religious, can be made intelligible without acknowledgment of these co-implicates and without rounding out our experience through the postulation of the "existence" of these "entities." There is, however, still another co-implicate of experience which, it has constantly been maintained, is equally

[1] Chapter VI, p. 263 ff.   [2] Chapter V, p. 218 f.

present in all experience and equally the object of necessary metaphysical postulation, namely, the "idea" of the infinite or absolute. It is important to determine whether this is so, and if so in what sense.

It has always been the contention of traditional metaphysics that the finite presupposes the infinite, the relative the absolute, and that the latter are as much a part of our experience as the former. You cannot experience the finite or relative, as finite and relative, except in so far as you also have as the co-implicate of that experience the notion of the infinite and absolute. For this reason the finite and infinite, relative and absolute, are among the most constant "philosophical words" in all developed languages, and belong peculiarly to what we call the metaphysical idiom *par excellence*.

It is, as we have seen, in religious experience, and in the numinous language which expresses that experience, that this co-implicate is most in evidence; indeed it is the reference to this co-implicate that gives it its numinous character. But this is but a special form of a more fundamental situation. As man's sense of his own limits and of his finitude is the fine innuendo by means of which he makes his immortal claim, so is the sense of the limited and finite, with which all experience is shot through, a still more significant innuendo by means of which a more far-reaching reference is made. The sense for the finite and the limited includes the sense for the infinite and unlimited, although "sense" in the latter case means awareness of a co-implicate.

The character of this co-implicate of experience is constantly misunderstood. For sensationalistic empiricism, from Locke on, it is precisely these words, the infinite and the absolute, which constitute outstanding examples of empty verbalism, and for the positivist, as we shall see when we examine the language of metaphysics in more detail, they make any sentence into which they enter nonsense. Such words indeed refer to no sensuously observable entity, but they have a reference none the less, namely, to a co-implicate of experience without reference to which the actual characters and distinctions within experience cannot be adequately and intelligibly expressed. When it is said that degrees of good imply perfection this is nothing less than literal fact, for without this notion all discourse involving degree or scale becomes unintelligible.

D
Conclusion: The Subject-Matter of Metaphysics

The conclusion to be drawn from all this is that metaphysics is both a necessary and a legitimate activity of human thought. It is not only possible but necessary. It is necessary in the sense that, in Kant's terms, it is a *Naturanlage*. It is such, not merely in the sense of psychology, as a disposition, the metaphysical instinct, to use Schopenhauer's term, but in the sense that it belongs to the nature of reason as such.

The position developed here has been well expressed by Kemp Smith. "Metaphysical postulation—if the processes by which we round out our experience may be so described—is legitimate, because only as metaphysically oriented is the human type of consciousness possible at all. Only by transcending the immediate can we apprehend the immediate."[1] There are two aspects of this formulation which should be commented upon. The first is the notion of "metaphysical postulation." Is this the term in which the processes by which we round out our experience should be described? Only, I think, in a certain sense. Actually the objects postulated—the self, the other, and the world (and any other objects which conceivably may be necessary to "round out our experience"), are co-implicates and as such parts of the experience itself. It is only when they are doubted that they become postulates. It is true, as we shall see, that the names which we give to these co-implicates, and the predicates which we apply to them, are "symbolic," and involve an element of postulation, but the co-implicates themselves are immediately known in the processes of experience themselves.

The second has to do with the notion of legitimate. That metaphysics is legitimate in one sense of the word no one would probably deny. The activities of the poet and artist, with which those of the metaphysician are often associated, are legitimate in this sense. It might probably be said with equal truth that only as thus oriented is the distinctively

[1] *Prolegomena to an Idealist Philosophy*, p. 175.

human type of consciousness possible. Those who would "eliminate" metaphysics in all probability in the main neither expect nor really desire to eliminate it as a part of human culture, any more than they expect or desire to eliminate all poetry or religion. But for them it is not a legitimate activity in a second sense. It is not legitimate as a form of knowledge. Here, of course, everything turns on the notion of knowledge. It may as well be admitted from the outset that a theory of knowledge which is "dyadic," to use the terms of a previous discussion, one which recognizes knowledge solely by simple acquaintance or by description, will almost inevitably deny to the metaphysical activity, although perhaps necessary and legitimate in the first sense, the character of knowledge. But if interpretation itself be a necessary part of knowledge—if no adequate notion of the relations of cognition to language can be developed except on the triadic theory—then the situation is wholly different. If interpretation, as we have defined the notion, is itself a part of knowledge, then the interpretation of the co-implicates necessary to experience and its communication is a legitimate part of knowledge.[1]

III

THE LANGUAGE OF METAPHYSICS

A

Our thesis thus far may be stated in several ways. We may say that only as metaphysically oriented is our human consciousness (as distinguished from the animal) possible. Or we may say, only through metempirical propositions can the empirical be made meaningful or intelligible; if science is possible metaphysics is possible. Or more fundamentally still, only when supplemented by metaphysical discourse can ordinary discourse, whether in poetry, science or religion, be made intelligible. It is the latter way of stating the position that now becomes of special interest.

It follows, in the first place, from this position that there will inevitably be a special "language of metaphysics." Meta-

---
[1] Chapter VIII, pp. 364 ff.

physical language, while part of the natural processes of linguistic development and construction (and thus sharing in the natural tendencies of language), will, at the same time, have its own characters, its own nature and, as it were, its own idiom. It is evident that it is this special character of metaphysical language that is significant, for it is by the logical analysis of *this kind* of language that metaphysics is to be shown impossible. It will be necessary therefore to examine the metaphysical idiom much more carefully than the language of the other symbolic forms. We shall have to examine metaphysical words or terms, metaphysical assertions or propositions, and above all metaphysical reasoning.

B

Metaphysical Language as a Form of Poetry

There has been, as we have seen, a general tendency to assimilate the language of metaphysics to that of poetry. This is partly due to the close relations between religion and metaphysics. To many the poetic or purely emotive character of religious language includes the purely emotive character of metaphysical speech and for much the same reasons. The impossibility of subsuming religious language under that of poetry has already been shown. The impossibility is even greater in the case of metaphysics. Nevertheless this view is widely held and has been maintained by all the historical forms of positivism. For Montaigne metaphysics was "sophisticated poetry," for Lange "justifiable poetry" and for Anatole France, as for many present-day philosophers, a "sorry sort of poetry." I shall let Anatole France speak. In his witty and brilliant way he expresses admirably both the standpoint and premises of the entire position.[1]

He has been reading a *Manual of Philosophy* and his eye

[1] *The Language of Metaphysics*, an essay in a volume entitled *The Garden of Epicurus*. The essay is in the form of a dialogue between Polyphilos and Aristos, the former upholding the naturalistic and positivistic philosophy of language, the latter maintaining in principle the position represented throughout this study. It is from every point of view the most incisive and significant discussion of this problem, for while it maintains the positivistic position it at the same time presents understandingly the opposing view, which most discussions of this question fail to do.

lights upon the following sentence: "The Spirit possesses God in so far as it participates in the absolute." These are typical metaphysical words. What do they mean? He proceeds, quite in the manner of Bentham, to carry them back to their original sensuous imagery—their "original and undefaced image," their archetypes as Bentham would say. What is the result of this reduction? According to France, instead of our original sentence we get the following: "the breath is seated by the shining one in the bushel of the part it takes in what is altogether loosed." What, then, have we here? Either nonsense or a sorry kind of poetry. This, I repeat, is the substance of the entire contention, whether voiced by a Montaigne and an Anatole France, or by the philosophical positivists. We shall presently examine certain details of the position more fully; here we shall consider merely the main contention.

Now, there can be no question that the language of metaphysics, no less than that of religion, is in many respects akin to poetry. The line, "Life, like a dome of many-coloured glass, stains the white radiance of Eternity," is both poetical and metaphysical. So also is Shaw's "Life is driving at its darling, brains." When Carlyle cries, "Force, force, everywhere force, illimitable whirlwind of force," he, too, is making a metaphysical assertion in a poetic or dramatic form. The very fact that the cosmological propositions of science, with their metaphysical element, are expressible only in the dramatic form shows this kinship. But while this is true, it is not true that metaphysical language is poetic in essence. For, whereas the sentences of the poets, in the majority of cases at least, have empirically experiencable entities as their subjects, the sentences of metaphysics, like those of religion, have as their subjects metempirical co-implicates of experience.[1] But there

---

[1] A. J. Ayer, *op. cit.*, p. 37, rightly denies that metaphysics may be subsumed under poetry and the language of metaphysics under the poetic type, but he seems to have done so for the wrong reasons. Whereas, he tells us, the sentences produced by the poets in the majority of cases have a literal meaning, but that meaning is false, the sentences of the metaphysician have no literal meaning and are therefore nonsense. Two errors seem to underlie this position: (*a*) that the sentences of the poets have literal meaning. Our examination of the language of poetry has shown that, with the exception of the intuitive meanings of poetic words, the sentences have metaphorical or symbolical meaning. (*b*) The second error arises out of the assumption that if sentences do not have literal meaning they are nonsense, or have no meaning at all.

THE LANGUAGE OF METAPHYSICS

is a further important difference. The language of metaphysics shares also, to a large extent, in the language of science. To this aspect of its language we must now turn.

C

Metaphysics and the Language of Science

Metaphysics, as previously defined, is concerned with the general ideas or principles which are indispensably relevant to assertions about everything which happens, or with the widest categorial connections possible. It follows from this that metaphysical words will, through a large range of expression, be identical with those of science. Words such as substance and property, quality and quantity, events and relations are both scientific and metaphysical. So also are such words as necessity and possibility, contingency and chance. Such categories are indispensably relevant for the expression of matter of fact, and in so far are scientific. They are metaphysical also, and become so precisely when we attempt to extend them as widely as possible, not only to everything which happens in the distributive sense, but also to everything in the sense of totality, not only to objects of experience but to the metempirical co-implicates of experience. It is for this reason that the doctrine of the categories cannot be separated from metaphysics itself. Part of metaphysical discourse is the question of the nature and application of the categories.

The language of metaphysics is partly the language of science, but part of it is neither scientific nor poetic. In order to round out our experience we postulate and acknowledge certain co-implicates of experience and in expressing these "objects" we develop an idiom which is neither scientific nor poetic. We use such words as phenomenon and noumenon, appearance and reality, existence and being, realism and idealism, etc. This is the metaphysical idiom *par excellence*. The development of such a vocabulary does not mean that our language has become either nonsense or a sorry sort of poetry, but rather that this distinctive idiom has become necessary to the adequate expression of meaning. The fuller development of this idiom and of its relation to metaphysical symbolism is a problem of a later context. Here we are concerned merely with stating the general relation of the **language of metaphysics** to that of science.

D

Metaphysics as a Hybrid of Poetry and Science

For the foregoing reasons it is not uncommon to describe the language of metaphysics as a hybrid of poetry and of science. As a result of this miscegenation it is said also to display the characters of hybrids—to have inherited the weaknesses of its progenitors without their good qualities. It is half poetic, but a very sorry sort of poetry. It is half scientific, but very bad science. Like all hybrids it is said to be infertile. Nevertheless it may be fairly questioned whether an adequate language, one which should adequately express reality in all its aspects, could be anything else than this; it may also be fairly questioned whether when its function is properly understood it can be truly called infertile.

It is important to recall here that a careful examination of the language and symbolisms of science discloses the fact that even science itself, if we take it in all its acknowledged range, is itself just such an hybrid, that it discloses a "double symbolism." The dramatic language of evolution, with its "struggle for existence" and survival of the fit, cannot be translated into abstract mathematical-logical relations without losing the meaning it seeks to convey, while, on the other hand, it is not until the mathematical-logical language and symbolism is translated into dramatic cosmological (therefore metaphysical) language that it says anything significant. In any case, whether we use the term hybrid or not, the language of metaphysics must have this double character and include the double symbolism. It must be related to poetry in so far as it deals with unique individuals and with meaningful wholes, it must be related to science in so far as it deals with relations. Bergson has caught and expressed aptly this difference. In so far, he writes, as the mind "works on concepts of **rela-**

tions it culminates in scientific symbolism. In so far as it works on concepts of things it culminates in metaphysical symbolism."

We may conclude, then, with Paul Valéry, that metaphysics is a "particular literary *genre*," characterized by certain subjects, and the recurrence of certain terms and forms, which mark it off distinctly from the types which we know as poetry and science. To subsume its language, with terms such as ideas, essences, noumena, etc., under poetry is to misunderstand both poetry and metaphysics. To subsume it wholly under science is to misunderstand both science and metaphysics. It is a particular literary *genre* because the subject-matter is particular. Metaphysics is not only a unique activity, a *Naturanlage* without which our human type of consciousness would be impossible, but it also, and for that very reason, represents a special universe of discourse, the contexts of all contexts, and thus demands a special language.

In summarizing his account of metaphysical language, Anatole France finds three characteristics of metaphysical words: (*a*) that they are largely metaphor; (*b*) that those which are not metaphor are abstractions and, finally, that a large proportion of them are negative terms. In Hegel's *Phenomenology*, out of twenty-six words taken as a sample nineteen are negative and seven affirmative. France has, indeed, seen the unique characters of metaphysical language, but he has failed to see their significance. It is only language so constituted that could possibly *express* the character and the products of the "metaphysical activity." All words are phenomenal in their origin—if they are to refer to the metempirical they must become metaphorical and symbolic. All words are concrete in their primary reference or intentions; if they are to become relevant to the maximum context they must be employed on the highest level of generality. All words are affirmative in their origin, but the very condition of their acquiring wider and symbolic significance is that their primary reference shall be negated. All these characters of metaphysical language are deeply rooted in the character of the metaphysical activity itself.

IV

METAPHYSICAL TERMS AND METAPHYSICAL PROPOSITIONS: THE NATURE OF METAPHYSICAL REASONING

A

So much, then, for the general characteristics of the language of metaphysics. A genuine understanding of this language, however, and of the issues which it raises, requires that we examine it in somewhat more detail. Any language contains words, sentences, and connected discourse, the latter involving, as we have seen, in some sense and to some degree, inference or reasoning. If metaphysics, as a human activity or *Naturanlage*, has the characteristics which have been ascribed to it, we may expect the elements of metaphysical discourse to be determined accordingly. Let us first look at metaphysical words and sentences.

A typical metaphysical sentence is, as we have seen, according to Anatole France, the following: "The Spirit possesses God in so far as it participates in the Absolute." Another sentence of the same type (given by Ayer) is: "the Absolute enters into, but is itself incapable of evolution and progress." Still another, which is often held to be scientific but is in reality metaphysical, is that of Spencer: "Evolution proceeds from the simple to the complex and from the undifferentiated to the differentiated." Still another (given by Carnap as typical) is that of Thales: "The essence and principle of the world is water." To this we may also add one of a similar kind, namely, the thesis of Schopenhauer that "the world is will and idea."

That which is common to all these sentences is, in the first place, the fact that the subjects of the sentences (the metaphysical substantives) are metempirical in the sense of our definition. The second character common to them all is that the predicates (metaphysical predicates), both attributes and activities, are all taken from the empirical domain or domains. This, I think, is always the character of a metaphysical sentence. The subjects of such sentences, whether "spirit," absolute, evolution, principle, are always entities (in the sense of

THE LANGUAGE OF METAPHYSICS   645

subjects of discourse) which are metempirical in the sense that they are not empirically observable, and therefore not verifiable in the sense of the empirical criterion. The predicates of these sentences, on the other hand, whether they be attributes such as water, will, or activities such as participate, enter into, proceed, are always characters or activities taken from various phenomenal domains. As such they are always empirically observable. For any word, such as water, will, possess, proceed, has reference or application to particulars which can be pointed to or "shown forth" in some fashion.

It is this peculiar character of the metaphysical sentence which raises the problem both of its meaningfulness and of the possibility of its being either true or false. In calling these metaphysical sentences it is not meant, of course, that sentences of this type are not also found in regions not normally described as metaphysical. We find them, as we have seen, in science no less than in poetry and religion. It merely means that when sentences of this type occur in any discourse, that discourse trenches on the metaphysical.

B

Metaphysical Terms: The Problem of Vocabulary

Any language consists of vocabulary and syntax. It consists of a collection of words which have meanings and of the rules which govern the building of sentences. There are, therefore, according to the critics of metaphysical language, two kinds of pseudo-propositions (*Scheinsätze*)—namely, those which contain words which appear to have meaning but which have not; and, secondly, those which are put together in ways contrary to syntax. The metaphysical propositions just considered are held to be pseudo-propositions for both reasons. Let us consider first the words that appear to have meaning but which have not.

Typical metaphysical words, according to France, are Spirit, God, Absolute. Those taken as typical by Carnap are of the same nature—principle, idea, absolute, infinite, God. The general thesis maintained in principle by both is that practically all words originally have meaning—namely, refer to sensibles, or observable entities. In the course of history they acquire new meanings and lose their old—some lose their meaning or reference altogether. Of this type are the metaphysical words. They are *Scheinwörte*; they appear to have meaning, but they have not.

Now the entire problem of empty words has already been considered in earlier contexts.[1] According to our view, the notion of empty words is itself a meaningless notion. The arguments for this general view need not be repeated here. Let us apply it specifically to "metaphysical" words. What, we asked, is the condition of the meaningfulness of any word? It is not, as we found, necessarily its reference to an observable entity. In order that a word may have a determinate reference, and therefore meaning, it is not necessary that there be an "index proper," an object to be pointed to outside the universe of discourse. All that is necessary is that the supposition of the universe of discourse in question be acknowledged. In general, it is true that there is such an index in the environment, common to speaker and hearer, but it is not necessary for intelligible discourse. Now, this "criterion of meaning" becomes of peculiar significance when applied to metaphysical words. Metaphysical words have reference and the reference is of this nature. The metaphysical substantives are, as we have seen, suppositions, or co-implicates of experience which must be acknowledged if communication and intelligible discourse are to be possible. There is reference to these entities in the case of every universe of discourse, although that reference is indirect, and it is this reference that gives them meaning.

So far at least as vocabulary is concerned, any one of the metaphysical sentences quoted is meaningful. Words such as the world, the soul, God, the Absolute or the infinite—the metaphysical substantives—are legitimate subjects of discourse —not because they refer directly to an empirically observable entity, but because they refer indirectly to the co-implicates of the experience of these entities. Another way of saying the same thing is to say that any one of the various laguages— the poetic, the religious or the scientific—must themselves, as language, contain words of this type if they themselves are to be ultimately meaningful. It is a mistake to think that any

[1] Chapter V, p. 190.

THE LANGUAGE OF METAPHYSICS

of these languages can function without words of this type. Poetry, science, and religion are all covert metaphysics, and when the hidden metaphysics is revealed it is found to be precisely these co-implicates about which metaphysics, as such, specifically speaks.

C

Metaphysical Sentences or Propositions

Metaphysical propositions are held to be meaningless because of the nature of their terms, but they are also meaningless because they are *syntax-widrig*, that is, the terms are put together in ways that violate the syntax of our language. Let us now examine this point.

That there are ways of putting words together which make nonsense is beyond dispute. Such, for instance, is the apparent sentence, Caesar is a prime number; it is, of course, untrue, but it is also nonsense. Such, it is believed, are also typical metaphysical sentences. For instance, those already quoted: the spirit participates in the Absolute; the Absolute enters into evolution and progress; the world is will; all is flux. Such sentences are meaningless, it is held, not only because there are no referends for the terms spirit, Absolute, evolution, the world, etc., but even more because they are made subjects of predicates in a way contrary to syntax. To talk in this fashion is of a piece with saying that Caesar is a prime number or that virtue is triangular. This phase of the general argument is more significant than the first and must therefore be examined with great care.

The issue here evidently turns upon two points: (a) what syntax is and what are the rules of syntax which such sentences are supposed to violate; (b) what is the unique character of these metaphysical sentences and the point at which they are contrary to syntax.

Syntax has to do with the ways in which words are put together in meaningful discourse.[1] The sole test of syntax is communication. Let us see from this standpoint what would constitute a wholly meaningless combination of words—there-

[1] Chapter VII, p. 292.

fore a syntactical nonsense. The pseudo-phrase, "large brown on" may perhaps be taken as the limit of syntactical meaning. It presents the semblance of a whole but conforms to no rule of syntax. The elements are significant, but the whole is nonsense. In contrast to this case, we have pseudo-phrases which have a seeming intelligibility as wholes, since they follow syntactical rules, but are meaningless because the elements have no meaning. Such are the classic lines of Lewis Carroll's *Jabberwocky*: "O frabjous day! Callooh! Callay! He chortled in his joy." So powerful is the sense of significance as a whole that the parts tend to derive meaning through their places in the whole.

Let us pass now from these cases of pure nonsense to the types of *"syntax-widrig"* propositions with which the metaphysical sentences are likened: Caesar is a prime number, virtue is triangular. These are not strictly nonsense in the sense of the previous illustrations, for while there are no objects which correspond to these expressions, yet the expressions are not totally without meaning. We have here passed over the thin line which separates pure nonsense from falsity and contradiction. The mere fact that we say that Caesar is a prime number and virtue is triangular are fantastic and absurd notions, shows that we grasp these expressions as meaningful, otherwise we could not attribute absurdity to them. A nonsensical expression, an utterly meaningless collection of words, could be neither fantastic nor false.

We may conclude, then, that even those cases to which the metaphysical sentences are likened are not wholly meaningless—are not syntactical nonsense—for the reason that by such combinations of words some meaning is communicated, and that ultimately this meaning is related to truth and falsity. What, then, is meant when it is said that they are contrary to syntax? The sentences, Caesar is a prime number and virtue is triangular, are said to be nonsense for the reason that the terms are taken from such widely different domains or contexts that the very attempt to put them together discloses an absurdity—in other words, the fantastic character of their error. They are not contrary to syntax but to our sense of probability and intelligibility.

With this view of the nature of syntax and of its relation to sense and nonsense, we may turn to an examination of the metaphysical sentences. They are said to be contrary to syntax, not because they do not follow syntactical rules, but because the predicates which are taken from empirical domains are applied to metempirical objects. Such objects do not exist, or at least are not verifiable, but even if they did exist, propositions about them would still be meaningless. This, then, is the thesis. It is our purpose to show that they are not contrary to syntax in any sense. In attempting to make our point it will be convenient to consider these sentences from the standpoint of both the subject and the predicate. The subject is in every case a metempirical co-implicate of experience: spirit, Absolute, the world. The predicate is in every case some aspect of experience such as "enters into," "proceeds," "will," "flux," etc. It is evidently this unique character of metaphysical predication which leads to the view that metaphysical sentences are contrary to syntax.

The first question, then, is whether to speak of a metempirical object at all is contrary to syntax. Most surely it is not. If it were so, it would be contrary to syntax to speak of electrons and quanta, the existential status of which is undetermined, and discourse about which some positivists would, as we have seen, exclude from science.[1] There is, then, no more reason why a sentence containing the word soul or God should be contrary to syntax than one containing the words electrons or quanta. And this is equally true of sentences containing the word "world" in the sense of the *omnitudo realitatis*. Sentences containing the partial wholes of physics are not syntactical nonsense; there is no more inherent reason why sentences containing the wholes of metaphysics should be. It is solely a matter of prejudice.

Clearly, then, it cannot be the unique character of metaphysical subjects that makes the sentences in which they occur supposedly contrary to syntax. The difficulty must lie, if it exists at all, in the predicates. Evidently the problem here revolves around the question of the syntactical validity of analogous predication. For in every case of a metaphysical sentence an aspect of experience is taken and predicated analogously of a metempirical subject. The question, then, is:

[1] Chapter XI, p. 548.

(*a*) whether analogous predication conforms to syntax or not; and (*b*) whether the special case of such predication in metaphysical sentences is contrary to syntax.

Now analogical predication itself can scarcely be said to be contrary to syntax. It is possible, of course, to argue that even the sentence, the priest is a physician of the soul, is contrary to syntax in that the two domains from which the subject and predicate are taken are too remote to be brought together meaningfully, and are therefore nonsense. But to say this is to enunciate a paradox of astounding proportions. For it not only involves the elimination of a large part of meaningful discourse, but also the setting up of an entirely arbitrary notion of syntax, namely, that only literal sentences are syntactically meaningful. Analogous predication, as such, can scarcely be said to be contrary to the syntax of language. The problem is rather that of the extension of such predication to metaphysical or metempirical substantives. With this we come to the nub of the matter.

The essential character of all metaphysical sentences is that predicates are taken from narrower empirical domains and applied to metempirical objects. Such objects are, as we have seen, of two kinds—those which make assertions about the metempirical co-implicates of experience and those which make assertions about the whole of reality. With respect to the first type of metaphysical sentences the situation is sufficiently clear. If, as we have maintained, the self and the other are known in experience and in its communication, they may be meaningfully talked about and predicates may be applied to them. But obviously these predicates must be taken from experience itself and can be applied only analogically. It was an entirely meaningful procedure for human thought in its beginnings to form the notion of the soul, and in speaking of it to apply the notion of psyche or breath to it, although with the development of thought the predicate would require "moulding" to make it applicable to, or expressive of, the object. The situation is not different in principle when we pass to the metempirical "wholes of physics." Here, too, as we have seen, analogous predication is meaningfully extendable into the realm of the metempirical. It is, however, when we come to metaphysical propositions of the second type, namely, those about the *omnitudo realitatis* that the problem of analogous predication becomes most serious.

The ultimate object of metaphysical discourse is to say something significant about the whole of reality and, since significance cannot be finally separated from truth and falsity, something that is true. Metaphysics seeks not only to discover categories that apply to every *thing*, but, since to find such categories means to say something about reality as a whole, to find predicates applicable to the *omnitudo realitatis*. Thus the discourse we call metaphysical is full of such propositions as the following: Everything flows or is in flux. All is matter or all is spirit. The world is will. Our problem here is not whether propositions of this type are true or false, but whether they are meaningless as contrary to the syntax of our language. This cannot, I think, be maintained. It is true that there are logical difficulties inherent in the notion of totality and of application of predicates to the whole. These difficulties we shall consider in a later context; here the problem has to do with syntax, for logic and syntax are not identical.

Metaphysical sentences of neither type can, then, be called syntactical nonsense. For one thing, they are not at all like those which are taken as examples of such nonsense. The sentence, Caesar is a prime number, is a nonsense because there is no analogy of being between the two. This is not at all the case in sentences of the type, all is flux, the world is will. In these cases fundamental aspects of our experience are taken and applied analogically to the whole. These aspects are of such a character that they are thought "to throw light" on existence in its totality and may be given a privileged position in our interpretation of reality as a whole. Such statements may be false, but they cannot be absurd in the sense of those to which they are likened. In any case, even the latter are not contrary to syntax and even these have a reference to truth and falsity. Truth and falsity are not irrelevant to metaphysical sentences. They may not be verifiable, although this is a matter for later consideration. Certainly they are not nonsense.

It is true, of course, that such sentences cannot have literal significance. They are metaphorical and of the type which we shall discuss presently under the name of fundamental metaphor. Analogous predication is, as we have seen, the germ of the symbol and wherever such predication, and with it the metaphorical, enters in, we have symbolic as contrasted with literal language.[1] It follows equally that, by virtue of the unique character of metaphysical substantives, the metaphysical symbol must have its own special characters. To the study of the metaphysical symbol we shall presently turn. For the moment we must consider the third phase of metaphysical language, namely, metaphysical reasoning.

D

Metaphysical Reasoning

Darwin modestly admitted that he was not accustomed to metaphysical "trains of thought." In this admission he recognized that which is an undoubted fact, namely, that in some way and at some point, metaphysical reasoning, although still reasoning, is different from scientific. He was, however, not presumptious enough to deny it the character of reasoning or to call it nonsense.

The trains of thought he had in mind were, as seen from the context, the kind of reasoning one finds in the traditional arguments for the existence of God and the arguments for the existence and nature of the self, as seen in Descartes, and the arguments for freedom or necessity. The difference which Darwin had in mind is clearly expressed in Kant's notion of the different kinds of "employment of the reason," the empirical, the transcendental, and the practical. It was the "empirical employment" to which Darwin felt himself alone accustomed.

---

[1] Mr. Ayer consistently adds *literal* in all cases. It is the "rules that determine the literal significance of language" that eliminate metaphysics. "Our charge against the metaphysician is . . . that he produces sentences which fail to conform to the conditions under which alone a sentence can be literally significant. No statement that refers to a reality transcending the limits of possible sense-experience can possibly have any literal significance" (p. 17). Again, in discussing the question of religious "knowledge" we are told that "there cannot be any transcendent truths of religion. For the sentences which the theist uses to express such truths are not literally significant" (p. 179). Finally, it is specifically said on page 214 that "the positivistic verification principle is a criterion of literal significance." When one follows the argument through one sees clearly that for him the opposite of nonsense or meaninglessness is not sense and meaning, but literal significance.

THE LANGUAGE OF METAPHYSICS

The programme of the anti-metaphysician is to show that metaphysical words are only apparent words, metaphysical propositions *Scheinsätze*, and metaphysical trains of thought pseudo-reasoning. Kant had already partly developed this programme by attempting to show that at least certain of these metaphysical trains of thought are paralogisms, although other non-empirical employments of the reason are retained. Logical positivism eliminates *all* metaphysical trains of thought.

Let us at the beginning recognize that if there is any such thing as metaphysics, it will necessarily contain trains of thought which are different in certain respects from those we find in the empirical employment of reason. This follows of necessity from the nature of the metaphysical activity. If the very nature of this activity consists in the rounding out of our experience by the "postulation" of metempirical entities, then, by that very fact, the reasoning by which we validate or legitimatize these postulates will differ from purely empirical reasoning. It will be of the nature of *argument to presuppositions*. Such a metaphysical train of thought, one indeed which is taken as typical by the anti-metaphysician, is the famous *Cogito ergo sum* of Descartes, upon which all the rest of his metaphysical trains of thought hinged. The existence of the ego or self is the necessary presupposition of, or follows from, the existence of thinking. It is not necessary to recall the well-worn criticisms of this famous assertion—that this is not a valid syllogism, that the existence of the self is not logically implied in the fact of thinking; or, still more fundamentally, that the existence of a metempirical object cannot be argued from the existence of any empirical fact. The essential point of all these criticisms is that the kind of "metaphysical" reasoning which would validate the postulate of a metempirical co-implicate of experience, is pseudo-reasoning, or as Kant would say, a paralogism.

The issue here involved has already been considered in the purely logical context.[1] Our conclusion there was, briefly stated, that implication in this sense is extra-logical, in the narrow sense of logical, and that the inference or reasoning involved contains in it extra-logical factors. But we also maintained that all genuine reasoning always contains factors of

[1] Chapter VII, pp. 313 ff.

this type. The assumption underlying Lewis's criticism of such reasoning is that presupposition, in the sense here used, is the same thing as implication in the sense of formal logic—in other words, that the problem is purely logical when as a matter of fact it is metalogical. After our discussion of the metalogical problems of language we may now state the difference more clearly. What I have called the necessary co-implicates of experience are presupposed in a different way from that in which one proposition is presupposed by another in formal logic. In the latter case, the relation of implication or presupposition is within the larger field of discourse and communication; in the former case the co-implicate and its acknowledgment is the necessary condition or presupposition of all discourse, and therefore of logic itself. This is what I mean by calling it metalogical.[1] What is meant here by presupposition is not "logically prior" but metalogically prior. In this latter case what is metalogically prior is presupposed, and denial of this presupposition does involve the denial of, and the ultimate meaninglessness of, that which presupposes it. This is true of all the metempirical co-implicates of experience and communication, and such reasoning to these co-implicates is valid reasoning.

The point I have been making may be brought out more clearly by comparing this type of reasoning with the types generally recognized. Ordinarily only two are admitted, the empirical and the *a priori*. The former, empirical reasoning and empirical proof, apply only to phenomena, the second only to relations of essences. The first applies only to observable entities and to hypotheses which conceivably could refer to observable entities. There is no empirical proof of metempirical objects, therefore no empirical reasoning about cosmological propositions (in science) which is not a paralogism. The second applies only to that which does not exist, and can therefore not demonstrate any propositions involving existence. This would, of course, exclude the type which we have been considering. Actually, however, there is this third type and, if my conten-

---

[1] This difference is tacitly recognized by Kant in his distinction between transcendental logic and ordinary logic. Kant made a mistake, perhaps, in speaking of the logical deduction of the categories, and the supposition that he deduced them in the sense of ordinary logic has led to widespread misunderstanding of his real position.

tions are sound, it cannot be excluded. Hartmann recognizes this third type, which he describes as *analytical*. It consists in the analysis of presuppositions and is really a combination of the empirical and the *a priori*. He applies it specifically to the proof of freedom, but it is really applicable to all the co-implicates of experience.[1] Returning then to our main thesis, metaphysical reasoning is in general of this type—namely, arguing from the possibility of experience and its communication to its co-implicates, or what it presupposes. Metaphysics is that activity which rounds out our experience—makes it intelligible by postulation of metempirical entities. In so far as this postulation is necessary, it is a legitimate activity and part of knowledge by interpretation. This is the peculiar "criterion of proof" of which Professor Lewis speaks. It is, perhaps, a question whether it should be called "proof" in view of the ordinary connotations of this notion. This is a question to be considered when we examine the entire problem of "verification" of metaphysical propositions.[2] The sole point of importance here is the consideration of metaphysical trains of thought as meaningful, as part of the general question of the meaningfulness of metaphysical language. On this question there can be no doubt. This type of reasoning is but an extension of the metaphysical activity. It is the way in which, in intelligible communication or discourse, we bring those who communicate to the acknowledgment of the postulates or co-implicates of experience.

One further point is of importance here. It is necessary to distinguish between these fundamental metaphysical trains of thought and the reasoning by which we argue as to the nature of these co-implicates. Although the "that" and the "what" are here closely connected, it may well be that concerning the latter our reasoning may contain paralogisms.

E

Metaphysical Language and Logical Analysis

We have now examined the language of metaphysics in its three aspects of vocabulary, syntax, and medium of reasoning.

[1] Nicolai Hartmann, *Ethics*, Vol. III, p. 140.   [2] Pp. 676 ff.

Our examination of this language has shown that its words, sentences, and trains of thought all have meaning when the criterion of meaning is properly formulated and the real nature of these elements in metaphysical discourse understood. Logical analysis cannot, as we have seen, legislate these meanings out of existence. Such analysis, when its true function is misconceived, leads, as we have seen, to the paralysis of speech and to the stultification of discourse.[1] Logic itself has its being wholly in discourse, and logic cannot legislate out of existence the presuppositions and postulates which alone make discourse, and therefore logic itself, intelligible. In that metaphysical postulation is necessary to round out our experience, metaphysical language necessary to make all other languages intelligible, the elimination of metaphysical language would mean the stultification of all discourse.

Metaphysical language has, then, significance, but it is still possible that it does not have *literal* significance. This is the form in which the anti-metaphysical position is stated by many. Stated in this form, however, the positivistic position makes two assumptions both of which are doubtful. It assumes that only literal propositions are significant and excludes the possibility that metaphysical propositions are symbolic and give us symbolic knowledge. In the second place, it assumes that no metaphysical propositions have literal significance at all, whereas metaphysical knowledge, while largely symbolic, may yet contain a non-symbolic element in it. Both of these assumptions are, I believe, unfounded. We are thus led to the second part of our study, namely, a study of the symbolic elements in metaphysics and of their relation to the non-symbolic.

V

SYMBOLISM AS A METAPHYSICAL PRINCIPLE

A

For reasons already indicated it was necessary to make a much more extended and detailed study of metaphysical language than of the other types. For the same reasons the study of

[1] Chapter VI, pp. 289 and 305.

THE LANGUAGE OF METAPHYSICS

the symbolism of metaphysics demands our special care and attention. Its distinction from the poetic and the scientific symbol is all-important. Metaphysics we shall maintain has its own form of symbolism, although it is defined by Bergson as the "science" that claims to dispense with symbolism. There is a sense in which this statement has a certain element of truth—and that sense will be considered presently—but in essence it is false, for metaphysics, properly understood, is rather, as we shall see, precisely that science or activity of man which carries symbolism to its highest development. In other words, *symbolism is a metaphysical principle.*

I shall develop this theme by recalling first certain conclusions which we have already reached. My first contention was, not only that if science is possible metaphysics is possible, but rather that science, unless it is truncated and caricatured, is possible only if metaphysics is possible. My second contention now is that, just as much of scientific knowledge is understandable only when it is recognized as symbolic,[1] so metaphysical knowledge is understandable only when it is recognized as having in it symbolic elements. As it is the literal or copy theory of scientific concepts that has broken down in modern science, so it is a similar treatment of metaphysical concepts that has led to the critique of metaphysics.

B

The Nature of the Metaphysical Symbol

The metaphysical symbol has already been distinguished in a tentative way from the poetic and the scientific in earlier connections.[2] In the terms of Höffding, already employed, the metaphysical symbol shares the general characters of all symbols, but differs from the others at one important point. It differs from them "in that it seeks to throw light on existence *in its totality or in its innermost essence* by figures which are taken from a single fact or a single side of existence as it appears in our experience."

The general truth of this definition has already appeared

---

[1] Chapter XI, p. 538 f. [2] Chapter XII, p. 581 f.

in our account of the language of metaphysics. Certain typical sentences or propositions already examined are clearly symbol sentences. In the earlier context our interest was confined to showing that these sentences are not contrary to the syntax of our language if the principles of that syntax are properly understood. Our present task is to examine their character as symbol sentences.

The predicates of these sentences, as in all symbol sentences, are always taken from some "single side of existence"—in terms of our earlier discussion from some single domain of experience; it is the subject of the symbol sentence which uniquely determines the difference in the way the predicate is applied. The application of the figure of the organism to the State, or of mechanism to the body, has as its object the throwing light on one part of phenomenal existence by predicates taken from another part; the application of these same predicates to existence in its totality makes of them figures or symbols of a significantly different character. An organic theory of the State is a symbol of social or political science; an "organicist" theory of reality is a metaphysical symbol.

The difference we are seeking to make clear may be expressed by the statement that the metaphysical symbol is *fundamental metaphor*. By fundamental metaphor I understand precisely that type of metaphor which is taken from the primary and irreducible domains of experience. Let us assume, for example, that the levels of being, or the "categorial scheme" represented by emergent evolution, does characterize fundamental aspects of being as experienced; that, roughly speaking, matter, life, mind, persons or selves are names or categories for irreducible qualities; that each level, while conditioned by the preceding, is not reducible to it. In that case, application of any one of these, as predicate, to the whole, or to the innermost essence, would be metaphorical. An organicist metaphysics would use the notion or category of life metaphorically; a spiritualistic or idealistic metaphysic would use the category of mind metaphorically.[1]

---

[1] A somewhat similar view is developed by Stephen C. Pepper in an article entitled "The Root Metaphor Theory of Metaphysics," *The Journal of Philosophy*, Vol. XXXII, No. 14, July 4, 1935. The notion of the origin of the metaphysical concept is roughly the same, but the symbolism of metaphysics is not related to

The metaphysical symbol, as fundamental metaphor, differs, then, in important respects from every other type of symbol, poetic, scientific, and even religious. These differences are due to the fact that it is fundamental. It is fundamental in the sense, first, that the subject of analogous predication is the *omnitudo realitatis*, and secondly in that, because of this fact, the predicates must of necessity be of a certain character. It is necessary, therefore, to examine more closely both the subject and the predicate of these symbol sentences. Let us consider the subject first.

C

The Nature of Metaphysical Subjects

As was pointed out in an earlier context, there is a real difference between the metaphysical elements or propositions in science and those which constitute metaphysics proper. Both deal with subjects of discourse which are limitless, inexhaustible and therefore indeterminate. Both speak of wholes or worlds which are metempirical, and therefore not "observable entities" to which propositions may be referred. But in the case of science they are always partial wholes; in the case of metaphysics proper it is the *omnitudo realitatis*. Now it may be that the first or scientific form of symbolism is legitimate and symbolic knowledge is here possible. It may be, however, that metaphysical discourse in the second sense is not meaningful and metaphysics, as genuine knowledge, is not possible.

So at least it is argued by many. The point at issue may be stated in the following way. To be able to predicate anything of the whole in a meaningful way it is required that this whole be envisaged as really not the totality of totalities, but itself a thing among other things. More technically expressed, if everything is a totality and this totality is itself not one of the everythings, then we have the totality of everything and *the* totality, and so on—so that there is no totality

that of science and the distinctive character of the metaphysical symbol, as I conceive it, is not made clear.

The term "radical metaphor" was used earlier (Chapter V, p. 176 f.) to describe the fundamental law of speech construction. It is for this reason that the term "fundamental" is here used.

except as a collection.[1] It is thus maintained that we cannot avoid a fallacy necessarily involved in the notion of a totality. Such fallacy is especially evident when it is expressed in terms of the notion of an all-embracing system. Such a system could not be enlarged, for it would already contain all that there is. If it can be enlarged it cannot be all-embracing, cannot be all that it claims to be. The very notion of system has therefore been rendered self-contradictory and fallacious by being made all-embracing. Neither can its claim to truth be absolute so long as it is possible to subject it to reinterpretation. An absolute system that is not final is a self-contradiction.[2]

The seriousness of the issue involved should not be minimized. It is true that the moment one begins to talk about totality, about the world or the universe, as we do about finite entities and partial wholes, one is "already on the brink of the unmeaning." To say that organisms develop or evolve is meaningful, to say that life evolves is still meaningful although its meaning is more difficult to determine, but what meaning is there in the proposition that the *world* evolves or indeed that everything evolves? And the same is true of all propositions of this type such as all is in flux, everything flows. Now, I think it must be admitted that we cannot speak about the whole without incurring just such difficulties, but I do not think that they are insuperable. The same difficulties inhere in the partial wholes of the sciences, both historical and generalizing. The fundamental presupposition of historical judgments is the notion of a completed series, although actually the series is never completed. The fundamental presupposition of the whole of physics—namely, the physical universe—is that, although it is also incomplete, significant propositions about it are possible. In these cases we escape the unmeaning by recognizing that our propositions are symbolic and that the greater the whole the more symbolic is our representation.[3] This is *a fortiori* true in metaphysics—in propositions about the

---

[1] See E. G. Spaulding, *op. cit.*, p. 283.

[2] Appeal is often made to the "logical theory of types" to prove the impossibility of metaphysics in the sense of propositions about the whole. The theory of types is, however, becoming increasingly unsatisfactory even from the standpoint of logic itself, and it is an open question whether its application to this type of problem is legitimate. In any case, it is possible to state the point at issue without appealing to this very debatable notion. [3] Chapter XI, p. 539.

omnitudo realitatis. Literal propositions are here, in the nature of the case, impossible. Such propositions are not only more symbolic than the propositions about the infinitely great and infinitely little of the physical universe, but, by reason of the nature of the subject of the proposition, symbolic in a different way. What this means will become clearer after our examination of metaphysical predicates.

D

The Nature of Metaphysical Predicates

The predicates of metaphysical sentences, like those of all symbol sentences, are taken from experience, but their character is determined by the nature of the subject to which they are applied. In that the metaphysical symbol seeks to throw light on existence as a whole, the metaphor employed must, as we have seen, be fundamental. This fact involves certain consequences with respect to metaphysical predicates which must now be explicitly stated. I shall emphasize two characters of metaphysical predicates which are most significant from the standpoint of metaphysical symbolism: (1) what I shall describe as the "moulding" of the predicate involved in metaphysical assertions; (2) the realm of experience from which, in order to be fundamental, the metaphor must be taken.

The fact that the subjects of metaphysical propositions are wholes, either partial or total, requires, of course, that the predicates must be taken from the most pervasive or most fundamental aspects of experience, but the fact that the subjects are metempirical and the predicates empirical requires that the predicates must be moulded, that is, used in a different sense from their literal employment. The subject to which they are applied being metempirical, although presupposed by experience, it is necessary that the predicates be "moulded" in significant ways. This requirement is, to be sure, but a special case of the phenomenon of moulding or distortion which we found to be characteristic of all types of symbolism and symbolic forms. In the case of the metaphysical symbol, however, this moulding involves despatialization and detemporalization of the predicates. Even in the case of the scientific symbol, we found that our space-time concepts must be moulded before they can be extended to physical wholes;[1] in the case of the *omnitudo realitatis* a further moulding is necessary. The character of this process we shall see in more detail in a later context.[2] Here our sole point is to emphasize the uniqueness of the metaphysical predicates as determined by the subjects to which they are applied.

All thinking, as Nietzsche rightly saw, is "*arbeiten mit den beliebsten Metaphoren.*" Even science works with metaphors and cannot indeed work otherwise. But the favourite metaphor here is determined by the purpose of scientific operation. If we use the metaphor of a machine—and that is of course what we do when we have a mechanistic notion of nature—we think of nature so, because only when we work with such concepts can nature be controlled. If we use the metaphor of will or purpose, it is because only by such metaphors can nature be understood or made intelligible to us. Operation and understanding are by no means the same thing. In metaphysics, however, the metaphor must be fundamental, that is, it must be taken from those ultimate and irreducible aspects of experienced reality without which experience could not be.

It is this that metaphysics has always tried to do, however imperfectly. It has sought to discover those aspects of experience which are all-pervasive and thus applicable to everything—in other words, "cosmic variables." One of the latest metaphysical attempts of this sort is that of Whitehead. His constructions are definitely guided by this notion of fundamental metaphor, and he recognizes, I think, the essentially symbolic character of metaphysical knowledge, although, perhaps, not with all its implications. I am glad to be able to quote a passage which seems to me to recognize this fact specifically. "Philosophers," he tells us, "can never hope finally to formulate these metaphysical first principles (namely the experience categories which he assigns to all the occasions in nature). Weakness of insight and deficiencies of language stand in the way inexorably. Words and phrases must be stretched toward a generality foreign to their ordinary usage; and however such elements of language be stabilized as technicalities, *they remain metaphors* (italics mine) mutely appealing for an imagin-

[1] Chapter XI, p. 540.   [2] P. 706.

ative leap."[1] The stretching of words and phrases towards generality means a moulding of our concepts into symbols. They remain metaphors and our metaphysical knowledge is ultimately symbolic in character.

I am not, it should be understood, either arguing for the Whitehead metaphysics or for his use of symbols. Indeed, I find great difficulties in this metaphysics and I feel that the imaginative leap for which his metaphors appeal (more particularly his use of feeling and value) makes too much demand upon us. All I am concerned to point out is that Whitehead's metaphysics is, when examined, an illustration of symbolism as a metaphysical principle.

The uniqueness of the metaphysical symbol in this respect may be seen by considering any one of the fundamental types of metaphysics. When Schopenhauer tells us that the world is, in its essence, will, he is not telling us that the things which make up the world—the stars, the mountains, animals and men—are all literally analysable into forms of willing in the sense of human will. That would be a cruder panpsychism than Schopenhauer would for a moment contemplate. What he is saying is rather that the fundamental aspect of experience which we know as striving, impulse, desire, will, is the best metaphor or symbol for the fundamental character of being common to everything that happens. In order to say this, however, he is compelled, as everyone knows, to despatialize and detemporalize the notion of will—to make the concrete forms of existence in space and time "objectifications" of a "will" which is spaceless and timeless. Now we are, of course, not concerned at all here with the question of whether this particular metaphysics is "true" nor indeed whether, or in what sense, it is "verifiable"—these are questions for a later context—our concern is with its meaningfulness. "The world is will" is a meaningful symbolic sentence. It has no literal significance—and indeed cannot have—but it is a fundamental metaphor which, by giving a privileged position to some fundamental aspect of experience, enables us to express in some degree the meaning of "reality." It is this that I meant by saying that by reason of the very nature of the metaphysical subject the predicate is symbolic in a "different way."

[1] *Process and Reality*, p. 6.

E

Symbols Normative for Metaphysics

Thus far in our treatment of symbolism as a metaphysical principle we have sought to establish two things: (*a*) In the first place, that while the metaphysical symbol, *eo nomine*, differs in important respects from the symbol of science, there is no crucial difference such as would make the latter possible and the former impossible. (*b*) In the second place, by reason of the difference between the two, the metaphysical symbol is of the nature of fundamental metaphor as above defined. In this notion of fundamental, however, is included an element which marks off the metaphysical symbol in a significant way from those of science. We shall call this the *axiological character* of the metaphysical symbol.

Metaphysics we found to be that fundamental activity by which we round out our experience through the postulation of metempirical entities. The legitimacy of this activity we found in the fact that without it knowledge and discourse cannot be made intelligible. When, however, we examine this experience which is to be thus rounded out, we find that, when taken in its totality or concreteness, it always contains *value* as a fundamental aspect. A fundamental metaphor must include this aspect, otherwise it is not fundamental.

In developing this point I shall make use of a well-known definition of metaphysics by Rickert. The task of metaphysics, he tells us, is the unitary interpretation of the total world in which there are both the real and the valuable. ("*Die Metaphysik macht es sich zur Aufgabe die gesammte Welt, in der es Wirkliches und Werthaftes giebt, einheitlich zu deuten.*") If, then, this is the task of metaphysics—and I believe that it is—it follows inevitably that to interpret the world as a whole—a world that actually contains both the real and the valuable—metaphysical concepts or symbols, in order to be fundamental—and *adequate*—must be, so to speak, value-charged. In other words axiological symbols must be normative for metaphysics.

That certain types of symbols are fundamental, and therefore normative, for science seems to be unquestioned by many. Thus it is frequently maintained that the universe is exhaus-

THE LANGUAGE OF METAPHYSICS

tively analysable in terms of pure mathematics and that only in so far as that analysis is carried out have we science. But to say that the concepts of the mathematical-physical sciences are those that are most suitable to the purposes of the biologist and psychologist—to say nothing of the historian—seems to be the very reverse of the truth. Organic wholes are, indeed, a part of nature, but the concepts of nature, the symbols by means of which their character as "living" is described, are certainly not mathematical.[1] However this may be (and it seems certain that even in science mathematical symbols are not normative, but that there is present what Bergson calls a "double symbolism") certainly in metaphysics a symbolism of an entirely different type is necessary. In the total world, which it is the object of metaphysical language to symbolize and express, the *Werthaftes* is as much a determining part as the *Wirkliches*. Metaphysical symbols, to be adequately expressive, must have an axiological aspect.

An essential part of the notion of fundamental metaphor is, then, that our metaphors or symbols must include the value side of experience. This fact may be described in two ways. We may say that the principle of the primacy of the axiological, the characteristic principle of all traditional philosophy, is determinative; or we may say that the language of metaphysics must inevitably be anthropomorphic and its symbols taken from the human and the personal, rather than from the abstract and impersonal, side of experience. The latter is the usual way of describing the situation, and there is no objection to thus describing it. For the critical mind, science itself is no less anthropomorphic; it merely takes its metaphors from another side of human experience, as in the case of the modern notion of "mechanism." The notion of the primacy of the axiological is, however, preferable. The symbols of metaphysics must be axiological for the reason that they cannot be fundamental unless they include the value side of experience. This is demonstrated by the actual history of metaphysical activity. The principle of "the primacy of value" which has dominated traditional European philosophy from Plato to Kant and Hegel is proof of this thesis. The primacy given to the axiological categories means, of course, many

[1] Chapter XI, pp. 523 ff.

things, but it means chiefly that in any attempt to express the "fullness of being"—not being as an abstraction, which is then the emptiest of all concepts—these categories must be given a privileged position. In this sense the "anthropomorphic" (or in terms of linguistic idiom, the "dramatic") is the condition of a meaningful metaphysic.

F
Can Metaphysics Dispense with Symbolism?

We have now developed in detail the notion of symbolism as a metaphysical principle and the unique character of metaphysical symbolic form. The converse of this principle would naturally be that metaphysics cannot dispense with symbolism. The Bergsonian view that metaphysics seeks to transcend and to dispense with symbolism would be shown to be untenable. This is indeed the case, but a brief consideration of Bergson's position, and his reasons for it, will serve not only to meet this issue more fully but further to confirm our preceding studies.

In order to understand the full significance of Bergson's contention it must first be clear what he means by symbolism in this connection. It is, briefly, "scientific" symbols that he has in mind. He is fully aware of the symbolic character of the basal scientific concepts. He knows perfectly well that these concepts are spatialized and that, while science strives towards a language of pure relations, these relations always have a spatial connotation. Logic, moreover, shares in this character, and logical thought, in so far as it is linear, can move only in logical space. It is *these* symbols that do not represent reality, and it is with these that metaphysics, as intuition, must dispense.

But—and this is Bergson's error—it cannot dispense with all symbolism. There is no intuition without expression; no expression without the beginning of representation, and no representation which does not involve the symbolic at some point. Bergson himself, in effect, admits this and his own metaphysical language is highly symbolic throughout. He himself gives us some hints as to the kinds of symbolism that metaphysics should use. "Metaphysics," he believes, "is never fully itself unless it emancipates itself from stiff and ready-made concepts and creates representations that are supple, mobile, almost fluid and are ever ready to mould themselves on the elusive forms of intuition." To his mind that language which is nearest to original imagery alone has this character. No image, he admits, can replace intuition. The freshest imagery has, so to speak, already wilted the moment it is separated from the immediate intuition. But the image has this advantage that it keeps us in the concrete. "No image can replace intuition, but many diverse images borrowed from very different orders of things, may, by the convergence of their action, direct consciousness to the precise point where the intuition may be seized. The single aim of the philosopher," and to this all his language should be directed, "is to promote a certain effort (of intuition) which in most men is usually fettered by habits more useful to life."[1]

Metaphysics, then, even for Bergson, does not really dispense with symbolism, and indeed cannot. In fact, for him, as for anybody else, knowledge is not really knowledge unless it is communicable, and there is no expression which does not involve symbolism in some form. The decisive proof, however, is the fact that all the fundamental intuitions of his own metaphysics are expressed in highly symbolic form. One could with advantage examine the entire *Creative Evolution* from this point of view. Even the notion of creative evolution itself is used in a symbolic sense. In any case, the language of the book is throughout dramatic. The account of the genesis of matter from life is as much a "myth" as any of Plato's. Metaphysics in the hands of Bergson does not, indeed, like "science," strive towards a symbolism of relations, but it strives towards a symbolism just the same. In that Bergson recognizes a greater kinship of philosophy to art than to science, he recognizes instinctively the sort of symbols with which he is dealing. Be that as it may, it is certainly clear that if metaphysics *claims* to dispense with symbols, it should not so claim. It is precisely this claim which, as we shall see later, has caused metaphysics so often to misunderstand itself and has led it into extremes of intellectualism or scepticism.[2] Metaphysics is rather that activity of the human mind—not "science"

[1] *Introduction to Metaphysics*, p. 16.   [2] Chapter XIV, p. 720.

in the narrow sense—which carries the inevitable element of symbolism, in all thought and its expression, to its highest pitch. As the metaphysical activity itself is inevitable, so symbolization is an inevitable part of that activity. This is not to deny, of course, that there is also a non-symbolic element in metaphysical knowledge—it is this element which Bergson has in mind in his doctrine of intuition—but rather merely that when this element is expressed it cannot be in other than in symbolic form. To this non-symbolic element we shall now turn.

VI

SYMBOLIC AND NON-SYMBOLIC KNOWLEDGE: THE "TRUTH" OF METAPHYSICS

A

The outcome of our preceding studies is the recognition of the fact that, even in metaphysics, our "knowledge" is to a large —and perhaps incalculable—degree symbolic. The question now arises: what are these symbols symbolic of? We have repeatedly seen that the idea of symbolic knowledge is meaningless except as contrasted with knowledge which is non-symbolic in some sense. There is, to be sure, no expression in language which is wholly literal, yet there is a significant sense in which certain aspects of knowledge may be called non-symbolic in contrast to symbolic, and certain forms of language literal in contrast to the symbolic.[1] Two further problems arise, then, out of this situation: (a) the question as to what elements in metaphysical knowledge are non-symbolic, and (b) the truth or verifiability of metaphysical knowledge in its two aspects of symbolic and non-symbolic.

B

Non-Symbolic Metaphysical Knowledge: The Co-implicates of Experience

The specific content of metaphysics, we have already seen, is certain co-implicates or presuppositions of experience. The

[1] Chapter IX, p. 435.

knowledge of these co-implicates, we shall maintain, is in part immediate and non-symbolic. The non-symbolic character of our knowledge here is to be found precisely in their status as co-implicates. They are given "with" or "within" experience, but not as objects "of" experience. To realize that they are thus given it is only necessary to remember that experience, in any sense significant for knowledge, is inseparable from discourse and communication. These co-implicates are made known or shown forth in the very processes of communication or discourse themselves. The postulation of their "existence"— and the metaphysical reasoning by which they are validated— are merely the expression of what is implicit in the experience itself. Metaphysical objects, as Hartmann points out, "are never given directly in the world of appearance; they come into evidence only indirectly. Hence there are no phenomena in which, without further ado, their existence would be manifest."[1] That is the important point. They are given indirectly in experience and come into evidence only indirectly, but they are *given*. There is, however, no intuition without expression, and the moment they are expressed the element of representation and symbolism begins. The fact that there is a self and another and an objective "world"—in other words, the *that* is non-symbolic knowledge. But the moment this knowledge is expressed—the *that* is really inseparable from the *what*— that moment symbolization begins. Kant called these metaphysical objects which enter only indirectly into experience, by reason of this very indirectness, regulative ideas as contrasted with constitutive principles. But for him they did so enter into experience; even experience itself, in so far as it seeks unity and intelligibility, cannot proceed without them. He should have seen that these co-implicates of experience, even though indirectly given, are equally constitutive of experience.

The existence of such non-symbolic metaphysical knowledge has been uniformly recognized throughout the history of traditional European philosophy. It has been described as *a priori* and intuitive knowledge, and with these conceptions has uniformly gone the notion of intellectual intuition.

The idea of a direct intuitive knowledge of the transcen-

[1] Nicolai Hartmann, *Ethics*, Vol. III, p. 139.

dental co-implicates of experience is a common one; the Cartesian intuitions of the self, the external world and of the infinite are typical. Nor is the notion lightly to be put aside if it is rightly understood. The notion of intuition, despite its many meanings, always has one common element, namely, that of immediacy and giveness. Now to be thus given it is not necessary that the object shall be given directly in sense experience; it may equally well be given indirectly as a co-implicate of that experience. In such a case it would not be a misnomer to call it intellectual intuition. In any case, it is partly this which traditional rationalism had in mind when it spoke of intellectual intuition.

It is wholly understandable that sensationalistic empiricism, when it is consistent as in the case of Hume, denies the existence of such co-implicates and therefore of an intellectual intuition. Kant also denied any intellectual intuition, but only with his lips and not really in his heart, for the essence of the Kantian critical philosophy is precisely the reinstatement of this notion in a new form. Both the transcendental self, as the presupposition of genuine knowledge, and the intelligible self as the presupposition of any genuine consciousness of obligation, are really intuited and acknowledged in the processes of experience themselves. They are both indeed *postulated* in order to round out our experience, but this postulation is really nothing more than the explicit acknowledgment of that which is presupposed in experience itself.

Non-symbolic metaphysical knowledge has also been traditionally described as *a priori*. This notion is also appropriate if the concept be properly understood. As was pointed out, the character of the *a priori* has been ascribed to certain things which are held to be true if they are the necessary presuppositions of some class of more particular facts or of experience in general—in other words if they are the necessary co-implicates of experience. This notion involves the conception of a material *a priori* as contrasted with a purely formal *a priori*. Sensationalistic empiricism also involves the denial of any material *a priori*. It follows that it must say that there are no necessary truths at all, or that they are merely formal. There is, strictly speaking, no material implication that is *a priori*. The question whether we may call these co-implicates *a priori* depends,

THE LANGUAGE OF METAPHYSICS

therefore, upon the question whether the relation between experience and its co-implicates is a necessary one. Now it is certainly not necessary in the sense that one proposition logically implies another. This we have seen in our examination of metaphysical reasoning. It certainly is not necessary in the sense that it "coerces" as does the sensuously given. But it is necessary in another sense. The necessary co-implicates of experience are necessary in the sense that, while they themselves are not directly given in experience, their acknowledgment is the necessary condition of experience itself and of its communication.

In sum, we may recognize in these notions of intuitive and *a priori* metaphysical knowledge attempts to characterize the non-symbolic element in such knowledge—the element of giveness which, while indirect, is no less a part of immediate experience than the experienced objects or entities themselves. We shall not make use of these terms for the very good reason that the ambiguities which have arisen in historical development lead to misunderstandings, but the essential notion which lies behind them we may, and indeed must, accept.

C

Metaphysical Knowledge: The Criterion of Intelligibility

Metaphysical objects are never given directly in appearance (sensation). They come into evidence only indirectly; but they do come into evidence. It is with the nature of this evidence, or verifiability in this field, with which we are now concerned. Since metaphysical objects are never given directly there is not, and never will be, any purely empirical proof of metaphysical propositions about them, for they are not the outcome but the co-implicates of experience. The empirical criterion, in its narrow sense, is here inapplicable. Evidence here consists in that "peculiar criterion of proof" of which we have already spoken. We shall describe it as the criterion of intelligibility.

We shall presently examine this criterion more closely. Here a single comment is in order. There can indeed never be any purely empirical proof for a metaphysical assertion, but it does not follow that such proof is *unrelated to* experience. We have repeatedly seen that it is impossible to separate experience from its expression and communication. We have seen no less clearly that the notion of experience cannot be separated from the co-implicates of experience which are given *with* it. The postulation of metaphysical objects is the necessary condition of making our experience itself meaningful or intelligible, and since experience is bound up with communication, it is within communication or discourse that intelligibility is determined. There is no wholly solipsistic verification anywhere—in any context or universe of discourse—still less is there such verification in the metaphysical universe which is concerned with "maximum context."

It is now necessary to develop the notion of intelligibility more fully and to show how it functions as a criterion of evidence. I shall start with the non-symbolic elements in metaphysical knowledge and then proceed to the symbolic.

Even the non-symbolic element is verified in this way. The metempirical co-implicates of experience come into evidence only indirectly; but they come into evidence. The evidence for their existence as co-implicates is that their postulation is the necessary condition of intelligible discourse—of rounding out our experience or making it intelligible.

The evidence for propositions *about* these co-implicates is but an extension of the same criterion. This could be shown for all the co-implicates of experience. Thus our discussion of intelligible communication and its conditions showed that such communication could not be made intelligible except on a certain theory of communicating minds and of the community. This was essentially and typically a metaphysical argument; empirical in so far as it is based upon the "facts" of communication, metempirical in so far as it involves argument to that which is presupposed by these facts. The attempts to characterize the transcendental self or the metaphysical community contained elements of figure and symbol, as we were fully ready to admit, but this is merely a necessary part of making the presuppositions of intelligible communication themselves intelligible.[1]

It is at this point that the general problem of symbolic metaphysical knowledge enters in. Propositions about these

---

[1] Chapter VI, pp. 255 ff.

metempirical co-implicates are, as we have seen, symbolic sentences. As such, they share in the general character of all symbolic knowledge, namely, that it is conditioned by our form of consciousness, by "community of subjective form." The metaphysical symbol is taken from some limited domain or category of experience and applied metaphorically to the metempirical. For the reasons already given, it must also be axiological in character and, to that extent, anthropomorphic. Symbolic metaphysical knowledge is, then, conditioned by subjective form, but it is conditioned in a unique way. The fact that it is so conditioned means, however, that there is no verifiability outside this community of subjective form and the processes of communication which take place within that form. We can at most speak of an authentic metaphysical symbol and of its authentication in metaphysical discourse.

This point may be illustrated by reference to any of the fundamental metaphors which are taken to "throw light on existence as a whole." The proposition that "the world is will" is a meaningful proposition, as we have seen, although there is no possibility of verifying it in the sense of the empirical criterion. There is no sensuously observable entity to which it may refer, no crucial experiment by which its truth may be determined. But while it cannot be verified directly in experience it is indirectly verifiable in the sense that it does or does not make our experience as a whole intelligible. It is in these facts, as we shall see presently, that the unique character of metaphysical "proof" consists.

D

The Notion of Philosophical Intelligibility

The notion of philosophical intelligibility is one that has become increasingly significant in recent philosophical discourse. We speak of intelligible and unintelligible world views, of intelligible and unintelligible philosophies, and we speak of intelligibility as a criterion of philosophical or metaphysical truth. In my *Intelligible World* this notion of philosophical intelligibility is the major theme, and I have sought to work out the conditions of philosophical intelligibility and the *form* which any metaphysics must take in order to be intelligible. For our present purposes I shall confine myself to certain aspects of this criterion which would, I think, be generally recognized as inherent in the notion.

We may, I think, distinguish two *main* conditions of philosophical intelligibility, which may perhaps be described as the linguistic and meta-linguistic. The first of these is closely bound up with problems of language and its use and has been insisted upon throughout our discussion. Metaphysics is discourse—discourse about the world. As such, it must conform to the conditions of all intelligible discourse. It cannot violate the "rules" of such discourse without paralysis of speech and stultification of discourse. It follows that any metaphysics which seeks wholly to extrude the subject-predicate notion, and the other categories bound up with syntax, tends to become unintelligible. The unintelligibility of certain outstanding forms of modernist philosophy illustrates this condition.

Linguistic intelligibility is a necessary condition of philosophical intelligibility, but behind the linguistic, or perhaps beneath it, lie more fundamental conditions. Here the dominating notions are coherence and adequacy.

Metaphysics is discourse and, like all discourse, to be intelligible, it must be coherent. This coherence is, in the first place, absence of logical contradiction. Logical form is, as we have seen, so interwoven with all our speech that to violate this form is to entail contradiction and incoherence. But this is only the negative aspect of the demand for coherence. As the condition of philosophical intelligibility coherence means much more than this. According to an almost universal feeling an intelligible world is a comprehensible world. Nothing is intelligible to us unless it is part of an organized and coherent whole of experience. Even in science intelligibility means, as we have seen, at least this. The fact is no longer isolated; therefore it is intelligible.[1] But for philosophical intelligibility coherence must mean more than this. Not merely absence of logical contradiction; nor merely necessary connections in the sense of science; but that more fundamental coherence which arises out of the demand to round out our experience and to make it meaningful as a whole. Coherence as a condition of

[1] Chapter XI, p. 536.

philosophical intelligibility is the reflection of the nature of the object of metaphysical activity, namely, the *omnitudo realitatis*.

With this conception of coherence we touch upon a further condition of philosophical intelligibility, namely, that of adequacy and adequate expression. We found reason to maintain that adequate expression constitutes the essence of the truth notion itself; it is, *a fortiori*, the condition of truth in the philosophical realm. In order to be adequate, philosophical discourse must be coherent, otherwise it cannot express the *omnitudo realitatis* which is its object. But the demand for adequacy includes more than coherence. This demand we have already seen expressed in the principle of fundamental metaphor. It is only in so far as aspects of experience are fundamental, "cosmic variables," that they are adequate to express the nature and meaning of the whole. The notion of adequacy in this sense is, if not the sole criterion of philosophical intelligibility and truth, its fundamental condition.

Out of this demand for adequacy arises the ultimate condition of all intelligibility—that "great metaphysical truth" as Whitehead calls it, that "all ultimate reasons (or intelligibility) must be in terms of aim at value."[1] It is, as I have pointed out in my fuller account of this principle, only processes oriented towards the "good" or value that have primary or intrinsic intelligibility—all the rest is secondary and derived. Purposive activity within our own experience, with its "links of intelligible connection," we in a very real measure understand, for we actually live through them many times a day. It is upon this that all other intelligibility depends. The only linkage of facts that is ultimately and intrinsically intelligible is one which is interpretable in terms of value. No relation within nature is really intelligible unless it can be understood as something analogous to relations within our own experience and its activity. This is what Renouvier has in mind when he says that the world is not really intelligible until it is "penetrable." Thus the concept of will alone renders that of force intelligible in any philosophic sense; but will itself cannot be defined by anything more primitive.

[1] See Chapter III, p. 127.

These, then, are the specific conditions or "notes" of philosophical intelligibility. Their significance will be seen more fully when we seek to apply them in detail in the following chapter. The notion or principle of philosophical intelligibility as a whole may, however, be made clearer in this context by bringing it into relation with the notion of truth as developed in an earlier chapter.

Our examination of this notion compelled us to find the essence of truth, not in any form of the copy theory—although some form of this notion is always present—but ultimately in that of adequate expression. In our further discussion of the relation of meaning to truth, we were likewise compelled to give the primacy or ultimacy to the notion of meaning. Finally we were led to a statement of the thesis, that the sum total of meaningful or intelligible discourse is the truth. This has, as its further consequence, the position that truth is ultimately immanent in discourse. It follows that intelligibility is the only possible criterion of truth in the metaphysical universe of discourse, for the subject of that discourse is in the last analysis the *omnitudo realitatis*. From the standpoint of language the significance of this criterion becomes even clearer. Metaphysical language is the language of all languages—the language necessary to make the other languages and symbolic forms intelligible. It may therefore be defined as the language of maximum context. It is for this reason that the criterion of metaphysical truth must ultimately be intelligibility.[1]

E

The Nature of Metaphysical "Proof": Verification and Persuasion

Many philosophers have recognized this unique character of metaphysical knowledge, and that "proof" here cannot be either of the nature of observation and crucial experiment or of formal logical necessity. It can only be of the nature of "persuasion." Thus C. I. Lewis writes: "Proof in philosophy is at bottom nothing more than persuasion. It is the essence of the reflective or dialectical method that proof should be recognized as this type."[2] Now I am not disposed to deny

---

[1] Chapter VIII, pp. 388 ff.   [2] *Mind and the World Order*, p. 23.

THE LANGUAGE OF METAPHYSICS 677

the general truth of the statement. I should merely wish to inquire more fully into the nature of such persuasion.

The truth of the statement itself can be easily shown. Suppose our metaphysical thinking is of the deductive type. If so, it must start from initial assumptions and these assumptions cannot *coerce* the mind. They can only be acknowledged. The fact is that there are no propositions which are self-evident in isolation. The deductively first propositions can be made significant and acceptable only by showing the cogency and general consonance with experience of their consequences. But suppose now that we proceed inductively and seek to construct a metaphysics on purely empirical premises. Here, again, the conclusions cannot *coerce* the mind. For the principles to be proved are already implicit in the assumption that the cases cited are typical and genuine instances of the category to be investigated. Here, too, an initial acknowledgment is presupposed and upon this acknowledgment everything else rests.

The indubitable fact is that in the universe of discourse of which we are speaking the mind cannot be coerced. It can only be brought to acknowledgment—to free acknowledgment of the premises, and consequently of the consequences which flow from them. It is also an indubitable fact that dialectical argument, metaphysical trains of thought, are of this type and always go back to mutual acknowledgment of presuppositions. There is no objection, to my mind, to calling such argument persuasion if the nature of the argument is properly understood, if, in other words, we recognize that persuasion is precisely this process by which we are brought to free acknowledgment. The only question is whether it can be called a kind of "proof."

I think it can be shown that all proof—even in science itself—rests ultimately upon such persuasion, upon premises or postulates that are not coercive but can only be freely acknowledged. This is seen in the fact that no conception of probability can be formed which does not contain the two elements of observation and "rationality," and that when the notion of rationality is examined it is seen to contain an extra-logical factor—a factor which is not coercive but can only be acknowledged.[1] The significance of this fact is often overlooked.

[1] Chapter VIII, p. 387.

It means, stated generally, that there is no empirical proof which does not presuppose postulates of the truth of which we can only be persuaded. An outstanding illustration of this is one to which I have already called attention. There is, we have seen, no empirical proof of the empirical criterion of meaning; it itself outruns verification in the narrow sense of the word and is, therefore, "meaningless on its own criterion." It can only be acknowledged, and the processes by which one is brought to such acknowledgment (if he is) are not coercive but persuasive.[1]

Behind this entire question of philosophic or metaphysical proof (this "peculiar kind of proof") lies a still more fundamental question, namely that of the "meaning of knowledge." We have had occasion earlier to distinguish between broader and narrower notions. Knowledge may, as Dewey says, "signify tested instances of knowledge" (in the sense of the empirical criterion); "but it also has a sense more liberal and humane." It signifies "things and events understood"; it means "inclusive reasonable agreement." If we include the latter in the notion of knowledge, then this "reasonable agreement" or mutual acknowledgment to which we come through dialectic is knowledge. The argument to show that it is—and must be—knowledge has been developed elsewhere[2] and need not be repeated here. No satisfactory theory of knowledge could, we saw, be found which was not triadic in character and which did not include knowledge by dialectic or by interpretation; on this third aspect of knowledge perceptual and conceptual knowledge themselves depend. It is with this third form of knowledge—knowledge by interpretation—that we are here concerned.

F

Metaphysics as Knowledge by Interpretation: Truth and Meaning

It is desirable in conclusion to comment briefly upon a widespread view of metaphysics and metaphysical language—namely, that it is interpretation of meanings, but that the notions of knowledge and truth are not applicable to it. "A

---

[1] Chapter V, pp. 219 ff.   [2] Chapter VIII, p. 364.

large part of our life is carried on," we are told, "in a realm of meanings to which truth and falsity are irrelevant." The aesthetic is, on this view, of course, such a realm of meaning, but it is with metaphysics as such a realm that we are here concerned.

This view has a certain plausibility for the reason that it contains an element of truth. Metaphysics is interpretation of meaning and the criterion of interpretation here is intelligibility. There is no knowledge—even that of acquaintance and description—which does not involve interpretation, but there is a third type which is wholly a matter of interpretation. Metaphysical knowledge is of this type. So much is true. Now let us turn to the element of falsity in the view. This lies in the statement that truth and falsity are irrelevant to such interpretation.

First of all, a large part of our study has been devoted explicitly to showing that in no realm of meaning are truth and falsity irrelevant—even in the aesthetic. But secondly—and this is even more important—meaning cannot "outrun verifiability." It may outrun the empirical criterion in the narrow sense, but if it outruns all relation to truth and falsity, it ceases to be meaningful and all discourse is stultified. Otherwise expressed, it is possible that "life may be *carried on* in a realm of meanings to which truth or falsity are irrelevant" (although I doubt that), but the *interpretation* of life cannot be. To call metaphysics an interpretation of meaning and to say that truth and falsity are irrelevant, is, then, to enunciate a contradiction in terms. To see the truth of this it is only necessary to recall our previous discussions of the notion of truth and of its relation to meaning. We shall therefore in conclusion attempt to relate the results of that discussion to the notion and criterion of intelligibility.

The thesis there defended was that ultimately the notions of truth and meaning coincide; that truth is ultimately immanent in discourse and that any completely determined meaning is the truth. The notions of truth and meaning do not necessarily coincide in limited contexts, but in the maximum context they do, and metaphysics is the "science" of maximum context. It cannot be denied that this statement of the nature of metaphysical truth raises difficult problems. Some of these have, it may be hoped, been already met by the analysis of truth in Chapter VIII, on which the thesis is based, but there are still certain points upon which further clarification is desirable.

The first of these has to do with the notion of context, itself already considered. Knowledge or "science" is ordinarily thought of as dealing with objects or with content. Thus physics deals with a certain limited content, while history deals with another limited content; metaphysics, if there be such, deals with maximum content. Now from a certain standpoint this is true. It is evident, for instance, that the content of physics and of history are quite different, and that this difference brings with it notable differences in the methodology of the two subjects. But there is a sense in which this does not properly describe the situation. There is a sense in which physics or physical science says something about everything that happens, including the things with which history deals. On the other hand, there is an historical element in physics, for the physical cosmos has a history in time also. The distinction of importance is, then, not so much one of content as of context in which the content is viewed. Thus metaphysics, if there be such, is the "science of maximum context," is concerned with the relation of what is said in these different contexts.

This is the significance of all those views which maintain that the deliverances of the sciences cannot be taken at their "face value," but that any philosophy of science involves a "higher criticism of science"—preferably the self-criticism of science itself—before these deliverances can be properly interpreted or evaluated. It is also the significance of our philosophy of symbolic forms. Both poetry and science—to say nothing of religion—say something about everything—including both nature and man—but they say very different things. What they say explicitly has reference to specific contents; what they say implicitly has reference to the contexts in which these explicit assertions are made. It is only when what they say implicitly is determined that they can be taken up into that higher synthesis which constitutes metaphysics. The problem of truth, then, cannot be separated from the context in which the assertion is made. It follows also that metaphysics, which is the language of maximum context, is concerned with contexts rather than with specific contents.

The reply to this objection does not, however, meet directly a second objection which will immediately be raised. How does this conception of metaphysical truth affect the truth of the minor details of the world—those details which must of necessity enter into the *omnitudo realitatis*, the total universe of discourse, no less than into the limited universes of discourse or contexts of which we have spoken? Or stating the same problem from another standpoint, what is said about the content in one universe of discourse, the scientific, may, as we have seen, conflict with what is said in another universe or context, the poetic or religious. Truth is truth, and there cannot be "kinds" of truth.

The force of this objection is undoubted, and yet it cannot be ultimately valid. Let us see what the real issue is. It is clearly the question whether science, poetry, or any symbolic form, is to be taken literally or at its face value. It involves the problems, already considered, of distinguishing between the explicit and implicit statements of these various forms. It is the explicit statements which constitute the contents or details of the world and these, as we have seen, do not always mean what they say. The minor details of the world must, of course, in a sense enter into the *omnitudo realitatis*. But it is a mistake to suppose that they necessarily enter into it in precisely the form in which they are described or expressed in a specific context, with its specific postulates and presuppositions. To suppose that they do is the grossest form of dogmatism. It involves taking one symbolic form dogmatically and giving a privileged position to its limited universe of discourse.

The point that I am making will, I think, become clear if we recall what is the essential issue of this section, namely, the nature of verifiability in the metaphysical sphere or context. Here, if our contentions have been sound, there is no purely empirical verification in the sense of the "empirical criterion." This criterion, however interpreted, is applicable only to "details" and their limited contexts, however large these details and partial aspects may be. Propositions about the whole could never be verified by reference to the parts, and there is no experience or observed whole to which the propositions could be referred. Either, then, there is no verifiability, and therefore meaning, in the case of these propositions, as the positivists hold, or else in this maximum context their meaning and their truth are identical. It is this latter proposition which we have chosen and have sought to maintain. This does not mean, of course, that metaphysical truth is unrelated to experience, for it has been shown, I think, that in experience intuition and expression are inseparable; it simply means that in this sphere verifiability is identical with the intelligibility of experience as a whole.

In view of all these considerations we must, then, reaffirm that the totality of intelligible discourse is the truth. It is this truth that metaphysics seeks, and truth in this sense can be determined only in discourse. This means that if a world view that is meaningful and intelligible—and is acknowledged as such—could be worked out, it would by that very fact be true. It is impossible that truth should mean anything else in this context. It is, I think, also what everyone really means by truth when he makes use of it in this context at all.

This position may be stated in another way. Man is so made that he cannot help trying to understand the world or universe in which he lives. Knowledge, in the sense of science, begins when he wonders about some particular object and tries to see how it fits into its surroundings of space-time. Even science cannot, however, as we have seen, wholly escape asking questions about the whole and making propositions about it. Science passes into explicit philosophy when the inquirer goes on to ask for meaning in the universe he is studying. Until the "how" passes over into the "why" all our previous inquiry is stultified. The only conceivable end to this process is the discovery of reality as self-authenticating, as that which we acknowledge as intrinsically significant and meaningful. In short, intrinsic intelligibility, self-authenticating rationality, is the only meaning of truth possible in this maximum context.

VII

SUMMARY AND CONCLUSION

The problems of the philosophy of language culminate in the problem of the language of metaphysics, those of the

THE LANGUAGE OF METAPHYSICS 683

theory of symbols in the problem of symbolism and metaphysics. This statement—with which we began the studies of this chapter—has, we believe, been fully justified. It is now possible in conclusion to see the significance of the study as a whole.

All knowledge of whatever kind is bound up with language and, since language is impossible without an element of symbol, all knowledge involves an element of symbolism. We may therefore speak of a philosophy of symbolic forms. If there were a field of knowledge, such as metaphysics, which could dispense with symbolism, such knowledge would be achieved by dissolving these forms into wholly non-symbolic intuitive knowledge. This is what certain types of metaphysics have claimed to do. This we have, however, found to be impossible. Such attempts, whether they be the negative theology and metaphysics of the ancients, or the more modern forms of a Bradley or a Bergson, do not leave us knowledge, but mystical feeling. We do not deny a non-symbolic element in metaphysical knowledge, but knowledge is not knowledge until it is expressed, and all expression involves a symbolic element.

Metaphysics, then, is not the "science" which claims to dispense with symbols. It is rather that activity of the human mind which carries symbolism to its highest point. In the narrow sense of science, as used in this discussion, it is not science at all, but, as we have said, an activity—precisely that activity which is concerned with the interpretation of various symbolic forms, including that of science itself. If we persist in using the term science for metaphysics, it must be used in the broadest and most humane sense and must not be limited by any of the specific definitions of limited universes of discourse.

Metaphysics, as a human activity expressing itself in language, can, then, no more than any other activity expressing itself thus, dispense with symbolism. But while this is true, it is also true that the symbols it employs—and must employ—differ in significant respects from other symbolic forms. The way in which they differ and the reasons for these differences have already been shown and need not be repeated here. At different points in the preceding chapter we illustrated the symbolism of metaphysics by reference to traditional metaphysics. An explicit study of this metaphysics, of *philosophia perennis* as I shall call it, will at once confirm the analyses of this chapter and afford us a further understanding of the metaphysical activity as such.

CHAPTER XIV

PHILOSOPHIA PERENNIS: THE "NATURAL METAPHYSIC OF THE HUMAN MIND"

I

THE preceding chapter was concerned with the examination of the language of metaphysics and with the symbolic elements which are part of that language. Our task was to show that the metaphysical activity, *as such*, is legitimate and that the language in which that activity is embodied and expressed is a meaningful or intelligible language. But this is in a sense but the first part of our general problem when viewed as a whole. There is the further question of a "true" metaphysic and of a valid metaphysical idiom.

Even those who admit the meaningfulness of metaphysical language and the possibility of metaphysical knowledge may, as we have seen, question the validity of our metaphysical idiom as it has actually developed. And it is here that a second problem emerges in connection with the language of metaphysics. It is maintained that any metaphysics that trusts to language at all is, by that fact, committed to the "verbalism of a false metaphysics." It is also maintained, according to three outstanding philosophies of language, that the natural metaphysic which grows out of this trust in language is such a false metaphysic. It is this second problem which constitutes the centre of the discussions of this chapter. We may speak of "a natural metaphysic of the human mind" and of the critical evaluation of this metaphysic.

Metaphysics, we have seen, is a *Naturanlage*. It is the inevitable process by which we round out our experience by postulation of metempirical entities. But not only is metaphysics in this sense natural, but the metaphysical activity expresses itself in a *natural metaphysics* of the human mind, and this metaphysics is to a large degree conditioned by natural language and its forms. It is with this natural metaphysic that we shall now be concerned. We shall seek to apply the principles of the preceding chapter to its interpretation and evaluation. Our task here is twofold: (*a*) that of description, and (*b*) that of critical evaluation. The descriptive task, to which we shall presently turn, consists in developing briefly this natural metaphysic, its basal elements and its essential structural form. This involves the thesis that there *has* been a *philosophia perennis*, and that this philosophy is identical with natural metaphysic in our sense of the term. The task of interpretation and evaluation, on the other hand, consists in determining what this natural metaphysic really "says" and in determining whether it speaks truly.

The critical evaluation of this natural metaphysic involves the application of the criterion of intelligibility developed in the preceding chapter. It has already been argued that in metaphysics the notions of truth and intelligibility coincide. Metaphysics is the activity which rounds out our experience and seeks to make it meaningful or intelligible; in so far as it does this it is true. In other words, metaphysics is the totality of intelligible discourse and it is this totality which constitutes the truth. The question, then, is whether "natural metaphysics" does this and whether other types of metaphysics are in greater or less degree unintelligible. This is the ultimate problem, but we must first show that there is such a natural metaphysic—describe its fundamental characters and form—and seek to interpret its significance.

II

PHILOSOPHIA PERENNIS: THE NATURAL METAPHYSIC OF THE HUMAN MIND

A

In the introductory chapter I called attention to the fact that more and more the notion of a traditional philosophy, of a *philosophia perennis*, in the sense of the Greco-Christian tradition, is being accepted as the true story of European philosophy. I also pointed out a fact which would also be generally accepted—that this tradition is based upon a high evaluation of natural language, or, as Bergson puts it, on "a trust in language."[1] It is with this tradition, and its relation to natural language, that we are first concerned.

[1] Chapter I, p. 23 f.

That there is such a *philosophia perennis* is, I repeat, generally accepted. The latest and in many respects the most significant statement of this thesis is A. O. Lovejoy's *The Great Chain of Being*. After treating of the "genesis of the idea" in Greek philosophy he concludes: "The result was the conception of the plan and structure of the world which, through the Middle Ages and down to the late eighteenth century, many philosophers, most men of science and, indeed, most educated men, were to accept without question—the conception of the universe as a 'Great Chain of Being,' composed of an immense, or, by the strict but seldom rigorously applied logic of the principle of continuity, of an infinite number of links, ranging in hierarchical order from the meagrest kind of existents, which barely escape non-existence, through 'every possible' grade up to the *ens perfectissimum* or, in a somewhat more orthodox version, to the highest possible kind of creature, between which and the Absolute being the disparity was assumed to be infinite, every one of them differing from that immediately above and that immediately below it by the least possible degree of difference."[1] The object of this quotation at this point is merely to emphasize the existence and unquestioned acceptance until recent times of a traditional metaphysic or *philosophia perennis*; the content of it, of which the quotation gives what is perhaps the central *idea*, will be developed presently. That which it here stated, and of which the entire book constitutes a demonstration, is that Western European thought developed a common way of thinking, a form of thought in which the world was made intelligible. Making use of a term which will be defined more accurately later, it was *the* "form of philosophical intelligibility."

This thesis—of the existence of a perennial philosophy and of a common form of philosophical intelligibility—is of great importance for the entire argument of this chapter. It may be held with a show of reason that to maintain this is greatly to oversimplify the history of philosophy; that the picture presented of a "single plan and structure of the world" does not sufficiently allow for the "strife of systems" within the stream

[1] *Op. cit.*, p. 59. The "genesis of the idea" in Platonism; its fusion with Aristotelean conceptions and transformation in certain respects by Neo-platonism; its development in mediaeval thought and continuation in Spinoza and Leibniz—even in Kant and the post-Kantians—is the underlying thesis of the book.

of European thought. This criticism is in part sound; the differences between a Plato and an Aristotle, a St. Anselm and a St. Thomas, a Spinoza and a Leibniz are real and should not be minimized. But it is only in part sound. In contrast with what I have called modernist tendencies in philosophy, this "single plan and structure of the world"— together with the fundamental characters which we shall find inherent in this structure—stand out with startling clearness. In any case this is the view of the situation which modern interpreters of European philosophy are increasingly taking.[1] Assuming this to be true, let us proceed to a more detailed examination of its fundamental character and structure.

B

Natural Metaphysic: Its Content and Structure

This *philosophia perennis* has been described by Bergson as the natural metaphysic of the human mind. It is now our problem to show by an examination of its content and structure that it is the natural metaphysic, or the one "to which the mind inevitably comes if it follows the "natural bent of the intellect" and of language to its conclusion.

The starting-point of this natural metaphysic, as indeed of all possible metaphysic, is what we described as the metaphysical activity—that activity by which we seek to round out our experience by the postulation of metempirical entities. It is entirely proper to say that metaphysical knowledge, like all knowledge, must begin with experience, but if so we must include in the notion of experience the necessary co-implicates of that experience. A natural metaphysics begins, then, with experience in this sense. The unnatural notion of experience which began with Locke and Hume and finds its culmination in positivism, admits, of course, of no metaphysics, natural or otherwise, for the simple reason that it starts with an abstract

---

[1] This criticism was quite commonly made on my interpretation of *philosophia perennis* in *The Intelligible World*. The appearance since then of Dewey's *The Quest for Certainty*, Lovejoy's *The Great Chain of Being*, and Von Rintelin's *Der Wert Gedanke in dem Europäischen Geistesleben*, have, I think, completely justified my interpretation.

and truncated notion of experience which excludes *ab initio* all metaphysical reference.

The experience out of which this natural metaphysic grows is, in the first instance, the experience of a living creature. It is, therefore, bound up with life in its concreteness and with language as the expression of life. Life itself generates the riddle of existence, carries in its own bosom "the burden of this unintelligible world." The metaphysical activity which seeks to round out this experience, the metaphysical instinct, is part of the life process itself.

It is for this reason that, as we have seen, poetry is "covert metaphysics" and the problems of the highest poetry and of the deepest philosophy are in essence one. The similarities between philosophy and meditative poetry, as Dilthey has so interestingly worked out, arise from their common starting-point and from the common form which it necessarily generates. It is for this reason also that, as we have seen, not only must poetry necessarily trench on the metaphysical, but the language of metaphysics must itself have some of the characters of poetry; metaphysical language is necessarily dramatic if it is to be intelligible.

To round out our experience—which is the character of metaphysical activity—means then inevitably, first of all, to round out the meaning of our own life and to make that life intelligible. All questions of life, however, revolve about problems of generation and death—beginning and end. Life is unintelligible unless expressed in these concepts and the form of reflection they generate. Without them and without this life form, the meaning of life is both unrealizable and incommunicable. We cannot think of life except as a centre of values and except as a movement towards the good. No intelligibility without finality. But it is equally true that we cannot think finality without origin. Origin and destiny are the same thing seen from two points of view. The essence and meaning of life involve both. To penetrate to and to express the meaning of life is impossible without these concepts.

This is the beginning of the natural metaphysics of the human mind, but it is only the beginning. To bring the ends of the life process together is the condition of its meaning or intelligibility, but the life process is part of a larger context, and to make life itself intelligible, the form of reflection just characterized must be extended to the cosmos as a whole. No intelligible theory of our own existence is possible that divorces it from this larger context; that divorces our *duration* from the context of eternity, our place in the cosmos from its infinity, man from his context in the totality of things. But can we make this larger context intelligible? Can we bring the ends of the world together? This, then, is the metaphysical problem. It may be incapable of solution—metaphysics may be impossible—but it is not meaningless. For it is the problem which life itself sets. Only by such rounding out of experience is our human type of consciousness possible. It may be that the ends of the world cannot be brought together and that all attempts to do so are but "rationalizations." None the less must they be brought together if there is to be any meaning or intelligibility in the philosophic sense.

In any case, we have here, as Bergson says, the "natural metaphysic of the human mind," that to which "everyone will come if he follows the intellect to its natural conclusion." Thus it is that "the identification of efficient and final cause" is not only the last word of Greek philosophy but, together with the concept of being it implies, the essence of the traditional form of philosophical intelligibility. We perceive God, or Idea or Spirit as efficient and final cause, according to the point of view, and it is this insight that alone makes the world intelligible to reflection. It is for this reason that "an irresistible attraction continually brings the intellect back to its natural movement and the metaphysic of the moderns to the general conclusions of the Greek metaphysist."[1] In my book, *The Intelligible World*, in which this natural metaphysic is developed more fully, I have described this structure of *philosophia perennis* as the form of philosophical intelligibility. By this I mean that the metaphysical activity, in its natural expression, must inevitably take this form. It does not follow, of course, that it is necessarily final in the precise form first worked out by the Greek genius. Many statements of it have been, if not actually refuted, at least surpassed in various ways. It does, however, represent the inherent and natural movement of human thought, and in so far contains that which is irrefutable.

[1] *Creative Evolution*, English translation, p. 329.

This will become clearer as we proceed to consider the fundamental characters of this metaphysic.[1]

C

The Fundamental Characters of Natural Metaphysic

The primary and outstanding character of this natural metaphysic is its recognition and acknowledgment of the metempirical co-implicates of experience. As Kant has rightly seen, the primary objects of any metaphysics are the soul, the world, and God. Certainly for this natural metaphysics, which Kant had clearly in mind, they are the primary objects, for while not the objects of sense experience, the soul, the world, and the infinite are so bound up with this experience that they constitute part of it—if only as regulative ideas without the use of which this experience cannot be rounded out, or made intelligible. As such, they are not only the objects of meaningful discourse—"things" or entities about which "something may be said," and to which predicates *may* be meaningfully applied—but they are also objects about which things *must* be said if our discourse about other things is to be ultimately intelligible.

This natural metaphysic, being, as we have seen, bound up with natural language, is characterized, in the first place, by the retention of the fundamental linguistic categories and their employment in a metempirical reference. In other words, it is a subject-predicate or substance-attribute metaphysic. This extension of the subject-predicate form involves, to be sure, more than this. Other basal linguistic categories, more especially those of activity, are also necessarily retained. This natural metaphysic is accordingly "realistic" as opposed to nominalistic. It retains as simples those entities which logical analysis dissolves into complexes. As opposed to science and logical

---

[1] In his review of *The Intelligible World* (*The Journal of Philosophy*, etc., Vol. XXVII, No. 4, May 22, 1930), John Laird chides me for the use of the expression "natural metaphysic of the human mind." "Was there," he asks, "ever a shabbier phrase?" I do not know why it should be called shabby except that it is very well worn. Kant, to say nothing of those before him, speaks constantly of *metaphysica naturalis* and Bergson, partly influenced by him doubtless, uses it constantly in *Creative Evolution*. I am quite willing to be criticized for the use of phrases made significant by such men.

analysis, it retains the intuitive meanings of words. If, to use the terms of Bergson, science strives towards a symbolism of relations, this natural metaphysic, as perhaps all metaphysics, strives towards a symbolism of things.

The second fundamental characteristic of this natural metaphysic is that it makes value categories *normative*, or gives to them the privileged position in its interpretation of the world. This we have already seen to be inevitable in our discussion of the language of metaphysics as *dramatic* in character and in our discussion of the metaphysical symbol. This character is, however, seen to be actually present when we examine the structure of *philosophia perennis*.

Nicolai Hartmann has recognized this fundamental character of traditional philosophy. "The great thinkers of European philosophy," he tells us, "with a correct feeling for the categorial superiority of values to principles of being," have given precedence in their systems to values. "Pre-eminently Plato, in that he raised the idea of the good to the apex of the realm of ideas, allowed values to rise above existence in strength and dignity; likewise Aristotle, in the principle of the *Nous* as the highest perfection and of the *Ariston*; so too the Stoics in the twofold conception of the logos as the primal principle both of morality and of the cosmos; in the same way the masters of scholasticism, in so far as they accepted the *ens realissimum* and the *ens perfectissimum* as identical. But even Kant with his primacy of the practical reason gave precedence to values as well as did Fichte and Hegel, who established on this basis the teleological dialectic of universal reason. Everywhere, except with difference of form, the axiological principle is made the foundation of the whole."[1] Everywhere except with difference of form—that is the point. The differences in form of expression between an Aristotle, a St. Thomas, a Leibniz, and a Hegel—differences which rise out of differences of cultural and scientific *milieu*—may easily disguise the common form, but the form is there and it is this form that gives the *structure* to this hierarchical conception of being.

This identification of the *ens perfectissimum* with the *ens realissimum* is the key to the understanding of this entire *philosophia perennis* and of the idioms which are characteristic of it.

---

[1] *Ethics*, Vol. I, p. 241, and other places in his three-volume work.

This philosophy is a value-charged scheme of thought and can only be understood as such. Plenitude, or "fullness of being," is a concept which arises only when value and reality are conceived as inseparable, and this inseparability is the axiom which underlies the whole of traditional philosophy. This is the fact. But the important point here is that it is the only natural metaphysics, for only a value-charged scheme of thought is natural. This we have seen in our account of its origin and source. A metaphysic which abstracts being from value is not only unnatural but in the end can only lead to meaninglessness and unintelligibility.

The third fundamental character of this metaphysic is that emphasized by Bergson, namely, the notions of efficient and final causation and their identification. I shall call it the principle of *intelligible causation*.

The rounding out of our experience through the postulation of metempirical entities leads necessarily to the extension of the causal notion beyond experience. Indeed this very activity of postulation may be described as determined by the principle of sufficient reason. The demand for intelligibility which compels us thus to round out our experience contains in it necessarily the notion that the ground or reason of that experience must contain in it "eminently" all that is found in the experience. It expresses itself in the two "axioms of intelligibility," *ex nihilo nihil fit, ex minimo maximum non fit*. The extension of the causal notion beyond experience is an expression of this principle of sufficient reason. In using the causal notion traditional metaphysics takes, as we shall see, concepts from the empirical or "phenomenal" world and applies them to the metempirical. In this procedure there is inevitably a process of "moulding" of the concept involved, and an element of symbolism is inseparable from such "transcendental" employment. But behind the symbolic lies a non-symbolic element, as we shall later see.

The relation of this character of natural metaphysic to the preceding aspect is evident. From the principle of the categorial supremacy of the good follows the principle that "all ultimate reasons must be in terms of aim at value," and that in any notion of intelligible causation efficient and final causation must ultimately be identical—two aspects of the same thing seen from different angles. In any case, intelligible causation is an essential part of any natural metaphysic. For this reason also the language of a natural metaphysic must be dramatic to be intelligible. Natural metaphysic is a value-charged scheme of thought, and any scheme that is value-charged must use dramatic language.

III

THE INTERPRETATION OF NATURAL METAPHYSIC: THE PRINCIPLE OF METAPHYSICAL SYMBOLISM

A

This, then, is the natural metaphysic of the human mind, and it is this metaphysic which we are now to understand and interpret. The problem before us is reasonably clear. The still more basal problem of the possibility or meaningfulness of any metaphysic—whether logical analysis of metaphysical language does not show that such language is meaningless—has already been disposed of. Our problem now is rather the meaningfulness or intelligibility—and therefore validity—of this special type of metaphysic.

To be sure, if this natural metaphysic is what it has been described as being—namely, that to which everyone will come if he follows the intellect to its natural conclusion—there is at least a certain presumption that it is necessary and, in a sense, final. This presumption is, I think, very strong; nevertheless it is possible that it may not maintain itself on more critical reflection. It is possible that, in the words of Bergson, we may have to "turn our backs upon the natural movement of the intellect." It is possible that, as many modern tendencies in philosophy maintain, the developments of science and more sophisticated logical analysis may compel us to do just this thing, and to develop what is in every sense an *unnatural* metaphysic. This metaphysic may be only that to which the mind *first* comes, when it follows the intellect, and the language bound up with the intellect, to its natural conclusion; a critical examination of both intellect and language may show it to be "the verbalism of a false metaphysic."

The critique of this natural metaphysic has been, as we

shall see, one of the main preoccupations of modern philosophy and the dissolving of this metaphysic one of the outstanding characteristics of modern culture. As is not unnatural, it is generally held that, while this critique did not begin with Kant, nevertheless it is in his *Critique of Pure Reason* that the essentials of this criticism are to be found and the death-blow to *philosophia perennis* was finally given. This I believe to be a false interpretation of the Kantian position, but a brief consideration of this critique will enable us to understand the modern movement.

For Kant dogmatism in metaphysics arises precisely through following uncritically the natural bent of the intellect, or the pure reason, to its natural conclusion—which is the same thing as saying, through following the natural tendencies of language into a realm where such language does not apply— the result being "transcendental illusion." Speaking generally, what this amounts to is that the three fundamental characters of natural metaphysic appear to be challenged:—the extension of the substance-attribute notion, of intelligible causation in both its forms, and above all, that ontologism which arises through the identification of the *ens realissimum* with the *ens perfectissimum*.

This, then, is the negative Kant. This negative criticism was, however, but a prelude to a reinterpretation of traditional metaphysic or to its reinstatement in a new form. Of this more presently. The important point here is that the Kantian critique of metaphysical language, together with other causes, has led to a widespread criticism of natural metaphysic as the verbalism of a false metaphysic. The points at which it has been chiefly attacked are precisely those points which we have found to be its fundamental characters—precisely those characters which make it a natural metaphysic—its substance-attribute character, its anthropomorphism as a value metaphysic, and its notion of intelligible causation.[1] Let us examine these in turn.

[1] A word should perhaps be said here on the Hegelian position regarding "natural metaphysic." For Hegel this metaphysic is the metaphysic of the "ordinary understanding." If reason is to concern itself with the metempirical, the categories of the mere understanding must be transcended or at least translated into ideas of reason. This the logic of Hegel in one of its aspects attempts to do. But here, too, as in the case of Kant, this is but a prelude to a reinterpretation of

B

Natural Metaphysic as Necessarily Substance-Attribute Metaphysic

The first fundamental character of natural metaphysics is that, by its very nature, it is, as we have seen, a substance-attribute metaphysic. Metaphysics "strives towards a symbolism of *things*." This is inevitable for the reason that the metaphysical activity consists precisely in rounding out our experience by the postulation of metempirical *entities*. It is impossible to express these co-implicates of experience otherwise than as entities, things or substances to which certain characters or attributes belong. It is possible that the notion of thinghood (*ens*) and the substance notion may require "moulding," reinterpretation, before its extension to the metempirical, but it cannot be eliminated from intelligible metaphysical discourse.

All discourse contains three necessary and inescapable elements—substantives, adjectives, verbs. It is impossible to express reality at all without the subject-predicate form. Denial of this form leads to the paralysis of speech and to the stultification of all discourse. This is the conclusion reached by the study of logic and language and of the relation of language to cognition. Now, metaphysics is no exception to this general principle. In *any* discourse there must be something to talk about and something that is said of it. It follows that any natural metaphysic must speak a subject-predicate language if it speaks at all. If it rounds out experience by postulating the existence of the metempirical co-implicates of existence these co-implicates must be subjects of discourse, substantives to which predicates are applied. The question now arises whether this character of natural metaphysic, thus developed, is a necessary character of any intelligible metaphysic.

So at least it is maintained by traditional philosophy. Unity—and with it the notion of substance which gives unity to any entity which can become the subject of intelligible

---

traditional metaphysics in a new form. It is precisely the thesis of Hegel that the categories of the understanding—substance, cause, etc.—are not annulled, but reinterpreted in the metaphysical context.

discourse—is the condition of intelligibility. To say of a being or entity that it is a substance is to assert that it remains one and the same among its multiple changes. And this is merely the same as to say that it can be intelligibly talked about. If the principle of identity and non-contradiction had no objective significance, becoming would be the fundamental reality, and about that which is pure becoming nothing meaningful or intelligible can be said. Becoming can only be an attribute of being, never being itself. To say that "to be is to become" or "change" is, as we have seen, to paralyse all speech and stultify all discourse. The axiom of intelligibility, as formulated by Thomism, enunciates this truth. *Quodlibet ens est unum, verum, bonum.* These transcendental predicates,[1] as they are called, constitute the conditions of intelligibility, and it is the first of these, *ens est res unum*, that formulates this first character of natural metaphysic.

It is, I suppose, facts such as these which lead the critic of natural metaphysic to say, with Whitehead, that the substance notion has "a sound pragmatic defence," expresses "a notion useful for many purposes of life," but still to maintain that in metaphysics it is "pure error." Our problem now is the extension of this notion to metempirical uses—to the metaphysical co-implicates of experience.

I think it must be clear that in order to talk about these "things" at all, they also must in some sense be things or entities to talk about. In other words, the same conditions of intelligibility hold in principle here also. *Ens est res unum.* Unity, as symbolized by the substance notion, is the condition of meaningful discourse here also. Critics of this position maintain that to use the notion of substance here is to introduce illegitimately a spatial image in a sphere in which it does not apply. To this it may be replied that such critics conceive of substance as position in space, whereas for traditional philosophy, with its intellectual point of view, substance is conceived of as a fundamental notion, belonging to a different order than quantity and sensible qualities. Being present in the whole and every part of it, it gives to the object its unity. It cannot be perceived by the senses as such but only by the

---

[1] The doctrine of the transcendentals is developed in the *De Veritate*. See especially Vol. I, Art. I.

intellect or reason. Now, I do not maintain that when the substance notion is employed in a metempirical sense the attribution is wholly literal. As a matter of fact, as we shall see later, it is employed in part symbolically. What I do maintain is that its employment, in some form, whether literal or symbolic, is the condition of intelligibility and intelligible discourse, whether empirical or metaphysical.

We have maintained that natural metaphysics must, by its very nature, be a substance-attribute metaphysic. This can be further shown by examination of the consequences of the extrusion of the natural categories of language. In our study of the three outstanding types of Neo-nominalism we found that one and all issued in the paralysis of speech and stultification of discourse,[1] or, in terms of our present context, in unintelligibility. Let us develop this aspect of the question. We have already examined these three types, logical atomism, Bergsonian dynamism, and Whitehead's philosophy of organism. In Appendix I we have further developed this thesis in more detail. Here we shall merely make specific application to the particular issue before us.

One of the classical forms in which this problem of a substance-attribute metaphysic appears is in connection with the metempirical notion of the Self or Soul. It was, for instance, precisely this problem which Kant had in mind in that part of the transcendental dialectic in which the paralogisms of the pure reason are treated. According to his view, the substance notion, which was made wholly for "empirical employment," cannot be extended without error to the metempirical co-implicate of experience, the Self. Nevertheless, as Kant clearly sees, the Self can be talked about meaningfully, and indeed must be talked about, if psychology itself is to be made intelligible. Nor can it be thus talked about except as an *ens*, except as a soul substance. It is therefore (the substance notion) a regulative idea, or in our terminology, a symbolic conception. Now it is interesting to see how Whitehead, with his abandonment of a substance-attribute metaphysic, handles this problem. He extrudes the notion entirely, either as literal or symbolic, with the result that his discourse about the self becomes wholly unintelligible.

[1] Chapter VII, pp. 289 ff.

Whitehead's philosophy, it will be recalled, is a philosophy of "events," and in that philosophy feeling, again a dynamic category, is fundamental. Every actual occasion, every prehension, has the element of feeling. Now in conformity with his principle of the redesigning of language, and his abandonment of subjects and substances, he must, as we have seen, turn ordinary language upside down. We are told that "the feeler is the unity emergent from its own feelings." Now this is, I think, unintelligible, both linguistically and materially. It seems difficult to think of feelings that do not presuppose the feeler. But this is not what I wish to emphasize here. It is rather that when he tries to talk intelligibly—that is, make the prehension of feeling itself the subject of meaningful discourse—it is to all intents and purposes made a subject with character and activities.[1] In other words, the substance notion is constantly introduced surreptitiously. The same general character of unintelligibility inheres, as we have seen, in the other two forms of Neo-nominalism, logical atomism, and the pure dynamism of Bergson.

But it is time to turn from the details of this argument to the general problem involved. A natural metaphysic is a substance-attribute metaphysic and traditional philosophy says that, to be intelligible, any metaphysic must be so. Modernism in its various forms says that such a metaphysic is erroneous.

When we consider again the premises upon which this critique is based we find that in all cases they are the same, namely, that the errors arise from following the tendencies of language, and that language was made for practice and is not moulded on reality. The false assumptions involved in this position have already been made clear.[2] Here we shall simply try to see what they mean in our present context. When viewed in this context they seem to be equivalent to the assumption of the *literal* character of metaphysical language and of the extension of the categories to the metempirical.

It may be admitted, I think, without further argument that

---

[1] This is an outstanding case of unintelligibility in Whitehead's philosophy. But *Process and Reality* is shot through with similar contradictions. This is especially true of his conception of God. Something of this he seems to sense when he says "the concept of God is the way in which we understand (?) this incredible fact —that what cannot be yet is." *Process and Reality*, p. 531. For a further development of these points, see Appendix III.   [2] Chapter VIII, pp. 372 ff.

the category of thinghood does break down when applied literally to the metempirical. In so far as the notion of substance is identified with this category it breaks down also. But this does not mean that it cannot be applied symbolically. There is undoubtedly a metaphorical element in these notions, due to the physical origin of all language and to the primarily spatio-temporal meaning of the notion of "thing" (*ens*); but it does not follow that because it is metaphorical and symbolical it lacks significance. For the fact that there is this symbolic element in it does not exclude the possibility that back of the symbolic there is non-symbolic knowledge. We shall presently consider these questions more fully. Here we shall simply reiterate our thesis that metaphysics necessarily strives towards "a symbolism of things."

C

Natural Metaphysic as "Value Charged." The Metaphysical Notion of the "Good"

The second fundamental characteristic of *philosophia perennis* or natural metaphysic is that, in the terms of Hartmann, it recognizes the categorial superiority of the "good" and therefore gives the primacy to value. It tends in the last analysis to identify the *ens realissimum* with the *ens perfectissimum*. Thus it is that this natural metaphysic is not understood at all except as it is seen to be, in its very nature, a value-charged scheme of thought. Such is "that plan or structure of the world" which has "dominated Western philosophy until the most recent times." The two determining notions in this worldview are those of plenitude and continuity, "plenitude of being" being identified with perfection and therefore essentially a value concept.

That this is a necessary character of any natural metaphysic we have already seen. The world contains both existences and values and it is the function of metaphysics to interpret the world as a totality. It follows from this that the symbols normative for metaphysics must be axiological.[1] It is, however, precisely at this point that this natural metaphysic is most bitterly attacked. Here too, it is held, its errors spring from

[1] Chapter XIII, pp. 664 ff.

following the natural bent of the intellect and the natural tendencies of language. The form which the criticism here takes is the charge that such metaphysics is anthropomorphic. It is important to realize that anthropomorphism here means two things, one more general and the other more specific. The first has to do with the categorial superiority of the good, and with it the extension of the value notion to reality as a whole—the *omnitudo realitatis*; the second has to do with the extension of the value notion in the form of finality or teleology.

The charge of anthropomorphism, in the more general sense, assumes that the "good" or value is an essentially subjective or human notion. It consists precisely in taking values from the human domain and applying them as predicates to the non-human, thus giving them cosmic significance. There are two aspects to be considered in this critique of traditional metaphysics. The first is the assumption that values are wholly subjective and "human," the second the assumption that the human notions of the "good" are applied literally to the non-human.

The first of these assumptions, namely, the subjective character of values, has already been dealt with in various contexts. In any case, the assumption of the objectivity of value has been the basal assumption of *philosophia perennis* throughout its entire history and must be an essential part of all natural metaphysic. Let us turn forthwith to the second aspect.

Nothing is clearer in the history of this metaphysic than that the human notions of the good are *not* applied literally, but symbolically. This is abundantly clear in religious philosophy and in the application of symbolism as a principle there. There is, indeed, an analogy between the human and moral good and metaphysical good as a "transcendental," but they are not identical. It is precisely the main contention of the doctrine of analogy and of the *via eminentiae*, that the human values must be "moulded" before they are applicable to the divine and that they are applied symbolically.[1] The same is true for *philosophia perennis* as a whole—for all those philosophies which maintain the categorial superiority of the "good" from Plato on. *Philosophia perennis* is, then, not anthropomorphic in any invidious sense. It is, however, when we come to the question of anthropomorphism in the second

---

[1] Chapter XII, p. 598 f.; also Appendix IV.

more specific aspect that the issues become completely clear and the problem most acute. It is the extension of the value notion in the form of finality or teleology that calls out the severest criticism.

Now it is evident that a natural metaphysic must do just this thing. It follows from the categorial superiority of the good that all ultimate reasons must be in terms of value. It is impossible to apply that notion, however, without the accompanying notion of teleology *in some sense*. The extension of the notion of ultimate end, no less than first cause, to the cosmos becomes a necessity of intelligible discourse. It is, indeed, precisely the necessary form of philosophical intelligibility. Here, too, it is quite possible that, as we shall see, the human notions of purpose, end, and goal must be moulded in order to be applicable in a metaphysical reference—that applied literally, they, like the substance notion, generate transcendental illusion; that, in other words, there is a symbolic element in them—but they cannot be extruded without loss of philosophical intelligibility. It is this that Bergson has in mind when he says truly that "the doctrine of final causes will never be definitely refuted. If one form of it is put aside it will take another."[1]

It is these considerations which lead us to maintain that, in this aspect also, the form of intelligibility of *philosophia perennis* is the form which conditions the intelligibility of any metaphysic. It would be possible here also, as in the case of the substance notion, to show the unintelligibility which follows upon the extrusion of the notion of finality. In fact, two chapters of *The Intelligible World* are more or less devoted to this task.[2] But to pursue this theme further would lead far beyond the space which can be legitimately devoted to this aspect of the discussion.

D

Natural Metaphysic and Intelligible Causation

The consideration of the notion of finality as part of the form of philosophical intelligibility leads naturally to the third

---

[1] *Creative Evolution*, English translation, p. 40. See also *The Intelligible World*, Chapter X.   [2] Chapters X and XI.

character of natural metaphysic, namely, that of *intelligible causation*.

This is in a sense its fundamental character. In describing it we have already seen the reasons for this—how it springs inevitably out of the nature of the metaphysical activity itself, and how it is related to the other characters of natural metaphysic. The question now is to interpret it and to show how it is a necessary part of any metaphysic.

Speaking of this very notion of intelligible causation, Lloyd Morgan has said that, while science has no need of the notion of causation in this sense, philosophy always has and always will.[1] What he means by this is that it is a necessary part of that notion of sufficient reason and intelligibility involved in the metaphysical activity. The meaning of this may be shown more clearly by reference to points made earlier in this book. The ideal of intelligibility in science is satisfied, as we have seen, by a symbolism of relations and to this science, in its ideal form, always strives. In the chapter on *Science and Symbolism* we saw that "intelligibility in science consists exclusively in necessary connections." Unless science trenches on the metaphysical and seeks to make cosmological propositions it has no need of the notion of intelligible causality. But the moment it does this the notion returns in all its force.[2] Here too, as we shall see, the causal notion cannot be extended literally to the metempirical context. It too must be "moulded" if it is not to lead to metaphysical error. Its application is also partly symbolic. But for that reason it is no less a part of the structure of philosophical intelligibility and as such presupposes an element which is non-symbolic.

E

The Principle of Metaphysical Symbolism

The task of this section was the interpretation of natural metaphysic, and this interpretation consisted in applying the principle of metaphysical symbolism worked out in the preceding chapter to the content of this metaphysic.

The assumption underlying the critique of this metaphysic

[1] *Emergent Evolution*, Chapter X.   [2] Chapter XI, p. 536 f.

is that its language is *literal*, that, in other words, it extends literally and uncritically the categories of the phenomenal to the noumenal world, the result being the generating of transcendental illusion or *Schein*. It is, as Bergson with great astuteness has said, precisely by taking the metaphysician literally that Kant was able to exercise his devastating critique on natural metaphysics. Now it seems quite clear that if this metaphysic is taken wholly literally it must lead to serious error. Our natural language, with its categories, was, from a genetic point of view, made primarily for dealing with the phenomenal world or, in Bergson's terms, to manipulate matter. In the extension of this language (made for "the empirical employment of the reason," again to use a Kantian phrase) to the metempirical employment of the "speculative" reason, there must inevitably be an element of fiction and to take this fiction for literal truth means serious error. But it does not at all follow that we are compelled to do so. It is precisely the character of any "critical" philosophy to distinguish between these two aspects. To make this distinction is to recognize symbolism as a metaphysical principle.

A parallel to this situation may be seen in the sphere of physical science. The extension of the concepts formed in the world of moderate dimensions to the infinitely small and the infinitely great involves a remoulding of the concepts and their application symbolically, not literally. To recognize this fact, as sophisticated science at least now does, is to acknowledge symbolism as a scientific principle. One of the subordinate notions in that principle is that enunciated by Jeans, namely, that the greater the whole with which physics deals the more symbolic the representation.[1] This is *a fortiori* true of the *omnitudo realitatis* of metaphysics. All this, then, is undoubtedly true, and no interpretation of this natural metaphysic is valid which does not recognize the element of symbolism in it. But our interpretation of it would be wholly false if we did not recognize that behind and underneath this symbolism is a structural element which is non-symbolic. This non-symbolic part is, to be sure, not wholly easy to disentangle, but we shall presently make the attempt. In the meantime we shall turn our attention to a closer examination

[1] Chapter XI, p. 539.

of the symbolic element in metaphysics. This we shall consider under the topic, *Natural Metaphysic as Symbolic Form; The Significance of this Form.*

IV

NATURAL METAPHYSIC AS SYMBOLIC FORM; THE SIGNIFICANCE OF THIS FORM

A

The conclusions of our study thus far may be summarized in the following way. There is a natural metaphysic of the human mind, natural in the sense that it arises necessarily out of the nature of the metaphysical activity itself. This natural metaphysic is identical with the essential form of *philosophia perennis*, with the fundamental plan and structure of Western European thought. The fundamental characters of this metaphysic, when examined and interpreted, show it to be not a wholly literal but a partly symbolic representation or rendering of reality. We may therefore speak of this natural metaphysic as symbolic form. We shall presently pass to a critical evaluation of this symbolic form. Before this is possible it is necessary, however, to develop this character of symbolic form more fully.

The unique character of metaphysical symbols and symbolism has already been developed in the preceding chapter. The metaphysical symbol is unique, we saw, in that, although taken from empirical domains, it is always applied to metempirical entities. The peculiar character of the subjects of metaphysical propositions requires certain special characteristics in the metaphysical predicates. For one thing, since the ultimate metaphysical object is the *omnitudo realitatis*, which includes both value and existence, metaphysical symbols must of necessity be axiological and not merely "logical." But there is another point which must here be emphasized. Since they are taken from various limited domains or contexts and applied to maximum context, they must be moulded as any other symbol. This moulding has, in the case of the metaphysical symbol, a unique character also and to this we must turn our attention.

We have already suggested this unique character in an

earlier context. We described it as the despatializing and detemporalizing of the predicates. The predicates are taken from various domains of the phenomenal or spatio-temporal world; in so far as they are to refer to, or be applicable to, the metempirical, they must be moulded, and this moulding takes place through a process of negation—negation of their spatio-temporal character.[1] One of the basal criticisms of natural language—that of Bergson—is that it spatializes reality and therefore "distorts" it; and, in so far as time is connected with space, it is also spatialized. Reality is spatialized by a subject-predicate metaphysics. Now that this is in part true we may readily admit. Natural language, when taken literally, does spatialize reality. But it is part of the essential character of language that it can transcend this spatialization. The law of the development of language—from copy to analogy and from analogy to symbol—is peculiarly exemplified in the case of space-time words.

B

The Metaphysical Symbol and the Spatio-temporal World

In an earlier context, under the caption "Space-Time and Language," we pointed out a special aspect of the natural development of language. Part of the upward movement of language, from the physical to the spiritual, is what we described as the despatialization and detemporalization of our space-time language. It was pointed out that all language is primarily spatial—even in the case of our words for time. In so far, then, as reality is represented by language it tends to be spatialized. But we also found that, with its development, language passes through an immanental logic or inner dialectic—from copy to analogy and from analogy to symbol. Language becomes both despatialized and detemporalized, in that spatial and temporal relations become symbolic for non-spatial and non-temporal relations. The concepts of space, time, and number furnish the actual structural elements of objective experience as they build themselves up in language, but they fulfil their task only because, according to their total structure, they keep in an ideal medium, precisely because,

---

[1] Chapter XIII, p. 663.

while they constantly keep to the form of the sensuous experience, they progressively fill the sensuous with spiritual content.[1] This despatialization and detemporalization of the "categories" constitutes, then, the unique character of the "distortion" which characterizes the metaphysical symbol. It gives rise to a form of language, of a metaphysical idiom, of a unique character—an idiom which, when closely examined, shows the symbolic character of this metaphysical language.

Two of these metaphysical idioms bring out this symbolic character in the clearest relief, namely, the idioms of "omnipresence" and of the "timeless present." The first of these embodies and expresses our experience or realization of the compenetration which negates the externality of space; the second the interpenetration which negates the mutual externality of successive moments of time. Without these forms of speech, this metaphysical idiom, it would be impossible to communicate man's experience when it is at its truest and at its "highest pitch." To the poet and religionist these idioms are familiar and wholly intelligible. "What could we do," asks Dean Inge, "with the entire higher range of poetry—with Shelley's *Alastor* or Wordsworth's interpretation of nature, for instance—if we did not understand these idioms? What could we do with the religion of a Plato or St. Paul or with St. John's life of Christ?" Literally nothing. Without an experience corresponding to these idioms they would all become nonsense, as indeed, they are to some. Philosophy must also understand and speak this non-temporal and non-spatial idiom, for without it philosophy would also remain stupid and dumb.[2]

These idioms then are meaningful. Yet they do not have literal significance. For omni-presence is a presence which is not a presence; literally presence means localization in space. A timeless present is a present which is not a present, for a present is that which is localized in time. These idioms are favourite terms with the metaphysicians; but it is not true of them, as Fawcett has said, "there is a voice in the study but no answering experience in the vasty deep?" This dictum the

---

[1] Chapter V, p. 185.
[2] For a fuller development of these points, see *The Intelligible World*, Chapter VII, especially pp. 262 ff.

most superficial examination of experience compels us to deny. For these idioms are an expression of authentic experiences which can be communicated, and which are confirmed or authenticated precisely in these processes of communication. The languages of poetry and religion are impossible without these idioms.

It is true that this metaphysical idiom has its difficulties, and the efforts to "rationalize" it have not been wholly successful. Over the attempts of the literal mind to do so, one scarcely knows whether to weep or to smile. The schoolmen, for instance, in attempting to express that *ubeity* which they called omnipresence distinguished three kinds of whereness, circumscriptive, definite, and repletive, the first being attributed to bodies, the second to souls and the third to God. With his characteristic wisdom and magnanimity, Leibniz however remarks, "that he does not know whether or not this doctrine deserves to be turned into ridicule as some people endeavour to do." It is indeed possible that in the attempt to give metaphysical language a literal significance people deserve our ridicule, whether they be metaphysicians or anti-metaphysicians, but in the case of the metaphysicians, at least, the effort seems to be deserving of our understanding rather than our scorn.

In any case, we see where the unique character of metaphysical language and symbol lies. In this omnipresence which is not a presence (literally), this timeless present which is not a present, we see the element of negation in metaphysical language. The excessive number of negative terms in this language was commented upon by Anatole France, and we now see the significance of their presence. The tendency to negation is present in all language and constitutes an important factor in the development and expression of new meanings. The metaphysician merely carries this tendency further. The poet speaks of light, but of "a light that never was on land or sea." The scientist speaks of "a machine that winds its own springs," therefore of a machine that is not a machine; of a "natural selection," therefore of a selection which is really not a selection. So also the metaphysician speaks of the world as will, but will that is not will in the ordinary sense. This general characteristic of metaphysical language expresses itself in a unique form, which I shall describe as non-spatial and non-temporal language. The negative element which is a part of all symbol function has, therefore, a special form in metaphysical language, namely, the despatialization and detemporalization of its concepts.

It is, then, this character of natural metaphysic as partly symbolic form which we shall emphasize in the ensuing studies. It is desirable, however, to consider first a further aspect of the metaphysical idiom, namely, the despatialization and detemporalization of the ontological predicates. The crucial point in the symbolic interpretation of natural metaphysics arises in connection with the predicate of existence. In order to round out our experience it is necessary to *postulate* metempirical *entities* which are given indirectly as the co-implicates of this experience. Part of this postulation is the ascription of "existence" or reality to them. For the literalist such ascription is always described as *hypostatization*. Hypostatization is, however, precisely what it is not. It would be this only if the notion of existence were applied literally. The metaphysical idiom does not really assert existence of its objects literally, but analogically or symbolically. In our discussion of the existential or ontological import of propositions it was made clear that existence or being may be predicated analogically.[1] The ideal existence ascribed to essences is not, as the nominalist supposes, an hypostatization or reification of ideas, but a symbolic use of the notion of existence, taken from the physical world. Thus the philosopher—to say nothing of the poet and religionist—speaks of the "things" that are temporal and of the "things" that are eternal, for he must use the only language which his primary intercourse with the physical world permits him, and that is a language of "things." He must speak in existential terms, even when it is not of existents that he is speaking.

The meaning of "existence" has always been the central problem of the metaphysician for the reason that it is the ambiguity in this notion which is the stimulus to all his thinking. If we ask the question whether Romulus existed or whether there are living creatures on Mars, the expressions "exist" and "are" are entirely unequivocal. But our troubles soon

[1] Chapter VI, p. 304 f.

begin. If we ask whether there is a soul or God, a devil or angels, whether there are forces, atoms, ether, a thing in itself, an absolute, our questions have no meaning until the sense in which the terms "exist" and "are" are used is defined. Such ambiguity is ordinarily cleared up by adding to the verbs exist, or to be, some qualifying adverb or adverbial phrase. The terms are used elliptically and the contracted symbol must be expanded. This expansion of the symbol generates all the typical metaphysical words such as existence and essence, ideal existence, of which the antimetaphysician says that they are meaningless. But the very fact that the symbol must be expanded shows that it is a symbol and that existence is used symbolically.

Existence in its literal sense is always spatio-temporal. It is precisely the postulate of the understanding, to use Kant's terms, that existence is bound up with sensation. When used in any other sense it is used symbolically. It is, however, as we have repeatedly seen, the essential character of language to develop from copy to analogy and from analogy to symbol, and this holds true of the ontological predicates no less than of others. It seems quite evident then, that the notion of existence in metaphysics must be applied otherwise than in the empirical or phenomenal domain. If in order to round out our *experience* we postulate metempirical objects or entities, these entities must indeed have being in the broadest sense of that word, but it is equally clear that if we apply the term existence to them, it must be with qualifying phrases which show its partly symbolic application. This does not at all mean, however, that any privileged position is necessarily given to the genetically first or literal meaning of the term.

The preceding considerations throw light upon a problem of fundamental import for the entire question of metaphysic and metaphysical language. It is frequently said—indeed it is one of the fundamental assertions of logical positivism—that the problem of reality, and with it such questions as those of realism and idealism, are meaningless questions. To this we can only answer—it is to be hoped with due modesty and courtesy—that they are meaningless only to those who do not understand the questions. The question of the nature of existence or reality is one of the most meaningful of all questions, for until its meanings are determined we cannot speak intelligibly.

C

Natural Metaphysic as Symbolic Form

With this understanding of the despatialization and detemporalization of metaphysical predicates we may now return to our main problem of natural metaphysics as a symbolic form and the significance of that form.

The idea of symbolic form is a familiar notion throughout our entire study. Poetry, science, and religion are all symbolic forms. They represent different universes of discourse and different ways of expressing "reality." The languages of these different universes say something explicitly, but when what they say is examined carefully it is found that they also say certain things implicitly; and these are always metaphysical. The question, then, is whether metaphysics (and metaphysical language) dispenses with symbolism or whether it is also symbolic form. For reasons which need not be repeated here we have decided that metaphysics is also symbolic form and symbolism is also a metaphysical principle. It is now necessary to develop this notion more fully.

The notion of symbolic form has already been applied by implication in our discussion of the three fundamental characters of natural metaphysics; it is now necessary to make the notion explicit. We found that such a metaphysic must necessarily take the substance-attribute form, but that it is applicable only symbolically, not literally. It must give the categorial superiority to the "good," but the good in a metaphysical reference is applicable only symbolically and not literally. The notion of intelligible causality is part of the form, but the notion of causality is again applicable not literally but symbolically. We may now see why this is necessarily so; what it is that makes these notions part of the general form of philosophical intelligibility, but also why it is that this form is symbolic form. It is the despatialization and detemporalization of these categories. The metaphysical idiom is symbolic of reality in the sense that while it uses the categories of the "phenomenal," it moulds or transforms them in a manner made necessary by their noumenal objects and their metaphysical reference. If, as we have seen, there were no non-symbolic "intuitive" knowledge of the metaphysical co-implicates, the predicates would not be symbols, but fictions.

This, then, is the general notion of symbolic form. We shall presently develop more fully the significance of this form by making clear the literal, non-symbolic element in it. Before passing to this point one special aspect of this form requires special consideration, namely, the notion of intelligible causation. Natural metaphysic extends not only the substance-attribute category (deriving from the noun) to the noumenal, but also the categories which spring from the verb, namely, those of activity.

Metaphysical language must, we have repeatedly seen, be dramatic. Even science when it trenches on the metaphysical, as it must inevitably do when it seeks to make propositions of a cosmic character, must also speak this language. Now, the essential character of dramatic language is that it is concerned with activities, not with relations. Included in this language is the notion of causality, both in its efficient and final aspect. Any language which is value-charged, any natural metaphysic which acknowledges the categorial superiority of the good, must include in it the notion of cosmic finality or teleology in some sense; for from its standpoint all ultimate reasons are of the nature of "aim at value." It follows from all this that natural metaphysic, as symbolic form, must include the notion of activity, and that any form of philosophical intelligibility must include the notion of ultimate cause and of ultimate purpose.

The terms cause or goal are evidently both taken from ordinary empirical contexts and applied to a wider context which is no longer empirical, and thus, on our definition, become symbolic. Their symbolic character becomes peculiarly evident when, in the rounding out of our experience, we postulate a first cause which is uncaused (*causa sui*), or, proceeding in the opposite direction, we postulate a goal which is without end, an infinite, "imperishable" goal. The idiom uncaused cause, taken literally, is a *contradictio in adjecto*. It does not mean that there is a cause, in the ordinary sense, that itself has no cause; it means rather that there is a cause or ground which is not like cause in the ordinary sense. It becomes then a symbol for a relation for which the causal terms are only imperfect expressions. The idiom, the imperishable goal, does not mean that there is a goal in the ordinary sense which has no consummation, but rather there is a goal, not like our human goals in the ordinary sense. It becomes then a symbol for a relation for which the ordinary teleological terms are only an imperfect figure.

The symbolic character of these notions was, *up to a point*, recognized by Kant. In the passage already referred to (On the Application of the Categories to God),[1] he writes, "On the contrary" (that is, in contradistinction to the application of the notion of cause to a body, an empirical object), "if I think of a supersensible Being as the first *mover*, and thus by the category of causality as regards its determination of the world (motion of matter), I must not think of its existing in any place in space nor as extended; I must not even think of it as existing in time or simultaneously with other beings. Hence I have no determinations whatever, which could make intelligible to me the conditions of the possibility of motion by means of the Being as a ground. Consequently I do not in the very least cognize it by means of the predicate of Cause (as first mover) for itself; but I have only the representation of a something containing the ground of the motions of the world." Here obviously the notion of cause as used symbolically is recognized. This interpretation is confirmed by his further statement that "by predicates which only find their object in the world of sense I can indeed proceed to the being of something which must contain their ground, but not to the determination of its concept as a supersensible being which excludes all these predicates." For if I can proceed to such a being by means of these predicates, then the very fact that I can do so means that they give us some knowledge. This is not literal knowledge, to be sure—not determination of the *concept* of a supersensible being, to use Kant's term—but it is symbolic knowledge.

In the context from which this passage is taken Kant deals, not only with the notion of first cause but also with that of final cause—in other words, with the notions of purpose and

[1] Chapter XII, p. 602.

goal—notions which likewise give us symbolic knowledge. When, in speaking of the teleological argument, he says of the notion upon which the argument is founded, that it is interwoven in the texture of all our thought, he recognizes that it is part of the form of intelligibility, part of the natural metaphysic of the human mind. If in his critique of natural theology he points out, with obvious regret, that we cannot use the notion to pass from the empirical to the metempirical, it is simply the same thing as saying that we cannot use it literally without creating transcendental illusion. The whole of the *Critique of Judgment*, in its latter part, consists in telling us that we can use the notion symbolically. And this is indeed inevitable on Kant's premises. For in the spirit of the *Great Tradition* he accepts the principle of the categorial superiority of the good, or the primacy of value. In his "Canon of Pure Reason" he recognizes that "the ideal of the highest good is the determining ground of the *pure* reason itself." Not of the practical reason alone—this is the constant misinterpretation of Kant—but of reason in theoretical and metaphysical employment also.

D

The Significance of Natural Metaphysic as Symbolic Form

Such then is, in briefest outline, the symbolic form in which the natural metaphysic of the human mind inevitably expresses itself. I have described it as the form of philosophic intelligibility. It is now necessary to consider the question of the significance of this form.

The question might be raised—and has indeed already been raised—as to whether its significance does not consist wholly in its being a temporary emotional substitute or surrogate for literal or non-symbolic knowledge—whether, in short, these symbols should not "be dissolved" before the greater light of literal knowledge; or whether, in still another form of statement, metaphysics is not that form of knowledge or "science" which seeks to dispense with symbols. Answers to both these questions have been already given and need not be repeated here. The notion of symbolism as a metaphysical principle is an explicit formulation of this position—the denial that metaphysical knowledge, any more than any other sort of knowledge, can proceed without symbolic representation and expression.

All metaphysic must be in part symbolic. The significance of natural metaphysic as symbolic form is that it is the necessary form of philosophical intelligibility. We have already seen the form which a natural metaphysic must take—the place which the notions of origin and destiny, of beginning and end, first cause and ultimate end, must have in such a metaphysic. Neither life nor the cosmos can be made intelligible without this form. It is this that created the plan and structure of Greek philosophy; it is this that continually brings the intellect back to its natural movement and the metaphysics of the moderns to the conclusions of the Greeks.

Now, it is possible to interpret this symbolic form in two ways. We may think of it as literal—as a supposedly literal representation of a transcendent reality—in which case it becomes *transcendentaler Schein* in Kant's phrase, or non-sense in the terms of the modern positivist.[1] Or we may interpret it as symbolic form, namely, as a necessarily symbolic expression of that which is in its essence non-symbolic. It is the latter interpretation which we shall seek to maintain.

The necessary presupposition of symbolic knowledge is, as we have seen in the preceding chapter, the existence of non-symbolic knowledge. The significance of symbolism consists wholly in the fact that it expresses what, by reason of the nature of language, would be wholly inexpressible literally. Now, the reality of such non-symbolic knowledge of metempirical realities we have already demonstrated. Is there any-

---

[1] It is a highly significant fact that Kant himself anticipates the logical positivist in calling metaphysical assertions "nonsense." In one context he speaks of such an assertion as *Sinnleeres*. For the pure understanding, that is for the reason in its purely empirical employment, metempirical propositions must be empty and meaningless. Why? Because it is a "postulate of empirical thought that the actual or the existent is bound up with sensation." But it is only in this context or universe of discourse, only on this postulate, that they are meaningless. There are other ways of employing reason—other postulates which make them entirely meaningful. By definition, "existence" is for the empirical employment the sensuously observable. But this definition is merely a postulate—a "convention," so to speak, of the reason in only one of its modes of employment. (See the *Critique of Pure Reason* (Kemp Smith edition), p. 326.)

thing corresponding to this form of knowledge in the case of this natural metaphysic and its symbolic form?

As one penetrates more deeply into this metaphysic it becomes increasingly clear that its driving force is the postulate of the transcendental validity of our intellect or reason and of its primary notions. To doubt the ontological validity of primary ideas or first principles ends, for this metaphysic at least, in making the intellect itself unintelligible and absurd. It simply means to doubt that the intellect and intelligible being are essentially related to each other. This relation is, however, included in the notion we have of reason itself, for otherwise there would be no intelligible object corresponding to the notion. Upon this *axiom of intelligibility* the entire form and structure of traditional philosophy rest.

This validity of the intellect and of its primary ideas and principles cannot, as for instance St. Thomas admits, be directly proven. We can only show that the denial of this validity leads to contradiction and unintelligibility. It is for this reason that, as we have insisted, in the ultimate metaphysical context truth and intelligibility are one, and metaphysical truth is immanent in intelligible discourse. But the point here is that it is upon this foundation that the entire symbolic form or structure of *philosophia perennis* rests. It is, indeed, this that makes it natural metaphysic, for nothing is more in accord with nature than this trust in natural reason and in natural language which goes with it. This trust in language is beautifully expressed by St. Thomas in his dictum that "we can give a name to anything in so far as we can understand it." Naming, language, is not separate from knowledge. To understand a thing is to express it and that expression, that naming, is as valid as the understanding with which it is bound up. It is, then, upon the axiom of intelligibility—and the trust in language which goes with it—that the whole of *philosophia perennis* rests. It is because of this foundation of natural metaphysic in the non-symbolic that the inevitable symbolic element in its idiom has both significance and validity.

This is the significance of natural metaphysic as symbolic form. This significance will become all the clearer if we study more carefully the critique which has been exercised upon this metaphysic in modern philosophy, and the gradual dissolution of *philosophia perennis* which has resulted. To this we shall now turn.

V

THE DISSOLUTION OF PHILOSOPHIA PERENNIS: THE "SELF-DESTRUCTION OF THE METAPHORICAL"

A

It need scarcely be said to those at home within the tradition of *philosophia perennis* that symbolism was a metaphysical principle throughout the whole movement of Greek and Mediaeval thought. Plato's use of myth and symbol was not the lapse of the inborn poet into his native dialect; it was rather the recognition on his part, as a phiolsopher, that only in such symbolic form could reality be ultimately apprehended and expressed. If the myth and symbol were not literally true, something like this must be true. This I believe to have been the underlying assumption of the entire European metaphysical tradition—until the most recent times.

That this was true of religious philosophy is, as we have seen, beyond question. The entire doctrine of the *via eminentiae*, with the still more fundamental Aristotelian doctrine of analogous predication with which it was bound up, proves this. Symbolism as a theological principle was part of this philosophy of religion.[1] But Dean Inge is right, I think, when in his *God and the Astronomers* he insists that the same assumptions underlie the conceptions of the world (as well as of God) in this metaphysics. We may summarize this point by saying, with J. Huizinga, that in this metaphysic "symbolism is the music of which the logically expressed propositions are merely the score." It is doubtful whether any of the great metaphysicians—any more than the great religionists—ever thought of metaphysical language in any other way. It was only with the increasing literalism of modern science, and its consequent dogmatism, that the literal and dogmatic character of metaphysics was assumed. It was on this assumption—of literal significance—that it has been attacked. Let us now turn to an examination of this critique of natural metaphysics.

[1] Chapter XII, pp. 598 ff.

B
The Critique of Natural Metaphysic

Ever since the beginning of the modern empirical movement this natural metaphysic has been under constant attack. Hume, of course, is the first really to see clearly both the premises of this attack and the conclusions which follow from them: For this he must ever be held in a certain dubious honour. Yet it is precisely he who wrote what is perhaps the most fatal passage ever written in the long story of human thinking. It is the passage with which he closes his *Enquiry Concerning the Human Understanding*: "If we take in our hand any volume of divinity or school metaphysics, for instance, let us ask, Does it contain any abstract reasoning concerning quantity or number? No. Does it contain any experimental reasoning concerning matter of fact and existence? No. Commit it to the flames, for it can contain nothing but sophistry and illusion."[1]

For Hume experience has no metempirical co-implicates; therefore there is no metaphysic. The thesis of Kant is more moderate. For him there are such co-implicates, but the reason in its purely empirical employment can say nothing meaningful about them. For both, this natural metaphysic seems to be taken literally, and as a result in the minds of both it is a dogmatism. For Hume it is both sophistry and illusion; for Kant, while empirically viewed it is transcendental illusion, from another point of view it is significant. Bergson has seen this point clearly in regard to Kant. In the passage already referred to, he tells us that "one of the principal artifices of the Kantian criticism consisted in taking the metaphysician and scientist literally and forcing both metaphysics and science to the extreme limit of symbolism to which they could go. Having once overlooked the ties that bind science and metaphysics to intellectual intuition, Kant had no difficulty in showing that our science is wholly relative and our metaphysics artificial."[2] It was indeed only by taking the meta-

---

[1] Hume to be sure did not carry out fully this extrusion of metaphysical elements, as Whitehead has pointed out (*Process and Reality*, pp. 80 ff.), the reason doubtless being that he could not do so without making himself unintelligible.

[2] *An Introduction to Metaphysics* (English translation), 1912, p. 80.

physician literally that Kant was apparently able to deal natural metaphysic such telling blows—blows from which it has not yet recovered; but it is quite possible that Bergson has not wholly understood Kant at this point. It is possible that Kant, instead of taking the metaphysician literally, was in fact showing that he *should not* be taken literally but symbolically; that *if* taken literally, natural metaphysics is transcendental illusion, while, if taken symbolically, it retains an external element of truth. This is my own view, and if it is sound it has great significance, not only for the understanding of Kant but for the entire interpretation of *philosophia perennis*. That this is Kant's position regarding that part of metaphysics known as rational theology, we have already seen. I believe it also to be true for the whole of metaphysics.

Kant's apparent ambiguity on the fundamental issue of metaphysics and metaphysical language is for many the scandal of modern philosophy. What he took away with one hand, we are told, he gave back with the other, and what he restored was precisely the essentials of natural metaphysic in another form. For him the status of metaphysics and of metaphysical language turns upon the significance of the basal metaphysical substantives, the Self (or Soul), the World, and God. So far as the "understanding" or empirical employment of the reason is concerned these are "empty words" and stand for nothing. Here Kant is apparently nominalistic and positivistic; these words have no literal significance. All metaphysical use of the categories, all application of them as predicates to the metempirical entities, is denied. But, curiously enough, he persisted in attributing meaning to them. As regulative ideas, with the necessary function of unifying and rounding out our experience, they have validity—even in the employment of the pure reason. In the sphere of the practical reason they not only have validity but reality, and propositions about them are meaningful and intelligible.

Had Kant stopped here we should have had the most ambiguous and sophisticated position in the entire history of philosophy—a chasm between meaning and reference which would make all thought contradictory and unintelligible. But Kant was too accomplished a thinker to stop here. Kant did not give back with one hand what he had taken away with the other—for he never took away metaphysics except in its form of dogmatism and literalism. It is precisely because metaphysics is a *Naturanlage*, because, as he says in the latter part of the first critique, metaphysics is "the crown and completion," the "full and complete development of the human reason," that natural metaphysics is, in its essence, valid and requires merely to be reinterpreted. This, according to my view, Kant attempted to do. His critique of metaphysics and its language—when taken as a whole—is not a break with traditional philosophy, but rather an attempt to restate its main concepts and principles in a more tenable form.[1] Nevertheless it cannot be denied that the chief effect was to give impetus to the dissolution of *philosophia perennis*. Unwittingly he gave aid and comfort to the metaphysical scepticism and positivism which, more than dogmatism, he deeply abhorred.

C

"*Die Selbstzersetzung des Metaphorischen*"

The gradual dissolution of *philosophia perennis* has been described by Mauthner as "*die langsame Selbstzersetzung des Metaphorischen*."[2] The slow but sure breaking up of natural metaphysic arose out of an increasing literalism. The assumption that only

---

[1] It is to my mind one of the fatalities of modern philosophy that Kant has been so grossly misinterpreted by the representatives of *philosophia perennis* themselves. They repeat over and over again in parrot fashion the antimetaphysical tendencies in Kant's thinking, when a careful reading, even of the *Critique of Pure Reason* as a whole, would correct that error. The real break with *philosophia perennis* did not come from Kant, but with the modernism which is a fusion of sensationalistic empiricism and Darwinian evolutionism and relativism. That surely by now should be fully understood. It is understandable, of course, that the neo-scholastics, for instance, should emphasize the negative elements in Kant, more especially his denial of intellectual intuition, which is the very heart of traditional philosophy, but these elements should not blind them to the fact that the primary objective of Kant was to defend against scepticism the main ideas of *philosophia perennis*. That he did this by recognizing the difficulties created by an uncritical dogmatism does not in the least affect his main objective. One of the latest illustrations of this fatal misunderstanding of Kant is found in Gilson's *The Unity of Philosophical Experience*. Neither the charge of "physicism," nor that of mere "moralism," can be maintained if the relation of the two *Critiques* is carefully studied.

[2] *Philosophie der Sprache*, Vol. II, pp. 489 ff. A very good account of a nominalist's view of traditional metaphysics.

words that have literal significance have significance at all, and that scientific concepts are literal copies, almost automatically turned all other concepts into anthropomorphisms. Thus it is that modern thought, like the fabled bird of old, has been eating out its own heart. For in tearing out all anthropomorphisms, all human metaphors, it has in the end cut the ground from under all knowledge. So long as the literal character of scientific concepts could be maintained, it was only metaphysical knowledge that was in question, but now that it is seen that science works with its own type of metaphors, that the concepts of science are themselves symbols, and in that sense anthropomorphic, scientific knowledge becomes likewise suspect.

The inevitably metaphorical and symbolic character of all language has been one of the main contentions of this study. As it is failure to recognize this fact that has led to the breaking up of natural metaphysic, so a return of understanding—perhaps through a more critical and sophisticated evaluation of scientific concepts themselves—may lead to a reinstatement of its essential characters in a new form. In any case, it is precisely this dissolution of *philosophia perennis* which is the outstanding feature of modern culture. The forces which have led to it have been described as modernism in philosophy and may be directly connected with the Neo-nominalism described in earlier contexts.[1] Nominalism in all its forms is the most terrible of all heresies, no less from a metaphysical than from a religious point of view. In so far as it concerns language, it leads, as we have seen, to paralysis of speech and stultification of all discourse. But in that language and intuition are inseparable, knowledge and language parts of one whole, stultification of discourse is but a reflection of a deeper unintelligibility at the very heart of knowledge and thought. This, it is increasingly realized, is the crucial problem of modern culture. It is for this reason also that this *philosophia perennis*, about which Western European culture was for so long organized, is being re-examined and evaluated anew. Let us attempt then, briefly, a critical evaluation of this metaphysic.

[1] Chapter I, p. 35 f.; Chapter VII, pp. 289 ff.; Chapter VIII, pp. 367 ff.; Chapter XII, p. 607 f.

VI

CRITICAL EVALUATION OF NATURAL METAPHYSIC; THE CRITERION OF PHILOSOPHICAL INTELLIGIBILITY

A

Now, it is apparent that an interpretation of this metaphysic such as the preceding is itself already in part an evaluation. An interpretation which shows that such a metaphysic inevitably grows out of the metaphysical activity, and that its fundamental characters fulfil the conditions of intelligibility and intelligible expression, is implicitly such a valuation. So also, by implication, is the criticism of modernist tendencies which shows their essential unintelligibility. All this is true, but it is still desirable to state these results in a more general form. We developed a criterion of philosophical intelligibility in the preceding chapter; it is now our task to apply it specifically to this natural metaphysic.

An evaluation of this metaphysic in its entirety would involve a restatement of its content in detail and a specific evaluation of its entire form and structure—a task which would require another book. Such a book I have in fact already written, *The Intelligible World*. At various points in the preceding discussion I have indicated how the three fundamental characters of natural metaphysic, its substance-attribute form, its claim to the categorial supremacy of the Good or Value, its principle of intelligible causation, are interpreted and evaluated in certain chapters of that book. All I shall attempt here is, then, to restate the criterion in its most general form and to indicate in a general way its application.

B

The Criterion of Intelligibility; as Self-Authenticating

The only possible *criterion* of metaphysical knowledge is, we found, that of self-authenticating intelligibility. In the maximum context which constitutes metaphysical discourse truth and intelligibility must ultimately coincide; the totality of intelligible discourse *is* the truth. It is not necessary to repeat the arguments for this position here but merely to recall the conditions of such intelligibility.

The first and most important point is the distinction between linguistic and meta-linguistic intelligibility. Metaphysics is discourse—discourse about the "world." As such it must conform to the rules of all intelligible discourse. It cannot violate these rules without paralysis of speech and stultification of all discourse. That *philosophia perennis* fulfils this condition of intelligibility we have tried to show. It is of necessity a substance-attribute metaphysic, for only such a metaphysic fulfils the primary condition of intelligibility and intelligible expression. It does not follow, as we pointed out, that this form has literal application, that it functions in precisely the same way as in the limited context of the spatio-temporal world. An inevitable element of symbolism inheres in all uses of language not confined to the "physical" context. But such symbolic use is valid, for the symbols in question refer to co-implicates of experience, knowledge of which is in part non-symbolic.

Deeper than linguistic intelligibility lies meta-linguistic, and the demands of intelligibility here are more far-reaching. The generic criterion here is adequacy of expression, or the inclusion of all the elements of experience. Internal coherence (in part logical coherence in discourse, but more fundamentally that coherence which expresses the demand to "round out" our experience and make it a meaningful whole) is a specific criterion which arises out of the first. Finally, the demand for a meaningful whole, precisely because of the nature of meaning, requires that such intelligibility shall include the demand that ultimate reasons, to be reasons, must refer to values.[1] The application of these criteria to *philosophia perennis* shows, I think, that this philosophy fulfils, in principle at least, these conditions; and suggests that any philosophy which shall fulfil them must take on its essential form. We have shown, not only that its form grows necessarily out of the nature of the metaphysical activity itself, but that precisely this form—with its

---

[1] This notion of the relation of linguistic intelligibility to philosophical intelligibility in general is further developed in my article, "Elements of Unintelligibility in Whitehead's Metaphysics," *The Journal of Philosophy*, Vol. XXXV, No. 23, where it is used as a criterion for the criticism of certain positions in *Process and Reality*.

three fundamental characters—is an expression of these demands of intelligibility. We have shown also that when this form is violated in any of its essential aspects the result is unintelligibility.

The more general criterion of adequacy is the result both of an analysis of the truth notion itself and of the conception of the function of philosophy as the interpretation of symbolic forms. Of the former enough has already been said. A word on the latter is necessary.

The point at which this demand became most apparent in our preceding discussion appeared in connection with the dilemma of religion. Religion, we found it maintained, must be dissolved either into poetry or philosophy. Instead we insisted that the *vis religiosa* of its language must be retained and interpreted in terms of metaphysics. But this demand is but a special case of a more general requirement which applies to all symbolic forms. Science and poetry are equally covert metaphysic and when their implicit assertions are made explicit they become metaphysical. In so far as the language of such interpretation is concerned, it must be, as we have seen, dramatic in character. Even science when it becomes cosmological employs a dramatic language. It is not an accident, therefore, that this natural metaphysic also employs this language, for any conception of intelligibility which conceives of ultimate reasons in terms of "value" must speak such a language. This character of metaphysical language is, accordingly, an expression of the general criterion of adequacy. If metaphysics is to serve as an interpretation of all symbolic forms, it follows that, in order to interpret them adequately, it must itself have a form which expresses explicitly what they implicitly say.

Of the specific criteria of intelligibility in the metaphysical sense, the one that is primary and determinative is, therefore, that all ultimate reasons involve reference to value. The demand for adequacy itself includes this requirement, for the *omnitudo realitatis* is a "world" that includes both "facts" and "values," and ultimate reasons in this context must take into account the values also. This criterion is met by traditional philosophy in its conception of ultimate reasons. This is brought out clearly in its notions of intelligible causation and intelligible finality. It is true that in the limited context which is science, intelligibility may conceivably mean only necessary connection and these value notions may be excluded as a matter of methodology—even the very notion of causality itself—but in the metaphysical context itself this is impossible. It is true that here also an element of symbolism is inevitable, as we have seen, but the symbolic element is easily distinguishable from the fundamental demands of intelligibility, and these cannot be eliminated.

It is the failure to recognize this necessary aspect of symbolism that has given rise to the constant charge of anthropomorphism in the application of these categories metaphysically. It is recognized, for instance, that teleology is a fundamental category of intelligibility within the sphere of the human—that without it we cannot even express or describe the human—but it is held that to extend it to the cosmos constitutes a reversal of the entire categorial scheme.[1] I should not deny that to apply this category literally—to read our limited human ends and values into the cosmos without "moulding" them—is naïve anthropomorphism; but I should insist that the human is part of a larger context and that no theory of our own existence is possible which divorces it from this larger context. Finality in man, divorced from this larger context, is left hanging in the air, and to insist upon its reality

[1] A recent illustration of this position is the argument of Nicolai Hartmann in his *Ethics*, Vol. I, Chapter XXI. He recognizes that teleology is a fundamental category of the human, but denies it all cosmic significance. I shall not attempt to meet his charge, that to give it cosmic significance is to deny it meaning for the human—that "the metaphysical humanization of the Absolute is the moral annulment of man." The facts seem to me quite the contrary, for it is only when men believes in a moral *world* order that he seems to have the courage of moral endeavour. My point here is a purely technical one, namely, whether to give cosmic significance to teleology violates the fundamental categorial scheme. It is true, of course, that the human, with its category of finality, is—to use a slightly different idiom—an emergent which, while conditioned by the lower levels, does not condition them; but it is also true that the lower levels of matter and life do not display what they really are until they have eventuated in the higher levels of mind and value. For understanding and interpretation of the lower levels the higher categories are equally necessary. I should say here of values and finality what Lloyd Morgan says about mind in general. In one sense mind emerges but in another sense it does not emerge, but is a correlate of the entire process. The point in this connection, however, is that Hartmann proceeds throughout on the assumption of the literal application of the human category of teleology to the cosmos, an assumption which a study of symbolism in science itself, no less than in other spheres, makes wholly unnecessary.

in a world where the notion itself is meaningless is the height of philosophical incoherence and unintelligibility. It is precisely such situations that the notion of metaphysical symbolism helps us to avoid.

The criterion of intrinsic intelligibility which is of next importance is, then, obviously that of internal coherence, but it is also the one which offers the greatest difficulties. Indeed this natural metaphysic has, from its earliest inception and first expressions, contained within it certain contradictory elements which it has never been able satisfactorily to resolve. Elsewhere we recognized that in this very tradition two apparently antithetic notions of God have been constantly conjoined, the God of religion and the Absolute of philosophy. These antithetic notions, as we have also seen, are closely related to two apparently antithetic notions of the Good, namely, self-sufficing Perfection and self-transcending fecundity or creativeness.[1] Now, nothing will be gained by refusing to recognize these apparent contradictions. If the criterion of coherence is interpreted in terms of absence of logical contradiction, then, I suppose that we must admit that the two notions cannot be literally true at the same time. If, on the other hand, we recognize the inevitably symbolic character of these notions and if, further, we recognize that deeper than the demand for absence of logical contradiction is the demand to round out our experience and to make it a meaningful whole, the situation takes on a different character. From such a standpoint the two notions are, as I have already said, virtually one, both psychologically and philosophically, although neither can be wholly dissolved into the other.

The contradiction here noted is closely connected with another difficulty which has also made itself felt throughout the entire history of Western thought, namely, the contradiction between the hierarchical conception of being which arises out of the nature of the good or value, and the apparently non-hierarchical conception which arises out of the notion of logical system. It is also at bottom a conflict between the notion of the categorial supremacy of value, characteristic of *philosophia perennis*, and the categorial supremacy of being. Out of the principle of the categorial supremacy of value

[1] Chapter XII, p. 627 f.

arises, as we have seen, the notion of a scale of values and with it the notion of a "chain of being" extending through every possible grade to the *ens perfectissimum*. In opposition to this is the notion arising out of the categorial supremacy of being. On this latter postulate, to be is to be, and the hierarchical concept is not applicable to the sphere of being. Now, I should be ready to admit that this apparent contradiction between "logical system" and the hierarchical conception of being has never been satisfactorily resolved. Nor do I think it can be resolved except by giving a privileged position to the hierarchical conception and subordinating the notion of system to it. This I have attempted to do in the final chapter of *The Intelligible World*—how successfully I cannot say. In any case this seems to me to be the only possible way, a way, moreover, which appears to be justified by our analysis of philosophical intelligibility. For if any one thing seems to be clear, it is that logical connection is a subordinate notion under the more ultimate criterion of a meaningful whole of experience.

C

The Essentials of the Form of Philosophical Intelligibility

The application of the criterion of intelligibility to perennial philosophy creates real difficulties, and I have no disposition to minimize them. Nevertheless, I should still maintain that the form of intelligibility, as we have described it, is the essential form and cannot be violated, *in its essentials*, without unintelligibility.

The term essential is here, of course, of the utmost importance. What I have said does not necessarily deny that much that is historically part of this natural metaphysic is open to criticism and requires restatement. Certainly, as I have already said, the form of intelligibility, as first worked out by the Greek genius, is not necessarily final. If not actually refuted, it has been in many respects surpassed. What I do maintain is that there is that in it which cannot be refuted because it is part of the very texture of reason itself. Much that is historically a part of this metaphysic is symbol and has been recognized as such. It would conceivably be the great *desideratum* for metaphysics to dispense with symbols and to intuit reality as it is, but that is impossible. Intuition is inseparable from expression and all expression involves a symbolic element. Metaphysics is also, partly at least, symbolic form. It is when this symbolic element is taken as literal that, as we have seen, the "refutations" become possible. But they are not really refutations, for the demands of intelligibility require that the essentials of this metaphysic be restated in another form. This, we have also seen, is the significance of the Kantian *Critiques*.

It is important that our position be not misunderstood at this point. To maintain that there is a philosophy, however perennial, which remains unchanged and unchangeable despite the changes and developments of the knowledge of the sciences, is to be guilty of precisely that dogmatism which Kant deprecated, and which it is the task of critical philosophy at any stage of history to reveal and transcend. Again, to maintain that this philosophy has been wholly intelligible, in the sense of being completely coherent and without logical contradiction, is to claim for it the status of a divine revelation rather than the product of human thought and its expression. But neither of these impossible positions have we sought for a moment to uphold. Far-reaching changes, both in our knowledge of the facts of nature and in our modification of scientific concepts and categories—such as space, time, substance, and causality —will affect the form of statement of our metaphysical positions; but no such changes, however vast, can affect the ultimate demands of reason and intelligibility, or justify any change in the fundamental categories of thought and its expression which stultifies all discourse. Coherence, in the sense of absence of logical contradiction, is a condition of all intelligible or systematic thought, but no resolution of contradictions is permissible which is achieved at the sacrifice of the demand for adequacy which is the primary condition of all intelligibility and intelligible expression. In short, whatever elements in this natural metaphysic time, and the knowledge which is of time, may refute, there is that in its form which is timeless and, in principle, irrefutable. Like finality, which is a special part of this form, if one form is refuted it will for ever take another.

D

The Intelligible World and the "Real" World

It is for these reasons that I closed *The Intelligible World* with this statement: "Philosophy is intelligible discourse about the world and the metaphysical idiom of the Great Tradition is the only language that is really intelligible." The present work might reasonably conclude with a reaffirmation of this belief. In thus reaffirming it, the underlying thesis of this entire book will also have been significantly reaffirmed—the thesis, namely, that language and cognition are inseparable, and that meaning and truth must ultimately coincide.

To this thesis, as to the final statement of the earlier work, one reply will inevitably be made. "You may have shown what are the conditions of intelligibility and what the conditions of an intelligible world must be, but you have not shown that the real world *is* intelligible." Now this may be— from one point of view—a just criticism, but from the standpoint of our studies of *Language and Reality* it is not only invalid but essentially meaningless. For it makes the assumption—one which we have contended throughout is essentially false—that apprehension of reality and its expression in language are separable things. If one holds that the notion of a *real* world, first known independently of all expression and then expressed in language, is a meaningful idea, then he may well ask that, after we have shown what an intelligible world must be, we should also show that this corresponds to the *real* world. If, on the other hand, such a statement of the problem seems, as it does to the present writer, meaningless, then meaning and truth must ultimately coincide, and the intelligible world *is* the real world in the only sense that real has any meaning for us.

The limits of my language *are* the limits of my world. This does not necessarily mean the dogmatic denial of anything beyond that which we can express, but it does mean—and indeed must mean—that it is only about that which can be expressed that questions of truth and falsity can be significantly raised. That being the case, it is in discourse—and discourse alone—that intelligibility and truth alike can ultimately be found. The totality of intelligible discourse *is* the truth.

APPENDIX I

THE DEVELOPMENT OR "PROGRESS" OF LANGUAGE

A

THE problem of the development of language is closely connected with problems of origin. With the advent of the evolutionary and genetic point of view of the nineteenth century, the older conceptions of an *Ursprache*, or natural universal language lying at the back of particular languages, received its death-blow and was replaced by the conception of development. This in turn has, as was pointed out, suffered more or less of an eclipse in recent linguistic theory, many linguists being, like Sapir, contemptuous of the notion.

The problem of development or progress arises in connection with two aspects of language—what Jespersen calls the "outer" and the "inner" side of language—the first having to do with external language forms, the second with meaning or reference.[1]

B

Development of Language Forms

When the notion of evolution was first applied to linguistics there was carried over with it the notion of development from the simple to the complex. On the basis of the earlier assumption of *Urwörte* or primitive roots, the development of language was conceived to be in the direction of the addition or combination of these simple or separate elements. On these assumptions the complex was represented by the inflectional languages and attempts were made to determine definite stages in the development of language.

It was formerly supposed by philologists that all languages could be classified under a few distinct types, the isolating, the agglutinative and the inflectional, and that these types represented definite stages in development. Thus the primitive form of all language was held to be the isolating type in which the words do not belong to fixed parts of speech but may serve indifferently as noun, verb, and adjective or adverb without internal modification, as in the case of the word *round* in English. From this supposedly primitive form, it was believed, language passed to the agglutinative stage, as some

[1] Jespersen has two books in which the notion of progress in language is discussed, namely, *Progress in Language with Special Reference to English*, Macmillan & Co., 1894; and *Language, Its Nature, Development and Origin*, George Allen & Unwin, 1922. It is primarily in the first that the distinction between inner and outer is developed. See p. 350.

of the terms lost their original independence of form and meaning, and became mere adjuncts to the more important words in the sentence. Thus Chinese, commonly cited as a typical example of an isolating language, has both "full" words which serve, e.g. as substantives and verbs, and "empty" words which serve as prepositions, or to indicate the syntax of the full words. From the agglutinative stage, it was believed, language passed into the "more perfect" inflectional form, in which the empty words have been welded as inflectional particles to the only true words.

This theory is, however, no longer held. The Chinese language, for instance, for long the chief example of the isolating type, no longer supports this theory. Further historical investigation seems to have shown that the strictly isolating character which to-day is the character of the Chinese, does not represent an original situation, but is itself the result of development. The belief, so long held, that in the Chinese we have a glimpse into the primitive formless character of speech has not maintained itself. In fact, philologists have come to recognize that these classifications do not represent any hard and fast divisions into which known languages can be classified. Sapir even doubts the validity of the classification itself.[1] To return, however, to the main point, for the philologist of to-day, speech, regarded as *external speech forms*, exhibits no single order of language development, no "law of progress" which applies to language as a whole. Indeed, if the inflectional were taken as the ideal language, certain modern languages would have to be viewed as regressive forms. Inflectional languages often lose their distinctive inflectional features and take on agglutinative, as in the case of the French. English has lost almost entirely its inflections and reached what closely resembles an isolating type of structure.[2]

The abandonment of this conception of the law of the development of language has not meant, however, the abandonment of all conceptions of development or "progress." Indeed, development, even in the matter of grammar or external language forms, is maintained by many linguists. According to this view, developed by Jespersen in his recent work on language, there has been development, but it is to all intents and purposes conceived in a contrary fashion. The farther back we trace the history of known languages, the more the sentence appears as one indissoluble whole, in which those elements which we are accustomed to think of as single words were not yet separated. He thus sums up this view of the evolution of language. "The evolution of language shows a progressive tendency from inseparable, irregular combinations to regular and freely combinable short elements." Assuming that changes in

[1] Sapir, *op. cit.*, Chapter VI.   [2] De Laguna, *op. cit.*, p. 111.

language have been in this general direction, the significance of the fact seems to lie in the inference that the direction of development has been, not so much from simplicity to complexity, as from less to greater determination and differentiation of meaning. The regular and free combination of short elements serves the meaning function of indication or reference—regularity of combination, definiteness of reference; freedom of combination, growing differentiation of reference.

C

The Development of Meaning: "The Inner Side of Language"

This progressive tendency in the development of external speech form is paralleled, according to Jespersen, by a development of inner meaning: "when we turn to the inner side of language, that is the meaning connected with the words, we shall find a development parallel to that noted in grammar." Here "the meaning connected with the words" has reference to the mutations of meaning connected with name transference and analogous predication discussed in Chapter V. With the manner in which he traces this parallel we are not here concerned—nor indeed with the question whether this parallel is quite so clear as he maintains. We are interested rather in the nature of this inner meaning and with the "law" of its development, if one may speak of law in this connection. Here the general tendency is that of movement from the physical to the spiritual and his conception does not differ in principle from that of Cassirer for whom the inner meaning of words develops from copy through analogy to symbol.

Cassirer's problem is the study of the *Aufbau der Sprache* in connection with the development of the varied forms of culture, more particularly science and art. He shows, in the first place, how this tendency manifests itself in the speech forms themselves—in the development of the parts of speech, including the copula, and then shows how this development makes it possible for speech to become the medium for the expression of conceptual thought and of pure relations.[1] It is indeed the very *Vieldeutigkeit* of the verbal signs, which appears on the analogical stage of development, that constitutes the real virtue of this stage. It is precisely this which "compels the mind to take the decisive step" from the concrete function of indication (*Bezeichnung*), which characterizes the early stage of language, to the general and more significant function of "meaning" (*Bedeutung*). It is at this point that language at the same time emerges

[1] *Op. cit.*, Vol. I, especially Chapter II.

from the sensuous husk in which it first embodied itself. The imitative and analogical expression gives place to the purely symbolic and thus becomes the bearer of a new and deeper spiritual content.[1] It is thus, and thus alone, that language becomes the "actuality of culture."

D

The Meaning of the Progress of Language

Many linguists are, as we have seen, contemptuous of this notion of evolution of language. Sapir speaks of "the evolutionary prejudice which instilled itself into the social sciences towards the middle of the last century, and which is now only beginning to abate its tyrannical hold on the mind." With this also was associated "the prejudice which arose from the fact that the majority of linguistic theorists spoke languages of the inflected type and to them this represented the highest development that speech had yet attained,"[2] a prejudice which gave rise to a false notion of development. None the less, there seems to be a valid and genuine meaning to this notion to which the philosophy of language may hold fast, namely, the linguistic development which parallels the historic growth of culture in its varied forms. Yet this sort of development, it is maintained by many, is but a superficial thing. "The fundamental groundwork of language—the development of a clear-cut phonetic system, the specific association of speech elements with concepts, and the delicate provision for the formal expression of all manner of relations—all this meets us rigidly perfected in every language known to us."[3] All this may be true—I am, of course, not competent to judge—and yet it seems to me scarcely to affect the issue as it presents itself to the philosophy of language. For the problem is not how "perfect" a speech structure is for the purposes of communication within a given speech community, but rather the manner in which speech has become a medium of communication of all the meanings, the references and the relations, which the growth of culture in its varied forms—science, literature, etc.—has discovered and revealed. From this point of view the linguistic development which parallels the growth of culture cannot be an artificial thing. It is, of course, precisely this development with which Cassirer is concerned.

No notion of development can, of course, be formulated without a criterion and a criterion always involves an evaluation. The ideal

[1] *Op. cit.*, Vol. I, p. 145. [2] Edward Sapir, *Language*, p. 130.
[3] Sapir *op. cit.*, p. 22.

of language thus formulated is, it is clear, inseparable from our own cultural context. It has been wittily said that when we speak of development from the amoeba to man, the amoeba has not been consulted. But the reply is obvious. We are not under any obligation to consult "him" for in the context or universe of discourse (!) in which he lives such questions have no meaning. This principle, it seems to me, is applicable to our present problem, as indeed to much of our present scepticism with regard to development or progress.

APPENDIX II

THE PROBLEM OF TRANSLATION IN GENERAL LINGUISTICS

A

TRANSLATION has always been a favourite topic of the student of language and raises problems of great complexity and difficulty. The question of what is translatable and what is not, in a given language, has been widely discussed, and linguists have developed "theories" of translation in order to solve these problems. A consideration of the phenomena of translation and the theories of translation developed serves to throw further light on the entire problem of communication, and is therefore significant for a philosophy of language. Problems of translation may be conveniently considered in connection with (*a*) primitive languages and (*b*) cultural languages. Let us begin with the former.

B
Translation and Primitive Languages

A

Comparative linguistics recognizes languages of widely varying types, of different natural origins and different historical development. The problem of conveyance of common meanings from one such language to another involves problems of "good" translation and of the limits of translation which lead us to the very heart of the philosophy of language.

It is often asserted that the conveyance of meaning from one language to another is very limited. The gap between primitive and developed languages, on the one hand, and the divergence in origin and development of the more developed languages, set very definite limits to the transfer of meanings. An illustration of this situation, in so far as it concerns primitive languages, is afforded by Malinowski's studies to which reference has already been made.[1]

In his attempt to translate his texts (magical formulae, items of folklore, fragments of conversations, etc., collected among the Melanesian tribes of New Guinea), he was faced with fundamental difficulties which he describes as of two kinds. One of these, which he characterizes as the subtler of the two, we may describe as linguistic form or context. "In a primitive tongue the whole grammatical structure lacks the precision and definiteness of our own, though it is extremely telling in certain specific ways. . . . In the structure of sentences an extreme simplicity hides a good deal of

[1] Chapter V, p. 197.

APPENDICES 737

expressiveness, often achieved by means of position and context." The second has to do with the meaning of words. Here translation is simply not possible by seeking equivalent words in other languages; the divergence of contexts is prohibitive. "In the primitive languages there exist conceptions entirely foreign to the developed language, let us say the English, and they exist in great numbers. All words which describe the native social order, all expressions referring to native beliefs, specific customs, ceremonies, magical rites—all such words are obviously absent from English, as from any European language. Such words can only be translated, not by giving their imaginary equivalent—a real one obviously cannot be found—but by explaining the meaning of each of them through an exact Ethnographic account of the sociology, culture, and tradition of the native community."

It seems possible to state, in a general form, at least, what is translatable and what is not translatable in primitive languages, what, in other words, is lost in translation. The difficulties occur at two points in connection with what we have described as the inner speech form of the particular language, but even more in connection with the "context of situation."[1] All linguistic communication takes place in a context of vital communication and it is this which sets limits to understanding. The divergence of contexts here is prohibitive. What is translatable—and in contrast with the untranslatable, it is by far the larger part of the total meaning—is describable as a certain "common record of human experience latent in all language." Behind the varying linguistic and grammatical categories are the notional categories of which we spoke in an earlier connection, and these embody a common record.[2] Again, similarity of reference in all respects is not possible in such communication—the divergence in vital context, the differences in the ways in which the common experiences are recorded in language, make that impossible. But these differences are irrelevant for the major purposes of communication. Here, again, the elliptical character of language becomes evident. So much more is understood than is expressed. It is the common suppositions with which the communicating subjects come to each other, however divergent in language and culture, which makes possible so large a degree of mutual understanding, however varied the linguistic medium.

There are then limits to the understanding of a primitive speech community. These limits are real, and yet, from the standpoint of the general problem of the range of communication, they can easily be exaggerated. In the primitive languages there exist conceptions

[1] Chapter V, p. 196.　　　　　　　　　　[2] Chapter III, p. 89.

entirely foreign to the developed language, as, for instance, English. They cannot be translated directly, but only by explaining the meaning of each of them through an account of the culture and tradition of the native community. Through this means the meaning can be conveyed. In other words, before the conveyance of meaning is possible the purposes and values of the culture, the suppositions which determine the universes of discourse in which the communication of the primitives takes place, must be understood and acknowledged. But such understanding and acknowledgment *is possible*.

C

Translation and Cultural Languages

The problems of translation become even clearer in connection with the conveyance of meaning from one cultural language to another. Here the question of what is translatable and what is not translatable has become a central problem of the philosophy of language.

It is often maintained, for instance, that a work of literary art in one language can never be *really* translated into another. Croce is a representative of this position.

In a sense, and up to a point, such statements are true. A literature is fashioned out of words that embody universal human experiences, but also out of the form and substance of a particular language. We speak of the "genius of a language" and, although a writer may seek to portray reality or express ideas while relatively unconscious of the peculiarities of the medium of expression, he is nevertheless guided by the medium, and when it comes to a question of translating his work, this peculiar genius makes itself felt and is with great difficulty carried over in the translation. This is true in a degree even of non-literary language. An Aristotle or a Kant may not be conscious of the rôle which the genius of the Greek or German languages plays in their analysis of categories and meanings, but when it comes to expressing the results of their analysis in another language, say the Chinese, this genius becomes evident. The difficulties of such translation are enormous, but Aristotle and Kant *do get translated*. Literature does get itself translated and "often," as Sapir says, "with astounding adequacy."

Sapir has attempted to solve this problem so far as literary expression is concerned. He assumes two kinds or levels of meaning—very closely intertwined, to be sure—one of which can be transferred without loss to an alien linguistic medium, the other of which cannot. To these correspond "two distinct kinds or levels of art—a

APPENDICES 739

generalized non-linguistic art which can be transferred without loss into an alien linguistic medium and a specifically linguistic art that is not transferable." "I believe," he continues, "the distinction is entirely valid, though we never get the two levels pure in practice. Literature moves in language as a medium, but that medium comprises two layers, the latent content of language—our intuitive record of experience—and the particular conformation of a particular language—the specific how of our record of experience. Literature that draws its sustenance mainly—never entirely—from the lower level, say a play of Shakespeare's, is translatable without too great a loss of character. If it moves in the upper rather than the lower level—a fair example is a lyric of Swinburne's—it is as good as untranslatable. Both types of literary expression, he adds, may be great or mediocre."[1]

I am inclined to think that the solution of the problem lies in this direction. We are already familiar with the notion of non-linguistic layers of meaning lying behind the linguistic.[2] In terms of these notions we may say that it is the latter that are translatable, the former that are not; and that this doctrine developed for the sphere of *belles lettres* may be extended, *mutatis mutandis*, to all fields of translation. That which created the difficulties of Malinowski's attempts to translate the language of the primitives is the particular conformation of the given language, the specific "how" of the recording of human experience.

Karl Vossler's philosophy of translation is interesting as confirming this point. He too takes issue with the position of Croce. He too distinguishes between that which is translatable and that which is not, and between levels of meaning. The "layers of meaning" distinguished by him are expressed by his distinction between "inner" and "outer" language form. The inner language form is untranslatable and always unique. He illustrates the distinction by taking two words for the same object from the two languages, English and Italian. "The being that in the external language form is called *cavallo* by an Italian and *horse* by an Englishman, in the internal sphere is an actual horse to the Englishman and an actual cavallo to the Italian." These names in the two languages are "by no means identical with the percept, the image or even the concept of horse. The translation of cavallo into horse may bring up all these—there is a common reference in both cases—but just *that part which is not identical is non-translatable or transferable*. Translation as an end, as an art, rests then," he holds, "upon the relation between inner and outer speech form."[3]

[1] *Op. cit.*, p. 238. [2] Chapter II, p. 88. [3] *Op. cit.*, p. 189.

On Vossler's theory, then, that which is untranslatable is the "inner speech form," the "specific how of the record of experience" of which we have spoken. What is translatable are the "identical elements" in all language, the latent intuitive content. In the case of the translatable the reference is similar in all relevant respects; the untranslatable elements are relevant only for that vital communication within a given speech community in which the wider intelligible communication is embedded.

D

Translation and the Philosophy of Language

A consideration of the problem of translation in its two main aspects brings to light certain points upon which the linguists seem to be agreed. What is translatable—and, in contrast to the untranslatable, it is by far the larger part of the total meaning—is "the common record of human experience latent in all language." What is untranslatable is the specific "how of the record of experience" or the "inner speech form" of the particular language. These conclusions—if valid—seem important not only for the problem of communication but for our entire philosophy of language. They seem to indicate that no account of translation is possible which does not postulate two things: (*a*) common notional categories lying back of the external linguistic forms and (*b*) the intuitive character of these elements. A study of the problem of translation seems, then, to reinforce two of the main positions maintained in our theory of language: the theory of the "parts of speech" in Chapter II, and the phenomenological analysis of the intuitive elements in language, in Chapter III. In so far as the problem of communication is concerned—the problem out of which our study of translation arose—it tends to confirm the view that some common latent content of language, some common intuitive record of experience, is a necessary condition of intelligible communication.

APPENDIX III

NEO-NOMINALISTIC PHILOSOPHIES OF LANGUAGE

A

In Chapter VII we considered briefly three typical modernistic philosophies of language and examined critically the assumptions which underlie them. We described them as (*a*) Logical Atomism; (*b*) A-logical Intuitionism; and (*c*) the Philosophy of Events, and took as the chief representatives of each, Bertrand Russell, Henri Bergson, and A. N. Whitehead.

We pointed out that these typically modern tendencies in philosophy and metaphysics all revolve about certain views of language and of its relation to cognition. These views are so important for the understanding of these tendencies and for the entire problem of language and metaphysics that it is desirable to present them in more detail. This is true of all three positions, but pre-eminently so of Whitehead's philosophy of language.

B

Logical Atomism

The first of these positions was described as logical atomism. It assumes that *fact*, to which language must correspond, that reality, on which language must be moulded, is a plurality of atomic elements. Obviously, ordinary language which expresses and reflects organization, cannot correspond to fact and must be irreparably infected with error. It is also clear wherein this error consists. All those elements in language which correspond to the organized and integrated elements of experience are fictions and in true nominalistic fashion described as hypostatizations. Language in both of its aspects, of vocabulary and syntax, thus misrepresents and distorts reality.

Logical atomism has aptly been described as "pulverizing the universe into nouns"; one might add "logically proper nouns." What is meant by this is that the ideal language would be one made up of irreducible linguistic atoms corresponding to the atomic facts that make up the universe. In order to represent an atomized universe of sense data, language itself should be pulverized into a collection of *nomina*. An illustration of this Neo-nominalism has already been presented in the quotation from Mr. Russell in which the type of language is described which we should use if we were true philosophers.[1] In such discourse we are no longer talking about selves and tables, but about "strings of events and spatial configurations." In science we are no longer talking about stars and organisms, for these are merely names for collections of sense data.

In a recent book, *The Scientific Outlook*,[2] Russell draws the logical conclusions from these premises, namely, that the more science succeeds, the less it says. It is for this reason also that he has himself been gradually passing from a representative to a purely operational view of the nature of scientific concepts. His earlier view was that there is a partial correspondence between the scientific concept and reality. In his later view he seems to accept the operational theory inseparable from nominalism. The result, as we have already described it, is a progressive paralysis of speech. For there can be no intelligible discourse in a language which is merely a collection of abstract nouns. Mauthner anticipated long ago the consequences of this neo-nominalism. Natural science, he writes, "at its present height of development, no longer knows what to do with the old categories of language. If our language were at the same state of development as our science all the old categories would be abandoned. We would then have a language in the making that only a small part of mankind could understand."

Now this is by no means as funny as it sounds. Much of modern science finds itself in the embarrassing position of being unable to translate its latest conceptions into the categories of ordinary discourse, of finding that the more it succeeds, the less it really has to say. At first sight this may seem to be a possible situation, but the more one reflects the more intolerable it ultimately comes to be. A final divergence between the "language" of science and the language of practice, between a symbolism of relations and a symbolism of things, cannot be contemplated without unintelligibility. It is for this reason that science must become metaphysical. For, as Bergson shrewdly says, science is a symbolism of relations; metaphysics a symbolism of things.

C

A-logical Intuitionism. Absolute Dynamism

The second Neo-nominalistic tendency in modern philosophy, that of Bergson, may be described as pure dynamism. This philosophy of language is, like logical atomism, equally strong in its condemnation of natural language, although for precisely opposite reasons. It

---

[1] Chapter VII, p. 290.
[2] Published by George Allen & Unwin Ltd.

assumes also that language is made for purely practical purposes and therefore misrepresents and distorts reality. For it language also is infected with errors, but its errors are of a different nature and origin.

A pure dynamism or activism, such as Bergson's, argues somewhat as follows: The mind, in order to grasp things, develops three kinds of representations or categories, namely, forms or essences, qualities, and acts. These three ways of seeing things correspond to the three grammatical categories, nouns, adjectives, verbs. Nouns and adjectives symbolize states; they can represent only the static. But if reality is not static, as Bergson holds it is not, nouns and adjectives can only misrepresent and distort reality. The burden falls, therefore, on the verb. The verb also, according to Bergson, when used as a symbol together with the other linguistic symbols, as in the subject-predicate form, also turns movement into a state, in order to apprehend or grasp it. The verb also is a name for a state. Bergson has an illustration of this point. We say, "the child becomes man." But in this proposition "becomes," he tells us, is "a verb of indeterminate meaning, intended to mask the absurdity into which we fall when we attribute the state man to the subject child." The truth is, he continues, that if language were really moulded on reality, we should not say this, but rather "there is becoming between child and man."[1] This line of thought, taken almost verbally from Bergson, expresses perfectly the thesis that language is not moulded on reality. For Bergson "to be is to become," and language, only in so far as it expresses becoming, in any way represents reality. The verb is the only part of speech that expresses or represents reality, and even the verb only when it expresses becoming, transitivity.

The true inwardness of Bergson's critique of language is apparent. Language, with its grammatical elements, was constructed merely to grasp states, or the static. It developed merely for the practical purpose of apprehending or grasping those aspects of reality which are useful, which are necessary for manipulation. In order to manipulate, we must turn movement or activity into static "things" or discontinuous states. But reality is not that. It is becoming, duration, continuity. Therefore language is not moulded on reality, and to know reality we must abandon language and the categories generated by language. Intellect and logic, which in Bergson's view are bound up with language, are wholly incapable of apprehending reality and must be abandoned for immediate intuition—not determined, and therefore distorted, by linguistic form. This is the meaning of a-logical intuitionism.

In many ways the very opposite of logical atomism, a-logical

---

[1] *Creative Evolution* (English translation), p. 303.

intuitionism is similar in its general assumptions and leads to the same general consequences. The consequences of logical atomism are, as we attempted to show, the progressive paralysis of speech. The same result follows upon a-logical intuitionism, although for somewhat different reasons. The only part of speech that expresses reality, as it actually is, is the verb, and then only in its aspect of intuitive expression of becoming and transitivity. Nouns and adjectives, essences and qualities, must all be "vaporized into verbs." Thus of necessity the distinctions between subject and predicate and between predicate and activity all break down. As Mauthner says, if we really wanted to express reality, we should no longer say, "the tree is green," but rather "the tree greens me." But even this does not go far enough. For there is no longer a tree to be green, just as, in Bergson's own example, there is no child to become man. There are only becomings, durations. By a different route we come then to the same general results as in the case of logical atomism. If there is no intelligible discourse in which the elements of discourse are merely a collection of abstractions, abstract nouns or names, equally there is no intelligible discourse in which there is nothing but verbs. As for the former there are no "I's" or "tables," no stars and organisms, but only collections of atomic entities, so for the latter there are no such objects but only becomings and durations.

Bergson indeed faces the consequences of his philosophy of language. Language does indeed misrepresent and distort reality. Reality cannot therefore be *expressed* in linguistic form. Though we may use language practically, metaphysically speech is paralysed. We should therefore—if we were true philosophers—not use it at all. We should be mystics and remain silent. This, however, we cannot do, and a way must be found out of this dilemma. This is found in his unique conception of language and metaphysics, as so eloquently developed in his *Introduction to Metaphysics*. In so far as we use language in metaphysics, it is not to represent or describe reality, but merely as a means, as a dialectical ladder, so to speak, to communicate intuition; to bring the hearer to the point where he may have the same intuition as the speaker. It is for this reason that, in the view of Bergson, metaphysical language is more akin to that of poetry than to the language of science.

D

The Redesigning of Language. Whitehead's Philosophy of Language

A third type of philosophy of language is that of Whitehead—a peculiarly interesting form, in that it combines elements of both of the preceding theories, just as Whitehead's entire philosophy is in a sense a fusion of these two points of view. It shares the same general assumptions as the preceding but, whereas the latter are pessimistic regarding language, and each in his particular way in principle proposes its abandonment, the former would remould or redesign it.

The mystic might indeed abandon all speech and remain silent, but not so the scientist and the philosopher. Science is knowledge that is verifiable and communicable. Communication is an essential element in knowledge, and some language, or rather language in some sense, is necessary for communication. Science is quite accustomed to the redesigning of language. Not only does it, in the interests of a purer notation, create artificial technical languages, but it also bursts through language in the ordinary sense and creates a special language of mathematics. It is accordingly but a short step to the proposal to redesign our natural language completely in the interests of philosophy, or, in other words, for a more adequate expression of reality.

The thesis expressed in this line of thought is actually developed into a philosophy of language by A. N. Whitehead in his *Process and Reality*. The basal assumption upon which Whitehead proceeds is the inability of natural language to express reality. It breaks down, we are told, precisely at the point of "expressing in explicit form the larger generalities." Thus, for him "philosophy must redesign language in the way that in the physical sciences pre-existing physical appliances are redesigned." "All modern philosophy," he tells us, "hinges round the difficulty of describing the world in terms of subject and predicate, substance and quality, particular and universal. The result always does violence to immediate experience."[1] Like many others, he tells us that "this language expresses a useful abstract for many purposes of life. But whenever we try to use it as a fundamental statement of the nature of things, it proves itself mistaken. For the employment of the subject-predicate notion there is a sound pragmatic defence. But in metaphysics, the concept is pure error."[2] This principle of the redesigning of language involves consequences of tremendous importance. It means a drastic revision of all the categories and an entirely new metaphysical language.

It is impossible in this context to treat exhaustively Whitehead's "new categorical scheme." It must suffice for our present purposes to suggest certain crucial points which indicate the character of the revision. For the category of substance we have the category of actual occasion, for the category of inherence that of ingression, for

[1] *Op. cit.*, p. 78. [2] *Op. cit.*, p. 122.

the category of thinghood that of concrescence. An examination of the results of this revision shows immediately the direction which it takes. In every case it is the substitution of "activity" for "states." Here, too, it may be said that the universe having been pulverized into events, language must be pulverized into verbs. Here, too, it is held, ordinary language is not "moulded on reality." We must try to remould our language so as to talk wholly in verbs, and if we cannot talk intelligibly in that fashion—as indeed Whitehead shows we cannot on almost every page of his book—we must constantly remember that we are speaking falsely. In Whitehead's philosophy there is, strictly speaking, "no thing" and nothing has or does anything. There is no thing and nothing has any quality or activity. I do not see green, for, strictly speaking, I am but a concrescence of my feelings—but green, so to speak, greens me. In sum we have a conception of language which shares in the assumptions of the other two forms and would redesign language in the direction suggested by these assumptions.

If anything were needed to bring to a final issue the basal problems of the relation of language to reality, this valiant attempt to create an entirely new language—and with it the designing of a new set of categories—should certainly accomplish that end. It would be easy to reply to such a proposal that the results of this redesigning have not been wholly happy, that *Process and Reality* which embodies these results is not precisely the most intelligible book in philosophy ever written, either verbally or materially. One might also say that a proposal such as this, which not only by implication but explicitly outlaws all that has been written in philosophy—including even the empiricists, Locke and Hume themselves, who are still under the dominance of the old subject-predicate language[1]—gives one furiously to think. It is not, however, my object to consider this attempt critically here. That has been done at various points in the body of the work. The object here is solely to describe in more detail this position regarding language as one of the three typical neo-nominalistic philosophies of language.

Its relation to the other two forms is obvious. Like them, it starts with the same assumptions regarding the nature of language and should logically reach much the same conclusions. The conclusions of the other forms were alike in this, the abandonment of natural language—the one, logical atomism, in favour of non-linguistic symbols, the other, a-logical intuitionism, in favour of poetry and mysticism. Whitehead will accept neither inference, but seeks rather to redesign natural language in such fashion as to avoid these con-

---

[1] *Op. cit.*, p. 80.

sequences and to retain the values of both of the other forms. We may well ask whether this is possible. I do not think so. The consequences of the other forms were, although for different reasons, describable as the paralysis of speech and the stultification of discourse. Can Whitehead's theory of language escape these consequences? Here, I think, our answer must in a sense be different. Speech is paralysed in a sense, but only in the sense that a language so redesigned, and which goes contrary to all natural speech and its forms, tends to become unintelligible, as a reading of *Process and Reality* will abundantly show. Our discourse does tend to become stultified, but in the sense that communication—carried on by means of categories which in ordinary language mean one thing, and in Whitehead's revision mean another—tends to become contradictory and incoherent. This, too, I think, a careful reading of *Process and Reality* will show. These positions have been worked out in considerable detail in a recent article, reference to which may here be made.[1]

The consequences for the philosophy of language which underlies these three types of metaphysics show then, more perhaps than any other considerations, the necessity of a scrutiny of the assumptions which underlie it and a criticism of these assumptions such as was attempted in Chapter VII.

[1] "Elements of Unintelligibility in Whitehead's Metaphysics: The Problem of Language in 'Process and Reality,'" *The Journal of Philosophy*, Vol. XXXV, No. 23.

APPENDIX IV

SYMBOLISM AS A THEOLOGICAL PRINCIPLE IN ST. THOMAS

One of the most important sources for the understanding of symbolism as a theological principle is to be found in St. Thomas's treatise on "The Names of God," which follows in the *Summa Theologica* immediately after the discussion of "How God is Known to Us."

The names of God do not refer to subjective experience but to an existent Being, the origin of all things. It is the classical formulation of "religious realism" in the sense of the reality of both substance and attributes.

The attributes of God are divided into absolute and relative, the former pertaining to God as He is in himself, the latter to the operations of God. The former, such as omnipotence, omniscience, and all-good arise from the nature of God as fullness of being, as *ens realissimum* and *ens perfectissimum*; the latter are determined empirically from the perfections in the universe of created things, and therefore on the basis of the analogy of being.

It is in connection with the relative attributes that the classical formulation of analogous prediction is developed. Distinction is made between the various forms which analogy may take. There is analogy of attribution, as when we say "the air is healthy," and there is analogy of proportion. Analogy of proportion may be proper analogy and analogy of metaphor. It is this latter distinction which is of main importance. Metaphorically we say that the lion is the king of beasts. So, too, metaphorically we say of God that He is angry. But since anger is a passion of the sensible order, we see quite well that it cannot properly belong to God. The analogy of proper proportionality, on the other hand, presupposes that the analogy is really found, in the strict sense, in each of the analogues and is based on a fundamental "analogy of being"—between the creator and the created.

The process by which we arrive at a conception of what God is, is, then, to quote the interpretation of a modern scholastic, threefold. "The first is a process of attribution. We attribute to God all the perfections we find in the universe. . . . Our second process is one of negation or elimination. In the universe there are many perfections which, while good and necessary for the beings that possess them, imply in their very concept limitations. We call them mixed or relative perfections. We do not attribute them to God because . . . the infinitely perfect cannot possess any but unmixed or simple and absolute perfections. The final process is one of ontological

APPENDICES

sublimation. We ascribe the simple and absolute perfections in the universe to God, not in the sense in which creatures possess them. His manner of possessing them is super-eminent and sublime because his is an absolute and necessary . . . possession."[1]

The treatise on *The Names of God* takes up and answers twelve questions, the third of which is of special importance in connection with our present study. It is whether any name can be applied to God in its literal sense. St. Thomas answers this question in the affirmative, but in answering it he makes a distinction of the utmost importance, namely, between the perfections themselves and their "mode of signification." What is significated by the names, good, wise, etc., belongs literally to God, who is the sum of all perfections, but their mode of signification, e.g. goodness, beauty, wisdom, as they appear in creatures, does not belong properly and strictly to God in whom these perfections are infinite. In this distinction are to be found the essentials of St. Thomas's use of symbolism as a theological principle. The names of God, although they give us an element of non-symbolic knowledge, nevertheless in the mode of signification are symbolic.[2] This distinction between the literal and symbolic marks the specific point at which symbolism as a theological principle becomes part of the Thomistic philosophy of religion. Some such application of the principle is inescapable in any adequate philosophy of religion. It is the loss of this distinction between the literal and the symbolic, and with it to a large extent the failure to recognize symbolism as a theological principle, that has caused so many difficulties in modern philosophies of religion. It is precisely by making theology speak literally, where it itself knows that it is speaking symbolically, that so many of the specious criticisms of the language of religion attain their apparent force.

It is, of course, true that many Roman Catholic theologians distinguish carefully the theory of analogy from the theory of symbolism. The former is sound doctrine, the latter is error. It must, however, be noted that when the symbolist view is thus denounced, it is the humanist theory of religious symbolism which the critics have in mind. The terms by which God is represented—wise, loving, just— are adopted, according to the "symbolic" view, we are told, simply

---

[1] See Charles Baschab, *Manual of Neo-Scholastic Philosophy*, pp. 419 ff.
[2] For further details on this question see *The Summa Theologica* of St. Thomas Aquinas. Literally translated by the Fathers of the English Dominican Province. Second and revised edition. Also Rev. R. Garriggou-Lagrange, *God; His Existence and His Nature*. Translated by Dom Bede Rose, O.S.B., St. Louis, 1934; Charles Baschab, *Manual of Neo-Scholastic Philosophy*, St. Louis, 1929; Etienne Gilson, *The Philosophy of St. Thomas Aquinas*, translated by Bullogh and Elrington, Cambridge, 1929.

to satisfy certain human cravings, as useful fictions, helping to produce desirable modes of conduct or sentiment. This, at least, is how the Dominican philosopher, Father Sertillanges,[1] describes what he calls the symbolic view. Now if symbolism means this, we can well understand that no form of Catholic theology could accept symbolism as a theological principle, but surely that is not what it has meant either historically or indeed among many Catholic theologians to-day. It is based on the belief in a concordance between things visible and invisible and where this concordance exists we have a metaphysical or anagogical, not a moral and humanistic theory.

Even in the Thomist school itself there is no unanimity on these points. Everything turns upon the degree of agreement between an attribute ascribed to God and that which the same word connotes when applied to man. If the agreement were complete we should have literal knowledge; if it is not our knowledge must be in some sense symbolic. On this point Thomists seem to differ. In any case it is scarcely necessary for us to enter into this controversy. We have been using the notion of symbolism throughout in a broader sense—in order to bring the symbolic element in religion into relation with similar elements in other forms of human experience and knowledge. In so far as St. Thomas himself is concerned, it seems to me that for him symbolism is a theological principle. In so far as the mode of signification cannot be applied literally to God, it would seem to follow that if it can be applied at all—and St. Thomas holds that it can—it must be applied symbolically. For that which is not a literal representation must be symbolic in some sense.

[1] A. D. Sertillanges, *Les grandes thèses de la philosophie thomiste*. For a critical discussion of this position see Edwyn Bevan, *Symbolism and Belief*, pp. 311 ff. (George Allen & Unwin Ltd.)

INDEX OF NAMES

Alexander, H. B., 241
Alexander, S., 457, 609
Ammann, H., 62, 91, 135, 149, 172
Aquinas, Saint Thomas, 600, 749
Aristotle, 174, 205, 351
Ayer, A. J., 220, 392, 640, 652

Bally, C., 89
Baschab, C., 749
Beatty, J. W., 479
Becher, O., 521
Bennett, 601, 625
Bentham, 183
Berdyaev, N., 588
Bergson, H., 55, 108, 342, 371, 525, 527, 629, 666, 690, 742
Berkeley, 28
Bevan, E., 614, 750
Birkhoff, G., 528
Bohr, N., 508
Bosanquet, B., 311
Braithwaite, R. B., 160
Bridgman, 532
Broad, C. D., 273
Brunner, E., 606
Bruno, F., 89
Buchanan, S., 183, 429, 432
Bühler, K., 98, 229

Carnap, R., 36, 161, 183, 209, 330, 634
Cassirer, E., 24, 48, 63, 67, 81, 93, 98, 106, 118, 124, 141, 145, 182, 185, 349, 402, 411, 453, 520, 535, 588, 592, 733
Chesterton, G. K., 475
Cohen, M., 271, 314
Coleridge, 457, 499
Couturat, L., 319
Croce, 100, 347, 455, 467, 626, 738
Cunningham, G. W., 116

Darwin, 30, 652
De Laguna, G. A., 67, 70, 78, 83, 117, 129, 732
Descartes, 26, 653
Dewey, John, 23, 228, 256, 265, 334, 368, 534, 688
Duhem, P., 519, 574
Dunbar, H. F., 414, 489, 596

Eaton, R. M., 103, 308, 422

Eddington, Sir A. S., 620
Einstein, 549
Eliot, T. S., 474
Erdmann, K. O., 139, 147, 193, 200

Feuerbach, L., 607
France, A., 57, 185, 693
Frazer, 589

Gardiner, A. H., 67, 82, 87, 200, 413
Garriggou-Lagrange, R., 749
Gilson, E., 611, 720

Haldane, J. B. S., 526
Haldane, J. S., 526
Hartmann, N., 327, 494, 632
Hartshorne, C., 224
Hegel, 29, 375, 695
Herder, 81, 128
Hertz, H., 47, 503, 508, 567
Hobbes, 170
Höffding, H., 408, 580, 622
Honigswald, R., 267
Hume, 28, 718
Husserl, E., 66, 115, 123, 135, 276, 320, 404
Huxley, T. H., 509
Huxley, Julian, 508

Inge, Dean, 707, 717
Ipsen, G., 62, 82

James, D. G., 501
Jaspers, K., 148, 254
Jeans, Sir J., 515, 539
Jespersen, O., 82, 87, 89, 170, 184, 731
Joad, C. E. M., 57, 524
Johnson, W. E., 295, 324
Jung, C. G., 419

Kant, 15, 104, 158, 256, 362, 404, 409, 491, 505, 602, 693, 713, 715, 719
Köhler, B. W., 79

La Mettrie, 515
Laird, John, 105, 126, 691
Leibniz, 28, 318, 324
Le Roy, J., 605
Lewis, C. I., 129, 211, 245, 274, 279, 314, 317, 329, 676
Lindemann, F. A., 321

Lloyd Morgan, C., 97, 240, 527 703
Locke, 27, 171, 412
Lovejoy, A. O., 576, 627, 687

Malinowski, 61, 197, 737
Margenau, H., 549
Mauthner, 368, 720
Mill, J. S., 139, 283
Montague, W. P., 205, 296
Müller, Max, 81, 176

Nietzsche, 189, 662
Northrop, F. S. C., 296, 497

Ogden and Richards, 37, 97, 103, 130, 161, 207, 231, 258, 465, 523, 739
Otto, R., 577

Paton, H. J., 316
Paul, H., 154
Peirce, 481
Pepper, S. C., 658
Perry, R. B., 160, 404
Plato, 24, 52, 350, 687, 692, 717
Poincaré, H., 503
Powell, A. E., 500
Prall, D. W., 160, 265
Prantl, 200

Ramsey, F. P., 171, 273, 353
Read, C., 448
Reichenbach, H., 540, 566
Reid, L. A., 449, 482
Richards, I. A., 137, 244, 250
  See also Ogden and Richards
Rickert, H., 276, 664
Ritchie, A. D., 386
Royce, J., 228, 258, 264, 339
Russell, B., 35, 41, 105, 279, 290, 356, 370, 553, 741

Ryle, G., 270

Santayana, G., 572
Sapir, E., 74, 86, 237, 734, 738
Scheler, Max, 162, 253, 579
Sertillanges, A. D., 750
Shelley, 359, 478
Sigwart, C., 303
Smith, N. Kemp, 104, 524, 637
Spaulding, E. G., 228, 263, 498, 633, 660
Stebbing, L. S., 121, 140, 273, 285, 294, 299, 303, 341, 479, 536, 568
Stern, Clara and Wm., 135
Stout, G. F., 144, 407
Streeter, B. H., 337

Taylor, A. E., 53, 180, 275, 304, 319, 618
Thompson, A. R., 495
Thomson Sir W., 518

Vaihinger, H., 369, 411, 491, 543
Valéry, P., 33
Van Gogh, 473
Von Humboldt, 29, 124
Vossler, K., 39, 64, 90, 94, 158, 234

Waerner, R. M., 467
Weyl, H., 538, 567
Whitehead, A. N., 51, 58, 114, 127, 323, 371, 377, 412, 451, 497, 632, 663, 698, 723, 744
Whitney, W. D., 73
Whittaker, T., 515
Willis, G., 88, 112, 184
Wittgenstein, L., 11, 41, 56, 333, 353, 357
Wundt, W., 76

INDEX OF SUBJECTS

Aesthetics (and Aesthetic meaning), 100, 457, 467
Ambiguity, 192
Authentic (and Authentication), 213, 219; and communication, in poetry and art, 485; in religion, 612
See also Verification

Behaviourism and Behavioural Meaning, 102, 129, 230, 243, 528
See also Naturalism
Bi-representationism, 237, 355

Cognition (and language), 44, 330, 370, 375, 392
Co-implicates (of Experience), 116, 212, 259, 633, 668, 689
Communication, 42, 229, 231; and the universal, 119; theories of, 243, 250; and knowledge, 261; and art, 264
Connotation, 137, 139, 141, 280
Context (linguistic), 116, 195; theories of, 203; maximum context, 303, 393, 679
See also Universe of discourse
Criterion (empirical), 208, 307; and authentication, 219; and communication, 383
See also Authentication

Denotation, 68, 137, 279
Description (knowledge by), 297, 337, 352, 357
See also Representation
Development (of language), 181, 731
Discourse (universe of), 115, 197, 200, 232, 240, 393
See also Communication and Context
Distortion, 427, 471, 541, 582, 663, 706
Dramatic language, 240, 464, 494, 528, 541, 557

Expression (and intuition), 347, 374

Idealism (and naturalism), 94, 132 (and realism), 263

Implication, 275, 310
See also Presupposition and Co-implicates
Inference, 275, 309, 326
See also Implication and Reasoning
Intelligibility (and meaning), 44, 231; and truth, 44, 392; and value, 128; types of, 240; criterion of, 671, 722
See also Understanding and Verification
Interpretation (as form of knowledge), 338, 360, 361; of symbols, 428, 487, 531; in metaphysics, 364, 678
Intuition (and language), 139, 143, 149, 159, 164, 288, 341, 344, 358, 408, 462, 467, 513, 608, 669
See also Expression

Knowledge (and language)
See Cognition

Language, definition, 64; and meaning, 68, 95, 107; and communication, 229, 264; and truth, 375, 380, 392; and reality, 50, 370, 374
See also Logic and Cognition
Linguistics (linguistic science), 38, 59, 92, 138
Literal (and symbolic), 382, 432, 543, 597, 612, 625, 640, 652, 668
Logic (and language), 43, 271, 328; and the metalogical, 305, 327; and symbolic logic, 316
Logical analysis (of language), 281, 293, 305, 655

Mathematics (language and symbolism of), 517
Meaning (and language), 64, 102, 107, 116, 120, 143; theories of, 102, 128; and truth, 226, 275, 388
See also Semantics, Intelligibility, and Verification
Metalogical (and the logical), 305, 327, 331
Metaphor, 156, 178, 358, 658; **and** symbol, 408, 432, 470, 721
See also Symbol

Metaphysics (language of), 631, 638; symbols of, 657, 664, 703; as symbolic form, 498, 563, 624, 705; natural metaphysic, 686
Myth, 586

Naturalism (and naturalistic theories of language), 59, 64, 82, 93, 102, 129, 189, 203, 243, 448, 452
See also Behaviourism
Nominalism (and neo-nominalism), 25, 35, 102, 289, 323, 367, 607, 721
Normative problems of language
See Validity (linguistic), *also* Criterion

Origin (of language), 71; and validity, 82

Parts of speech, 84, 149, 285, 292, 295
Phenomenology (and phenomenological method in linguistics), 134, 162, 167
Philosophia Perennis (and the problem of language), 23, 686, 717, 722
Philosophy (of language), 32, 36, 40
See also Linguistics and Linguistic Science
Picture (notion of), 337, 353, 358
See also Representation and Description
Poetry (language of), 145, 157, 457, 462, 570, 639, 642; truth of, 476; interpretation of, 487; metaphysics of, 492, 498
Positivism (logical), 36, 44, 161, 190, 208, 215, 220, 224, 244, 262, 284, 307, 330, 353, 386, 532, 548, 565, 609, 629, 634, 639, 640, 647, 652, 710
Predication, 68, 118, 288; analogous, 174, 301, 438, 597, 650, 748
Presupposition, 116, 211, 232, 249, 260, 313, 365, 493, 560, 621, 653
See also Implication, *Suppositio*, and Co-implicates
Propositions, 269, 292, 297, 347, 360, 378, 391, 483, 501; symbol propositions, 301, 437, 442; cosmological, 539, 557, 619; metaphysical, 644, 647

Realism, 94, 142, 162, 263, 326, 370, 608
See also Nominalism and Idealism
Reasoning (and language), 308, 320, 652
See also Inference
Religion (language and symbolism of), 571, 580, 595, 600, 603, 605; and metaphysics, 624
Representation, 66, 68, 100, 348, 353, 377, 422, 535
See also Description *and* Picture

Science (language of), 40, 506; symbols of, 417, 512, 546; theories of, 530, 551; literal and symbolic in, 542; and metaphysics, 564
Semantics, 38, 95, 109, 115
See also Meaning
Sentences, 269, 292, 310, 320, 386, 432, 548, 647, 732
See also Propositions
Sign, 96, 103, 108, 114, 121, 316; sign and symbol, 404, 407, 411
Space-time language, 42, 185, 706
Speech (and language), 67, 88
See also Language
Speech community, 109, 116, 228, 258
Speech-notion, 70, 80
Subject-Predicate (language), 86, 118, 295, 348, 350, 659, 661, 674, 696
Substance-Attribute, 291, 674, 691, 696, 744
See also Subject-Predicate
Suppositio, 125, 200
See also Presupposition
Symbol and Symbolism, 46, 402, 411; principles of, 421; interpretation of, 428; theories of, 447; in art and poetry, 415; in science, 417, 475, 513; in religion, 415, 580, 594; in metaphysics, 656, 664, 694, 706
Symbolic forms, 453, 492, 570, 621, 666, 705, 714
Syntax, 85, 283, 284, 292, 647

Terms, 149, 285
Translation (and communication), 235; theories of, 736

# INDEX

Truth (and language), 47, 375; definition of, 377, 380; and meaning, 44, 226, 388, 678; and intelligibility, 44, 226, 392, 549, 671, 675
See also Criterion and Intelligibility

Understanding, 120, 201, 233, 270
Universal, 116, 141, 287, 323, 368; and communication, 119, 233
See also Realism and Nominalism
Ursprache, 80

Validity (linguistic), 32, 168, 170, 187, 192, 208, 268, 326
See also Criterion
Value (and language), 159; and intelligibility, 126, 215, 239, 675; in art and poetry, 482; in religion, 605, 613, 622; in metaphysics, 664, 675, 692, 700, 724, 749
Verbalism, 190, 202, 285, 299, 303, 645, 656
Verification (and verifiability), 208; and meaning, 208; and communication and truth, 383, 442, 485, 545, 612, 668, 676, 729
Vocabulary, 284, 285, 645

GEORGE ALLEN & UNWIN LTD
London: 40 Museum Street, W.C.1

Auckland: 24 Wyndham Street
Bombay: 15 Graham Road, Ballard Estate, Bombay 1
Buenos Aires: Escritorio 454-459, Florida 165
Cape Town: 109 Long Street
Calcutta: 17 Chittaranjan Avenue, Calcutta 13
Hong Kong: F1/12 Mirador Mansions, Kowloon
Karachi: Karachi Chambers, McLeod Road
Madras: Mohan Mansion, 38c Mount Road, Madras 6
Mexico: Villalongin 32-10, Piso, Mexico 5, D.F.
New Delhi: 13-14 Ajmeri Gate Extension, New Delhi 1
Sao Paulo: Avenida 9 de Julho 1138-Ap. 51
Singapore: 36c Princep Street, Singapore 7
Sydney, N.S.W.: Bradbury House, 55 York Street
Toronto: 91 Wellington Street West

HUMANITY AND DEITY
by W. M. URBAN

Demy 8vo   25s. net

The topics on which the main argument turns in this important book by Professor Urban is the "intelligibility of the real." He criticises the present-day transcendentalist metaphysic and all forms of naturalism or humanism which think of God in terms of merely human projection.

BEYOND REALISM AND IDEALISM
by W. M. URBAN

Demy 8vo   18s. net

Whilst not overlapping *Humanity and Deity*, this volume extends the main argument to particular fields, and effectively illustrates the larger work.

THE WAYS OF KNOWING
by WILLIAM PEPPERELL MONTAGUE

Demy 8vo   *Third Impression*   30s. net

"An able and illuminating discussion of the most controversial topic in contemporary philosophy."—*Adelphi*

"A most attractive book. . . . The freshness of the author's imagination makes his writing always entertaining."—*Mind*

PHILOSOPHICAL ASPECTS OF MODERN SCIENCE
by C. E. M. JOAD

Demy 8vo   12s. 6d. net

"A book which will delight all lovers of mental gymnastics. But apart from the experience the hunt is really a good one, leading through a varied and exciting line of country under a guidance which is clear and determined."—*Manchester Guardian*

by **BERTRAND RUSSELL**

HUMAN KNOWLEDGE

Demy 8vo   *Third Impression*   *30s. net*

"His latest book is of peculiar importance in that it is an exemplar, for the general reader, of Russell's special contribution to human knowledge. In it he applies, with his usual lucidity and wit, the methods of inquiry, which he has done so much to develop, to the question of how we came to know whether we do know about the universe."—RUPERT CRAWSHAY-WILLIAMS in *The Observer*

HISTORY OF WESTERN PHILOSOPHY

Demy 8vo   *Sixth Impression*   *30s. net*

"One of the most valuable books of our time."—G. M. TREVELYAN.

"A monument of learning, written with clarity and grace, irradiated by those incidental flashes of humour and sharpened by those little cat-like touches of malicious wit by which the reader of Russell is perpetually delighted. Russell—one of the few writers who has known how to apply wit to philosophy."—C. E. M. JOAD

THE ANALYSIS OF MIND

Demy 8vo   *Eighth Impression*   *20s. net*

"This interesting and fascinating book . . . is a perfect model of what such books should be. . . . The style is so clear and technicalities so carefully explained that the reading of the book is an intellectual pleasure rather than a mental effort."—*Church Times*

INTRODUCTION TO MATHEMATICAL PHILOSOPHY

Demy 8vo   *Sixth Impression*   *18s. net*

"Mr. Russell has endeavoured to give in non-technical language, an account of his criticism as it affects arithmetic and logic. He has been remarkably successful."—*Nation and Athenæum*

TIME AND FREE WILL
by HENRI BERGSON

Demy 8vo　　　　　*Sixth Impression*　　　　　*18s. net*

"Prof. Bergson has done a very valuable piece of work. We know of no book which treats the question at issue with so much depth and subtlety or which deals with the special problems of psychological analysis with more fineness and accuracy."—*Speaker*

"We trust the foregoing inadequate summary of Bergson's position will prompt curiosity to pass on to the study of this most able work, which is very far removed from the forcible-feeble essays usually put forth by theological apologists . . . Mr. Pogson's translation is exceedingly well done."—*Literary Guide*

MATTER AND MEMORY
by HENRI BERGSON

Demy 8vo　　　　　*Sixth Impression*　　　　　*16s. net*

"Though it can hardly be claimed that Bergson has completely solved the extraordinary complex and difficult problem of memory and least of all the mystery of matter, it may be admitted ungrudgingly that he has clarified the obscurities of the former problem to a considerable extent, and has, above all, rendered great service by the masterly way in which he points out the insuperable difficulties of the materialistic position. . . . This excellent translation."—*The Quest*

"Appeals most to the educator because of the excellent treatment of the very practical subjects of memory and attention. We do not look for a final decision of such problems as are here dealt with, but no one can rise from reading this book and retain unchanged the views with which he began it. To say this of a book of psychometaphysics is to say much."—*Journal of Education*

THE PHENOMENOLOGY OF MIND

By HEGEL   *Translated by J. B. Baillie*

Demy 8vo   Third Impression Second Edition   35s. net

"It is impossible to speak too highly of the limpid translation, and the editorial aids which light up this famous philosophical treatise."
—*London Quarterly Review.*

THE CONCEPT OF MAN

Edited by RADHAKRISHNAN and P. T. RAJU

Demy 8vo   42s. net

In the contemporary climate of world thought, comparative philosophy has become increasingly important as a means to the mutual understanding of the world's cultures. Particularly since the last world war, East and West have come to realize that their traditional patterns of life and thought are not adequate and that each has much to learn from the other. Comparative philosophy has obtained a new impetus from thise sense of inadequacy; and in this field the comparative study of the concept of man with reference to his nature, his universe and his ideals is both urgent and fruitful.

The contributors to *The Concept of Man* are philosophers of both East and West, and write with authority on Greek, Jewish, Chinese and Indian thought respectively. This is the first work to bring the different concepts of man into systematic comparison, and it will appeal equally to the general reader, and to students of culture and philosophy.

GEORGE ALLEN & UNWIN LTD